GRUNTS

Also by John C. McManus

American Courage, American Carnage:
The 7th Infantry Regiment's Combat Experience, 1812 Through World War II

The 7th Infantry Regiment:
Combat in an Age of Terror, the Korean War Through the Present

U.S. Military History for Dummies

Alamo in the Ardennes:
The Untold Story of the American Soldiers Who Made the Defense of Bastogne Possible

The Americans at Normandy:
The Summer of 1944—The American War from the Normandy Beaches to Falaise

The Americans at D-Day:
The American Experience at the Normandy Invasion

Deadly Sky:
The American Combat Airman in World War II

The Deadly Brotherhood:
The American Combat Soldier in World War II

GRUNTS

INSIDE THE AMERICAN
INFANTRY COMBAT EXPERIENCE,
WORLD WAR II THROUGH IRAQ

John C. McManus

NAL
CALIBER

NAL Caliber
Published by New American Library, a division of
Penguin Group (USA) Inc., 375 Hudson Street,
New York, New York 10014, USA
Penguin Group (Canada), 90 Eglinton Avenue East, Suite 700, Toronto,
Ontario M4P 2Y3, Canada (a division of Pearson Penguin Canada Inc.)
Penguin Books Ltd., 80 Strand, London WC2R 0RL, England
Penguin Ireland, 25 St. Stephen's Green, Dublin 2,
Ireland (a division of Penguin Books Ltd.)
Penguin Group (Australia), 250 Camberwell Road, Camberwell, Victoria 3124,
Australia (a division of Pearson Australia Group Pty. Ltd.)
Penguin Books India Pvt. Ltd., 11 Community Centre, Panchsheel Park,
New Delhi - 110 017, India
Penguin Group (NZ), 67 Apollo Drive, Rosedale, North Shore 0632,
New Zealand (a division of Pearson New Zealand Ltd.)
Penguin Books (South Africa) (Pty.) Ltd., 24 Sturdee Avenue,
Rosebank, Johannesburg 2196, South Africa

Penguin Books Ltd., Registered Offices:
80 Strand, London WC2R 0RL, England

First published by NAL Caliber, an imprint of New American Library,
a division of Penguin Group (USA) Inc.

First Printing, August 2010
10 9 8 7 6 5 4 3 2 1

LIBRARY OF CONGRESS CATALOGING-IN-PUBLICATION DATA:

McManus, John C., 1965–
    Grunts: inside the American infantry combat experience, World War II through Iraq/John C. McManus.
        p. cm.
    Includes bibliographical references and index.
    ISBN 978-0-451-22790-4
    1. United States. Army. Infantry—History—20th century.   2. United States. Army. Infantry—History—21st
century.   3. United States. Marine Corps—History—20th century.   4. United States. Marine Corps—
History—21st century.   5. Combat—History—20th century.   6. Combat—History—21st century.   I. Title.
    UA28.M39 2010
    356'.1140973—dc22   2010009828

Set in Minion
Designed by Ginger Legato

Printed in the United States of America

To Michael and Mary Jane McManus, who made all of this possible

To Charles W. Johnson, who taught and led like a great general

To the infantry sergeants, lieutenants and captains of multiple generations who paid in blood, tears and anguish to teach us the lessons we all should heed

CONTENTS

Grunt: A United States Army or Marine foot soldier; one who does routine unglamorous work

—Merriam-Webster Dictionary

Introduction
Facing Our Fears

THE MOST POWERFUL, EFFECTIVE WEAPON in modern war is a well-trained, well-armed, and well-led infantry soldier. To some this assertion might seem naive, simplistic, or even antiquated, perhaps an appropriate statement to make back in Washington's or Wellington's day, but surely not in our own era of dynamic technical sophistication. After all, how can the average foot-slogging grunt with a rifle in his hands possibly compare with the malevolent power of technology's deadly birthlings? Indeed, the variety of modern space-age weapons is impressive: nuclear bombs and missiles with the power to destroy civilization; deadly gases and biological concoctions that could eradicate human life as we know it; super aircraft carriers; nuclear-propelled and nuclear-armed submarines; high-performance fighter aircraft; intercontinental bombers; computer and electronic eavesdropping technology; net-war computer hackers with the power to paralyze information-age economies; laser-guided smart bombs and unmanned combat aircraft, not to mention the bevy of land weapons (artillery, tanks, missiles, and so on) that tower over the infantryman like an NBA center over a toddler.

Each one of these weapons exudes a tantalizing, magic-bullet simplicity to fighting and winning wars. In other words, the side with the most sophisticated and deadly weapons should automatically win. The newer the technology, the more devastating the weapon, the more antiquated the infantry soldier should become. This self-deceptive thinking is nothing new. In ancient times, generals expected the chariot to sweep foot soldiers from the battlefield. In medieval times, the mounted knight and artillery would do that job. Later, in World War I, machine guns, frighteningly accurate artillery, and poison gas were supposed to make the infantryman obsolete. Of course, the rise of aviation created a powerful new brand of techno-vangelism. In the 1930s, air power enthusiasts, such as Giulio Douhet and Hap Arnold, argued that henceforth fleets of airplanes would bring war to the enemy's homeland, destroying his economy and his will to make war, thus negating any real need for armies.

The advent of nuclear weapons at the end of World War II seemingly elevated the "victory through air power" theory to an axiomatic level on par with Newton's scientific findings on gravity. Indeed, the mushroom clouds over Hiroshima and Nagasaki barely had time to dissipate before a new flock of futurists proclaimed this latest revolution in warfare. From now on, they claimed, wars would be fought by a combination of nuclear-armed airmen and push-button technicians collectively raining untold waves of destruction on the enemy's populace. "The day of the foot soldier is gone forever," one such visionary wrote in 1946. "He is as extinct as the dodo bird. Yet this rather elementary fact seems to have escaped the notice of the hide-bound traditionalists who still cling tenaciously to their predilection for swarming masses of foot soldiers." Writing a few months later, another self-styled seer (an infantry officer, no less!) agreed that "the days of the ground arms are ending. Warfare has changed. The scientists have taken over strategy and the military men have got to understand this sooner or later. The days of battles, as we know them and . . . have fought them, are gone forever."[1] I must risk posing an acerbic—or at least uncomfortable—question: How did those prognoses work out? The answer is obvious. They could not have been more wrong if they had said elephants fly better than birds.

Predictions regarding the demise of the foot soldier are always wrong because they are based on *theory*, not *actual events*. There is an old saying that rules are meant to be broken. Well, I would argue that theories are meant to be debunked, especially in relation to warfare. As a historian, I am, quite frankly, not interested in the theoretical world of jargon-packed war college papers, geopolitical treatises, and predictions about next war wonder-weapons or scenarios. Instead, I am interested in finding out *what actually happened*, understanding why it happened that way, and perhaps coming to some kind of conclusion on what this might bode for the future. This book, then, is about realities of the modern battlefield, not theories about it. On the basis of historical study, I can say this with absolute certainty: From World War II through the present, American ground combat soldiers, especially infantry-men, have been the lead actors in nearly every American war, at the very time when new weapons and technology were supposed to make them obsolete.

Thus, even in modern war, more is usually less. Since World War II, no one has, thankfully, ever used nuclear weapons. Instead, nukes settled into a useful role as a terrifying deterrent, assuring potential antagonists mutual destruction if they were ever actually employed. Their existence probably dissuaded the Cold War superpowers from making all-out war on each other. Both the Soviets and the Americans understood the pointlessness, and the horrible consequences for humanity, of nuclear war. The same has largely been true for every other nuclear power (of course, nuclear-equipped, fa-natical, extra-national terrorists would probably have no such compunc-tions). Saddam Hussein notwithstanding, chemical and biological weapons have also largely been absent from the modern battlefield. I am not arguing that this absence places them beneath consideration. I am simply saying that their existence does not negate the infantryman's vital importance. The same is true for the other techno-rich weapons I listed above. The armadas of bombers, ships, subs, missiles, and aerial drones, in spite of their staggering array of ordnance, and important though they are, have still never yet re-placed the ground soldier as the primary agent of warfare. From the inva-sion beaches of Guam in 1944 to sweaty patrols in twenty-first-century Iraqi heat, the guy with boots on the ground and a weapon in his hand almost al-ways takes the lead in carrying out the war aims of Washington policymak-ers, not to mention determining their success or failure. This is the pattern of recent history.

The American Love Affair with Techno-War

Since the beginning of World War II, no group of people or nation-state has invested more money, energy, and sheer hope in technology as a war winner than the United States. The belief that technology and machines can win wars of their own accord was prevalent as long ago as World War II and it still persists, argu-ably in even stronger form, in the twenty-first century. In 1947, S. L. A. Marshall, the noted combat historian, wrote: "So strong was the influence of the machine upon our thinking, both inside and outside the military establishment, that . . . the infantry became relatively the most slighted of branches." The country paid a high price in blood and treasure for this oversight in World War II, but very little changed in subsequent decades. In 2006, another erudite military analyst, Ralph Peters, wrote something eerily similar to Marshall's passage: "Too many of our military and civilian leaders remain captivated by the notion that machines can replace human beings on the battlefield. They cannot face . . . reality: Wars of flesh, faith and cities." Marshall and Peters both understood that flesh-and-blood human beings win wars. Machines and technology only assist them.[2]

Shrinking from the horrifying reality of war's ugly face (more on that later), Americans have a tendency to think of war as just another problem that can be addressed through technology, economic abundance, or political dialogue.[3] These are American strengths so it is only natural that Americans would turn to them in time of need. Nor is there anything inherently wrong with the idea of maximizing these considerable American advantages. But there is something more at work here. Reared in the comfort of domestic peace and prosperity, most modern Americans cannot begin to comprehend that, more than anything else, war is a barbaric contest of wills, fought for some larger strategic purpose. Victory in combat usually comes from the resolve of human beings, not the output of machines. Yet, the modern American war-making strategy invests high hopes in the triumph of genielike superweapons and technology. To some extent, this is because Americans took the wrong lesson from World War II. They erroneously believed that victory in World War II came mainly from Allied matériel, technological, and manpower superiority. This created a zealotlike faith that these advantages would guarantee victory in any future conflict.

Hence, ever since, the United States has had a persistent tendency to invest too many resources in air power and sea power, sometimes to the detriment of ground power. For instance, in fiscal year 2007, the Army and Marine Corps collectively received 29 percent of Defense Department budget dollars even though they were doing almost all of the fighting in Afghanistan and Iraq. The technology-rich Air Force and Navy received over 54 percent of the funding. In late 2008, even in the midst of two major ground wars, congressional leaders and Pentagon security "experts" were still talking about cutting, in future budgets, the ground forces in favor of wonder-weapon technology. Bing West, a leading American military commentator, even claimed that, as of 2006, the American armed forces contained more combat aircraft than infantry squads, "and more combat pilots than squad leaders." This in spite of the fact that, based on intelligence intercepts, insurgents in Iraq feared American infantry soldiers much more than American technology. One result of this misappropriation of resources was the sad spectacle of overstretched, overworked ground troops going into combat in Iraq without adequate personal armor or weapons.[4]

I want to state quite clearly that I am *not* arguing, in some sort of reactionary, antediluvian way, that modern technology, cutting-edge machines, firepower, sea power, and air power are unimportant for national security. All of these things are of tremendous importance. No serious person could possibly argue that the United States would have won World War II and prevailed in the Cold War without a preeminent navy and air force, not to mention a qualitative edge in weaponry, automation, engineering, economic largesse, communications, and supply. No rational individual would ever claim that there is no need for a navy or an air force, so why does anyone, for even a moment, confer any semblance of legitimacy on the view that ground combat forces are obsolete, especially when history proves that notion so absolutely wrong? It should be obvious to everyone that air, sea, and ground power are all vital. Indeed, Americans wage war most effectively when the services cooperate and fight as a combined arms team.

So, to be absolutely clear, I am not howling at the rise of the technological moon, pining away for a preindustrial time when small, well-drilled groups of light infantrymen decided the fate of empires. I am simply saying that, throughout modern history, no matter how advanced weaponry has become, the foot soldier has always been the leading actor on the stage of warfare. Further, I am contending that the sheer impressive power of techno-war leads to an American temptation to over-rely on air power and sea power at the expense of ground combat power. The problem is not the emphasis on technology. The issue is simply too much of a very good thing, to the exclusion of what is truly vital, at least if we are to consider actual history, not just theory. Embracing an expensive new brand of techno-war while impoverishing land forces is foolish and self-defeating, but it is too often the American way of war. Time and again since

World War II, American leaders have had to relearn one of history's most obvious lessons—*wars are won on the ground, usually by small groups of fighters, who require considerable logistical, firepower, and popular support.*

The question, then, is who supports whom. Modern American military strategists too often have fallen under the sway of the erroneous idea that ground forces only exist to support air forces or navies. That is exactly backward.[5] In 1950, Bruce Palmer, one of the leading Army intellectuals of the post–World War II era, wrote with succinct, prescient simplicity: "Man himself has always been the decisive factor in combat. Despite the devastating power of modern weapons, there are today no valid reasons to doubt the continued decisive character of the infantryman's role in battle. All indications are that the infantry will decide the issue in the next war as they did in the last."[6] Subsequent history proved him exactly right. Since World War II, nearly every American conflict has been decided on the ground, Kosovo being the lone, and debatable, exception. Even in the Gulf War, with the impressive, and devastating, performance of coalition air forces, the ground army had to carry out the actual job of pushing Saddam's armies out of Kuwait. So, at the risk of belaboring the point, we must consider not the theoretical but what has actually happened in recent wars. I realize that just because events unfolded one way in the past does not guarantee they will happen the same way in the future. That is quite true. But surely the patterns of past events indicate some level of probability that those same patterns will hold true in the future. If ground soldiers were of paramount importance in every previous conflict, isn't it reasonable to assume that they will remain important in any future war? After all, human beings are terrestrial creatures. They live on land, not in the air or sea. Doesn't this simple fact indicate a strong likelihood that land is the main arena of decision in war?

The trouble is that wonder-weapons and techno-vangelism push all the right buttons in American culture. Wonder-weapons are good business for defense contractors. They are career makers for field-grade military procurement officers. They appeal to the American public's fascination with high-tech gizmos (if you doubt that, take a look at the latest line of video war games, cell phones, or PalmPilots, and then get back to me). For Washington politicians, wonder-weapons hold an irresistible lure, in much the same way a brand-new casino or a full slate of NFL games hypnotizes an inveterate gambler.

For our friendly neighborhood congressman or senator, the latest supership, guided missile, or new-generation heavy bomber promises some very alluring prospects. They offer standoff weaponry that can supposedly protect the American people at home, as well as inflict surgical destruction on any enemy overseas, and they can do these wonderful things without requiring constituents to do much more than raise their television remotes for a collective cheer. More than anything, expensive new weapons systems offer precision war—desensitized, tidy, and impersonal—while risking the lives of, at most, only a few technical professionals who have, after all, signed up for this kind of thing. Best of all, for our national leaders in Congress and the White House, this version of techno-war is politically safe, negating the kind of soul-searching debates that naturally flow from the employment of ground troops. Of course, there is also the delightful prospect that said weapons system could be built in our congressman's district or our senator's state, creating local jobs. Needless to say, compared with the glitzy allure of the latest high-tech weaponry, there is little glamour (and usually not as much profit) for contractors and government officials alike in churning out rifles, machine guns, boots, and bullets for infantrymen. So priority often goes to the big-ticket stuff. I will readily concede that this mind-set has, in its own muddled way, somewhat enhanced American national security by making the United States the unchallenged world leader in military technology. However, the cost of this has been too great, and not just in dollars. The price of America's fascination with new age warfare is a fundamental misunderstanding of what war is and how best to prepare for it.

I will illustrate my point with one cautionary example of this misplaced thinking—namely, the planning for the Iraq War. Donald Rumsfeld's Department of Defense disregarded Army troop level recommendations and launched the invasion of Iraq without adequate manpower or planning for the ambitious mission of destroying Saddam Hussein's regime, occupying the country, and forging a democratic future. Rumsfeld and his partners mistakenly believed that overwhelmingly superior technology, "shock and awe" weaponry, and mobility would win this war, not ground soldiers securing terrain and people, especially in Iraq's many cities. Moreover, they failed to grasp that the effectiveness of technology and firepower is substantially diminished in urban areas, especially in the information age, when the killing of innocents by one errant bomb can cause a strategic setback. When one considers that, at the current rate of global urban growth, over two-thirds of the world's population will live in urban areas by 2050, this would seem to be an important point.

Alas, Rumsfeld's retinue simply figured, or hoped, that they would not have to fight in cities. They were dead wrong. In Iraq, the cities turned into the main arena of contention. Like many Americans, the Iraq War planners made the mistake of believing that, in war, technology trumps the human element rather than the other way around. They shrank from the fundamental reality that war is largely a contest of *human will*. It is also inherently ugly, vulgar, and destructive. Nor is this ever likely to change. When they dismissed the importance of these kinds of uncomfortable subjective realities that did not fit onto their spreadsheets, the terrible consequence was, of course, post-Hussein chaos, a pervasive insurgency, and a protracted, blood-soaked war.[7]

Humanity's Fatal Flaw

Humanity has a fatal flaw and it will probably never go away. That flaw is the propensity to make war. I offer no explanation as to why humans have this terrible flaw. Perhaps a psychologist could attempt to forge such an explanation. As a historian, I can simply state the fact that wars have marred the entire span of human history. They continue to do so today. There is no reason to believe that the future will be any different. In fact, one could argue that war has been the most powerful causative force in human history. At times war can act as a remarkably constructive force for humanity (the defeat of Nazi Germany leaps readily to mind).

Even so, war is like disease—a sad, immutable reality that is an inherent aspect of our troubled world. To ignore this reality and wish it might all go away is foolish in the extreme, quite similar to a cancer patient refusing treatment in the vain hope that the disease will disappear. It is far better to understand it and master it, much as doctors seek to triumph over a deadly disease. Only when we understand the true nature of war can we hope to prevent it. The nature of war is waste, destruction, barbarity, human anguish, depravity, and ultimate tragedy, not video monitors, joysticks, push buttons, and expensive gadgets. War cannot be sanitized or transformed, no matter how hard techno-warriors try to change it, from what it really is. War is an ugly beast that cannot be made to look nice through cosmetic surgery. War destroys youth. It destroys infrastructure. It destroys hopes and dreams. In its most common form, it is fought by small groups of frightened human beings (usually men), on the ground, in almost intimate fashion. Generally, war entails killing, the most taboo yet strangely all too common of human behaviors.[8] Citizens of a free society must understand all of this. We cannot afford the luxury of turning our eyes from these realities, any more than a health care professional can afford to be squeamish at the sight of blood. For if we succumb to the belief that war is simply a bloodless technological problem, to be dealt with at a safe distance, employing only machines and new-generation weapons, we will continue to court disaster.

In this book, I hope to make two major points. The first has to do with the importance of land power. In the late nineteenth century, Alfred Thayer Mahan, an American naval officer, wrote a significant book called *The Influence of Sea Power Upon History, 1660–1783*. Basically, Mahan argued that sea power equated to national power. The Royal Navy was his prime example, but he also clearly implied that the United States must follow the same path, especially through the construction of battleships. Mahan made his case by describing a litany of key naval battles. His argument for the importance of seaborne commerce, as protected by naval power, is indisputable.

However, he greatly exaggerated the importance of battleships and the *primacy* of sea power in modern war. While accepting Mahan's argument about sea power's vital necessity (along with the subsequent arguments of aviation advocates for the importance of air power), I am asserting that land power is the most important element in modern war. More than anything else, land power equates to national power. My most powerful evidence for this argument is the simple realities of America's recent wars. Obviously, American troops were highly dependent on air and sea forces for transportation, supply, and fire support. Planes and ships were of crucial importance in every war. I am not arguing otherwise. But the key word here is *"support."* Ground forces, while dependent on much support, still took the *lead* in the actual fighting against America's enemies. In fact, they did almost all the fighting and dying, even in World War II, when naval and air forces fought more battles than they have in all American wars ever since. In World War II, nearly two-thirds of American combat fatalities, and over 90 percent of woundings, occurred among Army and Marine ground forces. A generation later, some 58,193 Americans died in Vietnam. Over 53,000 of them died while fighting on the ground, in the Army or the Marines. Some 2,555 sailors lost their lives in that war, and it is a safe bet that a significant percentage of them were serving with ground forces as corpsmen or in special operations units like the SEALs. The unbalanced casualty ratios were even more pronounced in Korea, the Gulf War, Afghanistan, and Iraq (well over 90 percent of American combat deaths in those wars occurred among ground soldiers).[9]

These numbers simply reflect the obvious fact that, from World War II through Iraq, most of the fighting in America's wars took place on the ground. Is it not rational to say, based on these numbers, that in these conflicts land forces took a leading role? In my opinion, this is beyond question. Perhaps it is then reasonable to say that land power has proven to be the preeminent element of American power in modern times. I base this statement not just on casualty numbers but on the indisputable fact that when war has happened, ground troops, particularly infantry soldiers, have fought most of the battles. If this trend held up for more than sixty years, between World War II and Iraq, at a time of explosive technological growth, why would we have any reason to believe that the future will be any different?

The second point I plan to make in this book has to do with the reality of combat. In modern wars, the actual fighting is *the* story, not simply an antecedent to larger strategic considerations. I will use an example to explain what I mean by that. I bristle whenever I hear the orthodox explanation as to why the Allies won World War II. It goes like this. Once the Big Three (the USSR, Britain, and the USA) were in place, Allied victory was then inevitable. The matériel, manpower, technological, and transportation advantages that the Big Three and their partners enjoyed simply guaranteed an Allied victory. *No, they did not!* They swung the probabilities in favor of the Allies. They did not make victory inevitable. To say so is to deny the importance of what took place on the battlefield. The Allies could not have won the war if their soldiers were not willing to fight, die, and sacrifice, in large numbers, under the most challenging of circumstances. Can machines or warehouses full of supplies force men to move forward, into a kill zone, at mortal risk to themselves, in order to attack and destroy their enemies? Certainly not. Only good leadership and a warrior's spirit can do that. Material advantages can be very helpful (especially in the realm of fire support), but they cannot ever guarantee those vital ingredients of victory. From the Greco-Persian Wars through Vietnam, history is replete with examples of materially impoverished groups, kingdoms, tribes, or nation-states that triumphed over their better-heeled opponents.

That aside, I believe that too many American policymakers have sought to avoid seeing war as it really is, not just out of a natural preference for technological solutions to difficult problems, but also out of fear and disgust. Because American culture generally values individuality and the importance of human life, the truly awful face of war, as embodied in ground combat, is simply too ugly for many of us to behold. It is instead somehow more comforting, or humane, to assure ourselves that such unpleasant things are relics of an earlier, more barbaric age, easily suppressed under the weight of modern technology. War need not mean actual fighting and dying by ground soldiers. Instead it can be prosecuted from a distance, with smart weapons, and brought to an amicable conclusion with mutually reasonable enemies. Of course, the only problem with this well-meaning notion is that wars never happen that way. Once unleashed from its Pandora's box, the plague of war slimes us all, but none more so than the combatants themselves.

In 1976, John Keegan published *The Face of Battle*, a truly landmark book. By investigating the battles of Agincourt, Waterloo, and the Somme, Keegan delved, like no previous historian, into the stark realities of ground combat for the average soldier. He almost singlehandedly inspired the school of socio-military inquiry that focuses on the experience of the common soldier. Keegan made the salient point that firsthand combat accounts were rare until only the last few hundred years. The perspective of the average enlisted soldier was almost nonexistent until the nineteenth century. Instead we were left with traditional battle rhetoric—grand, sweeping charges, trumpets and glory, heroic generals, cycloramic drama. Keegan was one of the first historians to penetrate that battle rhetoric in search of the actual human story for the average participant.[10]

With full acknowledgment of Keegan's profound influence, I intend to employ the same approach to see how it holds up in a more modern time, for Americans from World War II through the present, at a time when there is definitely no paucity of sources from the common soldier. I have chosen to write about ten different battles or situations in recent U.S. history—Guam,

Peleliu, Aachen, and the northern shoulder of the Battle of the Bulge in World War II; Operation Masher/White Wing, the Marine Corps combined action platoons, and the Battle of Dak To in Vietnam; the combat experiences of infantry soldiers in the Gulf War, the urban struggle for Fallujah; and, finally, the world of one infantry regiment fighting the counterinsurgency war in Iraq. Each chapter is based on a diverse blend of primary sources, some of them coming to light for the first time. I make liberal use of after action reports, unit lessons learned, official documents, personal diaries, unit journals, personal memoirs, letters, individual interviews, and even group combat after action interviews I conducted with Iraq War infantry soldiers. These sources help us puncture the clichés of battle rhetoric and discover what the modern battlefield smells like and looks like, how killing and fear affect the combatants, and how Americans behave in battle.

I realize that I can be accused of stacking the deck in my favor by choosing only battles that illustrate my larger arguments. That is a fair point, even though my arguments evolved from studying these battles rather than the other way around. What's more, I could just as easily have chosen dozens of other battles or situations that would have illustrated my arguments every bit as well. In making my choices, one of my key intentions was to pursue variety. So I opted for a rich blend, from amphibious invasions to urban combat to pitched battles, to mechanized warfare and its diametric opposite, counterinsurgency. I chose no Korean War battles because I saw in them nothing tactically different from World War II. Only the reader can decide if this was an oversight. In any event, my goal is to illuminate, in the most unvarnished way, the troubling world of ground combat, as experienced by American soldiers of recent times. Mahan made his case by discussing naval history. I will make mine by writing about land warfare, in a way that I hope does justice to Keegan's methods.

I want to be very clear that I am not writing all this from the perspective of a professional soldier or statesman. I do not base my arguments on personal experience, military training, or in-depth study at any military college. I am only a historian, trained in modern American military history, offering a perspective on the basis of that expertise. As such, I have constructed my arguments around the lessons modern history has shown us, nothing more, nothing less. And what are those lessons? They can be summed up in the words of one World War II combat soldier: "There is no worse place than where the Infantry is . . . or what it has to do. A war is not over until the Infantry is done with it . . . finished moving on foot more than the other, finished killing more than the other. And when it is all done, and the Infantryman is taken home again, some of him will remain in that place . . . forever."[11]

CHAPTER 1
Guam, July 1944:
Amphibious Combat Against a
Self-Destructive Enemy

W-Day

THE UNDERWATER DEMOLITION TEAMS (UDTs) went in first. Their job was to blow holes through the coral reefs that served as a natural barrier for the American invasion force at Guam. With that accomplished, their next mission was to destroy obstacles and mines on the chosen landing beaches, and they were to do this in plain view of the Japanese defenders who sat in pillboxes, buildings, and bunkers, overlooking the beaches. Only a smokescreen and some covering fire from ships offshore would shield the Underwater Demolition Teams. Superb swimmers, trained explosives experts, and possessed of an adventurer's mentality, these intrepid souls were the ancestors of U.S. Navy SEALs. For nearly a week before the invasion, they swept the area, paddling or swimming ashore, setting explosive charges, scouting enemy positions. They were seldom molested by the Japanese, who were often too busy taking shelter from naval gunfire to deal with the UDTs. Sometimes, the Japanese were just plain clueless, exhibiting a self-destructive penchant that was to plague their defense of Guam like a veritable millstone around the neck. One group of Japanese soldiers was practically within spitting distance of a demolition team but did not fire a shot. "No one gave us orders to shoot," one of them later explained to his American captors. In the days ahead, of course, most of his countrymen would resist their American enemies much more forcefully, but always within the context of a deeply flawed plan that played to American strengths.

By the eve of the July 21 invasion (code-named W-day by the command-ers), the teams had accomplished all their missions with the loss of one man killed. They had cleared paths through the reefs, negating palm log barriers filled with coral cement, wire cable, and four-foot-high wire cages also filled with coral cement. They had also blown up, mainly with hand-placed charges, nearly one thousand obstacles on the beaches. They even had time to leave behind a nice message for their Marine brothers who would soon hit the beach. They nailed a large sign to a tree that read: "Welcome Marines! USO that way!" Rear Admiral Richard Conolly, commander of Task Force 53, whose responsibility was to transport, land, and support the invasion troops, later wrote that none of this would have been possible without the work of the UDTs and their "successfully prosecuted clearance operations." The only downside was that the UDTs, through the sheer weight of their efforts, made it quite obvious to the Japanese where the invasion would happen.[1]

In July 1944, the Americans wanted Guam for several reasons. It had once been an American colonial possession. The Japanese had seized it in 1941. The population, mainly Chamorros, had always been pro-American but were especially inclined toward the Americans after several years of difficult Japa-nese occupation. The locals were itching for liberation and the Americans intended to give them just that. Guam, with excellent airfields, anchorages, and hospitals, was a vital stepping-stone to Japan and ultimate victory.

The Americans planned a two-pronged invasion. In the north, the entire 3rd Marine Division, consisting of three infantry regiments and one artillery regiment, plus many attached units, would land between Adelup Point to the north and Asan Point to the south. The 3rd Marine Regiment would hit Red Beach on the left (north) flank. The 21st Marine Regiment would land in the middle at Green Beach. On the right (south) flank, the 9th Marine Regiment would take Blue Beach. The artillerymen would follow in successive waves. A few miles to the south, just below Orote Point—a fingerlike peninsula that jutted into the sea—the 1st Provisional Marine Brigade, consisting of the 22nd and 4th Marine Regiments, were to land at Yellow and White Beaches, respectively, near a village called Agat. They would be reinforced by the Ar-my's 77th Infantry Division, a New York National Guard outfit nicknamed the "Statue of Liberty" Division. All of these ground forces were lumped under the III Marine Amphibious Corps, commanded by Major General Roy Geiger, a judicious, meticulous Marine with an aviation background. The

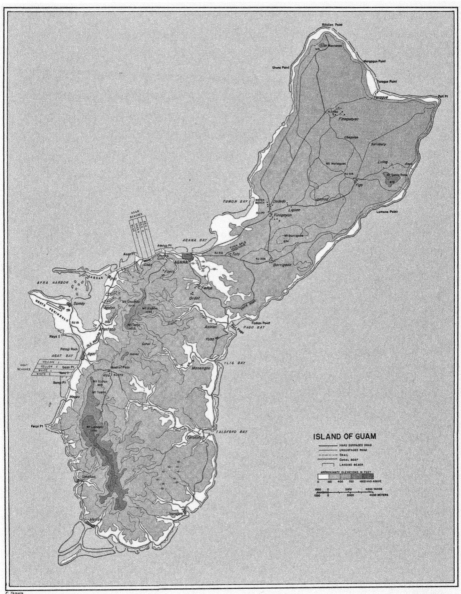

ISLAND OF GUAM

GUAM, 1944

USMC

obvious post-invasion plan for all of these units was to push inland, subdue Japanese resistance, and secure the island.[2]

Aboard the troopships that were cruising a few miles off Guam's shores in the early hours of July 21, most of the assault force Marines were actually eager to go ashore. Because they had comprised a floating reserve for the previous invasion of Saipan, they had been cooped up aboard their cramped, hot, austere ships nearly every day since the middle of June. Enlisted men slept belowdecks in cramped bunks stacked from the floor to the ceiling. The bunks inevitably sagged under the weight of their occupants. Only a few inches separated a man's nose from the hindquarters of the Marine above him. Showers were of the saltwater variety, making true cleanliness a veritable impossibility. The heads were usually crowded. Sometimes toilets overflowed, spilling a nauseating brew of salt water and human waste that flowed from the head into adjacent areas, including sometimes troop quarters. Navy chow was pretty good but, on most of the troopships, meals were only served in the galley twice a day. One ship was permeated with the stench of rotting potatoes in the galley "spud locker." Officers and sergeants put their Marines through physical training each day, but the fitness level of the men was bound to taper off in such conditions. Men passed the time by playing cards, writing letters, conversing with their buddies, or just plain thinking in solitude. Tempers flared and morale declined. "We were fighting each other," Private First Class William Morgan, a rifleman in the 3rd Marine Regiment, recalled. "We'd have fought hell itself . . . to get off that damned ship."[3]

Shrouded in inky darkness, the vast invasion armada settled into place off Guam's western shores. Admiral Conolly had amassed a powerful task force consisting of six battleships, six cruisers, seven destroyers, plus a dizzying array of aircraft carriers, submarines, support vessels, and troopships. At 0200, loudspeakers came to life aboard the troopships: "Now hear this, reveille, chow down for troops!" Nervous young Marines crowded into galleys, inching their way through steaming chow lines. On most ships, navy cooks served the traditional invasion fare of steak, eggs, biscuits, fruit juice, and coffee. Some of the men ate heartily. Some were too anxious to enjoy their meal or even eat at all. "There was very little conversation," one Marine later wrote, "many of the Marines were still half asleep. The rest of us were deeply engaged in our own personal thoughts."[4]

On a few ships, navy skippers heeded doctors' advice to feed the troops a light meal since patients with empty bellies were easier to treat than those with full stomachs. On one of those ships, the USS *Crescent City*, the Marines were surprised, and miffed, to be fed a meager breakfast of white beans, bread, and coffee. They complained loudly, and unambiguously, to their navy hosts, so much so that the ship's captain took to the loudspeaker to explain his rationale. After hearing the captain's announcement, Private Eugene Peterson of the 12th Marine Regiment snuck back into the galley and discovered that the cooks were serving meat loaf to the ship's crew. He asked for some of the tasty meat, but a sailor tried to shoo him away. "Beat it, Marine. We already fed you." But the chief cook witnessed this silliness and interceded. "Wise up, punk," he said to the cook. "This Marine is facing a day of bad news." The chief wrapped a large chunk of meat loaf in a towel, gave it to Peterson, and wished him luck. Peterson thanked the chief, hurried back to his unit, and found a way to wedge the meat into his pack.[5]

Meanwhile, aboard the myriad troopships, the assault troops were congregating topside, packs and equipment in place, rifles slung, anxiously waiting for orders to board their landing craft. The average infantryman was loaded down with about seventy pounds of gear. When the order came, they clambered, amid semi-organized chaos, over the sides of their ships, down huge cargo nets, into bobbing Landing Craft Vehicle Personnel boats (LCVPs), better known as Higgins boats. Having rehearsed this process many times, they knew to hold the vertical, not horizontal, grips on the cargo nets (so as to avoid having their hands stepped on by the man above them), while descending carefully step by step. At the bottom of the net, about three or four feet above the landing craft, they balanced themselves and then hopped into their waiting boats. One by one the Higgins boats filled up with Marines, then pulled away from the ships and circled in the darkness, waiting for the order to head for shore. Aboard the boats, the Marines, already wet from sea spray, jostled around, breathed stale diesel fumes, and tried to stave off nausea, whether sea- or nerve-induced.

By 0530, just before sunrise, even as the troops were loading into their landing craft, the preinvasion bombardment was in full swing. To the assault troops, the sheer pyrotechnics of the aerial and naval bombardment were awe-inspiring. The ships themselves appeared as nothing more than gigantic hulks in the darkness. When they fired, their muzzle flashes lit up the night, followed by waves of concussion. In that fleeting instant, the troops got all too

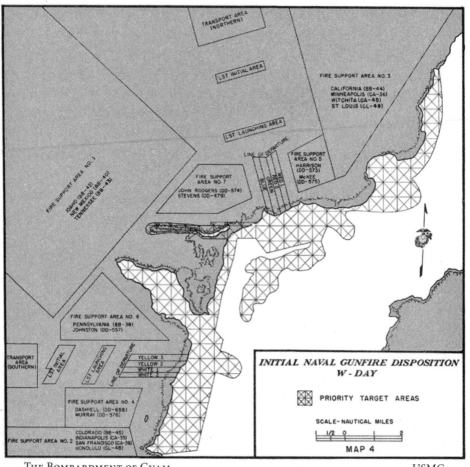

THE BOMBARDMENT OF GUAM   USMC

brief glimpses of the ships themselves or Guam's coastline. The bombardment was an overwhelming cacophony of sound and violence. The men could feel the concussion in their chests. Their ears were assaulted by so much noise that they had trouble hearing the engines of their landing craft. Battleships spewed sixteen-inch shells at the shadowy hills beyond the beach. Cruisers added hundreds of eight-inch shells. The explosions "sent fire and smoke hundreds of feet into the air," one Marine officer later wrote. "Small fires burned along the entire length of the beach. Destroyers were firing shells from close range. They roved back and forth, one firing a series of volleys, followed by another firing into the same area." Each battleship, cruiser, and destroyer bristled with multiple antiaircraft gun tubs. The crews lowered their guns to shoot in a flat trajectory and unloaded a dizzying array of small-caliber shells (mainly 40-millimeter) into preselected targets. Tracer rounds from these guns formed nearly solid orange and red lines that stabbed into the beach with seemingly geometric precision. As the sun began to rise, specially modified Landing Craft Infantry (LCI) ships hurried toward the shore and erupted in volleys of inaccurate but devastating rockets at Japanese pillboxes, command posts, and machine-gun nests. In total, on this day alone, they fired nearly 1,400 rounds of fourteen- and sixteen-inch shells, 1,332 rounds of eight-inch shells, 2,430 rounds of six-inch shells, 13,130 rounds of five-inch shells, along with 9,000 rockets.[6]

The sun had risen by 0630, ushering in a sunny, warm day with near-perfect invasion conditions. If anything, the barrage only intensified in the daylight, obscuring the beaches in plumes of grayish smoke. At this moment, carrier-based fighters and torpedo planes, mostly from the USS *Wasp* and *Yorktown*, swooped in and unleashed a wave of bombs and strafing, mostly on the invasion beaches. Japanese antiaircraft opposition was desultory at best. In all, the strike planes flew nearly five hundred strafing sorties. They dropped over four hundred tons of bombs and shot at anything that moved on the ground, disrupting Japanese communications and mobility, destroying gun positions, blasting troop concentrations. Above the strike aircraft, spotter planes flew in lazy circles. Inside these planes, trained observers radioed target information back to the ships, enhancing the accuracy of the naval gunfire.

Watching this grand spectacle from their landing craft, the assault troops were deeply impressed. The W-day bombardment was the culmination of seventeen days of aerial and naval pasting of Japanese defenses. "It made you wonder if anything could live through this pounding," Private First Class William Welch, a first scout in L Company, 9th Marine Regiment, commented. Hundreds of other Marines had the same impression, especially those who were new to combat. To Corporal Maury Williams, a recon scout with the 21st Marines (the Corps often referred to its regiments, but never its divisions, in this fashion), the bombardment was so intense that "it seemed that the island itself would sink into the depths of the waters from the terrific pounding it was taking. I was convinced that not many Japs could survive that fire."[7]

Others, especially those with prior combat experience, knew better. In previous invasions, they had seen similarly impressive bombardments that failed even to dent Japanese resistance. So, in reality, how effective was this preinvasion barrage? "I would say that the [preinvasion] fires were the most effective of any operation in the Pacific," Major L. A. Gilson, the III Marine Amphibious Corps naval gunfire officer, later wrote. Another Marine gunnery officer asserted that "when the morning of the landing arrived, it was known that the assault troops would meet little resistance." Of course, in this passive-voice claim, the officer did not outline exactly who thought this and why. Certainly, though, the assault troops enjoyed no such certainty (although they definitely hoped resistance would be light). Navy sources were equally effusive, claiming that, after the bombardment, the Japanese could defend Guam's west coast, where the landings were about to take place, with nothing bigger than machine guns.

However, Japanese sources indicated otherwise. After the war, Lieutenant Colonel Hideyuki Takeda, the highest-ranking enemy survivor, indicated that the bombardment had done considerable damage, but not enough to negate powerful Japanese resistance. Takeda estimated that the bombs and shells eliminated about half of the field positions along the coast, all naval gun emplacements in the open, and about half of the guns that the Japanese were hiding in caves. In addition, the aerial strafing restricted the movement of Japanese soldiers and demolished buildings that were not reinforced by concrete. Casualties from all this ordnance were surprisingly low, although some enemy soldiers were destroyed mentally—the Americans called this psychoneurosis or combat fatigue; the Japanese thought of it as a "serious loss of spirit." The American shells failed to do much damage to any emplacements with more than fifty centimeters of concrete. Nor did they disrupt enemy communications in any meaningful fashion. Basically, for the average Japanese soldier, it was possible to hunker down and wait out the bombardment, terrifying though it may have been.

Without question, the seventeen-day bombardment degraded Japanese resistance in significant ways, but it could not work the miracle of eliminating resistance altogether. Admiral Conolly's perspective reflected this reality of warfare: "Effectiveness cannot be measured . . . by a total absence of opposition but by what might have been had this [fire support] been lacking." The bombardment, he felt, was the best he had seen up to that time. Undoubtedly he was right. His task force did an outstanding job. But, even in the absence of any meaningful Japanese air or sea opposition, Conolly knew that American naval and air units could only assist the ground troops, not do the job for them. "The bombardment cannot attain physical land objectives. There always must be fighting by the troops on the shore to secure the positions," he wrote.[8]

At 0800, the landing craft began to head into the smoke-shrouded beaches. From LSTs some of the troops had boarded directly onto LVTs (Landing Vehicle Tracked), which would take them on their actual beach runs. These specially designed amphibious vehicles were often called amtracs or alligators. They were ideal for breaching the coral reef. Other Marines transferred from their shallow-draft, untracked Higgins boats by climbing over the sides and hopping into bobbing LVTs just before reaching the reef.

Now was white-knuckle time. Most of the boats had been circling in the water for several hours, giving the Marines plenty of time to get wet, seasick, and very nervous about hitting the beach. Faces were drawn and tight. Stomachs were queasy. The raw fear stimulated adrenal glands, enhancing the senses. "Your senses are different when you're about to invade," one Marine explained. "The sun is never brighter, the sky is never bluer, the grass, the jungle is never greener, and the blood is never redder. All your senses are just tingling."

Even as friendly shells shrieked overhead, exploding at unseen targets a few hundred yards ahead on the coastline, the Japanese began shooting at the vulnerable landing craft. The UDTs had done their job so well that there was little to fear from mines or obstacles. Instead, the Japanese lobbed a disconcerting number of mortar and artillery shells at the American invaders.

Machine guns splayed bullets along the line of boats, kicking up finger- and hand-sized splashes in the water from near misses. Marine infantrymen drew lower in their boats. Many of them could hear the pinging sound of bullets glancing off the protective armor of their LVTs. Gunners and coxswains had no choice but to remain in their exposed positions, swallowing their bile-globbed fear, praying silently that nothing would hit their boats. Corporal Williams could not resist the curious urge to peek over the side of his LVT to see what was going on. "Explosions and geysers were erupting all around us and I then came to know the fear that would live with me constantly, minute by minute, for the rest of that seemingly endless day." He watched in stunned silence as an enemy shell scored a direct hit on a troop-laden amphibious truck (DUKW, generally called ducks) some twenty-five yards away. "It was at that point that I realized . . . my life was not as precious to the Japs as it was to my family and myself." It was his disquieting introduction to the often impersonal killing of modern combat. All up and down the mighty lines of boats inexorably headed for Guam's coast, some took direct hits; most did not. Smoke wafted in plumes overhead, while water splashed everywhere in a confusing mishmash of boat wakes and near misses.

Aboard another LVT headed for Green Beach, radioman Jack Kerins glanced at his buddy Private Harold Boicourt and noticed how pale and waxy his face looked. Kerins reached out and touched Boicourt and the latter jerked in surprise "as if he'd been shot." Kerins tried to cheer him up by referring to a song they both liked. Boicourt only stared back with glassy, dilated eyes, almost as if he could no longer comprehend English. A few moments later, an explosion rocked the right side of the boat. "When we looked up," Kerins said, "our machine gunner was draped limply over his weapon . . . dead." In a nearby boat, Private First Class Bill Conley, a machine gunner in K Company, 21st Marines, popped up for a look around and was impressed with how many dead fish were floating in the water, including "a barracuda three or four feet long."[9]

Between 0830 and 0900 the first waves landed on their respective beaches against varying levels of resistance. To the south, at Agat, the 1st Provisional Marine Brigade took intense fire at Yellow and White Beaches. "The beach defenses were well organized and consisted of numerous concrete pillboxes built in coral cliffs and an elaborate trench system extending inland from the water's edge with many well-concealed machine gun emplacements and tank

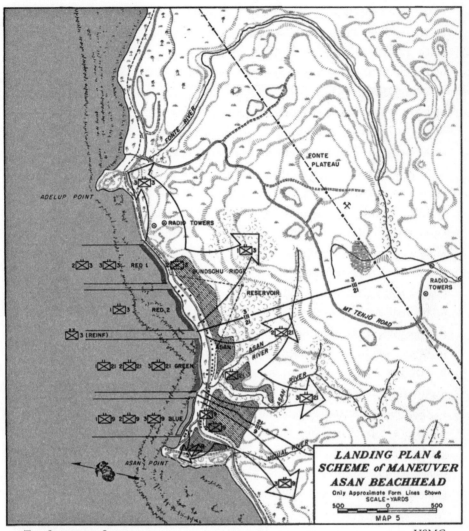

THE SOUTHERN LANDINGS USMC

traps," the brigade's war diary vividly recorded. "Heavy resistance was encountered from enemy small arms, machine gun and mortar fire." At Gaan Point, right in the middle of the landing beaches, a substantial blockhouse with one 37-millimeter gun and two 75-millimeter pieces savaged the approaching LVTs with enfilade (flanking) fire. "The blockhouse was covered by earth to form a large mound, and was well camouflaged," Lieutenant Colonel Robert Shaw, the brigade's intelligence officer, wrote. Protected by a four-foot-thick roof, and built into the very nose of the point, the blockhouse's guns picked off one LVT after another. The shells tore through the thin American armor, igniting fuel tanks, spreading deadly shards, burning men and tearing them apart. Staff Sergeant John O'Neill, a platoon sergeant in L Company, 22nd Marines, was riding in an LVT that churned right into the kill zone. He could see six nearby LVTs already burning and could hear enemy fire above the engine noise. "There was a sudden explosion, a searing blast of heat. The heat and acid smell of black powder was in the air." The LVT had taken a direct hit on the left side, igniting the driver's compartment into flames. One of the crewmen was badly wounded, blood pouring from open wounds. Staff Sergeant O'Neill ordered everyone to inflate their life vests and hop over the side. They waded through waist-high water, under fire, some five hundred yards to the beach.

The blockhouse guns continued pumping shells into the LVTs. They torched one boat carrying the 3rd Battalion, 22nd Marines, headquarters group, killing the battalion's executive officer. In total, the Americans lost two dozen landing craft from enemy fire and mechanical problems. Because of the way the enemy position was built, the Navy could not get a clear enough shot at it, meaning that the ground troops had to take it out. Those Marines who made it to the beach found themselves on the sloping ground just inland, involved in close-quarters firefights with entrenched groups of Japanese, killing the enemy soldiers at hand grenade range, then pushing farther inland as fast as possible. In one such firefight, Staff Sergeant O'Neill was organizing his platoon's movement when the man next to him suddenly got hit by enemy machine-gun fire. "I stood frozen to the ground and watched the burst take the top of his head off. It seemed like I stood there a lifetime before I could take my eyes from the horrid sight before me. I regained my senses and hit the deck." With the help of another platoon, they poured fire on the Japanese position, enveloped it, and killed the enemy soldiers.

The Americans also had to assault enemy-held caves, often with the help of tanks. One such cave contained a two-man machine-gun nest whose fire wounded thirteen Marines. American small-arms fire and grenades did nothing to the crew. A newly landed tank rumbled up and pumped three rounds into the cave entrance. One of the enemy soldiers ran out of the cave and sprinted successfully for the safety of another cave. His partner killed himself with a grenade rather than be taken alive. Behind Gaan Point, another group of Marines, augmented by Sherman tanks, maneuvered behind the infamous blockhouse and destroyed it from behind, mainly with tank fire. By early afternoon, the brigade had suffered 350 casualties but had carved out a lodgment a few hundred yards deep. The 77th Division's 305th Regimental Combat Team stood offshore, ready to reinforce the Marines. Burial parties later counted 75 Marine bodies at Yellow Beach alone.[10]

The northern landings were a mixed bag. Generally speaking, the bitterest fighting was in the middle to northern portion of the landing area, from Asan village to the Chonito cliffs near Adelup Point. On the southern end of the two-thousand-yard stretch of beach, near Asan Point, the 9th Marines enjoyed a reasonably smooth landing, although the initial waves were at times pinned down by withering Japanese machine-gun and mortar fire. "The best we could do was crawl forward until we could see an enemy position, then shoot, throw grenades, use flamethrowers, and any other method available to overrun or push back the enemy," Private First Class Welch recalled. According to one witness, the Japanese "clung tenaciously to installations such as caves, roadblocks, or dug-in positions. Very few surrendered, and it was necessary to destroy each individual in his position." Fighting in this fashion, the regiment secured most of its W-day objectives, including Asan Point.[11]

In the middle, at Green Beach, the 21st Marines assaulted in the shadow of an imposing cliff, some one hundred feet high, that loomed menacingly over the water and posed a seemingly impenetrable barrier. Regimental commander Colonel Arthur Butler and his staff had studied, in their preinvasion planning, photographs of two defiles that cut into either side of the cliff. Butler planned to envelop and scale the cliff by sending his 2nd Battalion to the left defile and his 3rd Battalion to the right. "It took ingenuity, back-breaking work under a blazing tropical sun, and a hell of a lot of fighting to do the job," one regimental officer said.

Indeed it did. When the first waves of the 21st waded ashore, they dodged

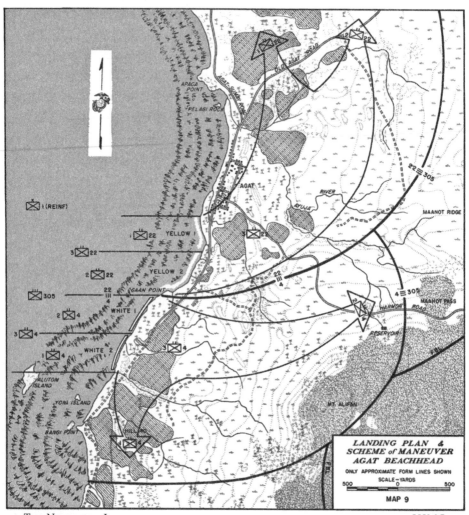

THE NORTHERN LANDINGS   USMC

in and out of shell holes made by the Navy's bombardment and took shelter in the lee of the cliff. The water from the reef to the edge of the beach was under constant mortar and machine-gun fire from unseen Japanese soldiers on the high ground. LVT coxswains, dodging the intense fire, gunned their engines to the beach, dropped ramps, and practically threw their Marines ashore. It took nearly two hours for Butler's officers to organize the battalions and make the movement up the cliffs. In that time, the fire grew more intense as the Japanese figured out where the Americans were hiding.

At last, the infantry Marines began their arduous climb, blending in, as best they could, with the thick green foliage and jagged brown ridges that ringed the defiles. Colonel Butler, from a ditch on the beach where he had set up his command post (CP) to avoid mortar fire, raised binoculars to his eyes and watched his men. One of his intelligence officers did the same: "Through field glasses they looked like so many flies crawling up the side of the living room wall. [They] slowly pulled themselves up the cliff, clinging to scrub growth, resting in crevices, sweating profusely in the broiling tropical sun." Private First Class Frank "Blackie" Hall, a twenty-one-year-old New Jersey native and first scout in F Company, was in the lead of the 2nd Battalion advance. "It was not all cliff. I don't mean we were hanging by our toenails and fingernails but there were times it was quite steep." The opposition was lighter than he expected, mostly just small-arms fire from handfuls of enemy soldiers in caves or gullies. The battalion did not reach the top until several hours later, well into the afternoon.

On the right, the 3rd Battalion Marines worked their way up the southern defile, across a small road, along the Asan River. Here too opposition consisted of small, disorganized groups of enemy soldiers. "They were dug in . . . under the ground everywhere," Private First Class Frank Goodwin said. "They had . . . trap doors that they could throw open and start shooting. We were taking mortar fire from the hills." A machine-gun nest opened up. Two bullets tore into Goodwin's buddy, hitting him in the chest, killing him instantly. Everyone else hit the ground. As was so common in these situations, most of the men hugged the ground and merely waited for things to quiet down, or someone to take charge. In the meantime, a few brave individuals maneuvered around, figured out the guns' location, and killed the enemy soldiers at close range, with grenades and small arms. In this manner, with plenty of stops and starts, the battalion reached the top of the cliff by midafternoon.

The 21st Marines had accomplished the amazing feat of taking the cliff in the face of enemy opposition. But they were exhausted from the heat, the sheer physical challenge of climbing such steep ground, and dealing with the stress of fighting groups of Japanese who could pop up anywhere. They were thirsty. They already missed buddies who had been killed or wounded in the course of the day. They were bruised and scraped from diving for cover and crawling along the earth. Their trousers and fatigue blouses were disheveled and torn. Even so, they knew they had to hold this newly won high ground. If the Japanese got it back, they could "place observed fire on all our beach installations, the Division command post and the Regimental Command Post," one officer later wrote. Tired or not, the Americans dug in a few hundred yards inland, along a prominent ridge that overlooked the cliff. Whether they liked it or not, they knew that modern combat was about physical endurance as much as anything else.[12]

Butler's Marines would have been chagrined to learn that their 3rd Marine Regiment comrades a few hundred yards to the left had an even rougher landing. Here too the terrain presented a major obstacle. To the left of Red Beach, Adelup Point (referred to as "the Devil's Left Horn" by the Americans) jutted gracefully into the sea, flanking the landing beaches. A massive seaside red-clay ridge, known as the Chonito Cliff, towered over much of Red Beach. Not far from the waterline, a seawall offered a bit of cover but also restricted movement for men and vehicles alike. Japanese mortar and artillery observers, augmented by machine gunners and riflemen, were holed up in caves within Chonito Cliff, overlooking the water. They had even built tunnel systems to connect caves. This afforded them protection from the preinvasion bombardment along with excellent sight lines and fields of fire. Farther inland, the cliff gave way to a dizzying array of rice paddies and ridges (the most prominent of which was named Bundschu Ridge after a company commander) that typified much of the terrain behind all the invasion beaches. "The innumerable gulleys [sic], valleys and ridges might as well have been gorges and mountains," the division after action report sardonically commented.

Colonel W. Carvel Hall, the regimental commander, planned a quick two-battalion attack, designed to get inland, envelop the cliff, and neutralize the ridge, all before the Japanese could recover from the shock of the bombardment. The problem was that the enemy soldiers had not been particularly hard hit by the barrage. They were alert and ready, waiting for the most advantageous moment to open fire. Artillery pieces on Adelup Point menaced the Marine LVTs as they closed in on Red Beach. Mortar shells and Nambu machine-gun fire greeted boats as they inched onto the bracketed beach. In one LVT, Corporal Pete Gilhooly, a squad leader in I Company, hurled himself over the side, steadied himself under the weight of his sixty-pound pack, and ran up the beach. "I was looking right into a Japanese bunker, right on the beach. Without further ado, I threw a hand grenade in there and took off." He and his comrades crossed a beach road, then turned to ascend the side of the cliff. At this point, I Company and the whole 3rd Battalion ran right into the cross fire of the concealed Japanese defenders. They were taking fire from cliff-side caves as well as the distant ridges. The result was horrible. "They attacked up a 60-degree slope," a Marine correspondent wrote, "protected only by sword grass, and were met by a storm of grenades and heavy rifle, machine-gun, and mortar fire. The physical act of forward motion required the use of both hands." In one company alone, half of the Marines were killed. "You could see little black figures crawling up the slope," one Marine witness later wrote. "You could see little black puffs of smoke coming out around them, which were grenades the Japanese were throwing at them. You could see the guys tumble up and roll back down the hill."

The beach itself was also under withering mortar, artillery, and machine-gun fire. Troops who were unloading supplies, litter bearers who were hauling wounded men, and carrying parties that were attempting to get ammo, equipment, and water to the forward Marines found that any movement could bring death. Pinned-down men lay in clumps, waiting out the shelling, resting, or steeling themselves for the courage to get up and move forward. The rotting, humid smell of death hung over the beach. In the tropical air, the dead were decomposing quickly. "Shore parties were working over the bodies as fast as they could under enemy fire, but it was a difficult job just to stay alive yourself, let alone identify a corpse and dig a grave in the beach for it," one Marine observed. Navy corpsmen scurried around, treating the growing number of wounded men lying on litters. Many were at the waterline, waiting to be picked up by LVTs that were themselves still under fire. In one part of the beach, a wounded Marine with a destroyed foot limped around, in a daze, whimpering for a corpsman.

The battle, like most, was not an organized, precise effort. It degenerated into a ragged contest of small groups, on-the-spot leadership, and physical probabilities. The caves were the main battlegrounds. Squad-sized groups of Marines, sometimes assisted by tanks, assaulted the caves. Flamethrower men took the lead. Stinking of fumes, bending under the weight of their cumbersome fuel tanks, they edged up to caves and torched them with two-second bursts. Nearly every cave had to be taken or sealed because, when outflanked, the Japanese would not retreat to their own lines. Instead they would stubbornly stay in place and fire on the Americans from the rear.

For the infantry, the day dragged on (at least for those lucky enough to survive), melting into one assault after another. Nothing could be taken without the foot troops taking the lead, yet often they could make little headway without tank support. The 3rd Marines took the cliff about midday, but they remained under intense enemy fire. In just one typical instance, mortar fire killed six men and wounded two others in Corporal Gilhooly's squad. A few hours later, the regiment took Adelup Point, following an intensive barrage by destroyers, rocket ships, and tanks. Resupply was now a problem since it was very difficult to haul crates of ammo, food, and water cans up the cliff. Any movement on flatter ground provoked enemy fire. Ingenious Marines rigged up cables to and from the cliff, in order to move supplies and wounded men. For a longer-term solution, engineers and Navy construction battalions (Seabees), with the help of bulldozers, scooped out a road at the tip of the cliff, all the while under fire. By the time the sun set on that horrible July 21, the 3rd Marine Division and 1st Provisional Marine Brigade had carved out shallow beachheads, none more than a few hundred yards deep. The 3rd Marine Division alone had suffered 105 killed in action, 536 wounded, and 56 missing in action. With every passing hour, though, the Americans grew stronger as reinforcements and supplies came ashore, all protected under the watchful gaze of a powerful, unopposed fleet.[13]

The Japanese planned to crush this lodgment before it could grow any larger. From the beginning, their intention was to defend Guam at the waterline, counterattack immediately with all-out banzai charges, and repel the invasion. Like Germany's Erwin Rommel, who had opposed the Normandy invasion the previous month, the Japanese at Guam believed that the Americans were at their most vulnerable during the invasion itself. If allowed to come ashore in large numbers and build up their awesome array of firepower and logistical capability, they would inevitably prevail. Imperial General Headquarters in Tokyo, and Lieutenant General Takeshi Takashina, the Japanese commander at Guam, believed that "victory could be gained by early, and decisive, counterattacks." For two years, since Guadalcanal, this had been the Japanese approach: defend at the waterline, counterattack, and overwhelm the Americans with all-out banzai attacks that epitomized the Japanese fighting spirit (*yamato-damashii*), and thus Japanese superiority. Guam was the classic case of this offensive mentality. "Counterattacks would be carried out in the direction of the ocean to crush and annihilate [the Americans] while [they] had not yet secured a foothold ashore," Lieutenant Colonel Takeda later wrote.[14]

On the evening of July 21–22, the Japanese began a series of such disjointed attacks against the American beachheads. Most of the attacks consisted of infiltration by individual Japanese soldiers or groups of a dozen, twenty, or thirty. This followed the tableau of the Pacific War. At night the Japanese liked to sneak into American "lines," which were usually nothing more than perimeters of loosely organized foxholes. "They come to you," one Marine commented, "especially at night. They infiltrate very well." The Japanese attempted to crawl close to the holes, surprise the occupants, and kill them at close range. Through long experience, the Americans knew to expect such frightening personal assaults. Men slept in shifts or in fits and starts. By and large, anyone moving at night outside of their holes was fair game. Navy ships assisted the ground troops by illuminating the area with star shells, bathing the landscape in undulating half-light all night long. "These would light up several hundred feet overhead, and slowly drift downward providing a light bright enough to detect anyone moving near you," Private Welch recalled.

Most of the Japanese activity on this night consisted of these sorts of terrifying but small-scale encounters. The exception was the 1st Marine Provisional Brigade sector, where Colonel Tsunetaro Suenaga, commander of the 38th Infantry Regiment, ordered a full-scale attack, with General Takashina's permission, to eliminate the American Agat beachhead. What is truly revealing is that both officers knew the attack would probably fail to annihilate the American beachhead, and would likely destroy the remaining combat power of the 38th. Yet they still decided, with little debate or caution, to do it. In this sense, they were facing a logical consequence of the decision Takashina and his superiors in Tokyo made to resist the American invasion at the waterline and push them into the sea with immediate counterattacks. They had designed their defenses, and deployed their soldiers, with this in mind. Now, with the successful American landing, they felt their best option was to carry out their original plan. But there was something else at work here. So powerful was the self-sacrificial suicide *yamato-damashii* cult among Japanese officers on Guam that such an attack seemed the only proper course of action. In so doing, they were, in effect, putting their heads in a collective noose and even fastening that noose in place.

That night, when the order filtered down the ranks, the Japanese soldiers took the news with sadness and stoicism. They were good soldiers who followed orders. Beyond that, though, they were products of a culture that placed a high value on meaningful gestures, personal sacrifice, and eternal honor. Some of the men cried. Most burned letters and mementos from home. The men of one battalion ate a last meal of rice and salmon, washed down with liberal quantities of sake. Colonel Suenaga burned the colors of his regiment lest they fall into enemy hands.

At around midnight on July 22, they unleashed a volley of mortar and machine-gun fire while the lead troops, screaming at the top of their lungs, rushed forward in waves, crashing into the American frontline foxholes. "The Japs came over, throwing demolition charges and small land mines like hand grenades," one Marine infantryman remembered. "Six Marines were bayoneted in their foxholes." The Americans opened up with machine guns, rifles, grenades, and mortars. Fighting raged back and forth for control of Hill 40, a prominent patch of high ground that overlooked the beach. In the eerie half-light, combat was elemental, often man-to-man, the sort of vulgar struggle that permanently scarred men's minds with the awful memories of intimate killing.

One key to the American stand was artillery. Since about midday, many batteries of the 12th Marines and the 40th Pack Howitzer Battalion had been in place, firing in support of the infantry. Now, in the middle of the night, the gun crews responded to fire mission requests, even though their positions were under attack. "Our battery fired between 800 and 1,000 rounds of ammunition that night," Lieutenant P. A. Rheney of the 40th recalled. In one gun pit, Captain Ben Read, the battalion's executive officer, spotted four shadowy figures following a line of communication wire. He challenged them and they rolled away, whispering in Japanese. A gunnery sergeant in an adjacent hole threw a grenade, killing one Japanese. Rifle fire killed the other three. "By about 0130, we were up to our necks in fire missions and infiltrating Japs,"

Read wrote. "Every so often, I had to call a section out for a short time so it could take care of the intruders with carbines and then I would send it back into action again [firing their howitzers]." In another gun pit, Private First Class Johnnie Rierson saw four enemy soldiers, exposed by the light of a flare, edging toward his position. He and another Marine opened fire with their carbines. "We killed one, but another one was only wounded. He kept trying to toss grenades into our gun pit before he died, but they hit a pile of dirt. That saved us." They later found two bodies a few yards away.

Night attacks are always among the most difficult of operations, even under the best of conditions, and for the Japanese, these were hardly the best of conditions. The Japanese attack quickly degenerated into a confused melee, with small fanatical groups wandering around, looking for trouble, then getting cut down by American firepower, particularly machine guns. In one instance, a Japanese soldier was silhouetted against a ridge, fully visible under the light of a flare, yelling at the Marines: "One, two, three, you can't hit me!" The Americans riddled him with a hail of rifle bullets. Elsewhere, Colonel Suenaga, brandishing a sword, was leading his men. He got hit by mortar fragments, staggering him. A rifle bullet finished him off. He went down in a lifeless heap.

The most serious threat to the U.S. Agat beachhead was an enemy tank-infantry attack on the Harmon Road in the 4th Marine Regiment sector. The Marines could hear "the elemental noise of motors and guns and tank treads grinding limestone shale. Banzai screams pierced the flare-lit night." There were four light tanks, with thin armor and small guns (so small they were derided as "tankettes" by the Americans). Private First Class Bruno Oribiletti destroyed two of the tanks with bazooka fire before he himself was killed. A platoon of Sherman tanks, augmented by howitzer fire from Captain Read's battalion, blew up the other tanks. Most of the Japanese infantrymen around the tanks fought to the death. By dawn, after a furious night of fighting, Colonel Suenaga's attack was over. The 38th Infantry had practically ceased to exist. Japanese bodies were lying everywhere, rotting in the rising sun. Captain Read found a dozen corpses near his gun pit. "The dead Japs did not have weapons, but were loaded with demolitions and grenades." They had intended to blow up the howitzers. Staff Sergeant O'Neill of the 22nd Marines also counted twelve enemy bodies near his position. "All night, the Japanese [had] probed our lines, first one place, then another." The American beachhead remained secure. All Colonel Suenaga had succeeded in accomplishing, besides his own demise, was weakening the Japanese ability to defend against American efforts to break out of the Agat beachhead. Dismal failure or not, the pattern was set. The Japanese on Guam now chose to succeed or fail with such counterattacks.[15]

Fright Night

The evening of July 25 was rainy and tense. For several days, the Americans had advanced incrementally, launching costly daylight attacks, enduring nighttime infiltrators and small banzai assaults. The two American beachheads still had not joined hands. Neither of them was any more than a couple miles deep. Casualties were piling up. Infantrymen dug shallow foxholes along ridgelines or any other high ground they could find. Frontline positions consisted of various holes, each one about three feet deep (at best), spaced several yards apart, with two or three men in each hole. Mortars and artillery pieces were in gun pits a few hundred yards behind the forward holes. In the 3rd Marine Division's beachhead, medics had set up a field hospital in a draw, just inland from the beach. Support troops were having a difficult time resupplying the frontline fighters because of bad weather, challenging terrain, and Japanese mortar and artillery fire. Guam was shaping up as a slow, bloody slog.

The Japanese were also hurting. Day by day the Americans were grinding them down with their relentless attacks and firepower. General Takashina had lost about 70 percent of his combat troops, along with many of his commanders. His units were immobilized during the day by pervasive American air strikes and naval barrages. By July 25, he believed that his men would not be able to stand the mental strain of the American attacks much longer. Takashina felt that, at this rate, he and his men were simply waiting for inevitable defeat and death. In the words of one of his officers, the general felt that "some effective measure was urgently needed."

For Takashina, that effective measure meant an attack. *Yamato-damashii* demanded aggressiveness, not passive defense. Takashina felt that the American lodgment was still vulnerable. He must eliminate it before the Americans had time to land more troops, more vehicles, and permanently entrench themselves with their incredible ability to build roads, organize their ground forces,

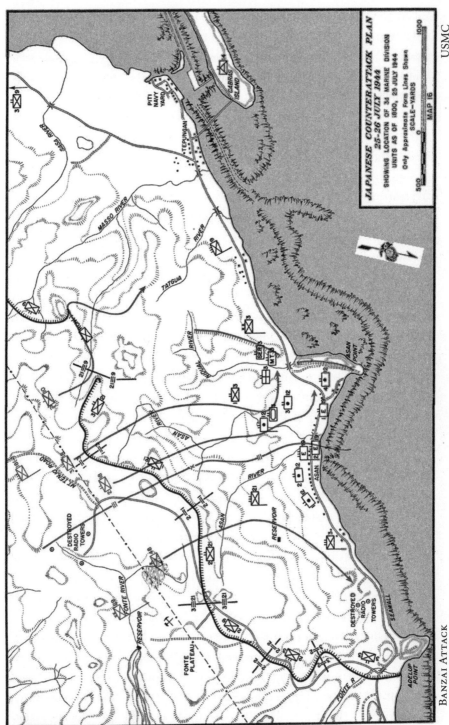

Banzai Attack

and employ superior technology. He made up his mind to gather his remaining strength and launch an all-out effort to push the Americans into the sea. Although this would be a nighttime banzai attack, it would not merely be a mindless suicidal gesture. Takashina planned to amass the remnants of his 18th Infantry Regiment, along with the 48th Mixed Brigade, and hurl them at the 21st Marines while exploiting the gaps that existed between the positions of the 21st and its neighboring regiments. Having breached the American lines, Takashina's stalwarts would then savage the American rear areas, thus extinguishing the Asan beachhead. Meanwhile, at Agat, the 38th Infantry's survivors, many of whom were bottled up on the Orote Peninsula, were to fight their way out and inflict devastating losses on the 1st Marine Provisional Brigade. The plan was a long shot, based on audacity and verve. It was the ultimate example of the prevailing Japanese notion that American invasions could only be defeated at the waterline by overwhelming, self-sacrificial counterattacks.

So, on the night of July 25, as periodic thunder showers pelted frontline Marines, filling their holes with water, the Japanese exchanged good-byes with one another and said final prayers in preparation for their sacred assault. The mood among them was one of sadness laced with grim determination. The word *gyokusai* (meaning death with honor) could be heard passing from the lips of many of these men. "Some took out photographs of their parents, wife, or children and bid farewell to them," Lieutenant Colonel Takeda wrote, "some prayed to God or Buddha, some composed a death poem and some exchanged cups of water at final parting with intimate comrades. All pledged themselves to . . . meet again at the Yasukuni Shrine [in Tokyo]." The men believed that their spirits would live on forever at this great national shrine. Most fortified themselves with generous quantities of sake. A few might even have dulled their fears with narcotics. Forward they went, into the night, in groups small and large, noisy and quiet.[16]

A few hundred yards—and another culture—away, many of the Americans could sense that something was afoot. Most expected the same sort of limited banzai attacks that they had absorbed, and defeated, the last few nights. This soggy, humid evening would be no different, or so they thought. The rain ended, leaving only the sounds of occasional firing along the front. Beads of water dripped from trees or the edges of foxholes. Young Americans settled in for yet another frightening evening of keeping watch for enemy infiltrators. One of those Americans, Frank Goodwin, an eighteen-year-old kid from Malden, Massachusetts, was sitting in a shallow fighting hole, atop a small hill, peering into the darkness. Around him other men of I Company, 21st Marines, were doing the same thing. At his elbow, his buddy was sleeping since it was Goodwin's turn to keep watch.

Goodwin was huddled behind the protection of several coral rocks that he and his buddy had stacked for protection around their hole. In front of the position, Marines had placed empty ration cans on sticks in hopes that anyone sneaking up on their holes would bump into the cans, thus making noise. Overhead a flare bathed the area in half-light. Goodwin looked down the hill and caught sight of what looked like four tree stumps a couple hundred feet away. He did not remember them being there in the daytime, but he knew the mind could play tricks at night. He woke his buddy and told him to take a look, but he saw nothing. "I stared out in that direction for a long time," Goodwin said, "and as nothing seemed moved I guessed he was right." Besides, if they were that close, they would surely run into the cans. Exhausted from several days of existence on the front lines, Goodwin dozed off with a pistol in his lap.

A couple thousand yards to Goodwin's left, Private First Class Ed Adamski was in a machine-gun nest that served as a forward outpost for F Company, 9th Marines, a unit that had spent the day in bitter combat to capture a patch of high ground known as the Fonte Plateau. The company belonged to the 2nd Battalion under Lieutenant Colonel Robert Cushman. They had been detached from their parent regiment and plugged into the 3rd Marines' sector because the latter regiment had suffered so many casualties.

Tonight was Adamski's twentieth birthday. He had once been an amateur boxer on the South Side of Chicago. Now he was a dog handler. He and about ninety other Marines and sixty dogs comprised the 3rd Marine Division's Provisional War Dog Company. The dogs and their handlers were sprinkled among the division's infantry units. Most of the dogs were Doberman pinschers, Labrador retrievers, or German shepherds. They were intensely faithful companions, superbly trained to detect the presence of the Japanese. Marines liked having them around because, during daylight attacks, they helped locate where the Japanese were. At night, they had an uncanny knack for knowing when infiltrators were approaching. For handlers like Adamski this meant round-the-clock work with little sleep. His Doberman, Big Boy, was fearless.

On W-day, he had steadied the young Marine during an intense enemy mortar barrage. Since then, Adamski's stomach had been tied in knots (a common symptom of fear), but Big Boy's friendship and fearlessness had kept him going.

Just before midnight, Big Boy suddenly jumped up and alerted them, pointing in the direction of the Japanese lines. The machine gunners with Adamski knew what that meant—the Japanese were coming. Big Boy settled down and then alerted them several more times. Adamski told the machine gunners to expect an attack any minute. With dilated pupils and racing hearts that pumped adrenaline-rich blood, they tensed and waited for the onslaught.

On the right flank of the 21st Marines' position, Private First Class Roger Belanger and his buddy Joe Babitz were walking warily through the dark, carrying out a contact patrol in the gap that existed between their regiment and the 9th Marines. Their job was to find where, exactly, the left flank positions of the 9th Marine Regiment were and then report that information back to their own unit. Before leaving for their dangerous patrol, they had smeared mud on their faces to hide their white skin at night. Up ahead they could see the 9th Marines trading shots with an unseen enemy unit. Knowing now the location of the 9th, they decided to turn around and go back to their own unit. They began to descend into a ravine. All at once, Belanger heard Japanese voices in the night. He and Babitz did not know it, but they were right in the pathway of Takashina's lead troops, who were carrying out the general's plan to exploit the gap between the two American regiments.

With every passing second, the Japanese were getting closer. Terrified, Belanger turned and whispered to Babitz: "Joe, take a couple of hand grenades, stick them in the mud with the pin off. Take your .45 [pistol], put it in your hand and have it cocked. I'll watch your back. You watch my back." Ever so quietly, they lay down on the grenades, pistols ready, watching the approaching enemy. There were about thirty or forty of them. Closer they came until they were almost right on top of the two Marines. Belanger's heart was beating so violently that he was sure the Japanese could hear it. "Then, all of a sudden, they stopped. One of 'em started pissing all over us. Then they were laughing. One of 'em gave a kick that hit me on the side of the . . . left rib. I was saying my prayers, to tell you the truth." Another one of the enemy soldiers was holding a bayonet. For a split second, it looked like he would drive the bayonet into Babitz's back but he did not. Belanger was tensed and ready to shoot him. "Then they went by. They kept chattering and chattering, Japanese lingo, and they went down that draw." When the voices died down, Belanger stood up, hollered, "Tojo eats shit!" and hurled all of his grenades into the ravine. Still shaking from their close call, he and Babitz made their way back to their 60-millimeter mortar position in support of C Company, 21st Marines.[17]

In these last few moments before the great attack, other Japanese were nowhere near as stealthy. Private Bill Karpowicz, who was peering into the night, aiming his Browning Automatic Rifle (BAR) in the general direction of the Japanese lines, could hear them "yelling, making noises like beating of metal drums, whistle blowing etc." Another Marine heard the enemy "laughing like shrill hyenas, clanging sabers against bayonets shouting 'The emperor draws much blood tonight.'" Other Americans heard the sounds of bottles shattering amid slurred bellows, shrieks, and screams. The Japanese soldiers hollered many chilling phrases: "Wake up, American, and die!" "Marine, you die tonight!" One even cried "Fuck Babe Ruth!" Sometimes they parroted the Americans, hurling grenades and yelling "Fire in the hole!" or "Corpsman!" The yelling was a classic example of posturing. Human beings, when facing a fight, will often scream, carry on, and strike an aggressive pose in hopes of forcing their opponent to flee. In this instance, though, the Americans were far from intimidated. Although the roaring enemy voices were eerie, most of the Marines were well used to this kind of thing. "It sounded like New Year's Eve in the Zoo," one of them sniffed. There was not one recorded instance of a Marine running away at the sound of the enemy screams.[18]

Supported by an intense mortar barrage, a wave of disjointed attacks hit the American lines just after midnight. Saber-wielding Japanese officers led the way. Enlisted men carried rifles, grenades, knives, bayonets, explosives, and even, in a few instances, pitchforks and baseball bats. Screaming "banzai," they hurled themselves across open ground, into ravines and gullies, over the tops of ridges and up hills, straight into American machine-gun fire. They went down in droves but, in no time, the frenzied survivors were among the American holes. Frank Goodwin was awakened by the bloodcurdling scream of a Japanese soldier who jumped right into his hole. Startled and terrified, he rolled onto his back and pointed his pistol, "firing at the same time, hitting the Jap in the face and he fell right on top of me." All at once, another enemy soldier was in the hole attacking Goodwin's buddy, a large man named

Jernberg. The big Marine grabbed the smaller Japanese soldier, "picked him right up by the crotch . . . and threw him out of the hole and then went after him. Somehow or other, he found a rock in the middle of this and smashed his head in. All along our lines the screaming Japs were making their assault. We fought . . . with anything we could get our hands on, entrenching tools, pistols, rifles, fists, and rifle butts as they were right in the holes with us." Some of the Japanese had explosive demolition kits strapped to their chests. They tried to jump into the American holes and detonate the explosives. "There were pieces of flesh flying all over the area" as Japanese soldiers detonated their kits.

Ed Adamski, the dog handler, saw Big Boy spring to full alert and emit a snarling bark. A split second later, the Japanese were running right at his machine-gun positions. As Big Boy lunged to attack them, the machine gunners opened up, mowing down rows of enemy soldiers. Adamski aimed his carbine at one man and hit him twice in the chest. But there were many more, all over the place, screaming, shooting, and trying to jump into Marine holes. "You could hear 'em popping the grenades on their helmets [to arm them] . . . then the explosion." Adamski was shooting at them with one hand and dragging Big Boy back into the hole with the other. A grenade exploded close, showering his chest with fragments, knocking him out from concussion. Big Boy somehow remained unscathed.

The same could not be said for Private First Class Dale Fetzer's dog, Skipper. When the Japanese attacked Fetzer's foxhole, Skipper obediently remained in the hole while his master fought hand to hand with a Japanese soldier. Another enemy soldier dropped a grenade into the hole. The explosion sent shrapnel into Fetzer's legs, knocking him into the hole. Skipper had massive shrapnel wounds. As the fighting raged around them, Fetzer tried to administer first aid to his beloved dog, but to no avail. The young Marine had his head pressed against Skipper's chest and listened as his companion's heart stopped beating. Rage engulfed Private First Class Fetzer. "I went crazy. I stood up there like a wild man shooting. Around my foxhole, there must have been eight or ten Japs laying there. They shouldn't have killed my dog. That was just like a piece of me."[19]

The situation was beyond chaotic. The fighting was personal, intimate. It was warfare at its most elementary and nasty. Baker Company of the 21st Marines was especially hard hit, and nearly wiped out, because the unit was right in the path of Takashina's main attack. Private First Class Mack Drake, a BAR man in the company, was on the unit's right flank, atop Bundschu Ridge, blazing away at Japanese shapes in the shadowy half-light of flares. A grenade exploded a few feet to the right, breaking his assistant's hip and lacing Drake's right ear, shoulder, and face with fragments. Still, the eighteen-year-old from Hendersonville, North Carolina, kept reloading twenty-round clips into his BAR and shooting. "I . . . shot several of the enemy in front of my position and their bodies were lying in front of me." A sword-wielding Japanese officer saw Drake and charged at him. "He tripped while swinging the sword and fell toward me. I was able to finish him off aided by my K-bar knife." Drake's use of the euphemism "finish him off" is revealing and typical. True, he did end the officer's life, but finishing him off really meant stabbing him to death, a traumatic method of extinction for killer and victim alike, so much so that it is hard for the killer to describe it without the emotional distance afforded by a euphemism.

Not far away, Private First Class Roger Belanger, the mortarman who had earlier bumped into the Japanese as they were infiltrating the American lines, was desperately fighting for personal survival (similar to every other American that night). "My carbine stock was broken [from using it as a club]. I bit one Jap's nose right off his face and spit it out. I had [a] Bowie knife and I used that. I took that Bowie knife and I grabbed him in the stomach and stabbed. We were using rocks or anything. I was taught to chew tobacco and I got to like it and I was spitting in their eyes. I did a lot of atrocious things. It was my life or theirs. It sounds like a movie, but it wasn't." Nearby, an enemy officer sliced open the abdomen of another Marine. The American lay badly wounded, his guts hanging out, creeping down his leg. The Japanese soldier went down in a hail of bullets.[20]

But the Japanese were still coming in ranks four deep. Private First Class Jim Headley, a member of an artillery forward observation team, mowed down several enemy soldiers with accurate carbine fire. He noticed a Marine just ahead, almost in the line of fire, and he kept yelling at him to move, but he would not. Just as Headley was about to run out of ammo, someone from another foxhole passed him a sock full of clips. Alongside Headley, Corporal Elwood Richter was firing with impunity at the approaching figures. "It was like shooting fish in a rain barrel," he later said.

This battalion, the 1st of the 21st Marines, was so hard hit that it was on the verge of total destruction. In this kind of devolving situation, a few courageous individuals can make a world of difference. One such person was Captain William Shoemaker, the commander of A Company. A retreat rumor, stoked by the chaotic fear that was unleashed by the banzai attack, circulated among some of the men. Wearing a captured Japanese trench coat, Shoemaker was all over the place, issuing orders, instilling confidence, telling his men they could not retreat. "Hold your lines, men. If the position falls, the whole beachhead will be endangered," he said. When he again heard someone screaming to withdraw, he stood up and yelled, "No, by God! We stay here and hold them!" His men held him in very high regard so they heeded his orders. In the estimation of Private First Class Walt Fischer, one of his telephone wire men, the captain was "a great guy" and a real leader. The captain asked Fischer to go on several ammo runs to the rear. Fischer braved intense enemy fire to do so. On one run, though, a rifle bullet slammed into him like a baseball bat. "It went along the side of my head and through my ear. It went down my cheek . . . out the back of my ear, out the back of my helmet." A corpsman bandaged his head and got him to the beach. Captain Shoemaker held his unit together, adding much to a stalwart American defense. "[He] contributed tremendously toward the defense of positions that night," the battalion executive officer later wrote.[21]

At the front edge of a sector held by K Company, 21st Marines, Private First Class Bill Conley was hurling grenades into the half darkness. Friendly mortar shells were hitting just ahead, undoubtedly inflicting casualties on the approaching enemy. In the light of the mortar and grenade explosions, he could see Japanese soldiers in crouched and crawling positions, edging closer. Conley looked to the right and glimpsed Japanese soldiers stabbing two riflemen in an adjacent hole. He sensed that the enemy was only a few feet in front of his own hole, but the .30-caliber machine gun was holding them back. Conley's crew ran out of fragmentation grenades so they threw a white phosphorous grenade. White phosphorous is designed to burrow into the skin, burning all the way through the body. Water only intensifies its heat. White phosphorous also emits white smoke. The Japanese saw this, screamed "Gas" to one another and abruptly ceased attacking Conley's hole. "We must have gone through about eight or ten boxes [of ammo], about two hundred fifty rounds in a box. The gun was so hot . . . you could . . . light a cigarette off the barrel." Conley could see enemy bodies lying in piles outside the hole. He estimated that there were about fifty of them out there. To Conley's right, Private First Class Karpowicz was at the end of the company line. Somebody had told him that he was the only man between the 21st and 9th Marine lines. Pointing his BAR to the right, he was shooting at running groups of Japanese. "With the flares bursting, lighting the area, I was able to see the enemy. As I saw, I raked the area. The noise was unbearable, our firing and the racket from the enemy." As fast as he expended magazines, his assistant loaded new ones for him.

Not far away, Lieutenant Bill Lanier was in another hole, confronting a horde of running enemy soldiers. Like nearly every other Marine, he hated them intensely. He saw them as "fiends," or "Japs, Nips," or even "diabolical animals." Like everyone else, he dehumanized them, not just out of hatred, but in order to justify killing them with impunity. Denying the enemy's essential humanity was as old as warfare itself, a crucial component to war's necessary killing. It was also an American cultural tendency, especially in the country's modern wars. As the Japanese charged at Lieutenant Lanier's hole, he and the Americans around him shot them down in droves. There were literally piles of bloody Japanese corpses around the holes. Still, their survivors kept coming, jumping into the Marine holes for death struggles. "Here truly is a personal fight for survival," Lanier wrote. "You are not fighting for glory now, nor for your country, nor your buddy. You are fighting to survive. You kill him by the quickest method you know, not because you are brave or heroic, but because you have no choice."[22]

Elsewhere, Staff Sergeant John O'Neill and his platoon were dealing with a similar situation. "They came in waves and like a solid wall, yelling and shrieking. Every gun we had was blazing away, but that didn't stop them. The first wave broke through." Sergeant O'Neill stood up and emptied an entire BAR clip of twenty rounds into several of them. The survivors dispersed a bit, gravitating away from his hole, attacking other Marines. O'Neill's foxhole buddy, Shorty Ferro, asked: "What are we gonna do?" "Pray that we'll see the sunset," the sergeant replied. O'Neill did but not Ferro, who soon got hit. "His face had been shot away." He sagged and died in the sergeant's arms. Soon American artillery began landing among the fourth and fifth waves of Japanese, inflicting horrible casualties. "Arms and legs flew through the air as thick as rain," O'Neill wrote. An officer, watching the same barrage, compared the flying arms and legs to snowflakes. "Japs ran amuck. They screamed in terror until they died."

The Japanese broke through in many places, so American artillery and mortar crews were often under direct attack themselves. Nonetheless, as the attack wore on, the American supporting fire grew steadily more accurate and more intense. The artillerymen fired twenty-six thousand rounds that night. Tanks also added devastating machine-gun and main-gun fire, cornering many screaming groups in the open. At times the enemy soldiers hurled themselves at the tanks. "Savagely they swarmed upon the mechanized vehicles, oblivious of the vicious machine-gun fire, and frantically pounded, kicked and beat against the turrets in an attempt to get the crew within," a witness recorded. Infantrymen blasted the enemy soldiers off the friendly tanks. One can only imagine how disquieting this experience must have been for the tank crewmen.[23]

Those Japanese who succeeded in breaching the front lines roamed the night, attacking the 3rd Marine Division's rear areas, including its hospital. Others holed up in caves, their courage diminished, waiting for the right moment to escape or to kill any Americans who wished to dislodge them. Confusion reigned supreme for both sides. But the Japanese could not exploit that confusion. Their assault was way too disorganized. Minute by minute, the Americans rallied, stood fast, amassed their firepower, and annihilated the Japanese attackers. "The enemy didn't seem to know what to do after he got behind us," the 3rd Marine Division's after action report accurately commented. A major reason for that was a lack of coordination because of the early loss of leaders. In general, the Japanese soldier depended heavily on his officers. Their army did not value individual initiative on the part of low-ranking soldiers. Draconian discipline was standard. Officers ruled their men with proverbial iron fists. They also were expected to set the example, and lead the way in every combat situation. "The [banzai] attack was led by officers," a 21st Marine Regiment post-battle report explained. "The result was that practically all of their officers were killed initially and the troops that penetrated our lines were 'lost' once they had broken through and lacked the initiative and leadership to carry out their attack."[24]

Thus, by the time the sun had risen, Japanese fortunes had set. In the gathering daylight, the Americans hunted down and killed the remaining

enemy. They killed them in caves and ravines where they had taken confused shelter, apart from their decimated units. Some of the Japanese killed
themselves by holding grenades to their abdomens, blowing out their intestines. The Japanese battalions no longer had any semblance of organization
or command unity. Nearly all of the commanders were dead. The vast majority of Japanese had died within sight of the original American positions. The
beleaguered survivors now found themselves trapped among the Americans, like veritable scorpions in a bottle. As an example, one group of enemy
soldiers was cornered near a gun position by a group of artillerymen from
the 12th Marines. Like most Japanese, they were more interested in death
than surrender. "We were set [upon] by an officer leading a banzai rush," one
of the Marines recalled. "About 10 ft. behind him was one Nip, and about
15 ft. behind him came three more. The officer was killed immediately, the
one behind him wounded and falling back about 20 ft. dying. The others tried
to retreat, but were killed." This deadly drama was repeated in at least a dozen
other spots.[25]

By noon, the crisis was over. Some seven thousand Marine riflemen had
successfully defended nine thousand yards of ground. General Takashina's
great attack had failed miserably. He himself had escaped, although he would
be killed a few days later. The putrefying corpses of his brave soldiers lay
everywhere in mute, ghastly testimony to the dismal failure of a flawed concept. "In some spots there were heaps of cadavers, with a sprinkling of arms
and legs that had been blown from bodies by mortars," a Marine recalled. "It
was impossible to walk two paces without stepping on an already bloating
body." They carpeted the entire battle area. They were tucked into ravines
and lying within strands of tall grass that were waving in the afternoon sea
breeze. They were heaped on the knolls and ridges as well as near American
foxholes. Some were lying half buried in the sand of the invasion beaches.

For fifty yards around Lieutenant Lanier's foxhole "was pile after pile and
row after row of the beasts in every conceivable stage of crawling and charging with arms, legs and weapons in grotesque positions." The lieutenant was
unmoved by the sight. Like most of the other Americans, he was infused with
the dehumanization of war. He hated the Japanese, seeing them as dangerous,
treacherous beasts that must be exterminated. "One never minds seeing dead
Japs—they're just like so many animals." Staff Sergeant O'Neill's platoon had
started the night with thirty-six men. Now fifteen were dead and another

eleven wounded. The ten survivors were "grimed with coral and mud, deep lines etched into young-old faces, the thousand-yard stare of battle shock in their eyes, cracked lips parched with dried blood." They stared dully at the nightmarish scene of slaughter around them. "The enemy dead laid two and three deep in front of our lines. There were many instances of Jap and Marine laying side by side. The ground was slick with blood. Water in the foxholes from the rain was a reddish brown muddy liquid."[26]

The stench was already considerable. The rotten, corrupting, languid smell of death ebbed and flowed on the breeze. Flies and maggots were already descending in pestilential droves to feast on the dead flesh. Private First Class Goodwin, who had fought much of the night with his bare hands, came upon a pile of dead Japanese. "The Japanese were very young and their eyes were wide open . . . and flies were all over them. It was just terrible. It smelled like garbage, rotting garbage . . . with a very sweet smell. Their bodies were all swelled up and black." His torso and his field jacket were covered with the blood of the man he had stabbed to death. He poured an entire canteen of water on himself, trying to wash the blood off, to no avail. He changed clothes but the stains remained on his skin. There were mental stains, too. For the rest of his life, he had trouble sleeping through the night.

At the division hospital, now secure after a horrible evening of fending off banzai assaults, doctors and corpsmen were totally absorbed in treating many hundreds of wounded men. Private Jack Kerins was passing the hospital's surgery tents, on his way to the front, when he noticed the survivors of B Company, 21st Marines, shuffling into the hospital area. He knew that these men were the remnants of a company that had been nearly annihilated. "They were filthy and ragged and wore blood soaked bandages at different places on their bodies. Some were openly crying. I never learned what happened to those Marines, but I do know I'll never forget them." The 3rd Marine Division lost 166 killed, 34 missing, and 645 wounded in the enemy attack.[27]

Ever the souvenir hunters, many of the Americans were already stripping the Japanese bodies of swords, pistols, binoculars, watches, rings, flags, pens, photographs, and other family mementos. A few Marines even carried pliers to remove gold teeth from Japanese corpses. Intelligence specialists combed the bodies for documents and other important military information. None of this would have been appropriate behavior in a "normal" situation. But, in the context of war, it was standard stuff. The same was obviously true for killing. Though the Americans viewed their enemies as animals, and knew they must kill them in order to survive, this still took a toll on everyone who had to take lives. Like other normal human beings, these Marines eventually carried some remorse over having to kill, even under such justifiable circumstances. "After the war was over, my thoughts on killing started to change," Jim Headley wrote. "As time went by, my attitude toward the enemy went from survival to regret—taking a life and sending someone into eternity. This bothered me and stayed on my mind."[28]

S. L. A. Marshall claimed that, in World War II, less than 20 percent of American soldiers ever fired their rifles in combat. He believed that the reluctance to shoot came from an unwillingness on the part of the average American man to kill. He further claimed that, even when men were directly in danger of being killed themselves, they still would not fire their weapons. Marshall was an excellent combat historian who did much pathbreaking work on the realities of battle for infantrymen. He was correct about the intrinsic hesitancy to kill, and he intuited something of the psychological cost of having to do so. However, he exaggerated this pacific tendency's effect on real battles. Moreover, he based his contentions on no verifiable evidence.

In actual combat, American troops did fire their weapons in large numbers and they did kill the enemy in order to survive. The banzai attack at Guam is a prime example of this. The Americans fought with whatever weapons they had in order to survive. If they had not done so, the beachhead would have been destroyed. In fact, rifles and grenades did most of the killing on the evening of July 25–26, not crew-served weapons. This meant that, contrary to Marshall's contentions, men killed their enemies at close range, with no unwillingness to shoot. The surviving accounts and records of the battle—and they are extensive—reveal no instance of an American refusing to fire his weapon, choosing his own death rather than be forced to kill the Japanese. This does not necessarily mean it never occurred, as perhaps this happened to some of the dead and they, of course, cannot contribute their perspective. However, one would think that if such reluctance to fight existed, it would feature prominently in survivors' accounts. Another important point to consider is that the Guam banzai attack was just one of many such similar attacks in the Pacific War, with generally identical results. At Guam and elsewhere,

American troops fought to the death and willingly obliged Japanese suicidal tendencies. With sardonic wit—an American cultural tendency—the Marines on Guam even circulated a handbill that described banzai attacks in the familiar terms of a carnival promotion: "Tonight: Banzai Charge. Thrills, Chills, Suspense. See Sake-Crazed Japs Charge at High Port. See Everybody Shoot Everybody. Come Along and Bring a Friend. Don't Miss the Thrilling Spectacle of the Banzai Charge, Starting at 10 P.M. and Lasting All Night. Admission Free."[29]

The failure of Takashina's Guam gambit destroyed the Japanese position on Guam. He had lost thirty-five hundred of his best soldiers. "The Jap charge had wasted the cream of the enemy troops on the island," the Marine correspondent Alvin Josephy correctly wrote. "After the failure of the charge, they had nothing more to oppose us with." They had lost 95 percent of their commanders and thousands of spirited soldiers, not just in the charge but also in resisting so stubbornly near the waterline since W-day. As a result, their offensive power was shattered. All they could do now was to withdraw their dispirited remnants to more defensible positions and wait for the Americans to overwhelm them. "From that day on, the campaign was all ours," the 3rd Marine Division's after action report succinctly stated. The Americans secured the island, against noticeably diminished resistance, within the next two weeks.

By giving in to their cultural vanity, the Japanese had played right into the American strengths of firepower and tenacity. Attacking Japanese soldiers were out in the open, calling attention to themselves (to put it mildly), thus making perfect targets. This practically guaranteed them a fatal beating from American firepower. In the close-proximity nighttime fight, personal weaponry did most of the actual damage. Had the attack come in the daylight, artillery, mortars, air strikes, and naval gunnery presumably would have decimated them. So, from an American perspective, the banzai attack was the best thing that could happen. "We well know that these night banzai attacks are the best and least costly way of eradicating the largest number of these fiends," Lieutenant Lanier explained. "This way they must come out into the open . . . where you have the protection of your own foxhole and organized fire." Combat infantrymen like Lanier knew that such attacks were terrifying and psychologically damaging, but they were preferable to assaulting strongly fortified Japanese positions full of fanatical enemy who would fight to the death. After Guam, the most thoughtful Japanese commanders understood that banzai assaults were foolish, wasteful, and counterproductive. Instead they now decided to entrench, fight defensively, force the Americans to come to them, and bleed them into nothingness. They would exploit what they saw as American cultural weaknesses—impatience and an unwillingness to suffer large numbers of casualties.[30]

CHAPTER 2
Peleliu, September 1944:
Amphibious Combat Against a Clever,
Defensive-Minded Enemy

The Decision

THE DEBACLE DID NOT HAVE to happen. There was nothing inevitable about it, nor anything truly necessary. With a few words, one man could have stopped it, but he could not bring himself to utter those words.

In late July 1944, Admiral Chester Nimitz, commander of the U.S. Navy's Pacific Fleet, met with President Franklin Roosevelt and General Douglas MacArthur at Pearl Harbor. Nimitz and MacArthur functioned as veritable co-commanders of the American effort in the Pacific. But they were more rivals than partners. They constantly competed for resources and influence with Washington power brokers. During the Pearl Harbor meeting, much to Nimitz's chagrin, MacArthur won the president's support for an invasion of the Philippines. MacArthur proposed to invade Mindanao in November and Leyte in December. Even though the admiral felt that these invasions were not wise strategic moves, he loyally pledged to protect the flanks of MacArthur's invasion force. One way to do that was to invade the Palaus, a Japanese-controlled chain of islands a few hundred miles east of Mindanao, the first Philippine island that MacArthur planned to invade in the fall. Because of a first-rate airfield, Peleliu was the most important island in the Palaus. Nimitz promised the president and MacArthur that he would invade Peleliu in mid-September in order to seize the airfield and cut off any Japanese naval or air threat to the general's Mindanao invasion. Subsequently, planners decided on September 15 for D-day at Peleliu.

A few days before D-day, the Americans discovered that Mindanao was only lightly held and need not be invaded. Aviators from Admiral William "Bull" Halsey's 3rd Fleet had raided Mindanao against almost no opposition. The aviation commander, Vice Admiral Marc Mitscher, recommended scrubbing the Mindanao invasion and Halsey agreed. Halsey felt that now it made more sense to step up the invasion timetable for Leyte to October. For several weeks, Halsey had actually been skeptical of the need for invading Peleliu. He thought the benefits of taking the heavily defended island did not justify the costs. Now, with no Mindanao invasion, he felt there was no purpose to invading Peleliu. He was right. Peleliu was now a strategic backwater. The Japanese garrison there could not hope to interfere with MacArthur's operations in the Philippines, especially if he did not invade Mindanao.

In the early morning hours of September 13, Halsey sent a message to MacArthur, Nimitz, and even Admiral Ernest King, chief of naval operations. "Am firmly convinced Palau not now needed to support occupation of the Philippines." He asked for permission to cancel the Peleliu invasion. MacArthur could not be reached directly. He was at sea with a fleet that was about to invade Morotai. For security reasons, that fleet was maintaining radio silence. Actually, his authority was limited to operations in the Philippines, not the Peleliu invasion (ominously code-named Operation Stalemate).

So the decision on Peleliu was really Nimitz's to make since he controlled most of the naval assets upon which the invasion of that island depended. A careful, pensive man, Admiral Nimitz deliberated for several hours before making a decision. "Carry out . . . Stalemate as planned," he told Halsey. That one fateful sentence consigned thousands to unspeakable misery and horror. Such is the crushing weight of life-or-death responsibility upon the souls of senior commanders. For the rest of his life, Nimitz never explained the reasoning behind his decision. Aptly summarizing the feelings of participants and historians alike, Samuel Eliot Morison, the great naval historian, referred to the Peleliu decision as one of Nimitz's "rare mistakes." During the war, the admiral kept a sign over his desk that read: "Is the proposed operation likely to succeed?" In this particular instance, an otherwise sage commander came up with the wrong answer.[1]

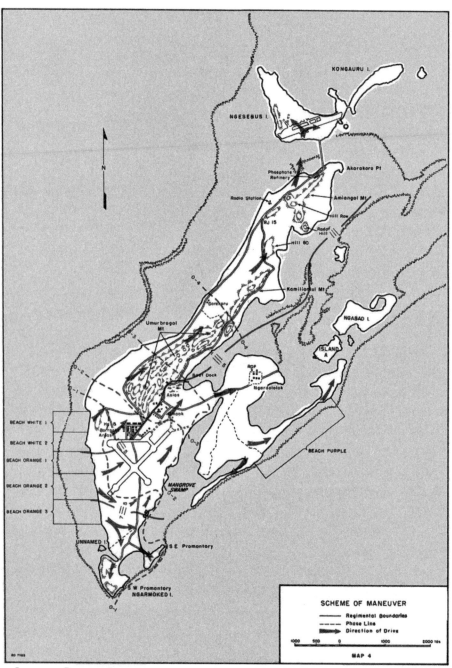

INVASION PLAN AT PELELIU   USMC

produced a bizarre Japanese command arrangement that remains something of a mystery to this day. According to all available Japanese sources, Colonel Nakagawa remained in command, but with a two-star general nominally assisting him. Given the rigid hierarchy of imperial Japan, this strains credulity a bit. The whole truth will probably never be known.

Despite their internal problems, the Japanese, by mid-September, had turned Peleliu into a death trap for the American invaders. The landing beaches teemed with mines, tetrahedrons, gun emplacements, antitank ditches, blockhouses, and machine-gun nests. Farther inland the Japanese had constructed a wide range of pillboxes and well-camouflaged gun positions, mainly to foil any American attempt to capture the airfield. The Umurbrogol now basically consisted of little else besides mutually supporting fortified caves, some of which were equipped with steel doors.

Thanks to documents they had captured on Saipan, the Americans knew much about the Japanese order of battle. But they had no clue about the true nature of Peleliu's imposing terrain, or even much appreciation for the true extent of Japanese defenses. Nor did any American have even an inkling of the new Japanese commitment to inland defense.[2]

The Brief Bombardment

The Navy's bombardment of Guam had been, in the estimation of most American officers, the most successful of the Pacific War. In that instance, the Navy had the rare opportunity to soften up Guam for seventeen days prior to the invasion. Even so, the bombardment did not diminish Japanese resistance enough to avoid major fighting once the Marines and soldiers came ashore. Peleliu was smaller than Guam, with fewer enemy soldiers, but it was much more intelligently defended. Carrier-borne planes raided Peleliu several times in the spring and summer of 1944, but the main job of softening up the island went, of course, to the Navy surface ships.

The original invasion plan earmarked only two days for Admiral Jesse Oldendorf's Western Gunfire Support Group (TG 32.5) to pound Peleliu with the usual array of fire from battleships, cruisers, destroyers, and smaller vessels. Major General Roy Geiger, commander of the III Marine Amphibious Corps, whose 1st Marine Division would assault Peleliu, pleaded with his naval colleagues for one more day and got it. Starting on September 12, Oldendorf's ships plastered Peleliu. His gunners focused especially on visible structures, such as blockhouses, barracks, hangars, administrative buildings, pillboxes, and gun emplacements. The airfield also absorbed a major drubbing. All hangars and buildings were in shambles. Pieces of dismembered aircraft were scattered all over the place. The bombardment also partially defoliated the island, exposing Peleliu's formidable coral ridges to American eyes for the first time (aerial reconnaissance photos had not even begun to do justice to the ridges). As Oldendorf's warships hurled steel at the island, the admiral stood in the combat information center aboard his flagship, the battleship USS *Pennsylvania*. One by one, as reports of destruction trickled in, he scratched each predetermined target off a checklist. The Japanese, true to their plan, did not even fire one round at the American ships. They huddled in their caves and bunkers, waiting for an invasion they now deemed inevitable. As at Guam, highly trained U.S. Navy Underwater Demolition Teams (UDTs) swam, under cover of the fleet's mighty bombardment, into the landing beaches to disarm mines, obstacles, and booby traps.

On September 14, Admiral Oldendorf made a stunning pronouncement. He had run out of targets and was ordering his gun crews to cease fire. The crews would resume their shooting the next morning, in support of the lead assault troops, but, for now, they were to stand down. Oldendorf believed he had destroyed every worthy target on Peleliu. To him it made no sense to "blast away at suspected positions and hope for the best." Better, he thought, to cease fire than waste ammunition. When news of his decision reached senior 1st Marine Division officers aboard their ships, they were shocked. "The dispatch sent by ADM Oldendorf was not only a surprise but was not understood by any of us on the Division Staff," Lieutenant Colonel Lewis Fields, the 1st Marine Division operations officer, wrote. Lieutenant Colonel Frederick Ramsay, another member of the division staff, described the reaction as one of "incredulity." Brigadier General Oliver Smith, the assistant division commander, understood that Oldendorf had hit many visible targets but "the cut-up, jungle terrain concealed many targets that the infantry had to overrun at heavy cost."

By and large, the Marines felt that Oldendorf's decision was calamitous and inexcusable. Their lives were on the line. They were the ones who would face the Japanese on the ground, in the toughest arena of combat, not the sailors. As such, the Marines expected the Navy to support them as fully as possible. Oldendorf's termination order, with his ammunition stocks far from depleted, was hardly the way to fulfill those expectations. Another naval commander, Rear Admiral George Fort, described Oldendorf's decision as "entirely correct." Fort acknowledged the infantry's difficult job but, to him, the idea of firing at an island with no visible targets was "an inexcusable waste of ammunition." Here was a classic difference in thinking between naval and infantry officers. The Navy commanders thought in terms of logistics because so much of their job was dependent upon manipulating cargo, fuel, and time schedules. Successful naval command demanded a strong technical mind and a keen understanding of how to utilize firepower. Marine officers existed in a more simplistic world of operations—closing with the enemy and killing him. All else was subordinated to that mission.

Something else was at work here, too. The naval officers, by the nature of their tasks (not to mention their distance from the battlefield), could scarcely conceive of what combat on the ground really meant. They rarely saw the actual results of their firepower. Few of them, even competent commanders like Fort and Oldendorf, truly understood the limitations of their weaponry. They did not fully realize that the Japanese could, and did, find ways to take shelter from the shells. The enemy hunkered down in caves, tunnels, or bunkers and waited for the shooting to stop. At Peleliu, very few Japanese soldiers fell prey to the pre-landing bombardment. The sailors had trouble realizing this. They thought in terms of hitting pinpoint targets, eliminating positions, and overwhelming the enemy with explosions. From the distance of a few miles offshore, it was hard for them to imagine that anyone, or anything, could survive under the avalanche of their shells. This was an inevitable consequence of their point of view. Inexperienced Marines who had never assaulted an enemy-held island often thought the same way. Only after they went ashore did they realize the terrible reality that enemy soldiers could remain alive and well in the wake of such terrible punishment. The bombardments, they came to understand, looked more impressive than they really were, but this realization only set in as a result of *experience on the ground.* "One must guard against the overenthusiasm of naval gunfire advocates who believe that nothing can survive the heavy preliminary bombardments," Colonel Walter William Wachtler, Geiger's operations officer, wrote.

A classic example of this juxtaposition is a conversation that Colonel

Lewis "Chesty" Puller, commander of the 1st Marine Regiment, had with the captain of his unit's troopship on the morning of D-day, as his Marines prepared to go ashore. "Puller, you won't find anything to stop you over there," the ship's captain claimed. "Nothing could have lived through that hammering." Puller, a commander with years of ground combat experience, demurred. "I doubt if you've cleaned it out. I believe they'll have pillbox stuff, fortifications like we've never seen before." Undeterred, the captain jovially predicted: "We'll expect you for dinner this evening." Puller assured the captain that he and his crew would be back in Hawaii well before the Marines were done with Peleliu.[3]

So, in view of firepower's limitations, was Oldendorf wrong to cease fire? Probably so. Although three days of bombardment could hardly be expected to neutralize Nakagawa's formidable defenses, it was still better than two and a half. If Oldendorf's ships could destroy only a few more enemy gun emplacements, or wound or kill a couple dozen more Japanese soldiers, the job of the ground troops would become just a little bit easier. Perhaps a few more American lives could have been saved. But, of course, no amount of bombardment could completely subdue Japanese resistance. The shooting could only help the Marines, not do the job for them. The Marines did not expect miracles from the Navy, just the absolute maximum level of support that the sea service could provide.

The Assault

The landing beaches stretched for a couple thousand yards along Peleliu's west coast. Puller's 1st Marines were to land on the left flank at White Beaches 1 and 2; the 5th Marines, under Colonel Harold "Bucky" Harris, would land in the middle at Orange Beaches 1 and 2; Colonel Herman Hanneken's 7th Marines would hit the right flank at Orange Beach 3. The airfield was, of course, the main objective. Looking like the numeral 4, it beckoned from just a couple hundred yards inland. Beyond it lay swamps and the dizzying network of jagged ridges, concealed caves, and open valleys that comprised the Umurbrogol.

At 0832, when the first Americans hit the beaches of Peleliu, Japanese opposition was intense. "My surprise and chagrin when concealed batteries opened up on the LVTs [Landing Vehicle Tracked] can be imagined," Admiral Oldendorf later said. The beaches themselves stretched for only about thirty yards before giving way to scraggly jungle foliage that made it difficult to see inland. Mines, obstacles, barbed wire, and booby traps were embedded all over the beaches. Fortunately, the UDTs and the preinvasion bombardment had disarmed and blown up many of the mines. The Japanese had also failed to arm quite a few of them.

Few enemy soldiers were on the beaches themselves. They were in caves, pillboxes, and concrete blockhouses beyond the foliage, just inland. They had pre-sited the entire landing area, from the beaches all the way to a prominent coral reef a few hundred yards offshore. In no time, an awesome volume of fire swept through the entire landing area, turning it into a ghastly killing ground. Artillery and mortar shells tore into amphibious trucks (DUKWs) and LVTs, setting them afire, burning the crewmen, blowing assault troops into the bullet-swept water. "The ammo which had been aboard them was exploding," the 1st Battalion, 1st Marines, history of events recorded, "and occasionally one of [them] would blow up, scattering burning debris over the beach." The 7th Marine Regiment's after action report painted a similarly grim picture of the beach assault: "Direct fire from heavy caliber anti-boat guns took an extremely heavy toll of landing craft. Many of the assault troops were forced to wade ashore without cover from the devastating small arms fire. Beaches . . . were also covered by pre-registered mortar and artillery fires which maintained a steady, unceasing barrage on the landing beaches . . . causing serious disorganization and inflicting heavy casualties."[4]

In fact, that dreary passage, written as it was by an officer after the battle, did not even begin to convey the full **horror** of the fighting. Mortar rounds exploded randomly up and down the beach, spraying fragments into the air, into the sand, and into bodies. Nambu machine guns chattered mercilessly, seemingly inundating the beach with bullets, kicking up sand and water, tearing into men. The bullets shattered bones, blew heads off, lacerated kidneys, and tore muscles into mush. Individual Japanese riflemen picked out unlucky Marines and shot them with impunity. Tanks came under immediate fire once they crossed the reef. "Over half of our tanks received from one to four hits during the ten minutes reef crossing, but none were knocked out," the division after action report related. The tanks were to provide crucial fire support for assaulting infantrymen, and even some measure of cover from enemy small-arms fire.

Ashore, smoke from the friendly bombardment and the burning amtracs wafted overhead in greasy shreds. Most of the Marines had already spent a long morning breathing stale diesel fumes, battling seasickness as their LVTs circled in the water, waiting for the signal to hit the beach. Those who were aboard LVTs that successfully negotiated the reef and made it to shore then jumped over the sides of their amtracs, ran up the beach, sensed the intensity of the fire, and took cover wherever they could. Few could see anyone, or anything, to shoot at. The Americans were caught in a skillfully pre-sited kill zone their enemies had spent many months perfecting. A more desperate situation can scarcely be imagined.[5]

Everywhere, individual Americans struggled to survive and fight back. Corporal Leo Zitko and his fellow Marines had shared a can of boned turkey aboard their landing craft as it roared toward the beach. Now they were pinned down alongside the landing craft, listening to machine-gun bullets clank off the side of the vehicle. "For the first time I began to realize there's a war going on," he wrote. He glanced to his right and saw an unexploded mine an inch away from his elbow. Also to his right, he spotted a blockhouse farther down the beach. The muzzle of a machine gun was poking out of the blockhouse. The muzzle flashed as the gunner depressed his weapon as low as he could and squeezed his trigger, spewing bullets along the ground.

This was called grazing fire. The purpose of the fire was to hit anything within two feet of the ground, especially prone men. One bullet smashed into the man next to Zitko with an ugly thud. "From then on . . . it was just a series of 'close shaves' and 'acts of God.'" Corporal Henry Andrasovsky's landing craft struck a mine and then got hit by a mortar shell. He and his squad scrambled over the sides of the LVT and into the water, just moments before another mortar round hit the amtrac and set it on fire. "A machine gun opened up on us in the water. I'd fire eight rounds out of my M1 [Garand] rifle and dive under the water. The water was about . . . chest deep. The machine gun . . . cut down just about everybody that was on the left side of that [amtrac]. I don't think any of them made it ashore." He ran into some underwater barbed wire, which tore at his clothes. Finally he and four other men made it to the beach. Their only option was to close with the machine gun and kill its crew, a classic infantry mission. Machine-gun fire from another amtrac forced the enemy gunners to duck their heads. Meanwhile, Corporal Andrasovsky and the others crawled close enough to pitch grenades at the gun. The grenades exploded, shredding the Japanese gunners with fragments. The Americans then leaned in closer and shot them point-blank, with no mercy or reflection. It was the very essence of the infantryman's decidedly personal war.

Corporal Alexander Costella's mortar squad landed in a section of the beach that was under intense sniper fire. "Our men were being picked off like flies. I ran up the beach dodging sniper and mortar fire—all the time firing my weapon into the trees hoping to hit some snipers." Costella dived face-down into a shallow shell hole. Gritty grains of sand irritated his eyes and lips. "One sniper got his sites [sic] on me. He did not miss by much. The bullet hit the sand in front of my face with such impact that it drew blood from my face." Joe Reid, a friend of Costella's, plopped down next to him in the hole. Reid was a popular guy, the sort of person who knew how to make everyone else laugh. Costella turned to warn Reid about the snipers. "Before I could finish my words he was hit in the middle of the forehead. The blood seeped out of a small hole. He had a blank stare. I knew he was gone." Costella felt horrible but he had no time to dwell on his friend's death. He sprayed the trees with fire from his Thompson submachine gun, got up and ran to another position. Out of his peripheral vision, he could see that the beach was littered with dead Marines. Nearby, Private William Martin was bending under the weight of a full field pack, ammunition, and a drum of communication wire. "A mortar shell exploded about three feet in front of me. It split in half. One piece went to the right of me and the other to the left of me." He lay stunned for a moment by the impact of the shell. He could hardly believe how close he had just come to having his head blown off. He quickly discarded the drum of wire and got away from that spot. [6]

In any amphibious invasion, assault troops are often most vulnerable right as they reach an enemy-held shore. At this point, they are disoriented. They are overloaded with equipment. They are probably seasick. They are riding aboard landing craft that make prime, and easily identified, targets for enemy gunners. Once out of the craft, the troops find themselves on open, sandy ground, in a pre-sited kill zone. Thus, Marines were trained to get off the beach as quickly as possible. The quicker they got off the beach, the sooner they could capture objectives and minimize their exposure to Japanese defensive fire. At Peleliu, in those first hours, almost every man—even those who were pinned down—kept thinking to himself: "Get off the beach!" That desperate thought kept flashing through Private Eugene Sledge's terrified mind as he crawled along the beach, watching the impersonal maelstrom of Japanese firepower destroy men around him. He saw a DUKW roll out of the water, onto the sand, only to be hit by a high-velocity shell. Pieces of the vehicle, and the men within, flew in every direction. He looked seaward and saw a group of Marines out on the reef, trying to exit a burning amtrac. "Their buddies tried to help them as they struggled in the knee-deep water," Sledge wrote after the war, in one of the most powerful combat memoirs ever published. Sledge saw splashes of water spout up as machine-gun bullets swept through the struggling men. New to combat, he was now filled with anger, revulsion, and abject frustration. "I had tasted the bitterest essence of war, the sight of helpless comrades being slaughtered, and it filled me with disgust."

Lieutenant Bruce Watkins lost six men from his platoon before the unit had even made it one hundred yards. "Still we hadn't seen an enemy soldier." He and most of the platoon made it to an embankment that overlooked the airfield. Waves of accurate, deadly machine-gun fire soon tore into them from the left. Lieutenant Watkins heard one of his privates calling to him: "Lieutenant, help me—I can't move." Watkins sprinted through heavy fire to get to him. "He was shot through the thumb and thigh, his leg broken, hugging the ground as best he could." The lieutenant picked the man up and, aided by the adrenaline that was coursing through his bloodstream, carried him to the embankment. A sergeant was lying there with his abdomen torn open, gushing blood. Watkins "saw them both onto stretchers and ready to be evacuated." This was humane but it was his job to lead, not care for the wounded.[7]

The problem was that casualties were piling up faster than Navy corpsmen could treat them. No group was busier, or more overtaxed, than the valorous corpsmen, many of whom were attached directly to the Marine infantry companies. "The cry 'Corpsman' and 'Stretcher bearers' became more nerve racking than the crump of mortar shells and the whine of bullets," an officer in the 1st Battalion, 1st Marines, wrote. Knowing their importance to the Marines' body and soul, the Japanese delighted in shooting at them. All along the hellish landing area, the corpsmen braved the worst kill zones, administering first aid to the wounded, under the most stressful circumstances. The best they could do for wounded men was to stop their bleeding, bind up their wounds, dull their pain with morphine, or treat the symptoms of shock.

Leslie Harrold, a nineteen-year-old corpsman with C Company, 5th Marines, was moving up the beach when he saw a man from his unit get shot in the mouth. "The guy's tongue was cut. He was choking to death on his own tongue and blood flowing down his throat. I got ahold of the guy's tongue and his bottom lip and I clipped 'em together" with a hemostat. Harrold then jammed several compress bandages into the Marine's mouth to further staunch the bleeding. "I dug out teeth and bits of gum. I did treat the shock by putting in a liter of blood plasma." He wrote down what he had done on a tag and pinned it to the wounded man, so that doctors aboard a hospital ship offshore would know his status. Then he flagged down an amtrac to evacuate him. He no sooner finished with this case than a bullet slammed into another Marine "right between the eyes. The bullet [went] in, hit something, turned and went out right in front of his ear. It was like hearing a cantaloupe dropped on the sidewalk." Harrold attended to him, tagged him, and sent him to an amtrac, all the while under withering fire.

As more men landed, the beach was soon a very crowded place, making it even harder to treat the wounded. Wounded and dying men lay everywhere. Corpsmen scurried around, listening to cries for help, working frantically to save lives. Adrenaline aside, the best way to move wounded men was on stretchers and this was an arduous, labor-intensive job. Generally, it took at least four able-bodied men to move just one wounded man on a stretcher. Some of the stretcher bearers were medics, but most were support troops of one sort or another who were now pressed into service to remove the growing number of wounded men. These litter teams only added to the crowded confusion that reigned on the beach.

Some of the bearers were African-American Marines whose bravery in tending to the wounded earned the universal respect and admiration of everyone on the beach that terrible day. In the opinion of one medical officer, the black Marines were "most proficient in this type of activity. All Unit Commanders praised their efficiency, zeal, and cheerfulness in performing their duties." Within an hour, the medical people had evacuated the first casualties to hospital ships. As the fighting raged, the evacuations took on a conveyor-belt quality as wounded Marines were treated by corpsmen, placed aboard amtracs, and then shuttled to the ships. According to a remarkably detailed, on-the-spot diary kept by Captain James Flagg, an operations officer in the 5th Marines, this regiment alone suffered 214 wounded during the assault. Among the corpsmen and the riflemen alike, he witnessed countless acts of anonymous heroism, certainly more than even he could ever document. "There were many examples of individual bravery. Some of these actions were never observed [by commanders] and will be forever lost." Flagg hit upon a great truth of combat. Decorations reflect only what survivors can see, hear, and record within the chaotic myopia of the fighting. Indeed, the same could also be said for battle history.[8]

One thing that is clear about D-day on Peleliu is that leadership was of vital importance. The 1st Marine Division was blessed with a large number of combat-experienced, dedicated small-unit leaders of all ranks. "We had plenty [of] good thinkers on the spot . . . making sense out of nonsense," one Marine infantryman commented. Throughout the morning, these "good thinkers" led mostly by example. In one typical instance, Private Charles Owen, a sixteen-year-old rifleman in A Company, 7th Marine Regiment, was lying among a clump of Marines, hugging the beach for dear life. The enemy fire was so intense that burrowing into the sand seemed the only way to survive. Every man knew that if he stayed here long enough, he would be killed. In fact, severed arms and legs were lying around them, grisly proof of imminent danger. However, rational calculation gave way to the direct fear of what that wicked fire would do to anyone who dared move a muscle. Beyond this, the inertia stemmed from something very common in combat—sheer confusion. Shells were exploding. Bullets were buzzing. No one could see the enemy. Few Marines had a sense of their location, or what direction to go. Basically, no one really knew what exactly to do next. Owen himself was in the grip of the sort of fear that induces sheer panic. This kind of fear has definite physical symptoms that affect the respiratory system, vision, and even a person's muscle dexterity. "Never before or since have I experienced such fright," he said.

He lay still and cursed at himself for lying about his age to join the Corps. He wished he were anywhere but here. Then, above the din of battle, he noticed a booming voice. "Down to my right, and at a point on the beach where the fearful storm of iron and lead was raging most furiously, there was a man coming up the beach toward us. He was the only person on his feet, as far as I could see." Private Owen could hardly believe that anyone could walk more than a few feet in the face of such terrific fire. The man was carrying a Thompson submachine gun and a Japanese shovel. He was covered with blood and mud, but Owen could see a major's insignia on his collar. He walked up to Owen's group and screamed: "Get the hell off this beach or I'll shoot your ass!" His rank was not necessarily what snapped them out of their fearful paralysis. It was his decisiveness along with his appearance and the determined look in his eye. They were convinced that he really *would* shoot them if they did not move, so he now became the greater danger. "When I got up and moved," Owen said, "so did others of my section and company, mortarmen and riflemen—everybody started moving off that beach. It was a complete exodus." A few minutes later a massive mortar barrage hit right where they had been. "If that major had not been clearing that beach . . . I would have been dead right there at the age of 16." The major was Arthur Parker, who, as a tank officer, had no direct authority over the infantrymen, but that did not matter in the heat of combat. "They had to be gotten off that beach or they would be killed," he later explained. "They wouldn't move so I screamed at them. I used all kinds of profanity."

Most of the myriad leadership events throughout the landing area were not so dramatic. Private Russell Davis, like so many others, was trying to figure out what was going on and what to do. He aimlessly wandered along the beach, looking for a close buddy, dodging near misses, before finally encountering a strong-willed NCO. "I saw a redheaded corporal, flailing his heavy arms and urging the men forward into the smoke at the edge of the beach. The corporal seemed to know what he was doing and I pressed toward him, happy to attach myself to anyone who knew what he was supposed to do." The corporal was striding around, bellowing at frightened men, even kicking some who refused to move. "Get forward!" he shouted. "There's a ditch ahead. Get into it. Stop bunching up on that sand like sheep." Davis and several others responded to him. Later, Davis watched as the corporal persuaded a demolition man to go forward with him and destroy a bunker.

Generally, this is how the battle went that morning. Frightened men asked corporals, sergeants, or lieutenants what to do and the leaders told them, thus giving them a job to focus on rather than their natural fear. The leaders understood that the situation was horrifying but not all that complicated. Staying on the beach meant death. So the best thing to do was move forward to destroy whatever, or whoever, was in the way. This was how the 1st Marine Division blasted out its bloody lodgment some fifteen yards inland at Peleliu.[9]

Life and Death at the Point

The worst fighting took place on the extreme left of the American beachhead, just on the northern edge of the 1st Marine Regiment's White Beach 1. Here a gnarled, thirty-foot-high ridge protruded, like a swollen knuckle, into the sea. Dubbed "the Point" by the Americans, this blunt ridge flanked the entire beachhead, allowing the Japanese to pour enfilading fire on nearly every Marine who was struggling ashore. Colonel Nakagawa understood the defensive advantages of the Point, and he fortified it heavily. According to a 1st Marine Regiment report, Japanese defenses consisted of "five reinforced concrete pillboxes housing a number of heavy machine guns and a 40mm [actually 47-millimeter] automatic weapon. Riflemen and machine gunners in spider traps or coral depressions gave close covering fire for the emplacements." The automatic weapon was an antiboat gun whose six-pound shells savaged the American DUKWs and amtracs. The pillboxes stood about five feet tall and were reinforced with steel rods and several feet of concrete or coral. The Japanese expertly concealed the pillboxes and their supporting positions within the jagged natural bramble of coral, sand, and foliage that blanketed the Point. Twenty-six-year-old Captain George Hunt, whose K Company drew the mission of capturing the Point, described it as "a rocky mass of sharp pinnacles, deep crevasses, tremendous boulders. Pillboxes, reinforced with steel and concrete, had been dug or blasted in the base of the perpendicular drop to the beach." Some of the pillboxes had coral and concrete piled as much as six feet high with small holes around them for supporting infantry soldiers. "It surpassed by far anything we had conceived of when we studied the aerial photographs."

In fact, the Americans had little idea of how strong the Point really was, because they could not see its defenses. "It was totally overgrown with little shrub trees," Sergeant George Peto, a mortar forward observer in K Company, recalled. "It was so camouflaged. It just looked like a bunch of brush. You couldn't really see nothing. It was one of the best fortified places I've seen or heard of." The pre-landing bombardment had not even touched the Point. The Navy had mainly fired at observable targets. They saw nothing to shoot at on the Point, so they left it alone. Only on the ground, then, could the Americans truly understand what they were up against. The Point's machine guns were raking the landing beaches. Japanese riflemen and light machine gunners even tied themselves onto the tops of trees. From that vantage point, they could pour accurate, aimed fire at the crowd of Marines all along the beach. "The entire beach was swarming with tractors, men evacuating wounded, and unloading supplies," one Marine recalled. "The sands were black with milling men."[10]

Basically, K Company had to take the Point or those milling men might well be slaughtered. When Hunt's outfit hit the beach, it was over-strength, with 235 Marines, plus a couple of radiomen, three Joint Air Sea Communications Operator (JASCO) teams, along with a few stretcher bearers and demolition teams. The captain would literally need every man to accomplish his challenging mission. Most of the company landed one hundred yards too far south. The 2nd Platoon pushed inland about seventy-five yards, right into a diamond-shaped ditch that the Japanese had dug to ensnare American tanks. The trap "was about 10 ft. high and 15 ft. wide and possibly 150 yards in length," Braswell Deen, a BAR man, wrote. He and the other 2nd Platoon men naturally gravitated to the trap for cover, only to find that it was a killing ground. Caught in the trap, Private Deen saw enemy bullets slam into his platoon leader and several other men. The Japanese small-arms and machine-gun fire was frighteningly accurate. Deen and the others were trying to fire back but they were pinned down "by a devastating cross fire from coral ridges, concrete pillboxes, caves and formidable fighting holes." Deen's assistant gunner took a bullet right between the eyes. His lifeless body slid down into the ditch. One by one, others got hit, many of them with mortal wounds. "Everybody was split up and separated," another private remembered, "and guys with blood on 'em were all over the tank trap. Any time anybody tried to climb out and keep attackin', they was shot." The temperature was hovering near one hundred degrees. Water and ammo were already running low. The platoon was combat-ineffective, pinned down, and cut off from the company for the rest of the day. Only with the support of Sherman tanks could the survivors escape that night.[11]

Minus his 2nd Platoon, Captain Hunt threw the rest of his company at the Point. Initially his men tried a frontal assault along the beach, but Japanese opposition was too intense, so Hunt's Marines, mainly in small groups, fought their way inland to attack the Point defenders from behind. "For nearly two hours they fought it out in a steady exchange of fire," the regimental after action report declared. "The protecting [Japanese] troops were killed or driven off first, leaving the pillboxes open to annihilation from their blind spots." That statement was accurate and straightforward, but it did not even begin to describe what the fighting was like for the infantrymen who had to do it. They fought the Japanese at close range, usually within twenty or thirty yards. It was personal combat. Men saw their quarry, aimed, and shot to kill. The main weapons of decision in this fight were grenades and small arms, not impersonal mortars or artillery pieces.

A few men did most of the grisly work. One such man, Private Fred Fox, noticed a stairway cut into the coral, leading to a dugout. He threw a white phosphorous grenade down the stairs. A couple other men threw fragmentation grenades. After the smoke from the explosions cleared, Fox raised his tommy gun and began edging down the steps. All at once, he saw a wounded Japanese officer at the bottom of the steps. "His left arm was burnt black but he was leaning on his right elbow with a Nambu pistol in his hand aimed at me. I pressed the trigger on the tommy gun firing four or five rounds into him." The .45-caliber bullets tore holes in the officer and he fell dead. Fox moved past him, into the dugout, where he found several bodies, including another officer who had apparently committed suicide by disemboweling himself.

Elsewhere, one of Hunt's platoon leaders, Lieutenant William Willis, led a group of Marines in assaulting the pillboxes that made the Point so formidable. One of his men, Private King, attacked one pillbox by himself. As he was hurling grenades at the pillbox's embrasure, a bullet tore through his helmet but, by some miracle, it did not hit his head. Another bullet caromed off his cartridge belt. Instead of fleeing, King stayed put and threw another grenade at the embrasure, killing most of the Japanese in the pillbox. The rest tried to flee. "My boys lined up as though they were in a shooting gallery at Coney Island and proceeded to pick them off with ease!" Lieutenant Willis later testified. "I remember one Jap who left a trail of smoke behind him, his pack evidently on fire. He was screaming like a frightened monkey. Then he fell down, still burning up, and didn't move." The monkey reference was no accident. Willis and the other Marines thought of the Japanese as animals, thus dehumanizing them. This stoked their own hatred and willingness to kill. Another one of Willis's men launched a perfect rifle grenade shot, right through the embrasure of the pillbox, scoring a direct hit on the 47-millimeter gun. The lieutenant watched in delight as the pillbox imploded. "After a big explosion, the pillbox burst into flame, and black smoke poured out of the embrasure and the exit. I heard the Japs screaming and their ammunition spitting and snapping as the heat exploded it." Three screaming Japanese "raced from the exit, waving their arms and letting out yells of pain. The squad I had placed there finished them off."[12]

As of 1015, the Americans controlled the Point. By Captain Hunt's estimate, he had lost about two-thirds of his company. His Marines had killed 110 Japanese soldiers. Already the steamy air was filled with the putrefying stench of the dead. Wounded men and dead bodies were strewn all over the shaggy, jagged coral of the Point. "The human wreckage I saw was a grim and tragic sight," the captain commented. "I saw a ghastly mixture of bandages; bloody and mutilated skin; men gritting their teeth, resigned to their wounds; men groaning and writhing in their agonies; men outstretched or twisted or grotesquely transfixed in the attitudes of death; men with their entrails exposed or whole chunks of body ripped out of them." The mere act of taking this position was a triumph of near epic proportions, and a testament to the potency of well-trained, well-led infantrymen who were determined to fight hard and work together as a team. With the equivalent of only a couple hard-pressed platoons, armed with only light infantry weapons, Hunt's men had taken five concrete pillboxes, numerous dugouts, and had killed over one hundred enemy soldiers, in less than an hour's fighting. They had done this with no fire support at all, not even mortars.[13]

K Company's ordeal was far from over, though. The men were exhausted and on the verge of dehydration from the intense heat of the tropical sun. Their uniforms were filthy, torn, and salt-encrusted. "Damn, it was hot and we were thirsty," one of the Marines later wrote. Some resorted to crawling into no-man's-land and stripping canteens from the maggot-infested bodies of their enemies. The Marines were also low on ammo and had little food. Hunt had so few able-bodied men left (thirty-eight, according to the records) that his fighting positions were spread quite thin, over the course of about eighty or ninety yards. Although K Company's possession of the Point had eliminated the deadly fire that had been saturating the landing beaches, the company was cut off. The men were under constant Japanese mortar and sniper fire. The mortars were especially effective. As the shells hit and exploded, they sent shards of rock and steel flying in all directions. At one point, a Japanese artillery piece lobbed heavier shells against the Point, wounding several men. Air and naval fire subsequently destroyed the gun. It was difficult to dig into the gnarled coral ridge, so the Marines stacked rocks and logs around their hasty fighting positions. Hunt was in radio communication with his battalion commander, but his radio batteries were running out of juice.

Fortunately for K Company, a supply LVT, crewed by four black Marines, made it into the Point just before evening. They dropped their ramp and unloaded boxes of ammunition, hand grenades, barbed wire, a flamethrower, and several surviving members of the 2nd Platoon. The LVT crew also brought a fifty-five-gallon drum of water, but this did not do much good. "The drum had not been cleaned," Private Fred Fox wrote, "and the water tasted awful, sickening. It was oil and water and no way could we drink it." For now, Fox and the others had to make do with captured Japanese canteens. K Company loaded several of their most seriously wounded comrades aboard the LVT, and it left.[14]

The resupply came just in time, because the Japanese fully understood the Point's significance and were determined to retake it. They had launched a few jabs during the day, but a sharper attack began at midnight with a ferocious mortar barrage, followed by a company-sized probe. Instead of hurling themselves forward with a wasteful banzai attack, the Japanese used the darkness to edge in close to the American lines. Their mortars forced the Americans to crouch low, behind their rocks, "like they were our mother's arms," in the words of one veteran, hoping the shells would hit somewhere far away. The shrapnel from the mortar shells showered the Point's scraggly trees and tinkled off the jagged rocks. The fragments also scored several hits on men and the air was filled with plaintive cries for corpsmen.

The Marines were very well disciplined. They did not give away their positions with wild, searching fire. Instead, they waited until the Japanese were within hand grenade range and then opened up. "We did a lot of shooting, a lot of grenade throwing," Private Fox recalled. "There was screaming and a lot of explosions." Sergeant Peto was on the extreme right of the company position, crouched behind a .30-caliber machine gun that he had taken from a disabled Sherman tank on the beach. Because the 81-millimeter mortars were not operational, he had become an impromptu machine gunner. By the light of flares, he fired at anything that moved beyond the rocks. "Whenever anybody heard a noise or there was some movement, everybody would open up. They were all around us. They were within ... fifteen or twenty feet of us." At this stage, the American fire was too much for the Japanese. "The attack subsided to occasional harassing mortar fire," Captain Hunt wrote, "and by 0300 there was quiet."

As the sun rose, the fighting once again intensified. The Japanese showered the American lines with mortar shells. Most of the enemy infantrymen were in a defiladed area within hand grenade range. Private Fox was manning a captured Japanese machine gun. Just to his right, a small group of Marines were hurling grenades at the enemy soldiers, who were about fifty yards away. "There was a big coral rock in front where our guys could stand up and get a nice throw at the Japs. The Japanese would throw back with their grenades hitting the rock, which would roll off to one side or the other." Captain Hunt was near the center of the company position, barking orders, radioing for help, managing the battle. "Our machine guns raked across the draw riddling any Jap that stuck up his head. I saw a hand rise to throw a grenade. Our bullets reduced it to a bloody stump. The fight became a vicious melee of countless explosions, whining bullets, shrapnel whirring overhead or clinking off the rocks, hoarse shouts, shrill-screaming Japanese." More and more Americans went down with wounds. Captain Hunt saw them walking, or being carried by stretcher teams, down to the beach, blood dripping from arms, torsos, and heads. Both sides continued to pour huge quantities of fire at each other. "I smelled the powder vapor, acrid, choking, could see it swirling white—sweat in my eyes, stinging—jacket was wet on my back—rock chips spattering at my feet."[15]

The fighting finally died down around 0730. The rest of the day was comparatively quiet. This gave Colonel Lewis "Chesty" Puller the precious time he needed to send help to Hunt's hard-pressed company. In the course of the day, the colonel sent more resupply amtracs, with reinforcements as well. Also, B Company of the 1st Marines attacked north and linked up with Hunt's K Company late in the afternoon on September 16. By then, Hunt had 60-millimeter mortars in his own position and 81-millimeters a couple hundred yards down the beach, at his disposal, plus some artillery, too. In that sense, his company was stronger than before but his men were now in the throes of total exhaustion. Knowing the Point's defenders were still vulnerable, Colonel Nakagawa amassed 350 infantry soldiers and launched a night attack. This was a well-planned assault to capture a key objective, not an immature banzai attack. Even so, the Americans, aided by the half-light of flares, mowed them down in droves. "Howls of pain which rose in front of our positions, dimly heard through the roar of our weapons, told us that we were hitting the mark," Captain Hunt wrote. The captain knew this was a fight to the finish. "Give them hell!" he screamed at his men. "Kill every one of the bastards!"

The Japanese colonel had committed another 47-millimeter gun to support his carefully conceived attack, but American artillery destroyed the gun and its crew. "The bodies were stacked 4-deep over the gun," Sergeant Peto wrote. Farther down the beach, the 81-millimeter mortar crews were firing at the absolute minimum range. "We were firing only 200 to 250 yards," Corporal Albert Mikel, a member of a mortar crew, said. "Our mortars were pointing almost straight up. In fear that the mortars might fall backwards, we placed sandbags on the barrels of the mortars." In spite of this blanket of firepower, some of the Japanese closed to within bayonet range. Several of them fell upon Private Fox, stabbing him repeatedly. He nearly bled to death but somehow held out in a delirium until another Marine rescued him.

By the early morning hours of September 17, the fighting petered out. The Japanese attack was a deadly failure. In a day and a half of fighting, some four hundred Imperial soldiers had been killed. Their torn, rotting corpses were draped all over the Point. They lay in mute testimony to the waste, vulgarity, and valor inherent in war. "They sprawled in ghastly attitudes with their faces frozen and their lips curled into apish grins," Hunt recalled. "Their eyes were slimy with the green film of death. Many of them were huddled with their arms around each other as though they had futilely protected themselves from our fire. They were horribly mutilated; riddled by bullets and torn by shrapnel until their entrails popped out; legs and arms and torsos littered the rocks and in some places were lodged grotesquely in the treetops. Their yellow skin was beginning to turn brown, and their fly-ridden corpses still free of maggots were already cracked and bloated like rotten melons." Such were the troubling realities of life and death at the Point. In securing it, the Americans had secured their beachhead on Peleliu.

Years later, Russell Honsowetz, a battalion commander in another 1st Marine Regiment unit that did not fight at the Point, smugly claimed that many Marines and historians "made a lot of ballyhoo" about K Company's desperate battle at the Point. Yet the company, he claimed, "was never in danger." This would have been news to the men who fought so desperately, and bled and struggled, and watched their buddies die in that awful place. Of the 235 members of the company who went into the Point, only 78 came out unscathed (at least in the physical sense). Hunt lost 32 men killed and another 125 wounded. "Imagine if an officer less brave than George Hunt had the job of securing the Point," Major Nikolai Stevenson, the 3rd Battalion executive officer, once said in tribute to the captain and his Marines. Knowing that K Company was fought out, Colonel Puller immediately placed the unit in regimental reserve. He knew full well that Captain Hunt's men had performed brilliantly. He and most other Marines rightly thought of the Point battle as one of the great small-unit infantry accomplishments in World War II.[16]

Sheer Misery

In the meantime, Peleliu was turning into a bloody slugging match of pure attrition, exactly the sort of battle the Japanese wanted to fight. The Americans were paying dearly for every substantial gain they made. On D-day alone, the 1st Marine Division suffered nearly thirteen hundred casualties. Late in the day, the Japanese launched a tank-infantry counterattack designed to push the Americans back from a shaky perimeter they had carved out at the airfield. This was a carefully planned albeit ill-advised assault, not a banzai attack. The Americans slaughtered their enemies in droves. "Here they come," Marines yelled to one another, even as they opened up with every weapon at their disposal. A combination of fire from Sherman tanks, antitank guns, bazookas, machine guns, and rifle grenades destroyed the enemy soldiers, and at least thirteen of their tanks, at close range.

The Japanese attack failed for two reasons. First, their tanks were small, thinly armored, and lightly gunned. They were no match for American antitank guns, especially the bigger Shermans. "Bazookas helped stop the assault, but it was the General Shermans that did the major portion of the damage," a Marine combat correspondent wrote. Second, the Japanese attacked over the relatively flat terrain of the airfield into a well-prepared defensive position, making perfect targets of themselves. When the fighting petered out, the shattered hulks of enemy tanks burned in random patterns all around the airfield. Treads and turrets were blown off. Side armor was peppered with holes. Flames consumed metal and flesh alike. Dead, half-burned enemy soldiers—some without legs, arms, or heads—were sprawled around the scorched vehicles, sometimes even wedged underneath their grimy treads. The following day the 5th Marines weathered heavy mortar fire to secure the airfield, the campaign's major objective. But this hardly seemed to matter. From the coral ridges beyond the airfield, the Japanese poured thick gobs of mortar, artillery, and machine-gun fire onto the vulnerable Americans. The American advance was slow in the face of such ferocious opposition.[17]

Moreover, the elements were emerging as a real problem. The heat was absolutely brutal. Temperatures reached 105 degrees in the shade, and there was precious little of that to be found anywhere on the beachhead. In the open, the temperatures were at least 115 degrees. It was, in the recollection of one Marine machine gunner, like a "steam room. The sweat slid into one's mouth to aggravate thirst." The surviving records most commonly describe the heat as "enervating," a word that means, according to *Webster's* dictionary, "to deprive of vitality." That certainly held true for many of the Marines. Robert "Pepper" Martin of *Time* had covered Guam. At Peleliu, he was one of the few civilian correspondents to see the battle firsthand. "Peleliu is a horrible place," he wrote. "The heat is stifling and rain falls intermittently—the muggy rain that brings no relief, only greater misery. The coral rocks soak up heat during the day and it is only slightly cooler at night. Marines are in the finest possible physical condition, but they wilted on Peleliu. By the fourth day, there were as many casualties from heat prostration as from wounds. Peleliu is incomparably worse than Guam in its bloodiness, terror, climate and the incomprehensible tenacity of the Japs. For sheer brutality and fatigue, I think it surpasses anything yet seen in the Pacific."

The stress of combat, combined with the unrelenting heat, made for a miserable combination. There was no way to escape the heat. The sun beat down relentlessly, turning the island "into a scorching furnace," according to one unit after action report. Everyone was sunburned. Jagged coral rocks poked painfully into tender, sun-baked skin. Men sweated profusely. Their fatigues were salt-stained, dripping wet from their smelly perspiration. Salt tablets helped a little bit, but supplies were low. Some Marines collapsed from heat exhaustion. One officer in the 1st Battalion, 7th Marines, saw many such men in his outfit "unable to fight, unable to continue. Some were carried out with dry heaves. Others had tongues so swollen as to make it impossible for them to talk or to swallow. Others were unable to close eyelids over their dried, swollen eyeballs. We lost their much needed strength in a critical phase of the operation."

Dehydrated, frightened, and exhausted, a few broke mentally under the strain of the heat. Private Russell Davis saw a big redheaded Marine, with dried lips and cherry red sunburned skin, completely lose his composure. "I can't go the heat! I can take the war but not the heat!" he screamed. Davis watched as "he shook his fist up at the blazing sun. Two of his mates pounced on him and rode him down to the earth, but he was big and strong and he thrashed away from them." Davis never knew the broken man's ultimate fate.[18]

To make matters infinitely worse, water was scarce. Each Marine came ashore with two canteens of water, a woefully inadequate ration for Peleliu's killer heat. Most of the men drank their canteens dry within the first few hours of the invasion. "We had practiced water discipline at great length . . . but the body demands water," Private Richard Johnston, a machine gunner in the 5th Marines, explained. "No matter how strong your will or how controlled your mind, you either drink what water you have or die in not too long a time." Medical corpsmen were covered with the blood of wounded men, but now had no water to wash that blood off their hands. With no other choice, they treated their patients with filthy, bloodstained hands. After the chaos of the beach assault abated, and the battle settled into a steady push inland to gain ground, shore parties hauled water ashore, mostly in fifty-five-gallon drums and five-gallon cans. By the second or third day, this water reached the frontline fighters. When a five-gallon can reached Private Sledge's K Company, 5th Marines, he anxiously held out his canteen cup for a drink. "Our hands shook, we were so eager to quench our thirst. The water looked brown in my aluminum canteen cup. No matter, I took a big gulp—and almost spit it out despite my terrible thirst. It was awful. Full of rust and oil, it stunk. A blue film of oil floated lazily on the surface of the smelly brown liquid. Cramps gripped the pit of my stomach."

The drums and cans had originally been used to carry fuel. Before the invasion, work parties had not properly cleaned the containers. Thus, when they were filled with warm water, the fuel residue mixed with the water, and the metal of the containers, producing a noxious, unhealthy, rusted, repulsive brown liquid. "Smelling and tasting of gasoline, it was undrinkable," Robert Leckie, a machine gunner in the 1st Marines, wrote. Nonetheless, many Marines, like Sledge, were so desperately thirsty that they drank the tainted water. Some vomited. Others were incapacitated with sharp cramps and had to be evacuated.

Word of the tainted water spread quickly. Soon the Marines began looking for other ways to slake their acute thirst. Private First Class George Parker's unit found two Japanese bathtubs filled with used bathwater. "It tasted a little soapy but we drank it. We had no choice." Private First Class John Huber, a runner in Sledge's company, was with a group of men who found a shell crater full of water and trash. "We filled our canteens and put in halzone [sic] tablets to purify it." Sweaty and thirsty, they chugged down the supposedly purified water. Then someone moved a metal sheet from the crater, revealing a dead Japanese soldier floating facedown in the water. A wave of nausea immediately swept over Huber and the others. "We soon started losing the water . . . and everything else we ate during the day." One of the men in Private Johnston's company took a canteen off a dead enemy soldier. Another Marine offered the man two hundred dollars for the canteen. Johnston was struck by how starkly different values in combat were in contrast to life back home. Fresh water was "something that in everyday life most people take for granted." On Peleliu, it was like gold. The man did not sell the water to his buddy. Instead he gave him a drink for free.

Engineers originally believed that Peleliu offered no sources of fresh water. Within a few days, though, they discovered Japanese freshwater wells. They appropriated those and dug several more of their own. By September 19, the wells were yielding about fifty thousand gallons of water per day, enough to sustain each man with a few gallons each day. In addition, the engineers brought desalination equipment ashore. "All we had to do was run this hose into the ocean," Private First Class Charlie Burchett, an engineer, recalled. "That thing would pump the water through this unit and it comes out nice, cool, just perfect drinking water." Within a few days, the water crisis passed. Infantrymen were not exactly awash in water, but they had enough to stave off extreme thirst and dehydration. The heat did not abate, though. Neither did Japanese opposition.[19]

The Destruction of the 1st Marines

Within three days of the invasion, the 1st Marine Division had already suffered over fourteen hundred casualties, in spite of the fact that the division had not even encountered the most difficult Japanese defenses. In the south, the 7th Marines were clearing out the swampy lowlands of the island. In the center, the 5th Marines were pushing from the airfield across the midsection of the island, fighting their way through plateaus, jungles, and swamps. In the north, the 1st Marines, having overcome the stoutest enemy beach defenses (including the Point), began attacking the daunting ridges of the Umurbrogol. This was the heart of Colonel Nakagawa's formidable inland defense.

Because of the limits of preinvasion photographic intelligence and inadequate maps, the Marines had little sense of just how daunting the Umurbrogol was until they were enmeshed in it. Already they were referring to this high ground as Bloody Nose Ridge, but it was more than just one ridge. "Along its center, the rocky spine was heaved up in a contorted mass of decayed coral, strewn with rubble, crags, ridges and gulches . . . thrown together in a confusing maze," the regimental history explained. "There were no roads, scarcely any trails. The pockmarked surface offered no secure footing even in the few level places. It was impossible to dig in: the best the men could do was pile a little coral or wood debris around their positions. The jagged rock slashed their shoes and clothes, and tore their bodies every time they hit the deck for safety." Even under ideal circumstances, in peacetime, the ground would have been quite difficult to traverse. "There was crevasses you could fall down through," Sergeant George Peto recalled. "It was a horrible place. If the devil would have built it, that's about what he'd have done."

What's more, it was very difficult to find cover, and the nature of the ground multiplied the fragmentation effect of mortar and artillery shells. "Into all this the enemy dug and tunneled like moles; and there they stayed to fight to the death," an officer in the 1st Marines wrote. To the Americans, the Japanese cave defenses were unbelievably elaborate. According to one Marine report, they were "blasted into the almost perpendicular coral ridges. The caves varied from simple holes large enough to accommodate two men to large tunnels with passageways on either side which were large enough to

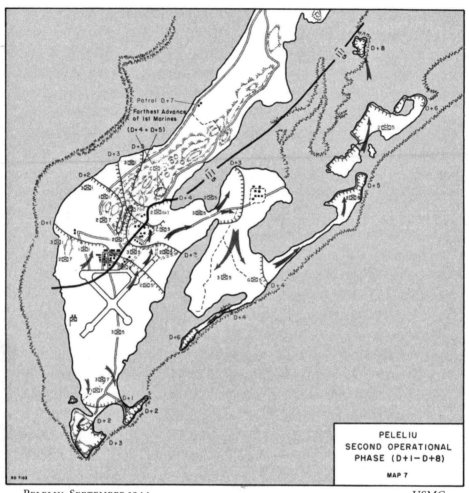

PELELIU, SEPTEMBER 1944   USMC

contain artillery or 150mm mortars and ammunition." Some of the caves even had steel doors. All of them were well camouflaged, with nearly perfect fields of fire. Naval gunfire, air strikes, and even artillery only had so much effect against these formidable hideouts. Only infantry and tanks could hope to destroy them, and this had to be done at close range, under extremely dangerous circumstances.[20]

On the day of the invasion, Colonel Puller's 1st Marines had 3,251 men. By the time the regiment attacked the Umurbrogol, the unit had already lost about 900 men, many of whom had fallen victim to heat exhaustion. Since most of the casualties occurred in the rifle companies, they were well under-strength now. This was scarcely a recipe for success, but Marines pride themselves on doing the unlikely, if not the impossible. Between September 17 and 21, Colonel Puller hurled his regiment, plus an attached battalion from the 7th Marines and a few tanks, into frontal attacks to take this high ground.

The true horror of this fighting is almost impossible to describe. The ridges were steep, so much so that some were little more than sheer rock faces, dotted only with fortified caves. The peaks of ridges were often so pointed that men could not stand on them. The rocky, crevassed ground was so un-stable that troops could not hope to keep their footing, much less maneuver in any coherent fashion. So the mere act of climbing the ridges, moving around, in suffocating heat, was challenging enough for the men. Under perfect circumstances, it would have been extremely difficult to overpower such a formidable network of caves. Under these conditions, it was a veritable impossibility, even for the gallant Marines. One of Puller's battalion commanders, Major Ray Davis, who would later earn the Medal of Honor in Korea and command the 3rd Marine Division in Vietnam, referred to the Umurbrogol as "the most difficult assignment I have ever seen."

As was usually true in any ground attack, the riflemen led the way and faced the greatest dangers. They climbed the hills in small groups, supported at a distance by machine gunners and mortarmen who generally fired from fixed positions. "As they toiled, caves and gulleys [sic] and holes opened up on them," a Marine, observing from the vantage point of a machine-gun post, recalled. "Japanese dashed out to roll grenades down on them, and sometimes to lock, body to body, in desperate wrestling matches." Private George Parker, a rifleman, was struggling up one ridge, dodging enemy grenades all the way. "All they had to do was give their grenades a little [heave] and they would go

100 to 125 yards down the hill onto us." Parker and the others could not hope to throw grenades high enough, or far enough, to do any damage to the enemy. They shot a few rifle grenades in response, but quickly took cover in the face of wicked machine-gun and mortar fire. Parker looked to his left and started to say something to a New Yorker, whose nickname was "Zoot Suit." As Zoot Suit turned toward Parker, "a bullet went through his nose from the side. The bottom part of his nose fell down onto his upper lip. I'm sure that turning his head to talk to me had saved his life." Zoot Suit was only too glad to get off the line. Elsewhere, a young private named Gene Burns leaned over to light a cigarette for a buddy. At the exact moment he did so, a Japanese mortar shell exploded in front of him, sending angry shards of shrapnel right where Burns's torso had been only a second before.[21]

They were the lucky ones. Many others were ripped apart by machine-gun bullets or fragments. Some died instantly. Others bled to death slowly, while calling vainly for help. Lieutenant Richard Kennard, a forward observer with G Battery, 11th Marine Regiment, was just behind the lead troops, calling in supporting artillery fire, watching so many young infantrymen get hit. "War is terrible, just awful, awful, awful," he wrote to his family. "You have no idea how it hurts to see American boys all shot up, wounded, suffering from pain and exhaustion, and those that fall down, never to move again." Many times he himself came close to getting blown to bits by uncannily accurate mortar fire. Unseen enemy snipers nearly blew his head off. Kennard's battery and several others were pounding the ridges and, by now, carrier-borne aircraft were even bombing suspected enemy positions along the Umurbrogol, but to no avail. The Japanese were too well entrenched in their caves, vulnerable to direct hits, but little else. For the Marines, there was almost no way to avoid the accurate enemy fire. Anyone spending enough time on the ridges got hit sooner or later. Any movement drew fire. One tank platoon leader from the division's 1st Tank Battalion watched helplessly as his tank's supporting infantry squad was decimated by mortar fire. Later, with bitter tears streaming down his face, the platoon leader told his battalion commander: "We couldn't do enough for them. We couldn't reach the mortars which killed them . . . like flies all around us." This was why, in the recollection of another tank officer, "the infantry inspired all who witnessed its indomitable heroism . . . to do one's damnedest."

After only a few hours, understrength companies of ninety men were down to half that size. Privates were leading platoons. Squads consisted of a few fortunate stalwarts. "As the riflemen climbed higher they grew fewer, until only a handful of men still climbed in the lead squads," Private Russell Davis, a member of the 2nd Battalion, 1st Marines, wrote. "These were the pick of the bunch—the few men who would go forward, no matter what was ahead. They are the bone structure of a fighting outfit." This was the military version of the old adage that, in any organization, a distinct minority usually does the majority of the work. Even in the World War II Marine Corps—a decidedly combat-oriented organization—small numbers of infantrymen did most of the fighting. These were the natural fighters who would always carry on, come what may. They were the minority, even in the Marines. This is not to say that others would not fight. They would and did. The majority fought hard, but the more intense the combat, the more of them fell by the wayside from wounds, death, and sheer exhaustion. The stalwarts, though, found a way to keep going. "They clawed and clubbed and stabbed their way up," Davis said. "The rest of us watched."[22]

Because of the Golgotha-like terrain, the terrible casualties, and the chaotic confusion of the fighting, many units lost any semblance of organization. They deteriorated into little more than random groups of survivors. "There was no such thing as a continuous attacking line," wrote Lieutenant Colonel Spencer Berger, whose 2nd Battalion, 7th Marines, was also being chewed to pieces. "Elements of the same company, even platoon, were attacking in every direction of the compass, with large gaps in between. There were countless little salients and counter salients." Commanders measured gains in yards. Anything in triple figures was a good day's work. At night, Japanese infiltrators, sometimes operating in squads, counterattacked the fatigued Americans. The eerie ridges rang with the desperate, animal-like cries of men struggling to kill one another. Veteran Marines expected and hoped that a "'banzai' charge would come to reduce the opposition," one of them wrote. "But the Japs were playing a different game this time."

It was a much smarter game. They stayed in their caves, making the Marines pay dearly for any advance. When the Americans were at their most vulnerable, usually at night, they would hit them with well-planned counterattacks, not mindless suicide charges. The experiences of C Company, 1st Battalion, 1st Marines, serve as a perfect example of this and, indeed, a microcosm of what happened to Puller's regiment at the Umurbrogol. On September 19, the company drew the assignment of taking Hill 100 (later renamed Walt Ridge after a battalion commander in the 5th Marines), at the southwestern edge of the Umurbrogol. Only through herculean effort and immense courage did the ninety survivors of this company climb the hill and finally take it at great cost, after several attempts. Once atop the hill, the commander, Captain Everett Pope, soon discovered that the Japanese were still holding an adjacent ridge from which they could, and did, pour withering machine-gun, mortar, and artillery fire down on the Marines. With night approaching, and having lost so many men to take this hill, Pope elected to stay in place. He and his men scooped out shallow fighting positions in a perimeter the size of a tennis court, and fought back as best they could. They were soon dangerously low on ammunition. "The line is flimsy as hell and it is getting dark," Pope radioed Major Davis, his battalion commander. "We have no wires and need grenades badly." Davis had no reinforcements to send, but he promised to get ammo to Pope, and perhaps string wires for phone communication.

After the sun set, the Japanese came for them. "A Marine unit can fight for a day or two with no food, an hour or two with no water," Pope later said, "but it's tough to fight with no ammo." With few bullets and only a smattering of grenades, the Marines were forced to fight hand to hand with the Japanese, kicking, stabbing, biting, scratching, struggling like animals to stay alive. The fighting was personal, primitive even. In some instances, the Marines used rocks against their enemies, and not just to beat them to death. They often threw the rocks in hopes of fooling the Japanese into thinking that they were grenades. Other times they literally threw their smaller attackers over the precipice of the hill. "The whole night was mixed up," Pope later said.

The gruesome sounds of C Company's bloody drama could be heard, quite distinctly, by other Marines below Hill 100. Private William Martin, a wireman in the battalion communication section, was approaching the hill, in the dark, with the intention of stringing wire for C Company. He could hear screams coming from the looming high ground. "All of a sudden a Jap stood up, took his rifle and directed it toward my helmet. He hit my helmet, lost his balance and landed on me. I swung my roll of combat wire and apparently hit him somewhere that made him roll off of me. I then picked him up and threw him down the path which I had just come from." Seeing this, a nearby American machine gunner opened up and killed the Japanese soldier. Not far away, in a captured Japanese bunker, Private Davis could hear the macabre voices, both foreign and domestic, in the tropical night. "We could hear them screaming for illumination or for corpsmen, as the Japs came at them from caves which were all around them. We could hear them crying and pleading for help, but nobody could help them."

By sunrise, Pope only had fifteen men left. Colonel Puller initially wanted him to keep attacking but, learning that C Company was basically destroyed, he rescinded the order. The captain and his survivors fought their way off the hill, leaving behind many of their decomposing dead, who could not be recovered for many days to come. Pope earned the Medal of Honor for his actions at Hill 100. The hill remained in Japanese hands. "It just seems impossible to get the Japs out of those coral caves," Lieutenant Kennard wrote his family, "and I don't know how the problem is going to be solved." By September 21, the 1st Marines had taken only a few hundred dearly won yards of the Umurbrogol. The regiment had suffered nearly two thousand casualties. Companies were down to ten men. Few platoon leaders or company commanders were still standing. Most of the sergeants were dead or wounded as well. Puller had culled out his rear areas of cooks, bakers, signalmen, litter bearers, and engineers to refurbish his line companies, but the Umurbrogol had consumed them, too. The 1st Marine Regiment was destroyed.[23]

Puller, Rupertus, and the Fatal Weakness of Strong Men

Chesty Puller was a legend in the Marine Corps. Even to this day, he looms as a larger-than-life figure, a fire-breathing, inspirational combat leader who exemplified everything a Marine officer should be. He had come up through the ranks, serving all over the globe with the Old Corps of the pre–World War II era. He saw as much ground combat as any twentieth-century American. Basically, he was to the Marine Corps what George Patton was to the Army—a colorful, unforgettable household name who embodied the aggressiveness of total victory. As with Patton, Puller believed in leading from the front. He was a warrior in the truest sense of that word (his detractors saw him as a "warmonger").

Diminutive and almost gnomelike, Puller always seemed to be wherever the action was thickest, talking to men, joking with them, inspiring them. His command post was usually close to the front lines, especially at Peleliu, where it was probably too near the fighting since many of his staff officers spent as much time taking cover as doing their jobs. To him, leading troops in combat was the highest calling.

He had a special connection with enlisted men, like Sergeant George Peto. At one point during the terrible fighting that followed D-day on Peleliu, Peto was feeling downcast, exhausted, and generally dispirited. Then he saw the colonel, who greeted him amiably: "Hi, son." Peto instantly felt better. "That encounter did more for my well-being than a good drink of cool water, which I was in bad need of. I would have followed that man to hell and that's exactly what we did at Peleliu." Pharmacist Mate 3rd Class Oliver Butler, a young Navy corpsman in E Company, 1st Marines, had been struggling for days to save more badly wounded men than he could ever count. As the sun set one night, he saw the colonel strolling the front lines as if out for an evening walk. Puller stopped at Butler's position and actually seemed to know him: "How are you doing, Butler?" Stunned and flattered, Butler replied: "I'm doing fine, Chesty, but we've sure lost a lot of men and I hope we get some replacements up here tomorrow." Puller seemed to understand completely. "I know, son, but hang in there and keep your eyes open and your ass down." He moved on, talking to other men as he walked the line. Butler later wrote: "Among the reasons Chesty Puller's troops liked him and admired him was the fact that he was a leader who actually and personally led and the fact that his personal courage was never in doubt." Puller often said that "no officer's life, regardless of rank, is of such great value to his country that he should seek safety in the rear."[24]

Inspirational though he certainly was, Puller's leadership at Peleliu left something to be desired. He was still carrying shrapnel in his leg from a wound suffered at Guadalcanal. The wound was infected, swelling his thigh to twice its normal size. He walked with the help of a rifle, a cane, or helping hands. His brother had recently been killed in another Pacific battle, and he burned with hatred for the Japanese, an enmity that perhaps took away some of his focus. He believed that the best way to win was through the pressure created by constant, unrelenting attacks. "He believed in momentum," General Oliver Smith, the assistant division commander, once commented. "He believed in coming ashore and hitting and just keep on hitting and trying to keep up the momentum until he'd overrun the whole thing [island]. No finesse."

In Puller's mind, the Japanese were no match for his Marines. He would defeat the enemy by overwhelming them. Although this aggressiveness was generally laudable, at the Umurbrogol it did not serve him well. By and large, he simply hurled his regiment into frontal attacks, with few adjustments and little maneuvering, "like a wave that expends its force on a rocky shore," in the estimation of one of Puller's officers. Chesty did this with utter, sustained ruthlessness, and not much in the way of fire support. To be fair, he did not have much of the latter to call upon, especially artillery. He might possibly have sidestepped the Umurbrogol, working his way up the west coast of Peleliu to encircle the Japanese in their caves, but that would have left the beachhead vulnerable to Japanese counterattacks. Still, with all that taken into consideration, he seemed to have little grasp of the utter impossibility of what he was telling his men to do. Day after day, he cajoled, threatened, and coaxed his commanders into launching more, and ever costlier, attacks. When Puller ordered his 2nd Battalion commander, Lieutenant Colonel Russell Honsowetz, to take a hill one day at all costs, Honsowetz complained that he no longer had enough men. "Well, you're there, ain't you, Honsowetz? You get all those men together and take that hill." Puller clearly wanted quick results regardless of the consequences. Amid the bloodbath, he simply would not admit to himself, or anyone else, that his regiment could not achieve the impossible.

Honsowetz was a great admirer of Puller, but others in the 1st Marines never forgave him for the losses the regiment suffered at the Umurbrogol. "Chesty Puller should never have passed the rank of second lieutenant," Private First Class Paul Lewis later said of his colonel. In Lewis's opinion, Puller wanted to earn the Medal of Honor and he did not care how many of his men died for him to get it, "just so long as he was still there at the end." Sergeant Richard Fisher thought of him as a tragic caricature of his own aggressive image. "All battles are 'training exercises' for men like Puller, and it was just another rung up his ladder. Puller was a man who could not live long without war." Captain Pope was anything but a fan of Puller, whom he thought of as a mindless butcher. "I don't think [he] was the greatest thing since sliced bread. I had no use for Puller. He didn't know what was going on, and why he wanted me and my men dead on top of that hill [Hill 100], I don't know." Pope especially resented Puller's enduring legendary status. "The adulation paid to him these days sickens me." General Robert Cushman, who served as commandant of the Marine Corps, believed that Puller was a great combat leader who nonetheless could not understand anything except constant attacks, regardless of circumstances. "He was beyond his element in commanding anything larger than a company—maybe a battalion—where he could keep his hands on everything and be right in the middle of it."

So, was Puller really at fault for the destruction of the 1st Marines at the Umurbrogol? To some extent he was. He demonstrated little imagination in maneuvering his units. He pushed his battered combat formations way too hard. He himself seemed to have little appreciation for the challenging terrain. He even turned down an opportunity to fly over it for a better look, saying he had plenty of maps. Nor did he truly understand the disquieting strength of the Japanese defenses. Sometimes positive characteristics can actually become a weakness. In this case, Puller represented aggressiveness, valor, and inspirational leadership, all ingredients that make the Marine Corps great. But he also demonstrated the tendency of Marine officers to over-rely on these strengths to the exclusion of all else. The repeated, mindless frontal attacks were the American version of banzai. They were almost as costly, and every bit as fruitless.[25]

It must be clearly understood, though, that at the Umurbrogol, Puller was only following the orders of Major General William Rupertus, his division commander. "The cold fact," one officer wrote, "is that Rupertus ordered Puller to assault impossible enemy positions . . . daily till the First was decimated." Puller might well have protested or demurred, but Rupertus probably would have relieved him. "It was more or less of a massacre," Puller later admitted. "There was no way to cut down losses and follow orders." Unlike Puller, the general had few good characteristics as a commander. A thirty-year veteran of the Corps, the fifty-four-year-old Rupertus had once been a champion marksman (he later penned "The Rifleman's Creed"). In the 1930s, while stationed in China, he had lost his wife and two of his children to a scarlet fever epidemic. By most accounts, he was never the same after that tragedy. He grew more reticent, more withdrawn, and more dour. Earlier in World War II, he had served as assistant division commander of the 1st Marine Division until being promoted to the top job in late 1943. He was aloof from his men and frosty with his staff, especially the able General Smith, his second in command, whom he treated like an unwanted disease. Cold and testy, Rupertus did not communicate well with his subordinate commanders.

He was a poor judge of terrain and tactics. He was rightfully proud of the Marine Corps, but allowed that pride to morph negatively into fierce contempt for the Army and the supposed incompetence of soldiers. At Peleliu, his men paid dearly for his interservice chauvinism. In short, he was completely out of his depth as a division commander.

Before the invasion, he had made the colossal mistake of telling his division that the fight for Peleliu would only take three days. Once the invasion began, he seemed entirely preoccupied with making this foolish and unfounded prediction come true. When the battle shaped up as a long slog, he at first denied the obvious, and then responded with ever more orders to attack, particularly in the Umurbrogol. Because he had broken his ankle in a pre-landing exercise, thus limiting his mobility, he was generally confined to his command post (CP). Like some sort of latter-day château general, he spent much of his time on the phone, snarling at his subordinates to "hurry up" and capture the island. As the casualty numbers piled up, he seemed divorced from reality. One day, during the height of the 1st Marine Regiment's struggle for the Umurbrogol, a newspaper correspondent came back from the front lines and told the general how many dead Marines he had just seen. At first, Rupertus tried to deny this, but realizing that the reporter knew what he was talking about, the general commented: "You can't make an omelette without breaking the eggs."

As the days passed and the casualty numbers grew, the general himself was on the verge of nervous exhaustion. In one instance, Rupertus sat, head in his hands, on the sleeping bunk he kept in his command post. "This thing has just about got me beat," he told Lieutenant Colonel Harold Deakin, his personnel (G1) officer. Deakin put his arm around the general and consoled him. "Now, General, everything is going to work out." Another time, later in the campaign, Rupertus summoned Colonel Bucky Harris, commander of the 5th Marines, to the division CP. Harris found Rupertus in there all alone, with tears streaming down his cheeks. "Harris, I'm at the end of my rope," he said. Rupertus told Colonel Harris that he was thinking of turning over command to him, but he later calmed down and nothing ever came of this.[26]

The general's main problem was stubborn, narrow-minded, self-defeating pride. The 1st Marine Division was part of the III Marine Amphibious Corps, under Major General Roy Geiger. The other major unit under Geiger's command was the Army's 81st Infantry Division. Even as the 1st Marine Division invaded Peleliu, elements of the 81st had secured nearby Angaur. By September 19, the division's 321st Infantry Regiment was available to reinforce the Marines at Peleliu. Rupertus was lucid and intelligent enough to understand how badly his division needed the Army's help at the Umurbrogol. Yet, for days he refused to even consider this option. He was absolutely determined that his division would take Peleliu alone. He was contemptuous of the Army and would not even think of asking for help from mere soldiers. He clung to his miserably wrong prediction of a quick campaign, each day expecting, and pushing mightily for, a battle-winning breakthrough. In other words, he was willing to squander the lives of his men in order to feed his own pride and prejudice. "This reluctance to use Army troops . . . was very noticeable to the Corps staff," Colonel Walter Wachtler, Geiger's operations officer, later wrote. "It is probable that he [Rupertus] felt, like most Marines, that he and his troops could and would handle any task assigned to them without asking for outside help." One Marine junior officer, writing to his family, put it even more succinctly. The brass, he said, "would never call in the Army like this, for it would hurt the name of the Marine Corps, I suppose, to let the world know that 'doggie' reinforcements had to be called in so early!!" This mindset has, at times, plagued Marine officers. The Corps inculcates the notion—crucial to the Marine identity—that Marines are tougher and simply better than soldiers. Marines can achieve most anything without much outside help, so the thinking goes. This is indeed what makes Marines so special, but in some instances, like Peleliu, it can also lead to a collective isolation in outlook, as if no one else is worthy to fight alongside Marines. Rupertus is the classic example of this insular mode of thought.

Geiger, however, was different. From D-day onward, he was ashore at Peleliu. Brave and energetic, he roamed the battlefield, constantly gathering information on what was happening. He had a low opinion of Rupertus, and had never gotten along particularly well with him. For several days, he watched as the situation at Umurbrogol grew worse. He considered relieving Rupertus, but did not like the idea of firing a Marine division commander in the middle of a fight. Instead, on September 21, he decided to take matters into his own hands. Geiger and his staff visited Puller's command post. Shirtless, with a corncob pipe in his mouth, Chesty limped around on his swollen leg while briefing the corps commander. Drenched in sweat, Puller's hair was plastered to his head. Colonel William Coleman, a member of the corps staff,

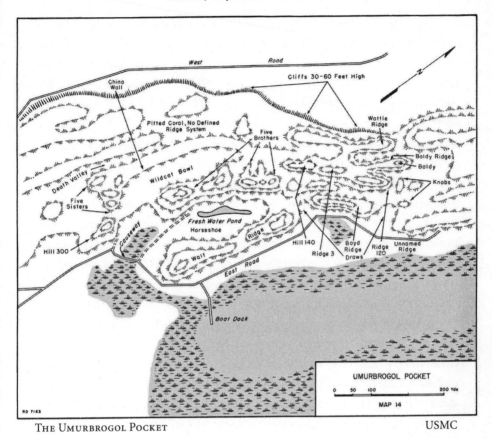

THE UMURBROGOL POCKET   USMC

had the impression that Chesty was completely exhausted. "He was unable to give a very clear picture of what his situation was." Geiger asked him if he needed reinforcements and Chesty "stated that he was doing alright with what he had." This was a crucial moment when Puller could have asked for the help he so badly needed but, like Rupertus, he could not bring himself to do so.

Puller's condition, and his tenuous grasp of reality, was the final straw for Geiger. The corps commander believed that Puller should have flanked and enveloped the Umurbrogol, rather than attacking it head-on. General Geiger proceeded immediately to Rupertus's command post and told Rupertus that the 1st Marines were finished as a fighting unit. The regiment had suffered 56 percent casualties. Davis's 1st Battalion alone had lost 71 percent of its Marines. Geiger told Rupertus that the regiment needed to be removed, not just from the line but from the battle altogether, and sent back to Pavuvu, where the unit could be rebuilt for future campaigns. He told Rupertus he intended to replace them with the Army's 321st Infantry. "At this, General Rupertus became greatly alarmed and requested that no such action be taken," Coleman wrote, "stating that he was sure he could secure the island in another day or two." Geiger overruled him. The battle was over for the 1st Marines, and the Army would replace them. The Marines of the 1st Regiment had literally given everything they could give at the Umurbrogol. They had fought, sweat, bled, and cried. They had performed with a gallantry that was nearly superhuman. Indeed, General Smith later wondered how they were able to capture as much ground as they did. Now, at last, thanks to General Geiger's intercession, their hell on earth was finally over. As they left the line, one of them said: "We're not a regiment. We're the *survivors* of a regiment." Another one later added: "We were no longer even human beings."[27]

Enter the Wildcats

The soldiers of the 81st Infantry Division were known as the Wildcats. Having seen limited action on Angaur, they were fairly new to combat, but not to soldiering. They had trained together for two long years. In contrast to the youthful Marines, the bulk of whom were in their late teens or early twenties, many of the Wildcats were in their late twenties and thirties. These Army infantrymen answered to a range of nicknames: doughboys, doughfeet, and dog-faces being the most common (the next generation would call them grunts, a name that stuck).

On September 23, they entered the front lines at the Umurbrogol. The soldiers immediately noticed the exhaustion in the faces of their 1st Marine Regiment comrades. The Marines were coated with coral grime. Their arms were marred by festering nicks and cuts they had gotten from diving for cover among the sharp rocks. Some had shaggy whiskers. Most had hollow, weary eyes, gazing dully ahead in what infantrymen generally call the thousand-yard stare. Their young faces looked strangely old, with lines caused by the constant facial muscular tension that resulted from abject fear. The Marines were worn down in less than a week by the unimaginable stress of bitter combat that caused "the constriction of the blood vessels in the stomach and the sudden whirling of the brain that occurs when a large shell burst nearby or a friend has his eyes or entrails torn out," one of the Marines later wrote. To Sergeant Thomas Climie, an older man in the 321st, these brave Marines were "dirty, scared kids. I felt so sorry for them. They were in shock." Filled with foreboding, he and the other soldiers stared, with anguish, at the Marines.

For their part, the Marines were bemused at how fresh and clean the soldiers looked. Sergeant Peto, who had come frighteningly close to death at both the Point and the Umurbrogol, watched as a burly Army captain led his troops into the line. When the captain saw how few Marines were left, "his face turned pale and he reminded me of a man that was told he was about to be shot and there was a good possibility that that is exactly what happened to him." A moment later, an awestruck Army tank crewman offered Peto some tomato juice. He drank some juice, but it no sooner hit his stomach than he vomited it up. "That pretty much tells the story of Peleliu." Amid the solemnity, the Marines kept their sense of humor. In one position, a sergeant, clearly thrilled to see the soldiers, smiled and quipped: "Here comes the Army, with the USO girls in tow."

The subtle differences between the two ground combat services were evident. Colonel Robert Dark, commander of the 321st, was shocked to find Colonel Puller so close to the front lines. When a confused Dark asked Puller several times for the location of his CP, an exasperated Puller spat and said, with emphasis: "Right here!" Dark ordered his adjutant to place his own CP one thousand yards to the rear. The story spread like wildfire among the Marines, who generally thought of themselves as tougher and truer warriors than soldiers. The soldiers believed Marines were overaggressive, to the point of mindlessness (hence the term "jarhead"). Lieutenant George Pasula, a young platoon leader in G Company, 321st, was stunned to find that the Marine company his unit relieved only had twenty-eight survivors. "Even I, as a young 2LT, began to wonder about the head-on attacks by Puller's 1st Marines." Pasula thought it made more sense to envelop the ridges and then use overwhelming firepower against the Japanese. This was the Army way.[28]

The 321st took its place in the line, on the western side of the Umurbrogol, alongside the 7th Marines. The two regiments repeatedly attacked the enemy-held ridges and caves. Most of the soldiers had already experienced combat on Angaur, but they were shocked by the bloodbath in which they now found themselves immersed. Like their Marine friends, they struggled just to keep their footing. They also got shot to pieces as they tried to assault caves and ridges. Lieutenant Pasula's platoon was working its way over a coral ridge, trying to push TNT pole charges into a cave opening. As several men were maneuvering the poles over the ridge, edging the charges in the direction of the cave, the lieutenant was talking on the radio with his superior officer. "I heard and felt a commotion, and looking up the ridge, I saw [a] Jap grenade just as it exploded." The grenade destroyed his rifle and his radio. "Blood was spurting from my right cheek." He caught fragments in his face, his shoulder, and his arm, but somehow the shrapnel did not break any bones. His radioman helped him across an open area, dodging sniper fire, to an aid station.

A couple hundred yards to the right, Captain Pierce Irby's L Company was trying to scale "a cliff of solid coral rock approximately 40 feet in height. The men had to pick their way very carefully up through the rocks. Often it was necessary for one man to climb to a place where he could get a foot hold and pull other men up to him with his rifle or foot. The progress was measured in inches." Not only were the rock-climbing soldiers in a terribly vulnerable position; they were really at the mercy of their enemies. Before the soldiers could get their footing, a shower of grenades exploded among them. Everyone hit the ground and tried to find someone, or something, to shoot at. Enemy machine-gun fire swept up and down the ranks of prone Americans. Men could hear the distinctive snapping sound of bullets ricocheting off rocks.

Every so often, the bullets struck flesh and bones. It sounded like a baseball bat striking a watermelon. "We just lay flat on the ground, and prayed that we survived the exchange," one soldier recalled. It was hard to make any headway under such circumstances.[29]

As the Marines had feared, a few of the soldiers were not up to the formidable task of assaulting the Umurbrogol. In one instance, Captain Thomas B. Jones, the commander of K Company, got orders from his battalion commander to take a key knoll. If the Americans did not take it, then the whole battalion, and the neighboring Marines, would come under suffocating enemy fire, and perhaps find themselves exposed to a Japanese counterattack. Jones's company had already lost many of its people in a direct assault on a pillbox at Angaur. He was in no mood for another such attack, so he refused the order on the grounds that attacking the knoll would be suicidal. The battalion commander relieved him. Then the only other surviving officer in K Company refused to take command of the company from Jones and carry out the order. He too was relieved.

Captain Irby was forced to transfer his 3rd Platoon leader to command K Company. "Some of the men were nearby and heard the statements made by their company officers," Irby wrote. "It was apparent that their morale had been greatly affected." The attack went nowhere. In the recollection of one Marine officer, the soldiers "moved forward along the ridge a few yards until they encountered the first enemy positions, then gave it all up as a bad idea." Marines from I Company, 7th Marines, ended up taking the knoll, but it cost them sixteen casualties, including the death of their company commander. Understandably, they were deeply angry over the incident, and the story spread quickly among the proud Marines, especially because the 7th was nearing total exhaustion after fighting for so long on the ridges. The problems with K Company seemed to confirm the opinion of so many Marines that the Army just could not fight like the Corps. When word of it reached General Rupertus, he smugly blurted: "There's the Wildcat Division of pussycats. Now I can tell Geiger 'I told you so. That's why I didn't want the Army involved in this in the first place.'" As if the situation would have been better without the presence of fresh reinforcements! Needless to say, Rupertus's statement revealed much about his pettiness and his myopic view of the battle. There is no record of him ever repeating his "I told you so" tirade to Geiger.

Marine frustration with K Company, 321st, was understandable, but blown out of proportion. The vast majority of the soldiers were fighting hard, doing their best, bleeding and dying alongside their Marine countrymen. As September turned to October, and the battle evolved into little more than a brutal struggle for each and every knobby ridge and fortified cave of the Umurbrogol, a distinct respect grew between the soldiers and Marines who were doing the real fighting, risking their lives in the daily crapshoot of combat.

By now, the 5th Marines had taken Ngesebus, a nearby island, and had secured the northern part of Peleliu. Battered though they were, they relieved the decimated 7th Marines and went into the line with the 321st at the Umurbrogol. All that remained in Japanese hands was the isolated inner ring of the Umurbrogol, a nine-hundred-yard-long, four-hundred-yard-wide pocket of ridges and caves. "We had everything . . . that was ever used by anybody," General Smith later said. "We had the beaches, we had the airfield, we were using everything that we ever wanted to use. All we didn't have was this darned pocket." With the airfield and the beaches secure from Japanese fire, and some of the high ground in American hands, there probably was not much point in trying to take the rest of the pocket. Better to let the isolated Japanese starve or die of thirst in their caves. But in World War II, American commanders generally liked to destroy all enemy pockets of resistance, especially in the Pacific, where the Japanese normally fought to the death rather than surrender. Wise or not—and it probably was not all that smart—this was the mind-set.[30]

So the bitter struggle for this strategically worthless coral mush continued, just as Colonel Nakagawa had foreseen. Day after day, groups of ragged American infantrymen attacked. To them, every jagged ridge and every looming cave looked alike, but they had nonetheless coined nicknames for some of the more prominent terrain features—the China Wall, the Five Sisters, the Five Brothers, Old Baldy, Hill 140, the Wildcat Bowl, and, of course, Walt Ridge. The 321st initiated an extensive sandbag-filling operation for their frontline soldiers. Carrying parties hauled the bags up to the Umurbrogol and plopped them down in rifle company areas on the front lines. Infantry soldiers then attacked by crawling forward, pushing the bags in front of themselves, affording some level of cover from the withering enemy fire.

The Americans also had plenty of fire support. Artillery constantly pounded the pocket. Sometimes bulldozers sealed caves, entombing the Japanese within. Marine F-4U Corsair fighter planes, operating from the airstrip, flew the shortest close air support missions of the war. They would take off, climb a few hundred feet, drop their bombs or napalm on suspected Japanese positions, turn around, land, and then do it again. Each flight lasted about two minutes. Some pilots did not even bother to raise their landing gear after they took off. In order to avoid friendly fire problems, "every member of the squadron was briefed in every detail of the terrain and friendly troop locations," one officer later wrote. "When the bombing run began, the frontline infantry units set off colored hand grenades to mark their lines." In many cases, infantry and air commanders flew joint reconnaissance missions together over the pocket.

Excellent and well coordinated though the air support clearly was, it could not destroy the Japanese caves. The only way to do that was through head-on assaults with direct fire support. Artillerymen from the 11th Marines, through superhuman effort, hauled their pieces to the high ground, within sight of the enemy. Sometimes they had to break their guns down into pieces, put them on pulleys, hoist them up the hills, and then reassemble them. They did this with 75-, 105-, and 155-millimeter guns. "To be effective it was often necessary to place the pieces within sniper range of the enemy," General Smith wrote. One battery set up three 105-millimeter guns and fired armor-piercing shells and white phosphorous rounds into caves at a range of only five hundred yards. The job of hauling ammunition up to the guns was arduous. "A 75 round isn't too heavy," Corporal William Burnett wrote, "but after you climb 300' [feet] with them and then have to run across 25' of open space with snipers you are pooped out." Because the infantry ranks were so depleted, many of the artillerymen stayed on the front lines, serving as de facto infantry.[31]

The most effective support came from tanks (both Marine and Army) and specially modified flamethrowing LVTs. Although the rough terrain limited the mobility of these vehicles, they worked closely with the infantry wherever possible. The LVTs crawled along, protected by the infantrymen. When the LVT crew, or a rifleman, spotted a target, the LVT belched a jet of flame in that direction. They were ideal for shooting flames into cave mouths and crevasses. "It is something to see," one soldier recalled. "They give it a squirt and the trees and brush disappear. And one sight I still can't get rid of is when a Jap appeared and the flamethrower hit him and you would see this big orange flame running and screaming and then no noise but still burning. It's terrible!"

The tanks would maneuver in front of the caves and blast them point-blank, sometimes even within a few yards of the cave openings. "Theirs was the mission of providing direct fire . . . to be used as close artillery," a tanker later wrote. One Marine recalled seeing a tank as it "rolled up to the mouth of a cave. The snout of its artillery piece swung into the hole. The piece fired shot after shot," dismembering the Japanese defenders inside. "Three . . . or four . . . rounds of HE [high explosive] bursting inside—topped off by a round or two of WP [white phosphorous] was standard tank treatment—and most effective indeed," a tank commander wrote.

In nearly every instance, the infantry stayed close to the tanks to protect them from assaults by extraordinarily brave Japanese soldiers wielding mines, torpedoes, and grenades. Private First Class John Huber of K Company, 5th Marine Regiment, was covering a tank when a Japanese machine gun opened up. He took cover next to the tank. "When the tanker spotted the Jap gun, it fired the 75 gun at it, and I took the muzzle blast of four rounds." It took him a few hours to get his hearing back, but the tank meanwhile had blown the enemy machine gunners into jagged pieces. The only trouble with the LVTs and tanks was that there were not enough of them. Because of maintenance issues, and the forbidding terrain, only a couple dozen were in operation at any given time, and that was always during the daytime.

So usually the attacks were carried out by dwindling groups of frightened, desperately weary infantrymen, carrying rifles, submachine guns, flame-throwers, and satchel demolition charges. Often, intense enemy fire killed and wounded many Americans, pinning assault elements down before they could get near the caves. Other times, the infantry was able to edge up against the openings. "We went from cave to cave, with small arms fire and grenades, to cover the men with the flamethrowers and satchel charges that would seal the caves," Private First Class Huber recalled. In an attempt to escape the flames and TNT, some of the Japanese ran from the caves, straight into riflemen like Huber, who shot them at close range. "As the Japs came running out on fire, we would have a field day finishing them off."

Sometimes, as the Americans cautiously advanced, they could hear the hidden Japanese talking or even smell their cooking. Private First Class Charlie Burchett and a group of Marines came upon one such cave and then "took a whole case of TNT and dropped it down with a rope. It quieted them down." After blasting another cave, Burchett and his buddies counted seventy-five dead Japanese. Like many of the caves, this one was part of an elaborate tunnel system that the Japanese had burrowed beneath the sharp rocks of the Umurbrogol. In the tunnels they stored food, ammunition, sake, and clothing.[32]

At night, some of the Japanese emerged from their caves. Some were looking for water, but most were intent on crawling into the American lines to kill a Marine or a soldier. Many companies strung barbed wire in front of their positions, but that was no guarantee of safety. By the glimpsing half-light of flares, the Americans fought off sleep (not to mention fear), and stared intently into the night, trying to spot them. "Their ability to creep in silently over rough rocks strewn with pulverized vegetation was incredible," one Marine said. Sergeant Francis Heatley, a machine gunner in the 321st, vividly remembered the rustling sound of rosary beads sliding across the rifle butts of prayerful men around him. The nights seemed endless. "Utter emptiness created a hole in my soul, as though life no longer had any meaning." His unit shot at anything that moved. The Marines tended to be more disciplined with their fire for fear of giving away their positions or hitting nearby friendly troops. When the Japanese did make it to the American positions, "they rushed in jabbering or babbling incoherent sounds, sometimes throwing a grenade, but always swinging a saber, bayonet, or knife," Eugene Sledge wrote.

Everything about the Umurbrogol was nightmarish and crude. It was ugly, foul, and wasteful as only war can be. Dante Alighieri or Jonathan Edwards, in their wildest imaginings, could hardly have conceived of anything more hellish. Four-man stretcher teams labored mightily to move wounded men down the steep slopes to the safety of field hospitals. Japanese snipers tried to shoot the bearers and, too often, succeeded. On the slippery ridges, it was easy to drop the wounded man onto the sharp coral, adding to his misery. The heat continued unabated. Grenades and mortar shells had to be kept in the shade lest they explode from the intensity of the sun. The twin stenches of death and rot were draped, like a suffocating, sewage-corrupted blanket, over the entire pocket. "It is difficult to convey to anyone who has not experienced it the ghastly horror of having your sense of smell saturated constantly with the putrid odor of rotting human flesh day after day, night after night,"

Sledge wrote. In such tropical heat, decomposition was quick. Dead bodies turned black and swelled up to twice their size. "Added to the awful smell of the dead of both sides was the repulsive odor of human excrement every-where." Rotting food, clothing, and vegetation only added to the hellish stink. Like so many others, Sledge felt as though "my lungs would never be cleansed of all those foul vapors." Some of those foul vapors emanated from the corpses of Marines whom the Japanese had mutilated, severing their decomposed penises and shoving them into fly-filled mouths.

Land crabs came out at night, skittering around, feeding on the dead. Swarms of flies bred with stunning alacrity, converging on the refuse and the decomposing corpses. They gorged themselves on so much blood and flesh that they swelled up to the size of bumblebees and were scarcely able to fly. When they did fly, they made a distinct humming sound. There were millions of them. "When you tried to lift food up to your mouth," Sergeant Climie explained, "before you got it there, it was covered with these flies. You could not brush them away, you had to snap them off with your fingers. We all got real sick and weak from diarrhea." The flies were bluish green colored and so aggressive that, in the recollection of one Marine, "if you had food in your mouth and if you opened it very wide, a fly would fly into your mouth. That's how bad those things were." The troops joked that the flies even had their own runway at the airfield. Sanitation teams attacked the flies with copious amounts of DDT, but the insecticide only worked on the adults, not the lar-vae. Still, the DDT helped reduce the fly population to some semblance of manageability.[33]

The Anticlimactic End

On October 15, after a month of horrible combat, the 1st Marine Division began withdrawing from the Umurbrogol. A few days later, these haunted sur-vivors boarded ships that returned them to Pavuvu. The division had suffered 6,526 casualties, mostly in the rifle companies. The 323rd, another regiment from the 81st Infantry Division, replaced the Marines. Together the soldiers of the 321st and 323rd overran the remnants of Japanese resistance in the Umur-brogol Pocket. In a tactic that was eerily reminiscent of the improvised explosive devices a later generation of American infantry soldiers would face, the Japanese booby-trapped much of the pocket. "In one of the valleys . . . 20 booby traps were found, the instruments ranging in size from the small 'Kiska Type' hand grenade to 100 pound aerial bombs," a 323rd Infantry intelligence summary reported. "Both trip wires and pressure type devices were used, as well as the trips being fired electrically." In one instance, dogfaces from E Company were moving through a draw when they ran right into a cleverly camouflaged trap. An electrically charged aerial bomb exploded, killing or wounding dozens of men. "Screams of pain and fright filled the air," the company history recorded. "The evacuation of the torn bodies of our buddies . . . was a hard grim task. Many of our closest friends could not be recognized. Many died in the arms of those who tried to ease their pain." Concussed men, with wide and hollow eyes, staggered down the ridges, toward the battalion aid station.

Mercilessly, and with careful deliberation, over the course of four weeks, the soldiers eliminated the Japanese defenders of the Umurbrogol. At last, on November 27, they killed off the last defenders. Colonel Nakagawa and General Murai burned the regimental colors and killed themselves. The Americans claimed later to have found their remains. The 81st Division had suffered 3,275 casualties, bringing total U.S. casualties at Peleliu close to 10,000. This was in exchange for the deaths of some 11,000 Japanese defenders, a nearly one-to-one casualty ratio.

Without a doubt, every Marine and soldier who fought at Peleliu was forever haunted, at least in some way, by the experience. Harry Gailey, the author of the best single book on the battle, properly wrote: "In terms of sheer heroism, every man who fought at Peleliu deserved the highest award his country could bestow." In the view of Gailey and almost every other historian of the battle, it should never have been fought. Possession of the island gained almost no strategic advantages for the Americans. Instead, Peleliu lived on as a cautionary tale of the price combat troops pay when senior leaders make poor decisions, based on faulty intelligence, interservice rivalry, and a lack of flexible response to a thinking, determined enemy.

By assaulting the Umurbrogol so vigorously, the Americans played right into Japanese hands. Colonel Nakagawa could not have planned it any better. The battle unfolded more or less exactly as he envisioned. It is true that the Americans took Peleliu, and thus won a "victory" of sorts. But the Japanese fulfilled their strategic objective of turning the battle into a bloody de-bacle for the Americans. Even though the Americans enjoyed total air and naval supremacy, the island could only be taken through the extremely val-iant actions, on a daily basis, of Marines and soldiers. Even then it was a nightmare of nearly unimaginable proportions.[34]

CHAPTER 3

Aachen, 1944:
Knocking 'Em All Down on a Politically
Unrestrained Urban Battlefield

The Setting

To THE GERMANS, AACHEN WAS a major political symbol of nationhood. To the Americans, it was little more than a collection of buildings. In the fall of 1944, as American troops approached the venerable western German city, Adolf Hitler ordered that it be defended to the last man. To him, and to many other Germans, Aachen was a cultural icon. This was where Charlemagne had once been crowned Holy Roman Emperor, creating what the Nazis later called the First Reich.

Aachen was the first major German city in the path of advancing American armies. Before the war, about 165,000 people had lived there. By the late summer of 1944, Allied bombers had raided the town no less than seventy times, damaging about half of Aachen's buildings, prompting wide-scale civilian evacuations. By September 1944, there were about 20,000 residents left. At that time, in the wake of a seemingly relentless American advance, German military authorities actually contemplated abandoning the town, partially out of concern for the speed with which the Americans were approaching, and partially because Aachen itself was located on low ground, in a basin, surrounded by imposing hills, making it hard to defend. Moreover, Aachen lay between two strong belts of fortifications to the west and to the east. These were the pillboxes, bunkers, tank traps, and minefields of the Siegfried Line, an imposing network of defensive fortifications that the Nazis had built to impede any invasion of their country from the west. But a combination of logistical problems, worsening weather, Siegfried Line fortifications, and German reinforcements slowed the whole Allied advance to a crawl in late September. Now the Germans settled in for a fight in and around Aachen. Hitler reinforced the Aachen garrison, ordered the remainder of the population evacuated, and told his soldiers to hold on to Charlemagne's city.

The Americans originally intended to bypass Aachen. "We had to weigh the value of the city of Aachen against getting a breakthrough of the Siegfried Line," Major General J. Lawton Collins said. Throughout September and early October, Collins's VII Corps slowly breached the Siegfried Line pillboxes to the north and south of Aachen. Two of his infantry divisions, the 30th and the 1st, were gradually enveloping the town—the 30th from the north and the 1st from the south. Collins's plan was for them to link up, besiege it, and force it to surrender. He and his division commanders initially agreed "not to get involved in the streets of Aachen." The key terrain, they thought, was the high ground outside of Aachen, especially the hills a few miles to the northeast of town, near Verlautenheide. The city of Aachen itself, they felt, was indefensible and next to meaningless. They were absolutely correct about the importance of the hills to the northeast, but mistaken in their assumption that Aachen itself had little meaning.

By early October, both divisions were involved in ferocious fighting for the hills. In the meantime, the Germans were hitting them with powerful counterattacks and had reinforced the city. In Aachen, the enemy now had five thousand soldiers, mostly from the 246th Volksgrenadier Division plus a few SS troops, entrenched in cellars and stone buildings. These men were supported by two platoons of 120-millimeter mortars, five Mark IV tanks, and over thirty artillery pieces. With the hill fights still raging, no siege yet under way, and such a powerful enemy force ensconced in the town, the Americans could no longer afford to ignore them. "These enemy forces . . . were a potential threat to our rear," one American officer later explained. Major General Collins and his immediate superior, Lieutenant General Courtney Hodges, commander of the U.S. First Army, reluctantly decided that Aachen must be taken.

This nasty job went to troops from the 1st Infantry Division, one of the most distinguished units in the Army. The 1st Division had been fighting since North Africa. The unit had assaulted Sicily and had led the way at

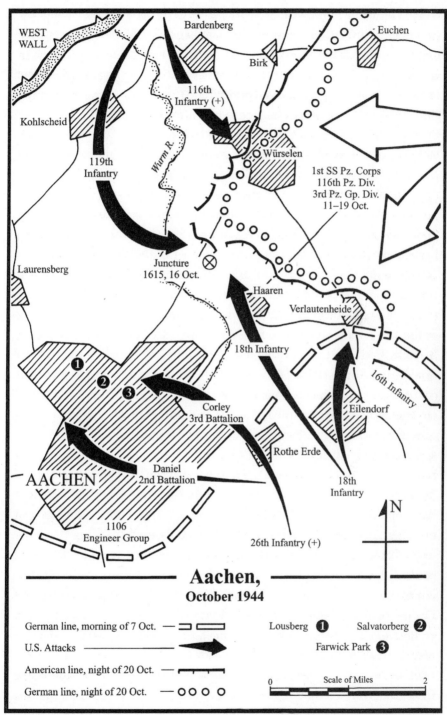

WEST WALL

Bardenberg

Euchen

Birk

116th Infantry (+)

Kohlscheid

Würselen

1st SS Pz. Corps
116th Pz. Div.
3rd Pz. Gp. Div.
11–19 Oct.

119th Infantry

Wurm R.

Laurensberg

Juncture
1615, 16 Oct.

Haaren

Verlautenheide

18th Infantry

16th Infantry

Corley
3rd Battalion

Eilendorf

Rothe Erde

AACHEN

Daniel
2nd Battalion

18th
Infantry

1106
Engineer Group

26th Infantry (+)

N

Aachen,
October 1944

German line, morning of 7 Oct.

U.S. Attacks

American line, night of 20 Oct.

German line, night of 20 Oct.

Lousberg **1**   Salvatorberg **2**

Farwick Park **3**

0   Scale of Miles   2

Omaha Beach in Normandy. Along the way, the division had suffered heavy casualties. Nonetheless, most of the commanders and staff officers were highly experienced. Their chronically understrength rifle companies were comprised of a mixture of veterans (most of whom had been wounded at least once) and replacements. Two of the division's regiments, the 16th and the 18th, were tied up in the fighting for the hills around Verlautenheide. To take the town, Major General Clarence Huebner, the division commander, only had two battalions, plus attachments, available from his remaining infantry regiment, the 26th, known as the Blue Spaders. This amounted to about two thousand soldiers against an enemy force over twice that size.[1]

Fortunately for the Americans, these battalions were led by two of the finest field-grade commanders in the entire U.S. Army. Thirty-eight-year-old Lieutenant Colonel Derrill Daniel, commander of the 2nd Battalion, had a doctorate in entomology from Cornell University. Before the war, he had worked as an insect control expert for the state of New York. He was also a reserve infantry officer who had been called to active duty in 1940, eventually ending up in battalion command. Nicknamed "Uncle Dan" (or sometimes "Colonel Dan") by his admiring men, he led the 2nd Battalion through the invasions of North Africa, Sicily, and Normandy, logging nearly two years of command time. He had proven himself to be an insightful, brave, and valorous commander. He already had four Silver Stars for bravery to his credit. His colleague, Lieutenant Colonel John Corley, commander of the 3rd Battalion, was every bit as distinguished. This Brooklyn-born son of Irish immigrants had graduated from West Point in 1938 and had been with his battalion since North Africa. Just thirty years old, he was infused with a youthful vigor and sheer force of personality that had become legendary in the battalion. He held his subordinate commanders to the highest standards, demanding excellence in combat leadership from them and showing them how to succeed. "I don't remember him smiling and I don't remember him shaking my hand," one junior officer later said. More than anything, he led by example. He had the rare gift of maintaining a commander's perspective while frequently fighting on the front lines like any everyday soldier. His bravery bordered on the maniacal. Between the North Africa and Sicily battles alone, he had been decorated no less than six times for valor, including the Distinguished Service Cross, the Army's second-highest decoration.[2]

Both Daniel and Corley had fought their way into Aachen's suburbs in the first week of October. Both had studied the terrain and prepared their battalions as best they could, under the frenetic circumstances of continuous operations, for urban combat. The inner ring of the city dated back to Charlemagne's time. It had narrow streets and crooked, close-packed buildings. To the north, along wider streets, were Aachen's hotels and spas, along with a stretch of high ground consisting of three hill masses generally called Observatory Hill or Lousberg that loomed, at the highest point, some 862 feet over the city. Surrounding everything were industrial suburbs of coal mines, factories, and homes. The Americans planned to assault the town from south to north. The 2nd Battalion's job was to capture the heart of the city. On the 2nd Battalion's right, the 3rd Battalion was to push northwest through the factories, the spas, and hotels, and then take all the hills of Lousberg.

Some of the troops had fought in towns during the battles for Sicily, Normandy, and in the drive across France. But no one had any experience fighting in a city of this size. The soldiers tended to call urban combat "street fighting," a moniker that revealed a certain level of ignorance since the open streets were often the last place an infantryman wanted to be during the fighting. The Army had almost no published doctrine on urban warfare, but this hardly mattered. The ability to improvise, under the stress of combat, was (and still is) a great strength of American ground combat troops, from privates to colonels. In this case, neither Daniel nor Corley had the time to deal with fancy field manuals or retrain their soldiers for urban combat. Instead, both men, in spite of their lack of experience with city fighting, intuitively understood how to approach it, as did many of their sergeants, lieutenants, and captains.

The key was to organize platoons and companies into combined arms teams. "Tanks and tank destroyers were assigned to each company," Lieutenant Colonel Daniel later wrote. "Artillery observers were to move forward as soon as ground was secured by the advancing rifle companies, meanwhile maintaining liaison with the rifle company commanders." Self-propelled guns and antitank guns also supported the riflemen, as did squads of engineers, mortarmen, and machine gunners.

Each group contributed its own unique strength to the team. The tanks, tank destroyers, and guns could pulverize buildings, ward off enemy armor, destroy German machine gunners, and even provide mobile cover for the infantrymen. Artillery could devastate entire city blocks, killing enemy soldiers or forcing them to move to safer places. The machine gunners and mortar teams lent even more accurate fire support. The engineers could deal with mines and booby traps. They also had the capability to blast German defenders in their cellars and bunkers. The riflemen, of course, were the lead actors in this urban choreography. They could protect the armor from the peril of enemy Panzerfaust antitank teams, whose warheads could puncture the armor of American tanks. The riflemen were also the ones who would carry out the actual assaults, securing buildings, killing the enemy at close range. These riflemen, according to one unit report, had to be "proficient in proper methods of moving along walls, advancing over walls and rooftops, firing from either shoulder, from the hip, and from covered areas, and rapid entry of buildings."

In the urban maze of rubble and ruined buildings, commanders might easily lose control of their soldiers. At Peleliu, the Americans had been hampered by poor maps. At Aachen, they were blessed with excellent, detailed maps of the city. In Daniel's case, he and his company commanders used those maps to establish "a series of checkpoints on street intersections and also in the larger buildings so that each unit knew where the adjacent units were on its flanks. Each company was assigned an area and generally each platoon a street. On cross streets, each platoon would go down about halfway, meeting in the middle."

The Americans did not have to worry about any political constraints. There were only a few thousand civilians in Aachen. The Americans had no wish to kill them, but, if they did, few would notice in the context of a world war that had already snuffed out the lives of more civilians than combatants. What's more, in Aachen the opposition would consist entirely of uniformed soldiers, making it easy for the Americans to determine who was a threat and who was not. The city was already in a decrepit state because it had been bombed so often. Thus, if the Americans unleashed wanton destruction on historical buildings, churches, and landmarks, they would suffer no political consequences in the court of world opinion. Indeed, the motto of the soldiers was "Knock 'em all down!" This applied equally to objects or people. Anyone, or anything, that even remotely threatened the Americans was fair game for the full range of U.S. firepower. In this pretelevision age, the Americans did not have to worry about the image-driven consequences of needless destruction or the killing of civilians. They could concentrate solely on the task of taking the city. The odd thing is that the Battle of Aachen was fought largely for political reasons, because of the city's cultural importance to German nationalism, yet politics had almost no impact on how either side actually fought the battle.[3]

Surrender or We'll Blow You Away

At 1020 on the morning of October 10, three American soldiers emerged from the cover of a building in Aachen's suburbs and began walking down Trierer Strasse (street), toward the German-held city. The man in the middle, Private Kenneth Kading, was waving a bedsheet-sized white flag attached to a pole. To his right was First Lieutenant William Boehme, an interpreter. To Kading's left was First Lieutenant Cedric Lafley, who was carrying orders straight from General Collins, demanding the surrender of the German garrison. The day was gray and overcast, with light rain pattering off the battered concrete. Much of Aachen was ringed by railroad tracks whose embankment rose up as high as forty feet. About fifty yards shy of a railroad underpass, several German soldiers materialized, waved the Americans over to them, and guided them through the underpass, into the German front lines. The Germans blindfolded the three Americans and led them up the street, first into an apartment building and then into a basement. Shorn of his blindfold, Lieutenant Lafley asked to see the German commander, but was told by two German officers that he was not there. Lafley gave them two envelopes containing the surrender ultimatum.

The Germans had exactly twenty-four hours to comply or else, the ultimatum decreed, Aachen would face "complete destruction." One of the German officers expressed a hope for good surrender terms. Another ventured to say that they would fight on regardless. A few minutes later, after some more desultory conversation and a polite exchange of cigarettes, the blindfolds were put back in place and the German guides led them back to the American lines. "On the way back our guides stopped briefly beside some comrades to take a nip from a bottle," Lieutenant Lafley wrote. "They would have liked to strike up a conversation with us but due to previous instructions they only spoke when necessary." The Germans led them past the underpass and nearly followed them back to the American positions. "It was necessary to tell them to stop and tell them to go back while we proceeded to our own lines." Later, the Americans broadcast the ultimatum by radio and loudspeaker. They also fired artillery shells full of surrender pamphlets into the city.

The Americans waited the requisite twenty-four hours and hoped for a German surrender. Few of the soldiers wanted to fight among Aachen's ruins. Although white flags did sprout from some windows and several dozen enemy prisoners filtered into American lines, most of the Americans were realistic enough not to get their hopes up. "Them bastards ain't gonna give up," a sergeant drawled on one street corner. "We'll have to root 'em out house to house style." He was exactly right. The German commander, Colonel Gerhard Wilck, never even replied to the ultimatum. His silence amounted to a contemptuous no.

In response, the Americans pounded Aachen for two days with artillery shells and P38 and P47 fighter-bombers. In the recollection of one witness, the fighters "came in at a 70-degree angle. You could see them strafing and then the two specks which were 500-pound bombs would cut loose and then a minute later there would be the explosion. Fires were started all over Aachen—there must have been a dozen large ones." Huge clouds of dust and smoke rose from the debris. Infantrymen watched approvingly and muttered encouragement to the aviators: "Go to it, you glamour boys!" The fighters dropped nearly 173 tons of bombs on Aachen. When the planes were gone, the artillerymen lobbed some five thousand shells at the city. At one point, as the shells exploded, scattering masonry, fragments, and dust, the Germans began playing waltz music over a loudspeaker they had set up. A bizarre voice spoke over the surreal music: "Hey, you dumb Americans, why don't you put your rifles down and come over and we'll have a party? If you will stop shelling we will play some music for you. We regret that we have none of your American swing records." When the shelling continued unabated, the voice said reprovingly: "All right, if that is the kind of music you like, that is the kind of music you shall have." Enemy mortar crews fired several rounds at the American-held buildings.

Engineers from the 1106th Engineer Combat Group added their own special flourish to the pounding. They actually built car bombs out of abandoned trolley street cars, placed them on their tracks, and used a bulldozer to push them down a hill at the Germans in Aachen. Each car bomb "was loaded with approximately a ton of enemy explosives made up of six German rockets, fifty 88mm shells, two boxes [of] 20mm shells, two boxes [of] 37mm shells and hand grenades and rifle grenades," one after action report said. The car bombs were the brainchild of Lieutenant Colonel Bill Gara, one of the engineer commanders. They did little appreciable damage. "I've always been disappointed that we didn't get better results from this ingenious scheme," Colonel Stanhope Mason, the division chief of staff, later wrote. As a whole, the bombs and shells rearranged the rubble, and jostled the Germans around, forcing them to take refuge in their cellars, but most survived the bombardment and were more than ready to fight when the assault on the city began on October 13. The incessant pounding did an effective job, though, of forcing enemy soldiers from the buildings that overlooked the railroad tracks.[4]

Plunging into the Concrete Jungle

Before launching their assault, the infantrymen hurled grenades over the railroad embankment. The grenade explosions sounded like a series of dull thuds. Men could hear shrapnel plinking off the piles of shattered masonry. As they hoisted themselves over the embankment, the city was eerily silent. The shattered hulks of apartment buildings loomed immediately ahead, brooding like some sort of disfigured ghosts. Jagged piles of rocks, support timbers, and other urban junk were heaped everywhere. Many of the soldiers took cover behind the piles or against the exterior of buildings, waiting for the supporting Shermans from the 745th Tank Battalion to negotiate their way over the tracks.

Lieutenant Colonel Daniel was impressed with the aggressiveness of the tank commanders in safely driving their vehicles over the embankment and positioning them for the assault. Daniel lined up all three of his companies, each with at least two tanks in support, and sent them forward into their assigned sectors. "Then began the slow mopping up of the buildings in the succeeding blocks," Daniel wrote. "The infantry had been instructed to avoid the open streets and work through the cellars with liberal expenditure of concussion grenades. The process was necessarily slow and methodical; it was found that in many blocks all cellars were connected, thus making it possible to clear the entire block without emerging on the streets."

Private Lauren Gast and his rifle squad found some of these pre-prepared tunnels and were only too happy to move through them. At times, though, they had to emerge from the tunnels to get into another building. "We would use a rifle grenade to blast the door open, then run across the street and enter through the open door." Most of the time, the buildings were empty. If there were no tunnels, the Americans created their own. "The area we were in was a lot of very small apartment buildings that one butted up against the next," Private Charles Dye of L Company said. "So we chopped holes through the walls and crawled through the walls. The engineers brought us up TNT and we would blow holes through the walls of these houses."

They could not take the whole city this way, though. Most of the time, they cautiously picked their way along the streets, using tanks, piles of debris, or doorways for cover. "In general a tank or a tank destroyer moved down each street with a platoon of infantry firing at the 2nd or 3rd house ahead," some of the soldiers testified in a post-battle historical interview. "When a house was cleared the infantry would signal that they were ready (and protected from muzzle blast); then and then only would the tank or tank destroyer fire its next mission. As the tracked weapons fired into a building they would force the enemy down to the cellar, where the infantry would toss hand grenades and immediately follow in." Often, the tankers fired high-explosive shells through windows and doors. Sometimes, they fired armor-piercing shells to punch a hole in a building and then followed that up with several high-explosive shells. The average tank crew fired fifty rounds of high-explosive ammunition per day.

Machine gunners set up their guns behind debris piles or in especially deep doorways about half a block behind the leading vehicles and riflemen. From there the gunners sent out volleys of bullets, down the street, ahead of their comrades as they advanced. Often the machine gunners shot up windows, especially on the upper floors of intact buildings, in hopes of killing snipers. Artillery observers moved with the infantry, calling down fire as close as two or three blocks away. The urban sprawl made radio communication spotty, so signalmen strung communication wire in the wake of the advancing infantry, allowing Corley and Daniel to stay in touch with their company commanders. Flamethrower and demolition men worked closely with the riflemen. "When a steel door was encountered," the soldiers said, "it was covered by infantry fire while the demolition man worked his way to it. At the same time, the flamethrower would work his way to a window through which he would throw a two- or three-second stream of fire normally 30–40 yards, thus forcing those inside to keep down, or driving them out." In the meantime, the demolition man would set his charge and blow the door open. Riflemen then ran forward, burst through the opening, and shot everyone inside at such close range that they could see the horrified expressions on the faces of their victims.

The Americans had to do quite a bit of "back clearing." This meant backtracking and clearing buildings they thought they had secured. "A group of enemy would work along the passageways in the sewer and then appear in areas that were thought secured," an after action report stated. "Each manhole had to be located, grenades thrown and the sewers thoroughly blocked and covered." The infantry soldiers also had to "search every building from cellar to attic, being certain that nobody, civilian or soldier, is left behind." Needless to say, this was time-consuming.[5]

Richard Tregaskis had covered the Pacific War, penning a famous book entitled *Guadalcanal Diary*. At Aachen, he tagged along with F Company, 2nd Battalion, as the men of that company fought block by block through the city. He was struck by how similar city fighting was to jungle fighting. "Windows are bushes, houses are trees. Every one of the thousands of windows, like every tropical bush or plant in the jungle, is a potential source of danger. And every house in a city, like every tree in the jungle, must be checked for enemy soldiers—probed by high explosive or an American foot soldier." As Tregaskis watched, the troops unleashed every implement of firepower in their arsenal, at anything or anyone they even perceived to be a threat. "The technique is to blast your way through the middle of a block of houses with high explosive when you can; just as you might carve a path through the solid wall of jungle with a machete."

Even with all the firepower, the process was exceedingly dangerous. The Germans could choose from a dizzying array of hiding places. Cellars with street-level windows were ideal locations for machine gunners, who spewed grazing fire along the concrete streets, or Panzerfaust gunners with perfect vantage points to hit the treads or side armor of tanks. Snipers favored upper-level windows because of the fields of fire and sight lines they offered. Sergeant Mack Morris watched, in disgust, as "a soldier stood easily in a doorway and a sniper two blocks away put a bullet through his head. The boy fell and lay quietly for a while. Then he bled from the mouth and groaned and died. His blood covered the doorway."

Elsewhere, at the leading edge of the 3rd Battalion's advance, Private First

Class Leroy Stewart, a scout in K Company, was crawling in a ditch alongside a curve in a street. Several machine guns opened up on him, kicking up mud and grass frighteningly close. He was an experienced infantryman who had joined his company in Normandy. Realizing that the road was completely covered by the enemy guns, he crawled back and looked for a concealed route to close with the machine guns. It occurred to Stewart that a tank could destroy the machine guns, so he sent back a request for one. "Word came back up. They didn't want to send up a tank because it might get knocked out. That made me mad. They didn't care if I got clobbered but didn't want to take a chance with a tank."

Stewart's attitude was very common among infantrymen. Nothing infuriated them more than this kind of situation. Their job was the most dangerous. They took the highest casualties. To them, it made sense to call on every measure of support, not just to accomplish the mission but to minimize their own danger as much as possible. But officers—especially tankers—often had a more cold-blooded point of view. To them, tanks were more precious than riflemen, especially in city fighting, where the armor was so immobile and vulnerable in tight spaces. As one such officer wrote, "It is not advisable to have [tanks] advance with the assault infantry. It would be very simple for the enemy to attack the tank" with a range of weapons. "A tank has no room to maneuver in a city street, and thus becomes very vulnerable to AT [antitank] fire."

Reflecting this viewpoint, Stewart's platoon leader came up and ordered him to get moving. Stewart tried to explain the situation to the lieutenant but he was unswayed. "He told me he was giving me a direct order to move up and not keep holding up things." Private First Class Stewart angrily refused. Here was a classic example of a crisis in small-unit leadership. Stewart had more combat experience than his lieutenant, affording him more status. In the Army's hierarchical structure, the officer's word should have been law. In garrison it probably would have been, but not in this life-or-death combat situation. Stewart knew that Army discipline and potential punishment paled in comparison to the grave danger posed by the machine guns. In real combat, American soldiers followed officers and sergeants because of confidence in their leadership, not necessarily because of their rank. The new lieutenant thus had no leverage. If he threatened court-martial, Stewart would probably have welcomed it as a chance to leave the front lines.

Stewart was a good soldier, though, not a malingerer. He offered to do what the lieutenant wanted but only "if he would go beside me." Again, here was another test of leadership, and the lieutenant failed. Instead of accepting this challenge, thus demonstrating his courage and a belief in his own orders, the lieutenant threatened to court-martial Stewart. As he did so, another soldier let the young officer off the hook by offering to carry out the lieutenant's order himself. The soldier made it to the bend in the road when, all at once, the guns opened up. Bullets tore into him. Stewart's squad leader tried to pull the wounded man back but he got hit, too. Chastened, the lieutenant called up tanks. The infantrymen used the tanks for cover. The tanks blasted the machine-gun-infested buildings, and the advance continued. In Stewart's opinion, "we had lost both of these men when we didn't have to." Such are the grave stakes of small-unit leadership in the infantry.[6]

Some of the heaviest fighting raged in several city blocks around a cemetery that was located immediately astride the 2nd Battalion's planned route of advance. Here the Germans had pillboxes, trenches, and antitank ditches, along with 20-millimeter and 75-millimeter guns hidden in several apartments. One platoon got caught in a cross fire of deadly machine-gun and mortar fire that killed two men and badly wounded eight others. A Panzerfaust streaked from a building and slammed into a tank. The ensuing explosion "knocked out" the tank. This was a boxing term favored by the Americans to describe a catastrophic kill. It was easier just to say "knocked out" rather than to describe the actual reality of twisted metal, burned crewmen, and exploding ammunition. For hours the two sides battered each other. Machine guns chattered. Tank guns boomed. Bazooka rockets smashed into walls. Rifles barked. American BAR men disgorged twenty-round magazines with a steady "tac, tac, tac" staccato.

The Americans steadily overwhelmed the German defenders, but doing so was a nightmare. One enemy-held building was really a reinforced steel and concrete pillbox. It contained four machine guns, protected by soldiers with Panzerfausts and MP40 submachine guns that the Americans called "burp guns." The burp guns were deadly at close range and could fire thirty-two-round clips at a rate of four hundred rounds per minute. At ranges greater than one hundred yards, the burp guns were useless. In tight spaces, they were quite deadly. The Americans brought up an antitank gun and battered the pillbox with several rounds, to no effect. In the end, according to a unit citation, "riflemen infiltrated under intense enemy fire that took its toll, and stormed the building, killing and wounding the entire German group of defenders." In other words, foot soldiers somehow worked their way close to the building as bullets hit many of them, probably killing a few (hence the phrase "took its toll"), until they were close enough to hurl grenades, burst inside, and shoot their enemies at close range.

Whoever wrote the citation did not mention the staggering toll this daring assault must have taken on the surviving American riflemen—the adrenaline rush, the gut-wrenching fear, the anguish of seeing friends torn apart by bullets and fragments, the guilt and helplessness of being able to do nothing to alleviate their suffering, and, especially, the trauma of killing fellow humans at close range, watching the life drain from their faces, hearing them cry for their mothers, listening to them beg for survival, possibly even finding family photos in their wallets, and knowing all the while who was responsible for killing them. This was the reality of urban combat for the 26th Infantry at Aachen.[7]

Experiencing the City

As the Americans drove deeper into the city, they encountered substantial numbers of civilians. Their presence only added to the stress of fighting in such an urban maze. To some extent, most of the soldiers held the German people responsible for the war, so they felt little sympathy for them. Nor did the Americans regret inflicting destruction upon such a shrine of German national consciousness. At the same time, though, few if any men wanted to kill or harm a noncombatant. "There were a lot of Germans still living in the town, in the basements," Private Dye said. "We did have to take some consideration for them. We tried not to hurt them. We weren't fighting the civilians; we were fighting the soldiers."

When the infantry soldiers flushed such civilians from homes and cellars, their first priority was to make sure they posed no threat. Very few did. Most of the Germans were frightened, almost desperate-looking. The vast majority were elderly people or children. "You want to get them out of the way so you can go on," one infantryman said. "Then some old lady . . . will remember that she left her kerchief, and of course she'll want to go back and get it. Or some little girl about six will have run off without her coat and her mother will want to go back to the house and get it or something. Damn it, that's a nuisance when you're fighting a war." Nuisance or not, the infantry showed remarkable patience with the civilians, if only because they were happy to spend a few minutes dealing with Germans who were not shooting at them.

In the wake of the infantry, civil affairs teams, intelligence specialists, and military policemen moved the civilians to the safety of barracks outside of town, cared for their basic needs, and debriefed them. "Normally people would march to the rear on foot, carrying what personal belongings they could," one civil affairs soldier later said. "At times they were loaded on empty trucks going to the rear, so that they would not interfere with transportation going to the front [lines]." The Americans issued them identification cards, fed them from food stocks they had captured in France, and gave them medical attention. On the first two days alone, the Americans evacuated 609 civilians. In the ensuing days, the numbers rose into the thousands.

Specially trained German-speaking counterintelligence teams—aided by German informers—circulated among the local men, making sure they were not Nazi spies. In one instance, Sergeant Dick Lang was interrogating a group of people in a church when he noticed a priest who, for some reason, did not look the part. Lang questioned him intensely and took an instant dislike to him, but the man answered all of his questions with no problem. He asked the other people about him and they said they had only known him for two weeks but he was okay. Lang still did not feel right about the man. "I couldn't really find anything wrong with the priest except I didn't like him." Another, less patient member of Lang's team shoved a pistol in the priest's face and demanded answers. "At this, our suspect stood up very straight, and at attention gave his true name and military rank. He was an SS spy, one of the first caught in Germany." He was, of course, a rarity. Most of the civilians were ordinary people who were glad to see the fighting pass them by. They were simply biding their time until they could return to their shattered homes and rebuild them.[8]

As German soldiers retreated at Aachen, they often left behind webs of booby traps and mines for the advancing Americans. Like Tregaskis's jungle, the urban wasteland was ideal for such traps. Slag heaps, hills of masonry, doors, window frames, and the assorted detritus of city life all made excellent hiding places. Earlier in the war, the German Army had done the same thing in the towns of Italy and France, so this was merely a continuation of their impersonal defensive warfare. In blocks where the Germans stood and fought, the Americans were reasonably sure to encounter few mines or booby traps because the Germans, of course, had no desire to trigger their own traps. But undefended areas fairly crawled with them. This was why Daniel and Corley attached teams of engineers to their rifle companies. As tanks and infantry soldiers carefully maneuvered along each street, engineers kept a wary eye out for mines and traps. "Certain houses had their doors wired to explosives in the mailbox," an engineer commander wrote. "A house yard was found to be mined and was carefully avoided throughout the operation. This small area was found to contain at least twenty-five booby traps, most of which were made of grenades with pull wires." Teller mines blocked some rubble-choked streets. Live grenades were placed in cupboards and drawers.

One thing that worked in the Americans' favor was that the Germans had to do almost all of their booby-trapping hastily at night. Also, Colonel Wilck needed most of his own engineers to fight as infantry, meaning he had few experts available for extensive booby-trapping. "Frequently trip wires were fairly obvious," the same engineer officer commented. Sometimes detonators were sloppily hidden or at times "not concealed or carried away." Quite often, civilians and prisoners revealed the locations of booby traps because they knew the Americans would defuse them, minimizing property damage and loss of life for everyone.

Most of the time, the infantry soldiers found more benign items in Aachen than mines. After all, thousands of people had once lived there. Their property was everywhere—clothing, jewelry, heirlooms, books, personal papers, cabinets, photos and the like. It was a strange mixture of the harshness of war with the comforts of home. The Americans rifled through many a family home. The soldiers were mainly looking for food, alcohol, money, valuables, and weapons. In the bombed-out kitchen of one shattered house, several soldiers from F Company found a tasty menu of food to scrounge. The kitchen, in the recollection of one witness, "was well stocked with rows of home-canned vegetables, a big barrel of hen eggs and another of goose eggs. There were various kinds of bread, cakes and preserves . . . all spread out by shelling." The soldiers promptly cooked themselves a meal of scrambled eggs, topped off by cakes.

At one point during the battle, Private First Class Stewart's K Company took a jam factory. "There were big wooden barrels full of fruit juice. We would shoot a hole in the barrel and drink all we could. There was fresh jam of all kinds waiting to be eaten. Close by was a ginger bread factory so we got a lot of the bread and made jam sandwiches." This rich food was rough on the constitutions of infantrymen who were used to eating canned C or K rations, causing some serious diarrhea. Toilet paper was already in short supply and, for obvious reasons, this made the diarrhea problem much worse. "We were using anything we could find for paper," Stewart said. "Curtains, bedding and anything we could find was used." In yet another abandoned house, Private Jim Curran's squad found a two-foot-high jug of wine. "It was the greatest wine I've ever tasted. We filled up our canteens and then went battling down the street." Most of Aachen was without electricity and water. Some of the American soldiers grew so thirsty that they took to dipping their canteens into the holding tanks of toilets.

There was simply too much rubble and broken glass for wheeled vehicles to move around in the city. Commanders and staff officers employed tracked M29 "Weasels" to haul supplies to the frontline rifle companies. They also used them to evacuate the growing number of wounded soldiers. In the opinion of one major, medics would "go anywhere, anytime" to get the wounded, many of whom would have died without quick, expert medical attention. At one street corner in Aachen, Tregaskis, the correspondent, saw a wounded lieutenant who had been stitched in the chest and abdomen by three burp gun bullets. The lieutenant was in shock, and his life was literally ebbing away with each passing moment. "His face was gray, and he had the stunned look of a badly wounded man. The human color had drained from his skin and his eyes were glazed." Blood from the bullet holes was seeping onto the sidewalk. Several tense minutes passed before finally a litter team retrieved the wounded soldier. "The wounded man's head sagged on his neck as he was lifted. His face was clay color and he groaned as if a wave of pain or fear had come over him." The litter team expertly lifted him up, comforted him, and hauled him away.

They were part of a clearly defined medical process. When a soldier got hit, his company aidman tried to get to him and administer first aid. Then litter teams came up, put the wounded soldier on a stretcher, and carried him back to the Weasels. The Weasels then carried them to aid stations that medics had set up in houses outside of town. Battalion surgeons, who were sometimes overwhelmed with wounded, nonetheless followed a checklist of their own. "The patient has all bloody and wet clothing removed," one surgeon wrote. "He is transferred to a dry dressed litter. He is given morphine. He is adequately bandaged and splinted and he is given plasma . . . and then evacuated" to a more permanent hospital.

The medics saved many more men than they lost, but casualties were still eroding the fighting power of the rifle companies. Within a few days, most were operating at half or two-thirds strength, proving the combat axiom that the closer to the sharp end of real fighting, the smaller the number of participants there will be. Each night, personnel officers fed brand-new replacements into the companies. This kept the rifle companies in operation, but they were always understrength, in constant need of reinforcements and fire support.

For the replacements, this was a rough way to enter the world of combat—friendless, in the middle of an urban brawl, engulfed in mindless destruction, engaged in the kind of fighting that took great savvy and wits for survival. The new men either adapted to their brutal circumstances or they died. "It would take a few days for a new man to get over the shock of being in combat and a lot of times they didn't last that long," one rifleman wrote. Private Dye welcomed many such newcomers to his L Company, and tried to teach them how to survive. "Follow me and do what I do," he told them. One time, he was leading four new soldiers to the collection of ruined husks that constituted the company positions, when he heard mortar rounds coming in. He hit the ground, huddled against a wall, and crouched for the impact. The four replacements stood staring at him in confusion. When the mortar shells exploded, though, their confusion evaporated quickly and they learned to hit the ground.

In the 3rd Battalion, a few of the rookies refused to go into battle. One shot himself in the hand, another in the foot. The veteran soldiers did not approve of this self-mutilation, but they understood why it would happen. Many of the old salts were suffering from combat fatigue and had to be medically evacuated. They were significantly more likely than new men to be affected by this combat-related psychoneurotic condition, mainly because they had seen too much, done too much, and were just plain exhausted (hence the word "fatigue").[9]

Killing for the Ruins

One of the most problematic aspects of the American situation in Aachen was that they went into the city without first isolating it. This afforded the Germans an opening (quite literally) to reinforce their hard-pressed defenders in Aachen. Isolating a city in urban combat is axiomatic: if the defending commanders can reinforce their garrison within the city, they can wage a protracted, attritional battle, grinding down the attackers, perhaps eventually destroying them in this way. Stalingrad is probably the best example of this nightmarish scenario. At Aachen the Americans did not face a situation of that gravity, but they did absorb major German counterattacks. Most of these attacks hit the 16th and 18th Infantry Regiments, outside of town, around Verlautenheide, where the Americans had not yet completed the encirclement of Aachen.

On October 15, amid ugly rain showers, some of the German attackers made it into Aachen itself, where they smashed into the right flank of Corley's 3rd Battalion. By now, Corley's men had taken Observatory Hill and much of the area, generally known as the Farwick Park, around the hill. "The Farwick Park area consisted of a dominating hill feature with a four-story observation building on top of the hill, a large building called the Kurhaus, and another called the Palace Hotel," Corley wrote. Jagged blocks of houses bordered the area on the southwest and northwest sides of the park, from a roundabout called Roland Circle to a street called Manheims Allee. "The Park was originally a hill. It had been gouged out to build gardens, an artificial lake, walks, tennis courts, and the two main buildings, the Kurhaus and the Palace Hotel. The forward slope of Observatory Hill was an abrupt slope covered with heavy underbrush. The ground next to the Palace Hotel was a rapid rising slope covered with scattered trees and slight underbrush."

The most powerful enemy attacks occurred late in the afternoon on the fifteenth, when a battalion of German soldiers—some of them teenaged SS troopers—with six tanks and self-propelled guns assaulted Observatory Hill. The noise, destruction, and chaos of the fighting were nearly overwhelming. Mortar shells belched from the hidden tubes of both sides, pelting the whole area, turning green grass into brown craters. A pair of German tanks with infantry riding aboard drove to within a couple hundred yards of the battalion CP. American M10 Wolverine tank destroyers from the 634th Tank Destroyer Battalion danced from street to street, trying to score kill shots on the enemy tanks. Corporal Wenzlo Simmons fired thirteen shots at one German tank. He thought he destroyed it but he probably just forced it to retreat because the tanks simply disappeared.

Some of the most desperate, close-in fighting occurred on the hill itself. A forward observer was in the tower, calling down 60- and 81-millimeter mortar fire on his own position, in hopes of stopping the German soldiers who were trying to negotiate the steep slopes. The Germans scored no less than thirty-six direct hits on the tower, but the observer continued his work. Some nine hundred U.S. mortar shells exploded all over the hill and the Farwick Park.

Combat raged at close quarters around the Kurhaus. The Germans were so close, and so determined to prevail, that most of the Americans ran for their lives, hoping that the mortar shells and some covering fire from a few stalwart individuals would save them. The infantry soldiers who were manning forward observation posts in select houses near Roland Circle were especially vulnerable. One of them, Private Curran, could hear "the krauts running up and down the streets there in front of us. There was about six of us at the outpost. I remember I was hit in the leg . . . by some shrapnel." Somehow they escaped, but Curran was never sure how. No doubt his conscious mind deliberately blotted out the horrible details, a common defense mechanism to minimize the damage of traumatic events.

As always in combat, the actions of a few individuals made a huge difference. In his battalion journal, Corley specifically mentioned two of his sergeants, Wise and Tomasco, for "brilliant qualities of leadership" and a "PFC [Jesse] Short of Co. K for single-handedly" holding off an enemy attack on his unit. Bazooka men risked imminent death by leaning out of windows to shoot at enemy tanks that they could only vaguely see advancing down the avenues toward them. No one knew if they hit any of the tanks, but they certainly warded them off. One BAR man alone fired fifty-nine magazines of ammunition at the Germans (further evidence, among volumes, disproving S. L. A. Marshall's dubious ratio-of-fire contentions).[10]

The fighting seesawed around Observatory Hill for most of October 15 and 16. In the opinion of Colonel John Seitz, the commander of the 26th Infantry Regiment, Corley's 3rd Battalion, in that two-day period, had "its toughest time" during the campaign so far in northern Europe. The German counterattacks were ultimately unsuccessful, but they did temporarily halt the American advance in Aachen. General Huebner waited until his division staved off the German counterattacks, then joined hands with the 30th Division, and isolated Aachen, before giving Seitz the go-ahead to resume his assault on the city.

The attacks resumed in earnest on October 18. Corley's battalion focused on clearing Observatory Hill, Farwick Park, and the area around the Kurhaus, particularly the Palace Hotel (also called the Quellenhoff), a beautiful, stately building that was perched atop the high ground. The aggressive battalion commander inadvertently strayed into the German lines during a pre-attack reconnaissance of the area and this, in his estimation, gave him "a hasty picture of the ground to the immediate front."

The Americans pummeled the area with mortar and artillery rounds on October 17, but went forward silently the next morning under cover of pre-dawn darkness. The battered German defenders could not hope to defend every building and avenue. Corley's men quickly infiltrated the enemy lines, surprising small groups of enemy soldiers, rupturing the center of the enemy defenses. Corley was convinced that the Palace Hotel was the key objective, so he focused most of his efforts on it. A few days earlier, in response to his request for more mobile fire support, a nearby artillery unit had sent him, and also Daniel, one 155-millimeter, tracked, self-propelled gun apiece. Corley made liberal use of the gun, battering enemy-held buildings. In one instance, the gun pumped fifteen rounds into several houses around Roland Circle, setting up a perfect assault by I Company. Later, he placed the gun on the tennis courts, assigned a platoon of infantrymen as security, and ordered the gun crew to open fire on the Kurhaus and the Palace Hotel. Each time the gun fired, concussion waves engulfed bystanders like an unseen wind. The sound echoed off nearby buildings, and even knocked down walls. Private Stewart was in a house adjacent to the gun. When the 155 fired, some of the house began to crumble around him. "I thought . . . a German tank had got to us."

Anyone standing too close to the gun risked getting knocked down, or even knocked out. The men could feel the concussion in their chests. But the shells were doing major damage, ripping through the walls, sailing through windows, exploding, showering anyone inside with a welter of deadly shrapnel. Tanks and tank destroyers added their lesser guns to the cacophony. Collectively, this firepower "forced the abandonment of a 20mm gun installed in an upper story of the Palace Hotel," Corley wrote. "It weakened all resistance to our front." The abandonment of the 20-millimeter gun was especially important because that rapid-firing weapon was so deadly to infantrymen, particularly those who were on the move, in the open. Under cover of the friendly supporting fire, groups of riflemen leapfrogged through ruined buildings. They crawled uphill toward the Kurhaus and the Palace Hotel, where Hitler had once stayed.

One platoon from L Company took the Kurhaus. Another, under the command of Lieutenant William Ratchford of K Company, burst into the lobby of the hotel. As was typical, Ratchford had mostly new men in his platoon. Many were tempted to think they had done their job simply by getting into the hotel, but Ratchford knew better. He divided them into small groups and told each group to secure every entrance to the basement, where he knew enemy soldiers would be hiding. "They threw captured potato masher grenades in on the enemy who was throwing his own out," a post-combat interview revealed. "Machine gun fire was also turned on the enemy, who by this time had had enough and was trying to get out of the building, pausing only long enough to set his ammunition on fire." Wherever they could, the GIs slaughtered retreating Germans, peppering them with machine-gun bullets, destroying them with grenades.

The luxurious interior of the hotel quickly became a wasteland of torn walls, shattered glass, shredded carpet, bodies, and bloodstains. The coppery stench of blood, along with the sulphuric odor of spent gunpowder and the dusty pall of fallen timbers and plaster, all permeated the hallways and rooms. "In peacetime it had probably been a nice [place]," Private Stewart later commented. "When we got done with it, it needed a lot of work done on it before it could reopen." Inside the hotel, the Americans killed twenty-five enemy soldiers and captured another twelve. They also found large amounts of food and ammunition. The hotel had, at one time, served as Colonel Wilck's headquarters, but he had since relocated to a large concrete air raid bunker several blocks away. By day's end, the 3rd Battalion had secured all of the key buildings on Observatory Hill, the whole Farwick Park area, and was now in the process of clearing some of the smaller hills and neighboring blocks of homes. In Corley's estimation, their success stemmed from the maximum use of firepower combined with quick, well-led, and coordinated assaults by the infantry soldiers.

A few blocks to the west, Daniel's battalion was also methodically fighting block by block in the medieval heart of the city, employing a similar blend of combined arms. The fighting ebbed through several venerable cathedrals in the city center. German artillery shells were falling in disquieting numbers. Many of them hit the ruined facades of tall buildings "with the result that the precarious walls collapsed" on anyone underneath, in the recollection of one soldier. Like his colleague Corley, Lieutenant Colonel Daniel made extensive use of his 155-millimeter self-propelled gun. At one point, he set it up at a crossroads, with perfect fields of fire, and watched as the crew disgorged shell after shell at German machine-gun crews in the ruined State Theater. The machine guns soon posed no further threat to the infantry.

As the foot soldiers advanced, they hugged close to accompanying tanks and tank destroyers. Both groups shot at anything that looked suspicious. "To discourage antitank crews or any enemy group, the infantry would toss assault grenades into each building whether they were fired on from that structure or not," an infantryman wrote. "In case the grenades did not secure the desired effect a vehicle would then pump a few rounds into the building. This usually brought a few Germans streaming from the building but, since the cellars of all the buildings were connected, the enemy often withdrew to the next structure; thus making it necessary to repeat this performance on each building." Sometimes the infantry soldiers spotted Panzerfaust-wielding German soldiers in windows. Riflemen peppered the windows, as did accompanying machine gunners. The tank crewmen, thus alerted to the danger, pumped their own rounds into the windows. Few of the enemy soldiers survived such onslaughts. When the infantry wanted to avoid moving on the open streets, they attacked through the back alleys. In many cases, bazooka men shot holes through walls, allowing infantry squads to outflank the Germans.

The bitterest fighting occurred in a technical school and in several surrounding houses, where young German soldiers were determined to make a final stand against an assault by F Company. "Machine gun, rifle and mortar fire hindered our advance," the company history recorded. "Several houses were bitterly contested room by room." This meant close-in fighting—hurling grenades, shooting people at point-blank range, sometimes even fighting to the death with fists or bayonets. It was the worst kind of traumatic, stressful, exhausting combat. "Driving hard against the outpost buildings before the school," one of the soldiers later wrote, "four squads worked from roof to roof clearing the machine gun nests which were sited to cross fire upon the approaches to the school."

Five horrendous hours of fighting ensued. It was an infantryman's fight all the way—personal, physically exhausting, and soul-stealing. For the most part, the soldiers of F Company had to fight room by room, against enemy soldiers who generally preferred to die rather than surrender. The tankers lent what fire support they could, but the closeness of the fighting often forced them to hold their fire. For the infantry, the killing took place at intimate range, in rooms, foyers, and basements. They watched their enemies die at close range. They watched them hurt. They heard them scream. They also watched their own friends get hit and go down, sometimes in silent, lifeless heaps, but usually with painful, surprised cries and bloody wounds. Corridors echoed with beseeching cries for medics. The reports of grenades, submachine guns, and rifles in such confining spaces assaulted the eardrums of everyone involved. No one who participated was unaffected. In short, it was awful in the extreme.[11]

Fortunately, the Germans were just about finished. With the fall of the technical school on October 20, along with much of the city center, and 3rd Battalion's seizure of the high ground in northern Aachen, Colonel Wilck's survivors could not hold out much longer. With the Americans in control of most of the city, German holdouts were scattered around, hanging on, but out of communication with higher headquarters (senior officers called these holdouts pockets of resistance).

Wilck, his staff, and many of his remaining soldiers were clustered inside a three-story-high, reinforced concrete air raid bunker that was straight in the path of Corley's relentless advance. Bunkers like this served as shelter, not just for German troops but also civilians. The Americans had already cleared several in Aachen. Mindful of Hitler's order to fight to the finish, Wilck sent his superiors several defiant messages, including one that reported that "the last defenders of Aachen are embroiled in their final battle!" Privately he was not as resolute. He knew the end was near, but he was concerned that if his garrison did not appear to be fighting to the end, Hitler would exact reprisals on the families of his soldiers.

On the morning of October 21, Corley's lead troops, augmented with the 155-millimeter gun, prepared to assault Wilck's bunker. The 155 crew fired several shots, battering the concrete, ripping big holes, but not otherwise penetrating inside. For Wilck, this was the final straw. He knew he had to surrender. He tried to send two of his men outside under a white flag, but in the fog of battle the Americans shot them down. So Wilck enlisted the help of two American prisoners, Staff Sergeant Ewart Padgett and Sergeant James Haswell. Both of these men were combat engineers who had been captured in Aachen a few days earlier.

Sergeant Haswell took the white flag and ran into the street, waving it vigorously. "There was a great deal of small arms fire at first, but I continued to wave the flag until the firing ceased." An American soldier leaned out the window of a nearby house and motioned Haswell to him. Haswell and Padgett then communicated Wilck's surrender message up the American chain of command to Lieutenant Colonel Corley's CP. Corley, Colonel Seitz, and Brigadier General George Taylor were all there. They insisted on an orderly, unconditional surrender. Haswell and Padgett dutifully returned to the bunker and relayed this to the Germans. Wilck and his staff were assembled in the colonel's room, waiting to surrender. As a sign that he accepted Corley's terms, Wilck took out his pistol, removed the clip and, in Haswell's recollection, "threw the clip under the bed, laid the pistol on the table, smiled and left the room." This was his way of accepting the terms.

A few minutes later, at 1000, Wilck and his men streamed out of the bunker, into captivity. Hundreds of enemy soldiers, a few with their hands on their heads, most with their hands at their sides, shuffled down Aachen's battered streets, past grubby-looking GIs. One of the American survivors, Private First Class Stewart, watched them walk by. They looked haggard but he and his buddies looked even worse. Stewart noted that he had not had a bath, a shave, a haircut, or a hot meal in thirty-seven days. Later, the Americans led Wilck and his officers to the pockets of resistance, where the colonel persuaded his remaining soldiers to lay down their arms. "The show is over," a 26th Infantry officer recorded in the unit's journal that afternoon. The Battle of Aachen was done.

The venerable city was almost completely destroyed. "The city is as dead as a Roman ruin, but unlike a ruin it has none of the grace of gradual decay," Lieutenant Robert Botsford wrote. "Burst sewers, broken gas mains and dead animals have raised an almost overpowering smell in many parts of the city. The streets are paved with shattered glass; telephone, electric light and trolley cables are dangling and netted together everywhere, and in many places wrecked cars, trucks, armored vehicles and guns litter the streets. Most of the streets of Aachen are impassable, except on foot. Piles of debris have been shored up along the gutters without much method."

This was the field of ruins that two battalions of infantry, augmented by armor, artillery, and engineers, had had to master. "Though the German garrison had fought courageously and skillfully, it had been beaten by a combined American force of half its size," one of the American officers recorded in the regimental records. Aachen demonstrated the potency of well-led combined-arms teams, as well as the remarkable versatility of infantry and the ability of ground soldiers to adapt to a confined urban environment. By all rights, two understrength battalions of infantry soldiers should not have been able to take a sizable city against a force more than twice their number. They did it through the manipulation and prodigious use of firepower, the aggressive zeal of riflemen, and the adept planning of commanders.

But they also had other advantages. Aachen was isolated for part of the battle, negating the enemy's ability to reinforce his garrison. More important, the fighting took place within a political vacuum. The American soldiers who fought there did not have to worry about any political consequences of their actions. Concern for civilians notwithstanding, the GIs were able to concentrate exclusively on the tactical challenge of taking the next building or the next block. They could destroy everything, and everyone, with impunity, as long as it enhanced the mission of seizing Aachen. No one cared if they did this with particular zeal, or even a lust for destruction—hence, "knock 'em all down." The media they dealt with were entirely friendly and supportive (Tregaskis even lived with the soldiers and told their life stories in his piece). World opinion had no impact on the battle. To the Americans, Aachen was just one more place to carry the fight to Nazi Germany, another piece in the strategic puzzle of victory. The city's annihilation held no significance to them whatsoever, nor to the overall strategic balance of world opinion. It was the classic example of a politically unrestrained urban battleground, one of the last such politically benign city battlefields in which Americans would ever fight.[12]

CHAPTER 4

Scenes from the Northern Shoulder of the Bulge: Men Against Tanks and Everything Else

Winter and Discontent

No ONE COULD DECIDE WHICH hurt more, the cold or the inertia. In December 1944, the western Allies were stalemated along the western frontiers of Nazi Germany. A fearsome winter had set in, blanketing much of the front with snow and ice, compounding the misery of frontline existence for American infantry soldiers. Most lived in crude, slushy holes or dugouts. If they were lucky, their holes had some overhead cover afforded by logs or scrap metal. A few soldiers enjoyed the partial shelter of ruined houses or barns. Foot gear was inadequate. Winter clothing was improvised from a mishmash of long underwear, sweaters, fatigue jackets, and wool gloves. Temperatures ranged from the teens to the twenties. Trench foot, frozen feet, and frostbite were distressingly common. Men went weeks without showers, haircuts, hot food, shelter, or any semblance of warmth beyond what a handful of pine needles set afire in an empty ration can offered.

What's more, they were sitting in place, defending fixed positions, instead of attacking, gaining ground, and hastening the end of the war. The combination of winter weather, supply problems, and stiffening German resistance had ground the previously inexorable Allied advance to a halt. So now they were defending. The average infantryman might have welcomed a respite from the dangerous routine of attacking, but each of them knew in his heart that only such a relentless advance would conquer Germany and end the war.

Because of this, the wintry inertia was disquieting for the American soldiers. Nazi Germany was on the verge of defeat, but the maniacal Adolf Hitler was not prepared to admit any such thing (proving the wise axiom coined by a later generation of American soldiers that "the enemy gets a vote").

Hitler decided to scrape together his last reserves, including his best armor and his most committed SS troopers, for a major winter offensive against a thinly held section of the American lines in the rough Ardennes Forest. In all, he had three entire armies, including more than eight armored divisions. His ambitious long-shot goal was to attack under a winter canopy that would negate Allied air superiority, gash a huge hole in the American front, drive a wedge between the British and American armies, destroy the fragile Allied coalition, and then negotiate a skin-saving end to the war. His main fist for this surprise sucker punch was the 6th SS Panzer Army under General Joseph "Sepp" Dietrich, an old Nazi party crony. Dietrich's army included four SS armored divisions. Led by these powerful units, he was to hit the northern shoulder of the American line in the Ardennes, knife into Belgium, and dash all the way to the vital supply port of Antwerp. A major portion of his attack was to hit the sparsely defended front of the U.S. Army's brand-new 99th Infantry Division.

The 99th had just arrived in November and had been holding defensive positions in the quiet northern Ardennes for about a month. The division was spread thin over a horseshoe-shaped nineteen-mile front of rugged terrain from Lanzerath in the southwest to Hofen in the northeast. This was twice as much ground as most American generals thought a division should defend, but with combat manpower at a premium in late 1944, this was the unhappy reality. Major General Walter Lauer, the division commander, had all three of his infantry regiments on the line. The 395th held his left (eastern) flank, which was anchored at Hofen. In the middle, east of the twin villages of Krinkelt and Rocherath, the 393rd was sprinkled among forest positions, facing east toward Germany. On Lauer's right (western) flank, the 394th Infantry Regiment defended the vital Losheimergraben crossroads, amid dense rolling woodlands.

In the U.S. Army, most infantry units have a distinctive culture that stems from tradition, the unit's leadership, and the men who populate the outfit. The soldiers of the 99th called themselves "the Battle Babies." The division was composed of an interesting mixture of men. The youngest soldiers were

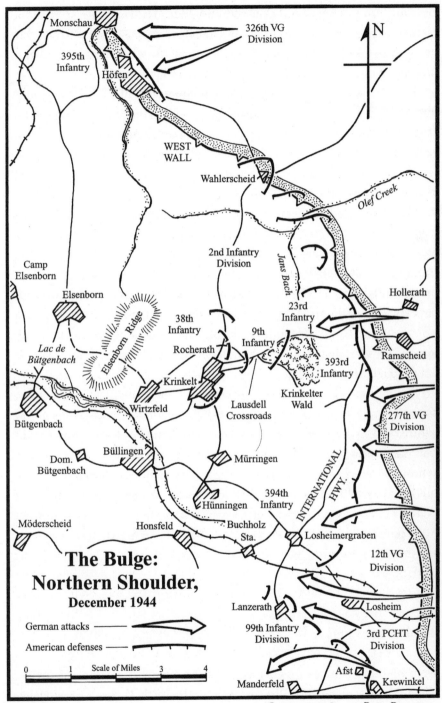

Monschau

395th
Infantry

Höfen

326th VG
Division

N

WEST
WALL

Wahlerscheid

Olef Creek

2nd Infantry
Division

Jans Bach

Hollerath

Camp
Elsenborn

Elsenborn

Elsenborn Ridge

*Lac de
Bütgenbach*

38th
Infantry

Rocherath

9th
Infantry

23rd
Infantry

Ramscheid

Krinkelter
Wald

393rd
Infantry

Bütgenbach

Krinkelt

Wirtzfeld

Lausdell
Crossroads

277th VG
Division

Dom.
Bütgenbach

Büllingen

Mürringen

Möderscheid

Honsfeld

Hünningen

394th
Infantry

INTERNATIONAL HWY.

Buchholz
Sta.

Losheimergraben

12th VG
Division

**The Bulge:
Northern Shoulder,**
December 1944

German attacks

American defenses

Lanzerath

99th Infantry
Division

Losheim

3rd PCHT
Division

0   1   Scale of Miles   3   4

Manderfeld

Afst

Krewinkel

COPYRIGHT © 2010 RICK BRITTON

academically bright, college-experienced men who had once been part of the Army Specialized Training Program (ASTP). The ASTP had offered them the chance to go to college, on the Army's dime, while they trained for future leadership or technical positions outside the world of combat infantry. However, the voracious combat needs of the fighting fronts had necessitated the program's cancellation in early 1944. As a result, many of these teenaged ex-ASTPers ended up in the 99th (and several other similar divisions), mixing with less educated men, generally in their early to mid-twenties, who had more experience in the Army. Forging a common identity as Battle Babies, they trained to a fever pitch back in the States.

By the middle of December 1944, though, they had seen no extensive action. They had patrolled, stood guard near their frontline holes, huts, or dugouts, and generally learned as much as they could about the ruthless world of frontline combat. Their vast sector consisted of "rocky gorges, small streams, abrupt hills and an extremely limited road net," according to a divisional report. Much of the area was blanketed with fir and pine forests that were now thick with snow and, on balmier days, mud. At this time of the year, there was only about seven hours of daylight in the Ardennes. Even at the height of the day, though, the trees made it almost seem like night. "Visibility was limited to 100–150 yards at a maximum," one soldier later wrote. "Fields of fire were equally limited and poor. Fire lanes for automatic weapons would not be cleared for any great distance without cutting down trees and thereby disclosing the position." It was a confining, almost claustrophobic environment. Throughout December, they could hear the Germans, several hundred yards to the east, moving large numbers of vehicles and soldiers. Patrols confirmed that the Germans were moving these men and this matériel into position, for what purpose no one really knew. The Battle Babies sensed that the Germans were up to something, but they had no idea they were right in Dietrich's path.[1]

Battle Babies Part I: The 394th Infantry at Losheimergraben

Precisely at the stroke of 0530 on Saturday, December 16, the Germans unleashed a monumental artillery barrage on the 99th Division lines. Unlike Guam, Peleliu, and Aachen, this time the Americans were on the receiving end of massive firepower. The shells poured in with "unprecedented ferocity," in the recollection of one soldier in the 394th Infantry. "Guns and mortars of all calibers, supplemented by multiple-barreled rocket projectors plastered . . . the area." So unaccustomed were the Battle Babies to large concentrations of German artillery that some of them initially thought the barrage was coming from American rounds falling short. Gradually, though, they realized that the shells were German, particularly when they recognized the familiar, and dreaded, crack of the enemy's 88-millimeter artillery pieces and the terrifying roar of Nebelwerfer rocket launchers. "It sounded like wolves howling," Private Lloyd Long, a BAR man in A Company, said. "[We] could hear incoming whistle and whoosh depending upon how close. Direct hits on the huge trees blew their tops off but also splattered shrapnel around." Huddling in a deep hole, Long heard pieces of shrapnel flying around outside. "It came down like deadly rain for what seemed like hours," Sergeant Milton Kitchens, a machine gunner in H Company, wrote. "My bunker sustained a direct hit, logs, timber and muddy snow flew everywhere." Blood was pouring from his mouth and his coat was shredded, but he was otherwise okay. His heavy, water-cooled machine gun was undamaged. Two men on his crew were wounded. Another was on the verge of a mental breakdown. "[He] was bawling like a baby and he looked finished but I kicked his ass up and ordered him to man that machine gun, which he did admirably."

At the crossroads, two gun crewmen from an antitank unit ran from their gun. They had failed to dig a proper hole for themselves and were frantically looking for cover. In the chaos of the moment, they ran into a line of foxholes manned by a platoon from K Company. The riflemen of this platoon did not know the crewmen. In the recollection of one witness, the crewmen were "oblivious to the several calls to halt, and tore off the cover of one of the foxholes. They were, of course, the instant target of the foxhole occupants." One of them was killed immediately, the other badly wounded.[2]

The pounding lasted for about ninety minutes, and inflicted surprisingly light casualties on the Battle Babies, mainly because most of the men enjoyed the shelter of deep, log-reinforced dugouts or holes. Some had even built sturdy log cabins for themselves. The enemy shells tore up communication wire and shredded many of the cabins, but they did little damage to the soldiers themselves.

The morning was dark and misty. Several inches of snow blanketed the ground. When the shelling ceased, an eerie, wintry silence descended. At 0800, just before sunrise, German infantry soldiers began moving toward the American lines. The darkness provided ideal concealment for them but, for obvious reasons, it also hindered their movement. The German high command arranged for legions of spotlights to bounce their beams off the clouds, thus providing the assault troops with artificial moonlight, which they used to infiltrate in and around the American lines. But the light also made them visible targets for the Americans, who now saw their adversaries emerging, like gruesome phantoms, from the predawn shroud.

At Buckholz, where the 3rd Battalion was in position astride both sides of a north-south railroad line at the extreme right of the 99th Division's entire front, soldiers from L Company were queued up in a chow line near the railroad station, waiting for breakfast. The company first sergeant, Elmer Klug, was inside the station, standing next to First Lieutenant Neil Brown, his company commander. At nearly the same moment, they saw several dozen men approaching, in march formation, on either side of the tracks. At first glance, they thought these figures in the darkness were men from the 1st Platoon, showing up for breakfast. Lieutenant Brown knew that it was not this platoon's turn to eat, though. He turned to his NCO and asked: "Klug, First Platoon is coming in for breakfast. What the hell is going on?" The first sergeant looked at them for a moment and exclaimed: "First Platoon my ass! Those are Germans."

Klug grabbed his M1 carbine, raced outside, ran toward them, and called for them to halt. In response, they stopped, as if shocked. One of them gave a command in German and they began to disperse on either side of the tracks. First Sergeant Klug shot the one who gave the command, and he dropped dead right on the spot. The others dispersed into the darkness. Klug ran back inside. By now Lieutenant Brown was on the phone to battalion, reporting the presence of the Germans. He did not know it, but these were the lead troops of a two-company attack on Buckholz. Within a few minutes, the American chow line quickly dissolved as men ran every which way, finding cover, shooting, trying to figure out what was going on. "Part of the Germans took cover in a railroad car about three hundred yards south of the station," one soldier recalled. "Others began to run towards this car and towards the woods to the south." Actually they took cover in at least one car. The cars, and many of the German soldiers, were actually to the north of—or behind—the L Company men.

Small-arms fire crackled as soldiers from both sides looked for targets and opened fire. A BAR man sighted in on one running figure, fired, and dropped him at a range of one hundred yards. The Americans fired several bazooka rounds at the trains but missed. Staff Sergeant Savino Travalini and two other soldiers unlimbered an antitank gun and shot at the boxcars, scoring several hits. The Germans, in or out of the boxcars, were in a difficult spot, exposed to American small-arms and mortar fire. Many of the enemy soldiers got hit and played dead in the snow. "I had a good position in the loft of . . . a barn," Private John Thornburg, a rifleman, wrote. "I was able to see the smashing of the railway car by the artillery [sic] piece. I could also see small figures, discernable as our riflemen, crawling in the snow and firing occasionally." An American M10 Wolverine tank destroyer rumbled up and fired several three-inch shells into the boxcars. A small group of enemy soldiers emerged from the trains and surrendered.

Soon German mortar and artillery fire screamed in. One shell scored a direct hit on the railroad station. A fragment from the shell glanced off T/5 George Bodnar and ripped into the head of Private Joe Ryan, killing him at once. The shelling continued unabated, prompting all of the men inside the station building, including Lieutenant Brown, to take shelter in a concrete bunker next to the station.

The Germans placed a machine gun atop a nearby water tower, as well as another one four hundred yards south of the station. The guns bracketed much of the open ground around Buckholz Station and the tracks with bullets. In the memory of one officer, they "beat the hell out of us." This was the officer's way of saying that some of those bullets struck men, usually with the now familiar sound of a baseball bat hitting a watermelon, spraying blood and tissue as they hit. The plaintive cries of the wounded rose above even the din of the shooting. "When you hear the painful cry of a wounded soldier," Private John Kuhn, a runner in K Company, wrote, "and you see his life's blood oozing out in the waist deep snow turning it to crimson red, whether he is friend or foe, it is not a thrilling experience or one soon forgotten." Captain Charles Roland, the battalion operations officer (S3), watched in horror as "a young lieutenant danced rubber legged until he twisted slowly and revealed a blue bullet hole in the middle of his forehead." Roland and Kuhn both saw the decapitated bodies—heads sheared off by shrapnel—of the regimental chaplain and his assistant, lying beside their jeep.

Once again, Sergeant Travalini was a difference maker. Somehow, he crawled to within striking distance of the machine gun south of the station and killed the crew with a grenade. In addition, he went back to the antitank gun and fired at least one round into the water tower. As if that were not enough, he took action when he found out that German soldiers had moved into a roundhouse only a few hundred yards from the station. In the recollection of several soldiers in a post-combat interview, Travalini "fired [a] bazooka several times into the roundhouse. This . . . flushed some of the enemy and as they came into view Travalini picked up his M1 and fired into them." For his exploits, he earned a battlefield commission. The fighting raged around Buckholz much of the day. The Germans were unable to dislodge the 3rd Battalion, so instead they found gaps in the thin American line and, dodging U.S. mortar and artillery fire, swung around to the battalion flanks, trying to cut the Americans off.[3]

A mile and a half to the east, much of the 12th Volksgrenadier Division was launching, in broad daylight now, another such relentless push for the Losheimergraben crossroads. This objective was important for the Germans. Taking it would give them a good avenue of advance north, toward the important towns of Murringen, Krinkelt-Rocherath, and the Meuse. Lieutenant Colonel Robert Douglas, commander of the 1st Battalion, had placed all of his companies in and around the crossroads. Company A was on the battalion's right, between Buckholz and Losheimergraben (which was little more than a cluster of farmhouses and barns on either side of the road). Company B was in the middle, astride the road. Company C held the east, or left, flank. Mortarmen and machine gunners from D Company were sprinkled around in support of the three rifle companies (lettered A, B, and C). The brunt of the attack hit the junction between B and C Companies. "'B' Company was overrun, with 'Jerries' all over the position using some of the foxholes which were in the area," Douglas later said. "There were more foxholes than there were American infantry to fill them."

The chaos and confusion were almost indescribable. Private First Class Carl Combs, a rifleman in B Company, was in a well-camouflaged, log-reinforced dugout about fifty yards east of the road, covering a 57-millimeter antitank gun. In the hazy daylight, enemy soldiers brazenly approached, in distressingly large groups. "German infantry showed up to our front and we opened fire, getting quite a few. After three or four such incidents, a tank moved up the road and at close range the 57 knocked it out. It was quite a sight with its ammo exploding." While the Germans were destroying some of the American dugouts, they had trouble locating Combs and his partner, Fred Robertson. Combs and Robertson kept shooting at large numbers of Germans who were crossing the road east to west, killing more than a few. "It was sort of like a shooting gallery."

Most of the defenders had a limited field of vision, obscured by the winter haze, the pervasive trees, and the myopic perspective inherent in any well-dug, fortified position. This created a sense of isolation, one so common to infantrymen in combat, who often see only a few yards to their left or right. At the crossroads (and, in fact, at many other spots along the northern shoulder of the Bulge), it was as if each group was fighting its own private war. The actions of NCOs were crucial. They were the ones who set the example, and they often did the fighting and dying. In one spot near the road, a squad leader saw his entire squad wiped out by a group of Germans. In a rage, he grabbed a BAR from one of his dying men and charged at the Germans, all the while firing the weapon on full automatic. The BAR's *dat dat dum* cadence petered out as the clip emptied. A German soldier killed him from a distance of no more than ten feet. Elsewhere, Technical Sergeant Eddie Dolenc set up a machine gun in a shell hole and zeroed in on an attacking enemy platoon. In just a few minutes, bodies, clad in Wehrmacht field gray overcoats, were literally piled up in front of the shell hole. The German tide swept past the hole. No one ever saw Dolenc again. In another spot, a BAR man climbed atop a log cabin and kept up a relentless fire on any Germans who tried to move within his field of fire. Several other men scurried back and forth, resupplying him with ammunition.

Much of the fighting was at such close quarters that mortarmen like Private Danny Dalyai pointed their tubes almost straight up, at nearly a ninety-degree angle, to hit Germans whom they could actually see, a rare thing for mortar crewmen. Dalyai's 60-millimeter mortar tube was nearly buried in snow, with only the top sticking out. Overhead, he had just enough of an opening between pine trees to get his shots off. "I had only 6 or 8 shells. I had no trouble getting all the shells off." They exploded among some Germans who were just beyond the tree line. In the next instant, as Private Dalyai watched in horror, an 88-millimeter shell scored a direct hit on the log cabin that was serving as B Company's command post. He ran over to check on the four men he knew were inside. "How I've wished to this day I never looked in! Blood was all over the place. Lieutenant Charles Butler got both legs blown off. You can imagine how very emotional and overwhelming this was for me." Aghast, Dalyai hurried away, only to stumble over a dead body. Another 88 shell exploded nearby, knocking him unconscious and destroying his hearing.

Not far from Dalyai, D Company's 81-millimeter mortars were dug into the tree-lined backyard of a farmhouse near the road. Private First Class Bob Newbrough was in a foxhole, observing for his fellow crewmen, when he actually saw a German soldier through a firebreak in the trees, no more than fifteen yards away. The two enemies were startled to see each other. The German was poised to throw a potato masher grenade into the mortar position but he ducked down, as did Newbrough. The American grabbed a rifle and opened fire. Just then, the mortar crewmen began firing their shells almost straight up, at the closest possible range. "I can remember hearing the burst of the mortar shells coming down towards me, ducking in the hole when the shells struck the woods" but still encouraging his friends to keep it up. The Germans, including the potato masher–wielding soldier, soon melted away.[4]

Although the Germans were hurling powerful forces at the 394th, their attack on the crossroads was bogging down. "The 12th Volksgrenadier Division was involved in heavy fighting for Losheimergraben, which was skillfully and bravely defended," a I SS Panzer Corps report stated. By and large, their armored vehicles were road-bound because of the rough terrain and, in some spots, the prevalence of snowy mud. To the south, a destroyed bridge at Losheim kept some of those vehicles waiting in place for many hours. Others made it to Losheimergraben, only to become embroiled in close-quarters fighting with the Americans. Antitank guns were not as big of a problem for them as bazookas. These handheld tubes were the great equalizer in any tank-versus-man confrontation. Even though most infantrymen were trained to fire this weapon, the majority did not possess the kind of courage it took to wield one, in real combat, against an imposing tank. That hardly mattered, though. The bazooka only required a two-man crew. This meant that, under the right circumstances, a mere handful of stalwart souls, brandishing a few tubes, operating from some semblance of cover, could make life very difficult for enemy tanks. The shattered cluster of houses that comprised Losheimergraben made good hiding places for bazooka teams, mainly because they were so close to the road.

Private First Class Ralph Gamber was in the cellar of one such house, facing the road. He and the men with him felt a rumble and saw a German tank right outside. In the basement was a bazooka with eight rounds. He loaded the bazooka while a forty-eight-year-old soldier, inevitably nicknamed "Pap," aimed and fired, even as Gamber studiously avoided the considerable backblast. The rocket streaked from the tube, sagged downward and struck the tank, stopping it cold. Pap fired again, scoring another hit. "When Germans crawled out, riflemen and antitank gunners shot them [with rifles]." Another tank tried to bulldoze the first one out of the way. "I told Pap [to] wait until it got broad side and then fire." They hit this one, too. It seemed that smoke came from the second tank but they were not sure. A third one appeared within their limited vision. Pap fired at it. The rocket hit the tread, damaging it. The turret of the third tank swung in the direction of the cellar, but before the enemy crewmen could snap off a shot, their tank lost traction because of the damaged tread. "It slipped over the bank; the territt [turret] gun was pointing down."

In the basement of another two-story house that was literally next to the road, Sergeant John Hilliard watched as enemy self-propelled guns neared a hidden bazooka team led by Sergeant Mel Weidner. "Weidner's platoon knocked out their vehicle first by making a direct hit on one of the treads with a bazooka rocket, and when the infantry unit moved forward to protect it, they were cut down by rifle fire and grenades. Weidner fired the rocket while one of his men [Private William Kirkbride] loaded." The heavy American small-arms fire forced the German infantrymen to move away from their vehicles in search of cover. Far too many tanks and guns were on their own. One of the self-propelled guns fired several shells into that house until it came into the range of another team that got "a clear shot at it and eventually knocked it out." Knocking it out, of course, normally meant setting it on fire, killing the crewmen, burning them, or forcing them to bail out so that riflemen could pick them off like clay pigeons.

A few of the bravest (or most desperate) Americans, like Sergeant Milton Kitchens and several helpers, even launched direct personal attacks on the

German armor. A lone enemy tank, in Kitchens's recollection, "was upon us and firing one round after the other. Suddenly it stopped right in front of our position." This was a terrifying but crucial moment. The first instinct for most of the infantry soldiers was to shrink deeper into their holes, as if they could cocoon themselves from the deadly peril the tank represented. That would have been the worst thing to do because it would have allowed the tank to blast their holes, machine-gun them, or even grind them into pulp. Instead of letting that happen, Kitchens and another man crawled out of their holes, working their way up to the tank. It was an act that required enormous courage, but they hardly thought of it that way. They simply knew that this was the best way to survive. After the tank fired, there was a slight pause as the gunner reloaded. During that time, Kitchens pulled the pin on a grenade and placed it in the muzzle of the tank's gun. The other soldier "smacked that grenade with the side of his rifle butt and it slammed up the barrel and into the inside of that panzer. All we heard out of that grenade explosion was a muffled poof, then silence. Soon that tank began exploding and we crawled back in the foxhole for cover."

In spite of the determined resistance of soldiers like Kitchens, the Germans steadily made headway. Hour by hour, through sheer numbers and relentless attacks, they found holes in the American lines, cut off small groups, and threatened to destroy the entire 394th Infantry. Hundreds of Americans were killed or captured. Within twenty-four hours, Lieutenant Colonel Don Riley, the commander of the regiment, decided, with General Lauer's permission, to withdraw. Riley ordered a fighting withdrawal to the north, in the direction of Hunningen and Murringen, for anyone who could still get out. The ultimate destination was Elsenborn Ridge, a prominent stretch of high ground several miles to the north.

At the Losheimergraben crossroads, a mixed force of infantrymen and antitank gunners under Lieutenant Dewey Plankers kept up steady resistance, while survivors retreated. "Many men who became separated from their own units joined with other outfits and fought wherever they happened to be," an after action report explained. "The situation was one of wild confusion." One of Riley's battalion commanders, Lieutenant Colonel Philip Wertheimer, added to the confusion through sheer cowardice. As the fighting raged, Wertheimer, a garrison martinet whose men disparagingly called him "Fainting Phil," cowered in the basement of his command post, totally unable to function. Like many other training ground tyrants, his supposed toughness melted in the face of real adversity. "The chief didn't know what to do," Private Steve Kallas, a BAR man, later commented. "He was smoking, walking around like a stupe. He wanted to surrender." Fed up with his cowardice and his whimpering entreaties to surrender, his staff effectively relieved him and continued the fight.

The retreat was generally marked by privation, hunger, and cold. There were also sharp firefights in some spots, especially Murringen, where some Battle Babies of the 394th clashed with lead elements of the two enemy divisions. In one incident at Murringen, Sergeant Harold Schaefer saw a man squatting next to a hedgerow, plopped down next to him, and said hello. "I . . . was looking into the blue eyes of a Jerry soldier. It's a tossup as to who was more surprised." Sometimes in such confrontations soldiers would choose to go their separate ways, embracing a tacit truce rather than kill face-to-face. Not this time, though. "The M1 is faster than the German rifle, or I was faster than 'Fritz,' because he got to die for his country."

One officer of the 394th bluntly, and aptly, summed up the regiment's fight at Losheimergraben. "Everything was all fucked up, we were all scared to death, and plenty of mistakes were made." In spite of these issues, the regiment, by fighting hard, held the Germans up for many crucial hours. The stubborn defense of the crossroads cost the I SS Panzer Corps, for the better part of two days, a badly needed route of advance north to Murringen, Bullingen, Malmédy, and points beyond. This job was mainly done by infantrymen, with some artillery, but little armored support.[5]

Battle Babies Part II: The 393rd Infantry in the Krinkelter Wald

Immediately to the northeast of the 394th, another Battle Baby regiment, the 393rd, also found itself in the crosshairs of the German offensive. These men, under pipe-smoking Lieutenant Colonel Jean Scott, were immersed, along a front of fifty-five hundred yards, in the Krinkelter Wald, a thick pine forest. From east to west, the forest had a depth of about four miles. Just to the west of the forest lay the vital twin villages of Krinkelt and Rocherath, farm towns through which an important north-south road ran. For the advance on the Meuse, the Germans had to control the road and the towns. First, though, they had to fight their way through the forest, and that meant assaulting the 393rd. The Battle Babies of this regiment, like their brethren elsewhere, were burrowed into the forest, manning a thin line of well-camouflaged dugouts, most of which had overhead log cover. Here and there, log cabins provided some semblance of warmth and shelter. All of the positions were oriented east, toward Germany.

As in other sectors, the enemy barrage inflicted few casualties on the 393rd, but it did disrupt communications. The real horror began just as the sun was slowly ascending over the eastern horizon, when soldiers from the 277th Volksgrenadier Division hurled themselves, under the cover of some supporting artillery fire, into the Krinkelter Wald. Many of the enemy troops wore white sheets to blend into the snowy surroundings. In the confusing half-light, they had little trouble, in most cases, penetrating to within a hundred yards of the American positions. "I had difficulty picking out targets," Private First Class Lionel Adda, an assistant machine gunner/rifleman attached to B Company, later wrote. "Tracers and one or two flares revealed bodies crawling towards us. I was firing my carbine more rapidly than I had ever done before." On either side of him, his squad's machine guns were pouring out withering fire. From only a few yards in front of his dugout, he heard someone holler "Heil Hitler!" In the next instant, a grenade exploded, followed by burp-gun fire. "The bullets dislodged dirt and stones in front of my hole, and they struck me painfully in my face." Then, after this near miss, the firing tapered off. As Adda's eyes adjusted to the gathering light, he could see twelve dead enemy soldiers heaped in front of his dugout, including one so close that he could practically touch the body (this was probably the one who had thrown the grenade).

Adda did not know it, but B Company and its neighboring unit on the right, C Company, were facing some of the most formidable German attacks. Colonel Hans Viebig, the commander of the 277th, threw the better part of two regiments into the fight. "Some of the Germans got into the same foxholes with our soldiers and several were bayoneted," surviving American soldiers related to a historian in a post-combat interview. "Others occupied positions adjacent to and in rear of our foxholes. The defense was spread so thin that our line was mainly a series of strongpoints with gaps between each." Consider, for a moment, what this really meant. Each foxhole contained, at most, three scared men. As the soldiers related, in some cases, Germans infiltrated the holes themselves, prompting a personal, bloody, ferocious struggle for life. They killed with rifles, pistols, bayonets, and even helmets. Here there was no retreat, no impersonal discharge of weapons at an unseen enemy. There was, instead, a personal struggle to the death, more akin to ancient combat than modern warfare. The vanquished lay bloody and bludgeoned in the snow. The victors were, in the short term, exhausted by their ordeal, owing to the post-combat depletion of adrenaline. Elation at survival quickly gave way to nausea at having to kill. In the long term, they would carry mental scars forever.

In the majority of cases, the fighting was not quite that close. More often, the Americans stood against the parapets of their dugouts and shot at whatever they could see. In the recollection of Technical Sergeant Ben Nawrocki, platoon sergeant of B Company's 2nd Platoon, he and his men "kept cutting them down. In many places, the Germans were piled on top of one another like cord wood." In a few cases, they got close enough to throw grenades inside the American cabins.

The BARs did tremendous damage. Nawrocki remembered seeing a bucktoothed BAR man, fighting barefoot in his hole—he apparently had his boots off when the attack hit—warding off the Germans with steady bursts from his fearsome weapon. "They were piled three and four feet high in front of his foxhole." To Sergeant Bernie Macay "it seemed like there were thousands. We could see them against the skyline. They were dropping like flies. There must have been hundreds of German dead in front of our positions." Macay's BAR man, Clyde Burkett, like many others of his ilk, did much of the killing. "He personally took a tremendous toll."

Corporal Alvin Boeger, a BAR man in C Company, was at first literally scared into paralysis by the menacing, tromping sound of approaching enemy boots. He cowered in his foxhole and found that he could not move his arms and legs. "I thought of my mother—how she would react to my death. I *saw* a gold star in her window." In World War II, a gold star flag signified the death of a loved one on some fighting front. Boeger was experiencing what one scholar called Condition Black, meaning a fear-induced shutdown of bodily functions. The limbs fail to respond. The heart rate shoots dangerously high. The blood vessels constrict, draining all color from the face (hence the term "white as a sheet"). Only the sight of German soldiers dropping grenades and shooting into nearby holes snapped Boeger out of Condition Black. He stood up, faced them, and pointed his fearsome weapon. "The enemy came on in waves and I fired my BAR until it was real hot. There were grey uniformed bodies everywhere."

Staff Sergeant Roy House, another BAR man, was part of a squad that was about to be overrun. He held off a company-sized group of Germans while his comrades withdrew. "I was able to hold off the attackers for about 10 or 15 minutes because they made no attempt at concealment. Finally one of the Germans was able to get to the left and shot me through my left arm." In spite of the wound, House escaped.[6]

The German attack had little ambiguity or complexity. They simply came forward in waves. Lieutenant Robert Dettor, a platoon leader in K Company, one of the hardest-pressed units, desperately tried to hold his platoon together in the face of a veritable avalanche of enemy soldiers. Small-arms fire was crackling everywhere. His communication wires to the company command post and his platoon outposts were completely out. In terse diary passages, he recounted the horror. "No contact with men except those in foxholes in immediate vicinity. Sgt. Phifer, Sgt. Surtorka, myself fighting from same emplacement. Sgt. Surtorka moved to foxhole on right to cover flank. Sgt. Surtorka yelled over grenade being thrown at my foxhole. Hunter hit by grenade. Sgt. Phifer wounded in the shoulder by rifle bullet. Enemy closing within 20 feet of foxhole." They were almost out of ammo. Hunter caught a burp-gun burst and slumped over dead. Lieutenant Dettor ordered all maps burned and food distributed evenly. Finally, when the lieutenant and his men ran out of ammo, the Germans overran the position. They jostled the Americans around, took their wristwatches, pens, money, and other valuables, and sent them east, behind the German lines. Half of K Company was overrun in similar fashion.

After such costly initial assaults against the American strongpoints, the German survivors began flanking them, taking advantage of many dead spots in the U.S. defenses, cutting them off. Units on both sides lost all cohesiveness. Most were out of communication with higher headquarters. The battle degenerated into clashes between isolated groups bumping into one another in the dark, bewildering forest. German mobility was dramatically restricted by the sheer volume of U.S. supporting fire. Fighting from deep holes, the Americans did not hesitate to call down artillery on their own positions since they knew the shells would do much more damage to the unsheltered enemy than to themselves. In one instance, a company commander and a forward observer, knowing they were in danger of being annihilated, called down 105-millimeter howitzer fire, literally on top of themselves. "The rounds burst in trees above their heads, and sprayed forward, piling up so many Germans in front of their positions that the attack failed," a unit after action report claimed. "It took guts, but it worked."

Mortarmen contributed their own fury. Working very carefully from their pits in firebreaks and clearings—mortar teams *never* set up their tubes underneath trees—they provided devastating close support for the hard-pressed riflemen and machine gunners. Sergeant Earl Wiseman and his 81-millimeter mortar crews from M Company laid down a steady curtain of shells in support of their buddies in the overwrought rifle companies. "I was proud then to be with these boys [of his crews] because the hotter the fight got, the better we functioned. Swinging one gun here, laying another there with azimuths continually shifting great distances and ranges steadily decreasing until they were down to 50 yards, and less." One section was even firing straight up "to put them right on top of Jerry coming thru those woods." The Germans breached the lines of Wiseman's platoon area, capturing several men in their holes. At that point, the platoon became part mortar unit and part rifle unit. Some of the men were fighting a deadly cat-and-mouse battle, stalking the Germans and vice versa. One man dropped a bloody enemy submachine gun at the feet of Wiseman's crew and said: "Here's a souvenir for you." The crews kept firing, eventually stopping the Germans in their tracks. "We stood the ground for that day tho and I dare say the Germans lost heavily for every step they'd taken." In fact, a company report later claimed that the unit's mortars and heavy machine guns had killed between two hundred and three hundred German soldiers.[7]

The 277th Volksgrenadiers utterly failed to take the forest by nightfall. They had breached the 393rd lines in many places, but had not dislodged the Battle Babies sufficiently to open the way to the twin villages. In snowy draws, and underneath snow-stooped trees, many maimed Germans lay fighting for their lives. Their anguished cries sounded like the wail of tormented souls. "The wounded could be heard hollering for hours and later a couple of German litter teams went out and picked up what looked like a number of bodies," an American soldier recalled. Lieutenant Colonel Scott's regiment was also in bad shape. The 3rd Battalion alone had already lost three hundred men. But, for now, the regiment was holding off the enemy. After the sun set, the fighting tapered off. Many of the dogfaces worried about a German night attack but it never came. Instead the Germans decided to bring up armor from the 12th SS Panzer Division and attack again at first light, mainly to take positions still held by the 3rd Battalion survivors. The Battle Babies had no tank support, no antitank guns, and a dwindling supply of ammunition. Artillery, mortars, and bazookas comprised their main weapons against the tanks.

Five Jagdpanzer IV/48 tank destroyers, accompanied by elements of an infantry battalion from the 277th, hit M Company. American artillery dispersed some of the infantry, but the lead tank destroyer kept coming. "One of our [machine] guns opened up on the tank and buttoned it up," one of the M Company sergeants wrote. "They also knocked out some of the infantry that followed the tank." As ever, "knocked out" was a euphemism for killing. Needless to say, the German infantrymen were not subjected to a standing eight count. They were ripped open by high-velocity bullets. Their lifeblood drained into the snow, turning it crimson, then rust as the blood dried.

The lead Jagdpanzer, invariably called a tank by the GIs, opened up with its own machine gun and a main-gun round, instantly killing one of the American machine gunners. The man next to him was, somehow, completely unscathed (and probably wondered for the rest of his life why). "The tank just kept coming, knocking out everything in its way," the company history recorded. Several of the Battle Babies, including Private First Class James Langford, crawled forward in the snow, bazookas in tow, trying to get a shot at the German armor. "We hit [it] a total of nine times with bazooka rockets and didn't even appear to slow it down," Langford wrote.

The other tank destroyers soon joined their leader. Together they spewed main-gun rounds and machine-gun fire at the GIs. "The bazookamen poured desperate shots [at the lead tank] and finally succeeded in hitting its tracks, immobilizing the vehicle. Otherwise it suffered no damage because the crew continued to fire their MGs." The Americans did destroy one other Jagdpanzer (thanks to the heroics of Sergeant Vernon McGarity, who earned the Medal of Honor), but the enemy attack was simply too overwhelming. In this terrain, the German armor had enough maneuvering room, along with cover and concealment, to foil the bazooka gunners. Those gunners had trouble finding ways to get close enough to the tanks, into advantageous positions, to hit their vulnerable side and rear armor, not to mention their tracks.

By now, Lieutenant Colonel Scott realized that the 3rd Battalion was almost surrounded. Against considerable odds, the 393rd had held off the enemy attackers for over twenty-four hours. With General Lauer's authorization, Scott ordered his battalions to disengage under cover of jeep-mounted machine guns and withdraw west, to a new defensive line between Rocherath and the forest. As best they could, the Battle Babies trudged, almost continuously under fire, away from their enemies, out of the menacing forest. Like the battle itself, the withdrawal was anything but orderly. It was more like a latter-year Trail of Tears, with battered, weary, hungry, scared, bewildered, cold survivors making their way west, usually in small groups, all the while worried about the possibility of being overtaken by the Germans. They had no idea that reinforcements were already in place.[8]

Enter the Indian Heads—3/23 Infantry in the Forest

The soldiers of the 2nd Infantry Division wore a unique Indian Head patch that portrayed a proud, fierce-looking Native American warrior adorned with battle headdress against the background of a large white star. The patch was the largest of any divisional unit in the Army. Somehow it symbolized the pride and resourcefulness of a division that had come ashore the day after D-day and had, for the most part, been in combat ever since. A hard core of experienced NCOs, staff officers, and commanders had held this outfit together through many waves of replacements. On the day the German offensive began, elements of the 2nd had actually been launching an attack of their own, at Wahlerscheid, just to the northeast of the 99th Division. In fact, officers of both divisions initially thought the German push was nothing more than an attempt to take the pressure off their comrades at Wahlerscheid. By December 17 they understood that they were facing an all-out, last-ditch enemy offensive that was coming right at them.

General Walter Robertson, the 2nd Division commander, had skillfully broken off his attack and rerouted his infantry regiments to back up the 99th. He understood that the 277th Volksgrenadier and 12th SS Panzer Divisions would eventually push through the Krinkelter Wald and into the valuable twin villages. He simply needed to hold them off long enough to place his units in and around the villages. One of his battalions, the 3rd of the 23rd Infantry Regiment, had moved through Krinkelt and Rocherath on December 16. From there they tromped into the western edge of the Krinkelter Wald to take up defensive positions that allowed them to block two key roads that led out of the woods and into the towns. Some of the soldiers had settled into existing dugouts with overhead cover. Others tried to scoop out shallow fighting positions in the frozen earth (digging true foxholes with shovels in the frigid ground was an impossibility). They had come from a rear area and thus had only a basic load of ammunition. Such was the confusion of the moment that, during the night, these men initially believed they would attack to restore contact with the 393rd. Instead their mission changed by morning to "hold at all costs," a desperate phrase that obviously held sinister connotations for the infantry soldiers, who might soon pay the ultimate price to fulfill the order.

The entire 3rd Battalion was supported by one platoon of Shermans, under Lieutenant Victor Miller, from the 741st Tank Battalion. "We were one rifle battalion thrust into a densely wooded area, with no terrain features that favored the defender, with orders to 'hold at all costs,'" Captain Charles MacDonald, the commander of I Company, wrote. "The defense was a single line of riflemen." His company was on the left (northern) flank, along the main road into the villages. There was a fifty-yard gap between his unit and neighboring K Company on the right. He had seven bazookas but only three rounds for them. Two of the tanks were in place to support him. Artillery support consisted of a few tubes from the 99th Division, whose observers MacDonald, of course, did not know.

As the sun rose, the 2nd Division men could hear sounds of shooting from the east, where the 393rd was fighting for its life. Soon, stragglers—both mounted and dismounted—from that embattled regiment began streaming through the makeshift lines of the Indian Head soldiers. The differing descriptions of this retreat are a classic example of the tendency of soldiers, even those with similar racial and cultural backgrounds, to perceive events according to their own assumptions, biases, and experiences. Nearly all of the 99th Division records and personal accounts speak of the 393rd's exodus as a "withdrawal," thus indicating some level of cohesion to the retreat with an ultimate purpose of setting up a new defensive line outside of Rocherath.

The 2nd Division accounts, coming from a more blooded division whose members were likely to look down on the less experienced 99th, paint a more mixed picture. Private First Class Edward Bartkiewicz, a rifleman in L Company, watched "American vehicles go by, jeeps, trucks, kitchen trucks pulling stoves . . . and it looked like some officers in jeeps going . . . right through us." Like many riflemen, he had no idea who they were, or what was going on. He just wondered why they did not stop and join L Company. Captain MacDonald, a bit better informed about the intense fighting to the east, saw them as the gallant survivors of a unit that had given its all. One of his platoon leaders, Lieutenant Long Goffigan, whose outfit was holding the extreme left flank, begged them for ammunition. Many of them complied, turning over grenades, ammo clips, and boxes of .30-caliber machine-gun bullets. Two of them even elected to join Goffigan's platoon. Elsewhere, in K Company's lines, First Lieutenant Lee Smith, a no-nonsense Texan with little appreciation for what the 393rd had just been through, saw them coming and tried to get them to halt and fight with his outfit. "They would not stop. They just seemed stunned." Smith even ordered them to halt and fight with his company. "I did so, but the next big bunch that came by were being led by officers who paid absolutely no attention. They were headed for town like trail cattle after water." Lieutenant Smith gave up, considering the effort useless, especially since "nearly all of them had thrown away their arms and equipment." To his dying day, Smith maintained, quite unfairly and ignorantly, that "the 99th Division crumbled completely." Such were the vicissitudes of just this one event.[9]

On one thing there was no confusion, though. As the number of stragglers petered out, every 2nd Division soldier understood that the Germans were close behind them and would soon attack. Shortly after noon, enemy infantry soldiers began clashing with all three of the 3rd Battalion rifle companies. Their attack was not unlike a quick-forming, violent thunderstorm. In a matter of seconds, the air was filled with bullets. One soldier described it as a "crackling crescendo." Anyone who raised his head risked getting it blown off. Tracer rounds bounced off trees. At the leading edge of L Company's line along a narrow forest trail, Private First Class Bartkiewicz saw the Germans erupt from the line of trees that were across the road. "There was all kinds of ammunition flying in all sorts of directions. Our machine gun could cut a person's body right in half if he was in front of it within about twenty feet. That's what happened." A German soldier tried to throw a grenade at the machine-gun team. The gunners cut him down before he could let go of the grenade. The ensuing explosion maimed the man's already cooling corpse. Bartkiewicz captured two survivors.

The Germans soldiers were close enough to I Company that Captain Mac-Donald's men could clearly see the billed caps indicative of SS infantrymen. The enemy troops were working their way through and up a slight draw in front of I Company's holes. "Wave after wave of fanatically screaming Germans stormed the slight tree-covered rise," Captain MacDonald later wrote. "A continuous hail of fire exuded from their weapons, answered by volley after volley from the defenders. Germans fell right and left."

German artillery and Nebelwerfer rounds were exploding behind I Company. In front of them, several rounds of U.S. artillery exploded among the attackers. "We could hear their screams of pain when the small-arms fire would slacken. But still they came!" The fire was so thick that Captain Mac-Donald was lying flat on his back in his shallow CP foxhole, with a phone to his platoons in one ear and a battalion radio in the other ear, trying to talk and hear amid the noisy maelstrom. Lieutenant Goffigan's platoon was bearing the brunt of the assault. He needed artillery support. Several men were wounded and the captain was calling for litter bearers. MacDonald was also talking to his battalion commander, Lieutenant Colonel Paul Tuttle, requesting more ammunition and artillery support. All he could get in response was a promise that "we're doing all we can" and another order to "hold at all costs." Goffigan was now reporting the presence of tanks in the distance.

To I Company's right, the Germans were also furiously attacking K Company. For the hard-pressed Americans, the stress level was extreme. When the shooting started, Smith was serving as executive officer, the company's second in command. Then Lieutenant Dillard Boland, one of the platoon leaders, came to Smith's hole and told him that he "couldn't take any more." He had been in combat for months and he had reached his limit. He left for the rear. Smith claimed that soon thereafter the company commander broke. "[He] . . . was hysterical. He was a martinet and I never saw a martinet that did well under fire. [He] chickened out and went to the rear."

Assuming command, Lieutenant Smith held K Company together the best he could in the face of unrelenting infantry and armor attacks. "Instead of running and falling the way we did they just walked and used marching fire. Then they would stop and fall down and the tanks would come on. Then the tanks would go back for them and they would mill around, then here they would come again." Like MacDonald, Smith spent much of his time talking with battalion, asking for help, listening to imprecations that he must hold on. All around him, he could hear "the crump of artillery . . . the high-pitched ripping sound of the submachine guns and the double rapid rate of the German machine guns as compared with ours." When soldiers got hit, they generally did not scream "or cry out or make any sort of audible sound." All the while, Lieutenant Smith was worried that his front could not hold out much longer, especially because he had few weapons with which to fight the tanks.

A few dozen yards to the left, the SS men were flinging themselves repeatedly at I Company. Captain MacDonald's men bitterly resisted each enemy push. "Seven times the enemy infantry assaulted, and seven times they were greeted by a hail of small-arms fire and hand grenades that sent them reeling down the hill, leaving behind a growing pile of dead and wounded." Each attack was poorly organized, with little artillery support, almost like a German version of banzai, yet with a distinct geographic objective. "There was only the suicidal wave of fanatical infantrymen, whooping and yelling and brandishing their rifles like men possessed." Many of these Germans were teenaged members of the Hitler Youth. With the oblivious idealism of youth, they were all too eager to turn the war back in their führer's favor. Some of them fell dead within ten yards of the company's lead foxholes.

As had been the case with the 393rd to the east, the presence of German armor was decisive against the 3rd Battalion of the 23rd Infantry. Five Mark V Panthers were closing in on Lieutenant Goffigan's platoon. In the lieutenant's recollection, the tanks "were firing into foxholes and cutting off trees like matchsticks." He called Captain MacDonald to plead for help. The captain arranged for some artillery fire but it did no good. A bazooka man in Goffigan's platoon fired two shots of precious ammunition at the lead tank but missed. Within moments, he was killed by enemy fire and the bazooka was destroyed. The tanks were now within seventy-five yards of the platoon holes. Lieutenant Miller's Shermans were the last hope of salvation for Goffigan's men. Half sobbing, Lieutenant Goffigan called Captain MacDonald:

"For God's sake, Cap'n, get those tanks down here. Do something, for God's sake." But the friendly tanks had moved south, closer to K Company, in search of a more advantageous position.

Goffigan's gallant infantrymen were left to fight the enemy tanks with little else besides rifles, machine guns, and courage. "Within a short time the tanks, with German infantry disposed on both sides of each tank, had approached where they could fire AP [armor piercing] ammo point blank into the foxholes," a post-battle report recounted. "A section of heavy machine guns held their positions and took a heavy toll of the enemy infantrymen until they ran out of ammunition."

At this point, when the Germans overwhelmed Goffigan's platoon, caving in the left flank, I Company's front began to collapse. The fighting was at extremely close range. The Germans were blasting everything in front of them, cleaning out hole after hole. "The sound of battle reached a height which I had never thought possible before," MacDonald wrote. "The burst of the . . . shells in the woods vied with the sounds of hundreds of lesser weapons." MacDonald was doing everything in his power to hold his outfit together, but events had moved beyond his control.

Throughout the forest, men were engaged in private death struggles. Private Hugh Burger was on the move, looking for a place to dodge the explosions. He jumped into a foxhole and literally bumped into an SS soldier. Stunned, the German staggered to his feet. The two enemies were now intimate participants in the evil of war. They could have mutually decided to live and let live, go their separate ways, but this was not the mood of the battle in the Krinkelter Wald. At this harrowing moment, Burger knew he had to act fast or die. "I grabbed his rifle with my left hand while gripping my knife in my right. I made a [lightning] thrust into his stomach and jerked up with all my strength. I felt hot blood squirt out on my hand and my arm as I pulled the knife out then rammed it home again as his body sagged and slid to the ground. To me it was sickening, but that was my job if I wanted to live." There were few more traumatic ways to kill than this, and Burger's nausea was standard for anyone having to take life in this elemental fashion. He wiped the blade of his knife against his pants, ran away in the direction of the villages, and later rubbed snow on his bloodstained arms and hands.

Captain MacDonald first attempted to pull the remnants of his company back to new positions, but in spite of the bravery of Private First Class Richard

Cowan, a machine gunner who held off the Germans for a few minutes, the situation was way too chaotic for that. Overhead the trees were bursting as artillery shells exploded. Machine-gun and rifle bullets were smashing into trees and men alike. The captain ordered his CP group to destroy their maps and radios and retreat. They made it as far as K Company, whose soldiers were also in close combat with enemy infantrymen and tanks. Lieutenant Miller's Shermans, having displaced here earlier, destroyed two of the enemy Panthers before German fire blew the American tanks up, killing Miller and several of his men. Some of the American soldiers were fighting the enemy with bayonets (the rarest form of combat in modern war) and using their rifles as clubs. One bazooka gunner swung his empty tube at a German, in an attempt to bludgeon him to death. Enemy soldiers with burp guns cut down the gunner.

The 3rd Battalion was disintegrating. Stragglers were already streaming out of the forest, into Krinkelt and Rocherath. Lieutenant Smith agonized over whether to keep trying to "hold at all costs" or retreat. His K Company soldiers held off the Germans as long as they could—helping many 3rd Battalion men escape—before Smith reluctantly ordered a withdrawal. The remnants of the company streamed west, out of the forest.

Captain MacDonald and a few of his men made their way west, somehow dodging intense enemy fire. Like Lieutenant Smith, the captain felt guilty for retreating. Moreover, he barely knew what happened to most of his men. His company had simply disintegrated under an avalanche of enemy pressure. MacDonald's clothes were soaking wet. His mouth was dry. He was sad and dispirited. He and his men made it to a farmhouse near Krinkelt, where Lieutenant Colonel Tuttle had set up his command post in the basement. The captain half expected to be court-martialed. Instead Tuttle greeted him warmly and said: "Nice work, Mac." The captain stood bewildered as Tuttle explained the big picture of the German Ardennes offensive and the true strength of their attack on the 3rd Battalion. "The Germans are throwing everything they've got. You held out much longer than I expected." MacDonald's company, along with the others, had held off the Germans for half a day, buying time for other Indian Head units to get into position in and around the twin villages. Moments earlier, MacDonald had believed that his beloved I Company had been lost for nothing more than his own failure as a commander. Now, though, he began to understand the important mission that his men had accomplished, many by making the ultimate sacrifice. Good news though this was, the thought of it all was overwhelming to him. He felt a catch in his throat. A moment later, the catch turned into deep, wracking sobs. In the dimly lit basement, he stood quietly, tears rolling down his cheeks, hands trembling, sadly contemplating his lost company.[10]

The Manchus at the Lausdell Crossroads

Captain MacDonald, and so many others like him, could at least take solace in the fact that the destruction of the 3rd Battalion, 23rd Infantry, had a purpose. Their self-sacrificial resistance (and the 393rd's determined stand) bought valuable time for General Robertson to arrange for the defense of Krinkelt and Rocherath. Every significant road in the area went through the two towns. If the Germans were to have any hope of carrying out a lightning advance to the Meuse, they had to control these roads, and thus the two little towns.

Throughout the day on December 17, the general disengaged from his attack at Wahlerscheid, personally supervised the southerly movement of troops to the danger area around Krinkelt and Rocherath, and deployed his men into defensive positions. For the 2nd Division soldiers, the process was exhausting and disorienting. One minute they were assaulting a line of pillboxes at Wahlerscheid. The next minute they abruptly ceased attacking, began a forced march several miles to the south, and soon thereafter they were fighting a defensive battle. Only a well-led unit like the 2nd could have pulled off this dangerous transition with any semblance of order.

As the sun set on December 17, ushering in a cold, dark winter night, this process was well under way, but the general was still scrambling to reinforce the twin villages. He planned to defend the towns with his 38th Infantry Regiment, a stalwart unit with the moniker "Rock of the Marne" for its part in blunting a major German offensive in World War I. Much of the 38th was still strung out in long columns along the narrow road that led into the villages. These soldiers were under enemy artillery fire, which, of course, inflicted casualties on them and impeded their movement. Moreover, retreating GIs and vehicles crowded the road and sowed confusion among the "Marne" soldiers. Robertson needed several more hours to sort this mess out and deploy the 38th's rifle companies, plus their armored support, in and around the villages. In the meantime, Robertson decided that soldiers from another one of his regiments, the 9th, absolutely had to hold a key crossroads—generally known as the Lausdell junction—about one thousand yards east of Rocherath, right in the path of the onrushing German advance. If the Germans captured the crossroads and succeeded in getting large numbers of troops and tanks into the village this evening, they could slaughter the 38th Infantry soldiers along the roads before they could hide in buildings or dig foxholes overlooking the road.

The 9th was one of the most storied infantry regiments in the Army. The unit had fought in nearly every war since its activation in 1812. In 1900, soldiers from this regiment had helped crush the Boxer Rebellion in China, earning themselves the colorful nickname "Manchus." Now, on this frigid Ardennes evening, they were once again at the center of momentous events. On the road north of Rocherath, General Robertson collared twenty-eight-year-old Lieutenant Colonel William McKinley, commander of the 1st Battalion, 9th Infantry, and gave him the job of defending the Lausdell crossroads. In the recollection of Lieutenant Colonel Ralph Steele, the regimental executive officer, the general emphasized that the battalion "must hold at all costs in order to ensure . . . an effective defense position."

It was like a father-son talk. The general, bald and in his late fifties, looked like the wizened elder he was. The youthful McKinley looked little different from the men he was leading. He was quite popular with his fellow officers and his soldiers. "He was a fearless and thoughtful commander," one of his soldiers said. "Our welfare was always his first consideration." He loved to sing, and had even written a 9th Infantry fight song. He was the grandnephew of President William McKinley, whose name he carried on. As a West Pointer who was born into an Army family, and an infantry officer who had earned many combat decorations, young McKinley was the embodiment of a warrior. Like any good officer, he never asked his troops to do what he would not. "Many times he did the dangerous himself, rather than risk the lives of his men," Steele later wrote. He had known General Robertson and Lieutenant Colonel McKinley for several years and greatly admired them. "Both Robertson and McKinley were soldiers all the way through and neither of them flinched or questioned the other. To me [watching them converse] was like viewing a movie."

When the conversation ended, Lieutenant Colonel McKinley placed his companies on a forward slope astride the crossroads. The soldiers dug shallow foxholes, through snow and earth, along little hedges that offered some bare semblance of concealment. Most of the men were in a foul mood. For almost five days they had been in combat, in the cold, with no hot food and little rest, watching their friends get killed or wounded. Now they had been sent on this boondoggle to stave off what they thought was only a local counterattack that some other unit could not handle. Combat units invariably see the world narrowly. Most believe they have a harder, more dangerous job than any other unit. They often perceive that it is their unhappy lot to succeed where other units have failed ("so then we had to bail out this other outfit" is an oft-heard phrase, as is "why do we always get the crappy jobs?"). Although these notions are usually false, built as they normally are on incomplete information, biases, and ungrounded assumptions, they do help build unit pride.

Hence, McKinley's men resented the situation they were now in, but they accepted it and were determined to do their job. If nothing else, they knew they must hold this position. McKinley had already lost almost half of his battalion in the Wahlerscheid attacks. His C Company was even down to fifty men. Fortunately, he had some help from K Company of the 9th, a unit that General Robertson had previously placed around a farmhouse near the crossroads. McKinley and his Manchus also had some assistance from a few machine-gun sections, along with three antitank guns from the 644th Tank Destroyer Battalion that were covering the road. In all, he had about six hundred soldiers. Among them, they had fifteen bazookas. Artillery forward observers had been out of communication with their batteries from the 15th Field Artillery Battalion farther to the rear for much of the day but, just as the battalion settled in, they reestablished contact and planned defensive fires along the likely routes of enemy attack. The infantrymen also had some antitank mines but they did not yet put them in place because they correctly believed that American armor and vehicles would still migrate along the road for much of the night.[11]

A shroud of foggy, inky darkness descended over the area. The air was cool and crisp, albeit fraught with the tension of anticipated combat. The dogfaces crouched in their holes and peered into the darkness. Shivering fingers hovered near triggers. Snot ran from noses. The body heat of each man caused the snow around him to melt, making it hard to stay dry. Some of the men lined their holes with straw in an effort to provide a semblance of dryness and warmth. They fought off sleep. Stomachs growled with hunger. In even more cases, stomachs were queasy with the bile of fear.

Some men, like Sergeant Herbert Hunt of A Company, hungered for tobacco. After digging in and lining his hole with straw, he was down to one soggy cigarette. He plopped to the bottom of his hole, placed his tommy gun on his lap, and lit the cigarette. "As I sat there, savoring each precious puff of the cigarette, I began to hear the distant rumble and clanking of moving tanks." Like many of the other men, Hunt had been told by his officers to be on the lookout for American tanks. But another NCO, Sergeant Billy Floyd, a combat-experienced man, peered into Hunt's foxhole and voiced the opinion that the tanks sounded German. The two sergeants walked a few dozen yards and stood by the side of the road, listening. A moment passed as the vehicle noises got closer. They could see a column of infantrymen approaching. Another moment passed. Then they heard German voices.

The truth hit Floyd and Hunt at the same time. They were actually standing right next to SS Panzergrenadiers who were walking along the road, with tanks rumbling right behind them. The two Americans stood frozen in place. Hunt's heart was beating wildly. "What followed made no sense. The German infantrymen passed by, scarcely looking in our direction. Some were laughing and joking. One German, with a very foul breath . . . leaned over and looked in my face as he passed. Then the German tanks passed by, splashing Billy and me with mud and slush." A German tank commander, standing in his open hatch, even flipped them off as his tank drove past them!

Stunned by this surreal experience, Hunt and Floyd took off to warn their company commander, Lieutenant Stephen Truppner. On the way they ran into another GI and, together, they heard the German tanks stop and shut off their engines. The three Americans got to Truppner's dugout, on the west side of the road, and told him what had happened. The lieutenant decided to radio for artillery and mortar fire while the three enlisted men warned the company of the German presence. Hunt and his friends left the dugout and took a few steps in the direction of the road. All at once, the night exploded with enemy fire. Machine-gun tracer rounds zipped along the road. To Hunt, it seemed like the tracers were about to go right through him. The other two men clutched their throats and fell dead to the pavement. Sergeant Hunt went back to the A Company CP and found out that Truppner could not get his radio to work. "Lieutenant Truppner wants you to go back to D Company and get the artillery turned on," one of the men told him. Their CP, he learned, was in a building behind a barn, just across the way.

By now, the shooting was intense. Tracer rounds were still buzzing in every direction. Sergeant Hunt heard the tanks firing their main guns, answered by American rifle and machine-gun fire. The barn was on fire (Hunt found out many years later that Captain MacDonald and a few of his men were taking shelter inside). Hunt made his way to a house behind it. "German tank shells were exploding against the front of the house, sending terrifying flames of light into the sky, and filling the air with hot, sharp, and deadly hunks . . . whirring shrapnel." Somehow, Hunt did not get hit. He made it to D Company and "told the company commander [Captain Louis Ernst] . . . that we had to have artillery, mortar, and tank support, immediately!" Ernst did so immediately and got quick results. A lucky shell scored a direct hit on one of the enemy tanks, cooking off the ammo inside. A spontaneous explosion blew the turret off.

From here, the battle turned into a confused struggle in the darkness and the shadows of burning fires. Generally, the Americans were fighting from within holes and buildings. The Germans were usually in the open, on the road, or outside of houses. American artillery and mortar shells were coming down on the whole Lausdell crossroads area. The effect was devastating, especially to the Germans. For instance, a new German armored column, with infantry, attacked B Company's position, immediately astride the junction. An American artillery forward observer walked his rounds up and down the road, toward the woods where the Germans were coming from. "This fire continued for about 10 minutes while B Company raked the infantry with machine gun fire," Major William Hancock, the battalion executive officer who helped coordinate the fire, later said. "The enemy tanks stopped when the artillery came in on them, and the defenders could hear the screams of enemy wounded." Fragments laced through the exposed infantrymen, cutting some of them into shreds. Others dispersed as best they could. Seldom did the rounds score direct hits on the tanks, but they did not have to. Near misses had the effect of spooking the enemy crews into immobility or retreat, especially when their infantry support melted away.

A couple hundred yards to the west, the same thing happened in A Company's sector. The shells even destroyed, or immobilized, four German tanks.

Three more kept rolling forward, like menacing nocturnal monsters, until they were among the company foxholes, shooting up the Manchu infantrymen with their machine guns and cannons. The explosions and anguished cries were horrible. Screaming into his radio, Lieutenant John Granville, a forward observer, made a desperate plea to the distant batteries for maximum support: "If you don't get it out right now, it'll be too goddamn late!" His ear was pressed to the receiver, but he could hear no response. Convinced he was dead, he leaned back and, in his own words, "reached out for God to take me by the hand." Three minutes later, a huge barrage from seven full battalions of artillery came cascading down, prompting the German tanks to retreat in a hurry.

Under the protective shelter of the artillery, the infantrymen dealt with the tanks as best they could—mainly with mines, rifle grenades, and bazookas. When Sergeant Ted Bickerstaff and Lieutenant Roy Allen of B Company heard the tanks in the distance, they placed mines on the road, right along their likely avenue of approach. "As we armed the eighth mine," they later wrote, "the German tanks were 400 yards away." They placed bazooka teams to cover the mines. "The tanks were stopped by the mines and the others proceeded to go around them through the fields." The bazooka teams destroyed them.

In a K Company foxhole about one hundred yards from the road junction, Private First Class Frank Royer, a rifleman, was awed by the sight of yet another attacking group of tanks. "They are big and really imposing to a Private in a foxhole with a rifle. I could make out the black hulk of a tank running over our foxholes and heading right for me." He and his foxhole buddy, Private E. J. Sanders, felt totally helpless. Just ahead, the tank ran over the foxhole of two other men from the company. Soon theirs would be next. This was like something out of a nightmare. Then something, or someone, hit the enemy tank, blowing it up. "It burst into flames. I could hear the crew screaming." The German tankers could not get out of the tank so they burned to death. Royer and his friend crawled closer to help a couple other K Company men dig out from under the burning German tank.

At the junction, in B Company's position, First Lieutenant John Melesnich, the company commander, personally destroyed one enemy tank with a bazooka. Two of his soldiers, Sergeant Charles Roberts and Sergeant Otis Bone, put their lives at extreme risk to attack a tank that was lacing the company with accurate fire. The two sergeants retrieved a can of gasoline from a nearby vehicle and then somehow sidled up alongside the metal monster. "[They] poured it on the tank, and set it afire" with thermite grenades. "The crews were picked off by American riflemen."

By midnight, the fighting died down a bit as the Germans withdrew, probably to reorganize for more coordinated attacks. Lieutenant Colonel McKinley sent a message to his regimental commander: "We have been strenuously engaged, but everything is under control at the present."[12]

In the morning, just before sunrise, the SS renewed their attacks, this time with even more ferocity. A chilly curtain of fog and drizzle hung over the area, concealing attacker and defender alike. The Germans threw nearly two battalions of tanks and two battalions of Panzergrenadiers at the Americans, particularly McKinley's hard-pressed outfit. American artillery and mortar shells practically showered the Lausdell crossroads. Some exploded as close as twenty yards in front of the American holes, if not even closer. "The men of the battalion engaged the tanks and infantry with every means at hand," a post-action report stated with laconic accuracy. As the report hinted, McKinley's infantrymen offered near-suicidal resistance, pouring machine-gun, rifle, and grenade fire at the approaching hostile shapes. "The riflemen of 'B' Company fired at the turret men of the enemy tanks as they proceeded to come down the road," Lieutenant Allen wrote. He watched as two enemy tank crewmen made the fatal mistake of abandoning their vehicle. "One was shot by 'D' Company and I shot the other." At this point, a bazooka gunner scored a hit on one tank but did no substantial damage. The menacing steel monster turned its turret in the direction of the bazooka men. "Four hits were obtained at a range of thirty yards without effect. Then one of my men approached the tank from the rear, poured gasoline on it, and ignited the gasoline with an incendiary grenade, thus knocking out the tank."

From the vantage point of a foxhole near the crossroads, Sergeant Hunt of A Company watched as German tanks, accompanied by groups of foot soldiers, cautiously moved west, right past the company holes. Some of the attackers were on the road, some not. All were under shell fire that Lieutenant Truppner was calling down in a last-ditch attempt to avoid being overrun. "Then ... the G.I.'s of A Company—all at the same instant—opened fire into the backs of the German infantrymen, killing them by the dozen," Hunt recalled. The terrified German soldiers careened around, looking desperately for cover. Few escaped the barrage of bullets. The .30-06-caliber rounds smashed into them, presenting the odd sight of torn holes in their winter uniforms (not to mention their bodies underneath). Threads hung crazily in all directions. Blood poured profusely from some of the worst wounds. Steam rose from others.

The shooting, though effective, gave away the location of A Company's positions. The enemy tanks, minus any infantry support, turned around, rumbled right up to the holes, and began blasting them with cannon and machine-gun fire. Hunt was transfixed by the horrendous violence of A Company's mortal struggle. "A G.I. leaped from his foxhole, lobbed a grenade onto the deck of a tank, and set it afire. Another G.I. was trying to rip open the hatch of a tank with his fingers. Three other G.I.'s were running behind the tanks, trying to set them afire with burning straw. Far to the right, a G.I. was trying to jam his rifle between the cleats of a moving tank." None of this extraordinary valor was enough to stave off the tanks. Two of them simply took up station adjacent to the foxholes and methodically shot up the occupants. Gradually the sound of American small-arms fire died off as, one by one or two by two, the soldiers of A Company got killed. Somehow, Hunt and a few others managed to escape to Lieutenant Colonel McKinley's command post in a dugout at the crossroads. The young commander draped his arm around Hunt's shoulders and exclaimed: "Thank God, Herb, you got out of there! I thought I had lost all of Company A." Hunt's eyes glistened with tears.

Elsewhere, Private William Soderman of K Company huddled in a ditch by the side of the road, pointed his bazooka at the lead tank of an enemy column, and fired. The rocket struck the tank and ignited it, forcing the crew to abandon it. The destruction of this tank created a roadblock that halted the column. The Germans could not quite see Soderman through the mist, but they poured heavy return fire along the road. He slung the bazooka over his back, grabbed his rifle, got up and ran away, in an effort to find a new firing position. All at once, he bumped into a platoon of enemy grenadiers. He raised his rifle, shot three of them to death, and took off, making it back to the remnants of his company in a cluster of houses. Once again, when enemy tanks attacked K Company, Soderman unloosed his bazooka and destroyed the lead vehicle (some accounts say he got two). As he displaced, a machine-gun bullet from a surviving enemy tank smashed into his shoulder, badly wounding him. He managed to crawl to the protection of a nearby ditch, where two of his buddies attended to him. "Guns were firing all around," Soderman later said. "The tanks were shooting. But everybody seemed too busy to pay any attention to us. I walked out of there upright. I guess I was too fuzzy to know exactly what I was doing." Medics evacuated him to the rear. He earned the Medal of Honor for his exploits.

His company was down to a handful of men, including Private First Class Royer, who was trembling in a foxhole, in the middle of a terrifying "friendly" artillery barrage that was designed to stave off the Germans and save K Company. "My ears hurt, head ached, and dirt crumbled into our hole from the shelling." The artillery slackened a bit, but not the German pressure. Royer heard a retreat order. He left his hole and started crawling west, but a fragment tore into his leg. Before he could even attend to his wound, German troops towered over him and forced him to surrender. Nearby, an enemy tank pointed its muzzle at the front door of a house that served as K Company's command post. Captain Jack Garvey, the commander, had seen the Germans capturing Royer and several others. He and his command group, including several refugees from I Company of the 23rd Infantry, surrendered before the tank could open fire. They ascended the basement stairs and filed through the front door. "We were marched out with our hands up—the most humiliating moment of my life," one of the NCOs later commented. Only twelve men from the company escaped death, wounds, or captivity.

The rest of McKinley's beleaguered battalion held on, thanks to a curtain of supporting artillery fire, not to mention sheer guts and determination. He was deeply worried, though, that his unit would be annihilated by the powerful enemy assault. Throughout the morning, his communications with regiment and division were spotty. He simply knew he must hold. Finally, late in the morning, he got authorization to withdraw west, into the villages, where troops from the 38th Infantry were now in place. McKinley's executive officer later said that the colonel was concerned that he would be "unable to get any of his troops out from the very close contact with the enemy." Fortunately for McKinley and his survivors, they were able to escape under the umbrella of the artillery barrage and some direct support from Sherman tanks of the 741st Tank Battalion.

McKinley and his operations officer were the last ones to vacate the battalion position. The Germans were so close that the two officers could hear them screaming for the retreating Americans to surrender. Six hundred men had gone into place at the Lausdell crossroads. Only 217 made it out. McKinley's dogfaces fulfilled their mission, destroying—mostly with bazookas—seventeen enemy tanks, halting the German push for the villages, and buying time for General Robertson to place reinforcements inside both Krinkelt and Rocherath. Colonel Francis Boos, commander of the 38th Infantry, even believed that McKinley's determined stand had prevented the destruction of his own outfit on the evening of December 17, when his men had filtered into the two towns. At midday on December 18, the grateful Boos told McKinley: "You have saved my regiment." The division operations officer chimed in: "You have saved the division." The Lausdell crossroads was arguably the Manchus' finest moment in World War II.[13]

The Indian Heads, and Friends, in the Twin Villages

Thus ensued, over the next thirty-six hours, a chaotic, hellish free-for-all within the villages. In the remains of what had been two quaint farm towns, the Germans found themselves enmeshed in a bitter block-to-block struggle that approximated urban combat. By and large, their attacks were violent but uncoordinated. They threw men and machines into the villages haphazardly, where they engaged in close-range death matches with their American adversaries.

To be sure, the conditions and terrain made it difficult for the German attackers to retain any semblance of organization. Most of the roads that went through Krinkelt and Rocherath were not paved. Vehicles, snow, and mud turned them into pulpy quagmires for the tanks of both sides. Houses were built from sturdy masonry. When artillery and tank shells hit these structures, roof shingles, bricks, and stones emptied rubble into the narrow streets, creating impromptu roadblocks. Some houses were intact, albeit with jagged holes in their roofs or walls where shells had penetrated the masonry. The presence of farm animals added to the chaos. Many were trapped in burning barns. Sometimes, the Germans, in an attempt to cover their assaults, herded animals into the streets. In the memory of one American, "cows lay dead all over the roads." Another soldier, from the 99th Division—many retreating stragglers from this outfit fought alongside their Indian Head comrades in the villages—never forgot the sight of "flickering flames illuminating a pen of abandoned bleating sheep. I was struck by the biblical innocence of the sheep and the violence of war."

The most prominent landmark in the twin villages was the battered Krinkelt church, located within the confluence of several roads. With a spire that towered over the landscape, the imposing stone church attracted artillery observers and vehicles alike. Truly, the fighting represented the full fury of industrial-age ground combat, but in a small-town setting. Tanks and tank destroyers yielded a bloody harvest. Yet, all too often the deadliest weapon in this environment was men with bazookas in their hands.

Using houses and rubble for cover, bazooka teams roamed this ruptured landscape, taking on tanks like modern-day duelists. Private Daniel Franklin, a rifleman in the 38th Infantry, was near the house that served as his company's command post when he heard that enemy tanks had overrun an adjacent platoon. Two of his buddies turned to him and asked if he had ever been close to a Tiger tank. In World War II, American soldiers tended to refer to every German tank as a "Tiger." In fact, bona fide Mark VI Tigers were fairly rare (a fortunate circumstance for the Allied war effort). More commonly, the GIs faced Mark IV medium tanks and Mark V Panthers. The surviving accounts of Krinkelt and Rocherath claim encounters with all three models, most notably plenty of Tigers. Franklin and the other two soldiers saw the enemy tank—which they believed was a Tiger—unleash a shell that tore through the attic of the command post. "We went around the building with a bazooka and hit the tank dead center in the rear." Nor were they the only ones in their unit to do so. "Lt. Bloomfield . . . and Sgt. Frank Little of N.C. [North Carolina] knocked out 2 tanks. They [the tanks] were all over us. Platoons were mixed. Radio operators were carrying bazookas. Lt. Richard Blankennagel . . . kept his platoon busy killing the Germans getting out of the tanks."

A couple blocks away, in another house, Private First Class Kenneth Myers's ears were assaulted by the overpowering explosions of enemy tank shells slamming into the building. "Bazooka men of all kinds moved to the windows and doors, firing right into the tanks of the enemy." Amid the racket, he could hear the screams of "soldiers and buddies with a half an arm or leg torn off, yelling for medics." Some were lying outside, in fields or along the roads. Some had been mercilessly crushed by the enemy tanks but were somehow alive "with half of their body left." Myers saw two German machine gunners and shot them to death.[14]

Elsewhere, Private Hugh Burger, the man in I Company, 23rd Infantry, who had killed an enemy soldier by stabbing him to death in the Krinkelter Wald, was now standing next to the second-floor window of a house, manning a machine gun with his buddy Private First Class Willie Hagan. They watched as an enemy tank cautiously rolled forward. The two made for an odd but synergistic pair—the sort of impromptu team that infantry combat often produces. Hagan was an irreverent career soldier in his thirties. To the eighteen-year-old, Bible-reading Burger, Hagan seemed impossibly old to be in combat. Hagan was on the gun and Burger was his loader.

All at once, a shell from a U.S. tank destroyer pierced the armor of the German tank, setting it afire. In the next moment, five German soldiers came into view alongside the burning tank. As their sergeant paused to give orders, Hagan opened fire. "I thought he would surely burn the barrel up before he stopped firing, but not a Kraut got up," Burger later wrote. Hagan turned to Burger and, in an almost clinical tone, said: "I got every one of the sonofabitches." They had also alerted any other Germans in the vicinity to their presence, so they decided to displace to the ground floor of the house. This was a smart tactic for any machine-gun team in this environment and, in this case, it probably saved their lives. "We were making our way down when a tank fired into the wall knocking it out, upsetting our machine gun and showering us with chips of bricks." This was the only shot, though, and they made it downstairs.

Later, the tank pulled into the house's backyard and sat there, its engine idling menacingly. The crew inside was probably searching for targets. Hagan and Burger found a bazooka and some ammunition. The sight for the bazooka was gone but the weapon still worked. Hagan loaded. Burger snapped off a shot. "The projectile hit the ground and skipped over the tank." Having missed so badly, Private First Class Burger felt like running away. His confidence was down. He was terrified of the tank's retaliation. Before he could run, though, Hagan tapped him on the shoulder, indicating he had loaded another round into the bazooka. In that nanosecond, Burger's attitude changed. Instead of panicking, he forgot his natural fear because of Hagan's quiet, unspoken determination. If Hagan could keep fighting, then so can I,

Burger figured. It was a classic example of the unspoken strength that infantry soldiers drew from one another under the most harrowing of circumstances. Burger aimed, fired, and scored a direct hit. "Hot metal sprayed like a cutting torch." Filled with the exhilaration that often overtook men in the immediate aftermath of such an impersonal kill, Hagan jumped up and roared: "You got him! You knocked hell out of the sonofabitch!"

This exhilaration soon gave way to horror. A hatch opened on the burning tank and a badly wounded crewman jumped out, collapsed, and lay writhing in the street. One of his hands was blown off and his face looked "like fresh ground meat." Hagan and Burger carried him into the house, put him on a cot, and tried to help him. The man was delirious and terrified. He kept screaming at the top of his lungs. Neither of the Americans spoke any German. For all they knew, the man was calling to his comrades to come get him. The wounded crewman simply would not shut up. What had started out as a mission of mercy turned into yet another moment of self-preservation. "He will bring every Kraut here in town in here on us," Hagan said. "If I stop that noise, you won't ever tell, will you, Burger?" The eighteen-year-old promised he would not. Hagan killed the man (in later years, Burger could not bring himself to say how his friend carried out the grisly business). In the shattered house, Burger hung his head to pray. The two men never spoke of this incident again. But, for Burger, the close-quarters killing brought back haunting memories of his own experience in the forest, when he had stabbed a young German to death. "Shooting a man from a distance is different [from] using a knife. I washed my hands over and over but I could still smell his blood."

A few blocks away from Burger, Sergeant John Savard, a Minnesotan, was also playing a cat-and-mouse game with the German tanks. He stepped out the door of one house and "found myself looking almost down the gun barrel of a Mark IV tank. I dived back inside and down the cellar as part of the building exploded. A bazooka team knocked out the tank and we killed the crew as they emerged."

In the attic of another house, Staff Sergeant Merrill Huntzinger, a machine-gun squad leader, was fighting as a rifleman alongside one of his section leaders, a man named Eddie. The two men were spread out on either side of the attic. Both had a panoramic view of the streets that led to the house. About fifty yards away, they saw dozens of German soldiers, augmented by a tank, apparently waiting to attack. Sergeant Huntzinger heard the tank engine start up. "Then the tank hatch opened. Someone stood up, took a quick look around, threw out an empty . . . shell casing, and I popped him. Then I opened up on crew members who were outside the tank." Huntzinger ran over to Eddie's position and saw him "dropping Germans left and right." The sergeant was worried that the Germans now knew their position and suggested they vacate the attic. "The hell with 'em," Eddie replied, "keep killing the bastards." Staff Sergeant Huntzinger could have ordered Eddie to leave but, like Private First Class Burger in the other house, he was emboldened by his partner.

No sooner did this thought flash through Huntzinger's mind than a tank shell hit the roof of the attic, close to Eddie's perch. The explosion staggered Huntzinger, making him feel "like my head was the size of a pumpkin. My ears were ringing, my head was thumping, my forehead and face felt like it had been sandblasted." The attic was enveloped in thick dusty smoke. Eddie lay unconscious. As Staff Sergeant Huntzinger tried to revive him, another shell exploded, knocking the sergeant down, giving him a bloody nose. With an act of sheer will, he picked himself up and rushed to the window he had manned a moment earlier. "Germans were kneeling outside our building directly beneath me." He aimed his rifle and fired. "It was like shooting fish in a barrel." This rifle fire, in addition to a well-placed grenade, prevented the German soldiers from assaulting Huntzinger's shattered house. A moment later, he heard a massive explosion as an American tank destroyer scored a direct hit on the German tank, setting it afire. By now, Eddie was barely conscious and moaning that he could not see. "He was seeping blood from several spots on his face and fluid was seeping from his eyeballs." Sergeant Huntzinger got Eddie out of the attic, to the medics, but Eddie's sight was gone forever.

In the heart of Rocherath, Lieutenant George Adams and several members of his 2nd Platoon, C Company, 38th Infantry, were holed up in a two-story house belonging to the Drosch family. On the street outside they saw eleven German tanks approaching, with infantry riding aboard. One of Adams's squad leaders, Sergeant Richard Shinefelt, fired several rifle grenades at them. The grenades did no damage to the tanks, but they reaped a grim harvest among the infantry. Time and again, the Germans in the twin villages attacked with infantrymen riding aboard tanks, making the foot soldiers ideal targets in such a contested, confined environment. They would have been much better advised to dismount their infantry and place them alongside the tanks, as protection from bazooka men (similar to what the Americans did at Aachen). The vaunted reputation of the SS aside, this revealed an amateurish ignorance among the commanders and troops of the 12th SS Panzer Division. The Americans made them pay by slaughtering the infantry soldiers with impunity.

Bereft of infantry support, the tanks rolled past the Drosch house. Adams's men showered them with bazooka shots but did no damage. At one point, several of the tanks stopped and unleashed three or four shots into the house. Masonry, walls, and stairs collapsed. In the recollection of Lieutenant Adams, "visibility was nil in the clouds of stifling smoke." The tanks moved on to points unknown. For a time, Adams and his men left the house, but they returned when the dust settled. Eventually, they were all that stood in the way of an enemy tank-infantry attack that threatened to overrun C Company's command post. Adams and his platoon sergeant, Rudolf Kraft, grabbed bazookas and climbed into what was left of the attic. Here was the ultimate infantry hands-on leadership. This platoon leader and platoon sergeant did not order others to do this dangerous job. They took it upon themselves and they did it together.

They both loaded and, at the count of three, pulled their respective triggers. Adams's misfired. Kraft scored a hit on the bogey wheels of the tank. Adams threw his defective bazooka aside and reloaded Kraft's tube. The sergeant fired a second shot that hit the turret of the enemy tank. The lieutenant bent over to reload. As he did so, two tank shells hit the attic, in quick succession. "The first round piled the wall, ceiling, and rubble on top of the two men so that the second which entered the attic and burst did no damage," a post-battle report later detailed. The tanks pumped round after round into the disintegrating house. As they did so, Adams, Kraft, and the other men simply took shelter in the basement alongside the terrified Drosch family. Between shots, the Americans went upstairs and manned their positions. The standoff benefited the Americans since they were the defenders.[15]

The problem for German tank crews in the villages was one of movement versus imminent danger. Their mission was to seize the towns quickly, yet they had to be wary of any forward movement because death could come from any direction. The ruined houses and rubble-strewn streets offered ideal cover for American tanks, tank destroyers, and bazooka-toting infantrymen. A tank crew could find themselves perfectly safe on one corner while their platoon mates a block away were in a kill zone. The streets around the Krinkelt church exemplified this unpleasant reality. As Staff Sergeant Willi Fischer's Mark V Panther neared the church, he watched American antitank fire hit the tank ahead of his. The commander managed to get out but his loader was cut down by American rifle fire as he tried to exit the wrecked tank. Fischer glanced in another direction and noticed another Panther in trouble. "Brodel's tank [was] burning slightly. Brodel could be seen sitting in the turret—lifeless. Ahead of me on the road, all tanks were shot out of action, some of them still ablaze."

Fischer gingerly withdrew his tank, dodging one near miss from an American antitank gun. A second shot hit his Panther's side and its track. Nobody was hurt, but the tread came off, miring the Panther uselessly in the mud. Fischer got out. Americans were still in the nearby buildings, shooting at anyone who moved in the streets. "Some of these killed our comrade Bandow . . . shooting him through his heart . . . right in front of my eyes." Nearby, another German tank commander, Sergeant Gerhard Engel, was gloomily looking at the destroyed remnants of several Panthers when, "at that moment a single Panther tank approaches . . . and, at a distance of a mere 100 metres [sic], turns into a flaming torch." In just a few hours, his company was almost totally destroyed. Near the church alone they lost five tanks. The Americans lost three Shermans and several other vehicles there.[16]

As the battle raged, houses changed hands several times. Some men, from both sides, were captured, liberated, then captured again. Infantrymen learned to take shelter in cellars. Tankers figured out how best to use the buildings and limited fields of fire to their advantage. According to one report, the Sherman crewmen "proved themselves adept at the art of waylaying and killing 'Tigers.' From well-camouflaged positions, by expert maneuvering and stalking, tank after tank of the enemy forces were destroyed by flank and tail shots."

Maneuvering for such kill shots took nerves of steel, alertness, and, most of all, patience. At times this led to significant tension between the tank crewmen and the dogfaces. The U.S. armor crewmen knew that the German tanks had better guns and thicker armor. They could not afford to go toe to toe with them. The consequences of failure were horrifying. The average tank carried

150 gallons of fuel and over one hundred shells, thus making an ideal tinderbox. If their tank was hit by an armor-piercing round from an enemy tank, they would probably be blasted, shredded, concussed, or, in all too many cases, burned. For these reasons, the crewmen were trained to employ extreme caution, especially within the confined environment of towns. "Some doughboys [infantry] don't seem to realize that the field of vision of a tanker is very restricted," a Sherman crewman commented. "Except for the tank commander, the crew have only a narrow slit to look through. This led the tanker to be a bit cautious. We tankers did not lack physical or moral courage. But there were times when courage simply wasn't the answer."

Most of the infantrymen did not appreciate, or understand, the kind of dangers the tank crewmen faced. Dogfaces knew that theirs was the most dangerous job. They had no protection except personal weapons and the clothes on their backs. So, in their view, the tankers were sheltered nicely behind several inches of armor, with the added security of a cannon and machine guns. As a result, they expected the tankers to always come to their aid, no matter the circumstances, just as a fellow infantryman might. "We in the infantry are screwed without you," an infantry officer once wrote in an article intended for tankers. In so doing he adeptly summed up the infantryman's mind-set. "You have to realize that your 'protection' means jack**** to me as an infantry soldier."

If the tankers did not provide the support that infantrymen, in their necessarily narrow view, expected, then trouble soon followed. Sergeant Hunt of the 9th Infantry blamed the loss of his company at Lausdell to the lack of tank support. He claimed that during the battle he only saw one tank. "That tanker stopped at my foxhole, looked down in the valley, saw the German tanks, spun about, and took off for the hills."

At one point during the fighting in Rocherath, Lieutenant Adams saw a German tank parked at a crossroads and asked a nearby tank destroyer crew to shoot at it. The destroyer's commander claimed that he could not see the German tank through his telescopic sights. Adams even offered to look through the sights himself and take the shot. The tankers demurred. Meanwhile, one of the infantrymen, a sergeant, grew so exasperated with this dialogue that he picked up a .30-caliber machine gun and took matters into his own hands. According to a unit post-battle report, the sergeant "draped a belt of ammunition around his neck and walked toward the enemy tank firing his machine gun from the hip." He did no damage to the tank, and he somehow escaped unscathed. Another time, Adams tried to get a Sherman tank crew to fire on a column of approaching troops. In the confusion of darkness, the tank commander could not tell if the troops were German or American, so he refused to shoot. As it turned out, they were soldiers from E Company of the 38th Infantry. "The tanker probably saved a friendly unit from suffering unnecessary casualties," Adams later admitted.

When a German tank closed to within a block of Sergeant Joseph Kiss's infantry squad, he ran to a nearby tank destroyer and ordered the crew to knock out the enemy tank. They refused, claiming they needed authorization from one of their own officers. "But we need you right now," Sergeant Kiss pleaded. Still they refused. He was so livid that he reported them to headquarters for refusing to obey orders. He also called them "yellow and other things." None of this had any effect.

Captain Halland Hankel, commander of M Company, 38th Infantry, had an ugly run-in with a Sherman crew during the fighting. Supported by a platoon of infantry soldiers, a lone German tank—Hankel claimed it was a Tiger—ended up perched right outside of his command post. Hankel's machine gunners and some service troops dispersed the enemy infantry troops with accurate fire. A Sherman tank was parked twenty-five feet away from the Tiger, in position for a perfect broadside shot against this vulnerable flank of the behemoth. The captain was standing right next to the Sherman and he expected to hear the friendly tank's main gun open up. Instead, he saw "the Sherman tank crew dismounting with well-practiced, precision drill, and explaining in terrified gesticulations that their armor was no match for the Tiger and that it would be suicide to stay in their tank." The captain had little sympathy for them. In his opinion, the crew was failing to do their job. He attempted to get the crew back in their tank "by physical persuasion." They resisted the unfamiliar infantry captain, refusing to get back in.

Meanwhile, other armored crewmen demonstrated more resolve, and this was typical. As Captain Hankel argued with the Sherman crew, an unseen American tank destroyer shot at the Tiger, missing it and hitting an unoccupied American jeep and trailer. The Tiger rolled forward. At that exact moment, the regiment's supply officer (S4) turned a corner in his own jeep and came face-to-face with the German tank. The officer and his driver ejected themselves "as if by jet propulsion" just as the tank ran over the jeep and completely flattened it.

The Tiger's gun was apparently damaged because it did not shoot. In the next few moments, as the tank flailed around, bumping into telephone poles, attempting to escape, it came under renewed assault from the unseen tank destroyer, an antitank gun crew, and a bazooka team. The destroyer scored a fatal hit, the Tiger bursting into flames. This was a rather typical instance. For every tank crew that refused pleas for help from the infantrymen, others remained on the job, helping in their own deliberate way. Together with the infantry soldiers, they all inflicted the proverbial death by a thousand cuts on the superior German tanks, peppering them with main-gun rounds, antitank shells, bazooka rockets, grenades, and even small-arms fire. Combined arms reigned supreme. It was rather like a pack of wildcats attacking an elephant. At the twin villages, it worked very well. For nearly three critical days, they held the Germans off in this fashion, wrecking their timetable completely.[17]

At midday on December 19, Generals Lauer and Robertson decided to withdraw north from the villages, to stronger defensive positions along Elsenborn Ridge. Thereafter, the survivors of both divisions gradually disengaged and withdrew. "On the night of 19–20 Dec., the 2nd Inf Div., plus . . . the 99th, executed a night withdrawal by phases, over a one-way secondary road to prepared and partially organized defensive positions," General Robertson later wrote. At Losheimergraben, the Krinkelter Wald, the Lausdell crossroads, and the twin villages, their troops had stymied a key route of advance that the Germans badly needed. The enemy made no subsequent headway against the new American defensive line at Elsenborn. This forced them west, to Butgenbach, where they were then stopped cold by the Blue Spaders from the 2nd Battalion, 26th Infantry Regiment, under none other than Lieutenant Colonel Derrill Daniel, whose outfit had figured so prominently in the capture of Aachen.

The cost was considerable. In a four-day period, the 99th Division lost 133 men killed in action, 1,394 missing in action (many of whom were POWs), 915 wounded, and another 600 nonbattle casualties to frostbite, trench foot, combat fatigue, and sickness. The 38th Infantry alone suffered 625 casualties at the twin villages; the 9th Infantry lost 664; the 23rd lost 773 soldiers. In the villages, the Americans inflicted over 2,000 casualties on the Germans. That damage, in tandem with the previous two days' grim harvest, crippled the 277th Volksgrenadiers and greatly weakened the 12th SS.

Weeks later, when the Americans retook the villages, they counted seventy-two destroyed enemy vehicles. Most were Mark IV and Mark V tanks. Tank destroyers had gotten nineteen of them. Shermans from the 741st Tank Battalion accounted for twenty-seven, while losing eleven of their own. Infantry soldiers with bazookas had killed almost half of the enemy tanks. "Determined infantry armed with its organic weapons can and will stop German armor, principally by use of the rocket launcher (bazooka) and by destroying the attack of the accompanying enemy infantry," Colonel Boos, the 38th Infantry commander, later wrote. At the villages, his Indian Head soldiers and their friends demonstrated the potency of resolute infantrymen on a confined winter battlefield.

The vulgarity and destruction they experienced were the very embodiment of modern ground combat. The horrors were nearly indescribable for most. The trauma of the fighting left deep wounds on the psyches of everyone who was there. "Man is mad, stark raving mad!" Private Harold Etter, a 99th Division soldier, wrote to his mother, after fighting in the villages. "Why must this mess go on, why can't I go home and raise my family like I should and [the] Germans do the same. This is war and I know that nothing is worse. If the sacrafices [sic] we have to put up with will end this maddness [sic] for all time, I guess it will be worth it. I am afraid it won't though, I am a little afraid for my own son." He was right to be fearful. In expressing his concerns, Etter sensed one of history's most enduring lessons and perhaps its greatest tragedy—the persistence of war. Like nearly every generation before, his infant son's life would not be spared.[18]

Operation Masher/White Wing: Air Mobility, Attrition, and the Big-Unit Grunts of Vietnam

Westy's Strategy

IN A SENSE, THE FIGHTING never really ended. World War II begat the Cold War. The Cold War begat limited, but costly, wars in Korea and Vietnam for the United States. Korea was predominantly a conventional struggle to prevent communist North Koreans and Chinese from taking over noncommunist South Korea. In that war, American infantrymen fought with largely the same weapons and tactics they had used in World War II. In 1953, the war ended in stalemate, which, for the Americans, was a victory of sorts because South Korea did not fall to communism.

Vietnam was quite different. By the mid-1960s, the United States was desperately trying to stave off a major communist insurgent effort to destroy the shaky noncommunist regime in South Vietnam. Communist North Vietnam, led by the charismatic nationalist Ho Chi Minh, was infiltrating large amounts of war matériel and thousands of well-trained North Vietnamese Army (NVA) soldiers into the South, where they made common cause with indigenous antigovernment insurgents commonly known as the Viet Cong (VC). Both China and the Soviet Union were surreptitiously aiding the communist effort in Vietnam with weapons, food, equipment, medical supplies, technical support, and even, in China's case, some soldiers.

President Lyndon Johnson wanted only to prevent a communist takeover of South Vietnam. He did not want the conflict to provoke World War III. He would bomb North Vietnam but he would not invade it. Nor would he authorize wide-scale invasions of neighboring Laos and Cambodia, where the communists maintained infiltration routes and built large base complexes in ostensibly neutral countries. For him, the endgame was a Korea-like stalemate that would secure South Vietnam for the foreseeable future. Thus, in his own words, he sought to do "what is enough but not too much" to win the limited war in Vietnam. In early 1966, that amounted to a dramatic escalation of the war, with more than two hundred thousand American troops in the country and more arriving every day (the communists were escalating just as furiously). Only this infusion of American soldiers had prevented a communist victory over the corrupt, hard-pressed South Vietnamese regime in 1964 and 1965. Having "stemmed the tide," in the words of one U.S. officer, the Americans in 1966 now went on the offensive.

General William Westmoreland, the American commander in Vietnam, concocted a strategy to achieve the limited victory that President Johnson so badly wanted. Nicknamed "Westy," the general's pedigree was second to none. A graduate of the West Point class of 1936 (where he had been first captain of the corps of cadets), he had served as an artillery battalion commander in World War II. After the war, he changed his branch specialty to infantry, became a paratrooper, and commanded the 187th Airborne Brigade in Korea. He made two-star general by the age of forty-two. In the late 1950s, he commanded the 101st Airborne Division. Later, he was superintendent of West Point and commanding officer of the XVIII Airborne Corps. He was a graduate of the Harvard Business School. Like so many other high-ranking Army officers in the 1960s, he was equal parts a commander, a leader, and a manager. A journalist who spent many years covering the war in Vietnam once wrote of him: "Westy was a corporation executive in uniform." Indeed, he was a classic example of a modern war manager. To Westy, victory in war was mainly a question of mobilizing resources for the proper application of overwhelming firepower and force.

True to form, in Vietnam, General Westmoreland's strategy for victory was attrition. He planned to launch big-unit operations, employing multiple infantry battalions, supported by copious amounts of artillery, air, and sea power to secure the countryside of South Vietnam. In this way, he would find the elusive NVA and VC insurgents, force them to do battle, and annihilate them with American firepower. "I elected to fight a so-called big unit war not because of any Napoleonic impulse to maneuver units and hark to the sound of cannon, but because of the basic fact that the enemy had committed big units [NVA and main force VC] and I ignored them at my peril," Westy wrote.

Seeing these big enemy units as the major threat to South Vietnam's security, his goal was to destroy them first and later mop up the smaller local force of VC guerrilla units that proliferated in many of South Vietnam's rural provinces. He often described the VC and their political subversives who were trying to destroy the South Vietnamese government as "termites persistently eating away at the structural members of a building." The enemy's big units were like "'bully boys' armed with crowbars and waiting for the propitious moment to move in and destroy the weakened building." To him, these bully boys were a bigger threat than the termites, so they had to be destroyed first.

With major communist forces thus swept away, the South Vietnamese Army (ARVN) would then occupy, and pacify, the rural villages, negating any possible attempts by the communists to return. He would therefore conventionalize an unconventional war in which the enemy made liberal use of guerrilla tactics. By exerting maximum pressure on them, Westmoreland believed that American firepower would eventually wear them down, inflicting a ceiling of irreparable losses, which he termed "the crossover point." At that stage, they would then have no other choice but to negotiate an end to the war, with South Vietnam intact. "By the time the war reached the final phase, I expected the bulk of the people to be under government control and protection," he later wrote. Westy's concept, then, called for large bases, extensive firepower, and rapid maneuver. Geographic objectives were not as important as killing large numbers of enemy soldiers. Woe to any commander who did not produce large body count numbers. To the infantry, all of this meant big operations.[1]

Infantry on Helicopters

In a road-impoverished country that was teeming with jungles, mountains, rice paddies, and river deltas, and where the identity and whereabouts of "the enemy" were often elusive, how could a modern army hope to fulfill Westmoreland's vision? The answer, according to many officers, was the helicopter.

This new type of aircraft, first used in Korea but perfected in Vietnam, gave the Americans considerable mobility. Helicopters could shuttle troops, move heavy weapons or equipment, provide fire support, resupply units in remote areas, evacuate wounded soldiers, and even conduct reconnaissance missions. In Vietnam, the Americans seldom knew the precise whereabouts of their adversaries. Helicopters allowed the Americans to project their power wherever the enemy might eventually appear (usually by ambushing a U.S. unit) on such a nonlinear battlefield. Helicopters afforded the Americans flexibility but also mobility. This was especially true for infantry soldiers, who could be loaded aboard helicopters and moved in squad-, platoon-, company-, or even battalion-sized units. The helicopter, particularly the versatile UH-1 Huey, gave infantrymen a new dimension of air mobility that was not dependent upon parachutes or fixed-wing aircraft.

The 1st Cavalry Division was the classic expression of this new form of airmobile infantry combat. Members of the unit thought of themselves as latter-day cavalrymen riding their helicopter steeds into battle. Many of them, particularly the helicopter pilots, assumed the persona and identity of cavalry (hence the prominent horsehead on the division patch). In reality, though, once the troops were on the ground, they walked, sweated, ate, and fought as infantry. They may have belonged to battalions that called themselves "cavalry" (such as the 1st Battalion, 7th Cavalry, or 2nd Battalion, 8th Cavalry), but they were really infantry.

By now, the World War II nicknames for infantry soldiers had given way to a blunt, yet respectful, term that has endured ever since—grunts. The infantry were known as grunts because they did the dirtiest and most dangerous job. In other words, they did the grunt work. The nickname had another origination, too. In Army and Marine circles, it was said that when an infantryman shouldered his heavy load of food, equipment, personal gear, and weapons, he let out an ever so audible, totally involuntary grunt.

True grunts took a perverse pride in their misery. They hated and loved their job. They disparagingly referred to outsiders as pogues ("people other than grunts"), another term that has stood the test of time. They often daydreamed about transferring to a pogue job, but few did anything about it. Their identity was built around the idea that they were the cutting edge, the toughest, most important, yet most abused soldiers. The hope for survival dominated their thoughts, even as the ubiquity of death draped over them like a heavy, stifling cloak. They knew levels of exhaustion and fear that few humans would ever experience. Most of them agreed that only a grunt could understand what that truly meant.

Equipped with over four hundred helicopters, the 1st Cavalry Division comprised a lethal blend of firepower, mass, and maneuver. "The helicopter allowed us to make the maximum use of the terrain and it certainly worked to our advantage," one of the division's company commanders later said. "We were able to approach areas from other than the direct road approach . . . or the direct trails, or networks that went into the areas." The commander of the division, Major General Harry Kinnard, had been a paratrooper in World War II. After his division deployed to Vietnam in the fall of 1965, he quickly grew very enamored of its versatility, especially the ability to "strike over very great distances, and to do that repetitively, and to hit and hit again. I was extremely impressed at the ability that the air assault capability gave us to mass in time and space against the enemy . . . even when he had an initial preponderance of force and even when he hit by surprise."

The birds also allowed Kinnard to expand the range of his artillery, since the pieces could be carried on slings by some of the bigger helicopters. Plus, the choppers enhanced communications throughout the division. In short, the helicopter was the perfect tool with which to implement Westy's big-unit war. Kinnard's outfit had suffered heavy casualties fighting the NVA at the Battle of Ia Drang Valley (of *We Were Soldiers* fame) in November 1965. Throughout December and January, the division incorporated replacements and prepared for more combat.[2]

At this point, General Westmoreland finally had the troops, logistical support, and aircraft to launch his large operations, commonly known as search-and-destroy efforts. The first such operation would take place in Binh Dinh province, located in the central portion of South Vietnam within the 1st Cavalry Division's area of operations. For several years, the communists had dominated this rich, rice-producing area. The Viet Cong had strong redoubts and much influence over the people. Some of the insurgents were locals who had gone north after the Geneva Accords split the country in the mid-1950s, only to return to their homes in the early 1960s to build a powerful VC infrastructure. In 1965, two North Vietnamese regiments, the 12th and the 22nd, infiltrated into the province, strengthening communist control that much more. These two regiments combined with the 2nd VC Regiment to

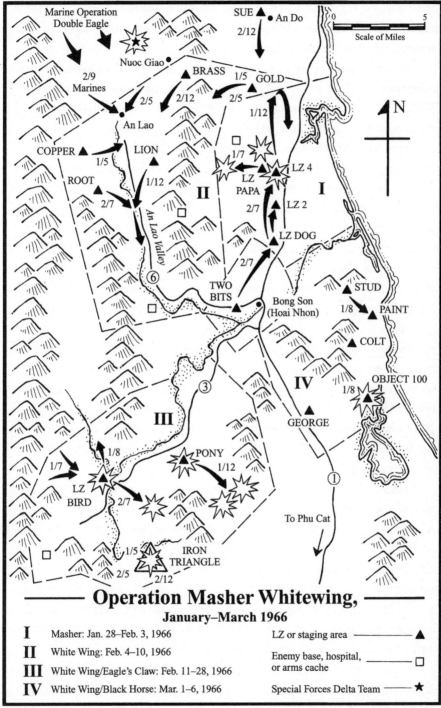

Marine Operation Double Eagle

SUE ▲ • An Do
2/12

Nuoc Giao •

2/9 Marines

BRASS ▲   1/5 GOLD
2/5 2/12 2/5
1/12

An Lao

COPPER ▲   LION ▲
1/5
ROOT ▲   1/12
2/7

LZ 4
1/7
LZ PAPA
2/7   LZ 2
LZ DOG
2/7

II   I

An Lao Valley

⑥

TWO BITS ▲

Bong Son (Hoai Nhon)

STUD ▲
1/8   PAINT ▲

COLT ▲

③

III   IV

GEORGE ▲

OBJECT 100
1/8

1/8
1/7
LZ BIRD ▲
2/7

PONY ▲
1/12

To Phu Cat

①

1/5
IRON TRIANGLE
2/5   2/12

N

0 — 5
Scale of Miles

Operation Masher Whitewing,
January–March 1966

I   Masher: Jan. 28–Feb. 3, 1966

II   White Wing: Feb. 4–10, 1966

III   White Wing/Eagle's Claw: Feb. 11–28, 1966

IV   White Wing/Black Horse: Mar. 1–6, 1966

LZ or staging area ——— ▲

Enemy base, hospital, or arms cache ——— ☐

Special Forces Delta Team ——— ★

COPYRIGHT © 2010 RICK BRITTON

form the 3rd NVA Sao Vang Division. Together the NVA and VC fortified villages with interlocking tunnels and trench systems. A CIA report in 1965 declared Binh Dinh to be "just about lost." The Americans believed that among the population of eight hundred thousand people, most either had direct ties to the VC or some degree of sympathy for them.

So, in January of 1966, Westy ordered the 1st Cavalry Division to sweep the communists from this troublesome but valuable agricultural province. In response, General Kinnard and his staff conceived of Operation Masher, a series of airmobile hammer-and-anvil assaults designed to find the enemy, disrupt them, and force them to move toward blocking forces that waited to annihilate them. While Kinnard's division took the lead in attacking the suspected communist strongholds within Binh Dinh, ARVN soldiers, Koreans, and U.S. Marines would seal off the roads and escape routes that surrounded the province. This would clear the Bong Son plain, the An Lao Valley, and the Kim Son Valley, the three terrain masses that dominated the area. One 1st Cavalry Division report described Binh Dinh as "a very rich, fruitful agricultural area. The terrain is open with watery rice paddies and palm groves in the lowlands and the mountains being very dense." According to the Army's official history, the highlands were honeycombed with spurs that "created narrow river valleys with steep ridges that frequently provided hideouts for enemy units or housed enemy command, control, and logistical centers." Late January was the perfect time for the operation because, by then, the Vietnamese holiday of Tet was over, as was a monsoon season that each year dumped many inches of rain on Binh Dinh.

General Kinnard chose his 3rd Brigade, under Colonel Hal Moore, to make the initial helicopter assault against the villages and rice paddies of the Bong Son plain. At Ia Drang, Moore had distinguished himself as commander of the 1st Battalion, 7th Cavalry Regiment (otherwise known as 1-7 Cavalry). He had since been promoted to full colonel and brigade command. In Vietnam, a typical brigade contained at least three infantry battalions. Brigades generally comprised about thirty-five hundred soldiers. Thanks to attached artillery battalions, aviation companies, and engineers, Colonel Moore's 3rd Brigade had about fifty-seven hundred men.

Moore was the epitome of a natural leader and a self-made warrior. As a high school kid in Kentucky, he had dreamed of going to West Point. To make this dream come true, he had moved to Washington, worked full-time in a book warehouse, finished high school on his own time, and knocked on the doors of countless senators and congressmen. Graduating from the academy in 1945, he was too late to see action in World War II. In Korea, he had served as a company commander in the 7th Infantry Division. A thorough military professional, he had read much about Vietnam's history and the reasons for France's defeat in the 1950s against the Viet Minh, the precursor to the VC and NVA. To Moore, Operation Masher was a "multi-battalion search-and-destroy operation in the vicinity of Bong Son." His plan was like the man himself—thoughtful, yet straightforward and uncomplicated. He intended to "air assault into various locations . . . on the Bong Son plain . . . find the enemy and engage the enemy, kill as many of them as possible and capture as many of them as possible." He planned to do this by placing one battalion on the northern side of the plain and another on the southern end, so they could squeeze the NVA and VC between them.

The ultimate strategic purpose of the operation was not just to kill or evict the enemy from Binh Dinh. The Americans believed that, in their wake, ARVN soldiers and South Vietnamese officials were supposed to occupy the province, reestablish Saigon's control, and care for the people. The operation, then, was an inevitable product of Westy's attrition strategy.[3]

Struggling for Dear Life in a Cemetery

Some units just have bad luck. Such was the case for Alpha Company, 2-7 Cavalry. Along with much of the battalion, the company had been ambushed and nearly destroyed by the NVA at Landing Zone (LZ) Albany during the ferocious fighting in November. Two months later, on the drizzly, overcast morning of January 25, 1966, the entire battalion, including Alpha Company, boarded Air Force C-123 transport planes at An Khe, the 1st Cavalry Division's base camp, for the short flight east to Bong Son and the beginning of Operation Masher. The soldiers were tense and apprehensive as they packed into the austere planes. "Everyone knew we were headed for some 'heavy shit,'" a soldier in another company wrote. Air Force loadmasters seated the troops on the floor, in rows, back to back.

One by one, the planes took off and climbed through the gray overcast sky, over the mountains that surrounded An Khe, and then flew east. A plane carrying Alpha Company's 3rd Platoon, plus a mortar squad, tried to take off and then aborted when the pilot could not get enough air speed. He tried again, this time successfully. The plane climbed through the clouds but then, in one awful instant, it turned downward at a forty-five-degree angle and plunged into a mountain. "I heard the tremendous crash and explosion as the aircraft augered into the side of the mountain," Lieutenant Colonel Kenneth Mertel, commander of the 1st Battalion, 8th Cavalry, recalled. The plane cartwheeled down the side of the mountain and exploded. The fire was intense. Grenades, mortar rounds, and ammunition were cooking off. Mertel's unit was responsible for securing the crash site, but his soldiers had to keep a safe distance for several minutes until the ammo finished exploding. When they went in, they quickly realized that there were no survivors. The crash killed forty-six men—forty-two from the 3rd Platoon, plus the four-man Air Force crew. "The bodies were badly torn," Lieutenant Colonel Mertel said. "They had to be placed in rubber bags and carried by the troopers several hundred meters to a spot where they could be evacuated by helicopters." Graves registration teams began the gruesome task of reconstructing the remains into some semblance of identifiable bodies.

When First Lieutenant Larry Gwin, the executive officer of the company, heard the terrible news, he was filled with disbelief. He was still hurting from the horrible experience of Ia Drang, as were most of the company's other survivors, and now this had happened. "I couldn't believe they were all suddenly gone, crashed into a mountain and obliterated," he later wrote. As the second in command, he drew the traumatic task of accounting for and identifying the remains. Very few were recognizable, except by their name tags. Gwin was devastated, but he somehow got the job done. The soldiers of the 3rd Platoon may not have been killed in combat, but they were just as dead, and their loss left the same kind of void in the lives of those who knew them. One of the dead men was Specialist-4 (Spec-4) Gary Bryant. His daughter Tammy later wrote that "his absence has left an unfillable hole in our lives."[4]

The crash was a troubling way to start the operation, but of course Masher went on nonetheless. For three days, Moore's battalions encountered little resistance as they hopscotched around the Bong Son plain in a series of heliborne assaults. On the rainy morning of January 28, troopers from the 2nd Battalion, 7th Cavalry, boarded their Hueys for an air assault on a series of hamlets that the locals called Phung Du. The Americans called it LZ-4. The differing names may seem like a small matter, but they illustrated a problem with the American big-unit war. To the Vietnamese, Phung Du was a singular place with history, identity, and a distinct soul. To the Americans, it was just another spot to disgorge soldiers, search for and destroy the enemy. The trouble was that, if places did not really matter, then perhaps the people within them might not either. Few of the Americans knew anything about Vietnamese history or culture. The Army had trained the grunts to fight a conventional war. Yet they were in Vietnam to secure the lives and loyalty of the South Vietnamese people, an objective more akin to counterinsurgency.

Packed aboard their Hueys, many of the troopers were especially nervous about this assault because their commanders had decided to forgo an artillery preparation on the landing zone. Pre-attack artillery bombardments were naturally a major element of the firepower-centered American way of war. Infantrymen were trained to rely on artillery support. Already, in the first few days of Operation Masher, against almost no resistance, the Americans had expended over two thousand rounds of artillery ammunition (mainly 105-millimeter howitzer shells). But, in a war with no front lines, and with observable targets scarce, it did not always make sense to precede air assaults with artillery barrages, especially in populated areas where innocent people could, and did, get hurt.

In one instance, early in the operation, Colonel Moore and his command group went into an area called LZ Dog, following a barrage. "We ran into a copse of trees and into a little village. There in the village was a Vietnamese family. There was a little girl about the age of my youngest daughter and she had been wounded by artillery fire. It broke my heart to see this beautiful little girl bleeding." Huddled inside their thatched-roof house, the girl's parents looked frightened and bewildered. One minute they had been living their normal lives. The next moment, the Americans had hurled explosives into their village, hurting their little girl.

Colonel Moore arranged for a medical evacuation (medevac) helicopter to pick up the girl and take her, along with her parents, to the 85th Evacuation Hospital. He was dismayed by the entire scene and what it said about the war effort. "It struck me then that we were not in Vietnam to kill and maim innocent men and women and children and tear up their houses. We were there to find and kill the enemy, and get them out of there." Quite true, but who was the enemy, where was he, and how could he be destroyed without the use of substantial artillery and air support? These were the troubling questions that bedeviled the American war in Vietnam, especially during the early years of escalation, when General Westmoreland launched his big-unit operations. In World War II, when American firepower hurt or uprooted civilians, even in pro-Allied countries such as France and Belgium, there were few strategic consequences. In Vietnam, when that same firepower injured ordinary people or damaged their property, it could turn them against the Americans and into the arms of the VC, with obviously adverse strategic consequences.

So, for fear of hurting innocent people, and because pre-assault bombardments often telegraphed the landing zones to the enemy, the Americans declined to soften up LZ-4 with artillery. The infantry soldiers were not pleased. "What stupid bullshit!" one of them exclaimed. It was hard enough for the men to face the dangers so inherent to combat infantrymen. To do that without maximum support was demoralizing, and even infuriating.

The hamlets that comprised Phung Du were bordered by palm trees, rice paddies, dikes, hedgerows, bamboo shrubs, and fences. At the southern edge of the village was a cemetery with raised burial mounds, reflecting local custom, which decreed that the dead must be buried sitting up.[5]

Charlie Company went in first. Almost immediately rifle fire pinged off the helicopters. Instead of flying through the intensifying fire and dropping the men in the village, the choppers generally dropped their troops off as quickly as possible, south of Phung Du, in the cemetery, where the fire was lightest. "We . . . landed in the midst of a North Vietnamese battalion that was reinforced by a heavy weapons company," Captain John "Skip" Fesmire, the commander of Charlie Company, recalled. In particular, they were up against the 22nd Regiment's 7th Battalion. Fesmire's company was scattered in isolated groups over several hundred meters throughout the graveyard and the southern approaches to the village. The NVA were shooting from pre-sited bunkers and trenches located mainly in the tree lines that ringed the village. "The company came under intense and effective automatic weapons and mortar fire," an after action report declared. Fesmire's company was in a cross fire, with no way out. Any movement could mean death. The men took cover behind burial mounds, paddy dikes, trees, or in muddy folds of ground.

The captain saw his radioman and one of his platoon leaders get hit. "We're in a hornet's nest!" he roared.

All around him, Fesmire's men fought for their lives, often within ten or twenty yards of their adversaries. About two hundred yards east of the captain, Sergeant Charles Kinney, the company's senior aidman, was huddled behind a burial mound, listening to the sonic crack that enemy bullets emitted as they barely missed him. His lift had come in at one of the hottest spots. Three of the other men on his chopper got hit before they even left the chopper. "They were riddled with bullets and dead before they hit the ground," he recalled. Although he was a medic, he carried an M16 rifle with several magazines of ammunition. He peeked around the mound long enough to see several NVA soldiers running for a bunker about thirty yards away. He squeezed off several three-round bursts in their direction. "At that distance . . . it was not hard to hit at least some of the numerous targets presented to me. They just kept coming laterally across my front weapon sight." Before he knew it, Kinney had expended four or five clips (about eighty rounds). An NVA soldier spotted him and poured AK-47 fire at him. The rounds shattered his M16, wounding him in the face, hands, and wrist.

To Private Charlie Williams, the horrific fighting was surreal, like something out of a movie. Grunts often compared combat with movies, revealing the cultural dominance of film in shaping the perspectives of Americans. This was the only way he could process the horror of watching several men get hit around him. Of course, he understood that, unlike the way many movies portrayed war, the merciless carnage around him was anything but glorious. "There's nothing exciting about seeing a guy ripped in two by a machine gun or torn in two by shrapnel. I was splattered with blood." He felt nauseous and wanted only to sit down and cry.

Elsewhere, Staff Sergeant William Guyer, who was in charge of the mortar platoon, was trying to get some rounds out while under intense enemy machine-gun fire. With no baseplate or plotting board, he propped the tube against a mound and fired several ineffective rounds at the NVA machine gunners. He took out his last shell, kissed it, and dropped it down the tube. The 60-millimeter projectile arced slightly and then exploded directly over the gunners, killing them. But another NVA soldier got on the gun and fired a burst. Guyer caught a bullet in the head and went down like a sack of wheat, probably dead before he hit the ground. Sergeant Jose Rivera, another mortarman, killed the new gunner, only to fall prey to an NVA mortar round that scored a direct hit on the shallow hole he had scooped out of the sand. The shell literally tore Rivera's body in half.

Artillery observers were calling in rounds on the various tree lines. Seeing the shells explode, many of the soldiers angrily thought to themselves that their situation would be much better right now if artillery had pounded the area prior to the landing, before the NVA entrenched themselves in their bunkers. Now, with the enemy undercover, the rounds could not inflict as much damage. Captain Fesmire hollered repeatedly for his company to rally on him. Some did, but the majority of his surviving troopers were pinned down, fighting intimate, private battles with North Vietnamese soldiers. The only saving grace was that the sandy soil absorbed many of the enemy bullets and, in Sergeant Kinney's recollection, "anything else the NVA threw at us, from hand grenades to 60mm mortar rounds."

Meanwhile, Captain Joel Sugdinis and the remnants of Alpha Company had landed a couple miles to the south, at a spot the Americans called LZ-2. He had lost his 3rd Platoon in the plane crash, but he was fighting with what he had left. Using fire and maneuver tactics, his two remaining rifle platoons fought their way through rice paddies, into the southern edges of the grave-yard. Like their friends in Charlie Company, they too were now in the cross fire, pinned down, fighting at close quarters with the NVA. One of the squad leaders, Sergeant William Bercaw, was seeing his first combat. Like so many other infantrymen, he was trained to close with the enemy and kill him. He told his squad to fix bayonets and charge a machine gun in a tree line. "I thought the shock effect of a well-determined force would turn the tables," he said. The squad made it to within fifty meters of the trees before taking cover in a sandy depression. Behind them, someone was calling them back, saying that artillery was on the way into the trees. Sergeant Bercaw covered his re-treating soldiers by rising to his knees and firing magazine after magazine on full automatic ("full rock 'n' roll" in soldier parlance). The enemy return fire came back fast and furious. Machine-gun rounds knocked off his canteen, creased his boot, and one even shattered the D ring that was holding the chin strap on his helmet. Then the enemy gun went silent. He beat a hasty retreat, proudly declaring to his men: "I had a duel with an enemy machine gun and I won."

In the early afternoon, Lieutenant Colonel Robert McDade, commander of 2-7 Cavalry, tried to reinforce his hard-pressed companies by helicopter under cover of a protective artillery barrage. The choppers took intense, accurate fire. Over one hamlet, Warrant Officer Robert Mason, one of the helicopter pilots, spotted an enemy machine gunner who had just shot and killed a pilot in another aircraft. The gunner was standing in the middle of a cluster of villagers, with his machine gun pointed upward on a mount. Not wanting to kill the noncombatants, Mason ordered his M60 door gunner to fire warning rounds, in hopes that the people would scatter. "The bullets sent up muddy geysers from the paddy water as they raged toward the group," Mason wrote. No one moved, even when the rounds hit within fifty feet of them. In that sickening instant, Mason realized that the people were not going to move. They were more afraid of the enemy gunner than the American helicopters. Mason watched as the door gunner reluctantly fired into the group. "They threw up their arms as they were hit, and whirled to the ground. After what seemed a very long time, the gunner, still firing, was exposed. [His] gun barrel flopped down on its mount and he slid to the ground. A dozen people lay like tenpins around him."

Over Phung Du, all six Hueys carrying soldiers from Bravo Company took hits. Two of them had to retreat. Only about a platoon of soldiers, plus Captain Myron Diduryk, their company commander, got into the uneasy perimeter that the Americans had cobbled together, mainly in the graveyard, over the course of several intense hours. Lieutenant Colonel McDade also managed to land, but he quickly got pinned down in a trench. "Every time you raised your head, it was zap, zap, zap," he said. "The dirt really flew." A stalemate had set in, ushering in a rainy, frightening night of desultory gun and grenade battles. At McDade's urging, Captain Fesmire gathered what men he could, including eight of his dead soldiers, and made it into the perimeter.[6]

Needless to say, Colonel Moore was frustrated with the situation at Phung Du. He was not pleased, in particular, with McDade. Moore was not quite sure that McDade was qualified to lead the battalion. "He had been a division personnel officer for a year or two. He was rewarded for his good service by the division commander who gave him the battalion." The debacle at LZ Albany back in November had partially resulted, Moore felt, from the fact that McDade did not, at that point, really know his troops. Now, in this operation, McDade just did not seem very aggressive or dynamic in resolving the stalemate at LZ-4. "I told him in no uncertain terms to get that landing zone cleared up, get that battalion organized, and get moving," Moore said. "I let him know I was very displeased with what was going on."

Throughout the night, Colonel Moore organized a relief force. Elements of the 1st Battalion, 7th Cavalry—his old unit—would maneuver north of the village and block the enemy's escape route from that side. Two companies from the 2nd Battalion, 12th Cavalry, would come from the south and reinforce the perimeter. The colonel decided to lead that part of the assault himself. After sunrise on January 29, artillery pounded the enemy positions. Then Navy A-1E Skyraiders and Air Force B-57 Canberras attacked the enemy-held positions north and east of the village three times with napalm and high-explosive bombs. This touched off secondary explosions in some of the NVA trenches. Sergeant Kinney, the wounded medic, was still pinned down outside the perimeter. He and several other soldiers, most of whom he had treated for wounds, were in hastily improvised foxholes, perilously close to the air strikes. Kinney was amazed at the courage of one NVA machine gunner, who waited for each plane to release its bombs and "then while it was in the process of upsweeping, he would fire a burst at the belly of the plane. Right before the bomb hit and exploded, he would duck into his fortified spider hole." After seeing him do this repeatedly, Kinney fired a 40-millimeter grenade from an M79 grenade launcher and killed the brave man.

At 1045, Moore and the 12th Cavalry soldiers landed south of Phung Du. "We came across a stream just to the south of LZ-4," Moore recalled. "We waded across the stream. It was up to our waists. We were under fire. I joined in the assault across the stream and we relieved the troops on LZ-4." Moore met with McDade, heard the battalion commander's situation report, and then strode around with his indomitable sergeant major, Basil Plumley, at his side. One trench was filled with wounded soldiers and a few Vietnamese women and children. Up ahead, scattered throughout the graveyard, he could see the bodies of several dead Americans. In Moore's opinion, far too many able-bodied soldiers were hunkered down, simply taking cover, rather than fighting back. "You can't do your damned job in a trench," he told many of them. Sergeant Major Plumley had known his commanding officer long enough to recognize his extreme displeasure with the situation. "The Old Man was not pleased. We talked to the men. They weren't in too deep spirits although they had lost quite a few men. The biggest thing they needed was leadership and guidance to move them out of there."

Moore had something in common with John Corley, the soldier who had commanded the 3rd Battalion, 26th Infantry, at Aachen. Both of them had a great knack for minding the big picture while staying close to the action, and without stepping on the toes of their subordinate commanders. In Vietnam, there was a great temptation for commanders at the battalion and brigade level to remain in their helicopters, where they could see much of the battlefield, and manage the fighting from on high. To some extent this made sense. From a helicopter, the commander could see the terrain well, often to the point of spotting the enemy, even as he remained in direct communication with subordinates and superiors alike. However, from thousands of feet overhead, he had little appreciation for the reality of what was happening on the ground. Terrain often looked quite different from the air versus the ground, especially in jungle-encrusted Vietnam. A man in a helicopter could not feel the heat, smell the smells, hear the screams of the wounded, gauge the mood of the troops. In short, he could become way too detached from his soldiers. In a helicopter, the commander was less of an infantryman and more of an aviator. If he spent enough time thousands of feet overhead, he often came to see the world of ground combat from a pilot's detached vantage point, rather than a grunt's intimate perspective.

For these reasons, and not out of any need for medals or personal glory, Colonel Moore liked to get on the ground during a fight: "You've got to be on the ground to sense what's going on, and the troops like to see you on the ground, sharing the risks too. It's not to be a hero. It just makes a hell of a lot of sense. You can't sail around in a helicopter on a radio and really know what's going on on the ground." At **Phung** Du, his personal presence was important to the outcome of the battle. He organized a counterattack that eventually overwhelmed the remaining enemy positions in hard fighting that lasted for the better part of another day as soldiers methodically assaulted the NVA bunkers, tunnels, and trenches. Much of the village was on fire and angry plumes of smoke wafted skyward. "As far as the eye could see the land was under assault," one witness related, "the full expression of the Army's war-fighting fury . . . as if waging war against the land itself."

The Americans captured a few prisoners, including one frightened man who relieved his tension in a unique way. "The first thing this guy did was squat down and take a crap," Colonel Moore recalled. "He thought we were gonna kill him. We gave him some water." They also reassured him that he would not be killed. Moore was a big believer that the better treatment prisoners got, the more information they yielded. This man divulged everything he knew.

As medevac helicopters swooped in to the now secure LZ to evacuate Sergeant Kinney and several other wounded men, he gazed at the dead, bloated body of one of his friends. "I was suddenly struck by the thought that for the rest of my life, I would be living on borrowed time . . . that had been given to me by all these men who had died on LZ 4 . . . while I had lived." This was not survivor's guilt so much as survivor's determination, and it had positive consequences. As Sergeant Kinney hopped aboard the medevac helicopter, he resolved to heal from his wounds, return to the company, save as many lives as possible, and then live his own life the best he possibly could. "It was the only way I knew to repay the debt I felt I owed."

That night, Colonel Moore and Sergeant Major Plumley stayed with the surviving troopers in Phung Du. "It helps the troops to see the colonel down there with 'em sharing the risks. They felt . . . more safe," Moore said. This command presence also gave the men a sense that someone was in charge, making decisions, looking out for their welfare. Moore's major concern was to keep the retreating NVA from escaping. On the morning of January 30, he ordered McDade's depleted companies and 2-12 Cavalry to move north, in hopes of pushing the NVA into the waiting muzzles of 1-7 Cavalry. In some instances, artillery fire, helicopter gunships, and fighters shot up dozens of retreating enemy, the exact sort of scenario Westy would have envisioned.

Moore's northward push also sparked a pair of sharp fights against company-sized NVA units in the villages of Tan Thanh and Luong Tho. In the latter engagement, three companies from 1-7 Cavalry were fighting so close to the enemy—ferreting them out of bunkers and spider holes—that, according to one after action report, "heavy fire support could not be used because of the close proximity of the engagement." Only by withdrawing from the village could the Americans make use of tactical air support and artillery. The communists had learned to negate American firepower by fighting at close quarters. The Americans came to call this enemy tactic "hugging the belt."

At Luong Tho, North Vietnamese opposition was so fierce that any helicopter that approached the area risked getting shot down. But, as the sun set on January 31, Captain Ramon "Tony" Nadal, the commander of A Company, had a dozen wounded men who needed immediate evacuation. Although the odds of getting in and out safely seemed minuscule, Major Bruce Crandall, who had performed numerous acts of bravery at Ia Drang, volunteered to fly his Huey through the darkness into a tiny LZ in hopes of extracting the wounded. The LZ was so small, and surrounded by so many trees, that Crandall had to descend vertically, all the while under steady enemy fire. Moreover, the night was so dark that Crandall could not see the trees or the ground as Captain Nadal talked him down. Nadal's soldiers laid down a powerful base of fire. The North Vietnamese responded with heavy machine-gun fire. Crandall could see their green tracers whizzing uncomfortably close. Somehow, he made it to the ground, picked up six wounded soldiers, took them to a base at Bong Son, and then came back in for another load. "Coming out was tough because I had to pull up and take those people out without any forward movement." Difficult or not, he pulled it off, saving many lives. Crandall willingly risked such danger not just out of a sense of duty, and not just because he and Nadal were friends, but out of deep mutual respect for the grunts. "You always had great confidence in the infantry. You supported those guys as well as they supported you."

The 3rd Brigade patrolled the Bong Son plain for several more days in early February, but the fighting died down into sporadic skirmishes with snipers. With the enemy seemingly gone, General Kinnard hoped that the plain was now secure. He ordered an end to this phase of Operation Masher in favor of a new push into the An Lao Valley. The vital calculus of casualties, of course, meant everything in these big-unit operations. Already, the Americans had lost 123 men killed (counting the plane crash), and another 200 wounded. Division records claimed 603 enemy killed, by actual body count. The reports also claimed, with no real basis whatsoever, that 956 other enemy soldiers were probably dead. The records were, of course, mute on how many noncombatants were dead or if, perhaps, on-site commanders counted some of their bodies as "enemy." Such were the vagaries and potential inaccuracies of the body-count war. Without question, though, the Americans had inflicted significant damage on the enemy's 22nd Infantry Regiment.[7]

When word of Operation Masher reached President Johnson, his first reaction was quite telling. Instead of asking about casualties, or what results the 3rd Brigade had achieved, he recoiled at the aggressive name the Army had given the operation. From the beginning of his escalation process, he had sought to downplay the size, scale, and violence of the military effort in Vietnam. He did not want the American people to think that their country was truly on a war footing. To his ears, "Masher" sounded too warlike. "I don't know who names your operations but 'Masher'?" he said to General Earl Wheeler, the Army's chief of staff. "I get kind of mashed myself," Johnson added. McGeorge Bundy, one of the president's security advisors, asked Wheeler to tell the commanders in Vietnam to come up with less provocative operational names so that "even the most biased person" could not use such names to criticize Johnson's Vietnam policy. Wheeler passed the request along to Westmoreland, who, in turn, told General Kinnard. The 1st Cavalry Division commander was stunned, and chagrined, by this political foolishness. In his recollection, he changed the name, "partly out of spite," to the most innocuous, peaceful moniker he could imagine—White Wing. So the campaign came to be known as Operation Masher/White Wing. This naming incident might appear minor, but it illustrated a fatal aspect of Johnson's war leadership that affected the way Westy carried out his strategy—all too often, Johnson was more interested in appearances than real results.[8]

They Must Be in the An Lao Valley

Once the fighting petered out on the Bong Son plain, General Kinnard felt that the An Lao Valley, a few miles to the northwest, was the logical place to clear next. Intelligence officers believed that the valley comprised an important logistics and transit point for the North Vietnamese. They had pinpointed it as the home for the Sao Vang Division's headquarters. An Lao was the likely place of retreat for those enemy soldiers who had escaped the fighting around Phung Du and the other contested villages of Bong Son. What's more, even as that fighting was going on in late January, Special Forces teams had run into a veritable buzz saw while they were reconning the area. They had found that the place was teeming with NVA and VC. One six-man team was lucky to be extracted intact. Two others became enmeshed in desperate firefights against overwhelming numbers of enemy soldiers. "We kept getting fire in on us," Sergeant Chuck Hiner, whose team was ambushed by the VC, recalled. All around him, his teammates got hit. Hiner got on the radio and called for fire support and a rescue attempt. "I could hear Dotson. He was hit through the chest and I could hear that death rattle. This other kid (Hancock) . . . they had stitched him from the ankle to the top of his head." Sergeant First Class Marlin Cook was nearby, lying still, paralyzed from a crippling, mortal wound. Air strikes by helicopter gunships came right in on his position. "It was either do that or get overrun," Hiner said. "We were fighting—I daresay the closest— within ten feet of each other. It was that tight."

Major Charlie Beckwith, the legendary Special Forces commander, was badly wounded by enemy machine-gun fire when his command helicopter approached the ambush site. Somehow, though, other choppers extracted the survivors. Of seventeen Special Forces soldiers who went into the An Lao, seven were killed and three others wounded. Three of the bodies were never recovered.

So General Kinnard expected a major fight when he sent Moore's 3rd Brigade and the 2nd Brigade, under Colonel William Lynch, into the valley on February 7. "Numerous valleys and draws were heavily forested, providing many areas in which concealment from aerial observation is afforded," a 2nd Brigade report stated. Helicopters landed most of the rifle companies on the ridges, from whence they worked their way down the steep slopes into the valley. The soldiers humped through this exhausting terrain, dealing with leeches, ants, heat, rain, mud, and abject weariness. "In a few days they were reduced to sodden, weary, leech-encrusted men," one soldier wrote. They found many abandoned enemy base camps, along with quite a bit of rice, salt, weapons, and tunnels. They also found plenty of evidence that the enemy dominated the area politically. "Moving through the villages, I was struck by how much anti-American propaganda I saw posted in them," a grunt recalled. "Some posters [showed] NVA or VC soldiers shooting down American aircraft."

But contact with the actual VC and NVA was sporadic to the point of nonexistent. "The hills were honeycombed with recently abandoned bunkers and caches which had to be destroyed before [we] moved on," the 2nd Battalion, 12th Cavalry's, after report recorded. The An Lao was typical of what field duty was often like for grunts in Vietnam. They spent most of the day cautiously walking, while carrying heavy loads of equipment, ammunition, and food, sweating in the beastly heat, all the while wondering when danger might beckon. The whole experience was grueling and exhausting, even if they never encountered the enemy, which they usually did not. The old cliché about combat being mostly an exercise in boredom, punctuated by fleeting moments of extreme terror, sprang readily to mind.

The Americans killed about a dozen rearguard VC. For the rifle company grunts, then, the An Lao was more a place of tedium than danger. Even so, a division report claimed that the operations in the valley "succeeded in throwing the enemy off balance," and added to "the general turmoil experienced by the VC during current operations." The author of the report even optimistically asserted that "the adverse effect on enemy forces will have a long-lasting effect in that area." This was staff officer spin doctoring. The Americans had not come to the valley to find nothing but abandoned camps and replaceable war matériel. Nor did the sweep have a substantial long-lasting effect.

In actuality, the elusive NVA and VC had somehow melted away, a common problem during the Vietnam War. Search and destroy meant nothing if the actual destroying never took place. General Kinnard and his brigade commanders decided to look for the enemy ten miles to the south in the Kim Son Valley, another obvious spot for base camps.[9]

The Crow's Foot

On the maps, and even from the air, the Kim Son Valley looked like a crow's foot (some thought of it as an eagle's claw). The Kim Son River and its tributaries snaked through a muddy sludge of inundated rice paddies. Brooding over the brownish mess were five jungle-packed ridges that comprised the various toes of the foot. "The ridges and valleys were covered with thick interwoven vines, rocks, crevices, along with leeches and snakes," Captain Robert McMahon, one of the rifle company commanders, wrote.

Colonel Moore devised a new way to ferret out the hard-core survivors of the Sao Vang Division. He air-assaulted all three of his battalions into the area. Some established company-sized ambushes "astride probable enemy escape routes in the valley fingers [ridges]." The rest of his brigade landed at LZ Bird, right at the hub of the valley, and established a firebase there from which the infantry then proceeded to "act as the 'beater' force, attacking out of the valley forcing the enemy towards the ambush sites." He called this new approach Hunter Killer. By now, the Americans were beginning to understand how predictable their loud, ostentatious helicopter insertions were to the enemy (that was probably one reason for the heavy enemy presence at LZ-4). So, during the Crow's Foot insertions, helicopter crews carried out many mock landings to confuse the enemy on the whereabouts of the rifle companies.

Moore's concept worked well. Almost immediately, the troopers clashed with the communists. Nearly every company was involved in firefights, often against platoon-sized groups of VC. In just a couple days, they had killed two hundred VC, captured several weapons caches, and overran a base camp, a hospital, and a grenade factory. Documents captured in the base camp revealed the location of a VC main force battalion staging area near the village of Hon Mot. Lieutenant Colonel McDade airlifted his B and C Companies near Hon Mot, just two and a half miles southeast of LZ Bird.

On the morning of February 15, Captain Myron Diduryk's B Company found the VC. His 2nd Platoon was moving through a rice paddy just outside of Hon Mot when they came under heavy small-arms and mortar fire. They took cover behind paddy dikes and returned fire. The experience of doing this was terrifying and nauseating. As enemy bullets snapped around them and splashed into the rancid paddy water, the grunts kept low, while propping their rifles and machine guns atop the muddy dikes to fire back. Everyone was wet, filthy, and rife with the fecal, moldy stench of the paddy. At first Captain Diduryk thought he was up against a VC platoon. Actually, he was facing two companies dug in along a jungle-covered embankment and hillside.

Diduryk had fought in the Ia Drang battle so he had a firsthand understanding of how effective American firepower could be in this kind of pitched battle. As his mortar crews pounded the enemy-held embankment, Diduryk's artillery forward observer called down 105-millimeter fire from tubes at nearby LZ Bird. "In the left sector of the 2d Platoon," Diduryk wrote, "artillery fire was brought to within 25 meters of friendly troops due to proximity of the enemy." The howitzer shells exploded up and down the length of the VC line. Air strikes from helicopter gunships firing rockets and A-1E Skyraiders dropping cluster bombs eventually followed. Under cover of this awesome array of weaponry, four Hueys swooped in to resupply B Company with mortar and small-arms ammunition.

Captain Diduryk planned an all-out assault, led by his 3rd Platoon, for the minute the bombardment lifted. Sure enough, at the appointed moment, his grunts rose up and went forward. They even had their bayonets fixed. "The platoon moved forward in determined, rapid and well-coordinated bounds employing the technique of fire and movement," the captain recalled. Infused with adrenaline, they soon began advancing at a dead run, screaming "like madmen" in the recollection of one soldier. This combination of posturing and aggressiveness overwhelmed the entrenched Viet Cong. As the 3rd Platoon soldiers approached them, firing deadly volleys from their rifles, the enemy soldiers broke and ran. As they did so, they exposed themselves to fire from the 2nd Platoon, which was still hunkered down in the rice paddy. Then, Captain Diduryk sent in his 1st Platoon, adding to the rout. Hollering groups of grunts spotted the fleeing VC and mowed them down. "The enemy was on the run," the captain commented. Those VC who stood and fought were slaughtered by the B Company soldiers. Many of those who took off, usually in groups of three or four, came under saturating fire from hovering helicopter gunships. The whole experience must have been awful beyond description for them—dodging the ubiquitous American fire, seeing comrades tattered by bullets or torn apart by shrapnel, fleeing from blood-crazed gun-toting Americans who were twice their size.

In two hours of one-sided fighting, two VC companies ceased to exist. Diduryk's grunts counted 57 enemy bodies and estimated, on a fairly sound basis, that they had probably inflicted another 150 casualties on the VC (counting wounded who escaped and bodies that were not found). "VC bodies were piled near a bunker," one soldier later wrote. "Some were missing limbs and heads. Others were burnt, facial skin drawn back into fierce, grotesque screams. [The grunts] were policing the dead for weapons and piling what they found in a growing heap. Most were smiling with victory. Wood smoke from the hootches mixed with the stench of burnt hair and flesh."

The company also captured four VC, including Lieutenant Colonel Dowwng Doan, the battalion commander. The thirty-seven-year-old Doan was a professional to the core. He had joined the Viet Minh in 1949 and had spent several years fighting the French. When Colonel Moore later interrogated him, he looked the American commander right in the eye and said through an interpreter: "You will never win." Doan firmly believed that his side would wear down the Americans as they had worn down the French. "He was a hardcore Viet Cong," Colonel Moore commented. "He was tough. He was not frightened a bit. I admired this guy for his absolute strength of spirit." He also respected him as a fellow military professional.

Doan was a prime example of the spirit and toughness that characterized many VC fighters. He and his comrades sought to win through superior human will. By and large, this was a successful formula for them. At Hon Mot, though, they ran into a lethal combination of American firepower and willpower that eclipsed the VC's strength in morale. Diduryk's B Company destroyed a force twice its size, at the cost of two men killed and six wounded. In the captain's own estimation, he was glad to employ "the overwhelming combat power provided by the artillery, mortar and TAC Air fire support systems." In his view, the supporting fire set the conditions for this major tactical victory, but they were not the most critical factor. "The most essential ingredient which contributed to the success of the battle consisted not of the tools of war but of the men of Company B. It was the leadership of its officers and noncommissioned officers; the gallantry and professionalism of its men; and, finally, its 'will to win'" that proved decisive. The lesson was that this kind of fighting spirit, supported by suffocating firepower, could be a formidable combination.[10]

Hon Mot began a series of running battles between the 1st Cavalry Division troopers and the communists in the Crow's Foot area. There were two types of engagements: clashes with retreating VC or NVA formations, and battles when the Americans found their base camps. In an example of the former, Bravo Company, 2nd Battalion, 5th Cavalry, on February 17 fought a VC heavy-weapons battalion not far from the site of Diduryk's battle. They battled along the valley floor among water-soaked craters created by Air Force B-52 bombers several days earlier on pre-operation bombing missions. "Two craters that were half filled with water were . . . full of semi-naked wounded with the medics administering morphine and changing bandages," Captain Robert McMahon, the company commander, wrote.

As was so often typical in combat, some men were paralyzed by fear, and others invigorated by it. McMahon saw his unwounded mortar platoon sergeant cowering among the wounded soldiers. The captain and his first sergeant gave the man "a severe chewing out" to force him back to the edge of the crater to call down fire on the enemy. By contrast, one of the other NCOs, Sergeant Gary Gorton, a mortar squad leader, was almost reckless in

risking his life. When his crews ran out of ammo, he bounded around, hurling grenades at the VC, firing clip after clip of M16 ammo at them. He personally killed and overran one enemy machine gun. Before he could get back
undercover, a VC sniper shot him through the head.

Captain McMahon was worried that his company was about to run out of
ammunition. He ordered his people to fix bayonets. Upon hearing the order,
Private First Class John Martin immediately thought of Custer at Little Bighorn. The enemy soldiers were so close, and so aggressive, that they were
rolling grenades into the American-held craters. Fortunately for Martin and
the other soldiers, McMahon was able to call down lavish fire support to keep
the enemy at bay. Air strikes were especially effective. "[A-1E] Skyraiders
dropped napalm so close that one white phosphorous bomb hit the edge of
[a] holed-up platoon and one officer threw himself back first in the mud to
douse his burning shirt," Martin said. White phosphorous burns straight
through skin, muscles, and bones. Water only feeds it with more oxygen,
making it burn more intensely. Mud, though, can douse it. Elsewhere, another soldier watched the planes swoop in for the kill. "The F-4 jets . . . were
coming in and they would make a steep dive and shoot these Gatling guns on
the front of 'em. It sounded like a cow belching. They were dropping some
bombs off their wings and they were dropping some white phosphorous."

In the end, the combination of air power, and a supporting counterattack
by Alpha Company against the rear of the VC unit, ended the battle. The
Americans counted 127 VC bodies. The grunts captured several recoilless
rifles and mortars.[11]

Meanwhile, the Americans began to unravel a network of enemy base
camps throughout the heavier jungles of the Crow's Foot that they came to
call the Iron Triangle. Ironically, they were aided in these finds by the testimony of Lieutenant Colonel Doan. Defiant and proud though he undoubtedly was, he also was garrulous in captivity, revealing much about how VC
units operated and, in this instance, the general vicinity where their bases
were located.

The fighting that eventuated from these base camp discoveries was ferocious. In most cases, point elements found the enemy the hard way—when
they opened fire from prepared, expertly camouflaged fighting positions. For
instance, Private Swanson Hudson's squad from Alpha Company, 1st Battalion, 5th Cavalry, was walking point one day for his entire battalion, follow-

ing a small trail in the jungle. "One second, everything was eerily quiet. The next second, enemy troops opened fire. They were hidden in machine-gun bunkers that had been dug flush to the ground. They cut my squad to ribbons . . . under deadly fire from 12.7mm machine guns, light machine guns, AK-47 assault rifles and some kind of anti-tank weapon—possibly a 57mm recoilless rifle." As it turned out, they were right at the edge of a major NVA base camp. The two men next to Hudson were killed instantly, as were the squad leader and three other men. The platoon leader was shot through the neck and arm. Hudson fired back as best he could until "my rifle was shot out of my hands. At the same time I was shot in my left thigh-bone."

In mere moments, everyone in the squad was killed or wounded. NVA snipers were strapped into the trees overhead, shooting anyone who moved. Bleeding and semiconscious, Hudson lay still, worrying that the enemy soldiers would soon come to finish him off. "I still remember the screams of those wounded guys, lying there helpless under the full firepower of both sides. I lay there on the hot, humid jungle floor with the smell of death all around me, a hot, sweet smell of blood." He and the other wounded soldiers were caught in a no-man's-land, as both sides poured relentless fire at each other. Lieutenant James Patzwell and several soldiers from another platoon eventually got them out. "They saved our lives that day." He and the others were later medevaced.

It is an axiom of combat that the experience of a battle can be radically different from unit to unit, or even person to person. Even as Hudson's squad was caught in the worst of the fighting, Private Joe Grayson's platoon from Bravo Company of the same battalion was a few hundred yards away, on the fringes of the battle. They got the word that another platoon from their company was in trouble and set out to help them. They could hear the popcorn-like crackle of the firefight in the distance. Grayson came to a sharp drop, when all at once "lots of bullets [were] flying all around me. I could look down and see a dry creekbed, a patch of sand, and I knew if I went there I would be shot dead." Needless to say, he stayed put. As he took cover and things seemingly calmed down, he had no idea what was unfolding literally within a stone's throw. "I didn't know it at the time, but Rip Rubeor, Richard Barnes and James Mize were some ten to fifteen feet in front and below me, taking some cover from the far bank of the creekbed and engaged in one hell of a fire fight. Most of the bullets flying at me were intended for them. Rip was the only one to make it out of there in spite of a bullet hole through his left side."

In another instance during the fight for the Iron Triangle, soldiers from Alpha Company, 2nd Battalion, 8th Cavalry, got pinned down in a rice paddy by accurate, sharp, small-arms fire emanating from a tree line. As at Hon Mot, the grunts took cover behind paddy dikes and shot back while submerging themselves in the disgusting slime of the paddies. One soldier remembered seeing a wounded sergeant bleeding enough that "the blood from his wound was turning the water and muck red."

Helicopter gunships screamed in and lit up the tree line with rockets and machine-gun fire, greatly slackening the enemy fire. In the wake of this supporting fire, the grunts picked up their wounded men, stumbled through the shin-deep mud, and made their way forward to the tree line. "Covering one another, we made it to the tree line on the edge of the rice paddy," Lieutenant Ed Polonitza recalled. "Everyone was covered with muck, soaking wet, bloody from gunshot wounds, or from the blood-sucking leeches that infested the rice paddy." As Specialist Garry Bowles, a medic, ran across the paddy dikes, "bullets impacted in the water all around me. I experienced a curious sense of exhilaration." This odd excitement came from the adrenaline high that occurs when the body goes into an accelerated state of fear-induced arousal.

Later, the company found itself in the middle of an NVA base complex, fighting untold numbers of enemy infantrymen. Bowles saw tracer rounds whiz past his face. He was trying to work on Specialist Dick Marshall, a badly wounded radio telephone operator (RTO), when he noticed the commanding officer, Captain James Detrixhe, load a fresh magazine into his rifle, rise up on one knee, and open fire. "His body suddenly lifted up and spun in midair. He landed on his back, facing me, but his helmet and the top of his head were both missing. He slumped to one side with blood pumping from what was left of his head spraying my face in a sticky mist." Specialist Bowles shook off his revulsion long enough to feel the pulse of the RTO. He was dead, too. Lieutenant Polonitza took a group of soldiers and maneuvered behind the NVA who had killed the captain and Marshall. The enemy chose to flee.

Later, the company had to clear out the complex bunker by bunker. "Once we started to advance," Lieutenant Polonitza recalled, "all hell broke loose, and you could see NVA soldiers all over the place. Their heads were popping out of their holes as they fired down on us. We were throwing hand grenades and firing our M16s at the bunkers as we advanced. Each time we passed a bunker, one of us would unload a magazine into the opening and then move forward, bunker by bunker. In some instances, our riflemen crawled into the bunkers and ripped the enemy virtually in two with their M16s firing on full automatic."

The Americans tried no less than thirty-three assaults, ranging from platoon to company size, on the Iron Triangle without fully overrunning it. Finally, the commanders decided to pull back and give the area a thorough pounding. Initially, fighter-bombers and helicopter gunships raked it over. Then Air Force B-52s disgorged hundreds of tons of bombs on the Triangle. When the grunts came back—sometimes aided by tear gas that planes dropped into the area—they hardly recognized the place. "Bomb craters were smoking everywhere," Private Bill Nixon recalled. "All the trees were down . . . not a bird, not even a bug was left alive. All the NVA had headed for the river nearby. There were so many bodies in the river that they formed a dam." Engineers actually had to blow the bodies up to get the river flowing again. The Americans counted 313 dead NVA. For the Americans, one brigade alone had lost 23 killed and another 106 wounded. Six of the dead men were in Private Hudson's squad. Contact with small groups of enemy survivors diminished and then died out altogether. An eerie stillness descended on the traumatized Iron Triangle, and indeed, all over the Crow's Foot.[12]

What If Winning Battles Doesn't Matter?

On March 6, soldiers of the 1st Cavalry Division were still looking for the remnants of the Sao Vang Division, but they were finding next to nothing. The fighting in Binh Dinh province was over for the moment. Sensing this, General Kinnard declared an end to Operation Masher/White Wing. This declaration made sense in the context of an operation like this, but really, the whole thing was a bit of an artificial construct. The Americans had, in a way, created their own battle narrative—conceiving of an operation, carrying it out in the way they hoped to fight the whole war, and then pronouncing an end when it suited them. The enemy obviously did not think of Masher/White Wing as a "battle" in the same way as, for instance, the Germans and Soviets would have acknowledged in World War II that they were engaged in battles for such places as Stalingrad or Kursk. To the NVA and VC, the six weeks of Masher/White Wing stood out only as a period of intense American harassment of their presence in Binh Dinh. Such temporary setbacks meant little to them. Only the long-term goal of uniting Vietnam under their control truly mattered.

Like any good narrative, the authors of Masher/White Wing pointed to supposedly dramatic results. General Kinnard correctly believed he had destroyed five of the Sao Vang Division's nine battalions. The 1st Cavalry Division records asserted that, in six weeks, the unit had killed 1,342 VC and NVA soldiers by actual body count, while capturing 633, including Lieutenant Colonel Doan and two other prominent officers. The reports also claimed—with no substantive corroboration—that the 1st Cavalry Division probably killed another 1,746 enemy. This may have been 100 percent true. It might also have been total fiction. Certainly other enemy fighters were killed besides those whose bodies the Americans found and counted. But one must be skeptical of any estimate, not just because of the inherent guessing nature of such permutations, but because it was so clearly in the interest of officers to inflate the numbers. Indeed, the Americans only captured 208 individual and 52 crew-served weapons, and that casts some doubt on even the confirmed body counts since the bodies of dead soldiers often lay next to their weapons. Undoubtedly, the enemy was able to recover many of their weapons, if not always their dead, but the gap between a few hundred weapons captured and over 1,700 bodies counted seems rather considerable.

For the Americans, the operation was quite costly. "We can have the best army in the world, with all the electronic gear, and yet, those little suckers could inflict unbelievable casualties upon you," one medic succinctly put it. Kinnard's division lost 228 killed and 788 wounded. Masher/White Wing lasted forty-one days, so that meant 25 American casualties, including about five men killed, per day. And, of course, this was just one operation, in one part of the country, at a time when fighting raged over much of South Vietnam.

The material expenditure revealed as much about the lavishness of the big-unit war as the impressiveness of American capabilities. During the operation, Kinnard's helicopter units flew over 73,000 sorties, amounting to some 26,000 man-hours of flying time. Helicopters and transport aircraft airlifted 93,351 passengers (most of whom, of course, were repeat travelers). Artillery units carried out 15,621 fire missions, shooting 141,762 shells. Tactical aircraft, mainly fighter-bombers, flew 600 sorties, dropped over 692 tons of general-purpose bombs, 165 tons of napalm, and 80 tons of white phosphorous bombs.

In an after action critique conducted a few days after the operation ended, General Kinnard told his commanders that he was delighted with what the division had achieved. "We struck a very hard blow at enemy units which had long threatened Bong Son" and the road network around the province. The general was impressed with his unit's airmobile capability and the valor of its soldiers. He was right to feel that way. His commanders coordinated air and ground operations very well. His soldiers fought with great bravery. When his units made contact with the enemy formations, they inflicted major damage on them.

But he was on shakier ground when he claimed, in another post-battle statement, that "as a result of Operation Masher/White Wing 140,000 Vietnamese were returned to government control. There is much evidence that the GVN [South Vietnamese government] intends to reestablish civil government in this area." In fact, nothing of the kind happened. The Saigon government was too corrupt, too ineffective, and too distant from Binh Dinh to succeed in that vital pacification task.

Nowhere was this more apparent than in the many refugees directly created by the operation. Here was an essential problem with the big-unit war. When the Americans fought within populated areas, they risked killing and wounding innocent people. In the words of one grunt, this "made the countryside less secure, and alienated the very people we were supposed to be helping." Whether correctly or not, Kinnard and his commanders believed that Operation Masher/White Wing accounted for remarkably few noncombatant casualties. Without question, the Americans tried very hard to spare innocents, but firepower could be merciless—with over one hundred thousand shells flying around, some inevitably hurt the wrong people, as Colonel Moore's experience so vividly demonstrated.

The other option was to uproot them from their homes and evacuate them to safer areas. During Masher/White Wing, the 1st Cavalry Division processed over twenty-seven thousand refugees. In the An Lao Valley alone, the

Americans evacuated, at the locals' request, about forty-five hundred of eight thousand people who lived in the area. Civil affairs officers tried hard to dispense food, water, and medical care to the refugees of Binh Dinh, but, in reality and of necessity, most of the divisional effort went into operations. South Vietnamese officials proved unable to fill the void.

For the unfortunate refugees, the experience was frightening, bewildering, and sometimes cruel. They were uprooted from the only homes they had ever known, where their ancestors were buried, where they generally had lived in some semblance of peace as small farmers. At times, their property was destroyed or damaged by vehicles, soldiers, or the fighting itself. John Laurence, a CBS news correspondent, remembered encountering an anguished group of about one hundred refugees at the edge of one village during the height of the fighting. "Their faces were twisted in contortions of grief, their mouths open, long strands of saliva spilling on the soil. Their noses dripped. Tears ran down their cheeks." Artillery boomed nearby, and the sound of the guns only added to their misery. "They shrieked and sobbed and wailed with choking throats and fluttering lungs, one after another."

Lieutenant Colonel Robert Craig, the division civil affairs officer, was trying to comfort them as best he could. Like so many other soldiers, his intentions were decent, but he knew next to nothing of the language, culture, history, and politics of Vietnam. Since there were so few interpreters in the division, he could barely communicate with the people. He gave them C rations and chocolate, but this hardly improved their mood. One of Laurence's Vietnamese crewmen spoke to them. The people understood that the American and South Vietnamese soldiers were moving them away from their land, and they were deeply upset about it. They wondered who would tend to their crops and the graves of their ancestors. No one had an answer for them. "To take them away from their land was to take away more than their lives," Laurence wrote. "It was to condemn their souls."

This group ended up in a spartan camp on the fringes of nearby Hoai An, packed in with six thousand other refugees. One week after Laurence had first encountered the little group, he saw them at the camp. "About thirty people shared each room. The insides of the buildings smelled of stale food and urine and wood smoke from cooking fires. Many of the people were sick. Some had wounds from shrapnel and bullets. Children cried. The stench was so strong it stayed in our noses when we left the building." The people were getting medical care, but they did not have enough food. By and large, they were sullen and deeply depressed.

This was the typical plight, at least in the short term, for many Masher/White Wing refugees, and it was emblematic of two major problems with the war effort. First, commanders were primarily concerned with operations—finding main force enemy units and destroying them. They were neither trained nor equipped for relief work. "I'm a soldier and my job is to beat the enemy," Colonel Moore told a reporter during the operation, and his colleagues would have readily agreed. They went into the operation believing that their main job was to sweep the enemy from the area, so that the Saigon government could then come back and reassume permanent control. Once they had done the hard part—fighting and dying—it was then up to someone else to take care of the population. So, in big-unit operations like Masher/White Wing, the Army apportioned comparatively few resources to care for refugees.

Second, the job of relief, resettlement, and pacification fell to a Saigon government that could not begin to handle it. Nor did the South Vietnamese authorities coordinate their efforts with Kinnard or other American commanders. Owing to Westy's strategy, commanders simply focused on the conventional war, often at the expense of pacification, which was, ultimately, the key objective. The result was a serious refugee problem, not just during Masher/White Wing but in nearly all the major operations. Because of all this, some of the refugees grew to distrust, dislike, and resent (to put it politely) the South Vietnamese government and Army, as well as the Americans, who were, after all, foreigners.

Infinitely worse than these issues was the fact that Masher/White Wing did not bring real security to Binh Dinh province. Less than a week after Kinnard declared a conclusion to the operation, intelligence officers were already finding out that the NVA and VC were coming back into the Bong Son plain and the An Lao Valley. They had simply waited for the Americans to move on, and then they returned to rebuild their camps, train replacements, and carry on the war indefinitely.

In fact, the 1st Cavalry Division was only beginning its struggle for the area. Troopers from this division would fight many more battles for Binh Dinh in the days, months, and years to come. Colonel Moore's brigade went back repeatedly in April and May of 1966, fought more battles, and lost more men. At that point, he began to lose confidence in the senior leadership, both Vietnamese and American, as well as the attrition strategy. "I want to make it very clear . . . that I was very disappointed at the end of that operation [Masher/White Wing] . . . when I'd lost all those men . . . and the enemy came back within a week or two," Moore later said. He wondered how the war could ever be won at this rate. "If they [U.S. and South Vietnamese] couldn't make it work in Bong Son—where the most powerful American division available had cleared enemy forces from the countryside—how could they possibly hope to establish South Vietnamese control in other contested regions where the American military presence was much weaker?" This was the key, and very troubling, question that vexed so many of the big-unit operations that followed Masher/White Wing.[13]

Masher/White Wing, then, was a discouraging tale. It illustrated that combat soldiers could fight, and win, battle after battle with a combination of firepower and valor, yet achieve no tangible results toward overall victory. In that respect, it truly was a microcosm of the way the United States Army fought its big-unit war in Vietnam.

CHAPTER 6

Counterinsurgency from the Barrel of a Gun: The Marine Combined Action Platoons

Westy Versus the Marines: Shoot and Scoot or Hearts and Minds?

WILLIAM WESTMORELAND AND HIS MARINE colleagues never agreed on a strategy for victory in Vietnam. As commander of Military Assistance Command, Vietnam (MACV), Westy believed that mobile big-unit search-and-destroy operations, massive firepower, and the destruction of NVA and VC main force battalions was the primary way to win. The Marines favored pacification—a stationary counterinsurgency struggle at the village level to destroy the influence of the local VC cells over everyday Vietnamese. Marines argued that this would isolate the bigger communist formations while securing the loyalty of the population. The Corps had a long history of fighting counterinsurgency wars in such places as Haiti, Nicaragua, and Santo Domingo.

This disagreement stemmed largely from genuine philosophical differences and not interservice rivalry. Westmoreland was too practical to indulge in such internecine silliness. His personal character leaned toward tolerance and broad-mindedness. His abiding love for the Army did not diminish his high regard for the other services. He understood the importance of cooperation and teamwork among the various branches of the military. He held the Marines in especially high esteem. He admired their bravery and resourcefulness. In the immediate aftermath of the Korean War, he had even briefly served with the 3rd Marine Division. A decade later, in Vietnam, that unit, along with the 1st Marine Division, was under his command. He deeply respected Lieutenant General Lew Walt (of Walt's Ridge fame on Peleliu), who, as commander of III Marine Amphibious Force, was the senior Marine in Vietnam. He also held a favorable, if not quite affectionate, opinion of Walt's superior, Lieutenant General Victor "Brute" Krulak, who, as commander of the Fleet Marine Force, Pacific, was responsible for all Marines in that part of the world. Their disagreement was professional, not personal or institutional.

The Marines were responsible for the five provinces that comprised I Corps, the northernmost section of South Vietnam. The area bordered North Vietnam and Laos. The terrain ranged from mountains and thick jungle to coastal flats, rice paddies, and coastline. Much of the population was clustered into various villages and hamlets, most of which were within a few miles of the coast.

Krulak, whose nickname derived from his habit of speaking bluntly—one of his fellow Marine officers even went so far as to describe him as "abrasive"—took the lead in arguing for a pacification-centered strategy in Vietnam. He did this in his own inimitable way, bending Westy's ear every chance he got. "I kept insisting to Westmoreland . . . and to anybody else who would listen, that . . . first and foremost, we had to protect the people," Krulak later said. In his opinion, General Westmoreland's attrition strategy was a recipe for failure. "I saw [it] as wasteful of American lives, promising a protracted, strength-sapping battle with small likelihood of a successful outcome."

In a 1965 strategic appraisal he wrote: "The conflict between the [NVA]/hardcore VC on the one hand, and the U.S. on the other, could move to another planet today, and we would still not have won the war. On the other hand, if the subversion and guerrilla efforts were to disappear, the war would soon collapse, as the VC would be denied food, sanctuary, and intelligence." He estimated that even if the Americans and South Vietnamese could kill the enemy at a ten-to-one ratio, which they almost certainly could not, the war would still be prohibitively costly, with no promise of victory. "The Vietnamese people are the prize. *If the enemy cannot get to the people, he cannot win.*"[1]

Westy was not necessarily opposed to pacification, but he saw it as subordinate to the more vital job of destroying NVA and VC main force units. These were the "bully boys" (to reiterate his metaphor mentioned in the pre-

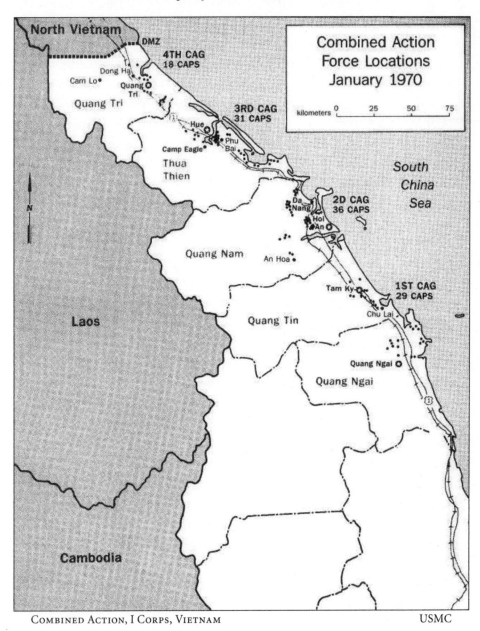

COMBINED ACTION, I CORPS, VIETNAM   USMC

vious chapter) who threatened to destroy the shaky "house" that was South Vietnam. The local VC who dominated many villages were like termites eating away at the house. In essence, Westy and Krulak were arguing over whether the bully boys or termites were the mortal threat.

Although most home owners would probably opt for termites as the greater peril, Westy saw it differently. In his judgment, the Marines' pacification, kill-the-termite-first approach was not aggressive enough. "They . . . established beachheads at Chu Lai and Danang and were reluctant to go outside them," he later wrote. This was not from lack of courage, but instead from "a different conception of how to fight an anti-insurgency war." Westy thought the Marines did not appreciate the potency of helicopters or mobile warfare in general. "I believed the marines should have been trying to find the enemy's main forces and bring them to battle, thereby putting them on the run and reducing the threat they posed to the population." He argued that this aggressive approach was especially important because of the close proximity to the Marine enclaves of NVA supply trails and infiltration routes.

The trouble was that, to some extent, search and destroy was the enemy of pacification. When Westy's battalions swept through the countryside or populated areas in search of the enemy, they could be quite disruptive of homes, property, and people. Inevitably, innocent people sometimes got hurt, uprooted, or inconvenienced. In the hearts of some Vietnamese, this bred resentment, fear, and anger toward the Americans. This, in turn, weakened the Saigon government and the American strategic situation in Vietnam. Thus, many of the big-unit operations were a classic case of more being less.

Indeed, Westmoreland himself, in a 1965 press conference, stated that his attrition strategy presented the average person in South Vietnam with three basic choices: stay on the land and risk getting killed by U.S. or communist firepower; join the VC and become the target of U.S. firepower; or move to areas under the Saigon government's control (in most cases, that meant a refugee camp). Quite a few, of course, chose option two. Many more took the unhappy third route. "I expect a tremendous increase in the number of refugees," Westy admitted to the reporters. This was, of course, exactly what happened. About one in four South Vietnamese became a refugee between 1965 and 1969. To the Marines, the disruptive attrition strategy was tantamount to making war on the people themselves.

Westy was always more than willing to listen to Krulak's ideas about this but he left no doubt whose view would prevail. "I happened to have the responsibility, not Krulak," Westmoreland once said. "The man who's got the monkey on his back, the man who's got responsibility, he's the one you got to listen to." In the end, they compromised. Westy carried out his big-unit war of attrition. The Marines pursued pacification in I Corps, but at the expense of their own intrinsic manpower and with no reinforcement, encouragement, or support from MACV.[2]

Rice Roots Infantry: The Birth of the Combined Action Platoons

In the summer of 1965, Lieutenant Colonel William Taylor had a problem. His 3rd Battalion, 4th Marine Regiment, was responsible for security in and around a Marine air base at Phu Bai. The base was quite vulnerable to mortar fire originating from the adjacent hamlets. Taylor's civil affairs officer, Captain John Mullin, knew that most of the hamlets contained Popular Force (PF) militiamen. These were poorly trained and armed locals who were under the control of the village, district, or province chief. Some of the PFs were veterans of the South Vietnamese Army (ARVN). Most, though, had little experience. The typical platoon consisted of anywhere from fifteen to forty men, normally led by the equivalent of a sergeant. Whereas the average ARVN soldier was a draftee who was conscripted by an abstract national government in Saigon, trained for military service, and probably sent to fight many miles away from his home, the PF was at least defending his village and family.

Poorly paid, and looked down upon by the Saigon government, the PFs' main job was local security against the VC. Needless to say, these militiamen were no match for the enemy (some of them were even sympathetic to, or even part of, the VC). Captain Mullin was a product of the Marine culture of pacification. Knowing full well the deficiencies of the PFs, he nonetheless wondered if it might be feasible to embed handpicked Marines with them in the hamlets around Phu Bai. Perhaps the Marines could strengthen the quality of the PFs and also benefit from their local knowledge. For all their problems, the PFs did offer one major asset—they had close ties with the people they were defending. Mullin believed that "combined action" Marine and PF units could provide security for the base and, at the same time, solidify the loyalty of the local people.

He proposed this to Taylor, who liked the idea. The colonel won approval from the local South Vietnamese authorities, and also his own superior, Colonel Edwin Wheeler. Wheeler forwarded the proposal to Generals Walt and Krulak. Naturally, they both saw the idea as a perfect way to implement their pacification strategy, so approval came fast. "Selected squads from each of the four Marine rifle companies [of 3/4] were organized into the 1st Provisional Platoon," a Marine report explained. "The platoon was integrated with a Popular Forces Company of six platoons, which then became the Combined Action Company. Each Marine squad was assigned to work with one of the PF platoons assigned to a village."

General Walt and Colonel Wheeler placed such importance on this that they personally chose the combined action commander, First Lieutenant Paul Ek, mainly because Ek could speak some Vietnamese and knew something about counterinsurgency war. The word circulated throughout the battalion, asking Marines to volunteer for this new initiative. Lieutenant Ek personally chose his people from this pool of volunteers. "Every man was handpicked," he later said. "Because of the magnitude of the job, I picked men who were mature, intelligent, who possessed leadership capabilities and tact." Ek felt that the latter quality was especially important because the combined action Marines would function not just as warriors but as everyday ambassadors among the people. He put his chosen group through a week of training in Vietnamese language, culture, and politics. They also brushed up on their patrolling skills. The brief training was, of course, barely adequate for this challenging mission, but it did at least give the Marines some level of preparation.

On August 1, they combined with their various PF platoons and began operations. The transition was difficult and awkward. Villagers and PFs alike were suspicious of the Marines. The Marine squad leaders had to work out tenuous command relationships with their PF sergeants. The two sides could not communicate well since most of the Americans knew little Vietnamese (a serious problem that would always plague the program and, indeed, the entire U.S. effort in Vietnam). Most of the Vietnamese doubted that Ek's Marines would stay in the villages long enough to truly protect them from the VC. Such skepticism was well founded. When the big units conducted operations, they rarely remained in one place for long since they generally spent most of their time trying to find the enemy. For the first week of the combined action program, even Ek's squads only patrolled their villages during the day. Soon thereafter, though, they patrolled round the clock, maintaining a constant presence.

These initial joint patrols with the PFs were an exercise in frustration. "When we first started going out on night patrols and ambushes, they [PFs] complained we made too much noise," Sergeant David Sommers, one of the squad leaders, recalled. "By slightly revamping our equipment, we were able to meet their standards of silence." The Marines initially saw the PFs as ill-disciplined pseudosoldiers. The Americans, for example, were shocked to see that the PFs seldom cleaned their weapons, something that every Marine was trained to do with an almost religious zeal.

Over time, though, the two sides learned much from each other, just as the program's architects had envisioned. The PFs learned better discipline and military skills. The Americans learned to proceed with patience and diplomacy. Also, the Marines came to appreciate and better understand the local culture. At first they were shocked by the poverty and primitive lifestyle of the villagers. Such was the case for Private Hop Brown, a rifleman in one squad, who came from a disadvantaged background in Harlem. "I didn't think I'd ever see people living in more squalid and degrading conditions than what I'd left behind," he said. Initially he was repelled by the impoverishment of the locals and what he perceived as laziness among the PFs. But, as time went on and the two sides formed relationships, his sympathy grew dramatically. "My attitude changed toward these people. As I got used to their way of life and started to see their customs and rituals from their point of view, I began to understand that things I took for granted as an American did not apply to this culture."

Most of the other Marines felt the same way. As the weeks unfolded, they came to appreciate just how badly the VC had sometimes terrorized the villagers, and they were determined to protect them. The various squads also developed an intuitive understanding of VC influence within their respective villages. "We found . . . that through the attitudes of areas we could pinpoint Vietcong activity within that area," Ek explained. "If you walk into an area and the people just go about their business and conduct normal daily routines with a fair amount of friendliness . . . things are pretty quiet." If the people were overly friendly, or distant or hostile, then the VC were nearby.

In spite of the challenges, it was clear by the end of 1965 that this first combined action company was a success. Security in the villages around Phu

Bai had improved significantly. The air base rarely came under attack. In the villages, firefights with the VC were rare. When they did take place, the Marines and PFs won. Intelligence tips on VC activity poured in from the locals, indicating a new level of trust on their part for the Marines. Many of the Americans had formed strong bonds with the PFs and some of the civilians, too. In December, when the battalion rotated home from Vietnam, forty of the sixty-six members of the combined action company opted to stay. Many sensed that they were at the leading edge of pacification. Working with the Vietnamese gave them a sense of kinship with them and awakened an obligation to protect them. In a way, they now had a kind of ownership in the war effort. It had a face and a purpose. It meant something beyond just humping around endless hills, jungles, and rice paddies, wilting under crippling heat, searching endlessly for an elusive, dangerous, faceless enemy.

The combined action Marines had become rice roots infantry. Curiously, they no longer thought of themselves as grunts, since they associated that term exclusively with the standard infantry mission of closing with and killing the enemy. They were wrong. They were the ultimate grunts. They were the tangible expression of everyday human will—defeating the enemy not just through combat power but through ingenuity, diplomacy, flexibility, decency, tact, practical know-how, and very basic cultural understanding. They carried out the mission as only human beings, not machines, could do it. They did it imperfectly, but effectively enough to make a positive contribution.

General Walt understood all too well what was happening. In January 1966, with the concurrence of his I Corps opposite in the South Vietnamese army, Lieutenant General Nguyen Chanh Thi, he expanded the combined action program. By the end of that year, there were fifty-seven combined action platoons (commonly known as CAPs) serving under various infantry battalions in the Marine areas of operation. In 1967, the combined action program became an independent command, separate from the infantry battalions. Eventually, by 1970, the program grew to 114 platoons, organized into twenty companies sprinkled throughout I Corps, under the control of four battalion-sized groups. At that point, the four combined action groups consisted of over two thousand Marines and Navy corpsmen plus, of course, thousands of PFs. Typically, Marine CAP squads were commanded by a sergeant, a corporal, or even, in some instances, a lance corporal. A squad normally contained anywhere from half a dozen to fourteen Marines, augmented by a corpsman.[3]

How to Get into a Combined Action Platoon

According to official program guidelines, CAP Marines were all supposed to be volunteers with at least two months in country, six months left on their tour of duty, combat experience, no disciplinary record, and a mature, open-minded attitude. Only the best Marines could be considered, especially the NCO squad leaders, whose personal responsibilities and daily autonomy were considerable. "The men I wanted to come into the Combined Action Program had to . . . know what it meant to take another human being's life, and how to shoot, move and communicate," Lieutenant Colonel William Corson, who ran the program in 1967, said. Such experiences would give them tactical proficiency, a proper understanding of war's tragedy, and an appreciation for human life. Corson was a counterinsurgency expert and a vocal proponent of the CAP concept. He had prior service in Vietnam dating back to the French war. He had also served in World War II and Korea.

As a Chinese-speaking intelligence officer with considerable field experience in Asia, Corson was adamantly opposed to Westy's search-and-destroy attrition strategy. He believed that the CAPs represented the best approach to victory. In order to succeed, he knew his program must have men who could, and would, kill the enemy but who also saw the Vietnamese as people, not "gooks," "slopes," or "zipperheads," to list just a few of the racist slang terms common at the time. "If they entered the job with an ethnocentric attitude, they would not succeed. They had to think on their own, be proud, loyal, and brave. And they had to have open minds to a new experience." In a squad, even one person who was prone to insensitivity, selfishness, racism, or offensive comments could undo the hard work of his entire team in winning the trust of the Vietnamese. So, Corson wanted the elite.

In practice, though, these lofty standards were difficult to maintain. Most of the time, the CAPs' manpower came from other in-country Marine units, especially rifle companies. Often, battalions were required to give up about twenty or thirty men per month to the CAPs. The commanders of these units obviously had no wish to lose their best Marines and receive nothing in return. They found ways to shunt men they perceived as misfits, rather than their most reliable people, into the program. Near the end of the war, men who were fresh out of training in the States were even assigned directly to the program.

The result was that men took a variety of paths, not all of them ideal, to their CAP. Private John Akins had the reputation of being a loner in his rifle company. When he got into a fight that he claimed another Marine provoked, his commanding officer immediately transferred him to a combined action company. "Ever heard of 'em?" the captain asked Akins. "They're those small teams that get overrun most of the time." Private First Class David Sherman's platoon got orders to give up several of its men to the CAPs. "There was a lot of hemming and hawing and maybe half of the needed men volunteered." Like several others, Sherman did not want to go because he liked the security of a larger unit. Nonetheless, his sergeant "volunteered" him. With no preamble, all of a sudden he and the other chosen ones became CAP Marines. "No school, no indoctrination, no nothing. Gather a bunch of Marines, stick us outside a hamlet, and we were a CAP."

Staff Sergeant Calvin Brown was assigned, seemingly out of the blue, to head up CAP-Alpha 3 when he got to Vietnam. "This was a relatively new program to me. I had no idea what it was going to consist of." Most of his previous training and experience did not apply to the job at hand. "I had to change my whole way of thinking. I was not really prepared for what I saw when I first went to the village" near Phu Bai. When Private First Class Thomas Flynn's battalion was scheduled to rotate out of Vietnam in 1966, his company commander arbitrarily assigned Flynn and several other men with little time in country to a combined action company. The young rifleman had never even heard of such a unit. "That night, as I lay on my cot, I kept wondering what [it] was all about." Some men in rifle companies, like Private First Class Jackson Estes, volunteered for the program because they were looking for a way to get out of combat, and they incorrectly perceived the CAPs as a soft deal. "I heard C.A.P. units are a lot easier," he wrote his wife as he awaited word of his potential transfer. "It would be safer too." Others simply wanted to escape close supervision and operate in a more autonomous environment.

More commonly, though, men did volunteer for the program because of a genuine desire to make a meaningful contribution to the war effort. Estes may have wanted a safer billet, but he also liked the idea of working closely with the Vietnamese. He wanted "a chance to live with [them] and get a clearer idea of what this war is all about." Lance Corporal Barry Goodson volunteered because, after several weeks of service in a line company, he liked the idea of getting to know the Vietnamese as people and helping them. "[I] signed up immediately, without question, and without going through proper military channels." Edward Palm was so eager to escape his boring rear echelon job and do something important that he embellished his service record during an interview with a gunnery sergeant who was recruiting for the CAPs. Impressed, the gunny accepted him on the spot. "I couldn't believe my good fortune, having just talked the Marine Corps into throwing me into the briar patch of my choice," Palm later wrote. Nineteen-year-old Sergeant Mac McGahan started his tour with a rifle company, fighting the NVA along the 17th parallel that divided the two Vietnams. He volunteered for a CAP because he liked the idea of improving the lives of ordinary Vietnamese. "We can see the progress being made," he told an interviewer. "Eight out of the fourteen men here [on the CAP] have extended for another six months. In a line company you're in a lot of combat and you're always tired. I went a month and a half averaging three hours sleep a night. You don't really care about the people. You just want to put in your time and get out. Here with the CAP you're not just killing the VC, you're helping people and you can see the progress you're making."

One of Corson's successors, Colonel Edwin Danowitz, personally checked the background and service records of potential CAP members, whether they were in-country volunteers or were assigned to the program directly from the States. "We scanned them to make certain the individuals had good proficiency and conduct marks." Anyone with disciplinary problems or the wrong kind of medical problems (for example, venereal disease) was out. Often he conducted personal interviews with the applicants. Danowitz claimed that he rejected about 30 to 35 percent of the interviewees. "We did have occasions where first sergeants would submit lists of people who were not volunteers and had no idea what the program was about; they were getting rid of their dead wood. However, once these people were interviewed, this was quickly determined and we sent them back to their units immediately."

With the expansion of the program, General Walt established a CAP school that most of the selectees went through before joining their new units.

The training was similar to the indoctrination Lieutenant Ek had given his original combined action Marines, mostly language and culture classes mixed with small-unit tactics and patrolling. Under the circumstances, this worked fairly well. Commander Richard McGonigal, a naval officer who actually visited every single CAP, marveled at how well the training, and service in the villages, changed the mind-set of the Marines. "When you take a group of civilians and transform them into Marines and get them to kill . . . and then somehow re-transform them into people that can kill discriminatingly and can go through some kind of identification with the people . . . to the point where they're willing to risk their lives to protect them . . . that's an amazing psychological trick." He believed that only the Marines, and not even the Army, could have pulled this off. "I'm quite certain the Navy couldn't, and the Air Force had no need to. They fought their war from thirty thousand feet. They never had to be accountable for blowing a hootch away." The CAP Marines were on the ground at the most basic level, though, and thus accountable for everything they did. Needless to say, substandard Marines did not usually last long in this demanding environment.[4]

Swimming in the Village Seas

Mao Tse-tung once famously said that guerrilla warriors must move among the people as a fish swims in the sea. The combined action platoon Marines were American fish in a vast Vietnamese sea. As the program grew, CAPs began popping up all over I Corps. "Marine members of the CAPs live in the same tents, eat the same food, and conduct the same patrols and ambushes as their Vietnamese counterparts," a 1967 report for General Krulak explained. The job was as much diplomatic as military. To the locals and the PFs, these Marines were the very face of America. The CAP members soon found that very little if anything they did escaped the notice of the Vietnamese. "They see everything we do—how we shave, how we dress, the way we talk to each other, the way we work," Corporal Joseph Trainer, a team leader in Thuy Phu village, told an interviewer. "If we give them a bad impression, that's the impression they'll get of all Marines, and Americans."

When Gunnery Sergeant John Brockaway established a CAP at a village in Quang Nam province, he found that the area had been under VC control for many months. The insurgents had told the villagers that U.S. Marines would rape their wives and daughters, steal their property, and kill their children. "When we first got there, you couldn't get within a hundred meters of these people without some of them going in the opposite direction." It took many weeks, and much good behavior, to loosen them up. Another Marine estimated that it took him about a month before he knew what was happening in his team's village. "When you first come here, it's hard, but then you begin to learn the customs and how the people operate . . . and pick it up eventually."

The Marines had to be very careful not to arrogantly foist American values and cultural norms on their new Vietnamese acquaintances. This took patience and tact. The rural Vietnamese did not share American ideas of time, labor, or money. They did not think in punctual terms of having to be somewhere at a certain time. They did not adhere to a time schedule for getting jobs done. They especially did not conform to American hygiene standards. Their personal bathing and dental standards were not to the levels that Americans took for granted. Moreover, many Marines were shocked, and nauseated, to see the people publicly defecate "right outside their homes, or right outside the street in front of their homes," in the recollection of one man. Quite commonly, the people also defecated in their rice paddies, combining waste disposal with fertilization. The Marines sometimes did, with local permission, build latrine facilities, but more commonly they had to accept such local customs or fail in their mission. For their part, the Vietnamese were a bit taken aback with the American penchant for using handkerchiefs. The idea of blowing one's nose into a cloth and putting it back into one's pocket was disgusting to them. "They wiped their noses on a banana leaf or just blew it on the ground," John Daube, a corpsman, recalled.

Sexual mores were markedly different, too. In rural Vietnam, sexuality was almost puritanical. Sex before marriage was forbidden. However, mutual masturbation by two men was widely accepted. The Americans could not begin to understand this concept (especially on the occasions when they caught PFs indulging while on guard duty). Among the Vietnamese, two men often held hands as a sign of friendship. Thus, if a Vietnamese man attempted to take a Marine by the hand, he was offering a significant gesture of trust and friendship. But the Americans saw hand-holding among men as homosexuality, at a time when American popular culture greatly frowned on same-sex relationships.

Hailing from a youth-centered culture, the Americans were slow to understand the importance of elders to the Vietnamese. So the Marines tended to interact with children—who were generally friendly and exuberant—more than adults, particularly elderly people. "With kids being kids, and Marines being Marines, you get attached to them," Lieutenant Thomas Eagan, commander of a combined action company named Delta-1, told an interviewer in 1967. Like many other Marines, he believed that making inroads with the kids would help the long-term effort in Vietnam. "They'll have a good many Americans that they can remember . . . this I think is definitely going to sway them to an attempt to hang on to the country as they know it." Perhaps, but this preoccupation with kids at the expense of elders sometimes cost them credibility with the average Vietnamese villager, until the Americans learned to reach out to everyone.

CAP squad leaders especially learned to cultivate village chiefs and district chiefs since both types of leaders were generally influential. Those who were not in league with the VC were usually in danger, so the security of a Marine CAP could be attractive to them. The mere act of sitting down, drinking tea with a chief, asking him how the Marines could help his people often held great sway. At times, it also yielded information on the VC or facilitated civic action projects for the village. Making this kind of headway with local leaders raised the status of the CAPs, and perhaps even legitimized them, in the eyes of villagers. Such on-the-ground support was, after all, a key objective of the combined action mission. When a CAP leader forged these relationships, it hardly guaranteed success, but he had little chance of accomplishing much without them.

Other cultural issues came from the unfortunate fact that some of the CAP Marines were boors who had no business being in the program. They dealt with people harshly, used racial slurs, broke squad rules about refraining from drinking and whoring, or just generally projected ill will. Most of these types did not last long on a team. Far more often, cultural problems resulted from simple American ignorance about local customs. CAP Marines, like most Americans, tended to pat kids on the head until they found out that many villagers believed this infested them with evil spirits. So, too, they had to learn to avoid crossing their legs or pointing their heels at their hosts when sitting in someone's home. To the Vietnamese, the pointed heel meant that the person at whom it was pointed would die the next day. Lieutenant Eagan found, to his chagrin, that he committed a gratuitous cultural insult one day. "All I had done was to walk into a hootch and said something to one of the old men in the ville and I turned my back on his family altar without paying any sort of respect to it." In a culture that was centered around ancestor worship, this was a grave offense indeed. It was no small matter tactically, either, because such an insult could easily cause the offended party to cast his lot with the VC, putting more American lives at risk.

CAP members also had to deal with the loss of face that resulted from errant firepower or damage inflicted by conventional units. When people got hurt or killed, it could unravel months of excruciating effort on the part of the CAP. Even when the damage was only material, tension was often high. Staff Sergeant David Thompson had to smooth over some very hurt feelings when a line unit carelessly destroyed a vase and several other sacred items in his village's temple one night. "Whatever the troops do . . . goes back on the American government, and this does not make for good relations [with] the people." These were the vagaries, and immense challenges, of operating in so alien a cultural environment.

Although some CAPs were aloof from their villagers, most did form some sort of relationship, many of which even culminated in strong ties of friendship. Generally, this happened quite gradually if the Marines behaved well and made an effort to insinuate themselves into the local customs and culture. The average Vietnamese peasant was caught in the middle of a vicious struggle that raged among the PFs, ARVN, the NVA, the VC (many of whom he probably knew), and the Americans. This meant that most of the people simply wanted the security to be left alone and live their lives in peace. "It's not that so many people in Vietnam are Viet Cong," one CAP leader explained as the combined action program was just starting to grow. "It's that most of them will swing with . . . whoever's got the strength. Because they don't have anything to lose by going over to the Viet Cong when the VC are in their village; or going back to the government when the government comes in the village. But now you've got a ville that's got khaki [a CAP] in it;

it's got medical attention there, it's got people that care and people that show some friendliness and some interest. So the villager like any other human being begins to develop loyalties."[5]

As foreigners, the Americans aroused a great deal of suspicion but also curiosity among the villagers. When the Vietnamese saw that the CAP Marines were willing to stay with them permanently, provide security, and blend in as best they could, they usually softened. One major indicator of this was when they invited Marines to share meals with them. This was such an important aspect of village culture that no American could turn down the opportunity. Thus, every CAP Marine had to be an adventurous eater. Corporal Michael Cousino found this out one day when a respected elder butchered a goat, drained its blood into a bowl, took a sip, and then offered it to Cousino. "I pretended to drink it by bringing the bowl up to my mouth and letting some blood form up around my lips. This way I wouldn't offend him. He accepted me into his family."

One time, the locals who lived near Thomas Flynn's CAP at Cam Hieu honored the Marines with an elaborate feast. With great fanfare, they arranged pots and baskets full of rice, with boiled chicken alongside trays of pig brains, intestines, jellied blood, and raw fish that still had their heads and scales. Flynn, a meat-and-potatoes Irish kid from New Jersey, was a bit reluctant to dive into the spread but he knew he had no choice. "As I picked up a piece of the pig brain, the people watched with anticipation. When I swallowed it and smiled, they clapped their hands and laughed. I wondered if they were happy because they thought I really liked their food or if they were laughing because they were thinking that this dumb bastard is really eating this shit!" These meals sometimes resulted in invitations to weddings, funerals, family gatherings and the like, for even more eating. The Americans learned to always leave something on their plates because, in Vietnamese culture, if a guest cleaned his plate, it meant that the host had not prepared enough food and he or she lost face.

Most of the Marines grew to like the local fare, especially the Nuoc Mam sauce with which Vietnamese flavored so many dishes. Corporal Barry Goodson made a point of buying sauce-soaked pork and fish sandwiches from nearby merchants whom he befriended over time. At times, a sandwich could be bug-infested, but Goodson hardly cared. "Eating it was a simple way to strengthen my bond with our Vietnamese counterparts." Sometimes, during day patrols, people invited the Marines to join them for lunch. Other times, they sat down together for full-fledged dinners of rice, fish, watermelons, and carrots. "After they eat they will sit and watch us, and laugh at the way we use their [chop]stick and eat their food," Sergeant Alexander Wert, a squad leader, said in early 1967. "It's all good natured. We laugh at them and they laugh at us, it's always a lot of fun."

Most commonly, the two peoples exchanged or mixed their foods. This was especially true among the Marines and PFs. The Marines were not shy about dispensing C rations, soda, and chocolate to their allies. When Sergeant Jim Donovan, who headed up a squad in Tuy Loan village, found out that his PFs liked Salem cigarettes and Orange Crush soda, he passed out these products as a reward for good behavior. He also loved Vietnamese food and enjoyed many mixed meals with the PFs. "I like rice and soup with the noodles. I ate at least one meal a day with a Vietnamese." They would mix C ration chicken and noodles with the local version. "They [PFs] would take the noodles and throw 'em away. Then they would make their own noodles and they'd eat the [C ration] chicken." Donovan was amazed that the PFs actually liked ham and lima beans, the most despised C ration meal for practically all Americans in Vietnam.[6]

The single biggest cultural problem was the language barrier. Even among the CAP Marines very few could speak Vietnamese with any semblance of fluency. Most knew only common phrases, slang expressions, and the odd word or two. Lance Corporal Richard Wildagel had thirty days of language training in Danang before joining his CAP, and the course was useful, but his communication with the people was still so limited that he often relied on hand signals and gestures. He found that he had to make a daily effort to be conversant. "Just by being in the ville, you can pick up a lot, just by listening to the people, or asking what something is." Corporal Dukin Elliot went to language school in the States for nearly a year. He was well ahead of his colleagues in his ability to communicate with people, but even he had troubles. "It's a difficult language to learn, because you can write a word the same way and it has different meanings." Only one man on David Sherman's team had any linguistic training and it was practically useless in Ky Hoa, their remote village. "His instructor was Saigonese. Vietnamese as spoken in Saigon is much different from what is spoken in the countryside. Out there dialects can change considerably in 10 miles."

Sergeant Donovan's squad even had an ARVN interpreter assigned to it. Of course, this yielded tremendous influence to this individual since he literally controlled the vital power of communication (a phenomenon familiar a generation later to many small-unit leaders in Iraq who also relied far too heavily on their interpreters). This meant he had to be reliable. Unfortunately, Donovan's ARVN was not. A visiting Special Forces major who knew some Vietnamese eavesdropped on the man as he questioned the locals and found he was feeding Donovan bad information. The interpreter ended up getting drunk and deserting. Fortunately for Donovan's team, he was replaced with a South Vietnamese Marine Corps sergeant who was loyal, courageous, and who spoke excellent English. "He gave me a lot of history of Vietnam. He got a lot out of people. They really liked him."

Most of the CAPs were on their own, though. The language barrier would have been a challenge even if the American preparation for it had been barely adequate. As it was, the Marines learned to get by as best they could. Those who at least made an attempt to speak Vietnamese tended to get along well with people. Of course, many of the Vietnamese, particularly the PFs, spoke some English. A surprising number of militiamen could converse to some extent. Children, always so adaptable, sometimes picked up English with stunning alacrity, and acted as vital go-betweens.

Even so, for most CAP Marines and their Vietnamese partners, everyday communication—such a crucial component of human understanding, empathy, and cooperation—was basic and tentative. The Marines and their PFs communicated by hand signals, common phrases, and even facial expressions. Given these constraints, it is remarkable how well they usually worked together.

Nonetheless, the inability to communicate in any kind of depth was a real hindrance for most of the CAPs. It limited how much intelligence they could pick up from locals. It intruded upon their cultural understanding. It curtailed the amount of in-depth joint operations or planning they could conduct with the PFs. It led to misunderstandings that could only be worked out through substantive conversation, as when someone from one group accidentally shot someone from the other, or when the PFs stole American property (as they often did). This language failure was a direct symptom of the flawed American approach in Vietnam—in a war whose outcome would be determined by cultural literacy, grassroots influence, and the local dominance that could only be forged by agile formations of light infantry, American strategists instead relied upon the bigness inherent in technology, material superiority, and firepower.[7]

With such deficient language skills among the CAPs, the team member most capable of bridging the cultural chasm was usually the Navy corpsman. "I think our Corpsmen, pound for pound, were some of the most important men we had," one commander asserted. Invariably known as "Doc" or "Bac si" (the Vietnamese word for medic), the corpsmen served as the on-the-spot medical face of the United States. Most of them were all of nineteen or twenty years old. In general, they worked with a PF who had been designated as a medic, either by his sergeant ("Trung Si") or the district chief. Quite often, the American corpsmen conducted medical civic action projects (MEDCAPs) for the villagers, treating everything from headaches to serious war wounds and contagious diseases. The corpsmen conducted close to two million MED-CAPs during the war. "Invariably surrounded by children, he seeks to advise and empirically treat whatever he encounters," Lieutenant Commander Lawrence Metcalf, who served as medical coordinator for the combined action program, wrote. "Identifying communicable disease and reporting it, acquiring intelligence information, and selecting for medical evacuation those patients whose conditions most warrant medical referral . . . are all part of the CAP Corpsman's routine."

By most accounts, they were even more effective than trained physicians. There were two reasons for this. First, they were less condescending with people and infinitely more patient. Second, unlike almost all the doctors, they lived among the people and developed some level of comfort with them. "Intestinal worms were endemic, and ringworm was common as well," David Sherman recalled. "Our corpsmen got the people disinfected, taught them rudimentary sanitation, cleared up some other minor medical problems, and introduced them to soap." Versatility, patience, and a true sense of compassion were qualities that all corpsmen had to possess. "I treated everything— boils, bunions, rashes included," corpsman John Daube explained. During his regular MEDCAPs, Jack Broz treated more babies than he could count. In many cases, their heads were covered with oozing sores from jungle rot and parasites. "I took some Furacin ointment and smeared it liberally all over the baby's head. Then I wrapped my own special bandage that I devised around its head, complete with chin strap." On one such MEDCAP, Wayne Christenson treated a boy who had severely lacerated his forearm in an accident. "I'd never sewed up anyone before. I injected the area with novocaine and sewed up the wound. This kid did not even whimper. The Vietnamese are a very stoic people."

For the corpsmen all of this was, of course, in addition to carrying out their primary responsibility of dispensing medical care to their Marine comrades. The worthy task of saving the lives of their friends, and caring for the Vietnamese, led to a high level of job satisfaction for the corpsmen. "I began to see myself less and less as a Navy corpsman and more and more as a Marine," Christenson said. Another corpsman came to think of the locals as part of his personal circle of friends. "There's a great deal of satisfaction in working with these people," he told an interviewer who visited his CAP one day. "I have gotten to know them all very well. There isn't one person in this ville I haven't treated yet." This corpsman, and dozens of others like him, were the cutting edge of the combined action program, particularly in relation to civic action. They helped break down barriers between the Marines and the Vietnamese. They also saved many lives.[8]

Turf Battles

Establishing ties and personal rapport with the Vietnamese villagers was of paramount importance for every CAP, but so was security. The most crucial step in earning the people's confidence was to provide them security. Without that, nothing else mattered. Defeating the VC, then, was the primary job of each team. Theirs was a war of wits and continuous tension, stalking and being stalked by shadowy groups of Viet Cong. Since the CAPs were so small in number, they were vulnerable (this was a major reason why Westy was always suspicious of them). Each team dealt with the constant danger that a large enemy unit, VC or NVA, might attack and destroy the entire CAP before nearby friendly conventional units could intercede.

Building a strong, defensible compound was important for the CAPs. Most constructed some sort of fortified area, complete with bunkers, concertina wire, claymore mines, and machine-gun posts. Patrolling, though, was the lifeblood of security. Patrolling is to an infantryman what skating is to a hockey player—it is the gateway to everything he does. On patrol, an infantryman gathers intelligence, projects power, assesses terrain, calms friends, intimidates enemies, outwits the enemy soldier or insurgent who would like to kill him, and, if necessary, gets into a life-and-death fight with that enemy combatant. In the CAPs, patrolling was the military version of the hometown policeman's beat. In a way, these patrols were the ultimate expression of ground power, depending as much on mere presence and relationships as overwhelming weaponry.

In the various hamlets and villages of I Corps, the Marines and their PFs spent much of their time on such patrols. Day after day, night after night, they roamed their respective areas, PFs in tow, usually in groups of less than ten, with several meters between each man, rifles and machine guns at the ready, always looking for danger. At night, amid darkness so vast that they could hardly see more than a few feet in any direction, they chose ambush spots among the rice paddies, within the jungles, or even at times in the hamlets. They hunkered down, tried to ignore mosquitoes, ants, the heat, and the persistent tension of the unknown, while they watched and listened for the VC. Sometimes they got into firefights with the VC. The vast majority of the time, they did not. When fights did occur, they usually lasted only a few minutes. The CAPs generally inflicted more punishment than they absorbed, but casualties among the Marines and PFs tallied up, normally in ones and twos, over the course of many such firefights. Most of the combined action Marines did not realize it, but casualty rates in the CAPs were actually higher than in the conventional rifle companies. As of 1967, each CAP Marine had a 75 percent chance of getting wounded and a 12 percent chance of being killed.

Good leaders, Marine and PF, knew never to set noticeable patterns. Patrols had to avoid using the same routes at the same times or perhaps the same ambush spots night after night, anything that might betray their location to the enemy. "To protect the people from Viet Cong terrorism and physical and economic harassment, the combined action units depended on aggressive patrolling and ambushing, superior tactical skill and a detailed knowledge of the local area and the people," a perceptive III Marine Amphibious Force report intoned. "[They] emphasized mobility, spreading their activity over thousands of meters to seek out and interdict the enemy."[9]

No matter how good the Marines were at patrolling, they could not be effective if they did not work well with the PFs. For one thing, the PFs represented the local people, whose loyalty must be won for pacification to succeed.

For another, even the worst PFs had unique skills that were crucial to the survival of any CAP Marine. The PFs best knew the terrain, the mood of the people, the whereabouts and perhaps even the identity of the VC. They also had an uncanny ability to sniff out booby traps. With experience, the Marines often grew proficient at all of these things, but, as foreigners, they could never know or understand the local situation like the PFs.

The Marines, of course, were much better trained and disciplined than the PFs. The Americans were physically stronger, more courageous, and they certainly took better care of their weapons. To these proud Marines, the PFs often seemed lazy, cowardly, and untrustworthy. "When we first came in," one CAP leader recalled, "it was a fight every night to get the people [PFs] to stand guard. They wanted to stand guard for two hours and go home and go to bed." Their reliability in showing up for patrols, as well as their noise discipline, were often substandard. Too often, they ran away when a fight loomed or even in the middle of firefights. One squad leader estimated that about 10 percent of the PFs in his combined unit were VC infiltrators who were simply gathering information on Marine weapons, procedures, and capabilities. In Edward Palm's CAP, the relationship with the PFs was marred by the fact that the PFs were unreliable and seemed to have an understanding with the VC not to patrol in certain areas. "A typical patrol began with Sarge, our squad leader, briefing the Trung Si the day before. Sarge showed him an overlay and requested that a number of PFs, usually twelve, be ready at the appointed time and place. If four or five showed up we were lucky. Despite numerous suggestions, complaints, and threats we were never able to form integrated, cohesive patrolling teams. It was luck of the draw every time out."

In the majority of cases, though, the PFs were good fighters. They simply lacked the formal training, good weaponry, and soldierly discipline that Marines took for granted. The Americans were often at fault for the problems that arose. For instance, Corporal Barry Goodson's combined action company commander, from the disembodied perspective of a compound miles away, decided to send a rear echelon man to join the team for a night in the field. The man was about to rotate home. The officer wanted him to earn some medals before he left and he could only do that in the field with the CAP. This was idiocy in the extreme. The frightened Marine was completely out of his depth. He knew none of the other men, and he posed a danger to the team because he did not know how to operate in this perilous light-infantry environment.

Sure enough, on ambush that night the rookie accidentally shot and killed a sixteen-year-old PF, thinking he was a VC. The brother of the dead PF, and many of the other militiamen, wanted to kill the Marine. Only the intercession of the Trung Si and the immediate removal of the offending Marine prevented them from doing so. The close relationship that Goodson's team had built over many months of shared danger with the PFs eroded literally overnight, and was never quite the same. "The air was filled with tension, distrust and fear," Goodson wrote. "During the day the villagers shunned us and refused our offers of help. They even refused our medical treatment. When we set up ambush, [the Trung Si] no longer mingled his men amongst mine. Time subdued the overt hatred and bitterness, but our relationship with all the Vietnamese people had changed. The distrust could not be shaken."

The Americans needed to understand that the PFs were in a perpetual state of war, struggling for their homes and families. Long after the Marines rotated back to the U.S., their fight would still rage on. This created a combination of fatalism and patience in most of the PFs, especially their leaders. The Americans had to accept this or fail. The typical PF leader was canny, courageous, and probably more combat-experienced than all the CAP Marines put together. It did no good to deal with him in a heavy-handed way, like a drill instructor berating a recruit. "He don't like the idea of some big galoot of an American walking in his ville and walking over to him telling him what he's gonna do and what he's not gonna do," Lieutenant Eagan said. "So . . . you have to deal with them as an individual and try to get him to come around to your way of thinking, or at least come to a point where you can compromise your thinking with his and come up with a mutual action patrol."

This could also mean looking the other way at their excesses. In this terribly personal war, what the Marines knew as torture was perfectly acceptable behavior to the PFs. A couple PFs from Sergeant Jim Donovan's team caught an NVA colonel one time and recognized him as the person responsible for obliterating a nearby village several years before. In a matter of minutes, they tortured and killed the colonel. "They chopped off a bamboo thing and stripped it. They soaked it in water and just started whipping him and screaming at him for questions. He wasn't gonna talk at all. I think his body turned out to be like jelly." Donovan contemplated interceding but he was concerned that, if he did, the PFs would turn on him. "This is people that have been at war for a hundred years and they didn't have any Geneva Convention shit."

Corporal Goodson encountered a similar situation one night—before the accidental shooting—when his PFs captured the Viet Cong girlfriend of an NVA officer. Everyone understood that she knew much about an impending enemy attack on the CAP. While in custody, she struggled mightily, "like a wild animal," in Goodson's memory. "The girl had hate in her eyes and continuously fought her captors, cussing us through her gag."

As the Marines stood aside, a team of PFs took her into a shack for interrogation. Goodson and the Americans heard shouts and the sound of slapping. Then, when Goodson heard her emit a bloodcurdling scream, he climbed the side of the shack and peered down from a ventilation hole. "The beaten girl was nude, lying in a pool of water on the floor. Wires, attached to every vital part of her body, led back to a hand-cranked generator. The hand on the generator cranked in rapid turns. The girl screamed again as her body jerked around on the floor." Sickened and haunted by the scene, he could watch no more. He contemplated doing something to stop this, but came to the painful realization that he was powerless. "It was their territory. It was their way. No one could interfere." The girl died in agony.[10]

Working with the PFs, then, was a constant process of accommodation, negotiation, and amalgamation. But when the Marines and the PFs clashed with the VC, or were attacked by them, they fought together as brothers. In the run-up to and during the major communist Tet Offensive of 1968, they made a point of attacking the CAPs with powerful formations. According to one study, almost half of all enemy attacks in I Corps from November 1967 through January 1968 were against the CAPs.

Even before the fighting intensified, many of the CAP Marines had picked up intelligence on the enemy offensive, as well as a foreboding mood among the villagers. "When we sent in reports" to higher headquarters, Private First Class Tom Krusewski recalled, "nobody believed us. That was one of the problems with the CAPs—we didn't have any officers with us. They thought we exaggerated. And they distrusted the Vietnamese." Indeed, NCOs had so much latitude and independence in running their CAPs that officers seldom had much impact on the day-to-day operations. To most CAP members, the officers were distant and out of touch, and generally held in contempt. "In our teams we were not listened to by higher command," one sergeant asserted. "We watched [enemy] heavy weapons squads come in, platoons come in [before Tet], and we called these [in]. And nobody would believe us. We watched them move in with rockets . . . and heavy mortars. We were told by higher-ups that, quote, 'we didn't know what the hell we were talking about.'"

Thus, the average Marine sensed what was in the offing, even if those at headquarters did not. While walking through his village one day, Corporal Igor Bobrowsky noticed that people were building coffins. Sergeant Keith Cossey watched as his village "had suddenly been filled with strange young men in civilian clothes." All of them carried South Vietnamese ID cards but they were actually the vanguard of a North Vietnamese Army regiment. "We had our hands full with literally hundreds of these characters just hanging around."

When the attacks started, they were especially violent. With terrible suddenness one night, the VC hit Private First Class Thomas Flynn's Tiger Papa Three CAP by bombarding their makeshift compound with RPGs. The tin and wood hootch where Flynn was sleeping collapsed on him. He got separated from his rifle. In the confusion, with bullets flying and the screams of Marines, PFs, and VC mixing together amid the noise, Flynn saw a Viet Cong soldier toss a grenade into an adjacent bunker, killing a Marine. "His body [was] twisted and his stomach was torn open from the explosion," Flynn wrote. As Flynn approached the enemy soldier, he turned and pulled a knife. "Before he could react, I grabbed his wrist and his throat and kicked his legs out from under him with a large sweep. We both went down on the ground with me on top. I disarmed him. With both hands on the handle, I thrust the knife into his chest."

Seconds later, a group of armed VC surrounded him. He lunged for one of them and, as he struggled for his rifle, another VC shot Flynn in the face. "My tongue was ripped. My mouth filled with blood, and I felt several teeth lying loose in my mouth." He could also feel a hole in his left cheek where the bullet had exited. As he vomited blood, the VC dragged him several yards by the hair. They bayoneted him in the hand and exploded a grenade against his leg. But they were either too distracted with the resistance offered by other CAP members or were perhaps unwilling to finish him off face-to-face. Eventually they retreated, the battle died down, and Flynn's buddies medevaced him. As was so common in these situations, the surviving Marines and PFs later rebuilt their compound and renewed their mission.

The enemy tactic was to strike swiftly with overwhelming force, attempt to overrun the compound, inflict maximum damage, and then withdraw before nearby conventional units could arrive on the scene. According to Lieutenant Colonel Corson, one 1967 assault was supported by "150 rounds of 82mm mortars, 40–50 rounds of recoilless rifle fire and multiple bangalore torpedoes to break the defensive wire. Once through the wire the assault forces moved rapidly against the pre-selected objectives of the dispensary, the command bunker and the ammunition bunker."

This particular attack lasted seven minutes. During Tet, most were longer. Often the enemy trained for their assaults on exact mock-ups of whatever compound they had targeted. Because of these elaborate rehearsals, the average enemy soldier was very well prepared to kill at close range. "At times the attackers advanced to ranges so close that hand grenades were employed freely by both combatants," one post-battle report stated.

In one such instance, a potent force of 150 NVA and VC assaulted a 3rd Combined Action Group CAP in the middle of the night. "As soon as the first [mortar] round hit the compound," Lance Corporal Frank Lopez, a rifleman, recalled, "they just put cardboard boxes and blankets and mats on the wires." This allowed them to breach the wire rapidly. They then set to work blowing up bunkers and exchanging shots with the Marines and PFs. "It looked like ants coming over a hill or just coming through the wire, towards the compound yelling and screaming," Lopez said. "Everyone was just yelling and getting hit." The CAP Marines and PFs had little illumination and no fire support because their supporting units were also under heavy attack. "The VC threw a lot of satchel charges that night," another Marine said, "within half an hour the entire compound was set on fire."

Men of both sides scattered in every direction, among bunkers and buildings, where they fought to the death in a personal fashion. The Viet Cong even taunted the Americans with bullhorns, naming individual Marines and promising to kill them (the VC often put bounties on the heads of CAP Marines). "They [VC] were every place," Corporal Arliss Willhite remembered. He himself heard his name over the bullhorn. "They had the Compound almost totally destroyed in twenty minutes. Why they did leave, and why they didn't kill everybody, I don't know. They just turned around and left when the sun started coming up." They probably withdrew for fear of getting annihilated by U.S. aircraft or rescue forces. As it was, they killed seven Marines and eleven PFs.

The next year, 1969, the communists launched another Tet Offensive. This one was not quite as potent as the one in 1968, but for the CAP Marines in the path of the attacks, this one was bad enough. Corporal Goodson's CAP, for example, knew from their many local intelligence sources that the attack was coming. Before the fighting started, though, they had the surreal experience of participating in a bizarre eve-of-battle Tet holiday banquet with the VC and NVA. In a situation that was probably unique in the entire history of the war, Goodson, the seven other Marines on his team, and the PF leader visited the enemy's remote camp, at their invitation, for a feast. "Every man in black PJ's and NVA uniforms nodded respectfully as we passed, giving us forced smiles that made no attempt at camouflaging the contempt and hatred they held for us. Yet even past the hatred you could sense a fear and reverence for our presence." At six feet three, Goodson towered over them, and made a point of stretching to his full height. Each Marine struggled to conceal his own fear, betraying no weakness in front of the enemy.

As the meal ended, an NVA officer stood up and spoke in English. "Welcome, gentlemen. I hope you have enjoyed your meal. You honor us with your presence as warrior honors warrior. You will all die tonight. Tonight, marines, some of our men will collect the bounty we have placed on your heads. Tomorrow we celebrate with same meal over our victory! But, today, enjoy yourselves. Eat as much as you like." Corporal Goodson sat listening and thought: "Hope we see you personally tonight."

When the banquet ended, the team left with little fanfare. The situation was nerve-wracking and strange in the extreme. Knowing full well that they would soon fight a battle of extinction, they had sat down for a convivial meal with the enemy, as if they were about to engage in nothing more consequential than a sporting event or a chess competition. Such were the psychological vagaries of combat, and the strong human connections that often existed between mortal enemies, even in this modern era when combatants sometimes cared little about old-world notions of honor.

Realizing that time was short, they retrieved their weapons, smeared themselves with buffalo dung to blend in with their surroundings, and settled into a predetermined ambush spot to wait for the communist attack. Sure enough, the assault came at about midnight. "It seemed like every tree and bush was alive with NVA and VC," Goodson wrote. "Brazenly they stepped into the light and opened fire with their AK's and machine guns. Green tracers and their deadly partners sliced away at the trees around us." American fire scythed through the enemy soldiers. In the weird half-light, the Marines could see some of them stumbling and falling.

The battle ebbed and flowed like this for an indeterminate amount of time. The team was running low on ammo. Goodson called his company commander, several miles away in a firebase, for fire support. The enemy fighters were within fifty meters of the team now. "They were coming from all directions like a pack of wolves moving in for the kill." Instead of arranging for artillery or helicopter support, the company commander accused Goodson of staging a fake battle for glory and medals. He refused to provide any help. Angry beyond description, Goodson hoped only to survive long enough to kill the CO. Once again, this was another troubling example of the disconnect between officers and enlisted men in the CAP program.

When the team was almost out of ammunition, and about to be overrun by the enemy, a sensible colonel got on the net, overruled the company commander, and came to the rescue with Hueys and helicopter gunships. The intense fire of the gunships kept the NVA and VC at bay, while the Hueys landed and resupplied the team with ammo. By dawn, the battle was over and the enemy was gone. The team had lost one man killed and another wounded. "Everyone was physically and mentally drained," Goodson later wrote. "Battles such as this one simply do not end with the last bullet. They are lived time and again in your mind as your senses attempt to cope with the horrors and the highs."[11]

Mobility, Agility, and Finality

In response to the Tet battles, the CAPs adopted new mobile tactics. As the furious onslaughts piled up, the program's senior commanders, such as Colonel Theodore Metzger, came to believe that the stationary CAP compounds were too vulnerable. After all, they were fixed targets. The VC knew exactly where they were and could easily gather intelligence on their defenses (as evidenced by the mock-ups they often built). Nor was it difficult, as Tet proved, for the enemy to amass powerful attacking forces to overrun a compound. If the CAPs became mobile, though, and never planted themselves in one widely known spot for any length of time, the VC lost the initiative. "With its mobility, the CAP can keep the VC guessing," Colonel Metzger said in early 1970. "They don't like to come after you unless they've had a chance to get set and do some planning. Mobility throws this off. It . . . means that the CAP can be found anywhere outside a village or a hamlet, and they [VC] don't like this when they're trying to come in for rice, or money, or recruits, or just plain coordination." Moreover, the mobile CAPs did not have to tie down a substantial portion of their limited manpower to the job of defending a compound. Instead they became stalkers, roaming daily and nightly throughout an area of operations, insinuating themselves into many villages, frequently clashing with the equally mobile VC.

By the middle of 1969, almost 90 percent of the CAPs were mobile. As Metzger put it: "CAP Marines literally went to the bush for their entire tours." At first, this could be quite a daunting challenge, especially for the newer men, who felt comforted by the false security of a compound. For many of the Marines—and all Americans in Vietnam, come to think of it—a compound, firebase, or perimeter meant security. This was actually one of the major problems with the war effort—namely, that not enough Americans were in touch with the people, or engaged in the job of providing them real security. Base camps were designed to offer safety to the Americans and no one else. Leaving that dubious security, plunging into the jungles, paddies, and villages among the people, seemed to augur great danger, if not guaranteed death. So the idea of permanently plunging into the world outside the wire was frightening indeed, a counterintuitive nightmare that portended a sort of bogeyman-inspired doom.

Perhaps this trepidation also stemmed from the natural human impulse to have a home, even in the most dangerous of situations. "I saw the mobile CAPs as extremely scary," Gene Ferguson recalled. "I didn't have the safety to run back to." He liked the idea of having a barbed-wire compound with mortars, machine guns, and bunkers around him. "In the mobile CAP they could just slaughter us like flies. I was so scared. When the weather got bad, we didn't get resupplied. There were times when we would go three days without any food." Like most newcomers, Barry Goodson was taken aback when he first joined his CAP and realized it was mobile. "You mean you don't have a compound to hide in case of an attack?" he asked his new friends. They assured him that they lived in the jungle full-time, moving to different ambush positions every night. A deep apprehension settled over Goodson and he wondered what he had gotten himself into. "Here I was with only five other men [Marines]. The *jungle* was our home!"

Goodson, like most of the other Marines, got used to the new ways, and came to embrace them. The mobile CAPs were indeed a potent weapon. In practice, they acted as stealthy hunter-killer teams, putting the VC on the defensive, forcing them to react to the Marines and PFs rather than the other way around. For the sake of sheer survival, they learned to blend in well with their surroundings. They were masters at patrolling because that was all they did.

They suffered fewer casualties than the stationary teams, and they inflicted more damage on the VC. "It was darned tough on the CAP Marines," Metzger said, "but it saved many lives and greatly enhanced our security capability." In 1969, at the cost of 117 Americans killed and 851 wounded, they killed 1,952 VC and NVA (by actual body count), while capturing another 391. They conducted about twelve thousand patrols or ambushes per month, most at night. They initiated two-thirds of their firefights (compared with a 10 percent rate in the line companies). In the first few months of 1970 alone they killed 288 enemy soldiers and captured 87. All of these numbers were improvements from the 1965 to 1968 phase of the program, when most of the CAPs were stationary.

The mobile CAPs were consummate, agile light infantry. They immersed themselves in the culture and the war itself. They arguably had more at stake than any other Americans in Vietnam because they were so close to the land and the people. Their lives were always at risk. "Ambushes, ambushes, ambushes; it seems like that's all we did in the CAPs I was in," Private First Class Warren Carmon recalled. "Our group ran them seven nights a week. My God, even the [line company] grunts got a chance to go to the rear for some rest." But not the CAP grunts. "Some of our ambushes were very successful. Like one night an NVA patrol, fourteen soldiers, entered our killing zone. It was perfect. We opened up on them, dropping eleven instantly. The other three tried to run but never made it. We moved around so much I can never remember the names of most of the villages. The people, at least to your face, were very friendly. They encouraged us to stay around their homes to protect them. We got along great with the kids."

The mobile CAPs did have one major downside, though. They enhanced tactical proficiency and security at the expense of civic action. With the teams on the move so much, they did not have as much time to devote to forging relationships with the villagers. They could not dig as many wells, share as many meals, conduct quite as many MEDCAPs, or share in village life to the extent they did before. For these reasons, Lieutenant Colonel Corson, the spiritual father of the program, actually disagreed with the change to mobile CAPs that happened after he rotated home in 1967.

In Corson's opinion, the vulnerability of the compounds should not have been a problem if the CAPs were doing their jobs correctly, winning the support of the people and thus finding out the enemy's every move from them. Corson believed that the CAPs had to maintain a visible presence in one spot, as an alternative to the VC. He believed that each CAP should, in the words of one scholar, "be a center of pacification; a place to which hamlet officials, elders and peasants could turn." Mobile CAPs could not do that quite as well as stationary CAPs. Overall, it is probably fair to say that the mobile CAPs were better at the mission of destroying the enemy and providing security (for both Marines and civilians) but at the expense of everyday grassroots influence within the villages.[12]

In 1970, not long after the program reached a zenith of 114 platoons that were covering about 15 percent of the I Corps population, the United States began its withdrawal from Vietnam in earnest. As this happened, Lieutenant General Ngo Quang Truong, the most highly respected ARVN commander of the war, pleaded with one Marine general: "I don't care what you do, but please don't take the CAPs." Nonetheless, the CAPs were disbanded and scaled back in the same proportion to other American forces in Vietnam. In 1971, the program came to an official end.

The CAPs were the most innovative aspect of the American pacification effort in Vietnam. They demonstrated the adaptable versatility of well-trained infantrymen, and the persistent tendency of modern warfare to devolve into a contest of will at the basic levels of home, hearth, and local economics.

How successful were the CAPs? The answer is mixed. The Americans lost the war in Vietnam, so the combined action approach could only have been so successful. Even at the peak of the program, only 2,220 Marines and corpsmen were a part of it, and, of course, some of them were administrative people who spent most of their time at a base. That number of 2,220 represented less than 3 percent of the Corps' strength in country. At any given time, no more than 10 to 15 percent of the population in I Corps was affected, in any way, by a CAP. And I Corps was just one part of South Vietnam, so the reach of the CAPs was not very extensive.

What's more, the presence of a CAP did not exactly guarantee success. Some never made any inroads with their PFs or the locals. Their relationships were chilly or downright hostile. James Trullinger, a scholar with many years of experience in Vietnam, spent much of that time in My Thuy Phuong, a village that hosted a CAP. Trullinger developed close relationships with people on all sides of the war, including members of the VC. Among the people he interviewed, he found that none of them had any close ties with or partiality to the CAP Marines. Outside of a tiny few government supporters, most of the people supported the VC, if not openly then surreptitiously. They thought of the guerrillas as courageous local boys who were standing up to the Americans and a repressive Saigon government. "The people were very happy after they saw how brave the Liberation Front guerrillas could be," one villager said. "Many of us thought to ourselves, secretly, that we must support the Liberation Front."

The other major issue was that, even when the people accepted a CAP and befriended the Americans, they seldom had any love for the South Vietnamese government. Often enough they hated and feared the VC, but they were put off by the poor behavior of ARVN soldiers, as well as the tendency of government officials to be corrupt and exploitive. So, often, the Americans earned their loyalty but not the Saigon regime, and that did not bode well because the Americans could not stay forever.

A few of the CAP Marines, like Edward Palm, believed that the program was a failure. "Combined action was merely one more untenable article of faith. The truth, I suspect, is that where it seemed to work, combined action wasn't really needed, and where it was, combined action could never really work." In his opinion, the VC infrastructure "was too deeply entrenched, literally as well as figuratively in some places. They had had more than 20 years to win hearts and minds before we blundered onto the scene. We were

naive to think 13 Marines and a Navy corpsman could make much difference in such a setting. The cultural gulf was just unbridgeable out in the
countryside."

Most of the other Marines disagreed. General Walt asserted that "of all
our innovations in Vietnam none was as successful, as lasting in effect, or as
useful for the future as the Combined Action Program." Lieutenant Colonel
Corson saw the CAP as a dramatic success and believed that, if it had been
expanded by fifteen thousand Marines, the VC would no longer have been
able to operate. "It would have taken two years [to eliminate the VC]. There
was no doubt in my mind about it." General Westmoreland would never have
approved such an expansion of the program. He admitted that the CAPs experienced some success at the local level, but as commander in Vietnam he
did not believe he had enough troops to sprinkle throughout the country in
such fashion. "I simply had not enough numbers to put a squad of Americans
in every village and hamlet; that would have been fragmenting resources and
exposing them to defeat in detail." One study estimated that in order to secure all of the unoccupied hamlets in similar fashion to the CAPs, over 22,000
PFs and 167,000 American troops would be required at the cost of $1.8 billion
per year. Not even the most ardent pro-CAP devotee would have argued for
such an expansion. Everyone acknowledged that the big units were needed to
fight major NVA and VC formations. Advocates like Corson and Krulak simply asserted that dealing with the big enemy units was not enough—in order
to win the war, the countryside also had to be secured through pacification
and the CAPs were, in their view, the best way to do that.

David Sherman noticed that his unit's village got stronger as time passed.
The people had more control over their lives and they grew more prosperous.
He was amazed that his makeshift squad and the PFs performed as well as
they did. "Either group could have been xenophobic about the situation. We
could have been more isolated than we were; they could have resisted all
change. Instead, we both managed to get our acts together. We found ways
to cooperate despite the cultural clash. It was, I think, an enriching experience for all of us." Tom Harvey, a platoon leader, held no illusions that
the CAPs had inflicted any sort of lasting defeat on the VC, but he still viewed
the program as quite effective for its size. "I think the concept of the CAP was
one of the best to come out of the U.S. effort in Vietnam, and one of the few

that wasn't counterproductive. I think we accomplished a lot with a relatively small cost to the U.S. taxpayer. We managed to keep the VC out of all the hamlets in Phu Thu District . . . with a force of probably no more than 75 Marines. Considering the number of kills, POW's, enemy weapons captured, chieu hois [ralliers], and intelligence, coupled with the relatively low cost to operate, I do not see how there could have been anything more efficient going for us."

Walt's III Marine Amphibious Force and General Krulak's Fleet Marine Force, Pacific, produced all sorts of graphs, charts, and statistics to measure this kind of success in the platoons. Much of this amounted to bureaucratic self-justification. It also demonstrated the overreliance on questionable statistics that warped the perspectives of American leaders, military and political, during Vietnam. After all, how could one really measure the level of loyalty and security among the people in a hamlet? Only those on the ground, round the clock, could offer any valid opinion, and even then the situation could change by the day. For this and many other reasons the high-level statistics are all questionable to the point of uselessness. The following facts are not, though. The combined action platoons reduced desertion rates among the PFs. In villages with CAPs, local leaders usually felt secure enough to sleep in their homes, a relative rarity among non-VC chiefs in non-CAP villages. Neither the VC nor the NVA ever displaced a CAP from a village. In 1999, Jim Donovan interviewed a former NVA division commander and asked him what he thought about the effectiveness of the CAPs. "In his opinion the hamlets where the Marines lived were of little help to his troops when they needed food, men or intelligence."

Over the course of nearly five years in existence, the CAPs killed 5,584 enemy soldiers and captured another 1,652. They also captured 2,347 weapons, a high ratio of weapons to enemy KIAs that lent credence to the body count numbers. They were 900 percent more likely than their colleagues in the big units to capture prisoners. They also sustained far fewer casualties from mines and booby traps. In terms of killing and capturing the enemy, they were per capita more potent and efficient than the line companies.

The effectiveness goes beyond these mere barometers, though. Many of the CAP Marines came to feel very strongly about their villages. They felt a commitment to protect the people, secure what they thought of as their freedom, and fight alongside their PF brothers. What other explanation could there be for the high extension rates among the CAP Marines? At the village level, the war made sense to them. Those who extended were committed to see the war through to a successful conclusion.

The CAPs conducted hundreds of thousands of patrols and ambushes. They spread immeasurable amounts of good feelings among tens of thousands of people. They built wells, schools, and homes. They helped farmers maximize their harvests. They taught fishermen to catch more fish. They dispensed medical care to the sick, wounded, and healthy alike. They shielded thousands from VC harassment, tax collectors, and recruiters. Their everyday bravery communicated something honorable about American culture to the Vietnamese—namely, that some young men could, and would, give everything of themselves for the betterment of others. By no means were they perfect, but their behavior was generally correct. Because of this, they established ties of friendship that never quite died away in the years since the war. "There is a residual of goodwill among the Vietnamese who were in contact with them," Corson claimed decades after the war. "It's there, because we have people that have gone to areas where they served as CAP Marines; and they found that the residual of goodwill was still there." Their other legacy is the Military Transition Teams (MITT) employed so effectively by both the Army and the Marines in Iraq in the twenty-first century. Like the CAPs, these teams embedded with their Iraqi Army counterparts, trained them, improved them, and established strong ties with the locals.[13]

More than any other modern combatants, the CAP grunts in Vietnam experienced the crucial element of human will in war. By necessity, they morphed into rural warriors. In retrospect, the CAPs were the least glamorous but probably the most effective aspect of the ill-fated American war effort in Vietnam.

CHAPTER 7

Attrition and the Tears of Autumn: Dak To, November 1967

"A Lousy Place to Fight a War"

The grunts called it "the Land with No Sun." This was Kontum province and it was the most challenging terrain in South Vietnam. Also known as the Central Highlands, the area around the valley village of Dak To and a nearby Special Forces camp of the same name teemed with thick jungles, foliage-covered mountains, and muddy valleys. "The mountainous regions are rugged and rise to heights of 2,400 feet," a 4th Infantry Division report, prepared in early 1968, stated. "They are normally covered with . . . thick jungle. The plateau area is intermittently covered with forests of 100–150 foot trees, grass and thick bamboo rising some 50–60 feet in the air. Except for the valley areas, 90% of the higher elevations are covered with dense close-canopy rain forests." Another soldier wrote of it as a "merciless land of steep limestone ridges . . . covered with double- and sometimes triple-canopy jungle. This nightmare vegetation reaches up to blot out the sun with teak and mahogany that tower 100 feet or more above the rot of the jungle floor. The draws between the ridges are dreary, tangled places of perpetual twilight, where a thousand growing things struggle to the death for light and air. The jungle is laced with vines and thorns, and in it live diverse snakes, a million leeches and about half the mosquitoes in the world." To the infantry soldiers, Dak To meant steamy, bone-weary humps, confining jungles, bamboo fields, wild streams, insects, exhaustion, and an eerie sense that they were treading on the enemy's turf.

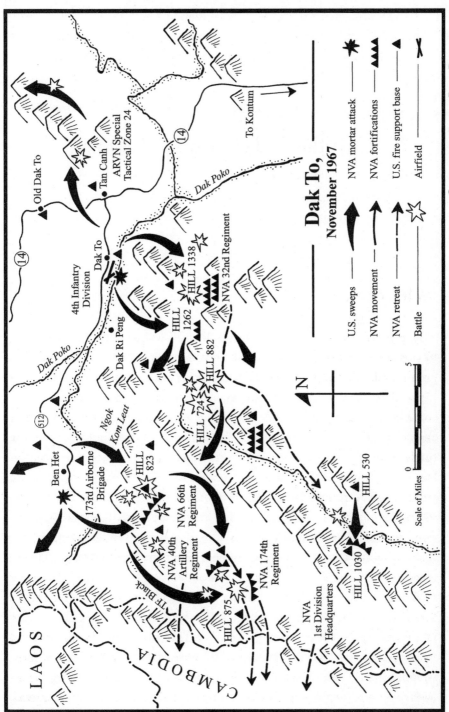

Dak To,
November 1967

U.S. sweeps ————
NVA movement ————
NVA retreat — — —
Battle ☆

NVA mortar attack ✵
NVA fortifications ◤◤◤
U.S. fire support base ◀
Airfield ✕

COPYRIGHT © 2010 RICK BRITTON

To Kontum

Old Dak To

Tan Canh
ARVN Special
Tactical Zone 24

Dak Poko

4th Infantry
Division

Dak To

HILL 1338
HILL 1262
NVA 32nd Regiment
HILL 882
HILL 724

Dak Ri Peng

Dak Poko

Ngok
Kom Leat

HILL
823

HILL 530

173rd Airborne
Brigade

Ben Het

NVA 66th
Regiment

NVA 40th
Artillery
Regiment

HILL 1030

NVA 174th
Regiment

HILL 875

NVA
1st Division
Headquarters

LAOS

CAMBODIA

N

Scale of Miles
0   5

In fact, just several miles away, in Laos and Cambodia, the North Vietnamese Army (NVA) maintained an extensive network of infiltration routes and base camps generally known as the Ho Chi Minh Trail. Shielded by the dense jungles, the North's courageous soldiers sallied forth from these routes into South Vietnam, often to fight as guerrilla warriors. In the fall of 1967, several regiments of these NVA regulars massed around Dak To, heavily fortifying many of the key hill masses. Their goal was to draw the Americans into a costly struggle for those hills. They hoped that the heavy jungle canopy, the dearth of roads, and the dizzying array of peaks would negate the firepower and mobility of American aircraft, artillery, and vehicles. The communists were planning a major offensive for early 1968 and they wanted to draw the Americans into such remote areas, away from population centers. If the Americans did not take the bait, then the NVA formations would push east, make common cause with Viet Cong (VC) insurgents, whose hidden supply caches would support the NVA, and fight a hit-and-run war near the country's population centers.

The Central Highlands, and specifically Dak To, presented General William Westmoreland, the American commander in Vietnam, with a vexing problem. He could not sit back and let the NVA move unmolested from their base camps into the rice-producing regions and cities of South Vietnam. Nor could he go after them in the exact manner he wished. He yearned to attack and destroy the Ho Chi Minh Trail sanctuaries. But President Lyndon Johnson feared the international political ramifications of invading such ostensibly "neutral" countries as Laos and Cambodia. That the North Vietnamese and their allies in the VC had already done so hardly mattered in the forum of international opinion, which viewed any American cross-border operations as aggression. For fear of this sort of backlash, and the possibility that hitting the communists in Cambodia and Laos would provoke a larger world war with China and the Soviet Union, the Americans, as of 1967, had straitjacketed themselves into fighting the ground war primarily on South Vietnamese soil. For Westmoreland, this meant he had to react to enemy incursions of South Vietnam, rather than take the fight to the communist bases or even North Vietnam itself. His avowed strategy for victory was, of course, attrition—fight the enemy's big units and savage them with overwhelming firepower until the communists could no longer continue the war.

Like most American commanders from World War II onward, Westy believed that aggressive attacks, the use of maximum firepower, and the relentless quest to annihilate the enemy's forces in battle all led to strategic victory. By and large, this had worked in the Second World War and it had produced some results in Korea, too. So, in Vietnam, Westy liked the idea of fighting such decisive engagements in the out-of-the-way Central Highlands, where he could employ the full range of his firepower without fear of inflicting casualties on noncombatants. This, he believed, was the place to pile up the large body counts he so badly needed for his strategy to work. If he could not go after the communist bases themselves, he could essentially head the enemy off at the pass—taking on NVA units when they crossed the border, around the hills of Dak To, before they could push east, get into the towns and cities of South Vietnam, and cause even more serious problems. Better, he thought, to fight them in the remote areas first.

He understood that the suffocating jungles and peaks of the border areas negated some of the mobility he so badly needed to carry out his search-and-destroy concept. But he felt that helicopters more than made up for whatever he might lose in ground mobility for his foot soldiers and vehicles. "I believe when the enemy comes forth from Cambodia or Laos with his principal formations looking for a fight we must go out and fight him," Westy once told one of his superiors. "We must strike him as soon as he is within reach, and before he can gain a victory or tyrannize the local population."

All of these ideas made some sense, but they also led to serious problems that Westy either downplayed or did not appreciate. If the United States was unwilling to invade Cambodia, Laos, or, for that matter, North Vietnam, then there was almost no way that the Americans could control the borderlands. The NVA knew the ground quite well, far better than the Americans. The communists could always retreat to their sanctuaries, where they could devise new plans, reinforce their combat units, and come back to South Vietnam whenever they chose. Ominously for Westy's attrition strategy, this also meant they could control the rate of their losses.

Westmoreland believed that by fighting the enemy in the border areas, he could "preempt his [the enemy's] plans and force him to fight before he is fully organized and before he can do his damage." This was highly questionable. One could actually argue that the NVA sought battle in exactly these spots and prepared accordingly. The thick terrain offered the perfect cover to conceal their movement. The "Land with No Sun" comprised the ideal place to construct well-camouflaged tunnels, bunkers, and spider holes that were often impervious to American bombs and shells. From here they would provoke American commanders, who they knew were so eager to find NVA units and pile up large body counts that they would do battle even when it was not necessarily to their advantage. As of November 1967, the NVA had fortified many of the hills around Dak To in just this fashion. Fighting there was more likely to play right into the enemy's plans rather than disrupt or preempt them. Not surprisingly, Westmoreland's in-house antagonist, Marine Lieutenant General Victor Krulak, opposed the commander's notion of fighting big battles in the Central Highlands. "Those battles were fought too often on the enemy's terms," he later wrote, "where close-quarters combat in the fog-shrouded hills, forests, and vine-thick jungles, with which he was familiar, stretched our logistic system and diminished the effectiveness of U.S. supporting arms, particularly air." Those indeed were the problems and, in the fall of 1967, they were about to coalesce in monumental fighting amid the unhappy hills around Dak To.[1]

The NVA blueprint at Dak To was similar to the Japanese inland defense at Peleliu. Both the NVA and the Japanese found ways to negate American firepower, mainly by digging deeply into favorable terrain and relying upon the willingness of their soldiers to fight to the death. They also both made use of the American tendency to overestimate the effectiveness of their firepower and engage in tactical assaults against heavily defended objectives of dubious strategic worth. They knew that, at times, the Americans squandered the incredible valor of their own combat troops for no ultimate strategic purpose (the Umurbrogol at Peleliu being a prime example).

In fact, even before the fall of 1967, the Americans had already fought the NVA in several sizable battles around Dak To. The most notorious clash took place on June 22–23, 1967, when the NVA succeeded in cutting off and destroying Alpha Company, 2nd Battalion, 503rd Parachute Infantry Regiment, 173rd Airborne Brigade, on a jungle hill in what the paratroopers called the Battle of the Slopes. Of the original 137 men in Alpha Company, 76 were killed and 23 were wounded. One post-battle examination revealed that 43 of the dead paratroopers had suffered fatal, close-in head wounds, indicating that the NVA had killed them execution style, probably as they lay wounded. Most of the Dak To fights were not this grim, but a clear pattern was set. The

NVA sought to draw the Americans into close-quarters battles, in the roughest terrain, where air and fire support were negated. Often this meant luring the Americans into costly assaults on heavily defended bunker networks. The enemy also tried to cut off and annihilate platoon- and company-sized units. With the exception of the the Battle of the Slopes, they usually failed. The Americans generally inflicted heavy losses on the NVA, but they were never able to win the decisive victory of annihilation they so badly wanted. Instead, combat would taper off into skirmishes as the surviving communists escaped across the border to their sanctuaries.

In October, after several months of uneasy calm around Dak To, American intelligence detected the new NVA buildup. Photo reconnaissance flights revealed enemy movement and fresh bunkers. Special airborne sensors that the Americans called "people sniffers" were flown over the jungles. They detected, by the sound of foot and vehicle movement as well as the odor of human urine and feces, the presence of new enemy regiments. The best information came from small, specially trained teams of soldiers who conducted long-range reconnaissance patrols (LRRPs) deep in enemy country. Amid constant danger, they spent their silent days skulking around the jungle, observing everything the enemy did. Patrols that made use of local Montagnard tribesmen were especially effective since the Montagnards knew the terrain and the enemy patterns so well. "Putting all that together, we could develop a pretty good pattern of where the enemy was and what he was doing," Major General William Peers, commander of the 4th Division, recalled.

In late October, based on this information, Peers moved his 1st Brigade to Dak To. Immediately the soldiers of this brigade detected even more NVA movement along the valleys around Dak To. On November 2, Sergeant Vu Hong, a member of an NVA artillery reconnaissance unit, turned himself in to an ARVN outpost. While operating as part of a scouting team that was plotting ranges and target information for mortar and rocket fire, he had apparently decided to defect. His knowledge of NVA plans was extensive (some thought suspiciously so for an NCO). Hong claimed that, in addition to his own 40th Artillery Regiment, four NVA infantry regiments—the 24th, the 32nd, the 66th, and the 174th—were positioning themselves for a major attack on Dak To, though many 4th Division senior officers were a bit leery of Hong, and suspected that he might be a plant, his information squared with what the Americans already believed. "All of our intelligence indicated that what he said was correct," General Peers stated. The general immediately arranged for the 173rd Airborne Brigade to reinforce his own 1st Brigade. Together, the two units were to push west, depriving the NVA of the key hills and ridges that overlooked Dak To before the four enemy regiments could take them. Within a few days, the 1st Brigade soldiers and paratroopers were involved in bloody fights with the NVA for Hills 1338 and 823, thus beginning the Battle of Dak To.

Did the NVA deliberately plant Vu Hong? Many years later, there is still no definite answer to this question. Hong himself has disappeared into the mists of time. Communist sources are mum on the subject (and on most other aspects of Dak To). Peers and his staff seemed to think that Hong was legitimate, as did their ARVN counterparts. The information he dispensed was certainly accurate, but perhaps that was the point. He had nothing necessarily new to say. Everything he told the Americans simply confirmed what they already thought, and reinforced their desire—inculcated in them by Westy's attrition strategy—to find the NVA regiments and fight them at Dak To. NVA commanders had so heavily fortified the hills around Dak To that it is hard to escape the conclusion that their goal was to lure the Americans into a major fight there. "The enemy continued . . . to choose the time and place in which decisive engagements would be fought," Brigadier General Leo "Hank" Schweiter, commander of the 173rd, admitted. "Only when and where the tactical situation, terrain, battlefield preparation and relative strengths of opposing forces favored enemy action were significant contacts initiated." In other words, at Dak To, the NVA commanders only fought where and when they wished to do so, leading to the conclusion that Hong might well have been a plant. As one grunt said, the area was "a lousy place to fight a war." Like it or not, though, they were in for an intimate showdown with their mortal enemies in this "lousy place."[2]

Ivy Leaves and Blood: Hill 724

The 4th Infantry Division had a proud history. Nicknamed the "Ivy Division" because of the way the number four looked in Roman numerals (IV), the unit had compiled a distinguished record in the Argonne Forest during World War I. Soldiers from the division had once stormed ashore at Utah Beach, liberated

Paris, and struggled through the hell that was the Hurtgen Forest. By the fall of 1967, the division had been fighting in various locales throughout South Vietnam for over a year. Most of the 4th Division grunts were draftees serving a two-year hitch in the Army. This was certainly true for one of the division's key infantry units, the 3rd Battalion, 8th Infantry, whose soldiers liked to call themselves the "Ivy Dragoons." The vast majority of the riflemen were between the ages of nineteen and twenty-one. Following their basic training, most had received subsequent light infantry training at the Army's Advanced Infantry Training Center, commonly known as Tigerland, at Fort Polk, Louisiana. These grunts came from all regions of the country. Whereas ground combat units in World War II had been all white, reflecting the racist segregation policies so prevalent in America at that time, in Vietnam infantry units were desegregated, with all races represented. This had been the case since the Korean War era, when President Harry Truman had signed an executive order mandating an end to racial segregation in the armed forces.

On the evening of November 8, two such companies of grunts, a couple hundred men, wearily settled into a knoll-side perimeter, not far away from Hill 724, their eventual objective. These troops from A and D Companies had been humping around this area for several days, engaging in periodic battles with the NVA. Most were carrying fifty to seventy pounds of equipment distributed among their metal rucksacks, their packs, and their web gear. They had already spent the better part of this day fighting hard to ward off enemy attacks before the shooting finally died down and they were able to cobble together defensive positions by hunkering down inside old NVA bunkers. These fighting positions were just over five feet deep and were reinforced with logs and sandbags. Both of the rifle companies were depleted enough by the fighting that they had trouble covering the whole perimeter. Forward air controllers arranged to cover the sparsely manned southern portion of the perimeter with their ordnance in case the enemy attacked there.

At 2000, to no one's surprise, the NVA attacked in force. "Supported by B40 rocket fire and mortar fire from the small hills to the west and northwest . . . the ground attack came suddenly from the south and east," a unit after action report stated. All at once, the night came to life with deafening fire and the screams of soldiers. Tracer rounds stabbed through the darkness. Mortar shells whooshed in and exploded. NVA soldiers were seemingly all over the place, running around and toward the perimeter. A couple of them were carrying flamethrowers. Before they could get close enough to roast the American bunkers, they were cut down by machine guns.

In one of A Company's bunkers, Specialist Fourth Class (Spec-4) Bill Vigil, a twenty-year-old draftee from Fresno, California, was standing alongside three other men, picking out targets and firing his M16 on full rock 'n' roll. He shot so much that he melted the barrels of several rifles. Still the enemy kept coming. "They were jumping around from tree to tree and you start popping 'em and getting in the hole," he said. "We were about eye level to their feet." Some of the enemy soldiers were only a few feet away. Somewhere to the right, he saw their fire shear off the head of an M60 machine gunner. NVA soldiers were throwing grenades into nearby bunkers. When the grenades exploded—usually with a seemingly innocuous pop—the NVA troopers tried to jump into the bunkers to kill the Americans at close range.

Vigil had been in country for about three months and he had seen his share of firefights. This one, he knew, would be a fight to the finish. The NVA meant to kill every last one of the Americans in that perimeter. To save ammunition, he and the others began firing single semiautomatic shots at the swarming enemy soldiers. They could only see what was in their immediate field of vision. They vaguely sensed that the fighting was raging all around the perimeter, but, as is so often the case with grunt-level fighting, they were only concerned with the struggle for their bunker and those around them.

Although he had not volunteered for the Army or Vietnam, Vigil was the product of much military tradition. His father had served in World War II, surviving serious wounds. His uncle had fought in Korea. One of his ancestors had been a Spanish conquistador. Standing in that miserable bunker, he was full of fear. He was angry, too. "You cry and laugh and all the senses humans have are just . . . running up and down your body." Adrenaline surged through his bloodstream. His stomach was tight and queasy with fear. But, like most of the men around him, he resolved to fight to the end. "We're not gonna say I give up. That's not in our deal. I never thought about me just laying down there and dropping my weapon and hanging my head and saying go ahead and kill me. If they're gonna take me, they're gonna lose a lot of people."

Not everyone was so determined, though. Inevitably, even in the best units, some soldiers will find close combat so traumatic that they will seize up with fear and quit, even if it costs them their lives. On the dirt floor of Vigil's bunker, a soldier whom he only knew by the nickname "Speedy" was lying down, curled up in a ball, crying uncontrollably. "They're gonna kill us, Vidge!" he screamed. "We're gonna die! What are we gonna do?"

Vigil glanced away from the bunker aperture for a second and hollered: "If you don't wipe your face and continue to load magazines, we're definitely gonna die! So load them goddamn magazines and let's keep going. I'm not asking you to put your head up here. I'm asking you to load the magazines."

This was a classic case of the merciless nature of infantry combat. Vigil's bunker, even with four resolute men fighting desperately, was still only as strong as its weakest man. In the end, through no fault of their own, their lives could have depended on whether Speedy would quit or fight.

Not far away from Vigil, Spec-4 Cecil Millspaugh was leaning on the trigger of his M60 machine gun. The twenty-pound gun—affectionately nicknamed "the Pig" by soldiers because it could eat up so much ammunition—spat out 7.62-millimeter rounds at a rate of over five hundred per minute. Millspaugh spotted a group of enemy nearing an adjacent bunker. He turned his gun on them and fired several bursts. All at once, he rose from his hole and rushed the NVA, firing all the way. Needless to say, the M60 was not designed to be employed in this fashion as an assault weapon. Like any machine gun, it was heavy and unwieldy, plus it went through ammo so fast that it generally needed to be fed belts by an assistant gunner in a fixed position. This hardly mattered to the adrenaline-crazed Millspaugh. He slaughtered the NVA soldiers at nearly backslapping range. The heavy bullets shredded them, spurting their blood in every direction. Several of them scattered or went down. Millspaugh jumped into the bunker they had assaulted and continued firing at other attackers, preserving that part of the perimeter.

At one point, the NVA took over the bunker next to Spec-4 Vigil's, about eight feet away, initiating his own personal duel to the death with a North Vietnamese soldier. Back and forth they went, firing their rifles, throwing grenades. For these Vietnamese and American men, who might well have been friends in another time or circumstance, the entire war boiled down to this personal struggle for survival, a struggle that meant literally everything to them but little in the big-picture context of the Vietnam War. Such is the ruthless calculus of modern combat. "We were playing peekaboo until I got him or he stopped or a frag [grenade] got him," Vigil recalled. "Something happened, but he stopped. He was laying there dead. There was two of 'em laying there on top of the GIs."

In another dugout, Private First Class Clinton Bacon saw a B40 rocket score a direct hit on an adjacent bunker. The logs and sandbags collapsed onto the men inside, wounding and partially burying them. Bacon surged outside and, while machine-gun and rifle bullets snapped around him, he crawled to the wrecked bunker and dug out the stricken men. "He began removing them, insuring that they received medical treatment," a citation later related. After that, he stacked some of the unscathed sandbags and resumed shooting back at the enemy.

According to one account, soldiers from Delta Company were "in close hand-to-hand combat" with the NVA. It is well to consider once again what this really meant. They were struggling at intimate, body-groping distance with other men, using any weapon at their disposal to kill them—bayonets, can openers, rifles, ammo boxes, helmets, anything. Death came in ugly fashion, with crushed skulls, severed larynxes, punctured abdomens or throats, gouged eyes, or from point-blank gunshot wounds. Warm, sticky blood bathed the victor and vanquished alike. The trauma was beyond description.

Because the fighting was going on at such close quarters, it was difficult for the Americans to employ artillery. This was no accident. The enemy liked to fight at this close range precisely because it could negate American firepower. Alpha and Delta Companies were forced to call down 105-millimeter artillery fire within their own perimeter. As long as the Americans remained in the bunkers, and the NVA continued to move about in the open, the shell bursts were likely to do more damage to the enemy than the GIs. Explosions mushroomed and flashed in seemingly random patterns, sending hot deadly fragments in every direction. In some cases, the fragments sliced into attacking enemy soldiers, killing a few of them, but wounding many more.

Air support only added to the carnage. "As the enemy crawled up the slope from the south, napalm was dropped in continuous strikes to within 25 meters of the perimeter," an after action report said. Guided by forward air controllers, Air Force F-4 Phantoms and other close air support planes screamed in and dropped large quantities of the jellied gasoline along every NVA avenue of approach. The ensuing flames consumed the jungle and men alike. "It takes . . . oxygen to make that napalm really work," one soldier said. "So if you're real close to it, you're gasping for air." Like the artillery shells, the napalm was especially deadly to troops on the move, rather than the Americans in their bunkers. In some cases, NVA soldiers simply expired in flames. Most of the time, the flames roasted them or even melted limbs or other body parts. The Americans could hear their bloodcurdling screams.

One napalm canister burst so close to Spec-4 Vigil's bunker that he could smell the acrid, almost sweet odor of the weapon's chemical ingredients (probably its benzene components). When the flames died down, he peered out of his bunker and saw, in the distance, an enemy soldier melted to the wheels of his .51-caliber machine gun. Other enemy soldiers were turned by the napalm into "frosty critters. They looked like charcoal. Some of 'em were even halfway running and then they're charcoaled. They were melted to the trees or wherever they were at."

The pilots were so skilled that they were dropping bombs, by the light of flares, on the edges of the perimeter. Sometimes, the grunts could see the bombs descend, and they generally looked to each man as if they would hit him personally. "I mean, the noise, it's unbelievable," Vigil recalled. "The ground would just jump up maybe two feet, right in front of you. The ground actually lifts so all that sand and dirt and everything is all over you. It just slaps you, like you're standing in a sand blasting machine." Undoubtedly the bombs, exploding as they were so close to the U.S. positions, wounded or even killed some Americans, but they did tremendous damage to the NVA.

At around 0200, the enemy attack tapered off. The NVA used long hooks to drag away their wounded and dead. After a lull, they hit the perimeter several more times, but never with as **much** ferocity as that first push. The next morning the Americans combed the area and counted 232 NVA bodies. Some had been killed by concussion and looked as if they were only sleeping. Others were torn apart by shrapnel or punctured with holes from rifle or machine-gun bullets. Some were little more than globs of dismembered flesh or, as Vigil mentioned, charcoaled remains of human beings. All of them emitted disgusting odors in the tropical heat.

Alpha Company had been decimated. Out of an original complement of more than 130 men, the outfit was down to 47; 21 had been killed. The rest were wounded badly enough to require evacuation. Even the supposedly "unwounded" had scratches, cuts, and bruises that in peacetime circumstances would require medical attention. A day later, Lieutenant Colonel Glen

Belknap, the battalion commander, decided to relieve Alpha Company. Although the perimeter was still under intense mortar and rocket fire, he airlifted his Bravo and Charlie Companies in and arranged for helicopters to remove the remnants of Alpha, including the dead and wounded. "We proceeded to pull the casualties out of the holes and get their bodies to the LZ, along with the surviving wounded," a Charlie Company soldier recalled. "Each chopper would be loaded with, first, the wounded, then the dead, as reinforcements arrived." One sergeant, coming upon the intermingled bodies of several soldiers—black, white, and brown—gazed at them thoughtfully and asked no one in particular: "How is it that men can die together, but find it so difficult to live together?"

The helicopters took the Alpha Company survivors and their fallen buddies to the American base at Dak To. Equipped with an airstrip and many buildings, the base was growing into the main American logistical and staging point for this intensifying struggle. Spec-4 Vigil and the other exhausted survivors from his company gazed at long rows of charcoal-colored body bags lying along the tarmac. Some of the misshapen bags held the remains of his buddies. Others contained dead soldiers from the intense fighting around Hills 1338 and 823. He paced around, staring at them, shaking with grief and anger, trying to comprehend that they were all gone. "I can still see . . . all those body bags. I think it was more to see than the battle itself. I was in a crouched position, walking around, just shaking." His nerves were shot. It took him several days to even resume eating again.[3]

In the meantime, Lieutenant Colonel Belknap resumed the push for Hill 724, a mass of high ground that was covered with a solid sheet of bamboo and tropical foliage. At sunrise on November 11, Bravo remained in the original perimeter to maintain a secure landing zone (LZ). Charlie and Delta set out for the hill, which was only about five hundred meters away. They made it, cut out a makeshift LZ, and sent word for Bravo to join them. This was the way the Americans generally operated in the Central Highlands. Commanders wisely sought to control the high ground. When they succeeded in doing so, they set up perimeters, like little American enclaves splayed into the heart of enemy country.

Later that day, just as Bravo Company was approaching the perimeter on Hill 724, the NVA attacked. "B40s were fired en masse, striking trees and showering positions with fragments," an officer later wrote. "Enemy mortar positions had been carefully prepared to fire from at least three directions. They continued to fire even under repeated air attack and counter battery." Some of the NVA soldiers had tied themselves into the trees, from which they could rain down withering accurate rifle fire upon the Ivy Dragoons. Others were pushing up the hill, assaulting, as usual, at close quarters. The grunts dropped their heavy rucksacks, fanned out into bomb craters, behind logs, in fighting holes or any other cover they could find and returned fire. From the vantage point of their perches in the trees, NVA snipers could clearly see some of the Americans, even if they were crouching behind trees or logs. This sniper fire was frighteningly accurate, ripping through the heads of several unsuspecting grunts. The Americans learned to spray the trees with automatic fire even if they did not see anything to shoot at.

Charlie and Delta Companies had already carved some semblance of a perimeter with holes and fields of fire from which to fight the NVA attackers. But the Bravo soldiers quickly realized that the NVA had gotten between them and their comrades in the makeshift perimeter. This put them in the desperate circumstance of taking fire, at close range, from all sides. With a flurry of AK-47 fire, the NVA overran several Bravo soldiers who were manning observation posts (OPs) to protect the company's flanks. The OP soldiers were in a hopeless position but they fought back with everything they had, especially Privates First Class Nathaniel Thompson and William Muir, who both were mortally wounded but remained in place, pouring out fire until the end. The NVA wiped out the OPs.

Several dozen meters from the OPs, Spec-4 Bob Walkowiak, one of the company commander's radio telephone operators (RTO), heard the shooting but did not know what was going on. He was helping the company medic attend to a badly wounded soldier. As the deafening sounds of shooting, explosions, and hollering raged around them, they came to the sad realization that the man was beyond hope. The medic moved on and Walkowiak tried to talk to the dying soldier and comfort him. "As I apologized for our inability to save him, the fight for his life ended. Hopefully, someday I'll know if he forgave us for failing." As the soldier expired, Walkowiak rolled over and looked at the clear blue sky above. The air was so thick with bullets and shrapnel that it was "like having stars or streaks in your eyes."

Medics were braving the worst of the fire, scurrying all over, treating and retrieving wounded men. They dealt with the horrible consequences of combat—the torn flesh, the jagged holes, the broken bones, the gushing blood, the internal bleeding, the crying and screaming of grievously wounded soldiers. With bullets zinging around and explosions cooking off, the medics could only hope to administer some first aid—keep the airways open, apply pressure bandages, stop the bleeding, give morphine shots to those who needed them—and hope for the best. One medic, Spec-4 John Kind, came under enemy attack as he was crouching over a badly wounded man, trying to save him. Kind grabbed the man's rifle and, according to one account, "began placing accurate fire at the advancing enemy." When the enemy attack failed, Kind resumed treating the wounded soldier. Another medic from Charlie Company, Private First Class John Trahan, was so busy that he personally treated eighteen wounded men in the first several minutes of the firefight. When he realized Bravo Company's predicament, he crossed a patch of open ground under intense fire to get to them, even though he himself was wounded, too. At that point, according to one witness, he took the lead in "caring for the wounded and evacuating them to safer positions."

Spec-4 Walkowiak, the RTO, found a bit of cover with two other men behind a small log. He cautiously peered down the incline of the hill at the foliage beyond and saw that the NVA was overrunning one of the platoons. "On the right, one man raised up to fire as he withdrew and was promptly shot dead. On the left a fellow with a pump shotgun retreated up the hill. He stood tall as he walked backwards, firing every few steps. No panic, just grudgingly giving up ground in that hail of bullets. As he raised his weapon to fire, a bullet went through his jaw." Enemy grenades soon followed, showering shrapnel in every direction. Employing M72 Light Antitank Weapon (LAW) rocket fire, machine guns, grenades of their own, and accurate rifle fire, Walkowiak's group managed to slow the NVA into a tense standoff.[4]

At about this time, an enemy B40 rocket exploded among Bravo's command group, killing twenty-eight-year-old Captain John Falcone, the commanding officer, who had been rushing all over the place, positioning his men, hollering orders, and trying to keep his soldiers as calm as possible. The well-liked former Marine and Army Ranger left behind a wife and three children. Lieutenant William Gauff, one of the platoon leaders, somehow made his way through deadly fire to reorganize the survivors around Falcone and assume command of the company, even though he was wounded himself. Another key leader, Staff Sergeant Raymond Ortiz, assumed command of his platoon when his platoon sergeant got killed. Ortiz manned a machine gun and poured belt after belt of 7.62-millimeter ammunition into attacking NVA soldiers. As was so often the case in this kind of desperate combat, the example of a tenacious NCO motivated other surviving members of the platoon to stay and fight. They laced the NVA with heavy fire until they ran out of small-arms ammunition and began hurling grenades at the enemy, finally forcing them away from that spot for good.

The Ivy Dragoon grunts were fighting tenaciously, but without some serious fire support the entire perimeter was in real danger of being overrun by the NVA. Mortarmen set up makeshift gun pits, pointed their tubes straight up, and fired their shells (NVA crews responded in kind). Aided by forward air controllers, jets screamed in to drop 500- and 750-pound bombs as close to the hill as they dared. In some cases, they dropped their ordnance within five hundred meters of the grunts. "They really lit the area up," Walkowiak later wrote. "The pilots put napalm and CBUs [cluster bomb units] directly on both sides of the perimeter of the hill behind my location." In one instance, he and several other grunts popped smoke grenades to mark their position for strafing planes. The fighter pilots swooped in and unleashed a stream of 20-millimeter cannon shells on a woodpile that was sheltering several NVA, leaving behind little besides boiling plumes of smoke, dust, and traumatized flesh. Walkowiak estimated that enemy fire diminished by one-third. Another soldier watched the planes drop cluster bombs full of 3-millimeter-long fléchettes or darts. "They'd come down through the trees and, holy cow, were they effective." Hundreds of tiny darts tore holes into any NVA soldiers who were unfortunate enough to find themselves in the kill zone of the cluster bombs. They died, literally, a death by a thousand cuts. In the recollection of one American, he and several others later found, in just one sector, "over a hundred bodies . . . with just little pinpricks over 'em . . . looking like a very fine shot from shotguns."

The aircraft were hardly impervious to enemy fire. Helicopter crews found it nearly impossible to even approach the hill, much less get close enough to unload supplies and remove the wounded. Enemy rifle, machine-gun, and rocket fire was just too intense. In the recollection of one man, the air was full of so many B40 rockets that "you could almost reach up and catch 'em." In one instance, Sergeant Steve Edmunds, a squad leader in Charlie Company, saw "a chopper, in an attempt to provide us with food, water, and ammunition was blown out of the sky by an enemy rocket, as it attempted to drop our supplies. The chopper exploded into flames and all the ammunition which was on board continued to explode." The enemy even shot down a CIA Air America T28 Trojan propeller plane that was operating as a forward air controller. The grunts were able to rescue the two pilots.

Artillery observers were constantly on their radios calling in fire missions. Several miles away, at various firebases the Americans had constructed, artillerymen hunched over their guns, in the synchronized choreography so necessary for well-trained crewmen to do their jobs properly, loading and firing their pieces. Everything from large-caliber eight-inch and 155-millimeter shells to the more common 105-millimeter howitzer rounds crashed into NVA-held portions of Hill 724 (and on some of the American positions, too). One of the observers, First Lieutenant Larry Skogler, was roaming around with his RTO and reconnaissance sergeant in tow, looking for good places to call down fire. From the lip of one bomb crater, he called in so many fire missions he lost track of how many. The low-key Minnesotan had once attended the state university in Minneapolis, but had gotten drafted in 1965 when he lost his student deferment. Well trained and experienced, he possessed the keen forward observer's feel for terrain, distance, angles, and the capability of the guns. At Hill 724, he had one battery of four guns at his disposal. "The trees were so tall, we couldn't get good artillery coverage on the ground," he said. "The one-oh-five rounds would burst in the trees and scatter all over creation. Ninety percent of it would be stuck in the trees." Even so, it was effective enough to wound and kill many NVA soldiers, if only because of the sheer volume of the American fire.

The more time that passed, the less chance the NVA had to overrun the battalion. Steadily, the Bravo survivors formed a continuous perimeter with hard-pressed Charlie and Delta Companies. With the NVA positions well known, the Americans could unleash a constant barrage of artillery, napalm, and bombs upon the enemy, at a minimum negating their movement. After dark, planes dropped flares to illuminate the area. C47 gunships (nicknamed "Puff the Magic Dragon") circled overhead, spewing forth laser-beam-like streams of Gatling gun rounds on the NVA. Farther away, B-52 heavy bombers unloaded many tons of explosives on suspected NVA strongholds.

During lulls, amid the dancing half shadows, the Americans heard NVA sergeants blowing whistles, organizing their men for new assaults on the perimeter. Over the course of the evening, they attacked several times. Those who could get close enough to the Americans fought it out in confusing, intimate firefights, with muzzle flashes winking like camera flashbulbs. The fighting was ghastly and brutal, sometimes even hand to hand. Because of the massive amount of American firepower that was raking every approach to the hill, the communists could not reinforce any of their attacks well enough to succeed in their goal of annihilating the hard-pressed American battalion. Gradually, the Americans fended them off and, by daylight, the battle evolved into a stalemate, with the NVA besieging the hill and the Americans keeping them at bay with firepower plus the sheer tenacity of their grunts.

The still-burning wreckage of the downed chopper blocked the small LZ that the soldiers had hacked out. Resupply helicopters could only swoop in and hover precariously several feet off the ground, all the while under enemy fire. The crewmen hastily threw out crates of ammunition, food, and water cans. If possible, grunts loaded the most seriously wounded aboard. Then the choppers took off. The whole process usually took less than a minute or two. The helicopters made operations in this remote area possible, but in such a heavy battle, they were a tenuous supply link at best. Control of all the ground around Dak To and the establishment of a secure land-based supply line was an impossibility under the circumstances (and a major reason why officers like Krulak thought it was folly to fight in the Central Highlands).

So the helicopter supply runs were only a temporary solution to this problem. In the words of one after action account, "Further support was impossible until the enemy could be driven far enough from the landing zone to deny observed fire." Captain John Mirus, the commander of Charlie Company, and Captain Terry Bell, Delta's commander, were the two highest-ranking officers left on the hill. Both of them understood that they must expand their perimeter to provide necessary breathing space for the choppers. If they did not, wounded men would die, and supplies of vital ammo and water would dwindle to dangerously low levels. They ordered their men to push the NVA back, away from the hill. "It took another two days of fighting out from the base to secure the area sufficiently to resume operations," a unit citation later stated.

In that time, the NVA gradually disengaged and faded away. The Americans later learned that they had destroyed the better part of two NVA battalions. They counted 300 North Vietnamese bodies. A prisoner told interrogators that his regimental commander had been killed. American losses were grim, too. When Bravo Company first went up Hill 724, it had 165 soldiers. When the fighting finally ended there, 19 of the men were dead and another 68 were wounded badly enough to require evacuation. Losses in the other two companies added several dozen more soldiers to the casualty rolls. As the survivors boarded helicopters and left the torn, pockmarked hill behind, their young filthy faces were tinged with the glazed, dazed, exhausted mask of heavy combat. Their bravery, combined with lethal fire support, had won a tactical victory at Hill 724, albeit one that did nothing to enhance American strategic aims in Vietnam. The Americans left the hard-won hill and resumed their pursuit of the NVA. The Dak To pattern was set.[5]

"I just knew that nobody was gonna get out of there alive": Task Force Black on Veterans Day

Most of them were volunteers. The 173rd Airborne Brigade was comprised of young men who had chosen to become airborne infantrymen. To achieve this status, they had endured rugged training. A few of them were draftees, but the vast majority had elected to join the Army, usually out of patriotism, machismo, or a thirst for adventure. Their nickname was "the Sky Soldiers," but in Vietnam they only made one combat jump. Instead, they functioned as the ultimate light infantrymen, grunts to the core. Their unit was arguably the hardest working in Vietnam. Since arriving in 1965, the 173rd had spent almost all of its time in the field, operating as a veritable fire brigade for Westy. Wherever the action was thickest, wherever the terrain was the most challenging, the Sky Soldiers were there. "We lived like animals," Private Ken Lambertson said. "We didn't go back to the rear. We didn't go back and party and drink and get high and all that." Sky Soldiers like Lambertson lived "in the elements, [with] the snakes, the critters . . . the leeches." In this unit, luxuries were unheard of. Troopers subsisted on C rations, coffee, and Kool-Aid. In a one-year tour of duty, a typical Sky Soldier spent all but a few weeks in the field, humping a sixty-pound rucksack, dealing with the heat, digging fighting holes, going without adequate sleep, facing danger day and night. "Such a rifleman was faced with so many hazards and hardships that the cards were completely stacked against him to ever make it out of that jungle without becoming a casualty to some degree or other," one of the unit's senior NCOs later wrote.

The paratroopers had fought around Dak To during the summer of 1967, so they knew the place was the NVA's backyard and that going back there would mean heavy fighting. Many of them had premonitions that they were getting into something terrible. "When we were told we were going back to Dak To, it got really serious," Sergeant David Watson later said. "We knew it was gonna be serious again." Now, in November, they were back to this foreboding, unhappy place, on the trail of their old NVA adversaries.

Like their comrades in the Ivy Dragoons, they had little trouble finding their quarry. On the windy evening of November 10, a company and a half of paratroopers laagered atop a hill mass close to Cambodia, over twenty miles west of Hill 724. Like the area that surrounded it, the hill was thick with bamboo trees, vines, and the moldy detritus of the jungle. This Sky Soldier group consisted of Charlie Company, 1st Battalion, 503rd Parachute Infantry, along with two platoons of the battalion's Dog Company. Collectively this force of just under two hundred paratroopers was known as Task Force Black. They were under the command of Captain Thomas McElwain, Charlie's CO, a self-made former enlisted man from West Virginia who had been in the Army for ten years but was still two weeks shy of his twenty-seventh birthday. Honest, fair, and professional, McElwain had been in command only a couple months but had already built up a strong loyalty among his men, who affectionately called him "Captain Mac."

He and his grunts knew the NVA were close. They had skirmished with them several times in the last few days. Moreover, as the troopers of Task Force Black had silently patrolled this jungle, they had found blood trails, empty bunkers, fresh feces, discarded equipment, artificial stairs cut into hillsides, and, most alarming of all, live enemy communication wire. Beyond all of these visual indicators, the paratroopers could just *feel* the presence of the enemy, particularly the spooky sensation of having eyes upon them. A few of the Americans could even smell the NVA. The mood among the grunts was tinged with the ambivalence of an impending fight. On the one hand, as aggressive combat soldiers, the men were excited at the prospect of a chance to destroy their elusive enemies. On the other hand, everyone understood that, no matter the outcome of the looming battle, death and wounds awaited many of them. "No one knew exactly what to expect, but we expected it would be something big," McElwain said.

November 10 was a tense but quiet night. In the morning, Captain McElwain received orders from Lieutenant Colonel David Schumacher, the battalion commander, to follow the enemy communication wire and hook up with Task Force Blue, a similar-sized element consisting of the battalion's Alpha Company and the other platoon from Dog Company. Unspoken was the expectation that the two task forces would draw the enemy into a sizable battle that would produce a big body count to fulfill the strategic expectations of General Westmoreland and his White House superiors.

Captain McElwain's plan was to send part of his Third Platoon, under Lieutenant Charles Brown, down the hill several meters to recon the laager site, as well as Task Force Black's anticipated route of advance, to make sure the enemy was not waiting in ambush. McElwain understood, and appreciated, that moving along trails was dangerous and to be avoided under most circumstances. But the vegetation in this part of Vietnam was so thick that his unit simply had to move along trails or any other small openings the jungle might occasionally offer. When Brown's patrol was finished, the captain planned to move his company along a narrow ridgeline while the two Dog Company platoons, under the control of their commander, Captain Abe Hardy, moved along a parallel ridgeline.[6]

At 0800, Brown and his men hoisted their weapons, spread out into a suitable patrol formation, and negotiated their way down the hill. They had not even gone fifty meters when the point man spotted an NVA soldier just down the trail. Intrepid North Vietnamese trail watchers such as this soldier often hid along obvious movement routes, watching, gathering information on the Americans, even shadowing them as they moved. The point man opened fire and wounded the enemy soldier, who then took off. Lieutenant Brown wanted to pursue the man's blood trail and radioed that request to Captain McElwain, but the captain told him to stay put. For all McElwain knew, the enemy soldier was luring Brown's platoon away from the company, into an ambush. At Dak To, American commanders constantly had to beware of these tactics, which, after all, were the product of the enemy's superior initiative and strategic position in the Central Highlands. Since they controlled most of the ground, they could usually do battle at the time and place of their choosing, for maximum

advantage. The Americans knew the enemy's goal was to separate and annihilate a platoon- or company-sized unit. To foil this menacing possibility,
good commanders like McElwain were intent on keeping their units together,
albeit at the expense of mobility and flexibility. What's more, on this morning he was mindful of his orders to link up with Task Force Blue, something
he could not do if his unit was absorbed in a rescue operation for a cutoff
platoon.

McElwain's most experienced platoon leader was First Lieutenant Jerry
Cecil, a member of the West Point class of 1966, a group made famous by a
Newsweek article (and subsequent book) on them. Twenty-four years old,
Cecil hailed from a rural Kentucky family with a long tradition of military
service. For him, West Point offered a free college education, a chance to serve
the country, and an exciting career as a soldier. He had thrived there and, like
many of his infantry officer classmates, he was a graduate of Ranger School,
one of the most formidable combat training courses in existence. He had been
in command of the 2nd Platoon since June. Knowing Cecil's background, his
experience, his knowledge of this terrain, and his quality as a small-unit
leader, McElwain decided to put his platoon on point after Brown's encounter
with the trail watcher. This decision reflected Cecil's excellence more than
any deficiency on Brown's part. Brown was a fine officer, just not as experienced as Cecil.

Lieutenant Cecil and the nineteen other men who comprised his platoon
slowly walked down the trail, passed Brown's group, and moved on. Like most
of the other men in Task Force Black, the 2nd Platoon had trained and fought
together for several weeks. They were as close as brothers, and they had developed a strong sense of teamwork in combat. The jungle they traversed grew
progressively thicker as they descended the hill, the trees taller, the shadows
longer. Cecil had several men deployed on either side of the trail in a cloverleaf formation to guard against ambush from the flanks. For several more
meters, the soldiers followed the communication wire. Then the point man,
Private First Class John Rolfe, spotted another trail watcher. Rolfe raised his
arm to signal for a halt and turned his head slightly back with a finger against
his lips to call for quiet. He turned back again to the front, took aim on the
NVA soldier, and fired one shot. The soldier went down.

The Americans moved a few more meters down the trail to look at the
dead man. Cecil radioed back a report to Captain McElwain and he came

up to have a look, too. Immediately the two officers and everyone else noticed how well equipped and fresh the dead NVA appeared to be. Lieutenant Cecil noticed that his AK-47 rifle had Cosmoline on it, indicating a brand-new weapon, and speculated that he had probably just come south. Captain McElwain knew that this probably meant that a new, reinforced enemy regiment was somewhere nearby. A chill ran down his spine. "They're out there, Jerry," he told Lieutenant Cecil. "This really is looking bad. I can feel 'em. We're gonna have to be really careful going down this ridge." Cecil readily agreed.

His platoon resumed its steady advance, in the same manner as before. The ridge narrowed. The sides of the trail grew steeper, making the footing tricky for Cecil's flankers. They covered several dozen more meters, to a saddle of low ground that formed at the bottom of the ridge, before the ground sloped upward into the next ridge. All around them were tree trunks, bamboo groves, and tangled green foliage. The sun could hardly penetrate this canopy. The air was moist and sodden. An eerie, unnatural silence hung over the jungle. "All the sights and sounds of the jungle just ceased," Cecil recalled, "you'd normally hear monkeys . . . walking through the jungle . . . you'd hear birds flying." Instead, now, there was nothing, as if the animals were hushed into an awed or frightened silence by something, or someone. The quiet was so alien it was almost earsplitting.

Every member of the 2nd Platoon knew that the silence meant big trouble, none more so than Cecil. He had learned much about ambushes at Ranger School, and had even taught ambush techniques at Fort Hood. He knew, with a powerful certainty, that danger was imminent. He thrust his clenched fist in the air, signaling his men to stop, and then twirled his index finger, ordering them to fall back into a mutually supporting semicircle. The lieutenant whispered: "Guys, I think we're in it. The gooks are here. When I give the signal, start . . . spraying at your feet like a garden hose." He figured this would kill any potential ambushers with grazing fire.

Lieutenant Cecil raised his CAR-15 rifle and opened fire, as did several others. At that exact moment, a host of hidden NVA soldiers began shooting, too. "You've never seen a Fourth of July display like this one—the noise was like ten million firecrackers," Spec-4 Ken Cox, a mortar forward observer who was standing a few paces away from Cecil, later commented. "They literally stood up in front of us," Cecil said. "It was like walking into a dark room, turning on a light, and seeing someone there. They literally stood up within arm's reach." The adrenaline rush was profound, almost like a narcotic, as the body's natural self-preservation mechanisms kicked in. Enemy soldiers popped out of holes and materialized out of the bushes. Everyone on both sides poured out as much fire as he could. Many of the platoon members were already on the ground when the shooting began. Those who were still standing flung themselves onto the trail and blazed away with their M16s. Quite a few of the NVA went down. Others tried to press forward, crawling or hurling themselves at the Americans. Intense enemy machine-gun, rifle, and rocket fire swept up and down the column. The AK-47 fire was so thick that the distinctive cracking sound of the enemy rifles sounded, to some men, like bullwhips snapping. Some of the fire hit home, wounding or killing grunts. One trooper caught a round in the face, instantly blowing out the back of his head in a red spray.

Spec-4 Jerry Kelley, one of Cecil's machine gunners, was with the point element, right in the worst of the kill zone. Most platoon leaders preferred to place their machine gunners in the middle of their formation for the sake of protection and flexibility, but on this day Cecil had fortuitously put Kelley's team up front where they were in a position to do major damage to the attacking NVA. The machine gunner was leaning on his trigger, pouring deadly fire into the shapes of enemy soldiers. "Oh my God, they're everywhere!" he roared. "Here they come!" He alternately stood and squatted along the trail, firing long bursts.[7]

In the meantime, Lieutenant Cecil was keeping his platoon together as best he could. With his RTO in tow, he lunged around, telling his men where to position themselves and what to do. In his recollection, he was attempting "to get some kind of perimeter that straddles the trail and hugs over to the right and left as it drops off. It's obviously pandemonium, chaos, shooting." Spec-4 Cox saw him repeatedly expose himself to enemy fire as he directed the battle. "This is when Lieutenant Cecil becomes the hero that he is, as far as I'm concerned," Cox later commented. "That guy stood up and placed everybody. He walked. He didn't run, but he walked fast and he placed everybody. He . . . made sure somebody was covering the wounded. He put that small perimeter in place, the whole time talking on the radio with the company commander." When it came to combat, infantry officers like Cecil were taught to guard against inertia, to do something—maybe even anything—no matter the circumstances. In this perilous situation, that philosophy proved appropriate. With his flurry of activity, the young West Pointer penetrated through the inherent confusion of this horrendous firefight and held the platoon together as a cohesive fighting entity. He also personally shot several enemy soldiers who were charging his position.

Lieutenant Cecil and his men did not yet know it, but they were at the open end of an NVA horseshoe-shaped ambush. The enemy had deployed the better part of a battalion along either side and in front of the trail where the saddle morphed into the higher ground. "Had we gone another thirty or forty yards, we would have been completely surrounded," Cox said. This would have put them right into the NVA kill zone. Few, if any, would have survived. Instead they had stopped short before the enemy could bait them into this trap. This was not the result of luck. These troopers were experienced, well led, and wise to the ways of the NVA. Because of deduction, prior experiences, and pure intuition, they stopped short of the kill zone, forcing the enemy to spring their ambush in the thicker foliage around the trail, where the Americans had a chance to fight back on something approaching even terms.

Even as the fighting raged, Lieutenant Cecil was on the radio, hollering over the din, reporting what was happening to Captain McElwain, who was about one hundred yards away, back up on the hill. At first, Cecil thought he was up against a squad, then a platoon, and then some sort of undetermined larger unit. When the enemy fire showed no signs of abating, McElwain grew concerned. He called Lieutenant Brown and ordered him to reinforce Cecil, but enemy opposition was so formidable that Brown and his people could only get within shouting distance of Cecil's platoon. Moreover, enemy rifle, machine-gun, rocket, and mortar fire was now coming from the front and both sides. This meant that the NVA was enveloping Task Force Black, attempting to surround and destroy the unit. "It was difficult to see the enemy," an after action report explained. "The jungle was closing in on the troopers as the enemy, completely covered with natural foliage, moved forward." Copying a tactic from their brethren at Hill 724, some of the NVA even tied themselves into the trees and poured intense fire down on Task Force Black. One of them dropped a grenade between Cecil and his RTO, Preston Prince, wounding both of them. Cecil got hit in the left hip, Prince in the right. They looked up and shot the NVA. His dead body tumbled out of the tree and hung several feet above the trail.

About half an hour after the battle erupted, Captain McElwain and his command group moved from the hill to link up with Brown's platoon. The captain could now see firsthand how desperate the fighting had become. He sensed that, somewhere out there in the trees, the enemy was moving along adjacent ridges, trying to get between the various American platoons to destroy each one of them in detail. This was exactly what they had done at the disastrous Battle of the Slopes in June. He understood that Task Force Black was now in serious danger of experiencing the same fate. To forestall such a bloodbath, McElwain knew that he had to get the entire task force together, into one continuous, defensible perimeter.

He actually found this to be a bit frustrating. McElwain, like many other combat arms officers of his generation, was taught to fight aggressively—close with the enemy and destroy them through fire and maneuver. "I was eager to . . . fight in battles instead of going into defensive positions. That's the way I had learned in all my experiences, was to fix the enemy, maneuver against him, and destroy him." In Vietnam's Central Highlands, though, that was not the name of the game. Here such aggressive tactics invited massacre because they made it easier for the NVA to surround units, fight them at close enough range to neutralize American firepower, and then inflict horrendous casualties on the GIs. Instead, the Americans, especially after the Slopes, learned, upon making contact, to peel back into a perimeter, hold it, and unleash their firepower at the communists, in hopes of keeping them at bay and inflicting a large body count. These tactics, effective though they undeniably were, reflected the unhappy reality that, in the Highlands, the enemy held the strategic initiative. By and large, the communists chose where they wanted to fight and they controlled most of the terrain. The Americans controlled only enclaves. Only in this sort of environment could such defensive tactics make sense.[8]

Be that as it may, Captain McElwain knew, on the morning of November 11, that Task Force Black's survival depended on forging and holding a strong perimeter. Knowing that time was short, he radioed Captain Hardy and had him move his two platoons back to Charlie Company's position. McElwain's Weapons Platoon, under Lieutenant Ray Flynn, and his 1st Platoon, commanded by Lieutenant Ed Kelley, were both still on the hill. He radioed Flynn and Kelley and told them to come off the hill and join up with everyone else at the base of the hill, where the perimeter was forming roughly around Brown's platoon. Ordinarily, Flynn's mortar crews would have had their tubes set up and firing. So far, though, they had remained inactive because the trees on the hill were so dense that the crews had no fields of fire. The situation was now so serious that Flynn's people buried their mortars, picked up their rifles, and dashed down the hill. They had to fight their way to the rest of the company. Most of the soldiers even left behind their rucksacks, taking only weapons and ammo with them.

The same was true for Kelley's riflemen and machine gunners. Knowing the company's predicament, they moved with great haste, in rushes, down the hill through the bamboo-riddled foliage. "We were in a . . . line going down," Private Lambertson remembered. "We'd stop and then move on a little bit. We could hear all the firing down below." Lieutenant Kelley constantly prodded his men to keep moving. The group was hunched over, pushing through the brambles, adrenaline coursing through their veins. "We literally fought our way down to where the rest of the company was," Kelley later said. "It was like a hundred damned Harley motorcycles all revving up. That's the only way I can explain the noise. It was absolute bedlam."

The volume of enemy fire was considerable. One of Kelley's most experienced men, Staff Sergeant Jerry Curry, caught some mortar shrapnel on the way down the hill. "Twenty-two months I never got a scratch until I got to that damned hill," he said. Curry was a prime example of a born infantryman. He'd been with the unit in combat almost continuously for that two-year period. A natural outdoorsman who had dropped out of high school and joined the Army in 1964, Curry had few equals when it came to combat savvy. He was so at ease in the jungle that he often led small groups of handpicked soldiers on recon patrols hundreds of meters away from Charlie Company, almost like a modified LRRP team. He liked combat so much that his greatest fear was being plucked from the unit and forced to go home. His admiring men referred to him as "Sergeant Rock" after the cartoon character. On this morning the shrapnel tore into one of his legs. "I just felt my leg kick up and it was numb the rest of the fight." Blood steadily trickled down into his sock but, true to form, the cigar-chomping NCO hardly paid any attention to his wound.

As the platoon moved and shot, some of the grunts even caught glimpses out of their peripheral vision of the enemy. At one point, Private Lambertson actually came face-to-face with two NVA soldiers. "We just looked at each other and kept going," he said. The odd moment passed quickly, as Lambertson hastened to keep up with his buddies. Why did the enemies refrain from shooting at each other? Perhaps they could not bring themselves to kill face-to-face. Or maybe the opportunity was so fleeting, and so instantaneous, that they scarcely had the chance to open fire.

Kelley was in such a hurry to reinforce the company that he bypassed an NVA machine gun. It was so close that the lieutenant could see "the grass in front of [it] parting" as the enemy gunner fired. "In retrospect, I should have gone ahead and taken care of that then because it was a thorn in our side the rest of the fight." The gun poured continuous and distressingly accurate fire on Task Force Black. In spite of this fire, Kelley and his people made it to the company, having fought there every step of the way. In the view of Sergeant David Watson, a fire team leader, it was like forcing the NVA to "open a door and then shut it."[9]

By about 1045, with the addition of Kelley's platoon, the mortarmen, and Hardy's Dog Company troopers, the Americans had established a makeshift perimeter about one hundred meters long and forty meters wide. Bamboo, tree trunks, and bushes offered the only cover. Lieutenant Richard Elrod, the company's artillery forward observer, and Captain McElwain both called down accurate artillery fire that played a major role in keeping the enemy at bay. Elrod, in particular, was all over the place, crawling and sprinting from one position to another. His RTO was killed and Elrod was wounded several times but, knowing the vital importance of the fire support to Task Force Black's survival, he kept at it. Many of his shells detonated within twenty-five meters of the American lines, even wounding some of the Sky Soldiers. Air strikes, coming in at greater range, only added to the devastation.

By now, Captain McElwain had ordered Lieutenant Cecil to fight his way back up the trail to the task force position. To cover the withdrawal, Cecil ordered his men to place claymore mines in front of themselves, crawl back as far as the detonation cord would go, and prepare to hit the clackers that detonated the mines. Each mine weighed about a pound and contained dozens of BB-sized steel balls. Many rifle platoons did not carry them on patrol, but Cecil's did. Against the objections of many in his platoon, he had forced his men to carry the mines. He himself carried two.

Here, in the middle of this fight to the death, the unpopular order paid off. When the soldiers detonated their mines, steel balls filled the air, shredding many NVA attackers. One enemy soldier was even in the process of trying to sneak up and turn a mine in the direction of its American owner when it exploded. The young North Vietnamese soldier literally disintegrated into nothingness, as if he had never existed. This and the other explosions staggered the NVA, giving many of the soldiers in Cecil's platoon some time to fall back. "I'm convinced, to this day, that me insisting on every man packing a claymore . . . saved us," Cecil later commented. "The claymores gave us some breathing room. When you hear that thing go off in the jungle and then smell the cordite, that's a deal breaker if you're the attacker."

This hardly guaranteed the 2nd Platoon's escape, though. The most difficult aspect of the withdrawal was moving the wounded and the dead, an awkward, dangerous, and physically exhausting task. Spec-4 Kelley, the machine gunner, bought his comrades precious time to drag away several wounded men who could not walk on their own. In the process, according to one eyewitness, "Kelley was suddenly wounded himself. He was out in front of the perimeter and moved back [twenty] meters, firing his machine gun as he moved. The enemy shifted their attention to Kelley, who was raising havoc with his weapon. He fired away with long, sweeping bursts." Other grunts laid down cover fire with their rifles for Kelley. The M60 gunner seemed oblivious to everything. With a look of intense concentration, he focused on shooting at a seemingly endless stream of NVA soldiers who were moving through the trees, trying to get him. "Kelley stayed with his weapon, cutting down one North Vietnamese after another as they charged him." They finally succeeded in cutting him off and killing him.

Lieutenant Cecil saw two of his men lying badly wounded several meters away, in what was now NVA territory, almost in the spot where the battle had originally begun. Two separate times, he made himself a prime target by crawling out to grab them by the armpits and drag them to safety. As he did so, he felt groggy from the concussion of several nearby rocket explosions and he flinched under the weight of more near-miss bullets than he could ever truly appreciate. "It's the typical adrenaline story," he said. "In normal times I couldn't have carried those guys from here to the door." After retrieving the first man, he was nearly overwhelmed with fear and wondered if he could bring himself to go back into the kill zone for the second man. "Of course there was . . . only one answer to that. You've gotta go 'cos you're the lieutenant." He did exactly that. Most of the 2nd Platoon soldiers made it back to McElwain's defensive position. Cecil had lost four killed. Everyone else, except for one man, was wounded.[10]

Within the perimeter, the remnants of Cecil's platoon were in the middle (most of his wounded men simply kept fighting). Brown was on the right and Kelley on the left. Task Force Black was surrounded but intact. Nearly everyone was hugging the ground, getting as low as possible. Much of the time, if they rose up even a foot or two, they risked getting blown away. The NVA attacked from nearly every direction. In the recollection of one soldier, these attacks "were characterized by an intense, concentrated barrage of rockets, mortar and rifle grenade fire immediately followed by a relentless infantry attack. The attackers surged through the bamboo toward [the] perimeter." The Americans unloaded on them with rifles, machine guns, and grenades in the direction of the movement. The troopers had to be very careful to make sure the grenades did not bounce off trees and roll back in their own direction. "An AK fired at me and four rounds . . . [went] in the ground along my leg," Sergeant Watson recalled. "We were fighting pretty heavily. Everybody [was], like, laying in a certain position, moving back and forth, trying to get lower. The leaves were covering us, which was probably a good thing."

Not far away, Watson's platoon leader, Ed Kelley, was imploring his machine gunners to fire short bursts and then displace before the enemy could pinpoint their location. Kelley's mouth was dry from fright or adrenaline, he was not sure which. Behind him, wounded and dying men were screaming in terror (the memory of their desperate shrieks haunted him for many decades). Now, he was humbled by the responsibility of command. "What do we do now, L-T?" many of his young soldiers kept asking. This was the essence of combat leadership. In life-or-death situations, soldiers follow an officer or NCO, not always out of military discipline but because they have confidence in their judgment. Lieutenant Kelley was frightened out of his wits but, like any good leader, he knew he could not show that face of fear to his soldiers. "I was just as concerned about how we were gonna get out of there as they were. But they were looking to me. I was moving about pretty much all the time, shifting people here, shifting people there."

His machine gunners were not following his orders quickly enough, and this allowed the NVA to zero in on them with B40 rockets. One of the rockets scored a direct hit on a team, vaporizing two men. "B40 rockets, you wouldn't believe the power in them," Staff Sergeant Curry said. "You get a direct hit, you're gone, ain't nothing left. They got hit and they just disintegrated." A mortar round came in and exploded close to Private Lambertson's head, bursting his eardrums, temporarily deafening him. Blood streamed from his damaged ears. The same round, plus an RPG, wounded Sergeant Watson, who had fragments in his jaw and an eye swollen shut. Sergeant Curry stayed close to the deafened Lambertson, pointing out where and when to shoot.

Most of the time, the NVA remained unseen, in the trees, like menacing apparitions. "The North Vietnamese presented an eerie picture as they moved ever so slowly," an after action report stated. "The enemy would spread apart branches, fire one round, and then freeze." Some of them even got into the American lines. One of them was running right past a shotgun-toting soldier. The American pointed and fired, cutting the NVA in half. Spec-4 Cox was lying on his back, against a log, looking for targets, when he saw two of them materialize right in front of his spot. In that instant, he was sure he would die. He only hoped the pain would not be too great when they shot him. "One of 'em looked right at me and I looked right back at him. We just sort of made eye contact. He was no more than . . . ten feet away." Before Cox could aim and shoot his rifle, the man and his partner took off into the trees.

Not long after this, Cox saw Captain Hardy walking toward him. The Dog Company CO was everywhere that day, braving the intense enemy fire, inspiring—and worrying—his soldiers with his courage. Tall and lanky, Hardy was the sort of person whose strides were so long that, when he walked fast, he almost appeared to be running. Several times that morning, his men and his fellow officers begged him to get down. As he loped up to Cox, the young mortarman could hardly believe that the angry enemy bullets and fragments missed the upright captain. The officer peered down at Cox and a nearby soldier: "How are you jaybirds doing down here?"

"We're doing fine, sir," Cox replied.

"That's good to know," he said breezily and resumed his odyssey, moving from one spot to another to make sure the line was intact. Captain McElwain later saw him running, shooting his rifle, and hollering obscenities at the enemy. When Hardy rested for a moment next to a spot where McElwain was lying, the West Virginian said to him: "Slow down, Abe. You can't beat them yourself." Hardy just smiled and took off in the direction of Lieutenant Kelley's platoon. One of the men was standing up, yelling at the NVA. Another was badly wounded, wandering around in shock, babbling. Kelley tackled both of them and tried to calm them.

Nearby, a gravely wounded man was sobbing and screaming: "I don't wanna die!" Lieutenant Kelley watched as Hardy stood up, trotted over to where Sergeant Watson was lying wounded and half dazed, and knelt beside the NCO. Watson greatly admired the young captain for his courage and his military bearing. He gazed up at Hardy. The captain yelled some instructions to a group of men, glanced down at Sergeant Watson, and stood up. As he did so, an NVA tree sniper, probably no more than a couple dozen meters away, noticed the movement, aimed at Captain Hardy, and squeezed off several shots. "He took three rounds," Watson remembered, "one in the head, the throat and the chest and he died on top of me and I couldn't move him with my arms." Somebody had to manhandle the captain's lifeless body off Watson. His dead eyes stared vacantly at Watson, whose trauma over the horrible incident never went away.[11]

The intensity of the battle ran in cycles. The North Vietnamese kept up a steady volume of rocket and mortar fire. They would attack one part of the perimeter, get repulsed, regroup, and then hit somewhere else. "Sometimes it was really, really intense," Private Lambertson explained. "Sometimes it wasn't that bad. When it wasn't that bad, you were moving around, collecting ammunition . . . getting guys to the middle of the perimeter where the aid station was. There was always something to do." Some soldiers tried to dig in, using their helmets, bayonets, or even their fingernails. Officers and sergeants were constantly reorganizing and shoring up the firing line. Men were packed close together, facing outward toward the mostly unseen enemy, waiting for bona fide targets before opening fire so as not to waste their dwindling stocks of ammunition.

As Lambertson indicated, medics had collected the wounded in the center of the perimeter only a few meters behind the main lines. Many on the firing line were wounded but could still fight. Those who were lying in the middle of the perimeter were only the most badly wounded. Some of the medics, like Spec-4 Ennis Elliott, who was lugging around a shattered forearm from an AK bullet, along with several other debilitating wounds, were themselves casualties. "When you see somebody else hit, it doesn't bother you," he said. "But when you look at your own arm and see the bone and blood, it's a shock."

The company's senior medic, Spec-4 Jim Stanzak, was a highly experienced soldier on his second tour with the 173rd in Vietnam. In that time, he had saved many lives. He had also seen quite a few soldiers die in his arms, their faces full of grief, shock, and sadness. Now he was dealing with more patients than he could handle. For him, the day was a whirlwind of responding to cries of "Doc!" or "Medic!" dragging wounded men to the middle of the perimeter and trying to save their lives. "I was getting guys hit one after another . . . and there was no way in hell that I could stay with [them] personally." He moved from patient to patient, fighting his own personal battle with death. He was also in extreme danger himself. In one instance, a man next to him took two machine-gun rounds to the head, exploding his skull and brains over Stanzak's shirt. "Of course, his head was pretty much gone."

Nearby, when a machine-gun team got killed, Private First Class John Barnes braved withering enemy fire to leap over to the gun and man it himself. The Dedham, Massachusetts, native was on his second tour. He was anything but a recruiting poster soldier, though. He was eager and affable, but he had a permanent slovenliness to him and he always seemed to be the last man ready to move out each morning. He was the type of person who would look dirty three minutes after he took a shower. His buddies liked to call him Pigpen. "[He] was a sad sack," one soldier recalled. "I mean, he was never shaven. He had no noise discipline. Lieutenant Brown had to put a man in charge of his rucksack just to keep it quiet."

What he lacked in field craft he made up for in courage. Several meters in front of Barnes's gun, NVA attackers were surging ahead, trying to overrun this part of the line. "He was inflicting heavy casualties on the enemy as they made one human wave assault after another," one nearby soldier recalled. In the recollection of Sergeant Robert Lampkin, his fire "turned back several enemy assaults, preventing that portion of the perimeter from being overrun." His accurate M60 fire killed between six and nine enemy soldiers (estimates vary). This fire was the only thing that kept the enemy from breaching the line and killing Doc Stanzak and the helpless wounded who were all just a few meters behind Barnes.

Suddenly, a well-camouflaged enemy soldier snuck to within a few yards and hurled a grenade through the dense bamboo. In one surreal moment the grenade somehow sailed through several stands of bamboo, over the machine gunner's head, and landed a few yards behind, right among the wounded. Spec-4 James Townsend, lying only a few feet away, saw the menacing grenade and noticed a flurry of motion from Barnes's direction. "[He] leaped from his position and threw himself on the grenade." Doc Stanzak had actually talked one time with Barnes about just such a situation as this. Barnes had assured the medic that he had too much to live for and would never hurl himself on a grenade. But, now, amid this anonymous stand of Vietnamese jungle and bamboo, when there was little time to mull over choices, Barnes made the ultimate sacrifice. Stanzak was only a few feet away. In the instant before the grenade detonated, the young New Englander happened to turn and look right at the medic. Stanzak saw "fright and fear" all over Barnes's face, but his expression also seemed to convey a question: "Doc, didn't I say I wasn't gonna do this?"

The grenade exploded, lifting Barnes's body about a foot off the ground, shredding his abdomen, almost cutting him in half. In a matter of seconds, he bled to death. Stanzak caught some shrapnel from the grenade, as did Sergeant Watson and a couple other men, but none of these wounds were life-threatening. Barnes had saved the lives of an untold number of his friends (one soldier estimated the number at ten). Why did he sacrifice himself to save the others? Perhaps out of love, perhaps out of obligation, perhaps just in the heat of the moment. His friends could never know for sure, but they were forever grateful to him. Glancing over at the brave man's body, Lieutenant Kelley was struck by how frail he looked. "The grenade had blown a huge hole in his torso and penetrated different parts of his equipment. His face was completely intact." For his heroism, Barnes earned a well-deserved Medal of Honor.[12]

Captain McElwain knew that, even though his men were fighting well, holding off powerful enemy attacks, time was not necessarily on their side. After all, they were surrounded, cut off from resupply, with many casualties, separated even from their rucksacks. Minute by minute, their stocks of water, medical supplies, and ammunition dwindled. Eventually, if Task Force Black did not get some serious help, the NVA would overrun the perimeter and probably kill everyone. Some of the men were down to only a few magazines of ammo, and were even saving their last bullet for themselves. "I just knew that nobody was gonna get out of there alive," one of them later said. Lieutenant Kelley, like many, believed he would certainly die and found a strange sort of peace in accepting that sad reality. "A calmness . . . came over me. I guess it goes along with pure acceptance of the fact that this is gonna happen."

McElwain was moving around frenetically, constantly on the radio, imploring higher command for help. On several occasions he had to personally fight for his life. "Each time the enemy carried the attack to the perimeter, CPT McElwain moved to the critical area killing the enemy when they started to break through and urging his men to hold the position," a post-battle report chronicled. "He personally killed six or seven North Vietnamese that day." In one such instance, several NVA soldiers came within fifteen feet of him but probably could not see him because of the dense bamboo. He raised his CAR-15 rifle and opened fire. "[The bamboo] was so thick in there that you could almost walk on top of somebody and not even see 'em," he said. "I hit four of them."

As McElwain's RTO, Sergeant Chuck Clutter's job was to stick close to him, no matter the danger. "I just never understood how anyone could pass through all that flying lead and . . . come out . . . unscathed," he said. "He was just living right that day, I guess. There's no answer to that." Clutter himself took an AK round to the leg, breaking a bone, and it felt like "a thousand volts of electricity . . . attached to a baseball bat." As medics tended to Clutter, Sergeant Jacques "Jack" deRemer, another member of the command group, took the radio from Clutter and gave it to another man. The wounded Clutter remembered that the fire around them was so thick that, as he lay bleeding, water from bamboo stalks kept splashing on him as bullets struck the stalks a couple feet overhead.

Employing the new RTO, McElwain remained in constant contact with Captain Ed Sills, the battalion operations officer, and Lieutenant Colonel Schumacher. By late morning, after passing along many conflicting reports on the size of the enemy force, McElwain was practically begging for help. Flying distantly in a helicopter thousands of feet overhead, and thus with no appreciation of the battle's ferocity, Schumacher thought that McElwain was overreacting. "First you report a squad, then a platoon, then a company," he said. "Now it's a battalion. Get up and go after those people."

McElwain was not a fan of Schumacher. In McElwain's opinion, the colonel was the type of spit-shined commander who was content to buzz around in his command chopper, rarely ever getting on the ground with his troops. The captain thought of him as a careerist who cared much more about his next promotion than the welfare of his soldiers. In McElwain's estimation, few things were so detestable as that. "He really didn't have any interest in anybody other than himself," McElwain said. This resentment, and the stress of the fight, boiled over into an argument. "Goddamn it, Six [radio lingo for the battalion commander]," he howled, "if you don't get us some fucking help down here, you won't have a Charlie Company! Listen to me, get us some help!"

Schumacher told McElwain to calm down and watch his language. The colonel still refused to send any substantial help. Fortunately, General Schweiter, the brigade commander, was listening to their radio communications. "You'd better listen to your man on the ground, Colonel," he told Schumacher. "If he says he's facing a battalion, he's facing a battalion." Only with that prodding from a superior did the battalion commander take action. He found that his options were limited. The logical force to relieve Task Force Black was Task Force Blue, since they came from the same battalion and were only a couple miles away. But they had run into an apparent enemy bunker complex and, according to Captain Jesmer, the outfit was pinned down by sniper fire. Schumacher told him to press through the complex and relieve Task Force Black. But Jesmer and his people remained pinned down by the snipers (actually this was just an enemy rear guard designed to hold off Task Force Blue while the main group finished off Task Force Black). Such was the intensity of the fighting going on all over the Dak To area that the only other unit available for an immediate rescue was Charlie Company of the brigade's 4th Battalion, several kilometers away at Ben Het. Just after noon, General Schweiter ordered Lieutenant Colonel James Johnson, the battalion commander, to get the company ready for a helicopter assault. Captain Sills found a small LZ for them about eight hundred meters north of Task Force Black's position.[13]

At 1300, even as McElwain and his people desperately hung on, Captain William Connolly and 120 of his Charlie Company troopers boarded their helicopters. After a short flight, the choppers dropped them off, one shipload at a time, in the LZ. "The company moved south, using trails and double-timing where possible to reach the embattled troopers of the First Battalion," a unit report later said. "The men carried a full basic load of ammunition for themselves and another basic load for [Task Force Black]." They moved as fast as they could but they had to be constantly wary of an enemy ambush. Most of Connolly's men knew that fellow paratroopers were in real trouble, so maintaining such a deliberate pace was frustrating for them. Sergeant Mike Tanner, a mortar forward observer with a radio strapped to his back, was especially impatient because he knew that his best friend from stateside training, Ben Warnic, was with McElwain's surrounded group. "So I was pushing the point team really hard," Tanner recalled. "I kept complaining that we were not going fast enough."

The point team's squad leader finally turned to Tanner and offered him point if he thought he could move so much faster. Tanner handed someone his radio and took the lead. He moved quickly and "recklessly not looking for booby traps or enemy ambushes." Several minutes after assuming the lead, he was delicately stepping across basketball-sized rocks to traverse a dry streambed. He happened to look down and saw "that the streambed was crawling with . . . hundreds or thousands of bamboo viper snakes. They were little hatchlings with . . . twenty or thirty adult snakes." The adults were a foot long and the babies about six inches. Hundreds of them slithered around the bottom of the rocks, a few inches from his boots. He kept going and the company followed him, but he soon yielded point back to the original group.

Before long, they could hear the distant sounds of Task Force Black's battle. Captain Connolly was in constant radio contact with Captain McElwain, informing him of his company's progress. Connolly's point elements made it to Task Force Black's original hilltop laager site and began to trade shots with groups of NVA. They also surprised and captured a couple enemy soldiers who were rifling through the rucksacks McElwain's men had left behind. The NVA had pilfered many packs for food and medical supplies and had even tried to employ the Americans' 81-millimeter mortars against them.

As Connolly's outfit began pushing down the hill, directly toward the Task Force Black perimeter, they ran into strong enemy opposition. After all, they were fighting through enemy lines to get to McElwain's position. Periodic firefights broke out as Connolly's men bumped into the NVA and fought it out. The captain was a West Pointer and a Ranger School alum who was totally dedicated to his soldiers. He was also highly experienced, having been in Vietnam for a year and a half. At just twenty-four years old, he was young for company command. He had trained his men to hit the dirt upon making contact, flip off their rucksacks, and use them as cover. Some would return fire. Some would dig in. During the rescue of Task Force Black, these tactics proved highly effective, partially because Charlie Company was dealing with quite a few tree snipers. The rucks provided a modicum of cover. The captain himself noticed a bullet in his ruck, looked up, and saw an NVA in a tree. "Sergeant [Janus] Shalovan, one of my platoon sergeants, was pretty close behind. I turned around and pointed to him and, next thing I know, that guy was falling out of the tree." In another instance, an NVA suddenly materialized a few feet away from the command group. Spec-5 Lynn Morse, the senior medic, blasted him with a shotgun. In Connolly's recollection, the fléchettes from the shotgun shell "actually stuck him to a tree. The NVA guy's toes were dangling."

NVA opposition was formidable, though, and several times Connolly's company had to retreat and regroup as they tried to make a last push to the perimeter. Part of the problem was that they were also taking fire from Task Force Black. "They'd tell their guys don't shoot . . . somebody's coming in," Connolly said, "then the enemy would shoot and somebody would return fire." Finally, he arranged with McElwain to have his guys completely cease fire for about a minute while Connolly's company charged through the NVA, into the perimeter. At Connolly's signal, they got up and sprinted down the ridge straight at Task Force Black's lines. "Bullets were flying everywhere and the men began yelling and shouting the running password to identify themselves in the confusion," one post-battle report stated. "They leaped and tripped over the dead and wounded as they broke into the perimeter." As they came in, they yelled "173rd! Don't shoot!" or "Geronimo!" or "Airborne!" Staff Sergeant Donald Ibenthal, one of Connolly's men, later said: "We wanted to make sure they knew we were coming and also so they wouldn't fire at us when we came in." He saw dead and wounded men everywhere. "The machine gunners we replaced were both shot in the head several times." The enemy fire slackened as Connolly's company made it through, either because the NVA were regrouping or perhaps because they were demoralized at the arrival of these newcomers.

The Task Force Black soldiers, many of whom had resigned themselves to imminent death, could hardly believe their eyes or contain their joy. "The emotion of knowing you only have a few more minutes or hours to live and you are helpless to do anything about it, being turned around to knowing that the bad guys are gone, Dr. Death is nowhere to be seen, and you have survived is impossible for me to describe," one of them later wrote. Sergeant deRemer, a white soldier, was so excited that he got up and kissed the first relieving trooper, "this big black guy. I refer to him as the first black guy I ever kissed on the lips," he said and laughed.

When Mike Tanner got through, he only saw four soldiers and feared these were the only survivors. To his relief, though, he saw that many other Task Force Black soldiers were still alive, including his buddy Ben Warnic, who was wounded but stable. Throughout the perimeter, officers and NCOs of both units coordinated a mutual relief and defense. For Lieutenant Charles Brown, the moment was perhaps the happiest of his life, even though his platoon had only six effectives left. A skinny, large-nosed sergeant first class brought his own platoon up to relieve Brown's. The young lieutenant thought that this grizzled sergeant was "the handsomest and bravest human on earth at that moment." The NCO lit a cigarette, stuck it in Brown's mouth, handed him a canteen, and said: "Tell your men to pull back and relax, we have everything under control now." The time was 1437.

The relief of Task Force Black did not end the battle, but it did mean that the NVA now had no real hope of annihilating the Americans and that was, after all, the purpose of their ambush. The Americans now had the initiative. They spent the rest of the afternoon gradually fighting their way back to the laager hill. McElwain did, though, have to leave many of his dead behind, including Captain Hardy's body. By nightfall, enemy attacks had ceased and the NVA contented themselves with lobbing mortar shells and rockets at the hill. This was not exactly a safe environment, but it was a veritable paradise compared with what Task Force Black had endured much of the day. The Americans were firmly ensconced on the hill. They had some helicopters coming in and plenty of supporting fire. Compared with the events of the day, the night was quiet.

The survivors were left to contemplate, sometimes through thousand-yard stares, the ordeal they had just endured. Almost everyone in Task Force Black had some sort of wound. McElwain's force had lost 20 dead, 154 wounded, and 2 missing. Connolly's company had 65 wounded, with no one killed. Sergeant deRemer, like most of the "lightly" wounded, refused evacuation (as did all of the company officers). His chore was to supervise the evacuation of the wounded and the dead. "One of my jobs was . . . to inventory each body bag and make sure that if it was a white body that all the other parts were white, and making sure we didn't have a bag with . . . two left feet in it." Sometimes he even had to move parts from bag to bag, a surreal and disturbing task.[14]

Task Force Black had survived, and won, not just because of the salvation given to them by their Charlie Company, 4th Battalion brothers, but also because of superb leadership and extraordinary valor. From the outset, Captain McElwain had recognized the extreme danger his unit was in, and took steps to avoid a repeat of the Battle of the Slopes. Most of his survivors believed that he and the other officers saved their lives because of their good leadership. McElwain saw it differently. He believed that he survived because of the bravery of his men. "I've always been thankful that I had that unit because they saved my life. If I'd have had maybe a different unit where I couldn't have controlled them as much or if they didn't have that esprit like paratroopers did . . . it may have turned out different, because we were very close to being overrun."

The sad postscript was that, in the context of the Dak To struggle, none of this meant enough strategically. The hill and the saddle were worthless. The surviving Americans were in no position to hunt down and destroy the battered NVA, whose 66th Regiment had sprung the ambush (they lost about a battalion in the fight). In the context of Westmoreland's attrition strategy, all that really mattered strategically was a high body count and a favorable ratio of casualties—kill way more of theirs than they do of yours.

Lieutenant Colonel Schumacher was a confirmed citizen of the body count culture. Like practically every other officer, he knew that his reputation and career advancement depended upon producing the right numbers. On the morning of November 12, he flew into the battle area and ordered McElwain to send patrols out to count the enemy dead. There was nothing inherently wrong with this order, as it made good sense to honestly assess the enemy's losses. The problem was the overwhelming emphasis he placed on producing numbers that sounded good.

McElwain's exhausted and sad survivors policed up their own dead and then fanned out, counting the decomposing remnants of their enemies—men who, like the Americans, also had families, homes, and much to live for. The stench was nauseating, like draping oneself in rotten meat. The troopers constantly had to be wary of booby traps and ambushes. The job was enervating and disgusting. "It was a very, very trying time for the soldiers there," McElwain later said. "It was an emotional event for them because they had so many of their buddies who'd been killed. I could just see it in their eyes how scared and tired and mad" they were. After an all-day search, they passed along a body count of sixty or seventy enemy. When McElwain reported that to Schumacher, he snapped: "Goddamnit, Captain, you lose twenty people and you expect me to accept a body count of seventy. Go back down there tomorrow and find me some bodies."

McElwain grumbled but he complied. After another nightmarish day of counting, identifying, and digging up enemy bodies in the tropical heat, the captain reported a find of ninety-five bodies. Still, this was not good enough for Schumacher, who clearly wanted something well into triple figures. "I can't believe you've had that many men killed and wounded and there's not any more enemy bodies down there so I want you to go back down."

McElwain had finally had enough. He was already angry at the colonel for his reluctance to send help during the battle. He was tired and sad and coursing with grief over his dead men. He bristled at the idea of his soldiers' valor being reduced to a mere casualty ratio for some bean counter at MACV. He knew that Schumacher was only motivated by his desire to produce a favorable body count so he would look good to his superiors, and the very idea of this angered him all the more. "Look here, Colonel," McElwain barked, "you tell me the fuckin' number you want! If you want a hundred and fifty, that's what the number is, but I ain't taking my men back down there again."

The two men bickered some more. McElwain told the colonel that if he insisted on pressing the matter, the captain would go down and count the bodies by himself, without risking his men. The colonel backed off when they settled on the captain's farcical suggestion of 150. The official records downgraded the total to 116, plus assorted strays. Either way, the ledger looked good to higher command. Schumacher had gotten his favorable body count.[15]

See the Hill, Take the Hill: The Horror of 875

The tension was palpable, jolting, like an electrical current. Here and there, morning fog hung in the valleys. For three companies of troopers, Alpha, Charlie, and Dog of the 2nd Battalion, 503rd Parachute Infantry Regiment, the order of the day from Major James Steverson, the battalion commander, was to take Hill 875. The hill was an unsightly, jungle- and tree-covered pile of woebegone earth a few miles east of Cambodia. It had no intrinsic value except that the NVA was there. The previous day, a Special Forces team had detected their presence and engaged in a brief firefight with them. The Americans had then spent much of the nighttime and early morning hours hurling the usual blend of firepower at the hill.

Now, after sunrise on this Sunday morning of November 19, it was time for the grunts to take it. This order came with little circumspection, no assessment of enemy numbers, no serious analysis of the strength of NVA defenses on the hill, nor any consideration of whether the hill was a worthwhile objective. In the war of attrition, Hill 875 was just one more place to find, fix, and kill the enemy. In the context of the episodic fighting that was raging around Dak To in November 1967, one hill was like any other. As at the Umurbrogol on Peleliu a generation before, American commanders had almost no idea what they were getting into.

But the grunts did. After several days of clashing with the enemy in his Dak To lair, the infantrymen sensed the danger that lurked on Hill 875. They had enough experience that they could sense the enemy's presence in such recent finds as spools of abandoned communication wire, steps cut into hills, vacant base camps, bloody bandages, and propaganda leaflets. Some of the soldiers even swore that they could feel the enemy's nearby presence. Many of the paratroopers believed this day would be their last day on earth. Before setting out for the hill, quite a few of them attended a Catholic Mass given by the battalion's legendary, universally loved chaplain, Father Charles Watters, a forty-year-old priest who made a point of spending most of his time in the field with the grunts. The respected priest even said Mass with camouflaged vestments and a portable altar. Like several other troopers, Sergeant Steven Welch attended the Mass even though he was not Catholic. "I figured I needed all the help I could get because things weren't looking good on that hill."

At 0943, the grunts began trudging up the hill, negotiating their way around felled trees and through scrub brush. "There was a heavy undergrowth of bushes, vines and small trees," a post-battle report stated. "Visibility was restricted generally to 5 to 15 meters and not more than 25 meters." Farther up the hill, the Americans could detect some gaps in the jungle where bombs and shells had impacted. Everything was quiet, unusually so, as if all the creatures of the jungle understood that the hill was pregnant with menace.

In column formations, Dog and Charlie Companies led the way with Alpha following behind in reserve. A small trail slashed down the hill, separating Dog on the left from Charlie on the right. About twenty meters separated the point squads of the two companies. A squad of scouts with specially trained dogs forged ahead, hustling up and down the hill, looking around for signs of the enemy. One of these soldiers picked up the harsh, sweet scent of marijuana smoke: "I smell Charlies," he said to another man. Neither he nor anyone else could see them, though. The scouts worked their way back down to the point men and warned them that NVA soldiers were very close. "Watch your ass, Zack," one of them said to Spec-4 Raymond Zaccone, a machine gunner, "the gooks are up there and they'll be after you." Zaccone and his squad leader, Sergeant Welch, were at the point of Charlie's advance. A shudder ran down their collective spines. To their left they could see Spec-4 Kenneth Jacobsen, Dog Company's point man, along with his slack man and his squad leader a few meters behind him.

About three hundred meters from the top of the hill, they came to a clearing that had been created by a bomb. Mounds of dirt and tangled brambles were heaped in random clumps. "At the edge of the treeline, when I looked out, I could tell . . . there were what looked like bunkers to me," Sergeant Welch said. "It looked like we were gonna walk into a kill area." Welch had been in Vietnam for eleven months. He knew an ambush when he saw one. He was sure the NVA were in those bunkers, waiting for him and the others to stray into their kill zone. He halted the point men and radioed his company commander, Captain Harold Kaufman, and twice asked for permission to recon by fire. The captain would not hear of it: "Negative. Move your men out now." In disgust, Welch flipped the radio handset back to his RTO.

Hearing the captain's order, Zaccone said: "This is stupid. This is fucking crazy." Welch nodded in agreement but gave the order to move out. A moment later, Spec-4 Jacobsen was stepping over a downed tree in the clearing when he smelled the enemy. He turned to his slack man and pointed at his nose. He lowered his hand and turned back again. Three shots rang out, ripping through Jacobsen, knocking him backward, probably dead before he hit the ground. One of the rounds tore through his head, spraying pieces of his skull and brain in a halo around him. In that instant, the world exploded as both sides opened up with everything they had. A medic named Farley ran to Jacobsen, hoping he could still be saved. Bullets laced through the medic, reeling him violently backward, killing him instantly. "We'd never seen anything like this," Spec-4 Zaccone later said. "I dropped down to one knee . . . trying to see something. The next thing I saw to my left, the brush was just being mowed down. Being a machine gunner, once the firing started, I couldn't make a move without being shot at."

The Americans were taking rifle, machine-gun, grenade, rocket, and even recoilless rifle fire. Men were getting hit left and right. "There is no sound in this world like a bullet tearing through a human body," Private Joe Aldridge said. "It sounded like slaps." Sergeants kept imploring their men to get up the hill, but that was impossible. The Sky Soldiers were actually right in the middle of a mutually supporting, expertly built NVA bunker complex, exactly where the enemy wanted to fight them. Some of the soldiers were no more than five meters away from bunkers. The enemy fighting positions were so well camouflaged in this mazelike jungle that it was quite difficult for the Americans to see them at all—at least until it was too late. Many of the bunkers were connected by underground tunnels. Even when the troopers succeeded in pitching grenades into apertures or killing enemy soldiers, others soon came through the tunnels, into the same bunkers, replacing their dead comrades. For the most part, the grunts were shooting blind. Many of them simply pointed their weapons in the vague direction of danger and snapped off shots.

Sergeant Welch was hugging the ground, listening to AK-47 and machine-gun bullets impact around him. In nearly a year in Vietnam, he had never experienced fire this intense. A medic crawled up next to Welch. The sergeant ordered him to go help a wounded man. He crept a few feet forward but got killed before he could get to the soldier. As in any firefight this serious, people were shouting, crying, and raging. The average soldier saw only a few feet in any direction and had no clue what was happening. "Everybody that moved seemed to get hit," Lieutenant Bart O'Leary, Dog Company's commander, recalled. "Progress sort of stalled at that time." Throughout the morning, at Major Steverson's behest, the paratroopers tried multiple assaults up the hill. Every one of them failed.

Finally, Captain Kaufman, the senior company commander, decided to call off the attack and pull everyone into a perimeter. While the soldiers laboriously extricated themselves from the kill zones of various bunkers and crawled back down the hill, fighter planes dropped bombs and napalm near the crest. Under fire all the way, the grunts managed to set up mutually supporting positions about twenty meters down from the initial point of contact. "The men began to dig in with knives, steel pots or anything else they could work with," an officer later wrote.[16]

A few dozen meters down the hill from them, Captain Michael Kiley, commander of Alpha Company, ordered his Weapons Platoon to cut an LZ and a collecting point for the wounded while his other platoons fanned out. His 1st Platoon protected the rear flank, closer to the bottom of the hill. The other two tried to tie in with Dog and Charlie Companies, a difficult task because the Alpha soldiers were spread very thin, mostly along the trail, in thick vegetation. They could hardly see the next squad, much less the other companies.

Nearer the bottom of the hill, about forty meters away from the company, four 1st Platoon soldiers were on OP duty, guarding the rear of the entire American force on the hill. Private First Class Carlos Lozada, a tough twenty-one-year-old kid from the Bronx, was lying just to the left of the trail, in a nice firing position, hunched over an M60 machine gun. Beside him was Spec-4 John Steer, his assistant gunner. His team leader, Spec-4 James Kelley, and Private First Class Anthony Romano were hiding behind some bushes to the right of the trail. Romano was incensed: "This is stupid . . . a fucking suicide mission," he huffed. The others shushed him and then he stalked away, back to the company. Soon thereafter they heard mortar shells exploding behind them. The rounds were detonating near the company command group, but the outpost men did not know that. The three men peered down the trail and noticed movement. A column of NVA soldiers emerged, no more than about twenty or thirty meters away, and walked right toward them. "They had on regular uniforms with bushes tied on them and black painted on their faces to camouflage themselves," Steer said. "Also, they had burlap sacks tied around their weapons."

Lozada waited until they were within fifteen meters and then opened up. "Kelley, here they come!" he yelled. He unloosed a long burst that caught the NVA by complete surprise and scythed through several of them. The rest scattered in every direction. On the other side of the trail, Kelley hurled two grenades and emptied a full magazine of M16 bullets in their direction. In spite of the heavy American fire, the enemy soldiers fired back with rifles and RPGs and kept coming. "They were trotting toward us in rows," Steer said, "they would run, drop down and get up and run some more. And they kept coming. They got real close." Steer kept feeding ammo into Lozada's gun. The two soldiers screamed at each other over the din of the weapons, intently looking for new targets. Steer saw an NVA only a few yards away. "I don't know how this guy got so close. I emptied an entire magazine into him."

By most estimates, Lozada alone killed as many as twenty enemy soldiers. Kelley and Steer killed six more. Still the NVA kept coming. These men represented the vanguard of two NVA companies that were leading a battalion-sized assault on the rear of the attacking American force. To get in position, they had moved along carefully prepared and concealed trails and hillside steps. The NVA was planning an elaborate bait and switch. While the American force was pinned down by the formidable nest of bunkers on Hill 875, these two NVA companies were to attack from behind, cut off and isolate the paratroopers, and kill them. The outpost men held them up for several valuable minutes while Alpha Company reacted to the surprise attack.

Several men from the 1st Platoon heard the sound of the shooting and ran to help the outpost men. At least three got wounded. Private First Class Romano carried one of them farther up the hill. He and several other soldiers yelled at the OP men to retreat. "They either didn't hear or refused . . . as they continued to fire and to throw grenades at the advancing enemy, who by now had gotten on both sides of us and threatened to surround us," Romano recalled.

At the outpost, the situation was getting critical. Spec-4 Kelley yelled for his machine-gun team to displace to his side of the trail. As Lozada kept firing, Steer dashed over to Kelley. Lozada stood up, held his M60 at the hip, and blazed away until he made it behind the log where Kelley and Steer had taken cover. The NVA were all over the place now and Kelley knew they had only moments to escape. "Lozada refused," Kelley said. "He would not pull back even when [the NVA] were just meters away." Kelley shot and killed one nearby camouflaged enemy soldier and then his weapon jammed. He got it fixed and hollered at his men to retreat. Lozada also had a jam but he cleared it, resumed firing, and told his buddies to fall back. In the confusion, as Steer was turning to go, he glanced to his right and saw enemy soldiers tromping past them. "Get down, Carlos!" he roared. In the next instant, two bullets slammed into Steer's back and his left arm. He spun around and saw Lozada up on the trail, starting to fall back. A bullet tore through the New Yorker's head and he went down in a heap. "He died in my arms," Steer said. "My eyes were wild and crazy. I was crying and saying how they had got Lozada." Kelley hurled a couple grenades, keeping the NVA at bay long enough to somehow collect the hysterical Steer and run up the trail, back to the platoon. Lieutenant Joseph Sheridan, leader of the 3rd Platoon, believed that the young machine gunner "gave the company the time to regroup and rejoin the task force." Lozada earned the Medal of Honor for his bravery in holding off the enemy attackers. In Kelley's estimation, the Bronx native "gave his life so that his comrades could be saved."[17]

In the meantime, the two NVA companies, with plenty of supporting mortar and rocket fire, were assaulting all out against the rear of the American perimeter, hitting Alpha Company especially hard. "Nothing was stopping them," Private Miguel Orona, a rifleman, recalled. "They kept coming. It was like we were shooting through 'em." Some of the NVA soldiers were emboldened by narcotics. "Several had strange grins on their faces," a paratrooper later wrote. "One trooper reported seeing an NVA charge into a tree, bounce off and continue his charge."

The situation was so desperate that they overran and killed the company command group, including Captain Kiley. They also executed several of the nearby wounded men. Lieutenant Tom Remington, the 2nd Platoon leader, led an abortive attempt to rescue Kiley and his men but ran into heavy opposition. Remington himself got seriously wounded. "I had a bad shrapnel wound in my leg and then a few seconds later, I was shot in the shoulder. Of . . . ten men with me, I think maybe five were dead and [the] other five were wounded. So . . . we never got to Captain Kiley." The company's survivors carried out a harried, fighting retreat up the hill, into the perimeter established by Dog and Charlie Companies.

They placed their many wounded in a bomb crater in the middle of the perimeter. Eventually there were close to one hundred wounded men in and around this spot. Some could still fight. Others were too badly wounded to do anything but lie still and cling to life. Men were crying, pleading for their lives, raging at the enemy or their wounds, and calling out for their mothers.

The medics had suffered devastating casualties. Many were dead. Others were wounded.

Father Watters was on a one-man mission of mercy, risking his life all over the hill, retrieving and tending to wounded men, whether in or out of the perimeter. He moved around so much, amid such devastating fire, that it hardly seemed possible he could remain unscathed. Lieutenant Bryan McDonough saw him scurry through snapping bullets and plop down beside one of the dying medics. "He cradled him in his arms, saying a quick prayer over him. After giving him last rites and blessing him, he moved forward toward the enemy to the next wounded man." He did this more times than anyone could count. In the lieutenant's estimation, the brave priest's actions inspired the soldiers "on to greater risks and very brave deeds."

He carried or dragged an untold number of wounded men to the relative safety of the bomb crater. He distributed ammo and water. In spite of the extreme danger he was in, he hardly seemed to notice. "He showed no strain or stress especially when among the wounded," one soldier later wrote. "The men talked to him freely and I'm sure he prevented several from going into shock." Several of the soldiers pleaded with him to get down but he paid them no heed. When Captain Kaufman urged him to take cover, he replied: "It is all right, someone has to do it." He moved among the wounded, dispensing water, praying with them, talking to them, keeping their spirits up. With water and medical supplies running perilously low, he used his holy water and wine to bring some relief to wounded soldiers. "He was my hero," one soldier later said. "He cared so much for us. He was always there. There was no task that was too difficult."

It is fair to say that no one was more inspirational that day than Watters. Although he was a man of peace who carried no weapon, no one instilled more fighting spirit in the troopers. He was the very embodiment of mercy, self-sacrifice, and duty. To frightened young men in a life-and-death situation, he was the face of God. He took crazy chances yet he did not get hit. To some, it seemed as if God was protecting him from the enemy bullets and fragments, as if a miracle was happening before their very eyes. At one point, Spec-4 Zaccone happened to glance over and see the priest with a dying soldier in his lap, administering last rites. "The sun happened to be shining down through the trees. He smiled at me. It was like this reassuring smile, his way of giving me some encouragement." The two men waved at each other.

Watters's smile was so peaceful, so reassuring, that it gave Zaccone some measure of peace himself, even amid such violent circumstances. "No one could quite believe the things that Father Watters did unless they had witnessed it," another man later said.[18]

As had occurred with alarming frequency throughout the Dak To campaign, the NVA at Hill 875 had forced a potent American ground force into an isolated, surrounded, hard-pressed perimeter. From well-hidden—and expertly displacing—positions on adjacent hills, NVA mortar and rocket crews hurled their deadly projectiles at the Americans. All over the perimeter, their comrades probed and attacked, provoking ruthless firefights between small groups of frightened men. "I was between two riflemen," Sergeant Welch recalled, "and I looked to one side and saw the right eye explode in the guy's head as the bullet went through it. Then, when I looked to my right, the other guy caught one in the forehead and he flopped down and . . . died." As always, the Americans fought back with stubborn determination and almost incomprehensible valor. They huddled in their shallow holes, picked their targets carefully, and held the line.

Try as they might, the NVA could not breach the perimeter. But they made it nearly impossible for helicopters to resupply the hard-pressed paratroopers. Any chopper approaching the hill flew through a gauntlet of small-arms, machine-gun, and rocket fire. The lower they flew, the worse the fire. Six helicopters were hit so badly that they were barely able to limp back to their base a few miles away at Ben Het. One crew did succeed in dropping, from an altitude of eighty feet, a couple pallets of ammunition into the perimeter. Sergeants distributed the ammo—mainly grenades and M16 magazines—as evenly as possible. Another pallet of ammo landed fifteen meters beyond the American lines on a downslope halfway between the opposing sides. Rushing beyond the perimeter, a recovery team attempted to recover the ammunition. The NVA reacted quickly, spraying machine-gun and rifle fire all around the pallet. Several soldiers tried to drag the crates back to friendly lines while Lieutenant Peter Lantz, another member of West Point's class of 1966, unleashed covering fire in the direction of the enemy. An NVA sniper squeezed off a perfect shot, killing the lieutenant instantly. The men had to leave his body where it fell.

As usual, another major factor in keeping the enemy at bay was prodigious supporting fire. Artillery shells, most commonly from 105-millimeter howitzers, burst all over the hill, wounding and killing NVA, disrupting their movements. Air strikes also did grisly, unrelenting work. In the recollection of one officer whose job was to coordinate air support, "pilots who had expended their ordnance would call back to their base and let them know [they] wanted [to be] rearmed as soon as [they] landed" because they were so badly needed at Hill 875. Many pilots flew three or four sorties over the course of the day.

As evening approached, the shooting quieted down a bit. The battered American survivors were deeply worried that the NVA was regrouping for a night attack. Air strikes continued to pound the NVA-controlled portions of the hill. At 1858, just as darkness crept over the unhappy hill, a lone American plane approached from the northeast, on course to pass over the shoulders of the Americans. Previous planes had swooped in from the other direction, over enemy lines. Noticing this, one of the first sergeants told his RTO to call the forward air controller and ask why. As he did so, the plane flew directly overhead. Many of the Americans thought the plane was a Marine jet. Others believed it was a prop-driven Air Force A-1E Skyraider. Such are the vagaries of eyewitness observations, especially in a combat setting.

Regardless of what it was, the pilot was clearly confused as to the location of the American lines. By the light of a flare, he dropped two 500-pound bombs over the American positions. One of them detonated, with a bright flash and a powerful wall of concussive sound, directly above Captain Kaufman's command post. The effect was nearly apocalyptic. In less time than it took to blink an eye, Kaufman and his command group were killed, as were many of the nearby wounded. Many of them were literally blown to bits, liquidated, as though they never existed. Father Watters was killed outright. So was Lieutenant Richard "Buck" Thompson, yet another member of West Point's class of '66. Some of the dead were blown to pieces. Hands, legs, heads, and torsos were scattered everywhere. "I could see the body parts on the trees," one survivor remembered. Those same trees were smeared with blood and flesh. In one position, a soldier looked up and saw a naked corpse hanging in the tree above him. Try as he might, he could not free up the corpse. Not wanting to attract enemy attention, he left the corpse alone, even though the bottom of the dead man's feet nearly touched his shoulders.

For about ten or fifteen seconds after the detonation, a stunned silence hung over the hill while the survivors shook off concussion and tried to figure out what had just happened. The only noise was the diffuse crackling of small fires. Spec-4 Ronald Fleming's eardrums were ruptured. Amid the drowsy world of silence around him, he kept screaming for someone to put out the fires. Blood was pouring from Spec-4 Steer's nose, mouth, and ears. "I noticed my right arm was gone because I went to pick it up and it was just hanging by some tissue. My right leg was almost gone." Thinking he was about to die, he cried out: "God, don't let me go to hell!" and then passed out. Lieutenant O'Leary, the Dog Company commander, had a sucking chest wound, but his first sergeant was hurt even worse. As O'Leary struggled to save the sergeant's life, he saw a man walk past holding the stump of his left arm with his right. "Will someone tie off my arm?" he mumbled to no one in particular and staggered away.

Sergeant Welch awoke to the sound of a man behind him screaming: "My legs are gone! Mom! Mom!" The man bled to death in his lieutenant's arms. Private First Class Clarence Johnson had been easing into a shallow fighting hole when the bomb hit, flinging him several feet in the air. "It took out my elbow and most of my left arm. My humerus bone and all the bones . . . closest to my shoulder down to the middle of my arm . . . were pretty much shattered." He lay quietly, fighting off concussion, with no morphine or medical care, all the while bleeding and in pain. Lieutenant Remington, wounded even before the bombing, was now hurt even worse, with shrapnel in his side and shattered eardrums. Even so, he had the presence of mind to crawl past horribly wounded, crying men and body parts to find a radio, get in touch with the firebase, and call off any further air strikes: "Stop those fucking airplanes," he roared. "Don't let 'em drop another bomb. They're killing us up here." The bomb killed forty-two Americans and wounded forty-five others. It was the worst friendly fire incident of the Vietnam War.

Of the 290 men who had ascended the hill in the morning, 100 were now dead and at least 50 more wounded. Even so, junior people took over leadership positions and began to reorganize the shattered remains of the unit. Within thirty minutes, they had reestablished the perimeter. With little water, no food, and a looming ammunition shortage, they held on, warding off several probing North Vietnamese attacks (by most accounts, the bombing had also hurt the NVA badly). Men slept or fought next to the corpses of their dead friends. Crazed with thirst, wounded troopers lapsed in and out of consciousness. The enemy well understood the importance of psychological warfare. They blew bugles and taunted the Americans with calls to surrender. A few of them got within ten meters of the American positions, but none broke through. "The night was absolutely hell on earth," Remington later said. "It was just desolate up there, scary, the smell . . . there was just death in the air."[19]

Knowing that the 2nd Battalion was in deep trouble, General Schweiter arranged for a relief force. He hopped on his helicopter and flew to see Lieutenant James Johnson, commander of the 4th Battalion. "Jim," he said, "you'll have to get your people to that hill. Get them there as fast as you can." Thus, for the second time in a week, troopers from this battalion were called upon to rescue a stricken group from another battalion. Lieutenant Colonel Johnson's companies had seen plenty of fighting themselves. They were spread all over the area. He got in touch with his company commanders and they spent the rest of the night hastily organizing a relief mission.

Johnson had less than three hundred men available within his Alpha, Bravo, and Charlie Companies. The situation was so critical that Johnson did not concentrate his companies and send them out as one large force. Instead, they set out as they were ready. Bravo was the first. Shortly after sunrise, about one hundred troopers from this company left Fire Base 16, a few kilometers to the northeast of Hill 875. They had spent a long, impatient night preparing for the rescue of their airborne brethren. "There was fear," one of them later wrote, "but on top of that fear was the driving force that we must get to and save our brothers." Knowing much about the 2nd Battalion's plight, they were laden down with extra food, water, and ammunition. Since a favorite NVA tactic was to pin down one unit and ambush a relieving force, Bravo Company proceeded very carefully along narrow trails, through thick jungle and bamboo, even employing a rolling artillery barrage ahead of their line of advance. The going was exhausting and tense. It took Bravo Company the entire day to make it to Hill 875. "We encountered sniper positions, commo wire, well-used trails and various other signs of a large enemy presence," Private First Class Rocky Stone, a machine gunner, recalled. They found several enemy base camps with bloody bandages, dead bodies, and even parts of bodies. They also discovered, and destroyed, several enemy mortar rounds.

By late afternoon they were finally within sight of the hill. All this time, of course, 2nd Battalion had continued to take accurate mortar and rocket fire, even as they fended off more enemy attacks. They were perilously low on water and ammo. Few of them had any food left. The Bravo Company troopers could hear the shooting. They also were engulfed in the powerful stench of death that permeated Hill 875. Fortunately, the NVA did not hold a continuous line around the hill. The Bravo Company men carefully ascended the ingenious steps that enemy soldiers had cut into the side of 875. Soon the relief force saw the grisly results of the previous day's fighting. "American bodies along with enemy bodies [were] all entwined on the jungle floor, covered in blood, some blown apart," Private First Class Stone recalled. "We saw bodies strewn all along our route. The smell of gunpowder, napalm, and death engulfed the hill and filled our noses." They found Private First Class Lozada's body, still at his gun, with NVA corpses all around him. Everyone was spooked by the sight of the bodies, so much so that some men wondered aloud if they would ever make it off this hill. The horrible cries of the wounded only added to the trepidation. The cries conveyed hopelessness, agony, vulnerability, and even anger. "This sound was one that none of us will ever forget," Stone said.

Somewhere between 1700 and 1730, Sergeant Leo Hill and his point element made contact with the 2nd Battalion. "There were tears in their eyes as they greeted their buddies from the 4/503d Inf.," one report claimed. The 4th Battalion soldiers passed out whatever food and water they had left. "It was like stepping into the third circle of hell," one soldier later commented. The cratered hill looked like a garbage dump, strewn as it was with discarded equipment, boxes, helmets, weapons, uniforms, and, of course, human remains. Felled trees lay crisscrossed in jagged patterns, making movement difficult. An odor of death, vomit, urine, and human feces blanketed the perimeter. Many of the filthy, dehydrated 2nd Battalion men were in a state of mental shock, gazing with listless, wide-eyed thousand-yard stares at their friends. In the recollection of one Bravo Company man, their faces communicated "relief at seeing us, yet a look of total terror, pain and disbelief." Bravo's medics began working on the many wounded. One of them treated badly hurt Private First Class Clarence Johnson and gave him some water, immediately lifting his spirits. "You knew you were gonna . . . live."[20]

Alpha and Charlie Companies stumbled into the perimeter a few hours later, after dark. Throughout the night, the three companies and the 2nd Battalion survivors manned the perimeter, expanded an LZ, dealt with the wounded, and called in fire missions on the NVA bunkers. The enemy responded with heavy mortar and rocket fire. The shelling was accurate enough to add to the list of American dead and wounded. In the darkness, some of the Americans, while keeping watch, inadvertently rested their weapons on dead bodies, thinking they were sandbags.

As the sun rose over the eastern horizon on November 21, the paratroopers were busy hacking out a new LZ, tending to the wounded, policing up weapons and bodies, setting up mortars, and planning their next move. Helicopters still had to run a veritable wall of fire to get in and out of Hill 875, but the gutsy crewmen did succeed in dropping off some supplies and evacuating the worst of the wounded.

Lieutenant Colonel Johnson was a no-nonsense, fair-minded leader who was well thought of by his men. Even so, he was not actually on the hill (yet another example of an absentee battalion commander). He was, though, in constant radio contact with Captain Ron Leonard, who was Bravo's commander and the ranking 4th Battalion officer on 875. At 0900, Johnson told Leonard that, in two hours, he wanted him to launch an attack to capture the summit of the hill. The captain was not surprised in the least by this order. In fact, he fully expected it and agreed with it. Yet, in retrospect, much can be read into this seemingly straightforward command. From Lieutenant Colonel Johnson's perspective, and that of nearly every trooper on 875, the hill had to be taken. Honor and pride demanded it. The idea of abandoning 875 was anathema to these proud airborne light infantrymen. To them, victory in war meant fighting tactical battles to destroy the enemy and take the ground he occupied. The hill represented a challenging task that must be accomplished, regardless of the cost. American culture frowned on the notion of leaving a job unfinished. In this context, Johnson's order made perfect sense.

However, from a bigger-picture, more objective point of view, the order was questionable. The NVA had already destroyed the 2nd Battalion. The 4th Battalion was hardly in good shape, having already fought for weeks. The NVA on Hill 875 were hunkered down in well-sited, heavily reinforced bunkers that were connected by tunnels. Some of the bunkers were strengthened by six feet of logs and dirt, and were thus impervious to artillery and air strikes. Nothing short of a direct hit from a B-52 bomber could destroy the bunkers. At any moment of their choosing, the NVA could use their tunnels to escape back into Cambodia. The hill itself was bereft of any strategic value. Taking it would mean nothing to the outcome of the war. Senior American commanders knew that they would eventually abandon it even if the 4th Battalion succeeded in taking it. Not to mention that doing so promised to be a bloodbath. In fact, the Americans were not even likely to compile much of a body count on the hill because NVA defenses were so strong and the enemy soldiers could escape so easily, probably after inflicting heavy losses on the Americans.

Basically, the North Vietnamese had baited the Americans into fighting for Hill 875. They well understood the American mania for body counts. They knew that the Americans would fight them anywhere in South Vietnam, even in places (such as Hill 875) where the communists enjoyed most of the advantages. At Hill 875, they also knew that, once the fighting started, the Americans would sacrifice heavily to take the hill because they believed this equated to victory. The enemy was quite content to let the Americans claim their pyrrhic notions of victory. Their aim was to goad the Americans into fighting for this worthless hill and either annihilate them or bleed them dry. To the NVA this meant victory of their own.

Hill 875, then, amounted to a fascinating but tragic dichotomy. From the ordinary paratrooper's point of view, the hill absolutely had to be taken—abandoning it would dishonor the memories of so many dead friends. Moreover, many of the troopers were angry at the enemy and wanted payback for the lives of their dead buddies (a common emotion in combat). But, from an outsider's point of view, taking the hill made no sense, and was actually counterproductive to the American cause. In essence, taking the hill amounted to an American banzai attack.

On November 21, the Americans postponed their attack several times while the choppers braved enemy fire to fly in more water, food, and ammo. All day long, NVA mortar crews, hidden on adjacent hills, hurled shells at the paratroopers. American artillery and air strikes continued to pound those positions and the NVA-held portions of Hill 875. Air Force F-100s and F-4s dumped nearly seven tons of napalm on the enemy bunkers. The stench of burning trees and benzene infused the air. As was so common, the Americans were convinced that their enormous firepower had killed most of the remaining enemy soldiers on the hill.

Just after 1500, the 4th Battalion companies started up the hill. Alpha was on the left, Charlie on the right, and Bravo in the middle. The footing was tricky. The soldiers had to step over and around fallen trees and foliage. In the process they made themselves ideal targets for the NVA, who were in their bunkers, just waiting for the Americans to enter their death zones. With devastating suddenness, they opened up with deadly machine-gun, rifle, mortar, and rocket fire. Several Americans were hit and went down in heaps. Others spread out, took cover, and returned fire, but they had great difficulty seeing the enemy. "The NVA were firing from six-inch slots in their bunkers," one after action report said. "The men crouched behind whatever cover they could find, small trees, logs, or mounds of dirt. The hill was soft from the constant bombardment that enemy rockets slid down the hillside among the troopers and exploded." Tree snipers added to the carnage.

In small groups, the Sky Soldiers poured out fire and advanced uphill in perilous rushes, all the while working against the formidable combination of gravity and savage enemy firepower. The bravest among them stood in the open and sprayed the trees, killing enemy snipers. The Americans tried to blow up the bunkers with M72 LAWs but the slits were so narrow that the M72 rockets bounced off logs, earth, or exploded among the mishmash of trees and other detritus. Mortar shells were also ineffective. The only way to destroy the maze of bunkers was up close, almost within hand-shaking distance, but this was difficult because they were mutually supporting, capable of sweeping every approach with deadly cones of fire. "They'd have three bunkers dug in the ground, maybe seven yards apart with a connecting tunnel," Lynn Morse, Charlie Company's senior medic, recalled. "They'd leave ammunition in each one of the bunkers. They'd shoot from this one and move to the last one or come to the middle one. You're still looking at the first one and they've got you in a cross fire." Some of the grunts got close enough to the bunkers to rake their narrow slits with rifle or machine-gun fire. A few even succeeded in dropping grenades inside them. They would no sooner kill the group inside the bunker than more NVA would move through a tunnel and replace them.

Private First Class Stone, the Bravo Company machine gunner, was wielding his M60 from the hip, "running up the hill and seeing men on my right, left and even behind me falling to enemy fire, their legs, arms and in some cases, heads blown off." Some of the bodies lay with their veiny guts spilled onto the ground. The air literally buzzed with the sound of bullets and angry fragments whizzing past him. Some of the rounds tore through his clothes and his equipment, yet somehow he remained unhurt. Intense though it was, he felt as if everything was happening in slow motion (the adrenaline rush and the reaction of his nervous system to extreme danger produced that effect). All around him, he saw his buddies go down. As they got hit, he could "see [them] fall, ever so slowly to the ground in a heap of blood; hear the screams [they] made as [they] hit the ground or the silence of [their] death. The roar of gunfire, theirs and ours, was deafening, yet, you could hear the sounds of bullets hitting flesh and bone, the last moan of the dying." Stone likened the awful experience to a movie, a common description among modern American combat soldiers whose cultural conceptions are, of course, so powerfully tied to Hollywood images.[21]

The NVA were rolling dozens of Chinese-made (Chicom) grenades down the hill. They bounced, rolled, and bucked malevolently downward. Often they exploded before the Americans could see them. One of the grenades burst under Private First Class Stone's M60, destroying it. He found himself pinned down by heavy rifle fire from an individual NVA soldier. Stone now had only a .45-caliber pistol. He fired back ineffectually. The AK bullets clipped perilously close to the young machine gunner. He glanced ten meters to his left and saw his platoon leader, Lieutenant Larry Moore, hiding behind a tree. Stone yelled at the lieutenant, asking the officer to lay down cover fire while Stone moved to a less exposed spot. "My pleas for help went unanswered as Lt. Moore never fired or attempted to fire at the enemy I was pointing out to him," Stone recalled. In such searing moments, a soldier's impression of a leader can forever be etched. As the lieutenant lay still, another soldier ran in front of Stone and promptly got killed by the NVA rifleman. Stone retrieved the dead man's M16, killed the NVA soldier with it, and then set off in search of another machine gun. Stone never trusted, or respected, Lieutenant Moore again.

About fifty meters to the right of Stone, another young officer was experiencing the extreme challenges of infantry leadership in heavy combat. Captain Bill Connolly and Charlie Company had saved Task Force Black over a week earlier. Now they were fighting among some of the best-hidden, deadliest bunkers. The trees and jungle were so thick that Connolly's troopers found it hard to move, much less fight. The captain was rushing around, RTOs in tow, constantly exposing himself to enemy fire, barking orders, talking to his lieutenants, trying to find a weak spot in the enemy defenses. "There was still a lot of mortar fire coming," he later said, "the bunkers were very well emplaced. They were situated so that they had interlocking fire. It was very difficult to go after one without getting hit with another one."

Hoping to build irresistible momentum in this attack, Captain Connolly kept pushing his platoons to clear out the bunkers. As he did so, squad after squad got decimated by enemy machine guns and mortars. Some of the men were literally shot to pieces. Others were shredded by mortar fragments. Quite a few collapsed under a flurry of machine-gun bullets. Their blood stained the trees and jungle floor. Medics crawled and sprinted everywhere, tending to screaming, crying men. Connolly believed that in order for the attack to have any chance of success, his 2nd Platoon, under Lieutenant Tracy Murrey, had to destroy one particular machine-gun bunker. "It had a commanding field of fire through the brush and debris," one Charlie Company soldier wrote. "Anyone trying to move forward was hit."

The gun had already cut down several men. The captain told Murrey to throw his last remaining squad at the gun. The bespectacled lieutenant had grown up with no father and had gotten through college on an ROTC scholarship. Most of his lieutenant's pay went toward his sisters' college education. As a platoon leader, he had struggled with land navigation and had sometimes clashed with the company NCOs. He hardly fit the recruiting-poster image of a gung ho airborne infantry officer. Connolly's order was deeply upsetting to him, tantamount to suicide. He pleaded with the captain to change his mind. Connolly appreciated the gravity of the command (he himself was only about fifty feet behind Murrey), but in the desperation of the moment, he felt there was no other option. In response to Murrey's pleas, Connolly barked: "That's an order! Out!"

Murrey may not have been the prototypical platoon leader, but he embodied the first principle of infantry leadership—never ask your people to do something you will not do yourself. Unwilling to send his men after the machine gun, he did it himself. He charged at the bunker, got within a few feet of it, and pitched grenades into it. The explosions killed the enemy gunner. Before Lieutenant Murrey could do anything else, NVA machine guns opened up from adjacent bunkers, ripping into the platoon leader. RPGs streaked from unseen positions, pulverizing Murrey. "The only thing left of him was his helmet and glasses," Morse, the medic, recalled. "I was one of the [men] that made out the reports of how his remains disappeared."

In spite of Murrey's valor, the 4th Battalion's attack was at a standstill. One platoon from Alpha Company did succeed in breeching the bunkers and nearing the top of the hill, but they were in danger of being cut off. Lieutenant Colonel Johnson, flying overhead in a helicopter, decided to call off the attack. Captain James Muldoon, Alpha's commander, and Connolly both believed that the hill could still be taken before nightfall, but the order stood. The battalion's survivors filtered back down the hill, yielding hard-won ground back to the enemy. The grunts were weary, frustrated, and anguished over the loss of so many friends. Another leaden night descended on Hill 875, practically dripping with the smell of death, tension, and desperation. In the darkness, Private First Class Stone, whose platoon had lost twenty-two men in the space of an hour, settled into a small hole. All around him, NVA mortar shells continued to explode. In the distance, he could hear the moans of wounded men. He felt a sharp pain in his back and thought he had been hit. He reached around to check this out and felt an object sticking in his back. He pulled the object out, only to discover that it was part of an American soldier's spine. The spine "had stuck in my back when I laid down on it." He had no time for emotion or reflection over the gruesome discovery. "I simply tossed the piece aside and lay back down."

For the next thirty-six hours, the Americans contented themselves with giving the NVA bunkers another pasting while they prepared for yet another assault. Artillery and jets repeatedly worked over the NVA sections of the hill. The bombs and napalm jostled the grunts around and took their collective breath away. Captain Leonard later called it "an absolute firepower display." Amid the endless sound track of explosions, Lieutenant Colonel Johnson finally made it into Hill 875 to meet with Leonard and the other two company commanders. He told them that there was still no doubt among the senior commanders (Schweiter, Peers, and the others) that the hill had to be taken. In fact, General Peers, commander of the 4th Division, was sending two companies from his 1st Battalion, 12th Infantry, to help out. The only question was whether the airborne commanders wanted their men to once again take the lead role in capturing the hill. Johnson felt that they should. Muldoon, Connolly, and Leonard agreed. If Hill 875 had to be taken, then Sky Soldiers should do it. For them, the hill had turned into a kind of holy grail, offering closure, redemption, and honor.[22]

On Thanksgiving morning, November 23, the costly quest for Hill 875 resumed. The attack was scheduled for 1100. The remnants of the 4th Battalion would attack straight up the hill, in the same place as two days earlier, with Bravo on the left, Charlie on the right, and Alpha following. On the other side of 875, Delta and Alpha Companies, 1st Battalion, 12th Infantry, would launch a supporting assault from the southeast. These two companies had air-assaulted onto the other side of the hill the previous day. In order to determine which of the two companies would lead the way, Captain George Wilkins, the commander of Delta, had drawn straws with his good friend Captain Larry Cousins, Alpha's CO. Wilkins had "won," so his men were in the lead with Cousins's people trailing behind.

Up until the last moment, the ubiquitous artillery and air strikes lambasted the hill. Some of the ordnance hit so close to the grunts that they had to dodge fragments. As the paratroopers of Charlie Company prepared to move out, Sergeant Mike Tanner, a mortar RTO, overheard Captain Connolly tell his command group that the hill had to be taken "at all costs." At that moment, the realization hit Tanner that he was probably about to die. A sad pride engulfed him and he sat down to write his wife a last letter. Many others did the same. Having experienced such horrors on this hill, most felt that they could not hope to survive another attack. But, when the word came to get moving, they stood and started up the hill anyway. Mortar crews walked rounds about thirty meters in front of them.

The grunts carefully worked their way over and around the mess of felled trees, shell holes, and other obstacles that honeycombed the ugly hill. They braced themselves for the NVA bunkers to come alive with machine-gun fire, but this did not happen. The Americans did not know it, but North Vietnamese commanders had decided to disengage at Hill 875. They had bled the Americans badly. Fighting to the bitter end for the hill served no further purpose for them. So most of the enemy survivors (from the NVA 174th Regiment) had previously exited the hill through their tunnels, then trekked back to Cambodia, surviving to fight another day.

Plenty remained behind, though, to make the Americans' final push for the top of the hill a very unpleasant quest. Enemy mortar crews on nearby hills hurled accurate mortar fire at the GIs. Well-concealed stay-behind snipers also opened up. Anticipating more close-quarters fighting among the bunkers, some of the Americans were carrying satchel charges of TNT. Several extraordinarily brave souls volunteered to lug flamethrowers, although no one really had much training in how to operate them. One mortar round scored a direct hit on Sergeant First Class William Cates, who was lugging a satchel charge. The shell disintegrated him and killed several men near him.

The flamethrower men were moving awkwardly under the weight of their smelly, heavy tanks of napalm, enhancing their vulnerability. As Captain Connolly moved up the hill, a flamethrower man named Flatley got slammed by a mortar. The round ignited the fuel in the tanks, detonating a fiery explosion. "He just basically evaporated," Connolly recalled. "I was very lucky. It threw me forward, ten, fifteen, twenty feet. I got up and I was fine." Not far away, Sergeant Tanner and another man slid into a bomb crater to avoid the heavy incoming mortar fire. "There was a flash and a blast of heat. We saw a [flamethrower] volunteer go down. He was struggling, all aflame. He crumpled in a blazing heap with the tanks on his back." In Bravo Company's line of advance, Private First Class Rocky Stone was walking uncomfortably close to Private Mike Gladden, a grunt who had volunteered for flamethrower duty. "A sniper shot the tank," Stone said. "I remember seeing the flame [shoot] out the tip, circle around . . . ignite the tank and totally engulf Mike in flame. I remember watching him spin in a circle totally covered in flames and hearing him scream for someone to shoot him. He was shot by his own men to save him a very painful, slow death."

Still the assault continued. Small, weary groups of paratroopers huffed and puffed upward, blasting snipers, shooting up bunkers, braving the deadly enemy mortar fire. At 1122, they finally made it to the summit of Hill 875. Stone and his buddy Private Al Undiemi led the charge. By now, Private First Class Stone was on his fourth machine gun since arriving at the hill. One had been destroyed by a grenade. Stone had warped the barrels on the other two from having to fire them so continuously. Brandishing his new M60, he jumped up, yelled "Let's go!" and ran for the top of the hill. He and Undiemi made it there and, finding no more resistance, they hopped into a bomb crater. All around them paratroopers were yelling "Airborne!" "Geronimo!" and "All the way!" in cries of victory. At last, Hill 875 belonged to the Americans.

The price was staggering: 158 killed and 402 wounded. Among the dead were all the members of Stone and Undiemi's squad, except for one man. When the terrible reality of these deaths sank in to Stone, he leaned, almost involuntarily, against a tree, his eyes cast downward, his mind trying to process what had happened on this troubled hill. "I had the feeling of total sadness as I looked around to see all the bodies and carnage around me and upon learning of the death of so many close brothers." He was proud to have taken the hill, but forever saddened, and troubled, by the irreplaceable losses his unit had suffered. Nearly every other survivor felt the same way.[23]

As the paratroopers focused on spreading out and setting up a defensive perimeter, the point elements of Delta Company, 1st Battalion, 12th Infantry, approached the crest from the south. They had received some sniper fire but little other resistance on the way up. In the confusing smoky haze that hung over the peak of Hill 875, Delta's point men could see soldiers moving around. "Just as we were preparing to fire upon these soldiers, someone yelled 'friendlies!'" Private Dennis Lewallen recalled. "The situation could have evolved into a very serious firefight where many more lives could have been lost. I think of this every time I remember or hear of the battle of Hill 875."

The other 4th Division company soon arrived. Together these Ivy Division troops extended the perimeter, circulated around, and attempted to comprehend what the paratroopers had been through. They were shocked at the sight of their hard-bitten airborne colleagues. "They were good guys but, boy, they were beat up," Captain Wilkins said. "That's a very proud tradition in that organization. They're pretty elite guys. You could tell they'd been in the fight of their lives." Even more troubling were the other sights that greeted them all over the hill. "Not one major tree seemed to be standing," Private John Beckman, a Delta Company rifleman, remembered, "and the whole side of the hill looked like toothpicks burning and smoking. It was the scariest sight I'd ever seen." Spec-4 Bill Ballard, an RTO, shuddered at the carnage and the putrid smell of death that engulfed the hill. "The upper . . . quarter of the hill was just totally nude. No trees, no stumps, no nothing, just dirt. It had been bombarded with artillery and air strikes so heavily that it was just clear." He and the others saw bodies and parts of bodies strewn all over the place, rotting in the midday sun.

Captain Larry Cousins, Alpha's commander, was in his second tour in Vietnam, but he had never witnessed anything like this. "There were helmets with heads in 'em . . . GIs, arms, legs, body parts everywhere," he said. He and his first sergeant saw the grisly remnants of a Sky Soldier's head hanging almost neatly from the twigs of a tree. "It was just like somebody scalped him right about where his ears were on both sides and just peeled all the skin off. You could see the eye holes. It was just sickening. It was kind of like a Halloween mask. It was . . . revolting to see Americans like that."

The hill was still under periodic mortar fire, but helicopters could now get in and out with some semblance of safety. The chopper crews evacuated many of the wounded and dead. They also flew in a special Thanksgiving dinner of turkey, gravy, cranberry sauce, mashed potatoes, and pie. Some of the men welcomed this meal as a morale booster. Others thought it was unthinkable, to the point of obscenity, to dine on such fare amid the dismembered, decomposing remains of their dead friends. Two days later, the helicopters came and took the paratroopers from the hill back to the main Dak To base, where they held a subdued ceremony to mourn their dead.

The 4th Division soldiers stayed on the hill for a few more days, taking casualties of their own from NVA mortar and rocket fire. Eventually, though, they abandoned the hill to resume the endless search for and pursuit of the NVA. The hard-won hill was now the enemy's to reclaim, thus illustrating the essential absurdity of expending so many lives for a worthless geographic objective. "A week or so later," Spec-4 Ballard recalled, "we were flying by that hill, going somewhere in our helicopters . . . and we could see 'em already up there, moving around, building bunkers, resettling." When paratroopers like Private First Class Stone found this out, they were understandably bitter. "This told us that all we had done, all we had gone through on that Hill was basically for naught," he wrote. "This . . . was an insult to us who survived and a bigger insult to those of us who gave their lives." The anger and bitterness never went away for him or for the other survivors of Hill 875. Fighting raged at 875, and Dak To, for the rest of the war.

Of course, American commanders could hardly have chosen to remain on Hill 875. It was deep inside enemy country, at the edge of a perilous supply line, and it had no intrinsic value. They only fought there because the NVA was there. When the NVA left, they had to as well. The Americans were much like tethered goats being led to and fro by their enemies. Nothing could illustrate the inherent worthlessness of the attrition strategy more than these unhappy realities. This cold assessment does not, in the least, diminish the extraordinary valor of the soldiers who took Hill 875. If anything, it only adds to it, since superhuman gallantry in the service of strategic aimlessness is even more impressive than bravery demonstrated for a clear objective, such as the Normandy beaches or Paris. The 173rd Airborne Brigade earned a well-deserved Presidential Unit Citation for its exploits on the hill and elsewhere at Dak To. The 4th Division's 1st Brigade also was a deserving recipient for its important part in the fighting.

The Americans found a grand total of 22 NVA bodies on Hill 875. Certainly they killed many more than that (probably about a battalion, according to captured documents), but the communists dragged most of them away. In the November 1967 battles at Dak To, the Americans expended over 151,000 artillery shells. Air Force, Navy, and Marine aviators flew nearly 2,100 close air support sorties for the grunts. B-52s even flew 257 sorties, blasting suspected enemy troop concentrations. By their own admission, the Americans lost nearly 300 men killed and about 1,000 wounded. The numbers were probably slightly higher than that since commanders notoriously tried to downplay their losses in hopes of showing favorable kill ratios. Every rifle company in the 173rd Airborne Brigade lost more than 50 percent of its troopers. The Army claimed that 1,644 NVA were killed in the battles at Dak To, but this figure is suspect. Westmoreland himself later put the number at 1,400. Many other officers, including one general, thought the number was closer to 1,000. Even if the high number is correct, the United States expended a monumentally inefficient 92 artillery rounds and one and a half air strikes for every enemy soldier killed.

As the battle raged, General Westmoreland was in the United States, briefing President Johnson, addressing Congress, and generally attempting to build public confidence in the administration's policy in Vietnam. General Westmoreland insisted that the United States was winning the war and he even optimistically ventured the possibility that, if the war continued to go this well, the troops might start coming home by 1969. In a press conference, when reporters asked the general if Dak To was the beginning of the end for the NVA, he responded: "I think it's the beginning of a great defeat for the enemy."

Sadly, the general was wrong. Dak To was not necessarily a defeat for the United States, but nor was it anything approaching a victory. It was true that the Americans decimated three enemy regiments at Dak To and foiled any communist plans to cut South Vietnam in two by pushing east from the Central Highlands. But the enemy's purpose was still served by fighting the Americans on even terms, bleeding them badly, and inconclusively. The longer the war dragged on, and the worse losses that piled up from such aimless tactical tests of bravery, the more the American public's appetite for the war diminished. In short, stalemate favored the communists and Dak To was, in the end, an inconclusive stalemate. Westy could inflict substantial casualties on the enemy, but not mortal losses, thus guaranteeing the failure of attrition. Dak To was the prime example of this unhappy circumstance. It was also a bitter tale of the price grunts pay for the poor strategic choices of their generals and political leaders. At Dak To, even the combination of extreme valor and overwhelming firepower could not produce any semblance of strategic victory for the United States.[24]

CHAPTER 8

Eleven Mikes and Eleven Bravos:
Infantry Moments in the Ultimate Techno-War

I Volunteer . . . Twice

THE WAR WAS LIKE A video game. Even its official moniker, "Desert Storm," sounded less like a real war and more like a cleverly packaged, and marketed, game—the kind that Americans of the early 1990s could find on the shelves of prosperous computer stores at a time of explosive growth in home personal computer ownership. The 1991 Persian Gulf War was the first conflict to be covered round the clock on television, most famously by CNN. It was information-age war, bombarding viewers with images and facts yet telling them surprisingly little about the real war. Footage-hungry television outlets broadcast the apparent new face of modern war—laser-guided munitions, "smart" bombs hitting precision targets, the "luckiest man in Iraq" scurrying away in his truck as an adjacent bridge implodes under the weight of new-age bombs. All of this made for great television, and presented modern war as technological, clinical, precise, at a distance . . . sort of like a video game, actually. It was vicarious, even voyeuristic. The images showed buildings and bridges going down in destruction, not people. There was no blood. There were no clumps of seared human flesh, no cries of agony, no sense of the profound, tragic waste that *always* accompanies war, techno or otherwise. It conveyed a sense of air power's invincibility and the individual soldier's irrelevance. It all seemed so clean. It reinforced the wrongheaded idea that wars can be fought exclusively at a distance, technologically, by small groups of highly trained professionals who assume minimal risk.

Stung badly by Vietnam-era media criticism, the armed forces during the Gulf War severely limited reporters' access to the fighting, especially ground combat. The vast majority of reporters got their information at military briefings, not from troops on the ground, particularly not from infantry soldiers. The briefing officers fed reporters carefully selected, and edited, images that resonated perfectly with a society already becoming inured to desensitized violence. Everybody was reasonably happy, though. The media got drama (and good ratings). Military authorities got to control the story of the war, with little probing or criticism. The sad result was a popular misperception that the war had been a detached experience, more of a spectacle than a traumatic event to the participants. "Oh yeah, I remember that," one civilian breezily told a combat veteran when the topic of Desert Storm came up, a mere two years after the war. Or, as one acerbic commentator wrote in the early 1990s: "Remember the Gulf War? Or was that last season's hit show?"

In the longer run, when most people thought of the war, they thought of the devastating effectiveness of air power, a notion reinforced dramatically by the video briefings. There was nothing inherently wrong with this conclusion. In the Gulf War, as always, the power of American air attacks was extraordinary. No one could reasonably deny that. The problem was in the unfair overestimation of this fearsome weapon. Fed by the usual yearning for bloodless wars of technology, the notion grew among Americans, from the ordinary person in the street to security experts, that air power and precision-guided munitions had made infantrymen obsolete. One advocate, in a statement typical of many others, asserted that "the Persian Gulf War ... confirmed a major transformation in the nature of warfare: the dominance of air power. Simply (if boldly) stated, air power won the Gulf War." Quite a neat trick! This author apparently missed the fact that, in spite of a sustained six-week aerial campaign, Saddam Hussein only exited Kuwait after the American-led multinational coalition defeated him in a decisive four-day ground war.

Such fallacious notions were eerily similar to those espoused by many military strategists in the immediate aftermath of World War II, when nuclear weapons were supposed to have banished riflemen from existence. "We have heard this siren song before," Colonel Daniel Bolger, an infantry officer, wrote in 1998. "The nukes meant no more infantry, no more mess and fuss, death from above. Instead, Americans inherited two very big, dirty Asian wars [Korea and Vietnam] that swallowed riflemen like Moloch. The great hydrogen bombs have yet to be used in anger. Now the snake oil salesmen are at the door again, this time hawking precision strike, victory through air-power. Nobody wants to pay for any infantry. Let the airplanes do it."

As Bolger indicated, the reality of the Gulf War was quite different from popular memory. In fact, 92 percent of munitions in the war were unguided. Indeed, a congressional investigation, conducted several years after the war, revealed that manufacturers and military leaders had significantly exaggerated the effectiveness of air attacks during the war. "Air power was clearly instrumental to the success of Desert Storm," the authors of the report wrote, "yet air power achieved only some of its objectives, and clearly fell short of achieving others. Even under generally favorable conditions, the effects of air power were limited. After 38 days of nearly continuous bombardment, a ground campaign was still deemed necessary." Lack of credible intelligence on targets—in other words, information on where to drop the bombs—also limited the reach and power of the American planes. The investigators found that, ironically, older-generation planes, such as B-52 bombers and A-10 Warthogs, inflicted more damage on the enemy than the newer-generation planes. They also found that precise accuracy was rare, even with guided munitions. "'One target, one bomb' efficiency was not achieved. On average, more than eleven tons of guided and forty-four tons of unguided munitions were delivered on targets assessed as successfully destroyed; still more tonnage of both was delivered against targets where objectives were not fully met."[1]

Packed with data and statistics, the report merely stated something that common sense should have made clear: air power was highly important but, by its very nature as a standoff weapon, air power was limited in its effect in achieving strategic goals, even in a war that conformed perfectly to American strengths. Combined arms was the key to success. Everyone was needed. Everyone contributed something valuable, especially the underappreciated ground units. In fact, ground forces inflicted the majority of the damage on Saddam Hussein's army, accounting for 79 percent of the tanks destroyed, 57 percent of the armored personnel carriers destroyed, and more than three-quarters of the artillery pieces eliminated by the coalition.

The truth was that, even with all the firepower of modern ground and air weapons, infantry soldiers played a significant role in the Gulf War. Every single one of these men was a volunteer. As an unhappy coda to the unpopular Vietnam War, Congress abolished the draft in 1973. From then on, the military would be stocked with people who chose to sign up. In fact, infantry soldiers volunteered twice, once for the Army and once for the infantry. In most cases, they had to actively try to get into the infantry, and then maintain high physical fitness and training standards to stay there.

In the 1980s, Congress and President Ronald Reagan made a point of compensating servicemen and servicewomen well, enticing them with such benefits as money for college, health, and family care. The result of all this was an educated, motivated, well-trained combat force. By 1991, 98 percent of soldiers had a high school diploma, three-quarters scored in the highest mental category on classification tests, and 41 percent were enrolled in the Army College Fund. More than one in four were African-American.

As always, infantrymen were in the minority. Indeed, the Army had more than 115 military occupation specialties (MOS), of which infantry jobs comprised only a few. Every soldier was trained as a rifleman, but few actually served in that capacity. The Marines had a higher percentage of manpower devoted to the infantry, but riflemen were still the minority. These late-twentieth-century grunts were armed with a new assemblage of weapons, including new-generation M16A2 rifles, M249 Squad Automatic Weapons (SAWs), and a variety of handheld and vehicle-mounted antitank missiles. They were outfitted with coal scuttle Kevlar helmets and sturdy battle dress utilities (BDUs).

In the Army, the infantry branch was divided into two major areas (some would argue two distinct cultures). Mechanized infantry formations were built around the Bradley Fighting Vehicle, the Army's newest armored innovation. To the average person, the Bradley looked like a tank. It was tracked and heavily armored. It had a turret, with a 25-millimeter main gun. It was equipped with a side saddle box that could fire TOW missiles (Tube-launched, Optically tracked, Wire-guided) to kill tanks. The thirty-three-ton Bradley was a formidable beast, but it was not a tank. It was an infantry carrier. Crewed by a driver, a gunner, and a commander, who themselves were infantrymen, the Bradley carried several more infantry soldiers in its crowded rear compartment. The Bradley provided these grunts—generally called "dismounts" in the mech world—with transportation and considerable fire support. Once outside the Bradley, their job was to fight as machine gunners and

Ground troops are crammed aboard a landing craft heading for the beach at Guam. Before these men went in, ships bombarded the beaches with almost thirty thousand shells and rockets.
US Army

W-day on Guam. Marines take cover beside a destroyed amtrac. Along most of the landing beaches, Japanese opposition was fierce.
USMC

This foxhole full of dead Marines on the beach at Guam provides a graphic look at the reality of combat. On W-day alone, the 3rd Marine Division lost 105 killed, 536 wounded, and fifty-six missing in action.
USMC

Marines haul wounded comrades back to the beach. From the first day of the invasion, casualty rates at Peleliu were devastating. The 1st Marine Regiment alone lost more than 56 percent of its men in less than a week of fighting.   USMC

A Marine sits beside a coral-and-concrete-reinforced pillbox on Peleliu. From positions like these, the Japanese inflicted massive casualties on the Americans.   USMC

A flamethrowing amtrac fires a long jet of flame into a Japanese-held cave in the Umurbrogol. One infantryman remembered seeing an enemy soldier "running and screaming and then no noise but still burning."   USMC

The charred remnants of a Japanese soldier who had been consumed by flames.   USMC

The ghastly face of violent death in combat. A Japanese soldier lies dead, somewhere on Peleliu.
USMC

A Sherman tank, probably from the 745th Tank Battalion, fires at potential German positions on Augustastrasse as infantrymen crouch in doorways and wait to move forward. Notice how the tank crewmen, wary of snipers, are also crouching low in their turrets.
US Army

Near the junction of the Zollernstrasse, riflemen pick their way through Aachen's rubble, toward the inner ring of the city. In general, the infantry avoided the middle of the streets, sometimes even clearing buildings with grenades, rifles, and submachine guns from cellar to cellar. US Army

Engineers clear debris from the Julicherstrasse. At the height of the fighting in Aachen, the streets were so choked with rubble and glass that only tracked vehicles could negotiate them. Notice the damage inflicted by shell fragments on the buildings.   US ARMY

A 57-millimeter gun crew, firing from a position next to Aachen's courthouse, supports infantrymen who are assaulting buildings a block ahead.   US ARMY

Two infantrymen in a foxhole outside of Rocherath. Men like these faced German tanks during the battle. Often they had only grenades and rifles with which to fight.   US ARMY

Moving into position in the Krinkelter Wald. Notice how the soldiers have spread out in case enemy shells burst in the trees above.   US ARMY

A soldier from the 2nd Infantry Division picks away at the earth, carving out a small dugout for himself. In December 1944, the infantrymen of this division occupied holes like this when the Germans unleashed their surprise attack.
US Army

Trucks and soldiers retreat through Wirtzfield on December 17. This retreat presaged ferocious fighting in the twin villages of Krinkelt-Rocherath, immediately to the northeast.
US Army

Infantry in the Krinkelter Wald. From these snowy positions, riflemen of the 2nd Infantry Division fought attacking Germans in December 1944.
US Army

Helicopters deposit grunts in a rice paddy during Masher/Whitewing. Typically, they would hover a few feet off the ground while the infantrymen jumped to the ground, formed a hasty perimeter, and then moved out.
US Army

Rice paddies and nipa palms. During Masher/Whitewing, a company of grunts struggles through the muck of a rice paddy toward an unknown objective. Each man is carrying everything he owns on his back.
US Army

Removing the wounded. The combination of helicopters and excellent medics saved many American lives in Vietnam. During Operation Masher/Whitewing, the Americans reported losses of 228 killed and 778 wounded while claiming to have killed more than 1,300 enemy soldiers. Like most operations of its kind, Masher/Whitewing was anything but decisive.
US Army

A combined action platoon (CAP) compound, Truoi Village, Loc Dien, in August 1967. The Marines and Popular Force militiamen have built sandbagged bunkers and tin-roofed hooches.

CAP Marines and their Popular Force allies enjoy a party and a meal. The man standing at the center is the village chief. It was highly important for the CAP Marines to accept the local culture, and eating Vietnamese food was a common way to do that.

A CAP team member tends to a local child. Beyond cultural understanding and a willingness to risk their lives to enhance village security, the Americans found that dispensing medical care was an effective way to forge friendships with Vietnamese villagers. Thus, each team included a Navy corpsman. COURTESY OF CHARLIE PANOSIAN

The very symbol of the CAP program. A CAP Marine sits at the ready, rifle in hand, protecting a small boy. Although the program was hardly an unqualified success, most CAP Marines believed that their own teams achieved good results. COURTESY OF MICHAEL MAJEWSKY

Airborne grunts in "the Land with No Sun," the unaffectionate name they coined for the triple-canopy jungles of Dak To. Notice the tall bamboo shoots surrounding these particular men. The soldiers found it very hard to move through these fields of bamboo because of their thickness and the sharp ends of each bamboo shoot. US ARMY

An equipment-laden airborne grunt fills his canteen in a jungle stream at Dak To. In the 173rd Airborne Brigade, the average infantryman spent almost every day of his one-year tour in the field, carrying heavy loads and dealing with difficult conditions and constant danger. US ARMY

The infantryman's greatest fire support: mortars. A mortar crew fires in support of the costly assault on Hill 875, November 1967.
US ARMY

A rare image of the Thanksgiving Day assault on Hill 875, November 23, 1967. The battle for the hill epitomized the bitter battles fought by paratroopers of the 173rd Airborne Brigade and the 4th Infantry Division for many similar hills in the Dak To area.
US ARMY

Rocky Stone at the trigger of his M60 machine gun during the battle for Hill 875. His assistant gunner is in the foreground. The fighting at Hill 875 was so intense that Stone went through four machine guns.
US ARMY

The Bradley Fighting Vehicle, home to many an infantryman during the Gulf War. The driver is visible in the foreground, just under his raised hatch. Atop the turret, the gunner is on the right and the commander on the left. The unseen riflemen and machine gunners are packed in the rear of the Bradley. US ARMY

A formation of tanks and Bradleys advances through the desert during the Gulf War. These combined arms teams inflicted devastating losses on Saddam's army. US ARMY

Mechanized infantry soldiers pose on and around a Bradley Fighting Vehicle during Desert Storm. By 1991, the Army's infantry was subdivided into two major branches: mechanized infantry soldiers, who rode inside Bradleys, and light infantrymen, who went into battle on foot, in Humvees, or aboard helicopters. Every single one of them was a volunteer.

COURTESY OF RICK AVERNA

Soldiers from 2-2 Infantry smash through a gate to take a building in Fallujah. In spite of an impressive array of supporting firepower and technology, much of the battle came down to this kind of arduous, dangerous work.
US ARMY

Lieutenant Neil Prakash, a tank commander, poses in his turret during the battle for Fallujah. Prakash and the other tankers lent vital fire support to the infantrymen, proving yet again the importance of combined arms in modern warfare.
US ARMY

A tank unleashes a 120-millimeter main gun round in Fallujah. In the confined urban environment, the concussion from each shot was such that it physically hurt to stand anywhere near the tank.
US ARMY

A rare image of opposing sides in the same picture frame. A pistol-wielding American soldier shoots an insurgent during the battle for Fallujah.
US Army

Fire and maneuver. One group of Marine grunts lays down fire while another rushes across a Fallujah street. These kinds of bound-and-overwatch tactics were a must amid the unforgiving cityscape.
USMC

The brotherhood of the infantry. A group of young grunts from 2-2 Infantry poses together toward the end of the struggle for Fallujah.　　US Army

Three soldiers stand beside a crater made by an exploded IED somewhere in Iraq. To create such an IED, insurgents needed only to bury an artillery shell, wire it up with a detonation system, and set it off near an American vehicle or soldier.
2-7 Infantry

Two soldiers from 3-7 Infantry patrol a street. While one advances, the other covers him from any potential threat in the adjacent buildings. A Humvee in the background lends potential fire support.
3-7 Infantry

A 3-7 Infantry Cottonbaler patrols a Baghdad market. The troops had to be constantly on the alert for trouble while maintaining some semblance of good relations with the locals.
3-7 Infantry

Ever vigilant, two Cottonbaler riflemen stand watch on an anonymous street corner. They symbolize the eternal importance of the infantryman, no matter how advanced modern weaponry and technology become.
3-7 Infantry

riflemen, the traditional role of the grunts. The Army MOS for mechanized riflemen was 11M, eventually spawning the nickname "Eleven Mikes." Similar to armor, the mech infantry world was about fire support, vehicle formations, gunnery, and cooperation.

Light infantry comprised the other half of the infantry branch. These were the traditional ground pounders who carried heavy rucksacks, usually walked wherever they went (at best they might have access to Humvees, the successor to the jeep), and fought as regular infantry. Some of them were paratroopers. Others were air assault specialists who rode helicopters into battle. They were the descendants of General Kinnard's 1st Cavalry Division troopers. Others served in straight leg infantry outfits like the 7th and 25th Infantry Divisions. The elite among them were Army Rangers. The MOS for light infantry riflemen was 11B, generally known as Eleven Bravo. Most of them were trained to manipulate a variety of small arms and antitank weapons. Theirs was a life of privation and deprivation, with long marches, patrols, small-unit live fire training events and the like. Light infantry units emphasized physical conditioning, discipline, camaraderie, teamwork, and patrolling. They were the purest of the pure, the last riflemen in a world full of wonder-weapons. Yet they and their mechanized brothers were among the central characters in the Desert Storm video game.[2]

Crammed in a Bradley and Acting Like Tankers

In a Bradley, everyone was usually uncomfortable. The driver was perched on a small seat, crammed into a narrow rectangle in the front left of the vehicle. In this cramped compartment, mobility was only a dream. Ventilation consisted mostly of an open hatch, although as he drove he usually had to keep the hatch shut. Mostly he just sweltered and focused on maneuvering the vehicle. A couple feet above and behind the driver, the gunner sat scrunched in the left hatch of the turret, with his thermal sights directly to the front of him. He could stand on his little seat, exposing about half of his torso, or he could sit down, button up his hatch, and squeeze himself into the turret's confined space. Immediately left of the gunner was the TOW box, arguably the most vital piece of equipment on the vehicle since it served as a launcher for the missiles that allowed Bradleys to destroy enemy tanks. To the gunner's right, the commander had about the same amount of limited space. Directly to his front was a coaxial 7.62-millimeter machine gun. When the vehicle was running, dust, dirt, and exhaust fumes blew into the faces of the gunner and commander alike. The three crewmen wore special radio-equipped helmets, rather like tankers.

The dismounts wore Kevlar helmets, BDUs, chemical overgarments known as MOPP (Mission Oriented Protective Posture) suits, and boots. They secured their M16s and machine guns and kept them pointed downward, at the ready. Jammed in the back of the Bradley, theirs was a life of cramped misery. During Desert Storm, a typical Bradley carried anywhere from four to six such infantrymen. In some vehicles they sat on hard metal seats; others perched on benches. Sometimes, in an effort to create more space, they removed the seats altogether and sat packed together on the floor. The unluckiest soldier (usually the junior guy) sat in the most confined area, right behind the driver in a spot known cheerfully as the hellhole. Personal space, as Americans generally think of it, did not exist in this enclosed world. The men sat draped against, sometimes even over, one another. Any movement affected the others. Few of these grunts were diminutive. One rifleman even remembered a squad mate who somehow wedged his six-foot-six frame into the unit's Bradley. The men had no windows. The only route of egress was through the rear ramp.

The Bradleys were crammed with an amazing amount of stuff: ammunition, cardboard TOW tubes, MREs (meals ready to eat), tools, water bottles, canteens, wrappers, books, magazines, and other assorted personal items. The Bradley's engine noise made conversation difficult. When the gunner shot the 25-millimeter gun, the whole vehicle shook. The noise of it all could be deafening. The stench of sweat, pungent feet, and gaseous emissions— of the human variety—mixed with engine fumes, weaponry, and metal to produce an unforgettable odor. Colonel Bolger wrote of the typical Eleven Mike: "He rides for hours and hours—often for days—in the back of a dimly lit metal box with five or more of his closest friends crammed into a space about equal to the back end of an average American family's minivan. As for heating, it exists . . . with two options: red hot and broken. If you want air-conditioning, take up a different line of work. The suspension system does what it can, but forget about a smooth ride. The track pitches and shimmies, jumps up and plops down. The men in the aft end hang on for dear life." The grunts sardonically referred to their Bradleys as "sardine cans" and "death boxes."[3]

By the late afternoon of February 26, 1991, the troopers of the 2nd Armored Cavalry Regiment had endured these conditions for more than two days. These soldiers, like Kinnard's people in Vietnam, called themselves cavalry (even referring to each company as a "troop"), but, in effect, they were mechanized infantrymen. In fact, during Desert Storm, commanders took the venerable idea of combined arms to a new level. They cross-attached infantry, armor, and artillery units into task forces and protected them with forward-deployed helicopter squadrons. Forward air controllers added to the party with a dizzying array of close air support planes, such as F-16 Fighting Falcons and A-10 Warthogs. Each troop in the 2nd Armored Cavalry Regiment consisted of thirteen Bradleys and nine M1 Abrams tanks, the veritable kings of the desert battlefield. The Abrams was, by that time, the most formidable tank in the world, with the best protective armor, the best suspension, the most effective flame suppression system, and the deadliest main gun in existence.

On that February afternoon, the lead vehicles of the 2nd Armored Cav were pushing east through the featureless desert, looking to cut off Saddam's line of retreat. Two days of ground war had beaten his forward-deployed units to a pulp. Many in those units had surrendered in droves to the 2nd Armored Cav and the other divisions that comprised Lieutenant General Fred Franks's VII Corps. Saddam had ordered his conquering legions out of Kuwait, and his elite units, most notably the Tawalkana Mechanized Division, were charged with the mission of holding off the advancing Americans long enough for the remnants of the Iraqi Army to escape. The Tawalkana soldiers were members of Saddam's vaunted Republican Guard. Most were from the Sunni tribes that provided a foundation of support for Saddam's Baathist regime. Unlike many of their Iraqi countrymen, they were determined to stand and fight.

At 1600 the lead tanks and Bradleys of the 2nd Armored Cav crested a slight rise in the desert and came upon a carefully prepared defensive position with tanks, infantry, personnel carriers, artillery pieces, and antiaircraft guns. Many of the enemy weapons were dug into cleverly concealed revetments. Most of the dismounted soldiers were in bunkers. The Americans were actually outnumbered, right in the middle of the Tawalkana's most powerful units. Both sides were surprised to see each other.

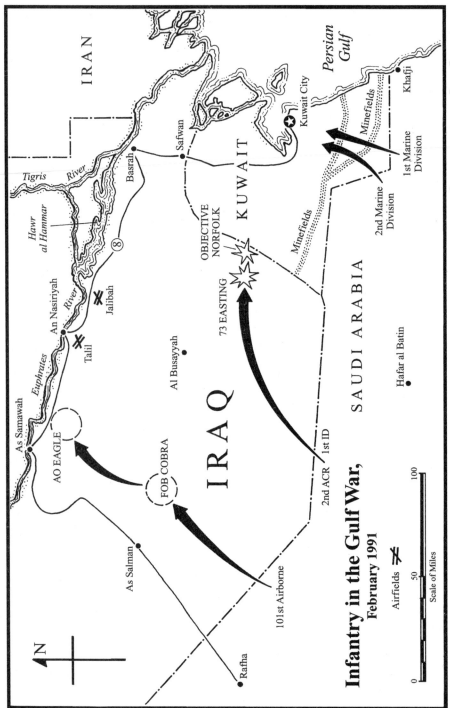

Infantry in the Gulf War,
February 1991

Airfields ⚔

Scale of Miles

0   50   100

COPYRIGHT © 2010 RICK BRITTON

Visibility was severely hampered by a raging sandstorm. Clouds of grainy orange and beige sand swirled randomly in whooshes. The two sides were separated by about fifteen hundred meters. Even with thermal sights and laser range finders, the American crewmen only caught glimpses of their prey. Iraqi artillery exploded overhead, forcing the Americans to slam their hatches shut.

Captain H. R. McMaster, whose Eagle Troop was in the middle of the American line of vehicles, ordered an immediate attack. He sensed that he was in a tight spot, almost within a U-shaped enemy ambush position, and his instinct was to be aggressive, to unleash the full killing power of his troop and all its supporting firepower before the enemy could adjust to the American presence. He had placed the troop's nine tanks, including his own, in the middle of his wedge formation. His Bradleys were on the flanks. At McMaster's command, his gunner, Staff Sergeant Craig Koch, and his loader, Specialist Jeffrey Taylor, fired two 120-millimeter main-gun rounds in less than ten seconds, destroying a pair of Soviet-made T72 tanks. "Two enemy tank rounds impacted next to my tank," McMaster recalled. Koch fired at another T72. "The enemy tank's turret separated from its hull in a hail of sparks. It burst into flames as the round penetrated the fuel and ammunition compartments." The heat was so intense that Captain McMaster could feel hot wind blowing into his face.

What did all this really mean for the Iraqi crewmen? In a word, catastrophe. They died horrible deaths, burned to a crisp, thrown from their vehicles, shredded by the shrapnel of the American shells and their own as well. Some died of blunt trauma, their heads exploding into little more than shards. One crewman, burning from head to toe, managed to exit his tank, only to go down in a hail of machine-gun bullets. The American Bradley and Abrams crewmen knew they had to work together quickly, almost perfectly, to avoid the same fate themselves. There was always a chance that, at any moment, an enemy shell or missile could tear through their own vehicle. The danger was especially real for the Bradleys since their armor was not as thick as that of the tanks.

In mere seconds, the encounter turned into a full-blown desert brawl with both sides firing everything at their disposal. The unit radios were clogged with excited voices as commanders and crewmen alike called out targets, bellowed orders, and relayed information. "All of the Troops' tanks and scouts [infantry

Bradleys] were now in the action," one of McMaster's platoon leaders later said. "Enemy tanks and BMPs [armored personnel infantry carriers] erupted into innumerable fireballs." A dizzying array of Iraqi military hardware went up in flames as depleted uranium, 120-millimeter Abrams rounds, and TOW missiles struck them. "Enemy tank turrets were hurled skyward," one soldier later said. "The fireballs . . . hurled debris one hundred feet into the air. Secondary explosions destroyed the vehicles beyond recognition."

The Americans maintained a disciplined formation, advancing and firing in rushes. Vehicles generally operated in pairs, employing Air Force wingman tactics. American artillery observers, riding in thinly armored M577 personnel carriers, called down devastating, continuous 155-millimeter self-propelled howitzer fire on the Iraqis. The M577s were buttoned up and almost unbearably hot. "We all stripped down to our boots and underwear, drenched with sweat," Specialist David Battleson, one of the crewmen, said. Another observer, Specialist Chris Harvey, peeked outside of his vehicle at the chaos raging around him. The panorama of destruction took his breath away. "All I saw were things burning. For three hundred sixty degrees. Nothing but action."

Several thousand meters to the rear, the howitzer crews worked without interruption, priming, loading, and firing. "No one could do the same job all night," Specialist Adeolu Soluade recalled. "I think I did almost every job on the gun that night." Some of the crews actually ran out of ammo until resupply convoys caught up with them. Flames shot as far as twenty feet from the muzzles of the guns. The noise and concussion waves of the shooting were immense, like an earthquake. "The guns had been firing so long that carbon was building up in the tubes," one soldier said.

While the tanks took the lead, the Bradleys pummeled the flanks. Their 25-millimeter rounds easily penetrated the armor of Soviet-made BMPs and even some of the tanks as well. Deadliest of all were their TOWs, which Bradley commanders fired at tanks, bunkers, and antiaircraft guns. One Bradley commander remembered rotating his turret just in time to see a T62 tank fire at his vehicle. "The enemy tank missed, throwing dirt in the air." The explosion was frighteningly close. "After we fired a TOW at the tank and destroyed it, we had to get out and clean off our weapons optics so we could continue." The Bradley crewmen, with help from their dismounts, had to do all this under extreme stress. "Violent explosions followed the impact of the perfectly aimed and guided fires," McMaster recalled. "All vehicles were suppressing enemy infantry to the front, who fired machine guns at us and scurried back and forth among the endless sea of berms which comprised the enemy position."

For the men in the Bradleys, the battle amounted to a constant struggle to keep up with the tanks, sight targets through the blowing sand, figure out their range, and engage them. The TOWs were like grim reapers stalking their prey. They flew within a few feet of the ground, trailing their guiding wires, seemingly picking victims with relish. One soldier saw a TOW score a direct hit on an Iraqi APC, exploding it "as if it were made of plastic. The metal armor shot up into the air accompanied by a fireball and it seemed to rise and fall in slow motion. In the blink of an eye a perfectly functional vehicle had become a burning heap of metal."

Lieutenant Daniel King and Alpha Troop, 4-7 Cavalry Regiment, were a few kilometers to the south, covering 2nd Armored Cav's flank. To the left of King in the turret of their Bradley, his gunner spotted, through the foggy mists of sand, a large heat blob on their thermal sight. "We raised our TOW missile, fired, and it exploded almost right away," King said. "I put my head up out of the turret and saw a T72 tank in a fireball about 300–400 meters away." Jumping up and down in the turret, he and his gunner exchanged high fives and whoops of pure elation. For them, the killing was impersonal, as if they had only destroyed a vehicle and not people. Armored combat tends to be that way. It also tends to be solitary, with crews in their own vehicular world.

But other men saw enemy soldiers and shot them, especially as Iraqis attacked from behind or fled when American columns advanced past destroyed vehicles. Amid the smoke and dust, Iraqi soldiers with machine guns, rifles, and rocket-propelled grenades (RPGs) found concealment from which to hit the Americans. Some of the Republican Guard soldiers even had Sagger missiles, capable of penetrating the armor of an Abrams if fired from a close enough range. McMaster saw his Abrams and Bradley crews "cutting down hundreds of infantry fleeing to subsequent positions. Some tried to play dead and pop up behind the tanks with rocket-propelled grenades. They fell prey to the Bradley 25mm and coaxial machine guns." Of course, "fell prey" meant that they got torn up by machine-gun bullets or blasted into pieces by the 25-millimeter rounds. "Men were cut in half right in front of our eyes," a soldier later wrote. One Bradley commander even mowed down several with an M16 rifle and a few grenades. For the Americans who unleashed this storm of death, the killing was personal. "They kept dying and dying and dying," First Lieutenant Keith Garwick, a platoon leader in Ghost Troop, at the northern edge of the American advance, recalled. "Those guys were insane. They wouldn't stop." The twenty-five-year-old West Pointer and his men mowed them down in droves, but still the Iraqis kept counterattacking or stubbornly defending revetments and berm-side bunkers. For Garwick and company, the horror of it all was deeply troubling. "A certain part of you just dies . . . somebody trying to kill you so desperately, for so many hours, and coming so close. I still don't understand it. I couldn't wait to see combat. What a fool I was." To another soldier, the experience was "intoxicating . . . also macabre."

The Americans dominated the battle, but they were hardly impervious to damage of their own. Lieutenant Garwick found that his company radio net was so jammed with frantic voices that he often had to dismount and run, under heavy fire, to the artillery forward observer's vehicle. In one instance, enemy artillery fire was so accurate that he and another man had to take shelter under the lieutenant's Bradley. "We just sat there crying, just shaken. The air bursts were coming right on top, ricocheting around us. We were in a corner of hell. I don't know how we made it out of there." Specialist Patrick Bledsoe, a Bradley driver in Ghost Troop, was absorbed with the movement of Iraqi infantrymen moving toward his track when a tank shell ripped into the turret behind him. "It was just like somebody hit us with a sledgehammer," he said. In the turret, the gunner, Sergeant Nels Andrew Moller, asked, "What was that?" A second later, another shell hit in nearly the same spot and exploded, killing Moller. Bledsoe got out of the destroyed Bradley and crawled to safety, as did the track commander.

Sergeant Roland Jones's Bradley in 4-7 Cavalry had dodged several near misses from enemy tanks or infantry, he was not sure which. As sparks and dirt kicked up around the Bradley, the engine got stuck in neutral. A track commanded by his platoon leader, Lieutenant Michael Vassalotti, drove up to shield him. Jones ordered his people to abandon the track. They no sooner got out than a Sagger missile struck it in the turret. "My whole right side felt it," Corporal Darrin McLane, Jones's gunner, said. "I caught some shrapnel in the arm. I . . . staggered a couple of steps, then started running." He and the others made it into the lieutenant's Bradley just in time for it to absorb two T72 hits just behind the driver, below the turret. "It was smoky inside," Jones said. "Everyone had been injured in some sort of way. I had flash burns to the side of my head and the back of my neck." Lieutenant Vassalotti and Corporal Jones also took flash burns to the face. Even as 25-millimeter rounds began to cook off in their casings, the men evacuated the Bradley. Not long after this, another tank round smashed through a nearby Bradley, shearing off the gunner's leg, mortally wounding him. The commander remembered experiencing "a big flash and a big wind, and the next thing I knew I was burning. I jumped out of the hatch." Other soldiers extinguished the fire. Fortunately the man's body armor absorbed much of the flames and shrapnel.

After dark, the battle petered out amid the horrendous stench of burning metal, rubber, fuel, and flesh. The noxious smoke of death—from men and vehicles—hung over the cold desert. The 2nd Armored Cav, and its friends from 4-7 Cavalry, had wrecked much of the Tawalkana Division. Infantry grunts herded thousands of enemy soldiers into captivity. There was little else to do with them except give them some water, MREs, medical care if they needed it, and wait for support troops to come up and take them away. For lack of any other defining feature or objective, American commanders called this engagement the Battle of 73 Easting, after the map coordinates of this otherwise nondescript patch of desert. In the battle, the Americans destroyed 161 tanks, 180 APCs, 12 artillery pieces, and half a dozen antiaircraft guns. Eagle Troop alone accounted for 28 tanks and 16 APCs. No one knew, or was much interested in, exactly how many enemy soldiers they killed—a telling contrast from the body-count obsession of the Vietnam War.[4]

Tawalkana was not finished yet, though. Like a runner accepting a baton in a relay race, the 1st Infantry Division's 1st Brigade advanced through the 2nd Armored Cav and kept up the pressure on the Republican Guards. Just after midnight, this combined arms force from the Big Red One collided with them at Objective Norfolk, another artificial American name for a patch of desert. The fighting was pure chaos, a three-hundred-sixty-degree struggle that was the very embodiment of modern combat. Commanders had a difficult time maintaining unit integrity and order of movement. The lack of navigational equipment on most of the Abramses and Bradleys made it easy to get lost. The night was windy and chilly, specked with sheets of light rain. These conditions, combined with the fire and smoke of burning vehicles, made it quite difficult for crews to identify targets through their thermals.

Visual identification was a near impossibility in the dark and smudge. "At night, war becomes even more difficult as you try to identify friend and foe," Father David Kenehan, the chaplain of a nearby cavalry unit, wrote in his diary. "Some guys will shoot first & question later in order not to endanger their crew."

The Republican Guards, in hopes of foiling the American heat-seeking thermal sights, shut their engines off or abandoned their vehicles until the Americans got within range or bypassed them. Then they attacked, either on foot or after jumping back into their vehicles. "They were shooting us from the rear, which is the only way a T55 or T62 [tank] can hurt an M1," a tank commander recalled. "We were 'coaxing' [machine-gunning] guys running between tanks, running between our tanks and bunkers, as we were moving through. It was really hairy. There were rounds flying all over the place." The Americans learned to shoot at all tanks and APCs, even those that looked empty because of cold signatures on the thermals. Surrendering enemy soldiers were sometimes interspersed with the attackers, making it very hard for the Americans to know when to shoot and when to hold their fire. "The passage into enemy-held territory was an eerie, almost surreal experience," Colonel Lon Maggart, the brigade commander, later wrote. "The night sky was filled with catastrophic explosions and raging fires the likes of which I had never seen before. Horrible fires roared from the turrets of Iraqi tanks with flames shooting high into the night air." He and the other soldiers were inundated with the unforgettable odor of burning oil, rubber, and flesh.

The air was thick with the thunderous booming of Abrams main guns and Bradley chain guns. Muzzle flashes and tracers flickered in the night like flashbulbs. Coaxial machine guns, firing at small groups of dismounted, RPG-toting attackers, could be heard chattering tinnily when the bigger guns paused for ammo. One Bradley gunner alone killed six attacking RPG teams. The American gunners blew up several ammo-laden trucks and dumps, creating dangerous fireballs and secondary explosions. Lieutenant Colonel Gregory Fontenot, commander of Task Force 2-34 Armor, finally ordered his crews to stop shooting up the trucks. "As we made our way through the trucks, many of which were on fire and a hazard to us, we found many enemy soldiers attempting to surrender." His armor heavy task force had few grunts to disarm the prisoners and move them to safety. Fontenot took to running over their discarded weapons with his tank.

"We were bypassing BMPs, MTLB [personnel carriers], trucks, and empty fighting positions," First Lieutenant Douglas Robbins, a Bradley-equipped scout platoon leader, wrote. "These vehicles were barely visible through our thermal sights." His platoon led the way for Task Force 5-16 Infantry, the main brigade grunt element. In an encounter typical of many that night, his gunner spotted two armored scout cars moving directly in front of them. "I halted the platoon, ensuring the four lead vehicles were on-line and ordered them to open fire" with 25-millimeter armor-piercing rounds. The Iraqi scout cars "blew up and began burning." Later they came upon enemy infantrymen in a bunker system. Lieutenant Robbins hoped they would surrender but they did not. As his vehicles laid down suppressive fire, a platoon of dismounted grunts assaulted the bunkers, killing anyone who resisted. Eventually, after enduring this lethal combination of mechanized infantry power, twenty of the Iraqi soldiers surrendered.

Another scout platoon leader adopted the risky but effective tactic of creeping to within a couple hundred meters of Iraqi infantry positions. "This kept the enemy soldiers from firing their RPG-7 antitank grenade launchers and machine guns until we were almost right on top of their positions." The sheer violence of these attacks, combined with concentrated firepower, was a deadly experience for the Iraqis. "We destroyed approximately 40 enemy infantry soldiers," the lieutenant wrote euphemistically, "including one RPG gunner who deployed less than 50 feet forward of my vehicle." The lieutenant's use of the word "destroyed" is revealing, as if he and his men had euthanized a lame horse rather than killing fellow human beings. Such is the emotional distance from killing that combat participants must sometimes forge in their own minds.

Throughout the night, the 1st Division tore through three lines of Iraqi defenses, consisting mostly of dug-in tanks and infantry. Like so many other Americans, Colonel Maggart employed movie and entertainment references to describe the carnage of the battle. In his recollection, when enemy vehicles got hit they "would explode in a huge fireball of flame and debris. These explosions were much like those seen on television shows, where space vehicles are vaporized by phasers or photon torpedoes. Metal particles were blown two to three hundred yards into the air. Often, each massive initial explosion was followed by two or three subsequent, but equally violent, secondary explosions as fuel and remaining ammunition detonated." Maggart constantly warned his crews to be wary of exploding ammo and fuel as they advanced past the funeral pyres.

For his tankers and infantrymen, though, their biggest danger came from so-called friendly fire, a significant problem in the Gulf War. In the confusion of the Norfolk battle, gunners sometimes snapped off shots at their own side. The Americans destroyed four of their own tanks and five of their own Bradleys. Main-gun rounds from tanks inflicted most of the damage. In at least two instances, these fratricidal shootings resulted in American loss of life. One such tragedy occurred when a tank gunner saw several RPGs crease a Bradley. Thinking the RPGs were muzzle streaks coming from an enemy tank's main gun, the Abrams gunner mistook the Bradley for the supposed Iraqi tank. He opened fire several times, destroying the Bradley and two adjacent ones as well. Sergeant Joseph Dienstag, a gunner on one of the wrecked Bradleys, escaped from his vehicle and went around to the back to help the dismounts get out. As the grunts poured out, Dienstag smelled the overwhelming stench of burning flesh. He pulled out a wounded radio operator who complained of pain in his chest and legs. "It was dark and I'm doing a lot of this by feel," Dienstag said, "and I put my hands at the end of his legs and there were no feet left there."

The Americans lost six men killed and thirty wounded that unhappy night. Medics had to use shovels to recover the charred remains of one dead infantry soldier. The dismounts were especially shaken by the unnecessary losses because they were often so helpless, crammed into the rear of Bradleys. "I felt drained," one of them said immediately after the self-inflicted killings. "I couldn't believe something like that could happen. All dismounts . . . were scared. Not only do we have to worry about T72s and T54s and 55s but we have to worry about M1 tanks too. The soldiers had a numb look." Father Kenehan assisted the medics as they treated one wounded Bradley crewman whose vehicle had been hit by American ordnance. "Part of his upper & lower lip on the right side was taken off & his jaw may have been broken." Another soldier was beyond help. "I anointed him & prayed for the repose of his soul."[5]

In spite of the losses, the Big Red One controlled Objective Norfolk by daylight and the VII Corps avalanche rolled east, seeking to cut the Kuwait City–Basrah road that served as the main Iraqi route of retreat. The Tawalkana Division had, for the most part, ceased to exist. The 12th Armored Division, another enemy unit that stood in the way of the American advance, was also decimated. At 73 Easting and Norfolk, mech infantrymen often fought as veritable tankers, adapting themselves to a desert tank fight in which shells and missiles, not mortars or small arms, did most of the killing at impersonal distances of several hundred meters.

As the VII Corps units attacked and overran the road, though, this was not always the case. In one instance, two platoons of Eleven Mikes from C Company, Task Force 3-41 Infantry, got the job of assaulting a heavily defended cinder-block police post on high ground that dominated a key portion of the road. Only riflemen could take this objective, known as the Al Mutlaa police station. Artillery, tank, and Bradley fire pounded the two buildings that comprised the police post. Iraqi soldiers fired back with rifles, machine guns, and RPGs. Finally, the grunts dismounted under a sky that was smeared with the ebony smoke of oil well fires—the Iraqis were burning Kuwaiti oil rigs as they retreated—and conflagrations from vehicles destroyed on the road by the Air Force.

Moving in urgent rushes, they assaulted west to east, across the road. "The company and platoon had rehearsed and trained for this mission so often in the last six months that everything was executed with the speed of a battle drill," Lieutenant Daniel Stempniak, whose platoon led the way, later wrote. Even so, once the lieutenant was on the ground, he was shocked by the unceasing noise of exploding vehicles. The explosions hurled metal fragments around, adding to the danger of the open ground. With only the cover offered by their fire support, he and his men had no choice but to brave an open kill zone for almost three hundred yards to the buildings. Using classic fire and maneuver tactics, they made it across the road to the westernmost building. Once inside, they pitched grenades and assaulted room to room, floor by floor. Sometimes they killed their adversaries face-to-face. At times, their uniforms were stained with the blood of their enemies. "That's where my infantrymen earned their money, fighting room to room," their brigade commander later said. "The Iraqis had AK-47 rifles and rocket-propelled grenades. They sprayed a lot of bullets around."

A couple dozen grunts spent hours clearing out the two buildings and an adjacent ridgeline of bunkers but suffered no casualties. The same could not be said for their enemies, who lost fifty-two killed and twenty-eight captured. "There was gore all over," one soldier recalled. "Many [dead Iraqis] were dismembered." Lieutenant Stempniak attributed the successful attack to the discipline and preparation of his grunts. "If not for the quality and training invested in the soldiers and NCOs the platoon would have suffered substantial casualties from friendly and enemy fire." The lesson, as he saw it, was that small groups of well-prepared and well-armed men, with superior will to their enemies, would always prevail, even against daunting odds.

To a great extent, the capture of the police post put the road firmly in coalition control. The road came to be known as the Highway of Death, not because of what happened at Al Mutlaa police station but because of the enormous destruction the Air Force unleashed upon retreating Iraqi columns of tanks, personnel carriers, and even civilian vehicles. It was almost as if the Eleven Mikes were never there.[6]

Marines in a Minefield and Screamin' Eagles on Helicopters: Job Opportunities for Eleven Bravos

As an amphibious expeditionary force, the Marine Corps was ill suited to desert warfare. War in the desert, with its great open spaces and flat ground, called for the mobility that came from fleets of armored vehicles. The Army of 1991 was designed for just this sort of mechanized conventional war, although most American leaders had believed this war would be fought in Europe against the Soviets. The Marines had no such capability. Outfitted, to a great extent, with an inadequate collection of amphibious light armored vehicles, older-generation M60 tanks, and thin-skinned Humvees, the Marines were not even as well equipped as the Iraqis. But they had something their enemies did not—superb light infantrymen. What makes the Marine Corps special is the recognition that the individual rifleman is the ultimate weapon of war. The Corps is built around that concept. In the Marines, the MOS for grunts is 0311. By the time a man earns that moniker, he has survived boot camp at Camp Pendleton, California, or Parris Island, South Carolina. Following boot camp, the arduous training regimen of the School of Infantry in California or North Carolina turns him into an infantry Marine.

In 1991, these Marines fought their war on foot, amid daunting circumstances. Specifically, they led the way into the most elaborate minefield in modern military history. During the many months of standoff that preceded hostilities, the Iraqis in southern Kuwait built two major defensive belts, consisting of millions of mines, augmented by bunkers, trenches, and barbed wire. Their hope was to pin down the Americans in the minefields and slaughter them with artillery, something they had often done in their war against Iran during the 1980s. For the Americans, the worst-case scenario was to get hung up in the minefields and come under chemical weapons attacks. "We were concerned about speed, and building momentum going north, to get through those two obstacle belts," Major General Mike Myatt, the commander of the 1st Marine Division, later wrote. "Because the worst thing that could happen was to get trapped between them." His division's job was to breach the mine belts and drive straight for Kuwait City. Myatt adopted an Army concept and divided his venerable unit into five task forces: Task Force Shepherd, a scouting force; Task Forces Papa Bear and Ripper, improvised mechanized outfits with light armor; and regimental-sized Task Forces Taro and Grizzly, the light infantry. Colonel John Admire commanded Taro. Colonel James Fulks was the CO of Grizzly.

Three days before the ground war was scheduled to begin, they learned from General Myatt that they would go into the minefield first. Their orders were to infiltrate, breach lanes through the first mine belt, and open the way for the armor. If the Iraqis counterattacked, as most expected them to do, the grunts were to hold them off, with a major assist from AV-8B Harrier close support aircraft until help arrived. Admire was flabbergasted, going so far as to call the news a "psychological shock" for his Marines. Although they did have some engineers attached to them, they had never trained for the task of infiltrating a minefield. They had no armor, few vehicles, and none of the sophisticated breaching equipment necessary to blow holes in the mine belts. "We would simply infiltrate at night on foot, with bayonets and rifles as our principal weapons," Admire later wrote. In Myatt's opinion, only foot troops could carry out the mission with the speed, stealth, and surprise necessary for success. When Corporal Michael Eroshevich of Task Force Taro and his squad mates heard the news, they exchanged death glances, as if to say "nice knowing you." With great insight, Eroshevich perceived the incongruity of the mission. "This was pretty much a Nintendo war. But we were going to walk thirty miles and go through a minefield on hands and knees." Another Marine believed that they would suffer a 70 percent casualty rate. "I didn't expect to come back alive," he said.

Indeed, the mission was a prime example of the difference between the Army and the Marines. Army commanders in the Gulf War assigned their breach missions to armored and mechanized units with mine-defeating explosives and equipment; in their wildest imaginings, they would never have entertained the risky, potentially casualty-intensive idea of sending foot infantry in first. They much preferred risking machines to destruction rather than men, plus they had more hardware to lose. For the Marines, the idea was daunting but not necessarily far-fetched. After all, good Marines with rifles in their hands were the Corps' primary asset, its best and its toughest people. Why not use the first team for what loomed as the greatest challenge?

Starting on February 21, both of the task forces infiltrated about eight miles into Kuwait on foot. Reconnaissance teams then approached the minefields with great stealth and caution. Their job was to find possible gaps in the layers of mines. Some of the recon Marines were so close to the Iraqis that they could hear and even observe them. "We could see the Iraqis walking up and down, and anytime a jet came overhead, they would sneak down into their holes," one of them recalled.

Under cover of the night and the smoggy black smoke emitted by hundreds of oil well fires, Sergeant William Iiams led one team from Task Force Taro up to a fence the Iraqis had built to mark the southern edge of the first mine belt. Through his night vision goggles he saw several antipersonnel mines near the fence and avoided them. Using specially modified wire cutters, he opened a hole in the fence and it fell down. "We went into the minefield for about ten or fifteen meters. We were side by side, shoulder to shoulder, because that's how we figured to clear a lane. We got up to the first real clump of mines. They were the Italian kind, with the clusters on top and trip wires all around. We tried to get through them, but they were just too thick in that one area." They turned around and quietly retraced their steps out of the minefield. At one point, his buddy grabbed him and pointed downward. Iiams glanced down and saw that he was standing right on top of a mine! Fortunately it was an antitank mine designed to detonate only with thousands of pounds of pressure. "I was kind of relieved," Iiams added with great understatement.

Safely away from the mines, he and the two other Marines on his team built a hide site inside an oil pipe, under cover of sand and burlap. They spent the entire day hiding and observing. The next night, Iiams and another Marine went back into the minefield and found a weak point where the mine layer was thin. Task Force Taro had found an opening to exploit.

As of the eve of the ground attack on February 23, Task Force Grizzly still had not. Nonetheless, General Myatt still ordered both of his task forces to go in that night. They had a few stops and starts because of a potential cease-fire the Soviets were negotiating with Saddam, but those peace entreaties fell through. Supported by only a few Humvees with TOW launchers, the Marines shuffled in long columns through the windy desert, in the flickering shadows of oil well fires, bound for the same jump-off spots where the recon Marines had entered the first mine belt. Each Marine was hauling at least seventy pounds of weapons, ammo, gear, and food. Dragon antitank gunners had a miserable time manhandling their unwieldy fifty-pound weapons. M60 and M249 SAW machine gunners also struggled. Some of the Marines, particularly mortar crews, dragged their gear on improvised carts. "These carts were the size of large wheelbarrows," Corporal Greg Stricklin said. "With all the gear loaded I figured a cart weighed between five and six hundred pounds." They had their MOPP suits on, but not their gas masks. The evening was chilly, causing many of them to alternately sweat and shiver. Only the best-conditioned troops could carry and maneuver such onerous loads and endure this strenuous march for miles. One of them called it "the most grueling physical experience of my life."

For Task Force Grizzly, two intrepid staff sergeants led the way, on their hands and knees, into the first mine belt, gently prodding with their bayonets, "old World War I style," in the estimation of one officer. The minefield was between one hundred and one hundred and thirty meters deep. "The majority of the [antitank] mines were exposed on the surface and very obvious," one Marine engineer recalled. "The majority of the antipersonnel mines were buried with the triggering devices exposed to be detonated [when] stepped on." Ever so carefully they crawled forward, gently poking with their bayonets. The job required total concentration. One slip, one moment of distraction, one mistake could mean instant death. Moreover, if the enemy did open fire with artillery or small arms, there was no cover to be had. "Once they found a mine, they just marked it and moved around it, leaving it in place," Colonel Fulk later said. "So they created a meandering path through the field." The two sergeants marked their finds with chemical lights. In their wake, the grunts carefully followed. Each man made sure to walk in the footsteps of the person ahead of him. It took nearly eight exacting, spine-tingling hours to forge a path through the minefield. By 0400, twenty-seven hundred Marines were through. Iraqi resistance was negligible. There were a few firefights, but most of the enemy soldiers quit when they saw that the Marines had gotten through the mines.

To the east, Task Force Taro, led by the intrepid Sergeant Iiams, entered the minefield in the gap he had found. Here, too, the Marines placed red and green chemical lights on the mines, creating an impromptu path that the heavily laden grunts followed assiduously. "We were so out in the open it was unbelievable," Captain Mike McCusker, the commander of India Company, recalled. "There was an oil well fire behind us that lit us up. We couldn't get away from it. They had so many mines stuck underneath [the sand]. Some were on top. Some weren't even opened, weren't even set, but we didn't know that at the time."

As the infantrymen gingerly worked their way through the minefield—struggling and cursing all the way—they were under constant pressure from higher command to move fast. The generals and colonels knew that speed offered the best chance of success. But, for the privates, lance corporals, and sergeants who were actually in the minefield, speed was a far lower priority than safety. It was an odd, and terrifying, situation for them, knowing they had to move fast, but realizing that no one could go through a minefield with any degree of quickness. "The blowing sand had uncovered some of the mines and it wasn't hard to spot them," Corporal Stricklin said. At times, though, the mines were only a couple feet apart, which made it hard for him to maneuver his cart safely. "We had to stop, back up and go around constantly." He heard incessant radio chatter from commanders, urging them to hurry it up. "I was tired of hearing that darned radio. We couldn't see . . . could hardly breathe . . . surrounded by mines that would send you home in pieces and someone was yelling about us slowing things down."

At last, by dawn, all of the Task Force Taro Marines were through. As in the Task Force Grizzly sector, Iraqi opposition was light, and prisoners began to stream in. Many of them had been pounded by American air attacks for days. When they realized that the minefields could not hold off the Americans, they gave up. Lieutenant Colonel John Garrett, whose 3rd Battalion, 3rd Marines, led the way for Task Force Taro, believed that the sheer audacity of the minefield breach, combined with the air attacks that clearly softened up the enemy, accounted for the Marine success. "I think they [Iraqis] were surprised by where we came through, when we came through, and the fact that we kept moving," he said. "It was really a combined arms operation." Like most Marines, Garrett understood the overwhelming power that resulted from ground troops and aviators working closely together.

As the sun rose on February 24, an exhausted Sergeant Iiams took a moment to look at the long line of two thousand grunts plus vehicles wending their way north. For the first time, the profound importance of his mission hit home to him. "It was a big responsibility on my shoulders. I didn't realize it until I looked back and all I saw was jarheads for miles." Against light opposition, the two infantry task forces began to dig in. As the morning wore on, Task Forces Ripper and Papa followed. They forged ahead and breached the second mine belt with their vehicles. From here they assumed the lead role in the push for Kuwait City, staving off several powerful Iraqi mechanized counterattacks. The 0311s were involved in some of this, but not as the leading actors. For one brief moment, though, in the ultimate techno-war, the entire Marine operation hinged on the courage and skill of a few brave men in a minefield.[7]

Even as the Marines did their thing, Army Eleven Bravo grunts from the 101st Air Assault Division (Screamin' Eagles) were jammed into Black Hawk helicopters, nearly two hundred miles to the west, carrying out an air assault sixty miles into Iraq. Their divisional forebears were paratroopers who had jumped into Normandy and Holland and had fought at Hamburger Hill in Vietnam. Since then, the 101st had been converted into a helicopter-heavy air assault light infantry formation, rather similar to the 1st Cavalry Division in Vietnam.

Black Hawk crewmen had removed the seats from their helicopters to accommodate as many heavily laden grunts as possible. On average, each helicopter carried fifteen troopers, who wedged together in spectacular discomfort. Weapons, rucks, boots, helmets, and fists splayed together in a confusing jumble of humanity. Some of the men were twisted into pretzel-like contortions. Most everyone had at least one limb that was asleep. Almost all of them could not wait to get off their helicopters, onto firm ground. Yet, they were also frightened of what might be waiting for them. "Everyone was a little on edge," Captain John Russell, a company commander, recalled. "You look around at your soldiers, and you're responsible for them. You want to bring them all back." The helicopters were flying one hundred fifty miles per hour in the post-dawn shadows, at nap-of-the-earth altitudes, ten or twenty feet off the ground, to foil any inquisitive Iraqi radar installations. Soldiers who were close to the open doors of the Black Hawks could look down and see miles of desert beige speeding by below.

These grunts were members of the 1st Battalion, 327th Infantry Regiment, nicknamed "the Bulldogs." Their mission was to lead the way on a deep penetration into Iraq, to secure the far western flank of General Norman Schwarzkopf's minutely planned ground offensive, and cut off a major enemy route of retreat along the Euphrates River. More specifically, their task was to seize control of a forward operating base (FOB), called Cobra by the planners, which would function as a refuel and resupply point for subsequent air assaults all the way to the Euphrates. Like all light infantry units, the 1st of the 327th required a great deal of fire support from a formidable blend of fighter planes, artillery, Apache attack helicopters, and giant, twin-rotor Chinook helicopters that carried many of the unit's TOW-mounted antiarmor Humvees and its supplies.

All of these helpers, except for the Chinooks, raked over the landing zone before the Black Hawks landed. In their wake, plumes of angry smoke boiled high into the sky. Lieutenant Colonel Frank Hancock, the battalion commander, had been told by his intelligence people to expect light opposition, maybe a platoon of enemy, but he did not buy that. He had a hunch that the planned landing zone (LZ) would be more heavily defended, possibly even by a battalion. So, the night before the assault he had decided to land his unit a mile and a half south of the original LZ. The decision was a nightmare for the mission planners but it was fortuitous for the trigger pullers. The billowing smoke was coming from a ridgeline of inhabited Iraqi bunkers, right smack dab on the original LZ. "Had we not shifted that LZ, we would have been in a major fight on literally the first ships going in," Colonel Tom Hill, the 1st Brigade commander—Hancock's boss—later commented. Instead they made a smooth landing, safely out of the range of Iraqi fire.

In mere moments, sixty Black Hawks touched down and disgorged nearly six hundred grunts, who quickly spread out into a defensive perimeter. Within half an hour, they had artillery in place, and many of the infantrymen had worked their way close enough to the ridgeline to call in more accurate artillery fire and air strikes on the entrenched Iraqi soldiers. For several minutes,

Hancock was content to let them work over the enemy trenches and bunkers. Then the first white flags appeared. Attack helicopters actually herded some surrendering enemy soldiers into the waiting muzzles of riflemen. "The airbursts over the bunkers and trenches helped to turn the tide," the brigade's command sergeant major, Bob Nichols, recalled. Dozens of the Iraqis streamed out. Many clutched white handkerchiefs. Others, though, stayed put and kept shooting at the helicopters. At this point, the infantrymen surged forward and attacked the recalcitrants at close range. "[They] were charging uphill toward the Iraqi trenches like Gettysburg," Nichols added. In the face of this aggressiveness, most gave up quickly, without much fighting.

Several thousand meters away, Lieutenant Colonel Hancock hopped aboard a helicopter at his command post for the short trip to the trenches, where he met with the Iraqi commander, Major Samir Ali Khadr, whose presence confirmed that the ridgeline was indeed defended by an infantry battalion. Hancock had never received a surrender before so he was not sure how to act. He did suspect, though, that there were more Iraqi soldiers farther to the north, at a potential logistics site. He turned to his interpreter and pointed at Major Khadr. "You tell this sonofabitch that he better surrender everyone or I'll bring the aircraft back and bomb again!" The major willingly complied. Over 350 soldiers surrendered and the Americans captured large caches of weapons, including small arms, mortars, and antiaircraft guns. FOB Cobra belonged to the Americans. The Iraqis admitted that the air assault completely surprised them, and they never recovered from the shock effect. The easy U.S. victory stemmed from the speed and boldness of the deep penetration assault, the aggressiveness of the riflemen, and the prodigious power of the close air support.

The capture of FOB Cobra allowed the American commanders to air-assault several more light infantry battalions, in the face of some nasty weather, to the Euphrates and Highway 8, severing a key line of withdrawal for the reeling Iraqi Army. The Eleven Bravos struggled through deep mud. Most of them were carrying about one hundred pounds of equipment, a crushing load for even the strongest of young infantrymen. "Such loads reduced their endurance, their ability to react quickly, and their ability to move great distances," one of their junior officers wrote. The heavy loads stemmed from the American tendency to reject austerity and rely upon heavy firepower and diverse logistical support. They also resulted from the American ability to put boots on the ground over long distances. After all, any grunt operating behind enemy lines needed to sustain himself until help arrived. At the Euphrates, commanders combated the problem by ordering their men to leave behind their rucks and instead carry only weapons, ammo, and food. The grunts were only too happy to comply.

The soldiers made it to Highway 8 and set up roadblocks. Their main worry was the possibility of an enemy armored attack, but fortunately that never materialized. They also had to be careful not to shoot civilian cars. Mostly they engaged retreating trucks and other light vehicles that were likely to carry Iraqi soldiers. Captain Mark Esper believed that his Eleven Bravo unit, the 3rd Battalion of the 187th Infantry Regiment (Rakkasans), stymied the enemy retreat because of four weapons. "The M60 MG [machine gun] was very effective at disabling or stopping moving vehicles; the LAW [Light Antitank Weapon] and AT-4 [antitank weapon] effectively destroyed moving targets; the 60mm mortar proved surprisingly effective at disabling the vehicles, and as we expected, killing soldiers; and the M203 grenade launcher was also an effective indirect fire, area weapon."

In one instance, a rifle squad placed two abandoned Hondas across the road as a roadblock obstacle. One night, an Iraqi military truck tried to ram its way through the Hondas. "I heard these guys [in the truck] lock and load," Sergeant Steven Edwards, the squad leader, said, "and that's when I gave my guys the [order to] open fire. We didn't get any fire back from them. We just shot 'em up." Edwards alone fired two full magazines into the truck. All thirteen enemy soldiers inside were dead. At another roadblock somewhere else along Highway 8, an officer came upon a small convoy that the grunts had thoroughly destroyed. "The scene . . . was right out of a movie." The grunts had shot up a couple of command cars, searched the dead bodies, and laid them out. "Farther ahead was a burning Mercedes truck towing an antiaircraft gun with the crew's bodies hanging out the doors. All of this destruction had been wrought by very disciplined, well-trained light infantry." In many cases, the Iraqi vehicles were full of loot from occupied Kuwait. Very often, the Americans captured retreating enemy soldiers, including many NCOs, who told their captors that their officers had abandoned them. "Leadership as befits a bunch of thieves," one grunt officer wryly commented. The light infantrymen were the ultimate nemesis of these "thieves."

The 101st's impressive leapfrog to the Euphrates elicited deep fear in Saddam that the Americans might push for Baghdad but, of course, that did not happen. Instead, the Highway 8 roadblocks had the effect of redirecting many Iraqi soldiers east, right into the main aerial attacks along the highway and powerful ground attacks by the 24th Infantry Division (Mechanized) and the 1st Armored Division. Highway 8 was part of the same road known as the Highway of Death. The American-led coalition succeeded in kicking Saddam out of Kuwait, but the dictator remained in power because of the coalition's reluctance to take Baghdad and overthrow him.[8]

Too many Americans learned the wrong lessons from their desert victory. Far too many believed that Desert Storm represented a new transformation in warfare. The natural American affinity for air power, technology, and intellectually appealing, clinical standoff war strengthened that belief all the more. Desert Storm belonged to tankers, close air support fighter pilots, attack helicopter pilots, and technicians. With inevitable advances in weapons and information technology, the future practically guaranteed more of the same. From now on, the transformation advocates argued, wars would be impersonal and clean, a simple matter of superior technology and logistical planning. The foot soldier supposedly had no major place amid such evolutionary sophistication.

But the techno-vangelists overlooked the fact that in the Gulf War, the Americans were lucky enough to grapple with an incompetent, ill-motivated, foolish enemy who indulged nearly every American strength. Saddam allowed the Americans plenty of time and space to ship their heavy armor and weapons overseas and put them in place. He ceded control of the air to them. He then made the colossal error of fighting them in the sort of set-piece, desert war of maneuver that conformed exactly to the American military's strong points of mobility, technology, professionalism, combined arms planning, and logistics. All in all, he was breathtakingly stupid.

Like all desert wars, though, the Gulf War was indecisive. People do not live in deserts. In the modern era, they live in cities. The vital center of gravity for most governments and political groups, then, tends to be in the cities, and that was quite true of Saddam's regime, which lived on to cause the Americans plenty more trouble. But too many late-twentieth-century Americans ignored, or overlooked, the urgent trend of global urbanization. With more and more people living in cities, the likelihood increased that future wars would be fought in populated areas, where American firepower and technology could be liabilities.

After the Gulf War, American leaders began to scale back the armed forces. The infantry, especially the Eleven Bravo units, suffered some of the deepest cuts from the economizing scalpel. Three entire light infantry divisions were phased out. Almost all remaining grunt units, mech and light, were chronically understrength. As always, Americans particularly underestimated the importance of their light fighters. "Light-infantrymen are a unique breed," the historian Adrian Lewis sagely wrote, "a unique national resource that has been continuously undervalued in American culture, in part, by the erroneous belief that anybody can serve as a combat soldier. The American fetish for advanced technologies further devalued the role of soldiers. This was no small loss, but it went almost unnoticed, until they were needed again." And, as Colonel Bolger sensed in 1998, they would be needed again—badly—in the urban battlefields that only infantry can truly master. "What will happen," he asked presciently, "in a future war when we have only the wonderful warplanes, we bomb and bomb, and the enemy does not crack?" Unfortunately, very few American policymakers in the late 1990s and early 2000s bothered to ask themselves this very same question. The sad result was old lessons learned by a new generation.[9]

CHAPTER 9

Grunts in the City:
Urban Combat and Politics—Fallujah, 2004

Welcome to the City!

DESERT STORM SIGNALED A REVOLUTION in warfare. From now on, wars would be fought at a distance with guided munitions, precision weaponry, and a full range of information-age technological weapons. America's enemies would be cowed into submission by the sheer ubiquity and lethality of guided bomb units, cruise missiles, laser-guided munitions, and other high-tech millennium weaponry. Rather than depend upon a slow-moving, difficult-to-deploy mass army with its attendant fleets of vehicles, American decision makers concentrated on creating a smaller, lighter, more agile ground force. In the future, most of the fighting would be done by the planes and ships with assistance from a small retinue of highly trained Special Forces and SEAL ground pounders. Modern technology had apparently made the infantryman obsolete, a quaint relic of a pre–information-age past. At least that was the thinking among far too many in the defense establishment of the late 1990s and early 2000s (Donald Rumsfeld being the most infamous example). As was so often the case, though, Americans were preparing for the war they wished to fight rather than the one they were likely to fight. The whole mind-set reflected the longtime American dream that wars could be fought from a safe distance, scientifically, rapidly, decisively, and logically, with little political strife. It was a veritable echo chamber, eerily reminiscent of similar claims made in the wake of World War II about the supposed revolution wrought by nuclear weapons.

The problem was that in the wake of the 9/11 terrorist attacks, the United States instead found itself enmeshed in counterinsurgent ground wars in Afghanistan and Iraq. In spite of the tremendous American technological and material advantage, a confusing stew of tenacious insurgent groups in both countries bedeviled America's strategic aims of rolling back Islamic terrorism and creating stable democracies. "In the United States, we've become so accustomed to high-tech weaponry, so assured of our own power, that we've become blind to who actually does the fighting and dying . . . infantrymen . . . twenty-year-old men who hunt other men with rifles," Owen West, a military commentator and former Marine officer, wrote, quite perceptively, as these wars raged. Indeed, these young volunteer riflemen of the early twenty-first century were bearing the brunt of both wars, serving multiple tours, patrolling endlessly, sacrificing more than those at home could ever begin to understand. The grunts of this so-called global war on terror were indispensable and, as usual, America did not have anywhere near enough of them.

This is not to say that American domination of the air, control of the seas, ubiquitous satellite imagery, and precision "shock and awe" weaponry were not important. They were all vital. But their techno-vangelist proponents had simply oversold the considerable merits of a good product. It was unfair to expect standoff weaponry to achieve anything more than limited strategic aims in Afghanistan and Iraq. A joint direct attack munition (JDAM), for instance, is an accurate and effective piece of aerial ordnance. These bombs can routinely hit targets with a margin of error under ten meters. But they cannot control ground or people; nor can they favorably influence popular opinion (indeed, the bomb's impersonal destruction usually tends to spike anti-American sentiment). Only foot soldiers can patrol an area, secure its infrastructure, develop relationships with locals, and defeat a guerrilla enemy. And only ground troops, especially infantry, can secure cities.

The war in Iraq was a classic example of this axiom. In 2003, President George W. Bush decided to invade Iraq to topple Saddam Hussein's odious regime, eliminate any potential threat that Saddam might employ weapons of mass destruction (an infamously unfounded fear, as it turned out), and transform a traditionally volatile, dictatorial country into a stable democracy. These were ambitious goals, far more challenging than the simple mission of throwing Saddam out of the Kuwaiti desert in 1991. Yet war planners in 2003 unleashed their invasion with less than half the number of troops that Bush's father had employed to win the 1991 desert war.

The twenty-first-century plan was to paralyze the Hussein regime with "shock and awe" guided bombs and cruise missiles while an armor-heavy ground force unleashed a lightning thrust through the desert to Baghdad. Their mission was to bypass the southern Iraqi cities, get to Baghdad, and decapitate the regime, before Saddam could recover and use the nukes and chemical weapons he did not really have. Once Saddam was gone, the country would then settle into a happily-ever-after coda with their American liberators. In the run-up to the war, Vice President Dick Cheney outlined this rosy scenario: "I really do believe we will be greeted as liberators," he told one journalist. "The read we get on the people of Iraq is there is no question but that they want to get rid of Saddam Hussein and they will welcome as liberators the United States when we come to do that." Norman Schwarzkopf, the commanding general for Desert Storm, later said, "I . . . picked up vibes that . . . you're going to have this massive strike with massive weaponry, and basically that's going to be it, and we just clean up the battlefield after that."

Basically, that was the plan, and it grew from many generations of wrongheaded thinking in America about what war is, how wars are fought and won, and what they truly cost. The Bush administration invasion planners of 2003 sought to avoid urban combat because it tended to be so bloody, protracted, and destructive. Also, they avoided the cities because they knew they did not have anywhere near enough ground soldiers to secure them. So, invading columns bypassed much resistance that later morphed into a full-blown insurgency. Yet the cities were *the* center of gravity for the Iraqi population. Indeed, 70 percent of Iraq's population lived in the cities. As a result, any invader who wished to control the country had to control those cities, not bypass them. Moreover, in an ominous harbinger, when the Americans in the spring of 2003 entered such cities as Nasiriyah and Baghdad, they found themselves involved in hard fighting.

What followed is, of course, well known. Some Iraqis, particularly Shiites and Kurds, did welcome the U.S.-led coalition as liberators. Others, especially Sunnis in Al Anbar province, were determined to resist the invasion. The coalition did overthrow Saddam's government. In the months that followed, though, the occupiers, through spectacular incompetence and lack of cultural understanding, were overwhelmed by the job of creating a new Iraq. The Americans did not have anywhere near enough troops to secure the country and rebuild it. Multiple insurgent groups—Sunni and Shiite—sprouted from the resulting malevolent seeds of unemployment, looting, discontent, and disillusionment. The sad result, by 2004, was a full-blown guerrilla war against elusive insurgents who sniped at the Americans, ambushed them when they could, curried world opinion with Net-centric, media-savvy information-age propaganda, and inflicted devastating casualties upon them with the improvised explosive device (IED), the terrorist version of a standoff weapon (and a chillingly effective one at that).

By this time, the main arena of contest was, ironically, the cities. Day after day, American soldiers carried out an unglamorous struggle to control the roads and the urban sprawl in such places as Baghdad, Najaf, Mosul, Kirkuk, Bakuba, Samarra, Ramadi, and Fallujah. The sad reality was that there were nowhere near enough troops to do the job. The war had devolved into a messy, unpopular counterinsurgent struggle for the urban soul of Iraq. Indeed, by the spring of 2004, many of the cities, including Najaf, the Shiite slums of Sadr City in east Baghdad, and Fallujah, were pregnant with menace, teetering toward an explosion of violence. In April, when the powder keg blew, these cities turned into full-blown battlegrounds. Once again, the Americans had to relearn the unhappy lesson that urban combat is an infantryman's game and that, technological advances notwithstanding, ground combat never goes out of style. The classic example was Fallujah.[1]

Vigilant Resolve?!

Since late April 2003, when American soldiers first entered Fallujah in substantial numbers, the town had bubbled with tension. This was a Sunni city with significant pro-Saddam sentiment. This was where imams controlled lucrative trading routes from Syria, where they dominated access to information and markets, and had done so for centuries. The people of Fallujah believed in their inherent superiority to their Shiite countrymen. They had dominated them for decades. The cruelty of Saddam's regime had worked in the favor of Fallujahns, empowering them. The democracy-minded Americans were a threat to this old order. They were also culturally ignorant, heavy-handed in the use of their firepower and in their relations with locals.

By the summer and fall of 2003, this combustible situation had boiled over into outright violence between Sunni insurgents and troopers from the 82nd Airborne Division. In at least two instances, the Americans opened fire on unruly crowds, killing civilians. The locals simmered with anger over American firepower (notice how this U.S. strength had turned into a liability in an urban, information-age environment). When the 1st Marine Division, of Peleliu fame, took responsibility for Fallujah in early 2004, the leathernecks hoped to pacify the situation there by adopting a more benign approach than their Army colleagues. But the mood in the city was not receptive to rapprochement and the situation was only growing worse by the day. Fallujah teemed with weapons and guerrilla fighters. By and large, the city had become "no go" territory for the Americans. In this sense, Fallujah was indicative of an anti-American revolt that was bubbling among many of the Sunni tribes all over Al Anbar province.

Very simply put, a major confrontation was brewing. In times like this, a flash-point event can sometimes touch off a larger conflict. On March 31, insurgents in Fallujah ambushed four American private security contractors from Blackwater USA. As the contractors (all of them former military) drove on Highway 10, the main route through the heart of Fallujah, insurgents machine-gunned and grenaded their cars, killing them. A venomous crowd then dragged their bodies through the streets, set them ablaze, and hung the charred remains from a bridge that spanned the Euphrates River.

The Marines knew who was responsible for this barbarous attack and they were determined to round them up at a deliberate pace, rather than react with overwhelming force. "Iraqis would see harsh reprisal as an act of vengeance," said Lieutenant General James Conway, commander of the corps-sized I Marine Expeditionary Force, which was responsible for Al Anbar. His immediate subordinate, Major General James Mattis, commander of the 1st Marine Division, concurred. He had no desire to make any attempt to seize Fallujah. He knew that fighting for the city would be costly. He understood that he did not have the resources or manpower to rebuild the city whenever the fighting did end, much less pacify and care for a quarter million hostile Fallujahns. What's more, any attack on Fallujah needed an Iraqi stamp of approval, and the shaky provisional government in Baghdad was hardly on board with the idea.

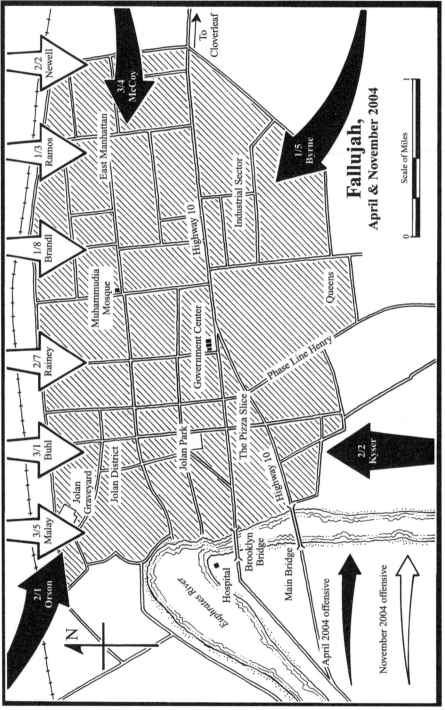

Fallujah,
April & November 2004

COPYRIGHT © 2010 RICK BRITTON

But American leaders, from Coalition Provisional Authority (CPA) head Paul Bremer to President Bush, found it impossible to ignore the disturbing pictures of the crowd and the burned bodies. The Fallujah attack was unique and visceral. Thus it had dramatic repercussions. Desecration of bodies is a major taboo in American culture. It had happened at Mogadishu in 1993, and Fallujah was an unwelcome reminder of this awful nightmare. In the view of Bush, Bremer, and Rumsfeld, the desecration represented a worldwide humiliation for the United States and a major challenge to the American presence in Iraq. So, the Fallujah attack could not go unpunished, mainly because of the power of the appalling images (notice the importance of information-age media in shaping strategic events). For these reasons, and out of sheer anger, Bremer and Lieutenant General Ricardo Sanchez, the ground commander in Iraq, ordered, with Bush's approval, the Marines to take Fallujah.

General Mattis may not have liked the order, but he was determined to carry it out. In early April, his Marines set up a cordon of nine checkpoints around the city to seal it off. Fallujah is wedged between the Euphrates to the west, a rail line to the north, and the desert to the south and east. The city only spans a few miles across, making it possible to cordon it off, even with the Marines' limited manpower. Engineers built berms to discourage movement at the edges of the city. The Marines only allowed food, water, and medical supplies to enter Fallujah. In early 2004, the population was probably about 300,000 people. Sensing what was in the offing, many of the locals began to leave in cars and on foot. The Marines screened them and allowed military-age males to leave only if they were with families. "The city is surrounded," one platoon leader at a checkpoint commented. "It's an extended operation. We want to make a very precise approach to this. We want to get the guys we're after. We don't want to go in there with guns blazing."

However, the pending attack, dubbed Operation Vigilant Resolve, was much more ambitious than that. Any attempt to take the city would require much in the way of blazing guns. The politicians and the brass provided very little strategic direction to Mattis beyond orders to take the town. Mattis filled the vacuum by laying out the objectives: apprehend the perpetrators and the many foreign fighters who had been massing in Fallujah for months, clear out all the heavy weapons, and reopen Highway 10 to American traffic. Four battalions, augmented by Army Delta Force and Special Forces soldiers, in all comprising about two thousand troops, would carry out the main assault, knifing into Fallujah from the northwest, northeast, southwest, and southeastern corners of town. The battalions comprised Regimental Combat Team 1, the modern incarnation of the old 1st Marine Regiment, with Colonel John Toolan, a reserved Brooklyn native of Irish heritage, in command. His ground troops could call upon support from AC-130 Spectre gunships, attack helicopters, unmanned aerial observation aircraft, and Air Force F-15s. As the assault proceeded, the Marines planned to inundate the city's inhabitants with leaflets and loudspeaker pronunciations that emphasized the Americans' strength and benevolent intentions. As one officer put it: "This is a flash bang strategy. Stun the bad guys with aggressive fire, then psyops [psychological operation] the shit out of them, always coming back to the theme of the inevitability of the superior tribe."[2]

On the evening of April 4, after listening to a slew of fiery pep talks from their commanding officers, the Marines began their push into the city. Opposition consisted of about two thousand insurgents of varying quality and commitment. They were a mixture of Saddam loyalists, members of local tribes that opposed the American presence, youthful adventurers, former Iraqi Army soldiers, and hard-core jihadis, both local and foreign. They were armed with AK-47 rifles, RPK machine guns, mortars, and copious amounts of RPGs. Rather than one entity with one commander, they were a patchwork of insurgent organizations under the loose control of various leaders. The insurgents usually fought in teams of five to ten men. The Marines generally referred to them as "muj," short for mujahideen, or holy warrior.

Fallujah's narrow streets, sturdy buildings of brick, mortar, and concrete, and even many of its historic mosques comprised ideal fighting positions for these men. "Generally, all houses have an enclosed courtyard," one Marine infantryman wrote. "Upon entry into the courtyard, there is an outhouse large enough for one man. Rooftops and a large first-story window overlook the courtyard. Most houses have windows that are barred and covered with blinds or cardboard, restricting visibility into the house. The exterior doors of the houses are both metal and wood." Often the doors were protected by metal gates. Most of the structures were two stories and had only a couple of entry points. The rooms were "directly proportionate to the size of the house." In some cases, cars and buses blocked the likely avenues of the American advance.

The first night featured many sharp clashes, but the fighting intensified after daylight on April 5. Clad in body armor, laden down with weapons, ammunition, and equipment, the infantry Marines arduously worked their way block by block, deeper into Fallujah. The enemy fighters mixed with noncombatants, creating a broiling, confusing mass of humanity. One group of Marines saw an RPG-toting man stand among a crowd of women and children, aim his weapon, fire, and then run. Reluctant to fire into the crowd, the Marines chased him but he disappeared into the urban jungle. This scenario repeated itself countless times. Quite often, the Marines took to the rooftops and traded shots with insurgents across the street, or a block or two away. The key for the grunts was to stay away from the streets and crossroads.

When clearing buildings, the Marines spread themselves into a staggered, linear stack formation, against an exterior wall, near a door or other entryway. In the recollection of one grunt, as the point man burst into the house, "each Marine in the stack looks to the Marines to his front, assesses the danger areas that are not covered, and then covers one of them." They held their rifles erect, at their shoulders, ready to fire. Each man covered a corner of the room they were clearing. The key was to spend a minimum amount of time in "fatal funnels"—doorways, hallways, and other narrow spots where they were especially vulnerable to enemy fire. All too often, in this three-dimensional game of urban chicken, they came face-to-face with bewildered, frightened civilians. In most cases, the Marines did not speak Arabic and had no translators with them. They tried to tell the people to leave town, that the Marines were there to apprehend terrorists (or "Ali Babas" in local parlance), but communication was limited. Some of the people did leave. Others did not wish to leave their homes unprotected from the excesses of both sides. Most had no love for the Americans.

By midday on April 5, firefights were raging all over the city. "There was nothing fancy about this," an embedded correspondent wrote. "This was the classic immemorial labor of infantry, little different from the way it had been practiced in Vietnam, World War II, and earlier back to the Greeks and Romans." Lieutenant Christopher Ayres and a squad from Weapons Company, 1st Battalion, 5th Marines (1/5), cornered a sniper and dueled with him in an alleyway. The lieutenant, a Texan who had entered the Corps as an enlisted man, came face-to-face with the sniper. "We both emptied a magazine, but didn't hit each other." The insurgent's AK rounds whizzed past Ayres and bounced off the alley walls. Chips from the wall nicked Ayres in the face. The sniper ran away, with Ayres's squad and another group of Marines in hot pursuit. As they did so, they came under more fire from a house. An enemy riflemen shot one Marine in the throat and another in the thigh. Using the stack method, the Marines assaulted the enemy house with grenades and rifle fire. In the melee, they captured three enemy fighters who were carrying grenades and rifles. There were also two women and five children in the house, but somehow they did not get hurt.

In the kitchen, a stalwart guerrilla shot First Lieutenant Josh Palmer, hitting him three times in the side, killing him. One of Palmer's squad leaders put a bullet through the insurgent's head. When Ayres arrived in the kitchen, he recognized the dead man as the sniper he had dueled with in the alley. "When they were searching the dead guy, they pulled up his shirt and found a pull cord attached to a white canvas suicide vest packed with blocks of C-4 explosive," Ayres said. "Thank God a Marine dropped the sniper dead in his tracks before he could pull the cord." The Marines left the kitchen, rolled a grenade in there, and bolted from the house. The explosion detonated the man's suicide vest, blowing him to bits and leaving a three-foot-long trench in the remnants of the kitchen floor.

Ayres and his cohorts were part of a battalion effort to sweep through the industrial sector of southeastern Fallujah. The shabby streets teemed with run-down factories, warehouses, garages, and junkyards. Faces covered by keffiyehs, insurgents darted from structure to structure, snapping off RPG shots, spraying wildly with their AKs. The RPGs exploded twice—once when the gunner pressed the trigger and then again when the warhead impacted against its target. "We all crouched up against a wall as bullets whizzed by," Robert Kaplan, a leading military commentator who had embedded himself with Bravo Company, 1/5, recalled. "As the marines consolidated the position, the whistles turned to cracks and we stood up and relaxed a bit." Through binoculars, they could see the enemy fighters some one hundred meters away. "Men armed with RPG launchers, wearing checkered keffiyehs around their faces, could be seen surrounded by women and children, taunting us. Only snipers tried to get shots off."

A few blocks to the west, Lance Corporal Patrick Finnigan and his fire team from Charlie Company were in the middle of a whirlwind firefight with a dizzying array of muj fighters. "They had . . . sniper teams, machine gun teams, guys that were organized in four-man groups with Dragonovs [sniper rifles], RPGs," he said. "They had homemade weapons too that would shoot rockets that were just obscenely big, but not very accurate."

Finnigan was an Irish Catholic kid from suburban St. Louis who had joined the Corps after 9/11 for a complicated blend of reasons—patriotism, his parents' impending divorce, and because his college career had stalled. He was a veteran of the initial invasion of Iraq the year before. Like most every other Marine in his outfit, he had heard about the mutilated Americans and he was excited to take Fallujah and destroy the insurgency there. "It was basically an all-day fire exchange with the enemy, pushing 'em back. That was pretty crazy. We were getting attacked from buildings, so we were taking positions behind . . . dirt mounds returning fire, doing fire and maneuver . . . and trying to close with them as much as we could." At one point, an RPG streaked past him and hit a Humvee behind him. Small fragments sprayed him all over his body. Each of the hits felt like "somebody holding . . . some fire on your skin." Corpsmen evacuated him to an aid station, where doctors gave him morphine and carefully picked out each fragment they could see. After the morphine wore off and the doctors had removed as many pieces as they could find, he returned to duty.

By and large, grunts like Finnigan were on their own during the push into the city. Their fire support came mainly from mortars as well as the Mark 19 grenade launchers, .50-caliber machine guns, and shoulder-launched multipurpose assault weapons (SMAW) from the battalion Weapons Company. Air support mainly consisted of Cobra helicopter gunships. The entire regimental combat team had only one company of M1A1 Abrams tanks from the Marine 1st Tank Battalion. They generally operated in pairs, helping the infantry wherever they were needed. Tank drivers sometimes had difficulty maneuvering their formidable beasts through the city. Tank commanders often had problems pinpointing the location of enemy fighters, even when taking fire from them. "It was very difficult to determine the direction, distance, and location of enemy rifle fire," Captain Michael Skaggs, the tank company commander, later said. "These sounds echoed around buildings, and the enemy remained concealed within dark areas. For tankers, muzzle flashes and rifle firing signatures were difficult to locate unless they had a general location to look." Usually, they were dependent upon the infantrymen to point out targets, often by firing rifle or machine-gun tracer rounds at the targeted building or street. At times, the tanks could be vulnerable to close-quarters enemy attacks if they did not have infantry support. For instance, Lance Corporal Finnigan was behind a mound, covering one tank that was close to a house, when he saw a teenager attempt to drop explosives down onto it from a rooftop. "It was only a hundred-meter, or two-hundred-meter . . . shot. I just put the triangle on the square and squeezed the trigger and he fell instantly." The ensuing explosion collapsed the entire roof of the building, but the tank was unscathed.[3]

The fighting raged on like this for three more days, with the Americans inflicting serious punishment on both the insurgents and the infrastructure of Fallujah. Militarily, the Americans were winning. General Mattis estimated that he needed only two or three more days to take the entire city. Politically, though, the Americans were on the verge of a catastrophe because of the unfair perception in Iraq and elsewhere that the Americans were unleashing destruction with impunity. In general, they tried to launch air strikes as judiciously, and with as much precision, as possible. They attempted to limit the destruction wrought by tanks, mortars, and other weapons. They especially hoped to avoid shooting at mosques, but when they took fire from the mosques, they returned it. Those journalists who were embedded with Marine infantry units attested to American restraint, although they were not in a position to see what was going on beyond the Marine lines.

The sad fact was that it simply was not possible to assault a sizable city without killing innocent people and wrecking private property. "Civilian casualties are accepted as inevitable in high-tech, standoff warfare," the military analyst and Marine combat veteran Bing West once wrote. "The infantryman does not stand off. The grunt must make instant, difficult choices in the heat of battle." For the average Marine infantryman, it could be quite difficult to determine who was a noncombatant and who was not. Men of all ages sometimes took potshots with RPGs or rifles, discarded the weapons, and then melted into crowds or buildings. Unarmed people, especially teenagers, watched the Marines and relayed information to the insurgents in person or on cell phones. Even women sometimes gathered intelligence in this fashion. Other unarmed men hid in buildings, spoke with mobile mortar teams on cell phones, and called down fire on the Americans. For the Marine grunt, any Fallujahn who was capable of walking and talking could potentially be a threat. How could he know which Iraqi was simply talking to a friend on his phone and which was passing along information to insurgents on the next block? Needless to say, the environment was unforgiving.

As the fighting raged, General John Abizaid, the theater commander, claimed that the commanders at Fallujah had "attempted to protect civilians to the best of their ability. I think everybody knows that." But everyone did not know or believe that. Quite the opposite was true, actually. Worldwide media reports teemed with claims that the Americans were wantonly killing large numbers of civilians in Fallujah. One *New York Times* report, filed from Baghdad, told of a wounded six-year-old boy whose parents had been killed by American bullets. The boy told the *Times* reporter, Christine Hauser, of seeing his brothers crushed to death when their house collapsed under the weight of bombs. "Iraqis who have fled Falluja [*sic*] tell of random gunfire, dead and wounded lying in the streets, and ambulances being shot up," Hauser wrote. A subsequent story, filed this time from Fallujah itself, reported one gravedigger's claim that, in the town cemetery, "there are [two hundred fifty] people buried here from American strikes on houses. We have stacked the bodies one on top of the other."

Arab media outlets, such as the notoriously anti-American TV network Al Jazeera, carried the most incendiary declarations of American-led destruction. As the fighting raged in Fallujah, the insurgents welcomed Al Jazeera reporter Ahmed Mansour and his film crew into the city. Mansour and his crew filmed many scenes of wounded Iraqis at Fallujah's largest hospital. The images were awful—mutilated children, sobbing mothers, horribly wounded old people, blood-soaked beds, harried doctors and nurses, and dead bodies, including babies. The ghastly scenes ran continuously in a twenty-four-hour loop. The clear implication was that the Americans were wantonly killing and maiming. Hospital personnel claimed that the Americans had killed between six hundred and a thousand people. Because any Western journalist entering the insurgent-held portions of the city risked being kidnapped and beheaded, the Al Jazeera footage and claims comprised the main image of Fallujah before the world. Thus, the insurgents controlled the crucial realm of information, shaping world opinion—and more important, Iraqi public opinion—in their favor.

As with so much media reporting in the Internet age, the problem was lack of context. The visceral hospital scenes were horrifying to any decent human being. But the circumstances that caused this death and destruction were vague. Were these people deliberately targeted by the Americans? Had they actually been wounded and killed by American bombs, shells, or small arms? Or had the insurgents done the damage? Were the civilians perhaps caught in the middle of firefights raging between the two sides? Had they clearly indicated their status as noncombatants? The pictures answered none of these reasonable questions. They only stood as accusatory portraits, with no corroboration, against the Americans, for the human suffering they had allegedly caused. By this time, insurgent groups in Iraq were masters at controlling information, using the Internet to spread anti-American propaganda and shaping the world's perception of the war in their favor.

The result of all this was anger in Iraq over Fallujah. American policymakers, often troubled themselves by the pictures, did little to counter the Al Jazeera story line of U.S. barbarism. After a year of occupation, many Iraqis, Shiite and Sunni alike, were already boiling with bitterness against the Americans for a litany of problems, including chaotic violence, lack of electrical power, lack of potable water, nighttime raids against private homes by the Americans, and a slew of cultural tensions. The pictures from Fallujah made it seem as though the Americans were systematically destroying the city and its inhabitants, simply because of what had happened to their four contractors. Resentment morphed into abject hatred and hysteria, especially among those who had always opposed the U.S. invasion. One anti-American cleric, for instance, screeched on Al Jazeera that the Americans were modern-day Crusaders who intended to slaughter all Iraqis. "They are killing children!" he wailed. "They are trying to destroy everything! The people can see through all the American promises and lies!"

Even moderate Iraqis were outraged by what they saw on Al Jazeera. "My opinion of the Americans has changed," one Shiite store owner in Basra told a journalist. "When [they] came, they talked about freedom and democracy. Now, the Americans are pushing their views by force." Another middle-class man was so angered by the video he saw of Fallujah that he declared: "We came to hate the Americans for that. The Americans will hit any family. They just don't care." This was hardly the reality in Fallujah, but it became the perception among far too many Iraqis.

Consequently, as April unfolded, many of Iraq's cities were on the verge of a total revolt against the Americans. Iraq was coming apart at the seams.

Heavy fighting raged, not just in Fallujah but in Ramadi, the largest city in Al Anbar. Not only were the Sunnis rising up, but also some of the Shiites, particularly Moqtada al-Sadr's Mahdi Army militia. In Najaf and the Sadr City section of Baghdad, his militiamen were fighting bloody pitched battles against the U.S. Army. The situation in Iraq was so bad, and the American control of the urban roads so shaky, that commanders worried about the possibility that their supply lines would soon be cut. The Iraqi Governing Council (IGC), a provisional body that Bremer's CPA had devised to hasten the transition of Iraq from occupied country to a new sovereign democracy, was on the verge of dissolution. Several of the Council's twenty-five members condemned the invasion of Fallujah and threatened to resign in protest. At least two members actually did resign. When the Americans attempted to legitimize the battle by sending Iraqi Army soldiers to help out, they mutinied. Nationwide, desertions among soldiers and policemen skyrocketed to 80 percent.

To top it all off, the political situation in the United States was also volatile, and in a presidential election year, no less. Antiwar sentiment was hardening. Governor Howard Dean, an avowed peace candidate, came close to winning the Democratic Party nomination before Senator John Kerry finally outpaced him. Kerry's position on the war was ambiguous, but he was a harsh critic of the Bush administration's handling of the conflict. He lambasted Bush for bungling the war and portrayed the war as a disaster. The Fallujah mess only added ammunition to Kerry's arsenal. His candidacy reflected a significant component of the American electorate that had lost confidence in Bush's leadership and viewed the war as a foolish, costly mistake, a bloody quagmire in the making. All of this threatened to severely damage Bush's chances for reelection.

Under threat of this potential strategic meltdown, Bremer and Abizaid felt that they must halt the Fallujah operation or risk a massive political defeat in Iraq. On April 9, they ordered the Marines to hold in place. Mattis and his leathernecks were incensed. They yearned to finish the job of taking Fallujah. Instead, Bremer, Abizaid, and other American authorities began an on-again, off-again, dizzying series of negotiations with the IGC, local sheiks, Fallujah city fathers, insurgent groups, and any other Iraqis who seemed to offer the possibility of a favorable resolution to the situation.

The Marine grunts could not understand why the brass was restraining them. The infantrymen's dangerous reality was quite distant from the back-and-forth political maneuvering that had come to dominate the Fallujah story, but what they did know disgusted them. One grunt expressed their prevailing sentiment with a contemptuous parody of the negotiations: "Hey, Sheik Butt Fuck, will you please, please, pretty please turn over those naughty little boys who slaughtered our people, burnt their bodies, and strung them up from that bridge?" Even more frustrating for the Marines, the negotiations took place against the backdrop of a supposed cease-fire, which existed only in name. Throughout April, plenty of fighting raged with much loss of life on both sides, but with no decisive result.

In fact, the end of American offensive operations provided a major respite to the guerrillas. They now had plenty of time to rest, rearm, reinforce, and carry out deliberate, calculated attacks on the Marines, and on their own turf, no less. "The Muj inside the city . . . just dug in deeper, slabbing up their machine-gun bunkers and mortar pits with fresh concrete," a Marine infantry platoon leader wrote. "They had plenty of food—most of it relief aid—and all the water in the river to drink."[4]

Each day the Marines hoped and expected to receive the order to renew their attack. It never came. Instead of advancing block by block, working toward the finite objective of taking the city, the frustrated Marine grunts found themselves stalemated, holed up in buildings, trading shots with any insurgents who messed with them. Snipers did much of the fighting. The urban jungle was a paradise of targets for them. "It's a sniper's dream," one of them said. As precision shooters, they were the perfect antidote in an urban setting to the excess of American firepower.

In a way, the snipers were also the ultimate manifestation of Marine Corps ethos. They were riflemen par excellence, masters at the art of precision killing. They embodied the notion that even in modern war, the individual fighter is still the ultimate weapon. This is the foundational philosophy of the Corps and it was on full display in Fallujah. In modern combat, snipers are the most personal of killers. They track, stalk, and spot their prey. They sometimes can see the expression on the faces of their victims—and even know something about their personal habits. This is rare in modern war, when soldiers shoot powerful weapons at their enemies but often do not know for sure if they ever hit or kill anyone. This is one reason why it is foolish and invasive to ask a combat soldier if he ever killed anyone. He probably does not know or, more likely, he does not want to know. If he has killed, then asking him that question is like asking him to reveal intimate secrets about himself, almost akin to demanding explicit details about his sex life.

Every sniper has to embrace an equilibrium in his attitude on killing or he simply cannot do the job. He has to avoid identifying or sympathizing with his victim too much, or he will be reluctant to kill him. On the other hand, he must guard against becoming drunk with the power of life and death, thirsting to kill anyone who enters his sights, regardless of whether that person is a threat or a valuable military target for the larger goal of fulfilling the mission. Striking the proper balance requires great strength of character and mental clarity. Each Marine sniper at Fallujah had to come to terms with becoming such a killer.

They set up in well-hidden positions on rooftops and near windows. They maintained a vigil, searching for insurgents day and night. Some of the shooters were graduates of the Marine scout sniper school's rugged program. These craftsmen were often armed with M40A3 bolt-action rifles designed specifically for sniping. Other shooters were just good riflemen from infantry platoons. Lance Corporal Finnigan fit the latter category, although he had trained with the snipers on Okinawa for a few weeks before deploying to Iraq. Armed with an M16 that had an Advanced Combat Optical Gunsight (ACOG) mounted on its sight rail, Finnegan was ensconced on a rooftop, along with a machine gunner and a Mark 19 grenadier. "We had a couple of sandbags," he said. "We actually had a bunch of alternate positions, from different windows in the building. We had a chair set up." The chair was positioned about ten feet from any window or hole so as to shield the barrel of the rifle and provide some cover for Finnigan. The ACOG allowed him to see for many hundreds of meters, deep into enemy territory.

His best friend and several other platoon mates had been killed on the first day of the offensive, so he was itching for some payback. The rules of engagement were flexible. Anyone who was armed or moving military supplies or even pointing their fingers at the Marine positions was a legitimate target. The negotiations notwithstanding, Fallujah remained a war zone. Round the clock, plenty of shooting raged back and forth all over the city, and Finnigan's spot in a section of the city the Marines called Queens was no different. Periodically they got shelled by 120-millimeter mortars. They also took muj machine-gun and rifle fire.

Finnigan operated in twenty-minute shifts, giving his eyes plenty of time away from the gun sight to rest. "It's not like you're just sitting there behind the scope for hours at a time. That's impossible. Your eye will get really tired. Everybody takes a turn." Many times, he spotted insurgents on the move and opened fire. "Most of these idiots would just be walking . . . and they had no idea where we were and they would have their weapons and neat little uniforms on or whatever. They'd just be walking down the street having no idea they were about to enter a killing zone." In all, he estimated that he killed fifteen of these armed men.

A couple dozen blocks to the north, in the Jolan district, Corporal Ethan Place, a trained scout sniper attached to the 2/1 Marines, was also hunting for targets. Like all scout snipers, he worked with a spotter, who helped him find targets, figure windage, and protect him from enemy snipers. Place and his partner spotted a group of insurgents rushing toward their positions, ducking through alleyways. The attackers would peek around a corner, launch an RPG in the Marines' direction, and then scramble back out of sight. Place concentrated on one especially active corner. Sure enough, an insurgent with an RPG started around that corner. Place squeezed the trigger of his M40A3 and hit the man full in the shoulder. Unlike Hollywood movies, the round did not knock him off his feet. He simply crumpled, twitched, and fell. Another enemy fighter, wearing a black ski mask, glanced around the same corner. Place waited until the man moved into the open and then shot him in the chest, killing him instantly. In the next few hours, he killed several more. "They look up the street and don't see anyone," he said. "They can't believe I can see them." When a white car with three armed men approached at three hundred meters, he killed all three of them. Needless to say, the enemy attack went nowhere.

In subsequent days, he killed numerous guerrillas who were trying to drag away the dead bodies of their comrades. He personally shot and killed at least thirty-two insurgents. His spotter got several more. The streets in their range of vision were strewn with maggot-infested, swollen, stinking carcasses. There were so many flies feeding on the head of one body that it created the appearance of a full beard. At night dogs and cats tore at the corpses, sometimes eating all the way to the bone. The incessant howling and moaning of the animals provided an eerie sound track to the evening shadows. Overhead, AC-130s raked enemy-held buildings with cannon and Gatling gun fire. Psychological operations teams played heavy metal music by the likes of AC/DC and Drowning Pool. The muj countered with fiery anti-American rhetoric blared from the speakers of mosques: "America is bringing Jews from Israel and stealing Iraq's oil. Women, take your children into the streets to aid the holy warriors. Bring them food, water, and weapons. Do not fear death. It is your duty to protect Islam." The competing sounds symbolized this epic clash of cultures. The irreverent Marines dubbed this surreal environment "LaLa-Fallujah" after a popular rock festival.

For the muj, the Marine snipers were the most terrifying weapon of all. They seemed to be everywhere, all-knowing and all-seeing. They meted out death so swiftly and so personally that they created great mental strain among the enemy fighters. They were so effective that Fallujah's city elders and IGC negotiators began demanding their withdrawal as a precondition of any settlement in Fallujah. "I find it strange," Lieutenant General Conway replied to one such demand, "that you object to our most discriminate weapon—a Marine firing three ounces of lead at a precise target. I reject your demand, and I wonder who asked you to make it."[5]

But, by early May, that was about the only demand the Americans had rejected. By now, the Abu Ghraib scandal was in full bloom, only adding to the American strategic woes in Iraq. So, in spite of their obvious military successes in Fallujah, the Americans were now on such weak political footing that they agreed to a withdrawal. As a fig leaf to cover this obvious reversal, the Americans agreed to turn over the city's security to the so-called Fallujah Brigade, a unit that was comprised mainly of former Iraqi soldiers and even some insurgents. The brigade would be armed and supported financially by the Americans. In exchange, they were to enforce a cease-fire and maintain peace in Fallujah. In reality, the Fallujah Brigade had no such capability, mainly because its members sympathized with, or were even part of, the insurgency. Turning over the city to them was tantamount to giving it to the guerrillas.

When the grunts heard the withdrawal order, they felt betrayed, bitter, and very angry. Many felt that they were being cheated out of a victory that they and their fallen brother Marines had earned. Thoroughly disgusted, Lieutenant Ilario Pantano, a rifle platoon leader in Echo Company, 2/2 Marines, turned to a *Time* magazine reporter who had covered many wars and asked: "Does this remind you of another part of the world in the early 1970s?"

The allusion to Vietnam was clear. Like every other Marine in his company, Lance Corporal Finnigan was peeved and frustrated by the order. "It was bullshit. It was a tough pill to swallow. It just wasn't much fun to hear that." Major Dave Bellon, the intelligence officer for RCT-1, knew the realities in Fallujah as well as, or better than, any other American. His assessment was dead-on: "We're letting the muj off the canvas. They'll use Fallujah as a base to hit us."

As the Marines left, their supposed Fallujah Brigade "allies" jeered and glared at them. Some turned and pantomimed defecating in the direction of the Americans. Others jubilantly waved Saddam-era flags. "They [Americans] told us to change our uniforms," one of them told a reporter, "but we refused. We are not with the Americans. We are Iraqi fighters." Another brigade member said of the Americans: "They lost. They should leave." One of the insurgents crowed that "this is a great victory for the people of Iraq. The mujahideen and the Falluja [sic] Brigade are brothers." Many of the Fallujahns agreed. A triumphal mood permeated much of the city. Armed men in pickup trucks honked their horns in celebration. Groups of men and teenagers stood together cheering on street corners. "We believe God saved our city," one of them said. "And we believe they [Americans] learned a lesson . . . not to mess with Fallujah." Storefronts featured signs with such pronunciations as "We have defeated the devil Marines!" and "Jihad has triumphed!"

They were wrong, though. They had not defeated the Americans. The Americans had defeated themselves. Their self-imposed reversal was the result of their strategic fecklessness, their vacillating political and military leadership, their cultural ignorance, and, most of all, their fatal willingness to allow the enemy to shape world opinion in an information age. For a nation that pioneered the concept of mass media, the American inability to competently tell their own side of the Fallujah story and thus counter the endless drumbeat of insurgent propaganda was both stunning and unacceptable. The sad result was an artificial defeat and a city thrown to the metaphorical wolves.

At Fallujah in the spring of 2004, the Americans carried out 150 air strikes that destroyed 75 buildings with about a hundred tons of explosives—hardly an excessive onslaught. The number of dead civilians ranged between 270, according to the Iraqi Ministry of Health, and somewhere just north of 600, according to Al Jazeera. Insurgent losses have never been pinpointed but they were probably well into the hundreds (of course, part of the problem in calculating the casualties is figuring out who was truly a noncombatant and who was not). The Americans lost 27 killed and over 100 wounded, essentially for no tangible results. Fallujah in the spring of 2004 could not have contrasted more sharply with Aachen in 1944, when American soldiers fought an urban battle with no political constraints and no world condemnation. At Fallujah, politics and popular perception shaped everything. In the end, the Americans lacked the strategic clarity and force of leadership to attain their objectives. Rarely has an operation been more poorly named than Vigilant Resolve in April 2004.[6]

Timing Is Everything: Back to the Malignant City in November

Fallujah grew much worse as 2004 unfolded. As many of the Marines had feared after the cease-fire settlement back in the spring, Fallujah's various insurgent groups solidified their hold on the city. They used it as a sanctuary and a launching point for attacks on the Americans in Al Anbar. Practically every day, they attacked the Americans with a vexing mix of IEDs, Vehicle Borne IEDs (VBIEDs), suicide bombings, mortars, rockets, and shootings. The Americans responded with raids, targeted air strikes, cordon and searches. The casualties piled up on both sides. In Fallujah, there were, according to Marine intelligence sources, seventeen separate insurgent groups and about a dozen important leaders, the most notorious of whom was Abu Musab al-Zarqawi, the Jordanian who headed up al-Qaeda in Iraq. Together they co-opted the traditional influence of local tribes in Fallujah.

Like a tumor, the power of these terrorist gangs metastasized into a malignant growth on the Iraqi body politic. Even as Al Anbar burned with resistance to the Americans and the new Iraqi Interim Government (IIG) the Americans had created in June, Fallujah stood out as a no-go area of special defiance. It was essentially a city-state of its own, a hostile challenge to a fledgling, Shiite-controlled Iraqi government that was struggling for legitimacy in the eyes of its own people, especially Al Anbar Sunnis.

By summer's end, local imams and guerrilla leaders, many of whom were foreigners, had imposed hard-line Islamic strictures (known as sharia law) on the city. Operating from one of the city's numerous mosques, a ruling council known as the Mujahideen Shura enforced this radical interpretation of Islam, sometimes with harsh punishment. This witch's brew of local insurgents, sheiks, imams, and foreign terrorists imposed a Hobbesian sort of gang rule on Fallujahns. Alcohol of any kind was forbidden. Anyone caught selling it or consuming it was flogged or spat upon. Western-style haircuts, CDs, music, and magazines were all forbidden, sometimes on the threat of death.

The terrorists often watched the American bases throughout Anbar and took note of which locals worked there. When they left work, the insurgents would abduct them, take them to their strongholds in Fallujah, and kill them. "Summary executions inside Fallujah happen with sobering frequency," Bellon, newly promoted to lieutenant colonel, wrote in the fall. "We have been witness to the scene on a number of occasions." He was still serving as RCT-1's intelligence officer. Thanks to camera-equipped unmanned aerial vehicles (UAVs) circling over Fallujah, he sometimes saw these murders happen in real time. "Three men are taken from the trunk of a car and are made to walk into a ditch, where they are shot. Bodies are found in the Euphrates without heads washed downstream from Fallujah."

The most gruesome murders were the beheadings that went on in various torture chambers the terrorists established among Fallujah's many anonymous blocks of houses. The most infamous example was Zarqawi's beheading of Nicholas Berg, an American hostage, on May 7. In Berg's case, and in many others, the killers broadcast their grisly handiwork to the rest of the world via the Internet and Al Jazeera. In another instance, hooded terrorists stood before a camera and forced a kneeling man to confess that he had helped the Americans. They then cut his head off. Chanting and praying, they plopped the bloody severed head back onto the victim's torso. The editor of this particular execution video interspersed the beheading with Al Jazeera images of American air strikes and the women and children who had allegedly been killed as a result of them.

"I don't think we could overstate . . . the presence of that city as a sanctuary for terrorists, criminal groups, Muslim extremists, [and] indigenous members of various resistance groups," Lieutenant Colonel Willie Buhl, commander of 3/1 Marines, told a historian in October. "The presence of that sanctuary has done more to impede the progress we're trying to make here than anything else I can think of." He was especially distressed by how easy it was for Zarqawi and other thugs in Fallujah to "pull on historic ties and bring the tribe leaders and hold them accountable, coerce them, to intimidate them."

In many cases, the imams, who were supposed to act as moral leaders in the community, eagerly abetted the work of the terrorists and profited from their dominance. "The imams use the mosques to gain control over ignorant people," Lieutenant Colonel Bellon said. "They preach hate, and that's not a religion. I keep the book on these guys. Most of them are criminals. They own the real estate, they send out thugs to shake down the truck drivers doing the run to Jordan, they fence the stolen cars and organize the kidnappings. They get a cut of every hijacked truck. They could teach Al Capone how to extort a city. They use young, gullible jihadists as their pawns." It was as if Fallujah was now run by an especially malevolent combination of Cosa Nostra and the Taliban.[7]

Basically, the situation was intolerable. In January of 2005, Iraqis were supposed to go to the polls to elect a permanent government. Continued status quo in Fallujah could threaten the legitimacy and security of those elections. Prime Minister Ayad Allawi and his interim government in Baghdad spent much of 2004 ignoring Fallujah and then attempting to negotiate some sort of peace settlement with the city fathers. By the fall, though, Allawi knew that he could no longer allow the insurgents to flourish there. If he did, he would steadily lose face, and power, with the Iraqi people.

American leaders, military and political, knew by the fall that the withdrawal from Fallujah had been a terrible mistake. They knew they must take the city, and they now understood that timing was everything in this regard. Learning from their mistakes, the Americans spent much of the fall cultivating a suitable political environment for the violent urban battle they were planning. They lined up the support of Allawi and his allies. They arranged for reliable Iraqi troops to participate in the assault. They established checkpoints outside the city in order to control access in and out of Fallujah. To avoid potential supply problems, they secured all the roads around the city. Utilizing a nice blend of aerial photographs, local informant reports, and reconnaissance patrols, they gathered a wealth of good information on the insurgents, their methods, their weaponry, their defenses, and their whereabouts.

They estimated that the city was defended by about two to three thousand fighters of varying quality and commitment. About a quarter of these men were hard-core foreign fighters who had come to Iraq for a showdown with the American infidels. On satellite and UAV surveillance photographs, the Americans even assigned a number to every one of Fallujah's thirty-nine thousand buildings. Perhaps most important of all, they were much more aggressive, and effective, at dealing with Fallujah's noncombatant population and shaping popular perceptions of their intentions. "We had public affairs, civil affairs, and IO [Information Operations] all sitting down at the same table, working through the themes, to make sure we were getting the effect that we wanted," Lieutenant General John Sattler, who had succeeded General Conway as commander of I Marine Expeditionary Force (MEF), said.

In September and October, American and Iraqi officials repeatedly urged the city's civilian population to leave town before the impending battle. "We . . . used radio messages, some of which were generic to Al Anbar province, but a lot of them were targeted to the people of Fallujah," Major Andy Dietz, an Army information operations officer attached to RCT-1, later said. "We would do loudspeaker broadcasts from the periphery of the city, especially on Fridays doing counter-mosque messages. We would pass out handbills in places we knew people were transiting into the city." The Americans also dropped leaflets blaming the guerrillas for Fallujah's sickly economic state. "We would . . . tell the people of Fallujah that you would have had a water treatment plant this month except that your city is full of insurgents," said Major General Richard Natonski, who had taken over command of 1st Marine Division when Mattis was promoted in August.

In addition to explaining how terrorist control of Fallujah was hurting them, the leaflets outlined the American rules of engagement in the coming battle. Because of the threat of VBIEDs and SVBIEDs (suicide car bombers), all vehicles would be considered hostile, as would anyone with a weapon. The leaflets and other announcements communicated an air of inevitability about the notion of Fallujah's return to coalition control. "[We] let the people in Fallujah know we're coming," Colonel Craig Tucker, commander of RCT-7, said. "We're not telling you when we're coming, but we're coming. And they left. And what you had left in there was those guys who were gonna fight you."

The insurgents still enjoyed some popular support among the people, but many months of repression had taken its toll, ebbing the anti-American euphoria of the spring. Most Fallujahns had no wish to fight alongside the jihadis or to take their chances of avoiding American bombs and bullets. They voted with their feet. As of early November, almost 90 percent of the population had left the city, thus creating an isolated urban battlefield in which the Americans could liberally use their massive firepower. They had essentially emptied the city in anticipation of turning it into a battlefield, an unprecedented feat in modern military history. The exodus did have a downside, though. Some of the terrorists, including Zarqawi, escaped from Fallujah. They evaded the American checkpoints by blending in with the crowds.

By November, whether President Bush won or lost his election contest with Senator Kerry, he had decided to take Fallujah. When he defeated Kerry on November 2, the victory only added that much more urgency to the impending offensive, as well as a more stable political environment for Allawi's government. The prime minister declared a state of emergency in Iraq and, on November 7, after one last failed attempt at negotiations with Fallujah's leaders, he ordered the assault to commence. In a strategic sense, this dotted the last political i's and crossed the final t's. Of course, this did not necessarily mean that politics were no longer a factor. The Americans initially dubbed the assault Operation Phantom Fury but Allawi renamed it Operation Al Fajr (The Dawn), a moniker he felt was less vengeful and more appropriate to the circumstances.[8]

The Breach

The insurgents may have been cruel, but they were smart and determined. They spent months fortifying Fallujah and its approaches. American intelligence analysts identified 306 separate strongpoints throughout the city. The mujahideen used half of Fallujah's seventy-two mosques for military purposes. They lined the streets with car bombs. Other cars and pickup trucks blocked the roads and entry points to the town. They placed IEDs in every imaginable spot—houses, curbs, manhole covers, telephone poles, and any other likely American transit point. They wired up entire buildings with hundreds of pounds of explosives. They dug holes, trenches, and house-to-house tunnels to create good fighting positions and escape routes for themselves. "Fallujah is a city designed for siege warfare," a sergeant said. "From the studs to the minarets, every goddamned building is a fortress. The houses are minibunkers with ramparts and firing slits cut into every rooftop. Every road into the city is strong-pointed, mined, and blocked with captured Texas barriers [full of dirt]."

The jihadis used bulldozers to build a ring of mined berms around the city, especially to the north along a five-foot-high railroad embankment (quite similar, actually, to the railroad that bordered Aachen). In the days leading up to the American assault, the most dedicated foreign fighters stationed themselves on the outer edges of Fallujah, in the upper floors of multistory buildings, in ideal position to launch RPGs, call down mortar fire, or snipe at the Americans. In some spots, the insurgents stacked tall heaps of tires in the streets. American commanders feared that when the attack began, the enemy would set fire to the tires, similar to what Mohammed Aidid's militiamen had done at Mogadishu in 1993, to create clouds of black smoke that could negate the effectiveness of UAVs and other supporting aircraft. By now, the number of enemy fighters in Fallujah ranged between twenty-five hundred and forty-five hundred men (estimates vary). Overall, it is fair to say that their defenses in November were far more elaborate and formidable than they had been in April.

Fortunately, so was the American battle plan. By and large, this plan was the brainchild of Generals Sattler and Natonski. As the corps-level commander of I MEF, Sattler concentrated on cutting off Fallujah from the outside world. He borrowed a brigade-sized combat team from the Army's 1st Cavalry Division to secure every external approach to Fallujah. A battalion from the British Army's Black Watch regiment also assisted in this mission. Natonski, the division commander, focused on taking the city itself. He pulled a bait and switch on the enemy. Through a series of raids and feints, he led them to believe that the main assault was coming from the south and east of Fallujah. They deployed many of their fighters to those areas, all the while "in a heightened state of paranoia and anxiety," according to General Natonski. Cell phone intercepts confirmed their great confusion. The fact that the Americans had previously cut off the city's power supply only added to the disarray.

In reality, Natonski's main punch was coming from the exact opposite direction. The night before the main assault on Fallujah began, he sent the Iraqi 36th Commando Battalion and its American advisors to capture the Fallujah

General Hospital on a peninsula west of the Euphrates. During the April fighting, the insurgents had masterfully used the hospital to trumpet their claims that the Americans were butchering civilians. This time, they did not get that chance. The commandos took the hospital easily. Marine reinforcements from the 3rd Light Armored Reconnaissance Battalion and a company of soldiers from the Army's 1st Battalion, 503rd Infantry, quickly seized the Euphrates bridges, including the infamous "Brooklyn Bridge," where angry fanatics had hung the burned remains of the contractors back in the spring. Securing the hospital and bridges had the extra benefit of confusing the insurgents even more. It convinced some of their commanders that the American assault was coming from the west, across the bridges, and they moved more people to cover that approach. But the main attack was coming from the north. Throughout the day on November 8, Natonski and his staff moved two regimental-sized combat teams, RCT-1 and RCT-7, into position, mainly by vehicles.

RCT-1, of course, was the modern descendant of the 1st Marine Regiment of Chesty Puller and Peleliu fame. RCT-7 equated to Herman Hanneken's 7th Marine Regiment, which had also fought on that terrible island in 1944. RCT-1, under Colonel Michael Shupp, consisted of three infantry battalions: 3/5 and 3/1 Marines and the Army's Task Force 2-7 Cavalry (a mechanized infantry battalion). Colonel Craig Tucker's RCT-7 was similar. He had 1/8 and 1/3 Marines, along with Task Force 2-2 Infantry of the Army's 1st Infantry Division. Both regimental combat teams were augmented with tanks, engineers, psyops, medics, forward air controllers, artillerymen, Navy SEAL sniper teams, and other special operators.

Army-Marine relations had come a long way since the Peleliu days. Whereas in 1944 General Rupertus was loath to even share the same battlefield with the Army, in 2004 at Fallujah Marines and soldiers served together in the same regimental-sized units, effectively fighting side by side. In fact, General Sattler specifically requested, and received from his superiors in Baghdad, the two Army mechanized infantry battalions for the Fallujah assault.

Although rivalry still existed, soldiers and Marines generally had deep respect for their counterparts as professional warriors. Some of their officers had even been through the same training schools at Fort Benning, Fort Leavenworth, and other posts. In essence, the two ground combat services were melding their own unique institutional strengths together for this battle. Both 2-7 Cavalry and 2-2 Infantry as mechanized units possessed Bradley Fighting Vehicles, Abrams tanks, and other armored vehicles that were ideally suited to a politically neutral urban environment. Their armor provided vital protection for their grunts against enemy IEDs, car bombs, mortars, and small arms. Plus, the vehicles lent perfect fire support for them when they were clearing buildings. The Marine battalions had the usual blend of Light Armored Vehicles (LAVs), Armored Amphibious Vehicles (AAVs), and Humvees, along with a passel of Mark 19s, TOW missile launchers, .50-caliber machine guns and SMAWs, but they were basically composed of light infantry. The Marine grunts would be needed to clear buildings—only infantry could do that—but they needed protection and fire support from the vehicles and heavy weapons.

So the Army's job was to act as a wedge-busting force, leading the way into and through Fallujah. They were to smash through enemy defenses, blow up strongpoints, maintain the momentum of a steady advance, and force the insurgents to choose between retreat and destruction. At the same time, the Army grunts would take buildings under the protective snouts of the Bradleys and Abramses. Even more than the Army, the job of the Marines was to go block by block, clearing every room, killing the muj at close quarters. They would advance both adjacent to and in the wake of the Army.

Aside from the bait and switch, there was nothing fancy about Natonski's battle plan. Both regimental combat teams were to push straight into Fallujah and clear it from north to south, block by block, until they reached the desert that bordered the southern edges of the town. RCT-1 would capture the western part of the city. RCT-7 would take the eastern section. Behind the American advance, several battalions from the newly formed Iraqi Army would back-clear buildings, find hidden weapons caches, and interrogate prisoners and noncombatants alike. Their role was to solidify their fledgling government's control of Fallujah once the Americans cleared the city of insurgents. In all, General Natonski had about twelve thousand troops, of which half were earmarked for the actual assault on Fallujah. Air support would consist of helicopter gunships, Air Force, Navy, and Marine fighter jets, along with AC-130s (now appropriately code-named Basher) and UAVs.[9]

By late afternoon on November 8, as the encroaching shadows of the coming evening lengthened, both regimental combat teams were in position north of Fallujah. Amid the seemingly endless desert landscape, hundreds of vehicles were stretched out "like long trails of ants," in the recollection of one NCO. The soldiers and Marines had spent the day going through the usual military hurry-up-and-wait routine. As in April, they also heard many pep talks from their officers and senior NCOs. "This is as pure a fight of good versus evil as we'll probably see in our lifetime," Lieutenant Colonel Pete Newell, commander of 2-2 Infantry, told his soldiers, a few of whom were female medics and intelligence specialists. Newell's experienced and universally respected command sergeant major, Steve Faulkenberg, told the soldiers, in a voice that was uncharacteristically dripping with emotion: "I could not be more proud of you if you were my own kids." After hearing Colonel Shupp deliver a similarly moving speech, Marine Private Andrew Stokes recalled "getting chills, being all motivated. I made peace with God in case I died." Thousands of others did the same. They tried, though, not to dwell on the unpleasant reality that death or serious wounds might beckon for them in Fallujah.

Staff Sergeant David Bellavia, a history-conscious rifle squad leader in Alpha Company, 2-2 Infantry, was determined to remember every detail of the coming battle. He peered at the many vehicles around him and at the battered city he and his men would soon attempt to take. "This is the moment we've trained for since we were raw recruits," he thought. "I've got to be able to tell my grandkids someday. I need to be able to tell them what this day meant to all of us." Like an electrical current, a ripple of eager anticipation pulsed through the troops. "It was something to see," Lieutenant Colonel Bellon later wrote. "You could just feel the intensity in the Marines and Soldiers. It was all business." The troops were excited, on edge, nearing a fever pitch as they waited tensely for the word to attack.

They were like actors waiting for the curtain to rise on opening night or football players gathering in the locker room before the Super Bowl. Only this was not a performance or a game; it was life and death. After so much preparation and anticipation, they had reached a state of total impatience, a point at which facing imminent danger becomes more desirable than even one more minute of inconclusive, but safe, waiting. Rather than sit around much longer and contemplate their uncertain future, they wanted to take action and end the cursed anticipation, a common human emotion when facing danger. "Come on, what the hell are we waiting for, let's get moving" was a common thought among the grunts. To make matters worse, a misty curtain of light rain began to descend.

The railroad tracks and embankment ringed this northern approach to the city. The Fallujah side of the embankment teemed with mines and IEDs, as did many of the first streets and buildings the Americans would attempt to capture. The initial stage of the Fallujah assault called for the engineers to breach this formidable belt of deadly obstacles (in stark contrast to the Gulf War, the breach would not be made this time by knife-wielding Marines on their hands and knees). Blowing an opening into Fallujah was dangerous work and the engineers needed a great deal of fire support to prevent the enemy from pinning them down among the IEDs, raking them with RPG and machine-gun fire. The grunts liked to razz combat engineers for being demolitions nerds but, in truth, as one infantry soldier indicated, they deeply respected them as "the intellectuals of the combat arms branches. They have a million crafty solutions to problems that would make us knuckle-dragging infantry types scratch our heads and pause."

In the weeks leading up to Operation Al Fajr, the Americans, for political reasons, actually refrained from pasting Fallujah in the same way they had bombarded objectives in earlier wars (Guam, Peleliu, and Aachen, for instance). Every fire mission and air strike had to be approved at I MEF level or above. Because of this, some of the ground troops were concerned that they would pay a fearsome price in blood for the conniving of the politicians. By the time they were about to tear through the breach, though, the restraints were long gone. Artillery shells, fired from 155-millimeter self-propelled Paladin howitzers a few miles away, tore into houses. Plumes of smoke and dust billowed in the gathering darkness. Masonry flew everywhere. The air was filled with a low but steady rumble of detonating shells, so many that the ground seemed to be quaking. "The Air Force, Navy and Marines send waves of F-16 and F-18 fighter jets," Staff Sergeant Bellavia wrote in a present-tense format. "They whistle over the city to drop laser-guided bombs and satellite-guided Joint Direct Attack Munitions. The *whomp-whomp* of their detonations can be both heard and felt, even at this distance. Fallujah is smothered in bombs, shrouded in smoke. Buildings collapse. Mines detonate."

In many instances, the bombs set off a chain reaction of explosions as lines of IEDs and car bombs cooked off. Attack helicopters swooped in and disgorged rockets and 30-millimeter shells anyplace that the pilots spotted enemy fire. Propeller-driven AC-130 gunships hummed overhead, unleashing their terrifying panoply of cannon and Gatling gun fire. Distinct lines of blue tracers slashed from these planes to the ground, creating a sight reminiscent of a light show. Tanks, Bradleys, AAVs, and other supporting vehicles shot up any building that overlooked the railroad tracks, adding to the pyrotechnics. "The results were exactly as we had hoped, creating massive casualties and chaos within the enemy ranks, disrupting their ability to defend against the breach," Captain Paul Fowler, a tank company commander, said.

Even so, the insurgents unleashed a disconcerting amount of RPG, machine-gun, and mortar fire as the engineers rolled their D9 armored bulldozers and other vehicles up to the embankment. Bullets sparked off the dozers and up-armored Humvees. There was so much rifle fire coming from the buildings that it reminded Colonel Shupp of camera flashes at a big sporting event. "The whole city was lit up with those flashbulbs, but the flashbulbs were actually small-arms fire coming against our forces." The bullets smashed into the embankment and whizzed past vehicles. Many of the Americans were observing the city through night vision goggles, but the light of so many flashes and explosions almost made those devices useless. "There were red streaks which were RPGs coming from the city and going over our trucks [Humvees]," Lance Corporal Sven Mozdiez recalled. He and the Marines around him saw a three-man RPG team huddle together in a hole as they got set to fire. Their weapon malfunctioned, emitting a flash out of the back but not the rocket. The surprised muj stared at one another for a long moment. A Marine Mark 19 gunner spotted them and showered their hole with 40-millimeter grenades, killing them all. Mozdiez saw another fighter lean over the third-story railing of one house and spray his AK-47 in the direction of the Americans. "We got a bead on him and Lance Corporal [Kevin] Weyrauch fired a TOW missile in that level of the building and we didn't receive any more fire from that position. The problem was taken care of."[10]

To forge their respective breaches, the engineers employed mine-clearing line charges (MICLIC, or "mick lick"), a weapon that had worked well in the Gulf War. The MICLICs were anything but elaborate. Each one was nothing more than a one-hundred-meter-long rope adorned with about one thousand pounds of C-4 explosive affixed to the rope in clumps. A trailerlike vehicle with a hydraulic launcher propelled the rope deep within the minefield.

"When detonated, anything surrounding the MICLIC gets vaporized," one soldier explained. "What the explosions don't destroy, the concussion waves finish off." The MICLIC would basically set off a chain reaction of mine and IED detonations, clearing paths three meters wide and one hundred meters long through the obstacle belt. In this case, the explosions would also punch holes through the embankment and railroad tracks.

When the engineers were finally ready, they radioed all the units with the message to button up inside their vehicles. Then they blew their MICLICs. Multiple explosions detonated. Roiling orange balls of flame lit up the night. A massive concussion wave shook vehicles. Debris flew in every direction. A chain reaction of sympathetic detonations touched off as IEDs and mines exploded. "There were at least five daisy-chained IEDs that went off," Major Lisa Dewitt, the battalion surgeon for 2-2 Infantry, recalled. "When that big boom occurred, there was a collective celebratory shouting and cheering, like somebody scored a touchdown." The engineers then marked the new breach lanes with chem lights and special tape.

In a few spots, the Marines experienced difficulty in getting across the tracks and exploiting the breach lanes, mainly because of equipment problems. RCT-1, for instance, was delayed for several hours because one of its engineer vehicles tipped over. For the most part, though, the advance through the breach lanes was rapid as tanks, Bradleys, armored bulldozers, and AAVs began rumbling into the gaps. The crew of one Bradley had painted the nickname "Bada Bing!" on their Bradley in honor of the strip club in *The Sopranos*.

The soldiers of Lieutenant Colonel Newell's Task Force 2-2 Infantry were leading the way for RCT-7. They were the first Americans to enter the newly created lanes and head straight for the muzzles of insurgents, who had weathered the bombardment by hunkering down in sturdy buildings. Newell had arranged for the Big Red One's 3rd Brigade Reconnaissance Troop to cover his vulnerable lead vehicles as they negotiated their way through the narrow lanes. East of the city, on high ground at a crossroads known as the cloverleaf, Bradleys, tanks, and Humvees equipped with special long-range surveillance equipment (known as L-RAS) kept the insurgents at bay with devastatingly accurate fire. "Their whole job in life was to get in position where they could see deep into the city, behind where we were moving," Newell said. "[They] pretty much destroyed a platoon's worth of insurgents right at the breach point. You couldn't move within a hundred meters of that thing without somebody in Recon Troop shooting you."

The L-RAS resembled a square box. Mounted atop a Humvee, its thermal laser could identify enemy fighters several kilometers into the city. Once an enemy was identified, a soldier would simply push a button to target the insurgent. "Hit the laser button and it'll give you a ten-digit grid and direction—basically everything you need for a perfect call for fire to take them out," Staff Sergeant Jimmy Amyett, a section leader in the troop, recalled. "And the whole time they have no idea you're watching them." They called down accurate artillery and mortar fire. They also shot enemy fighters with a blend of 25-millimeter and machine-gun fire.

In the meantime, Newell's Bradleys, accompanied by escorting tanks, gingerly rolled through their slender lanes. Staff Sergeant Bellavia was packed inside one of the Bradleys with his rifle squad. They were laden down with M16A4 rifles, M4 carbines, M249 Squad Automatic Weapon (SAW) machine guns, grenades, shotguns, body armor, Kevlar helmets, and a variety of other weapons and pieces of equipment. They were hot, sweaty, and generally uncomfortable. The air was stale, leaden with body odor and foul exhalations. "Our asses grow sore," he wrote. "When we try to reposition ourselves, we squash our balls." The sergeant and his men could hear mortar shells exploding outside, uncomfortably close to their track. They also heard the booming of friendly artillery shells and Abrams main guns. The Bradley started and stopped several times, nearly driving them crazy with anticipation. At last, the driver gunned the engine. "As our Brad works up to its top speed, we're thrown around like bowling pins. My head cracks against the bulkhead, then I'm thrown against the ramp. Gear starts flying around us. Outside, the explosions grow in volume and intensity." Some of the explosions were from nearby IEDs.

Bellavia was sitting in the very rear of the Bradley, near the ramp. He leaned forward and looked through the periscope viewer and saw tracer rounds sailing past his own vehicle and nearby Bradleys. The world outside was little more than a blur of muffled explosions, smoke, and swirl. He could see well enough, though, to spot the engineer's chem lights and tape. A few seconds later, the track was through the breach lane, and with several tanks and other Bradleys it began rolling toward the city. RPGs streaked out of the urban haze. One scored a direct hit on the turret of the platoon sergeant's

Bradley. "Fire scorches its flanks as the vehicle lurches forward," Bellavia remembered. "Seconds later, it runs across an IED, which explodes with such force that the entire back end of the Bradley leaves the desert floor."

The resilient Bradley crashed back down and kept going. Then, a second later, Bellavia's Bradley hit an IED. "A shattering blast engulfs us. The back end of our Bradley is thrown upward. Dust and smoke spiral around us. I choke and gag and try to scream for my guys." The compartment was full of smoke and dust. Temporarily deafened and disoriented by acoustic trauma, Bellavia could not hear or see his men. All he could hear was a high-pitched buzz, although he was aware that the vehicle gunner was firing the 25-millimeter chain gun. He screamed at his men to tap his knee if they were okay. One by one, they did so. As the seconds passed, his body recovered from the shock of the explosion and his senses returned. The battered but intact Bradley kept rolling.

Finally, they reached the edge of the city and dismounted. As Bellavia descended the ramp, he felt like he was setting foot on Omaha Beach. "My stomach's in a knot. I feel like my grandfather in World War II, like I'm literally living in a historical moment." Instead of running into a wall of fire, he and his soldiers took cover behind their vehicle, flipped their night vision goggles into place, and, for the first time, studied Fallujah from close range. "All around us, the darkness is broken by fires of all sizes and shapes. Buildings blaze. Rubble smolders. Debris burns in the streets. Houses have been cleaved in two, as if some sadistic giant had performed architectural vivisection on the entire neighborhood. Floors and rooms have been laid bare, exposed by the ravages of the night's shelling. Furniture is thrown haphazardly about. Smashed desks, burned-out sofas, faceless TVs lay in heaps within these demolished homes."

Bellavia noticed globs of white phosphorous clinging to the ground around the buildings like "manna from hell. It reminds me of the burning liquid metal of *Terminator 2*." The artillerymen had employed the white phosphorous to spark building fires and force the insurgents into the streets, where high-explosive rounds would engulf them in shrapnel. Other than the fires and the intermittent but considerable booming of tank guns, all was silent. Bellavia's squad was surprised at the relative tranquillity. Under the watchful snouts of their vehicles, they maneuvered, with one fire team of four soldiers covering the other, into the nearest buildings.

All up and down the northern edges of Fallujah, the Americans were fil-
tering through their breach lanes into the city. Just as the heavily mechanized
2-2 Infantry led the way for Tucker's RCT-7, Colonel Shupp chose 2-7 Cavalry
to go in first for RCT-1. "We [had] two lanes open," Shupp said, "so now 2-7
[was] into the city and fighting, destroying everything on the route that could
be a possible IED. Basher . . . above us [was] firing into everything that they
possibly could, attacking the enemy on strongholds for a possible IED . . .
[and] VBIED cars that could have been on the routes . . . and . . . getting big
secondary explosions off them." Each of the explosions detonated an IED or
car bomb that could have caused many grunt casualties.

In the wake of the heavy mechanized forces, the Marine light infantry
units rolled through in AAVs and Humvees accompanied by psyops teams
blaring Richard Wagner's famous symphony epic "Ride of the Valkyries." The
Marine grunts dismounted, against surprisingly light resistance, and seeped
into the first ruined blocks of drab, wrecked, sand-colored structures. The
situation was one of controlled chaos. Units were mixed up or dumped into
the wrong spots. Grunts eyeballed windows and doorways for hidden insurgents. The light of fires and flares created weird shadows that bounced off
buildings and streets. The well-trained infantrymen knew to avoid standing
in open areas so they gravitated to the buildings. "We ran as fast as we could,"
Sergeant Shawn Gianforte recalled. "To my surprise we made it through the
breach with very little resistance at all. We went in one building and got set
up and let everyone figure out where we were." All around him, hundreds of
Marines and soldiers were doing the same thing.

The mujahideen had spent five months building a fortified barrier that, in
the end, held up the Americans for five hours—at the most. By 0200 on November 9, both of General Natonski's regimental combat teams were through
the breach and into Fallujah. The preliminaries were over. The fight for the
city was on.[11]

2-2 Infantry and the Wedge

They were nicknamed "Ramrods" but they were more like sledgehammers.
Their proud lineage spanned nearly two hundred years of American military
history. Soldiers of the 2nd Infantry Regiment had once fought in such legend-

ary battles as Gettysburg, Normandy, and the Battle of the Bulge. At Fallujah, they were the embodiment of mech infantry. Their job was to blast their way through the enemy's cleverly placed strongpoints, dash down the streets, seize Highway 10 (now known to the Americans as Phase Line Fran), force the insurgents to displace from the cover of their fortified houses, and then either annihilate them with the synchronized firepower of several dozen armored vehicles or push them into the not-so-welcoming arms of Marine light infantrymen. General Sattler opined that they were "critical to quickly slicing through the insurgents' defenses and disrupting their ability to conduct coordinated counterattacks." As Lieutenant Colonel Newell succinctly put it, "a Bradley and a tank can take an RPG shot in the face and keep moving and still fight. A dismounted infantry squad cannot."

Because of this simple reality of urban combat, it simply made good sense for 2-2 Infantry to take the lead in Fallujah. "The plan before we put any dismounts on the ground or in the buildings," one NCO recalled, "was to use our 120s on the Abrams or our 25-millimeters on the Bradleys" to shoot up any house that might contain enemy fighters. The battalion was the perfect blend of armor and firepower. Because the city was almost completely free of noncombatants, they could spew out death and destruction with impunity. "My goal . . . [was] not to clear every single building," Newell said. "The job was to break up any organized resistance. Any platoon-sized resistance . . . destroy it, break it up so that it couldn't function . . . use speed and firepower to get through the northern part of the city as rapidly as possible."

His mission, basically, was to take the enemy's heaviest punches and, in return, grind the insurgents up with the many weapons at his disposal. He had to do this with only half of his battalion. Newell's outfit only came to Fallujah a few days before Operation Al Fajr. Their main area of operations in Iraq was a portion of Diyala province, north of Baghdad. Participation in Fallujah did not relieve Newell of responsibility for Diyala. This absurd situation, "a royal pain in the ass" in his recollection, was a symptom of America's paucity of ground troops in Iraq. This, of course, was a by-product of the shock and awe techno-vangelism of those who had launched the war. Like it or not, though, Newell had to leave behind two of his rifle companies. At Fallujah, his attack force consisted of two main components—a tank company on loan from another unit and his own Alpha Company. In all, Newell's task force had only about 450 soldiers, most of whom were not dismounted trigger pullers. Even Alpha, the battalion's main infantry assault force, had only about fifty or sixty dismounts to perform the nasty business of clearing buildings and thus do the worst of the fighting. These lonely riflemen and machine gunners represented the sharp tip of a very long spear.

For these grunts, like Staff Sergeant Bellavia and his squad, the fighting that unfolded in Fallujah was personal and visceral. Just before dawn on November 9, Bellavia and his people were in a house, scouting for any sign of the enemy. They were shrouded in a silence that struck the Buffalo native as incongruous because he could almost feel the presence of the jihadis. With nine months of combat experience in Iraq, he had developed that sixth sense about impending danger that often characterizes good NCOs. He decided to order one of his men, Private John Ruiz, to fire an 84-millimeter AT4 rocket at a propane tank on the next block. Hopefully this would provoke a response from any nearby insurgents. But, just as Ruiz was about to lean out the doorway to shoot, Sergeant Bellavia heard footsteps in the street. Someone was coming. By the sounds of his approaching footfalls, crunching off the shards of glass and rubble that blanketed the street, the person was heading straight for them. Bellavia peeked out and saw a man with an AK-47 slung over his shoulder. He was carrying a car battery, a common tool for setting off big IEDs. He was about fifty meters away and approaching quickly. "He's got a big bushy, mountain-man beard and is covered with filth," Bellavia wrote. "His clothes are smeared with gunk. His face is splotched with grime. He looks like a street person . . . just two eyeballs walking."

A spasm of terror shot through Bellavia, nearly debilitating him. This was a typical self-preservation instinct in the presence of a live enemy. For most humans, the normal reaction to such mortal danger was to run away, but soldiers must be different, even counterintuitive. As a way to conquer fear, they are intensely trained to focus on specific tasks, especially in the face of such danger, so that fear will be forgotten or sublimated to the job at hand.

So, for Bellavia, the moment of abject terror passed quickly as he focused on his prey. He raised his M4 carbine and prepared to fire. Unlike many early-twenty-first-century American grunts, he had little interest in hunting. But he knew that hunters often emitted a quick noise to startle their prey into stopping short or turning toward the shooter. Sergeant Bellavia called out casually: "Hey." Sure enough, the insurgent stopped and looked at Bellavia, presenting a perfect target. The twenty-nine-year-old squad leader squeezed off two tracer bullets that streaked into the man's chest and shoulder. Both hits produced "a puff of smoke, like exhaust from a cigarette." As the wounded man stumbled around, his eyes bulged and he screamed in agony. "He howls, a long mewling, pain-wracked scream." Staff Sergeant Colin Fitts, a fellow squad leader, swung his shotgun into position atop Bellavia's helmet and laced the man with two slugs, tearing one of his arms off, knocking him down. A SAW gunner on the roof added several bullets that tore him up even more. When several of the machine gunner's bullets missed, they bounced up and down the street and off nearby houses. Then all was silence again.

A surge of adrenaline-laced excitement swept through Bellavia. He was so euphoric at killing the insurgent that he felt as if his vital organs were rearranging inside of him. His triumph instilled in him a keen sense of masculinity, as if he had now proven himself a better man than the insurgent. He felt powerful, almost invulnerable. He cupped his hand to his mouth and emitted an animal-like cry of victory: "You can't kill me! You hear me, fuckers? You will never kill me!" He was excited to be alive. He was also overcome with relief that he had what it took to kill another human being in such a personal fashion. "Combat distilled to its purest form is a test of manhood," he wrote. "In modern warfare, that man-to-man challenge is often hidden by modern technology—the splash of artillery fire can be random, a rocket or bomb or IED can be anonymous. Those things make combat a roll of the dice. But on this street and in these houses, it can be man-to-man. My skills against his. I caught him napping and he died."

In such instances, when soldiers kill face-to-face, euphoria can erode quickly into guilt over taking life. The perceptive Bellavia expected this contradiction and even welcomed it. "Combat is a descent into the darkest part of the human soul. A place where the most exalted nobility and the most wretched baseness reside naturally together. What a man finds there defines how he measures himself for the rest of his life. I embrace the battle. I welcome it into my soul." By doing so, he was probably trying to master the guilt that often leads to post-traumatic stress disorder. PTSD is, to a great extent, a product of guilt—survivor's guilt, guilt at not measuring up to one's self-image or the expectations of others in combat, most of all, guilt at having killed. Staff Sergeant Bellavia knew all the risks. Every bit a professional grunt, he was determined to overcome them.

As it turned out, the insurgent had been in the process of laying a horrifying trap for 2-2 Infantry. The battery he was carrying was meant to touch off a colossal amount of explosives that were packed into a house that the grunts were about to clear. "The whole thing was wired to blow," Bellavia recalled. "I've never seen that much C-4 [explosive] in my entire life. It looked like a log cabin, that's how many bricks were all taped together on the walls." Propane tanks and even a fuel tank from a jet aircraft were cleverly arranged among the whole deadly bouquet. When Bellavia had first spotted the insurgent, he had been heading for a nearby fighting hole. His mission, the soldiers soon understood, had been to wait for the platoon to enter the house and then touch the battery to wires leading away from the house, into the hole. The ensuing combination of flames and powerful explosives of this BCIED (building-contained improvised explosive device) would, most likely, have killed everyone in the platoon. With this chilling discovery, Bellavia and the others felt anything but guilt. They were pleased, and relieved, that they had killed the bearded man.

Creeped out by the thought that other BCIEDs might await them, the Ramrod grunts spent the rest of the night clearing houses. Their knees and elbows were already raw from scraping against rubble and glass. They encountered more booby traps but none so elaborate as the notorious first BCIED. At each house they expected major resistance, and there were a few firefights, but most of the buildings were unoccupied. Newell's battalion was moving so quickly that they were already closing in on Highway 10. The speedy advance had a downside, though. As the pre-assault plan had envisioned, Newell's assault platoons were smashing through the enemy's prepared defenses, disrupting their movements, and killing some of them. But there were no front lines and 2-2 Infantry was deeper into the city than the neighboring Marines. This meant that the insurgents were all around Newell's men, capable of popping up anywhere.

After sunrise, when the Americans no longer enjoyed the advantage of their night vision devices, the enemy fighters grew more aggressive. Sergeant Bellavia's squad was on a rooftop, looking south, when, from all around them, they heard a chorus of voices hollering to one another in Arabic. The voices trailed away and a single whistle blew. As the whistle tapered off, he and his men heard the sound of several dozen feet tromping through the dizzying warren of streets and alleys around them. "They're coming for us," Bellavia thought.

The squad's supporting Bradleys and tanks were, for the moment, occupied elsewhere. Although it would take them several minutes to work their way into position, around buildings and through streets, they could help if need be. The sergeant turned to his men: "We're not gonna bring any Brads up," he said to them. "We're gonna make them think they've trapped dismounts in the open without support. They're gonna rush us, and we'll fucking take them out. Hooah?" His grunts all replied with "Hooahs" of their own. In the early-twenty-first-century Army, this ubiquitous word had many meanings, ranging from "okay" to "gung ho" to "I agree" or even "I understand." The soldiers were arrayed in a firing line, covering every angle of approach, with SAWs, M4s, and M16s at the ready. Bellavia, ever the conscientious NCO, reminded his shooters to aim low and adjust high for maximum accuracy. The air was dusty and thick. Visibility was good. They could see for several blocks in every direction, although the sight revealed little more than the typical mishmash of drab, sandstone-colored buildings that characterized much of Fallujah.

The attacking insurgents soon ran into serious trouble. From the vantage point of a nearby house, Fitts's squad opened fire through windows and doors and slaughtered several of them. In the stunned aftermath, Fitts moved his people out of that house and linked up with Bellavia. All was quiet now. No one was in sight. The two sergeants estimated that somewhere out there was a force of about fifty or sixty mujahideen. They were desperately looking for the Americans but they did not know exactly where they were. They were probably spooked by the ambush Fitts had just sprung on them.

Suddenly, from about one hundred meters to the north (behind the line of the American advance), they heard a voice crying "Allah!" The grunts peered in that direction and saw a man in the middle of the street, aiming a machine gun, with an ammo belt wrapped around his arm, Rambo style. He was walking toward the Americans, chanting "Allah!" and mumbling to himself. "The muj are probing us," Bellavia wrote. "This lone fighter is a sacrificial lamb, baiting us to open fire and reveal our positions. It is a chilling way to employ a comrade." Still the courageous man kept coming. His tone was resolute, defiant and passionate.

Bellavia, like most of the Americans, was contemptuous of the enemy's fanaticism and cruelty, but he could not help but respect the insurgent's valor and belief in his cause, odious though the sergeant believed that cause to be. Bellavia's ambivalence was quite similar to the way Marines had felt about their Japanese enemies at Guam and Peleliu. When the machine-gun-wielding man got too close for comfort, Sergeant Bellavia ordered his machine gunners to open fire. Their staccato bursts spewed bullets into the pavement around the man. He looked right up at the Americans and roared at them in a tone that quaked with rage. Just as he opened fire, the machine-gun bullets tore through his legs like a saw. "White bone exposed, the insurgent collapses onto his severed legs," Bellavia recalled. "He screams in agony, but refuses to give up the fight. Blood pools around him in the street." Still the man leaned on his trigger. His rounds smashed into the American-held building with dull thuds. Another American burst engulfed him. "The insurgent is ripped apart. Chunks of flesh spray across the road."

He had done his job, though. Within a minute, the Americans began taking intense machine-gun, rifle, and RPG fire. "The enemy is hitting us with everything he has," Bellavia wrote. "Our wall becomes torn and pitted along the west and north sides. Figures dart between buildings and race across the street below." Some of them were in and around the houses across the street, no more than thirty meters away. In the recollection of one witness, they wore "tracksuit pants and the uniforms of the Iraqi National Guard." The Americans laced into them with everything at their disposal. The heavy cyclic bursts of machine guns melded crazily with the semiautomatic, throaty cracking of rifles. Plumes of smoke rose from the feed trays of the SAWs. Empty brass casings tinkled onto the ledge of the roof and spilled downward into the street or onto the rooftop. A fragment from a tracer round hit Sergeant Warren Misa in the face. Bellavia fished it out. Misa was okay but his face was swollen and infected where the fragment had burrowed into the skin.

The two sides screamed and cursed at each other. One of the Americans stood up, shouted "fire in the hole!" and fired an AT4 rocket at an insurgent taking cover behind a gate below. Someone let out a whoop, like a child exulting over fireworks. The gate exploded. Two machine gunners followed with several bursts, killing the enemy shooter. An RPG exploded just below the ledge, shaking the entire roof with concussion. Many others streaked by, "flying left and right, impacting buildings," in the recollection of one soldier. The firefight was evolving into a standoff. At this rate, though, the Americans risked losing fire superiority to the more numerous insurgents.

Fitts and Bellavia decided to play the mech infantryman's ace in the hole.

One of them got on the radio and called up a Bradley commanded by Staff Sergeant Cory Brown, a man nicknamed "Grizzly Bear" by his platoon mates because of his personal courage. The two rifle sergeants asked Brown to attack alone down the insurgent-held street. The intrepid Bradley commander readily accepted the challenge. "The Bradley rolls forward down the street and straight into the insurgents," Bellavia recalled. "At first, they're astonished the Brad is counterattacking by itself. But they quickly swarm the Brad with tracers. RPGs strike the road around it." The Bradley responded with a steady barrage of 25-millimeter. The abrupt sonic booming of the rounds slashed the air as the shells smashed into rooftops, windows, asphalt, and, most likely, people. Each round evoked miniwaves of shock and assaulted eardrums.

An IED exploded near Brown's Bradley, obscuring it in dust and smoke. The mujahideen thought they had crippled the Brad. A group of them rushed down the street, trying to close the distance to Brown's vehicle, destroy it at intimate range, and kill the three crewmen. On the rooftop, the grunts had a perfect view of the enemy's movements (thus personifying the military term "overwatch"). Several of them had M203 grenade launchers attached to their rifles. They dropped 40-millimeter grenades among the enemy, pinning them down while the riflemen and machine gunners scythed them with bullets. A few went down and did not get up. Others scrambled for cover.

Brown's Bradley rolled warily in reverse down the street, back toward the friendly support of Bellavia's group. An enemy RPG team materialized next to a cistern and snapped off a shot. The warhead exploded next to Brown's battered and scarred Bradley but did no major damage. In response, Staff Sergeant Brown raised his TOW box and unleashed the fury of this fearsome weapon upon them. "When it comes to urban fighting," Bellavia commented, "a TOW is a gift from the Pentagon gods." The TOW hurtled down the street and exploded next to the cistern, killing the RPG men. Bellavia saw other enemy survivors making a run for it. "Our guns cut down seven of them. [One] insurgent runs out of his sandals before Ruiz shoots him in the belly. Our men cheer wildly and shout taunts."

The longer the battle raged, the more it favored the Americans. With the insurgent locations pinpointed, the dismounts began to work closely with tanks and Bradleys, devastating the enemy with coordinated fire. Once pinned down, it was hard for them to escape. The Brigade Reconnaissance Troop, still fighting from the cloverleaf outside of town, added still more Bradley, tank, machine-gun, and sniper fire, killing even more enemy. The muj could not hope to succeed against this effective blend of armored firepower and quality dismounted infantrymen. "We . . . scored a significant victory," Bellavia said. "We suffered only one slightly wounded and killed many, many bad guys. We withstood a multidirectional attack for over three and a half hours."[12]

Under the weight of this combined arms power, 2-2 Infantry kept advancing swiftly. In one instance, they spotted large numbers of armed insurgents moving into a mosque that was located in neighboring 1/8 Marines' area of responsibility. The soldiers radioed the Marines and asked for permission to fire artillery at the mosque. Since 1/8's rifle companies were still a considerable distance from the mosque, they finally assented after about an hour's worth of cautious conversations about the political wisdom of shelling such a holy site. Firing from Camp Fallujah several miles away, Paladin 155-millimeter howitzer crews unleashed a staggered pair of twenty-round barrages right onto the mosque and its surrounding area. "Some hit the building and some hit just south of it," Lieutenant Neil Prakash, a tank commander who helped call in the rounds, later said, "but every explosion went off, and it was like a volcano: three to five guys shot up like they'd come out of a geyser." Prakash's tank was near Highway 10, a couple thousand meters from the mosque. In his turret, he leaned forward and gazed at the flying bodies through his commander's sight. He had done much of the spotting for the artillerymen. Now he surveyed the gruesome results of his competence as bodies flew in every direction. "They were perfectly still, not waving or fanning their arms or anything. They were already dead as they were going airborne and blossoming out. I was looking at this place and it was just smoldering. There are very few times that I've ever felt sorry for the enemy, but this time they just got slaughtered."

Back at the cloverleaf, one of the reconnaissance scouts peered through his L-RAS and saw a round impact "on the left side of the building and I saw three bodies fly into the air. It was awesome." Several of the Americans saw bodies hit the ground and bounce two stories into the air. Some bounced as high as five stories. "It was the most insane, surreal thing I'd ever seen, just watching these bodies fly," one of them said. "They looked like dolls." They may have looked like dolls, but they were flesh-and-blood men, destroyed with ruthless finality by modern firepower. It was the essence of the violent horror that characterizes modern war.

As the shells exploded against and in the mosque, survivors poured outside in hopes of escaping. "[They] were stumbling out, coughing from the
smoke," Captain Chris Boggiano of the Brigade Reconnaissance Troop recalled. A fresh barrage landed among them, blowing some to pieces. Arms,
heads, and pieces of flesh flew in all directions. Lieutenant Prakash watched
one enemy fighter emerge "out of the gray smoke, and he's holding his stomach, dragging his AK by the sling, and he's gagging and retching; and just
then . . . ten more rounds landed right on top of his head." The shelling
killed between forty and seventy insurgents, including one of Zarqawi's top
lieutenants.

By late afternoon on November 9, 2-2 Infantry had secured Highway 10.
Many of the 2-2 grunts yearned to continue their advance and keep the enemy
in disarray. They wanted to push across the highway and clear the industrial
areas of south Fallujah. But they were too far ahead of the Marines to do that,
so they paused at Highway 10. To some of the soldiers, the Marines seemed
slow and deliberate, too preoccupied with clearing every last building before
continuing the advance. "You could see the differences in how we fight,"
Major Eric Krivda, the XO of 2-2, said. "We'd do whatever we could to drop
[a] building first" with tanks and Bradleys. "The last possible resort is we send
an infantry squad in to clean up the remnants." Captain Fowler, an Army
tanker, even claimed that the pause allowed the insurgents "to move back
behind our lines. We ended up forcing them out again, but we don't like to
pay for the same ground twice." Some of the Marines, conversely, thought the
Army was moving so fast because they were simply riding around in armored
vehicles, shooting at targets and moving on, without dismounting and truly
eliminating resistance.

Both perceptions were wrong. For the most part, the battle was unfolding according to plan. In a figurative sense, the Army was shattering the enemy's wall; the Marines were cleaning up the rubble. Each and every building
did have to be cleared or the insurgents would infiltrate back into them.
Marine light infantry and the Iraqi battalions were best suited for that time-
consuming, exhausting task. By the same token, the Army's mechanized capability was ideal for urban fire support and mobility, so it was not the least
bit surprising that Lieutenant Colonel Newell's 2-2 Infantry moved faster
than the Marines. Newell's small number of dismounts, and not any deficiency on the part of the Marines, meant that 2-2 would have to do much

back-clearing of areas the unit had already traversed. "We do have some disadvantages in not having lots of dismounted infantry," Newell said, "so that's why . . . there needs to be a balanced organization. It's a complementary relationship." At Fallujah, the concept of melding Marine light infantry dexterity with Army mechanized brawn worked very well, and with an amazing minimum of friendly fire problems.

Thus, Newell's grunts began clearing buildings on either side of Highway 10 "to destroy pockets of enemy resistance bypassed during the attack south," the unit after action report said. By now, hungry packs of stray dogs and cats had learned to follow the Americans as they assaulted the buildings, because they left behind so many bodies in their wake. One soldier witnessed a cat eat the lips off a dead insurgent. Sergeant Bellavia saw several hungry dogs feeding on the remains of a dead enemy fighter. "The dogs gnaw and tear at his flesh. One comes up, his snout smeared in gore. My stomach flutters." In some cases, the animals ate all the way through to the bone.

Covered by Abramses and Bradleys, the Army grunts kicked in so many doors, cleared so many houses, dodged so many booby traps, and destroyed so many weapons caches that they lost count. Time after time, the grunts lined up in a stack, on either side of a doorway, hugging the wall, each man orienting his weapon to cover a different sector, each wondering to himself if he was about to enter a BCIED or a house full of jihadis. The skin of the grunts was peppered with nicks and cuts. Their eyes were rimmed with dark circles. They stank of dust, cordite, stale MRE crumbs, body odor, and soiled underwear. The sweaty T-shirts that hugged their irritated skin had given many of them prickly heat. They were irritable and surly. They were coated with the disgust and cynicism of infantrymen in combat.

Firefights erupted on various blocks. The Americans annihilated anyone in their path. On one street, an enemy machine gunner opened up on a group of Americans just as they rammed through the door of the house he was defending. He wounded three of them before the grunts pulled back and a Mark 19 gunner blew the enemy gunner to pieces. Sergeant Bellavia came upon another muj gunner lying in rubble alongside his weapon. The sergeant and one of his team leaders opened fire. "I hit him twice in the back and hear his lungs expel a sudden rush of air. Was it a death rattle? I'm not sure." A pool of sticky, dark red blood engulfed the fighter. The other soldier shot him in the head. Bellavia nudged his legs apart and kicked him in the groin, just to make sure he wasn't playing possum. The sergeant's boot sank deep into his leg cavity and he realized that the man had no scrotum or penis left. Needless to say, the man was very dead.[13]

A few minutes later, as the clock neared midnight and the men were on the verge of exhaustion, the platoon assaulted a handsome two-story square-shaped home. Behind the house was a nice courtyard garden. Bellavia figured that the house and garden must have belonged to someone with money. He knew that this was the Askari District, where many of Saddam's military officers had lived.

The lead soldiers found the front door unlocked. In the stack, there were men from both Bellavia's squad and Fitts's. With Sergeant Misa in the lead, they surged into the dark front room of the house. The only illumination came from the SureFire flashlights they had fastened onto their rifles. Beams of light bounced along the walls and corners as each soldier cleared his respective sector. Bellavia was outside, in the courtyard, watching this through a window when, all of a sudden, he heard shooting and a lot of it. He rushed inside, just in time to see tracers ricocheting off the floor and walls. There were so many that, to Bellavia, it looked like someone had thrown a telephone pole on top of a big campfire, sending embers flying in all directions. The tracers sizzled and hissed. They touched off little fires in piles of garbage and papers strewn about the house.

The shots were snapping off quickly, fast and desperate. The noise was deafening. Confusion reigned supreme. At first the sergeant thought his men were shooting at nothing so he screamed at them to cease fire. But, in reality, they were in heavy contact, pinned down in the living room by withering fire from well-hidden insurgents. The term "pinned down" is, in essence, a slice of military vernacular that means the enemy fire is so accurate, so deadly, so thick that any movement can bring instant death.

Two jihadis were hunkered down in the middle of the house, near a central stairwell, with well-sighted fields of fire into the living room and the foyer of the house. The truly amazing thing was that, with hundreds of bullets buzzing around, no one on either side had gotten hit yet. Bellavia chanced a look through the foyer doorway and saw the two muj shooting from behind "a pair of three-foot-high concrete Jersey barriers with little more than their heads and shoulders exposed. One of the insurgents holds an AK-47 against each shoulder with the barrels resting on one barrier. The other man has a

Russian belt-fed PKM machine gun perched atop the other barrier." Fitts and several other soldiers were pinned down opposite the doorway, on the other side of the living room.

A round grazed Private First Class Jim Metcalf, one of the SAW gunners, right under his body armor. He stumbled and cried out: "I'm hit!" The Americans heard the insurgents laughing above the din, mocking Metcalf, taunting him: *I'm heeet!!* At the same time shards of glass and debris practically filled the air. One of the soldiers took some fragments to the eyes and hollered: "My face! My eyes!" The insurgents laughed some more and wailed in mock distress: *Ohhhhh, my feeece! My eyes!* The sound of their voices made the hair on Bellavia's neck stand up. It was as if they were questioning the manhood of the Americans. The sergeant was filled with rage and fear, and it is safe to say the others were, too. As a leader, he tried to remain calm enough to consider what to do. He realized that, with several men pinned down inside the house, the supporting fire of tanks, Bradleys, artillery, and close air support were all useless. The enemy had designed their fighting position for just this type of close encounter. "This ambush is the product of study," he wrote, "an enemy who has thoroughly analyzed our strengths and weaknesses. They've created a fighting position that negates our advantages of firepower and mobility. All we can do is fight them at point-blank range with the weapons in our hands."

This was exactly the sort of mano a mano situation that, according to the techno-vangelists, was supposed to be a relic of the past, but it was all too real and, in Fallujah, all too common. The two sides would fight to the finish with whatever weapons they had at their disposal. Wits, presence of mind, and valor counted for much in this terrifying environment. Here, weapons were the tools of fighting spirit.

Bellavia was in the best position to lean into the foyer and open fire on the insurgent position. This would put him squarely into a fatal funnel but it had to be done if Fitts and the other men were to have any chance to escape the house. Bellavia loved Fitts like a brother. The two men had been through nine months of combat together. Their feelings of brotherhood, combined with the squad leader's heavy sense of responsibility, extended to every man inside the house. Bellavia dreaded the idea of exposing himself in the fatal funnel, but he knew he must do it.

Hollering back and forth, he and the others worked out a plan. When Bellavia stepped into the doorway and opened up with his SAW, the others would vacate the house—quickly. The New Yorker readied the SAW. He was still enraged, yelling insults back and forth with the muj. His breathing was jagged and nervous. His palms were sweating. A thousand thoughts raced through his intelligent brain, but a line from *The Exorcist* came to dominate: "The power of Christ compels you!" As a somewhat religious man, he was fascinated that this, of all things, would come to him during such a moment of peril. Perhaps it was because he equated his struggle against the insurgents to the movie priest's epic battle with demons. He muttered a short prayer, stood up, and opened fire at the stairwell: "Go! Go! Go! Get out!" he screamed.

Sergeant Bellavia stood in the doorway and pointed his weapon at the Jersey barriers. The SAW can fire over seven hundred rounds per minute and Bellavia had a full drum of two hundred 5.56-millimeter bullets to cook off. As he leaned on the trigger, the insurgents did the same. "Bullets bash into the wall to my left. The doorframe splinters. Tracers hiss this way and that, bouncing off the bricks and ceiling. Bullets slam into the Jersey barriers and penetrate to their hard foam centers. Hunks of foam pop out of the holes I've made and cartwheel across the room. I can see their faces and they're angry but they're smiling; they look completely evil."

He caught his glimpses of their grinning visages against his own muzzle flashes and the streaking lights of tracer rounds. Behind him, Fitts and the others scrambled out of the house. Bellavia's SAW fire was so overwhelming that the insurgents had to duck or risk having their smiling heads blown off. "Get out there," he thought. "Clear the room and juice these guys." But it was as if his legs were cemented in place. He could not bring himself to walk up on them and kill them at point-blank range. He did not know why. Perhaps he was afraid of pushing his luck any further. Perhaps he was repelled by the idea of snuffing out their lives at handshake range. Regardless, when he ran out of ammo, he bolted from the house, enraged at himself for not finishing them off.

He found Fitts and several other men just beyond the garden, taking cover behind a wall. Bellavia was absolutely disgusted with himself. He paced around roaring and cursing. "There's no escaping this: I cut and ran. When shit got hot, I ran. I'm an NCO. I'm supposed to lead by example." He felt like a fraud and a coward. He had joined the Army, in part, to prove to himself that he was no such thing. Like any good sergeant, he felt a strong obligation to lead his soldiers. To him, running from an enemy-occupied house was not the way to do that. The insurgents were still spewing fire from that house. Near misses sparked on the pavement all around the Americans. "We're all gonna die," one frightened man said. "We're not going to die!" Bellavia shouted back. "They're gonna fucking die!" He was calming himself as much as he was calming the scared soldier.

A Bradley came up and raked the house with 25-millimeter and coaxial machine-gun fire. As much as the soldiers hoped that the supporting fire had killed the insurgents, most everyone, including Bellavia, understood that someone would have to go back into the house and kill them face-to-face. The sergeant knew that he had to lead the assault, even though he believed he would not survive. The very thought of it all frightened him to death, but it had to be done. "If I don't go in," he later wrote, "they'll have won. How many times have we heard that American soldiers rely on firepower and technology because they lack courage?" From studying military history, he knew that America's enemies always made the same claim. He was determined to disprove it.

Gathering several of his soldiers, he prepared to make a coordinated assault. All the while, he kept psyching himself up and projecting a fearless persona to his men by telling them "you were born for this moment . . . you were born to kill these evil motherfuckin' terrorists . . . we're gonna eat their flesh and send them to fucking Lucifer." Every man believed that death waited in the house. Another squad leader, Staff Sergeant Scott Lawson, sidled up to Bellavia and told him: "I'm not going to let you go in there and die alone." Bellavia was overwhelmed by the nobility of Lawson's statement. Bellavia's feeling of brotherhood for him was so powerful that he felt "closer to Lawson than to my own kin." Here was a prime example of an enduring truth about American combat soldiers: they fight, die, and sacrifice for one another. For them, no other motivation to face danger is ever as powerful. "I just wasn't gonna let him go in there by himself and die," Lawson later said. "That night it was hectic, crazy. You lose your mind a little bit."

After hurling some grenades, the squad crept through the courtyard, with Bellavia and Lawson in the lead. Michael Ware, an Australian reporter, was among them, observing everything. The Bradley fire had not killed the muj but it did force them to abandon the windows and take shelter in the house's interior. It also punctured a water tank, coating the floor of the building with a quarter inch of dank water. Bellavia and Lawson entered the house and carefully moved along the foyer wall, toward the stairwell. The house stank of moldy water and rotting fish. They could hear the enemy fighters whispering in Arabic. Bellavia was carrying an M16A4 with a 203 grenade launcher attachment—not an ideal weapon for close-quarters battle (CQB) because of its size and weight. Lawson had a 9-millimeter pistol.

Bellavia was peering through his night vision goggles, looking for the insurgents. Then, confusion reigned as shooting broke out. Bullets whizzed past Bellavia, so close he could almost feel the wind of one as it snapped past his helmet. Others tore chunks from the walls. The fire tapered off and the insurgents began chanting *"Alahu Akbar"* (God is great) over and over, in a frightened tone, almost as if calming themselves. Through the haze, Sergeant Bellavia could see them now, and they were still behind the barriers. One of them looked very young. He bent down to prep an RPG. The other one had a neatly trimmed beard and was wielding a machine gun. Behind them, propane tanks lay in piles. Bellavia was praying to himself now. He tried to clear his mind but again all he could think was "The Power of Christ compels you!" He screamed that aloud, brought his weapon to his shoulder, and rushed toward them. "Close-quarters combat is instinctual, fought on the most basic and animalistic level of the human brain," he wrote. "Body language, eye contact, the inflection of voice can turn a fight in a heartbeat." The younger insurgent looked up in surprise. His eyes met Bellavia's and, with venomous emphasis, he spat out the word "Jew!" Bellavia put a round into his chest and his pelvis. The jihadi spun around, fell down, and his blood poured into the water, spreading red pools outward from the dead form. The other man ran for the kitchen. Bellavia and Lawson shot at him and scored several hits, as evidenced by his intense moaning, but he kept returning fire from the kitchen. Lawson ran out of ammo. Outside, soldiers were screaming in confusion. Some thought Bellavia had been wounded or killed.

At this point, for Bellavia, the battle became a one-man struggle. Chaos ensued as, throughout the dark house, he engaged in a personal duel to the death with the insurgents. In two instances, he had to shoot them multiple times before they died. Many times, he yelled at them in Arabic to surrender. One of them responded with taunts. "I will kill you and take your dog collar," he said. "Mommy will never find your body. I'll cut your head off." For the American, the creepy voice was unnerving to the point of sheer panic, but he suppressed his natural fear and kept fighting. He stalked one wounded insurgent up the stairs onto the upper floor. He and the man had awkwardly exchanged shots in a bedroom, stumbling around an armoire where the bearded man had been hiding. This fighter had a thick beard, he was middle-aged, and he stank to high heaven. Bellavia thought of him as the bogeyman because he looked so bedraggled and had emerged from the armoire, like something out of a child's nightmare of monsters in the closet.

As Sergeant Bellavia ascended the wet stairs in search of the enemy fighter, images of his wife and son kept flashing through his mind. In his mind's eye, he saw a casualty notification team coming to the door of his home. He imagined his wife as a widow, his son growing up with no father. He saw his own tombstone. He was filled with a strange combination of fury and regret. Like nearly every infantry soldier, he was torn between an obligation to his actual family and his military family. He loved them both with an intensity that was hard to describe. Both of them needed him badly. Right now, in this horrible place, though, his military brothers needed him more.

Near the top of the stairs, he slipped on a pool of blood and fell forward a bit. At that exact moment, the bogeyman opened fire. The bullet whizzed overhead, right where Bellavia's head would have been if he had not slipped. A chance incident, a slip of one mere foot, had saved his life and left him always to wonder why. The sergeant straightened up and sputtered: "You're gonna fucking die, dude." He shot and missed. In the muzzle flash, Bellavia could see fear in the eyes of his enemy. The man fled to a room. The New Yorker found him, threw a grenade in there, and wounded him again. Just as Bellavia was about to open fire and finish him off, he noticed propane tanks and a smoky fire burning up a mattress in one corner of the room. Bellavia could smell natural gas. Concerned that one of his tracer rounds might touch off an explosion, he held his fire. "I step forward and slam the barrel of my rifle down on his head. He grunts and suddenly swings his AK up. Its barrel slams into my jaw and I feel a tooth break." Bellavia's father was a dentist and all the squad leader could think of right now was how angry his dad would be that he had cracked a tooth. "These are the irrational thoughts that come into your mind at this moment," he later said.

In fact, these were the first blows in a desperate fight to the death. Bellavia tasted blood in his mouth and throat. He swung his rifle like a baseball bat and caught the man full in the face. The bogeyman still had the presence of mind to kick the sergeant in the crotch. His M16 clattered onto the floor. Bellavia tried beating him with a small-arms protective insert (SAPI) plate from his body armor and then his Kevlar helmet, too. The two struggled back and forth, kicking, clawing "like caged dogs locked in a death match. We've become our base animal selves, with only survival instincts to keep us going. Which one of us has the stronger will to live?"

Bellavia kept yelling in Arabic and English at the man to surrender, but to no avail. With his right finger, he gouged the man's left eye and was "astonished to discover that the human eye is not so much a firm ball as a soft, pliable sack." The gouging of an eye is highly unsettling to most all human beings, even a trained warrior like Bellavia. Even with his life on the line, and wearing Nomex gloves, he could not bring himself to plunge his finger deep into his enemy's eye socket. He withdrew the finger. The man fired a pistol shot that just missed Bellavia's head. "I thought . . . I'm done." In that moment, he suddenly remembered that he was carrying a knife. "That knife was the only thing that was gonna make me live." As he rose slightly to grab it from his belt, the man bit him in the crotch. Paroxysms of pain and rage coursed through Bellavia. At first he used the blunt end of the knife to batter the man's gray-flecked hair, but still his teeth clenched into Bellavia's crotch. "His breath was horrible, just stale, nasty breath." The American could feel warm blood running down his leg but fortunately his vital parts were intact.

At last, he locked the knife blade into place, rolled heavily onto the muj, and stabbed him under the collarbone. The man was crying, struggling and wailing. One of his hands kept beating Bellavia's side but the blows steadily weakened when the knife nicked an artery. Bellavia heard a gurgling, liquid sound. Both of them were bathed in the warm arterial blood. Bellavia kept pumping the knife blade "like Satan's version of CPR." A powerful smell, much like rust, emanated from the blood.

Bellavia saw fear and then resignation in the eyes of his enemy. "Please," he said to the American. With tears of his own, Bellavia replied, "Surrender!" "No," the man said with a smile on his face. With one last spasm of strength, he reached up with his right hand and caressed Bellavia's face. "His hand runs gently from my cheek to my jaw, then falls to the floor. He takes a last ragged breath, and his eyes go dim, still staring into mine. Why did he touch me like that at the end? He was forgiving me." The two enemies had shared a supremely ironic killer-and-victim intimacy, almost sexual in its intensity, that only they could understand. Bellavia was anything but exhilarated. He was exhausted from his postfight adrenaline crash, aching from his wounds, and wrung out from the awful experience of killing face-to-face, in an animal struggle. He lay still, shivering, cold, nauseous, coated with the dried blood of the man he had just stabbed to death.

When, at last, he collected himself, grabbed his rifle, and left the room, he heard American voices downstairs. He stumbled into the hallway and almost bumped into another enemy fighter. In the confusion, the muj lost his AK-47. Bellavia fell on his rear end but held on to his M16. "The dregs of my body's adrenaline supply shoots into my system." He shot the man several times. The wounded muj dragged himself to the roof of the house and flung himself into the garden below. An unseen SAW gunner finished him off. Bellavia shuffled to a corner, sat down heavily, lit a cigarette and took a deep drag. As he contemplated what had just happened to him in this hell house, it occurred to him that today was his birthday. "I've had better birthdays," he thought. The other grunts came upstairs and asked if he was okay. "Yeah, I'm good," he replied bravely. He knew that was not true, though. In fact, he doubted he would ever be the same again.[14]

Nor was the battle anywhere near finished for him and the other grunts. Task Force 2-2 Infantry pushed across Highway 10 and continued methodically clearing block after block of urban sprawl. "They would dismount and clear a building to the roof to get eyes into the next block, or the next intersection," one officer remembered. "Then they'd move the Bradleys around to get some suppressive fire, bring the guys down off the roof, down into the next block, and then do it again." Newell eventually had to use soldiers from the Brigade Reconnaissance Troop as dismounted infantrymen. In addition to local resistance, often these men and the everyday grunts fought face-to-face with foreign insurgents who had come to Fallujah from such countries as Yemen, Saudi Arabia, Afghanistan, Pakistan, and Sudan to martyr themselves.

The process of seizing buildings was exhausting and deadly. Alpha Company lost its commander, Captain Sean Sims, and its executive officer, First Lieutenant Edward Iwan. Sims was shot at point-blank range by a hidden insurgent inside of a building he thought was clear. Iwan took a direct hit from an RPG as he stood in the turret of his Bradley during a major insurgent counterattack. The warhead embedded in his abdomen, nearly severed him in two, but did not explode. Dr. Dewitt's aid station was close to the fighting, maybe about a kilometer away. She did everything she could to save him, and even got him to the operating table at Camp Fallujah, but he died there. As Iwan lay dying and unconscious, Lieutenant Commander Ron Camarda, a chaplain, sang hymns to the young lieutenant. "I was singing 'O Holy Night' when he shed a most awesome and beautiful tear." Camarda believed that the tear came from Iwan's sadness at his imminent death and the profound love he felt for his soon-to-be-grieving family.

According to Task Force 2-2's after action report, "The speed and shock effect of the task force attack south cornered the insurgents into their last strongholds in the southern corners of the city and prevented them from reorganizing or developing a coherent defensive plan. These fighters fell back to prepared defensive positions, including spider holes, underground tunnels connecting basements of houses, IEDs along roads, houses rigged with explosives, and defensive positions on rooftops." Newell's formidable force steadily battered them to death. In the meantime, the Marines were also fighting house to house.[15]

Door to Door with 3/1 Marines in the Jolan and Queens

Young and cocky, they were the unit descendants of the men who had fought at the Point and among the terrible Umurbrogol caves on Peleliu. Born in the 1970s and 1980s, they were products of America's postindustrial, information-age culture. They loved video games, guy movies, reality TV shows, porn, and glam magazines like *FHM* and *Maxim*. They called one another "dude" and "dog." Even officers and sergeants routinely employed these ubiquitous monikers when talking to their young Marines. They were tech savvy and very bright, though they could sometimes be ignorant of grammatical niceties and basic geography. Modern American entertainment culture was so powerfully ingrained in them that they generally referred to their enemies as the "bad guys" and themselves as the "good guys," as if the Iraq War was merely a giant action film. Many of them coated themselves with tattoos. Their music was a blend of country, hard rock, and rap. They no longer referred to their NCOs as "Sarge." They called them "Sar'nt," as if saying the full title might absorb too much time and energy. Their officers used words like "battlespace" instead of "battlefield" and "challenge" instead of "problem." Like their World War II ancestors, the grunts smoked cigarettes in distressingly high numbers. But, unlike the Old Corps Marines, they knew all about the dangers of smoking and still did it. Even more commonly, they dipped snuff, mainly as a means to combat exhaustion, the favorite brands being Skoal and Copenhagen.

In some ways, they were societal anomalies. In the midst of postfeminist America, they were unapologetically macho and homophobic. Paragons of physical fitness, they fought for a country with a serious obesity problem. They swore so creatively and with such frequency that polite conversation with a civilian could be a greater challenge for some of them than the boot camp they had all endured and mastered. To put it mildly, they were politically incorrect and proud of it. Like almost all infantrymen, they were irreverent on the outside, reverent on the inside. They were a fascinating blend of hard-bitten cynicism and tenacious idealism.

They had more in common with their 3/1 Marine predecessors than otherwise. As with the 3/1 Marines at Peleliu, they loathed their enemies and everything they stood for, but respected their fanatical courage. Their weapons were different from the World War II Marines', but their spirit was the same. They were grunts to the core—lean, aggressive, sour but good-hearted. They were among the finest light infantrymen in the world. Their competence and skill underscored the generally unappreciated reality that not just anyone can become an infantryman. "There is a certain amount of natural talent that can't be created," one Marine officer wrote. "When that talent is there it can be nurtured, but it can't be created where it doesn't exist." A rifle platoon leader added his opinion that "there are probably few jobs in the Marine Corps . . . that are more challenging than being an infantry squad leader."

In western Fallujah their job was to go door to door, cleaning out every building, in the Jolan and Queens, a pair of terrorist strongholds. "Clearing buildings is combat at its most primitive," one embedded civilian historian wrote. "The fighting is up close and personal, not the pushbutton warfare that many Americans hear about and see on television." This meant ending the lives of other human beings with a staggering degree of personal violence and trauma. "You're just acutely aware of what war is about," Major Joe Winslow, a Marine combat historian with 3/1, later said, "finding and violently killing other people as best you can and you're exposed to the results of that . . . Marines being killed or injured, dead enemy body parts, bodies stuck everywhere, just death in general. It's very earth shattering." In fact, American intelligence officers believed that the Jolan was where many of the most hardcore insurgents, including Zarqawi's crew, were headquartered. The area was also known for its narrow streets and dense, sturdy structures.

As with 2-2 Infantry in eastern Fallujah, in this western section of town the Army's 2-7 Cavalry, under Lieutenant Colonel Jim Rainey, led the way through the breach as an armored fist. They cleared the streets of IEDs and VBIEDS. They destroyed RPG and machine-gun teams. Their grunts cleared plenty of buildings. More than that, though, the sheer force of their tanks and Bradleys shocked the enemy into immobility. "The 3/1's mission was to flow behind 2-7 after they entered the city . . . and start clearing the enemy right behind the penetration," Colonel Shupp, commander of RCT-1, later said. "I can't tell you how happy we were with Jim Rainey and 2-7. These guys are fighters. They're the best soldiers I've ever seen in my life." Lieutenant Colonel Buhl, 3/1's commander, was grateful for the armored screen that the tanks and Brads provided his Marines. "I'm very thankful for everything 2-7 did for us. I'm impressed with that battalion. They were a seasoned battalion. They really . . . attacked, aggressively. Their leaders were squared away."

In the wake of this powerful wedge, covered by the watchful eyes of Marine and SEAL snipers, Buhl's rifle companies plunged into the close-packed jungle of sandstone-colored buildings. They were aided by satellite photographs and even some real-time images from UAVs flying overhead. The drone of their engines became a constant sound track. At ten thousand feet, fighter jets loitered, waiting to help. The supporting fire of artillery and mortar crews was readily available. But it was up to the grunts to clear the buildings. In general, they carried about forty or fifty pounds of gear, consisting of fresh magazines for their rifles, water, grenades, body armor (IBA), Kevlar helmets, weapons, and assorted specialty items like bolt cutters, shotguns, or sledgehammers.

Most of the city blocks were about two hundred meters long, with an average of one hundred structures on each block. A house might contain nothing or it might teem with jihadis looking to martyr themselves. "It would seem that the first block was always clear," Lance Corporal Dustin Turpen of Lima Company said, "and they let us think there was nobody there, and we started to get complacent. After you kick fifty doors in, and there's nobody there, it starts to become normal. It's like the fiftieth house you clear that day, and you're just trying to get it done, and that's when the shit happens." As Turpen indicated, the job of assaulting the buildings was up close and personal, a high-stakes jumble of kicking in doors, rushing through rooms. The repetitiveness was mind-numbing. There was a definite Russian roulette feel to it. Danger could come from any direction in the urban morass. "You have to cover everywhere," First Sergeant Brad Kasal of Weapons Company said. "You had a guy pointing [his weapon] in the front, a guy pointing high, guys covering high in other directions, a guy covering the rear. The fire can come from anywhere . . . up high, low, down in a sewer . . . a window."

Each fire team and squad had to perfect a distinct choreography and chemistry, with a man covering each sector, reacting instantly to the person next to him, covering his every movement, proceeding as smoothly as possible into the dark interior of the building. They draped their rifles over their armored vests, always orienting them forward, braced expertly against their shoulders, ready to shoot. Every man's rifle was secured with a three-point sling, preventing slippage off the shoulder. Each room presented the possibility of close contact and a personal fight to the death. "I'm the assault team, so I'm always the first one in the house," Corporal Matthew Spencer, a fire team leader in Kilo Company, told a historian. "Once we're in the stack, we're all ready to go. We can read off each other. Most of the time the door is straight in front. We'll go in . . . and from there, you take your immediate danger areas and your doorways and we're pretty much split from there and we don't really see each other until we meet up in a bigger room or we're coming out."

Corporal Francis Wolf, a squad leader in the same company, always ordered his Marines to shoot up the house first and then assault. "And once we enter the house, just basically, hard, fast, intense . . . frag every room you can . . . sometimes two to three depending on the room." They found that grenades were not all that effective because the rooms offered so much furniture and debris for cover. Moreover, the insurgents often anticipated that the Marines would use grenades, so they stacked mattresses and tables near windows and doors to absorb grenade fragments. So, Wolf and his people killed almost exclusively with rifles. "The SAW is not very maneuverable inside of a house. The only time we'll ever use a SAW in a house is if we have to clear by fire. If we know that there's insurgents in the rooms, we'll poke the SAW around the corner and lay . . . a one-hundred-round burst and just light the room up." Most of the time, though, they killed the enemy fighters with multiple aimed shots from their M16s. Frequently, through the smoke and dust, they watched the life ebb from the eyes of their enemies. With firefights taking place in such small rooms, the grunts were inundated with the acrid stench of cordite and gunpowder, to the point where they could taste it in their mouths.

Often it took many shots to kill a jihadi because they were under the influence of adrenaline, cocaine, amphetamines, or other drugs that gave them extra staying power. "The terrorists just wouldn't die unless you removed their brains from their skulls," one grunt NCO said. Houses, streets, and rubble were riddled with spent needles and drug paraphernalia. One mujahideen took a shot to the face, point-blank, and stab wounds to the chest but kept fighting. "His brains were out on the floor," Corporal Bill Sojda recalled. "A normal person would have died with a bullet in their head and multiple stab wounds." So, even grievously wounded insurgents could present a deadly threat. "I know of several instances where near-dead enemy rolled grenades out on Marines who were preparing to render them aid," Lieutenant Colonel Bellon wrote. "It was a fight to the finish."

The Americans did take prisoners, but in this unforgiving, stressful environment they were usually inclined to shoot anyone who offered any semblance of a threat (they were especially leery of suicide bombers). In one well-known instance, when the Marines took a mosque after heavy fighting, they encountered a badly wounded insurgent. One of the riflemen thought that the man was a threat and he shot him to death, right in front of a camera-toting reporter. The graphic footage was beamed to the world, generating controversy and even an official investigation of the shooter's actions. The brutal reality was that every encounter with the enemy portended imminent death. Life-and-death decisions had to be made in a split second. "There is no one technique for house clearing," another squad leader said. "Sometimes I'll be noisy to draw fire, sometimes I'll sneak in. I'll climb over a roof and come down the stairs, or feint at the front door and enter through the kitchen. Training gives you the basics. After that, you have to adapt." The most important thing was to avoid being predictable.[16]

Regardless of how professionally the squads assaulted buildings, the job was time-consuming and very dangerous. The goal of the jihadis was to lure the Marines inside the buildings, where they could inflict casualties on them at close range. All too often, the insurgents intended to die and simply wanted to take as many Marines with them as they could. This was especially true in the heart of the Jolan and Queens, where many foreign terrorists made their last stand. "Their discipline throughout the battle still amazes me," Gunnery Sergeant Matthew Hackett of Lima Company said. "They just sat in the house and waited, kind of like spiders; they waited for the perfect shot, our faces or necks, since our body armor and Kevlars . . . protected our bodies."

With distressing frequency, they would hole up within a house chosen for its excellent fields of fire on every avenue of approach and also for its sturdy interior. They covered every window and door. "They knew what we were doing," another NCO said. "They studied our tactics, sitting there, waiting to kill us before they died." When the Marines plowed inside, the muj opened fire from point-blank range. Then the Marines would find themselves trapped inside the house, usually with some of their own men dead or wounded, involved in a room-to-room fight to the death. Supporting weapons were often no help in these situations because the Americans obviously could not blow up houses where Marines were trapped. The focus then changed from clearing the house to extracting the casualties. Most modern American infantrymen are taught to avoid open streets during urban combat. But when Marines got pinned down inside buildings, the streets outside, ironically, became the safe spots, the very place where Marines sought to make their escape.

Hackett's Lima Company had several such incidents. In one instance, a squad assaulted an auto repair shop, right into the waiting muzzle of an RPK machine gun in an adjacent room that covered the door. The squad leader was the lead man. He quickly ducked away and shouted "Get the fuck out!" to his guys, but it was too late. Several of them were already piling inside. The enemy gunner unleashed a stream of bullets, one of which caught Lance Corporal Nicholas Larson in the jugular vein, killing him. As Larson's blood poured out onto the floor, several others fought back with grenades and rifles, but they were pinned down. "I've never seen so much blood in my life," one of them recalled. In an effort to distract the machine gunner long enough for his buddies to beat a hasty exit from the repair shop, Private First Class Nathan Wood charged the enemy gunner's room, hurling a grenade inside and spraying it with his M16. The machine gun killed him, too. The other Marines threw grenades at the room and dodged a hail of bullets to exit the shop.

They summoned a SMAW gunner to blow up the shop, even though the dead bodies of their comrades were inside. The shoulder-launched SMAW fires an 83-millimeter rocket and can puncture eight feet of concrete. It creates massive overpressure capable of collapsing a building and crushing a person. The room where the rocket explodes can heat up to fifteen hundred degrees Fahrenheit. The gunner pumped two rockets into the shop, turning it into jumbled rubble. As it turned out, there were three mujahideen inside. Not only did they survive the SMAW rounds, but they kept fighting, even though they were wounded and pinned in place by rubble. The Marines had to kill them with point-blank rifle shots before they could recover the bodies of their dead friends.

Another time Lima Company's 1st Platoon ran into a well-hidden group of hard-core Chechen insurgents who were just waiting to ambush them. One squad had three men wounded inside of a building, fighting room to room against the disciplined Chechens. They managed to get their wounded Marines out. Another squad was approaching an adjacent building. The squad leader, Sergeant James "Bennie" Conner, cautiously skulked into the courtyard, making it as far as a window on the house's southern side. Several yards away, behind the courtyard wall, Lance Corporal Michael Hanks was covering him. Conner chanced a peek into the window and came face-to-face with a man who looked like "Yasser Arafat in his younger days . . . red towel on his head . . . dirty, dark-green coat on." The man had several rifles and two RPGs arranged around himself. He and Conner both opened fire. Neither had a very good angle to shoot the other, but Conner got hit in the arm. Enraged, the twenty-seven-year-old sergeant emptied an entire magazine into the window. "I'm hit, dude," Conner told Hanks. "I got to come by the window, so cover me." Hanks replied, "Okay, dude."

Hanks lunged forward. Behind him, taking cover behind the wall, was Patrick O'Donnell, a civilian historian who had embedded himself with the platoon. He thought about following Hanks into the courtyard. At that moment, though, a presence told him: "Don't go any farther, you aren't trained to clear a house." An instant later, he heard a long burst of RPK machine-gun fire and then someone screamed that Hanks was dead. Machine-gun bullets had torn into his face. "Michael Hanks's bloody head was lying next to my boot," O'Donnell wrote. "There were still a lot of bullets flying, but for a second everyone stopped. The moment seemed to last for an eternity." The platoon leader, Lieutenant Jeffrey Sommers, ordered everyone to pull back. "They started . . . firing and throwing grenades at the house. Since I thought there was a tiny chance that Hanks was still alive, I grabbed the back of his flak jacket and started dragging him to the rear. A Marine came to help me. I was dragging Hanks with my right arm. Hanks's lifeless body weighed a ton." The blood of the fallen Marine soaked the historian's boots and the incident marked him for life, hardening his resolve to tell the story of such valorous men. "When you're in the middle of this, it all becomes so personal," he later said. The 1st Platoon alone suffered thirty-five casualties, including four dead.

In another telling incident, three Kilo Company Marines were trapped inside of a house that was defended by several insurgents (probably Chechens). First Sergeant Kasal of Weapons Company and seven other Marines heard what was going on and came to the rescue. Kasal had once served as first sergeant of Kilo. He was determined to do all in his power to save the three Marines. "All I could think about was three of our own getting captured by the bad guys and beheaded . . . on TV." Kasal and the others burst into the house and began methodically clearing it. They found one wounded Marine and two dead insurgents. The walls of the house were smeared with the crimson red blood of the mujahideen.

As the other Marines fanned out to clear each room, Kasal noticed one open room near a staircase and two adjoining rooms. He told two Marines to cover the staircase. Then he told Private First Class Alexander Nicoll to cover him as he cleared the room. Kasal did not just charge through the doorway. The first sergeant had twenty years of infantry experience. He knew that the most effective way to enter a potentially hostile room was to "pie" it. In other words, he stood in the doorway and visually inspected each part of the dark room in slices. This technique focused his eyes, steadied his weapon, and minimized his exposure to anyone in the room. The knowledge saved his life. Just as he looked to the near wall, he saw a crouching man, at handshake distance, with an AK-47. As the man raised the weapon, Kasal backed up and shouted "Bad guy!" to Nicoll, who was standing right behind the first sergeant. Just then the jihadi fired a burst that barely missed Kasal. He could feel the sonic whoosh of the bullets as they flew past his chest. "I placed my weapon over the top of his rifle and stuck my barrel straight into his chest and pulled the trigger. I emptied 8 to 10 rounds into his chest before he went down." Even then the man was still moving, so Kasal fired two more bullets into his head. His body collapsed in the doorway.

Kasal and Nicoll did not know that the two Marines they had posted at the stairwell were no longer there. There were insurgents all over the house and they had gone off to fight them. Meanwhile, a muj snuck down the stairwell and opened up on Kasal and Nicoll from behind. Bullets tore into Kasal's right leg. Nicoll caught a round in his left leg. Kasal painfully crawled, dragging his right leg behind him, around the dead man's body, into the room. Then he came back for Nicoll and pulled him in as well. He did all this under fire, as rounds impacted around the two Marines. They were both bleeding badly, pinned down inside of the room. Both of them were carrying a pressure dressing, designed to stanch the flow of blood from open wounds. Kasal decided to use both dressings on Nicoll, "so that at least one of us could live," the first sergeant later said. "I was bleedin' pretty bad by this time. Blood was spurting out of my leg. I was kind of getting weak and starting to lose consciousness." Even so, when the insurgent snuck close to the door and pitched a grenade to a spot about four feet from them, Kasal pushed Nicoll down and draped his body over him, shielding him from the blast. "In all honesty, I thought I was going to bleed to death from severe wounds and lack of medical treatment anyway." The NCO figured if he himself was going to die, he might as well save Nicoll's life. The grenade sent hot fragments into Kasal's legs, buttocks, and lower back, "causing my head to spin and my ears to feel like they had just burst." His gear absorbed much of the blast, though, and many of the fragments went upward.

It took thirty or forty minutes for other Marines to rescue the men who had originally been trapped and then turn their attention to extracting Kasal and Nicoll. As several Marines, including Lance Corporal Justin Boswood, unleashed a wall of covering fire, Lance Corporals Christopher Marquez and Dan Schaeffer ran in and pulled the first sergeant and Nicoll from the house. "The whole house was just shaking with 5.56 rounds, just SAWs going off with a two-hundred-round burst and the [M]16s as fast as you could pull the trigger," Boswood said. The Marines blew up the house with a satchel charge of explosives and, in Boswood's recollection, "a door was about one hundred feet in the air . . . and pink mist was underneath the door." Even amid this destruction, the muj were not all dead. From the rubble, one of them tried to pitch a grenade at the Marines. They pumped hundreds of rounds into his remains. Nicoll survived but lost his left leg. Kasal lost 60 percent of his blood and endured over twenty surgeries, but he kept his leg. One Marine was killed in the house and eleven others wounded. Several men were decorated for their part in this "Hell House" fight, including a Navy Cross for Kasal.[17]

As the battle unfolded, the Marines learned to avoid such costly encounters and make better use of supporting arms, regardless of how much damage they did to Fallujah. "Our young men are trained to run through walls," Lieutenant Colonel Buhl said, "so we had to teach them that when you got bad guys in a house, not to just send in people." As at Peleliu, too often the first inclination of tough young Marines was to close with and kill the enemy wherever they found them, regardless of whether it was advantageous to do so. Buhl and many of his junior officers and NCOs told their Marines, "The minute you get in contact [with a fortified house] back away, cordon, coordinate, and drop it." When the casualty numbers began piling up, the grunts were only too happy to comply.

This meant using combined arms. At Aachen, combined arms teams had been vital to American success. The same was true at Fallujah. Marine battalions like 3/1 were dominated by light infantrymen, but they enjoyed the support of a marvelous array of effective weapons and learned to use them quite well. "I believe that the . . . greatest . . . combat power of a Marine infantry battalion is tied to its employment of combined arms," Buhl commented. "In an [urban] fight . . . combined arms is everything . . . tanks . . . bulldozers . . . engineers . . . indirect fire . . . aviation fire." Artillery and mortar crewmen laid down a curtain of fire ahead of the attacking infantry squads.

Most of the time the rifle companies were also supported by a nice array of vehicles, including machine-gun-toting AAVs, plus Humvees equipped with Mark 19s, .50-caliber machine guns, or TOWs. The Mark 19s and .50 cals were capable of tearing chunks out of buildings. The TOWs, of course, could collapse them altogether or, at the very least, punch entry holes into them for the riflemen.

The grunts especially loved working with tanks. Buhl's battalion was supported by one company from the Marine 2nd Tank Battalion, plus whatever assistance 2-7 Cavalry could provide. "It was like going on an evening stroll in a dangerous neighborhood with a Tyrannosaurus Rex," one Marine wrote. In addition to its 120-millimeter main gun, each Abrams had a coaxial machine gun and a .50 caliber. RPGs could damage the optics, the treads, or set fire to the carrying racks on the tank's turret, but they could not penetrate its thick Cobham armor. Nor could the vast majority of IEDs do much damage to them. So, the Abrams truly was like an impervious dinosaur, or at least the baddest kid on the urban combat block. In one instance, a tank was moving down an alleyway with some grunts. Standing in his turret, the tank commander peered over a wall just in time to see insurgents pitch grenades over it. The grenades exploded harmlessly against his armor, shielding the grunts. His driver swiveled the tank back and forth, smashing the walls, and then his gunner unloaded on the insurgents with his machine guns, shredding them.

Four tanks supported each company. "We used the tanks a great deal in terms of prepping buildings before we'd go in with Marines on the ground," Lieutenant Timothy Strabbing, a platoon leader in India Company, recalled. "We'd have a tank supported by an AAV and two vehicles behind [it]" as they moved warily down each street. The infantrymen positioned themselves alongside or behind the tanks. The grunts could point out targets for their tanker comrades by simply opening fire or talking into the phone on the rear of the Abrams. But they had to avoid standing directly behind the powerful turbine engine because it generated so much heat and such a high-pitched whining noise.

Because Fallujah was almost entirely empty of civilians, the tankers made liberal use of their considerable firepower, spraying rounds wherever the infantry might need them. "I fired twenty-five to forty-one hundred twenty-millimeter rounds each day," Master Gunnery Sergeant Ishmael Castillo, a tank commander, said. "Every tank did." In Fallujah, Castillo and his fellow tank crewmen shot approximately twenty-five hundred main-gun rounds at targets within one hundred feet. The concussive effect (not to mention the blast and shrapnel) of each shot was immense. When the Abrams fired its main-gun round, anyone standing near it risked being knocked down, knocked out, or deafened. It was like standing in the middle of a thunderclap. It physically hurt to be anywhere near an Abrams when it fired its main gun. For obvious reasons, the insurgents usually tried to avoid confrontations with the tanks, but many of them failed. Tank shells dismembered them, shredded their limbs, collapsed buildings onto them, and, in a few cases, disintegrated them.

Close air support was available in large quantities for the Marines. Each company had an actual fighter pilot attached as a forward air controller. In some cases, they called in strike missions from their own squadron buddies. The Marine grunts especially liked their own F/A-18 Hornet two-seaters, Harriers, and Air Force F-16Cs. According to Captain Pete Gallogly, the 3/1's air officer during the battle, the battalion called upon "91 laser-guided 500-pound bombs and 35 GPS 500-pound bombs. We dropped two 1,000-pound GPS bombs on a large complex—they flattened it. We dropped 10 laser Mavericks, called in 119 AC-130 strikes, 21 Hellfires [missiles], 4 TOWs, and 9 fixed-wing strafing attacks."

The infantrymen especially loved the AC-130 Bashers. "I'd fuck that plane if it was a woman," one of them said. In fact, at least one of the AC-130s was commanded by a woman. Few Marines knew that, but among those who did, heartsick rumors circulated that she was sultry and beautiful. This, of course, only added to the black widow mystique of the plane. The jihadis were absolutely terrified of it. Several prisoners testified to that fact. "They really feared Basher, because the aircraft flew at night and was basically invisible to them," one Marine officer later commented. "They could hear 'em [flying], and they could hear . . . when they fired." The muj called the plane "the Finger of God" because of the accurate, withering line of tracers that, in darkness, looked like a vengeful finger pointing to the ground.

Basher's infrared optics allowed the crew to see almost any night movement in Fallujah. Night after night, they flew circles above the Marine infantry positions, killing any insurgents who dared move in their direction with a combination of 105-millimeter howitzer fire and 20-millimeter Gatling gun fire. This afforded the Marines night security, allowing them to rest, and it limited jihadi movement, a real asset because, throughout the battle, insurgents tended to re-infiltrate areas the Americans had previously cleared. When Basher fired, it sounded as though the air above was literally being torn apart like a flimsy piece of cloth. For the grunts, nights in Fallujah were chilly and creepy. Psyops teams roamed around, playing hard-core rock songs such as "Bodies" by Drowning Pool, along with the sound of crying babies, the meowing of cats, and even the menacing laugh of the beast in the movie *Predator*. Amid this phantasmagorical environment, Basher was always a comforting sound.

Engineers tagged along with the infantrymen, playing a vital role. They used a combination of C-4 explosives, satchel charges, and old-fashioned bangalore torpedoes. They threw or placed their goodies into windows and doors, or alongside insurgent-held buildings. In one typical case, a young engineer hurled a bangalore through an open window. The ensuing explosion literally lifted the building off the ground. The grunts rushed forward, only to find, in the recollection of one man, "a terrorist's bloody arm sticking up in the rubble almost like it was reaching for the sky." Another time a bangalore collapsed the front of a house, touched off a fire and burned several mujahideen to death as they frantically tried to escape. "We realized that demo was the way to go," Lieutenant Jeffrey Sommers declared. "Rockets and bangs go where we shouldn't."

The engineers also made extensive use of armored D9 bulldozers, which were equipped with large blades and bulletproof glass. They were resistant to small arms, RPGs, and even IEDs. Throughout the Jolan and Queens, the loud clatter of their engines, accompanied by beeping as they raised their blades, could be heard. Time and again, the Marine engineers used the dozers to clear rubble and crumble fortified buildings on top of their defenders. "The D9 would come up and . . . would just start pushing stuff over, and if they ran out, they got shot," Gunnery Sergeant Duanne Walters, an engineer, recalled. "If they stayed inside . . . the house dropped on 'em." Lieutenant Strabbing saw one insurgent perch atop a balcony and fire his AK-47 on full automatic point-blank at a D9. Like some sort of impervious monster, the dozer kept demolishing the house. A tank then pumped a shell inside. The lethal combination "annulated [sic] the house and the area that individual was in with rubble and that was that." Another time, Lance Corporal Justin Boswood's fire team pulled back from a strongly held house and watched in delight as a D9 "pushed over the gate to the courtyard and then . . . went through and just started leveling [it]. None of the insurgents ran out of there. [It] was pretty cool just thinking that the last thing they heard was the methodical beep [of] a dozer."

The most common helpers were SMAW gunners, commonly known among the Marines as assaultmen. Whereas a rifleman's MOS was 0311, an assaultman was 0351. Each company had half a dozen two-man teams and they were worth their weight in gold. "The 0351s . . . were tasked with SMAW gunnery, explosive breaches, demolition of structures, and destruction of captured enemy weapons, and, in rare cases, unexploded ordnance," Lieutenant Carin Calvin, who commanded several assaultmen in Lima Company's Weapons Platoon, later wrote.

The SMAW itself was about two and a half feet long and weighed sixteen pounds. Many of the assaultmen strapped their tubes onto their backs and fought as riflemen until they were needed as rocketeers. On average, they fired about ten rockets per day. Before firing, the teams made sure to clear anyone standing behind them because the back-blast could be deadly. Commanders liked to put them on roofs where they could fire down onto buildings. Quite often, they aided the infantry not just by shooting known insurgent-held buildings but by punching entry holes (mouse holing) into structures the riflemen were about to assault. This gave them different entry points besides a window or door that might be covered by the enemy. It also could kill any insurgents who might be in the house. "We found that our assaultmen had to first fire a dual-purpose rocket in order to create a hole in the wall or building," Lieutenant Calvin said. "This blast was immediately followed by an NE [thermobaric novel explosive] round that would incinerate the target or literally level the structure." The Marines learned to fire sequential shots at the same spot, enhancing the overpressure and explosive power of the rockets and punching bigger holes into the buildings. In retrospect, the use of the SMAWs at Fallujah was rather similar to the way American soldiers used bazookas at Aachen.

Day by day, the Marine grunts arduously blasted and cleared their way through the Jolan and Queens, making increasingly free-handed use of every supporting weapon they could. "This was a grueling, on the ground, dirty, extended period of combat and manual labor," Major Joe Winslow, a Marine historian who was with the grunts, commented. "Day after day of blocking off these city blocks, small houses, different types of neighborhoods, breaking down the door, pushing through the door, going upstairs, breaking down the windows, moving the furniture . . . in addition to being shot at . . . lance corporals, corporals and sergeants . . . extremely infantry intensive. I don't care how many Scan Eagles you have or Predators [UAVs], or whatever, if you don't have some Marine peering under that cabinet, it's not gonna happen. They cleansed that city." Besides killing nearly one thousand insurgents, the Marines found several torture houses (and even some live victims), dozens of weapons caches, and Zarqawi's headquarters.[18]

Fighting to the Loose Ends

On November 16, after nearly a week of bloody fighting, Allawi's Iraqi government declared Fallujah secured. Pure and simple, this was political posturing. It was true that coalition forces had advanced through the whole city and controlled most of it. But plenty of hard fighting lay ahead for the grunts as they turned north and back-cleared block after block of demolished buildings, where small groups of insurgents patiently waited to make their last stand. Allawi was eager to rebuild the city and open it up again to its residents. The American generals wanted to stoke the perception that they had won a quick victory. They and Allawi knew that, in the information age, the longer the battle appeared to drag on, the better the chance that world media outlets would portray it as a stalemate or even a defeat for the coalition. Actually, Allawi's declaration was similar to the American tendency during the Pacific War to declare that islands were secured when much hard fighting remained to be done (Peleliu being an infamous example). The spirit of the announcement was usually correct—the enemy was defeated strategically—but many enemy holdouts remained in place to fight to the death, inflicting many casualties on the Americans. Indeed, the Japanese rarely if ever surrendered at the end of an island battle. Fallujah was like that, too. Unlike Aachen, there was no central enemy authority to declare surrender and lay down arms. The muj simply fought to the death or faded away. It was a fight not to the bitter end, but to the loose ends. In fact, the Americans did not even allow Fallujahns to return in any serious numbers to the city until December 23.

So, at Fallujah, the grunts hardly noticed the political machinations of Allawi and their own military superiors. For them, the daily grind of clearing buildings and risking their lives remained unchanged. As far as they were concerned, as long as someone was still shooting at them, then the battle was not over. Most of the infantry units spent the rest of November and even parts of December sweeping through the city, methodically destroying any remaining resistance. "It was really about having a tremendous amount of physical stamina," Winslow, the Marine historian, asserted. "Somebody's gotta go up every flight of stairs, gotta go through every steel gate and gotta break down every single door, gotta open up every roof in every alley." Most of the time, they found nothing. Sometimes they fought it out with hidden insurgents.

Almost always, they killed them. At times, they lost some of their own. In all, during November and December, they cleared close to twenty thousand buildings, often two or three times apiece. Often, when they cleared a building, they spray-painted an X on it. They were supported by 540 air strikes and over fourteen thousand mortar and artillery shells. They found over six hundred separate weapons caches, including several car bomb factories. They killed at least two thousand insurgents and captured another twelve hundred.

In total, the Americans lost 95 killed and 560 wounded over the two months. The Iraqi Army lost 11 killed and 43 wounded. The assaulting force of 6,000 troops, then, suffered an 11 percent casualty rate. Of course, some wounded soldiers and Marines did not report their injuries, so the rates were probably even higher. As always, the rifle companies—especially the Marines—suffered the most. The first sergeant of Kilo Company, 3/1 Marines, said his unit awarded eighty-four Purple Hearts, including thirty-two to Marines who were wounded badly enough to require evacuation to the States. This represented a casualty rate of over 45 percent. From November 8 to 25, the two Army battalions lost five soldiers killed. During the same time, 46 Marines from the four assaulting battalions were killed. The 3/1 lost 19 killed, the most of any battalion in the battle. Throughout 2004, 151 Americans were killed in and around Fallujah and another 1,000 wounded.

The survivors were grateful to have lived, but forever marked by their experiences. Staff Sergeant Bellavia vividly recalled, near the end of the battle, how physically wrecked he and his squad members were after many days of intense urban combat. In his recollection, he and his unshaven buddies were "ragged outlines of what we had once been . . . our uniforms . . . covered in dried gore, blood, grime, concrete dust, and smoke stains. All of us [had] brown slicks of diarrhea pasting our pants to our backsides . . . we were so sick that some of us [could] hardly walk." The physical toll generally faded with proper rest, food, and hygiene. The mental toll was more enduring. Some had trouble dealing with the trauma of having seen their friends die. Others were bothered by having had to kill, sometimes in very personal fashion, a common by-product of war for infantry grunts. Their struggle for peace was just beginning.

The city was also profoundly damaged. By most estimates, about 60 percent of the buildings were destroyed, not to mention the infrastructure of sewers, telephone wires, and the like. Lance Corporal Boswood, like nearly everyone else, was awestruck at the destruction. "This city was just in shambles, telephone wires just hanging everywhere, houses blown up, cars, huge craters, everything." After the battle, one general stood among the ruins and took in the overwhelming sight of overturned cars, half-crumbled homes, sagging roofs, cratered streets, shattered telephone poles, demolished storefronts, and simply muttered to himself in awe: "Holy shit."

Upon returning home, many of the residents were heartbroken at the destruction and bitter at the Americans for doing it. "There was no food, no water, no electricity—just the smell of gunpowder," one Jolan resident said. "This is the American way of democracy?" Another man, a shopkeeper, bitingly said: "The resistance didn't destroy houses. They didn't harm people." The former point was valid. The latter claim was laughably false. "You never want to destroy someone's city like this," Staff Sergeant Bellavia said, "but this was the only way to eliminate those fanatics." Almost all of the Americans would have agreed and eventually some Fallujahns, too. Even before the fighting was finished, Army engineers and Navy Seabees were busy rebuilding. The Americans subsequently pumped millions of dollars into Fallujah (the Iraqi government's contributions were minor and feckless). The reconstruction effort would take years. The elections of January 2005 took place more or less unhindered, although only a few Fallujahns and Anbaris participated.

After the battle, Lieutenant General Sattler claimed that "we have . . . broken the back of the insurgency." He was wrong. Fallujah did not come close to ending the insurgency in Iraq. The war would rage on for many more years. Those insurgents who escaped Fallujah often relocated to Ramadi and other spots in Al Anbar to cause much more trouble in the months and years to come. Nor did the fighting in and around Fallujah completely cease. To be sure, the Americans had absolutely eliminated it as a terrorist sanctuary, but IED bombings, sniping, and firefights were all too common by 2006, even though the Americans found and killed Zarqawi that year. Only after the Anbar Awakening, when the Sunni tribes finally turned against al-Qaeda in Iraq and cast their lot with the Americans, did Fallujah calm down for the long haul. The Battle of Fallujah was merely a small step in the direction of the Awakening, not the cause of it.

Hamstrung by their own mistaken preconceptions of modern war, buffeted by world opinion, the Americans had eventually prevailed in an urban setting, but at great political and military cost. As one military commentator adeptly put it, "The Battle of Fallujah was not a defeat, but we cannot afford many more victories like it." In the end, the battle was a brilliant combined arms and interservice operation, one that featured incredible valor at the grunt level. The performance of the infantry soldiers and Marines was among the best in American military history. Unlike Aachen, though, Fallujah was only a partial strategic victory for the United States. The controversial Iraq War would grind on, demanding many more sacrifices from the grunts.[19]

CHAPTER 10

"Watch Out for IEDs!"
Twenty-First-Century Counterinsurgent Warfare
Through the Eyes of One Infantry
Regiment in Iraq

Shock and Flaw

FALLUJAH WAS NOT TYPICAL. THROUGHOUT Operation Al Fajr and even to some extent during the fighting in April, the grunts were free to employ a wide variety of weapons whenever they felt threatened. The November fighting, of course, took place within an empty city, a unique circumstance that could obviously not be replicated with any degree of regularity. Far more commonly infantry grunts in Iraqi cities had to be more restrained. Amid the crowded streets and densely occupied buildings of the typical Iraqi city, infantry soldiers could hardly shoot first and ask questions later. Although danger could lurk anywhere in such an urban morass, the Americans had to be very careful about unleashing their firepower, even when that meant assuming more risk themselves.

Intellectually, every soldier knew that shooting up buildings, cars, and the inevitable innocent bystanders would derail their mission in Iraq, even if they also killed bona fide terrorists. This knowledge, though, did nothing to dampen the immense frustration, fear, and stress of struggling each day against an unseen enemy who dealt out impersonal death and destruction, then blended in with the population. Such is the nature of counterinsurgent warfare. Less is often more, but it is also incredibly hard on the soldiers. They must fight by a clearly defined set of rules against enemies who follow no rules or moral laws whatsoever.

In Iraq, by 2005, the Americans were deeply enmeshed in this kind of desperate, deadly counterinsurgent war. They often felt, and acted, as though they were grappling with phantoms in a pitch-dark room. In spite of Fallujah and the successful January 2005 elections, the insurgency was growing stronger and the American death toll was rising in Iraq. Commanders were finding that they had nowhere near enough troops, particularly of the infantry variety, to maintain stability in their areas of operation. "The lack of Army dismounts . . . is creating a void in personal contact and public perception of our civil-military ops," one general stated. Somehow, a ragged ensemble of third-world insurgents was withstanding the might of the world's leading military power.

The soldiers were now paying a steep price for the catastrophically wrong ideas their leaders had embraced about war. The flawed 2003 Rumsfeldian vision of a shock-and-awe, techno-rich, lightning-fast war in Iraq had given way to an unglamorous, complex, politically controversial, troop-intensive guerrilla slog in 2005. "In struggles of this type there are seldom suitable targets for massive air strikes," one military commentator wrote. "Ground forces geared and equipped for large-scale war are notoriously ineffective against guerrillas. Militarily such forces cannot bring their might to bear, and their efforts are all too likely to injure and alienate indigenous populations and thus lose an equally important political battle."

The stunned Americans—in political and military circles—were ill prepared for this most human of conflicts. This was particularly true of the Army, upon which the greatest burden of the war rested (as usual). Although the service had a long tradition of fighting, and mostly winning, guerrilla wars, the Army had de-emphasized counterinsurgency studies after the painful experience of Vietnam. The Special Operations School at Fort Bragg had even thrown away its counterinsurgency files after Vietnam, an act that was roughly analogous to a group of attending physicians throwing away all case history information on a disease that had just claimed the life of a beloved patient. The Command and General Staff College at Fort Leavenworth, along with most every Army development school, offered few if any courses on irregular war. The Army prepared itself to fight conventional wars against similarly structured adversaries. Reflecting the outlook of American policymakers, the Army was preparing for the war it wanted to fight rather than the one it might fight. The 1991 Gulf War only exacerbated the yawning gap in counterinsurgency studies. So, by the Iraq War, the armed forces as a whole were poorly prepared to fight a war against insurgents. "The only way to fill the void was through a career of serious self-guided study in military history," wrote Colonel Peter Mansoor, a brigade commander with a Ph.D. in military history from Ohio State. "The alternative was to fill body bags while the enemy provided lessons on the battlefield."

And, tragically, the body bags were being filled, largely because of improvised explosive devices (IEDs). Through hard experience, most of the insurgents had learned to shy away from pitched battles with the Americans. Instead they sowed the roads and alleys of Iraq with IEDs. Simple and lethal, an IED was often nothing more than a mortar or artillery shell hidden among roadside debris, dead animals, or dug into a spot alongside or even under the road. Sometimes they were pressure-detonated. More often, a triggerman waited for the Americans to enter a kill zone and then detonated the IED by wire or the electrical signals generated by such mundane items as a cell phone or garage door opener. At times the IEDs were wired up to propane tanks. When the IEDs' ordnance exploded, the propane ignited, along with the targeted vehicle's fuel tank, badly burning the victims. IEDs ranged from crude and easily spotted grenades or mortar shells to elaborately prepared traps with daisy-chained artillery shells or hundreds of pounds of explosives capable of destroying a Bradley or even an Abrams tank.

For insurgents, IEDs were perfect standoff weapons, inflicting death on the Americans from a safe distance, impeding their mobility, and eroding their morale and resolve. Insurgents in Iraq used IEDs in much the same way the Viet Cong had used booby traps in Vietnam, but with even greater effect. Whereas 20 percent of American casualties in Vietnam were caused by mines and booby traps, in Iraq IEDs were responsible for more than 50 percent of American deaths by 2006. "They [Americans] are not going to defeat me with technology," one insurgent told a journalist around this time. "If they want to get rid of me, they have to kill me and everyone like me." Car bombs and suicide bombers (called VBIEDs and SVBIEDs by American soldiers) only added to the bloody harvest.

All of these frightening weapons were indicative of two undeniable facts. First, there was considerable opposition to the American presence in Iraq. To a distressing extent, insurgent groups reflected the murderous anger and frustration of substantial numbers of Iraqis, or at least their willingness to tolerate such shadow warriors in their midst. Second, they represented the latest illustration of human will in war. They showed that human beings themselves are the ultimate weapons, not machines, no matter how clever, technologically advanced, or useful those machines may be. How, for example, could any machine possibly negate a suicide bomber who was determined to blow himself up because he believes that this was the path to paradise?

Opponents of the American occupation understood that they could not hope to defeat the Americans in a conventional fight, so they adapted, using their own standoff weapons, negating American technological and material advantages. Using the Internet and mass media, they waged information-age political war. Their targets were not just the American soldiers who traversed the roads each day. In a larger sense, they were targeting the will of the American people to continue this faraway war in the face of rising casualty numbers. Day by day, the guerrillas were demonstrating anew one of history's great lessons, summed up perfectly by Adrian Lewis: "War is ultimately a human endeavor. War is more than killing. And the only thing that technology will ever do is make the act of killing more efficient. Technology alone will never stop a determined enemy. The human brain and the human spirit are the greatest weapons on the Earth." Indeed they are, and the experiences of one American infantry outfit, circa 2005, illustrate that vital lesson quite well.[1]

2-7 Infantry in Saddam's Backyard

They called themselves the Cottonbalers. Unit lore held that their regimental ancestors had once taken cover behind cotton bales to fight the British during the Battle of New Orleans. In reality, the soldiers of the 7th United States Infantry Regiment probably fought that battle from behind the cover of earthen embankments, but the nickname stuck nonetheless. Proud owners of more battle streamers than any other regiment in the United States Army, the 7th fought in every American war, from 1812 to the twenty-first century. Even a cursory look at their combat history read like an honor roll of U.S. battles—Chapultepec, Gettysburg, Little Bighorn, El Caney, the Marne, Argonne Forest, Sicily, Anzio, Chosin, Tet '68, Desert Storm, to name but a few. World War II Cottonbalers had fought from North Africa through Italy, France, and Germany all the way to Berchtesgaden, where they captured Hitler's mountain complex in May 1945 (contrary to popular myth, the *Band of Brothers* paratroopers were not the first into Berchtesgaden).

The Cottonbalers of the early twenty-first century were Eleven Mike (11M) mechanized infantrymen. In April 2003, as part of the 3rd Infantry Division, they had led the way into Baghdad. In January 2005, two of the regiment's battalions, 2-7 Infantry and 3-7 Infantry, returned to Iraq and were assigned responsibility for different sections of the country—Tikrit for 2-7 and western Baghdad for 3-7. Their war this time was radically dissimilar to their April 2003 dash to Baghdad. This time, they were immersed in counterinsurgency.

Located on the Tigris River about eighty miles north of Baghdad, in Salah ad Din province, Tikrit was Saddam Hussein's hometown and a place dominated by Sunni tribes. This river town of a quarter million people sprouted some of the dictator's key advisors and many of his elite Republican Guard soldiers. This was especially true of Saddam's al-Nassiri tribe. In spite of the ties with Saddam's regime, Tikrit was not a focal point of resistance to the initial American invasion. Only later in 2003 and 2004, partially in response to the occupying 4th Infantry Division's heavy-handed tactics, did insurgent violence begin to grow. "A budding cooperative environment between the citizens and American forces was quickly snuffed out," one historian wrote.

By the time the Cottonbalers arrived in 2005, the Americans had begun to reach out to the locals but the insurgency was still going strong. Car bombs, suicide bombings, IEDs, mortar, and rocket attacks were all too common. In Tikrit (and Iraq, for that matter), there was no central resistance group such as the Viet Cong. Instead, there were a dizzying variety of cells, some with only a few members, others numbering in the dozens, with names like Juyash Mohammed, Taykfhrie, Albu Ajeel, and Ad Dwar. Some of the guerrillas were former regime loyalists. Some were Sunni opponents of the Shiite-dominated regime in Baghdad. Some simply resented the American presence in their homeland. Others were part of organized crime groups that had operated in the area for many generations. A comparative few were hard-core al-Qaeda operatives and even some jihadi fugitives from the Fallujah fighting. Most, though, were average people just trying to survive in trying times. "We had a few people that were the hard-core old regime members," Lieutenant Kory Cramer, a platoon leader in Charlie Company, said. "They were cell leaders. But the majority of the people doing the attacks were normal citizens.

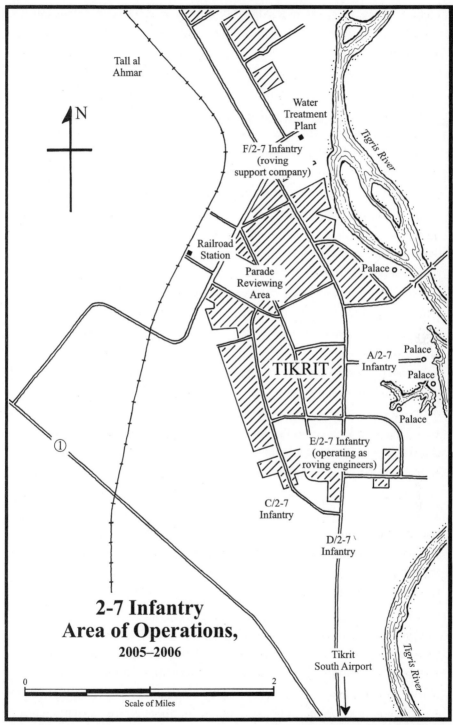

Tall al Ahmar

N

Water Treatment Plant

F/2-7 Infantry (roving support company)

Tigris River

Railroad Station

Parade Reviewing Area

Palace

TIKRIT

A/2-7 Infantry

Palace

Palace

Palace

E/2-7 Infantry (operating as roving engineers)

C/2-7 Infantry

D/2-7 Infantry

Tikrit South Airport

Tigris River

**2-7 Infantry
Area of Operations,**
2005–2006

0   2

Scale of Miles

They were broke, poor and needed to put food on the table for their families. The cell leaders would pay these guys . . . if they would go out and plant something [IEDs]." The company kept finding mines on one road, only to find out later that a mentally handicapped child was planting them. "His brother or father . . . was telling him to go put these [mines] out there."

Just before this deployment, known as Operation Iraqi Freedom III to the soldiers, 2-7 Infantry had been reorganized into a combined arms battalion, a typical process for mechanized infantry battalions by this time. Alpha and Bravo Companies were straight mechanized infantry. Charlie and Delta were armor companies. Easy was engineers and Fox consisted of supporting mechanics, trucks, recovery vehicles, and quartermasters. In practice, out of sheer necessity, most of the soldiers, at one time or another, functioned as dismounted infantrymen, even the tank crewmen and engineers. This was the trend all over Iraq by 2005.

Lieutenant Colonel Todd Wood, a gentlemanly Iowan and former college baseball player with nearly twenty years of experience in the infantry, was the commander. He had about eight hundred soldiers under his charge. They were stretched quite thin in their area of operations because they were responsible for more than just Tikrit. The battalion's area of operations (AO) also encompassed Bayji, an oil town about forty miles to the north along the river, and most of the desert that led west out of Tikrit, many miles to Lake Tharthar. Lieutenant Colonel Wood spread his companies throughout the AO to cover it as best he could. Alpha Company was in the heart of Tikrit. Bravo Company was in Bayji. Charlie Company covered the outskirt towns of Owja and Wynot, plus the desert where weapons traffickers often operated. Delta had Mukasheifa and another slice of desert. Easy Company operated as roving engineers, infrastructure specialists, and additional infantry. Wood also had, at various times, a light infantry company from the 101st Air Assault Division or a Pennsylvania National Guard mechanized infantry company from the 28th Infantry Division to patrol Kadasia, on the northern outskirts of Tikrit.[2]

The soldiers did not live among the people. That approach was an effective counterinsurgency tenet implemented later, during the surge phase of the war. Instead, in 2005, Wood's troops were housed in forward operating bases (FOBs) with such names as Remagen, Danger, Summerall, and Omaha. They ate and slept in the FOBs and then ventured "outside the wire" to patrol their areas. The typical FOB was located within preexisting buildings, most of which featured the sturdy beige brick structure so common to Iraq. The buildings ranged from old houses to palaces. Each FOB generally consisted of living quarters, a chow hall, a motor pool, a command center, a gym, perhaps even surrounding walls and guard towers. Meals were nutritious and plentiful, offering a variety of foods that grunts of previous wars could only have dreamed about.

Soldiers typically lived in the buildings, or in trailers, two or three to a room. Officers and senior NCOs sometimes had their own rooms. Almost everyone had air-conditioning and, given Iraq's brutal heat, that was a big deal. "I had a nice room to myself," Lieutenant Kramer said. "It was about the size of my bedroom back home but I didn't have to share it with my wife." Lieutenant Casey Corcoran's Delta Company was based in a palace called FOB Omaha, though it was anything but lavish. "It didn't have walls and . . . there were birds and rats living in it with you and the electricity was on and off. But you could say you lived in a palace."

Power came from a combination of the local grid and generators but it could be very spotty. "The generator to our buildings broke down and has left us at the mercy of the city's power," one Alpha Company soldier at FOB Danger wrote to his family and friends on July 25. "So, we have power for roughly 3–4 hours on and 3–4 hours off. It really isn't too bad at first, but after an hour or two of no power (hence no air-conditioning) during the middle of the day, the temperature starts to creep its way up." Just as the FOB got uncomfortably hot, the power would come back on.

Often, multiple units rotated through a FOB, so the Cottonbalers often shared theirs with other outfits. As had always been the case from World War II onward, the American war effort required tremendous logistical and administrative support. This meant that the majority of soldiers, especially females, served in noncombat units. Although the nature of the guerrilla war in Iraq often created great danger for combat and "noncombat" units alike, many of these support soldiers performed jobs that kept them safely in the FOB. Grunts generally look down on anyone who does not face as much danger as they do (and usually that means everyone else). They especially resent when support soldiers have better weapons and equipment. In Tikrit it was not at all uncommon for the Cottonbalers to patrol in unarmored, dilapidated Humvees while soldiers at the FOB had brand-new rifles and up-armored

Humvees. The resentful infantry soldiers disparagingly called the FOB-bound support troops "pogues" and "fobbits."

Sometimes this clash of cultures led to tension when the infantrymen came back to the FOB after a hard day of patrolling. "We were in full battle rattle—goggles, knee pads, elbow pads, looking like a shooter," Sergeant First Class Kenneth Hayes contemptuously said. "Then you'd see a guy laying out in the sun across the street or walking around in PTs [shorts and T-shirts] with no Kevlar [helmet] on." Another Cottonbaler NCO, Staff Sergeant William Coultrey, was flabbergasted and angered by their lack of understanding for the exhaustion the combat troops felt after a mission. "We'd come back in . . . and you'd take your vest off and you're all sweaty. They tried to tell us at first that we [couldn't] come in the chow hall sweaty." The Cottonbalers simply refused to stand for such nonsense.

For the infantrymen, the FOBs offered a reasonably safe sanctuary from the dangerous unpredictability of Tikrit. Insurgents sometimes lobbed mortar shells and rockets at the various FOBs, but most of the time the fire was ineffective. Even so, the Americans had to expend quite a bit of manpower to protect their bases. "It was a force protection nightmare having folks at all different places [FOBs]," Lieutenant Colonel Wood said. He and his personal security detachment spent a lot of time driving in up-armored Humvees from sector to sector, visiting the various companies. "We had a lot of soldiers that pulled a lot of guard duty." The security of each FOB came only through such constant vigilance. Every soldier knew that, even as he slept, others were guarding the base. So, at the FOB, a grunt could relax, get a shower, cool off, catch some sleep, eat a good meal, and rejuvenate himself until it was time to strap on his body armor, his weapons, and the rest of his sweaty gear to venture out for yet another mission.

They were almost like aviators—venturing forth from a secure base, facing danger, and then going back home to their base. This reflected the American strategy at this point in the war to protect themselves in big bases and keep as low a profile with the Iraqi people as possible. It was the exact wrong way to fight a counterinsurgent war. "The first rule of deployment in counterinsurgency is to be there," Lieutenant Colonel David Kilcullen, the Australian guerrilla warfare expert, wrote. "This demands a residential approach—living in your sector, in close proximity to the population, rather than raiding into the area from remote, secure bases. Movement on foot, sleeping in local villages, night patrolling: all these seem more dangerous than they are. They establish links with the locals, who see you as real people they can trust and do business with, not as aliens who descend from an armored box."[3]

The fact that the Americans did not live among the people guaranteed that their influence would be limited, mainly to the duration of their patrols. It also meant that they were usually reacting to the insurgents rather than the other way around. When the Americans went back to their FOB, the insurgents filled the void, much the same way the VC had re-infiltrated villages in Vietnam after General Westmoreland's battalions moved on to different areas. In Iraq, even when company commanders devised schedules that guaranteed that at least one platoon would be out in sector at any given time (as the Cottonbalers often did), their influence could only reach so far. The insurgents always knew that, eventually, at some point each day, the Americans would retreat back to the security of their FOBs. To the average Iraqi, this made the Americans seem aloof, concerned more with their own comfort than the security of the area. Anyone who considered helping the Americans knew that, when the GIs went back to their FOBs, they were at the mercy of insurgent reprisals.

To minimize this problem as much as possible, and because the Americans had such limited ground combat manpower in Salah ad Din province, the operational pace for 2-7 Infantry was frenetic. On average, each soldier participated in at least three patrols, raids, or outpost (OP) operations per day. It was not at all unusual for the men, especially in the infantry and armor companies, to do five or six missions per day. "There were times when you'd go on a six- or eight-hour patrol and then come back in, maybe get an hour's rest, and then it's right back out there again for an all-night OP," Sergeant Kevin Tilley, a sniper, recalled. Every company commander maintained a quick reaction force (QRF) that was ready to scramble out of the FOB at a moment's notice in case of trouble anywhere in the sector. "If you were on the QRF," Tilley said, "God help you, because you may roll out of the FOB between ten and fifteen times."

A typical mounted patrol in Humvees, Bradleys, or tanks consisted of driving around the streets, the alleyways, the back roads, the dirt trails, maintaining a strong presence. At times, they raided the homes of suspected insurgents. There were even rumors that the infamous al-Qaeda leader Abu Musab al-Zarqawi was operating in the area. Several times, the Cottonbalers responded to supposed Zarqawi sightings. The soldiers spent a lot of time dismounted from their vehicles, talking to the locals, mainly through Iraqi interpreters. At any moment during a patrol, an IED could detonate, an RPG could whoosh out of any building or from any corner, or a suicide bomber could strike. OP duty generally meant keeping watch over a section of road to prevent guerrillas from placing IEDs, or it might mean watching a house where they might be hiding. It was tedious, tiring, and often quite boring. "When you're sitting for hours, it really gets to you," one grunt said. "You're just sitting there thinking about how you wanna go home or you're thinking about how hot it is."

The dizzying number of missions could be especially hard on the men in the armor companies because, with a strength of only about seventy soldiers, they were roughly half the size of the other companies. Frequently, the tankers patrolled as de facto infantrymen in stripped-down Humvees instead of in their armored behemoths. At full strength, a tank platoon had sixteen soldiers. Usually a few men were gone on R and R or other assignments, so it was not unheard of for a platoon to roll out of the FOB with nine or ten soldiers. "You can only run your guys so much before . . . they break," a tank platoon sergeant in Charlie Company said. "We didn't have enough guys to do the mission sets they wanted us to do. Pretty much from the day we stepped on the ground until the day we stepped off to come back, it was a hundred percent balls to the walls." In and around Tikrit, it took enormous amounts of concentration and work just to maintain the status quo. The tankers of Delta Company, for example, spent much of their time patrolling Highway 1, the main supply route (MSR) through Tikrit, to keep it free of IEDs. "Delta MSR sweeps patrolled over 70 kilometers down and back twice a day," the company after action report declared. "Delta Company ensured the MSR stayed 'Green' [clear] with these painstaking, long, slow IED sweeps."

No matter which company a soldier came from, almost all of them, at one time or another, functioned as a dismounted infantryman or a gunner on a vehicle. "There were few opportunities for traditional engineer missions," one Easy Company engineering officer wrote, "but the company had plenty of Infantry type missions." The regular Eleven Mike riflemen and machine gunners, of course, crewed the vehicles and patrolled as dismounted infantrymen all the time. "We have conducted operations of almost every kind," Lieutenant Colonel Wood wrote in the summer of 2005. "We have done river raids from boats, Air Assaults . . . from helicopters, and of course traditional operations using our Tanks, Bradleys, and Armored HMMWVs [Humvees]." In all, they conducted over one hundred raids, six thousand patrols, detained 171 suspects, found and destroyed sixty-two weapons caches.

At the height of the summer, temperatures soared to 120 degrees and beyond. The tension inherent in the threat of potential danger, combined with the hellish heat, was exhausting. "You've got all that crap [equipment] on," one rifleman complained, "and it's a hundred and thirty degrees. You're . . . mentally exhausted 'cos . . . any window a guy could stick an AK[-47] out. The next vehicle coming down the road could be a VBIED. That pile of trash right there could be an IED." Since the soldiers knew that every vehicle might contain a suicide bomber, any car that came within one hundred meters of the Americans required great scrutiny. The rules of engagement always seemed to be in flux (a source of great agitation for the troops) and were always seemingly handed down by lawyers who rarely went on patrols (a point of even greater perturbation). But, in general, if an Iraqi vehicle was heading straight for an American and did not heed a signal to stop, the soldier would fire one warning shot in the air, then another in front of the car, then another in the engine block. and, finally, if the vehicle kept coming, he would put rounds through the windshield. The privates, specialists, and sergeants had to make life-and-death decisions—with strategic implications—in mere seconds. Did the unheeding vehicle contain a distracted parent with a car full of screaming kids or was it a suicide bomber? The soldiers were well disciplined, but they were only human. They could not be right all the time. Sometimes they prevented bombings. Other times they killed innocent people. The insurgents' strategy was to create this sort of uncertainty, the kind that led to tragic deaths that would alienate the population from the Americans.

To avoid dehydration, the grunts drank copious amounts of water, often to the point where they felt that their bladders might explode. Soldiers would discreetly duck inside their Bradleys or Humvees, urinate into an empty water bottle, tightly replace the cap, and then resume their duties. In one instance, a Humvee gunner had to defecate so badly that, in the middle of a patrol, he hopped down from his turret and did his business in the middle of a street.[4]

The Tikrit area could actually be quite calm, so the vast majority of the time the patrols were uneventful. As the days wore on, monotony could set in, especially as the soldiers came to know their AOs like the proverbial backs of their hands. Each day secmed to be a blur of driving or walking down the same streets, talking to the same locals, chasing the same elusive "bad guys." Firefights and pitched battles of any kind were very rare. Without the give-and-take of conventional combat, the grunts could sometimes lose their edge and settle into a dangerously false sense of security. Commanders expended much time and effort to keep their men from getting complacent. "Tikrit was a place where, if you let your guard down, you might get away with it for one day, you might get away with it for a whole month and then, bang, you'll get hit by a VBIED," Lieutenant Lane Melton, a rifle platoon leader in Alpha Company, said. "These guys . . . were trained to go out there and pull the trigger and you had to convince them that this isn't the fight. You have to convince them that we're out here to make this place better and it's not gonna happen by shooting up [the town]. There's not a lot of terrorists out here. We're gonna win by building up their schools . . . and things like that." It was a tough sell, especially when the men faced so much danger from impersonal, but deadly, IEDs. They yearned to hunt down and kill those responsible. That was part of their mission, but not always as important as the peacekeeping job of fostering good relations with Tikritis.

To relieve the stress and buck up morale, Wood implemented a patrol rotation policy for the companies. Every month, each company enjoyed a two-day stand-down with no mission responsibilities. The soldiers could eat, relax, sleep, watch movies, read, play video games (Ghost Recon was a favorite), phone their loved ones, have barbecues, play sports, or do whatever else they wanted to do. The forty-eight hours off were heavenly, but the days leading up to and after the stand-down were onerous for the soldiers because of the need to cover for other units that were resting. At times, sergeants and lieutenants would sense that the stress or exhaustion of constant missions was getting to a soldier and give him a day off to recover.

Even amid the hectic pace of operations, the troops found enjoyable ways to fill up their downtime. Fox Company held a weight-lifting competition. Delta Company ran kick ball, volleyball, and basketball tournaments. Charlie Company played dodgeball. On several occasions, Lieutenant Matt Woodford, a platoon leader in that company, bought steaks and grilled them for his guys. "We're a tank platoon so I only had to get sixteen steaks," he said and laughed.

The fun and games ended when it was time to leave the FOB and go back out in sector. In spite of the fact that little happened most of the time, danger was ever present. In October alone, throughout 2-7's AO, there were twenty-two IED attacks. "We heard an explosion once an hour for three hours straight and found ourselves glued to the radio listening for the report to come in on what happened and if everyone was okay," one soldier said from the perspective of an FOB. Soldiers found and destroyed another fifteen IEDs that month. There were nine mortar attacks and three rocket attacks, as well as five grenade and four small-arms-fire incidents.

One of the IEDs—a double-stacked land mine—claimed the life of Private First Class Kenny Rojas. Another terrible concoction, consisting of a mine and several 155-millimeter artillery shells, killed Specialist Joshua Kynoch, a Bradley driver. Seven other soldiers from the battalion were killed in the course of the year. Sergeant Daniel Torres and Staff Sergeant Steven Bayow of Bravo Company were the first two soldiers to lose their lives. In early February, they were riding in the back of an open-topped Humvee as it left FOB Summerall in Bayji. Almost immediately they ran into an IED. The explosion killed both of them instantly. In May a fanatic drove a car bomb into a Bravo Company Humvee, flipping it over three times, killing Private First Class Travis Anderson and wounding four others. Another car bomb killed Sergeant Carl Morgain, a Pennsylvania National Guardsman attached to the battalion. That same month, an IED that was concealed underneath a tire exploded and killed Delta Company's Private Wesley Riggs as he was pulling the tire off the road. In August and September, respectively, IEDs killed Lieutenant David Giaimo and Sergeant Kurtis Arcala. In many cases, the Cottonbalers, through good intelligence work and targeted raids, apprehended the killers.[5]

This was satisfying but it was also reactive. The core of the battalion's mission was not really to kill terrorists; it was to prevent their existence. Mirroring the overall American strategy in 2005, 2-7 Infantry attempted to do that by turning over security responsibilities to the new Iraqi Army and the local police. "I came here with a very myopic focus [that] success equals the defeat of the bad guys through shooting bullets," Lieutenant Colonel Wood said in late October. He came to find out that the mission was much more complex than a situation where they could "kill enough terrorists and then peace was gonna break out." The goal was not just security, but also economic growth. "The insurgents will be defeated through economic, government and military means. We are trying to provide an environment that would allow [Iraqis] to create a system to self-govern."

To do this, he and his soldiers had to reach out not just to local government leaders but to the local tribes. To a great extent, the foundation of Iraqi society is built upon family honor and long-standing tribal loyalties, especially in midsized cities like Tikrit. Many of the tribes even predate Islam. In Tikrit, the al-Duri, Jumalee, al-Jabouri, al-Nassiri, and Albu-Ajeel tribes are preeminent. The tribal leaders, known as sheiks, hold great power and influence.

In 2003, when the Americans first occupied Iraq, they naively expected to co-opt the tribes, especially in the Sunni areas, to create a federal democracy. By 2005, they had come to understand the error of their ways. Army commanders now knew that stability in Iraq could only come through the tribes. Fortunately for the Cottonbalers, the previous unit in their AO, the 18th Infantry, had enjoyed reasonably good relations with the tribal sheiks, and this established a nice foundation for the 7th. Wood and his officers spent much of their time meeting with the sheiks, often eating lavish meals of rice, flat bread, lamb, and pastries, drinking chai tea, discussing a myriad of issues. In his recollection, the typical topics included "assisting the local government in accomplishing tasks . . . assisting in the building of local infrastructure . . . [and] generally helping the local population with every task they need help with, i.e. school, hospitals, businesses."

They learned patience. Iraqis do not value punctuality or time management in the same way as Americans. In their culture, directness is impolite, a stark contrast with American norms. Even in business meetings, it is customary to engage in many minutes of idle conversation before getting to the issue at hand. The Americans learned to filter out much of what they heard. Any tip-off or insider information about the identity and location of a terrorist had to be thoroughly vetted. Too often, the Iraqis simply denounced people whom they did not like, people who owed them money, or people with whom they had long-standing feuds.

For the Cottonbalers, every meeting and every meal was an unglamorous exercise in diplomacy and restraint. Lieutenant Colonel Wood spent significant amounts of his time dispensing aid to the sheiks and their key power brokers, while encouraging them to help him with security. He also sometimes had to smooth over the angry feelings that resulted from accidental killings, even though, in most instances, the Cottonbalers did not do the shooting. Too often, supply convoys that regularly drove through Tikrit shot at any perceived threat. "I was more afraid of them than anything," Specialist Dan Driss, a member of the battalion mortar platoon, commented. "They would shoot at anything." Wood defused the angry feelings that eventuated from such killings by talking with the sheiks and the affected family members. Following local custom, he usually paid $2,500 to the aggrieved parties. This blood debt would then relieve the family members, and their tribal allies, of their honor-bound duty to avenge the death of their loved one.

In a couple of instances, Lieutenant Colonel Wood had to smooth over some serious cultural problems relating to gender. On one raid, a Special Forces team detained their female informant at her own request. "My life is not safe here," she told the team. "Take me somewhere and secure me." They did so without any assistance from the Iraqi Army or female U.S. soldiers. This was completely unacceptable in the local culture. The erroneous word spread among the Iraqis, particularly the soldiers, that the Americans had abducted and violated her. It took many weeks to dispense with that falsehood.

Another time, Lieutenant Lane Melton's infantry platoon was supposed to set up an OP atop the roof of a male dormitory at the local college but mistakenly established their OP on the roof of the female dormitory a block away. The next morning, when they saw quite a few young women emerging from their building, they discovered their mistake and quickly left. "But the word went out immediately that U.S. soldiers were inside the female dorm doing who knows what," Lieutenant Colonel Wood said. "We [brought] in key leaders and put out our version of the truth as quickly as we could. The perception was what was tough. For five months we fought the rumors of U.S. soldiers . . . routinely going up there and violating women. It was a onetime thing but we fought the rumor the whole year." Wood even made regular appearances on local radio to debunk such rumors and shape public perceptions as positively as he could.

Some of the sheiks could not be trusted. "There was always bias in everything," Lieutenant Corcoran commented. "You couldn't take anything they said . . . at any sort of face value." Some were playing a double game, maintaining ties with insurgent groups and the Americans. A few were funding insurgents or had family members involved in cells. Arresting these veiled enemies usually caused more trouble than it solved. Few of the sheiks were indomitable allies. That simply was not the culture of the place. The tribes' loyalties were to themselves, not any outsider, whether that was the government in Baghdad, Americans from the other side of the world, or al-Qaeda, for that matter.[6]

For the Cottonbalers, the crux of their plan to turn over the security and economic growth of Tikrit to the Iraqis revolved around the Iraqi Army and the police (collectively called Iraqi Security Forces or ISF by the Americans). Among the many bad decisions the Americans had made in 2003, the disbanding of Iraq's army was one of the worst. It eroded the security of the country and dumped many thousands of disaffected, militarily trained, unemployed, angry Iraqi young men into circulation. Realizing what a colossal screwup this had been, the Americans had since re-created the Iraqi Army and, by 2005, as the war grew more unpopular in America, they invested most of their hopes in turning the war over to this new security force. Thus, the soldiers of 2-7 Infantry spent much time and effort training Iraqi soldiers and assisting the local police with security. Wood established a Military Assistance Transition Team (MITT), parceling out his soldiers to work on a daily basis with the Iraqi Army. The Americans also launched a public information campaign to support this transition effort. They broadcast radio messages, handed out leaflets, and even rented billboards to post glossy ads featuring images of dedicated, professional soldiers and policemen.

Compared with the overall poor quality of the army and the police in Iraq at that time, the Cottonbalers were fortunate to work with soldiers and policemen who were at least reasonably proficient and reliable. The soldiers were mostly Sunnis from the province. They wore desert camouflage utilities (DCUs), helmets, boots, and a range of military equipment. Many had military experience in Saddam's army, especially the officers. The Iraqis had little regard for NCOs (a major reason why Saddam's army had been weak), so the Americans emphasized the importance of sergeants and tried to build an NCO corps essentially from scratch. "They tried," Staff Sergeant Kenneth Hayes, an MITT team member, said of the soldiers he assisted. "There's some clowns and then there's some good soldiers actually trying to do the right thing. There was a dropout rate. We'd lose guys. But most guys were trying to do the right thing." In characteristic American fashion, few of the U.S. soldiers knew the local language, culture, or customs. They communicated with their charges through interpreters or they would speak to the Iraqi soldiers who knew some English. As was typical in Iraq, corruption could be a real problem. One time, for example, the Americans supplied their counterparts with brand-new AK-47 rifles, only to find out that the Iraqi commander had stolen the rifles from his men so that he could sell or give them to his family members and fellow tribesmen.

Over time, the corruption ebbed a bit and the army units got better. Eventually, after much intensive training from the Americans, the Iraqi soldiers ran their own operations without all that much assistance except for logistical support. "It was nice to have them because they did a lot of raids . . . that were in farmlands so we didn't have to worry about getting anybody in our company to go out there and do it," Sergeant First Class Michael Deliberti of Charlie Company said. "Then they started taking MSR [main supply route] OP [outpost] for us." The sergeant's company commander, Captain Jason Freidt, felt that "a lot of 'em not only built confidence in themselves but the population developed confidence in them as well." Captain Kelvin Swint, who headed up a MITT team and worked every day with the Iraqi soldiers, believed that "they were committed to cleaning up that area." Throughout 2005, the Cottonbalers' Iraqi Army partners conducted multiple operations and even assumed responsibility for the security of one FOB. This did not necessarily represent victory, but it was a step in the right direction.

The blue-shirted police, of course, were local men and not as well trained, well armed, or reliable. In some ways they were more important than the Army, though. The soldiers represented outside, American-sponsored authority, mainly at the province level since few of the Sunni soldiers had any love for the Baghdad government. Like the Americans, the Iraqi Army could, of course, enhance security wherever the soldiers went, but their influence was still limited because most were not from the areas where they operated. The police, as local men with the same tribal and family ties as everyone else, represented the best hope for stability. They were of mixed quality because some were insurgents, had ties with insurgents, were ambivalent about the situation, or, most commonly, they were frightened of reprisals. "When I first got to Owja," Captain Freidt said of the section of Tikrit that his company patrolled, "the only police station I had, guys would be doing guard outside and they would be wearing ski masks. None of the policemen wanted anybody else to know that they were part of the Iraqi Security Forces."

The situation did get steadily better, but the police and the soldiers were always prime targets for the insurgents, especially in off-duty hours. The insurgents, of course, were confined by no rules of war and virtually no human decency. Like mafiosi, they would hunt down the off-duty ISF members and their families and kill them. In one attack, an Iraqi Army officer's brother got his legs blown off, and, in the memory of a Cottonbaler sergeant, "all he [the brother] was doing was coming outside to go to the hospital 'cos his wife was pregnant." A terrorist walked up to another off-duty staff officer and pumped nine bullets into him. Insurgents killed the wife and brother of one police chief.

In fact, while most of the IEDs were meant for the Americans, the majority of car bombs and suicide bombings were directed at the police or the Army because they represented such a mortal threat to the predominance of insurgent groups in Tikrit. Throughout the spring and summer, the bombings happened with terrifying frequency. "At one point we had one going off every three days," Lieutenant Colonel Wood recalled. These bombs killed three hundred civilians and inflicted one hundred casualties on the Iraqi police and soldiers. The most infamous such bombing took place on February 24 at a police station the Americans thought of as the best in the whole province. A car bomb took the lives of ten policemen at the station and wounded several others. Another time, insurgents detonated a car bomb in a crowd next to a police station, killing thirty-one people and wounding eighty-one more. The aftermath was truly horrible. "The ambulances were cramming as many wounded and dead as they could hold," Lieutenant Jon Godwin wrote. "The air was so thick in some areas with fumes of burnt rubber and fuel mixed with the smell of burnt human flesh it was suffocating. Several bodies were still on the ground and had been covered with burkas. The surrounding businesses and apartments had the windows blown out of them. After the fire trucks had put out the flames, the water had mixed with the puddles of blood and turned gutters into small streams tinted red." Another time, at the site of a suicide bombing, he saw the remains of four victims who looked as though they had been petrified in ashes, similar, he thought, to those who died in the volcano at Pompeii, Italy. Charged with gathering forensic evidence, he "found the bomber's face a block from the explosion and I collected it into a garbage bag." An Iraqi policeman then led him to a spot where the rest of the bomber's head was lying grotesquely in a blob. "Even though I didn't make any actual contact with the remains, I think I used a whole bottle of hand sanitizer after the incident."

In spite of the gruesome bombings, the Americans never had trouble recruiting men for the security forces. These men were motivated by a combination of financial need, personal pride, protection of their turf, and some level of loyalty to the Americans. The Americans provided medical care, financial assistance, and security for the police after the bombings and this solidified a bond of sorts between them and their Iraqi colleagues. This, in turn, produced some tangible results. The police and the army both steadily improved, although never to the level of proficiency where the Americans thought they should be. Still, security was getting better and economic growth soon followed. By the fall, bombings were in steep decline, although IEDs and kidnappings were on the rise, so Tikrit remained dangerous. Elections went off with no substantial problems. For 2-7 Infantry, the record in Tikrit was mixed. The population still held no special love for the Americans or strong allegiance to them. There were no dramatic failures or successes, just steady, albeit glacial, progress that redounded more to the tactical than the strategic advantage of the American position in Iraq. Such were the complicated realities of pre-surge counterinsurgency in a midsized Sunni city.[7]

3-7 Infantry in Western Baghdad

Without control of Baghdad, the Americans literally had no chance to succeed in Iraq. The capital city was a megalopolis, with a 2005 population of 6.5 million and growing quickly. Baghdad was so large, so profoundly central to Iraq's economy, and so central to Iraq's vexing political situation that it was at the very center of the fighting. The city teemed with insurgent groups of all shapes, sizes, and agendas—Shiite militiamen, Sunni rejectionists, Saddamist stalwarts, foreign jihadis, organized crime, al-Qaeda butchers, and most commonly, half-interested anti-American neighborhood resistance fighters. "You've got Mustaafa and Muhammad who are just pissed off," one intelligence officer said in describing the latter type of insurgent. "They're not getting enough water. They're standing in a line and they can't get a job." So they lashed out. The population density and the concrete jungle of neighborhoods comprised

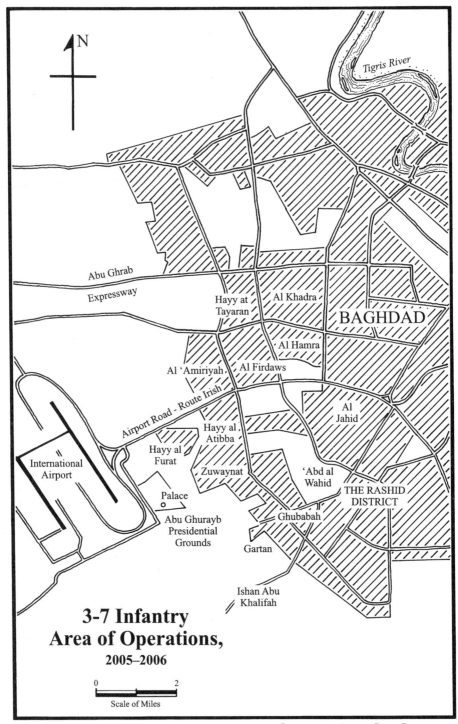

N

Tigris River

Abu Ghrab
Expressway

Hayy at
Tayaran

Al Khadra

BAGHDAD

Al Hamra

Al 'Amiriyah

Al Firdaws

Airport Road - Route Irish

Al
Jahid

Hayy al
Atibba

International
Airport

Hayy al
Furat

Zuwaynat

'Abd al
Wahid

THE RASHID
DISTRICT

Palace

Ghubabah

Abu Ghurayb
Presidential
Grounds

Gartan

Ishan Abu
Khalifah

**3-7 Infantry
Area of Operations,**
2005–2006

0   2

Scale of Miles

the perfect environment for insurgents to operate, like proverbial fish in water. Baghdad made Fallujah look like a rural hamlet. By 2005, the capital city, similar to other parts of Iraq, was plagued with daily violence. Some of it was internecine, Sunni versus Shia. Much of the violence was directed against the Americans, the Iraqi Army, and the police. IEDs, car bombs, and suicide bombings were predominant; firefights and pitched battles were comparatively rare.

Amid this chaos, Lieutenant Colonel Dave Funk and his 3-7 Infantry Cottonbalers assumed responsibility for the Rashid district in southwest Baghdad. This AO included the Baghdad International Airport and Route Irish, an extraordinarily dangerous, IED-infested highway that led from the airport into the heart of the city. The 3-7 was configured like the 2-7, with the same combined arms mix of infantry, armor, engineers, and support troops, many of whom functioned as dismounted infantrymen. This battalion of 800 soldiers was charged with the task of controlling a district containing about 800,000 people (and growing by the day), an area of operations that two battalions had previously covered. Rashid featured a mixture of Sunnis and Shiites. Transient groups of poor squatters were growing in size and scale. Most of them were Shiites attracted to the area by the possibility of finding menial jobs in the growing city. Funk divided Rashid into sectors and assigned each of his companies a sector to cover. Quite commonly, platoons were responsible for several blocks, containing tens of thousands of people.

As in Tikrit, the soldiers lived in an FOB and commuted to war. Later, during the surge, the Americans would learn that the only way to defeat the insurgents was to live (and sometimes die) among the people by spreading out into combat outposts throughout Baghdad's many neighborhoods. This wise but painful approach dramatically diminished the influence and potency of insurgent groups. But, at this point in 2005, the United States was still fighting its ineffective FOB-centric war. Most of the 3-7 Cottonbalers lived in FOB Falcon, a sprawling, dusty, walled base with tents, barracks, a motor pool, an excellent dining facility, and the usual amenities. "There is plenty . . . the soldiers can do to relax their minds and bodies," Lieutenant Reeon Brown, an infantry platoon leader, wrote in a letter. "The gym here is as big as a warehouse. It is opened 24 hrs a day as well as numerous Internet cafes, where soldiers can e-mail loved ones. Every soldier stays in a two man room with ac [air-conditioning]." They also had satellite television and sufficient opportunities to watch movies or play video games.

Sallying forth from their remote base, these very few would have to decisively influence the very many, a daunting job indeed. The 3-7's herculean task was merely a symptom of what was going on in Iraq as a whole—the Americans had nowhere near enough ground troops, especially infantrymen, to pacify the country and achieve their ambitious objective of transforming Iraq into a peaceful democracy. This difficult situation was a direct consequence of overreliance on air and sea power, at the expense of ground power, a mistake American policymakers had been making time and again since the start of World War II.

The previous outfit in Rashid was a cavalry battalion with plenty of vehicles but very few infantrymen. As a result they rarely ever got on the ground to speak with people. They would drive from place to place, at high rates of speed to avoid IEDs, always careful to stay away from areas they thought of as too dangerous. "Their method [of] relationships with the community was to wave to 'em from the vehicles," one Cottonbaler infantry platoon leader related. As a cavalry unit miscast into an infantry role, this was all they were equipped to do. Moreover, they had bought into the notion so common among Americans in Iraq that personal safety necessitated the protection of armored vehicles or an FOB. In their view, getting on the ground was way too dangerous.

The Cottonbalers were not comfortable with this. Regardless of the initial dangers they might face, they believed in getting to know the locals and establishing a strong on-the-ground presence in every area. "We thought the decisive terrain was the people," Funk said. The colonel was a six-foot-five giant of a man with a sizable personal presence and a wry sense of humor. He knew that, in southwest Baghdad, personal relationships would help his people accomplish their mission like nothing else could. "We have to develop a level of trust in the people and they in us and we have to develop in them the confidence that we are there to do good for them. So the notion of speeding around at Mach Seven, gun ablazing . . . wasn't getting the results . . . that we all thought we needed."

Thus, the 3-7 soldiers spent many hours on the ground, patrolling the streets. They had a bit more time off than their counterparts in 2-7, but the pace of operations was still similarly hectic. On average, a grunt enjoyed a day and a half off per week. Often, on dismounted patrols, they were protected by up-armored Humvees with .50-caliber machine guns or M240 machine guns mounted in their turrets, or Bradleys or even the occasional tank. Most of the time the patrols had a defined purpose, such as visiting a certain person, checking out a certain neighborhood, or apprehending a wanted insurgent, rather than just riding around waiting to get attacked.

Ever vigilant, the infantry soldiers circulated up and down the crowded commercial streets and among the diverse blend of neighborhoods. Every earth-toned house, large or small, seemed to have a satellite dish perched atop its roof. Many of the men marveled at this weird blend of space-age technology with old-world poverty. "They introduced themselves to local power-brokers and imams [religious leaders], visited schools, police stations, and mosques, and went door to door introducing themselves and passing out contact information," Alpha Company's unit history declared. "There were some very wealthy neighborhoods as well as some brutally poor ones. Where former regime officials lived the infrastructure was relatively good, whereas in other areas sewage clogged the streets and created small lakes." The sewage created the powerful stench of human waste, dust, and rotting garbage that soldiers grew to associate with Iraq. Experiencing the smell was like standing in a landfill, next to a sewage treatment plant, on a hot day. It was nauseating but the soldiers grew used to it. "You noticed where the corruption really was," Specialist Javier Herrera, a machine gunner from Miami, Florida, recalled. "Some neighborhoods looked pristine. Others . . . looked like everybody from this [nice] neighborhood just picked the trash up and put it in their neighborhood." He and the other soldiers were especially amazed at the resourcefulness and abject poverty of the squatters. They would collect aluminum cans, pack them with mud, and build small houses with them. "Then they would tarp . . . a blanket or something . . . and make a roof. It rarely ever rained during the summertime so they were good to go."[8]

After many months without much of an American presence, quite a few of the Iraqis were shocked when the soldiers began to mingle with them. "They looked at us like we'd just come out of a space ship," Lieutenant Kevin Norton, a platoon leader in Bravo Company, quipped. "To actually walk up to a café . . . dismounted, on the street, in a security posture . . . but walking down the street . . . where you can get close to people and wave to 'em, say hi to 'em . . . to them was unbelievably shocking." Some people were so excited to see the Americans that they hugged them and gave them flowers. To them, the Americans represented a new way to solve local problems and enhance security. Others were more reticent or suspicious. Few, if any, were overtly hostile. One street might be full of friendly residents. The next block might be empty or packed with sullen people. "Daily patrols would visit homes and talk to families about . . . what the Iraqi government was doing for them and improvements in the ISF," Alpha Company's history said. "Each patrol leader had his own business card that he would pass out with contact information."

They also gave out their cell phone numbers and flyers that described all the work the Americans were doing to improve living conditions. Through interpreters and an assortment of halting Arabic and English, they conversed with scores of people on nearly every patrol. As time went on, the soldiers' understanding of Arabic increased and, of course, many of the people knew some English. Children tended to have the best linguistic skills. They would often translate in exchange for chocolate. "Everyone out there is a potential informant or a potential insurgent," Captain Ike Sallee, the commander of Alpha Company, asserted. "If you really want to get this place secure, you've got to change perceptions. You've really got to focus on changing people's minds."

The Cottonbalers understood the vital importance of human intelligence. In essence, they were soldiers doing a policeman's job. Only by cultivating local informants, building trust and rapport with the people in their respective neighborhoods, and gathering good information from them could they foil the insurgents. Only ground troops could do this very personal job. The 3-7 Infantry basically had to start from scratch in this regard. "Beyond overall demographics of the area and figures [power brokers] at key locations, we really had nothing," Lieutenant Ben Follansbee, an infantry platoon leader in Alpha Company, explained. Lieutenant Colonel Funk was shocked to learn from his predecessor that almost 90 percent of that unit's intelligence information was coming from higher headquarters rather than from everyday soldiers on the ground. "Well, geez, I think that's backwards," he thought.

He was absolutely right. It is an incontrovertible fact that, in combat, the best intelligence information comes from on-the-ground sources—human contact. The higher up the chain, the more distant intelligence analysts tend to be from their subject, and the more reliant they tend to be on such technological sources as satellite photos or audio intercepts rather than bona fide human contacts. Human informants can sometimes be of questionable reliability but, in a counterinsurgency war, they are vital. After all, in such a war, knowledge is practically everything: Who is an insurgent, what motivates them, when and where will they strike, what is an acceptable counterinsurgency approach within the constraints of the local culture? All of these are central questions. "As the S2 [battalion intelligence officer]," Captain Steve Capehart said, "when we . . . got on the ground and gathered information and built a rapport, it made my job a hell of a lot easier." Truly, counterinsurgency is an intelligence officer's game. Indeed, as the Iraq War unfolded, infantry companies began using their artillery forward observation teams as company intelligence specialists. "Nothing beats having your own informal network down at your level that helps you develop something," Funk said.

Over time, through sheer repetition and endless human contact, the soldiers of 3-7 developed these sorts of relationships with Iraqis, Shiite and Sunni. "You were a detective," one small-unit leader said. "You'd go out there and you were questioning, on the ground. You're an ambassador. You're going out trying to fix what's broken, trying to help the people, win their affection, see if you can get 'em on your side. At the same time, though, you're also a combat patrol leader." This meant that they always were on the lookout for any threat, especially suicide bombers. They also made sure to maintain good discipline—soldiers covering corners, covering each other's movements and the like—to project an aggressive posture. This deterred many of the insurgents, who were more inclined to attack soft targets.

As mutual trust accrued, the locals began passing along good information. Over 90 percent of the battalion's intelligence data eventually came from such sources. As the Americans got better information, it minimized one major by-product of poor intelligence: the disruption, and popular resentment, caused by raids on the wrong houses, or the incarceration of innocent people. "I would say that maybe half of the IEDs we found was because a local . . . would say 'Ali Baba' and actually point out where it was," Lieutenant James Cantrell, a platoon leader in Delta Company, said. One friendly local kid, whom the soldiers called Johnny, regularly pointed out the location of IEDs. "Every [weapons] cache we found was from somebody calling in the information," Lieutenant Follansbee said. Before long, tips began pouring in by phone and personal contact. The majority of the time, the information was correct. One of Follansbee's squad leaders, Staff Sergeant Michael Muci, found that acting with restraint, even on raids, counted for a lot with the Iraqis. "We knocked on the door. We didn't go crashing in. That saved a lot of hassle. You're a foreigner and you come into these people's house because someone said something . . . so our platoon always knocked. The people liked that. We gave 'em courtesy" and respect. They also made sure to give any women in the house plenty of privacy. As a result, the platoon's area was usually very quiet.

Like their regimental brothers in Tikrit, the Cottonbalers of 3-7 also worked closely with the Iraqi Army and the local police. In a way, the Americans felt sorry for them because they were in so much danger from insurgent reprisals. "It took a lot of guts for them to be in the military," Sergeant Jason Wayment said. "They would stay in their compound for three or four days and then go home for two days. If anybody saw 'em leaving the place, going to their house, then they'd get killed." Wayment personally knew of several soldiers whom insurgents killed while they were on leave. Specialist Herrera knew one NCO who was so concerned for his safety and that of his family that he did not go home for six months.

The army compounds and the police stations were sometimes attacked by insurgents. By and large, the ISF men were brave, but not very skilled or savvy. "They're not very disciplined people," Specialist Joshua Macias, a mortar platoon soldier who often worked with the Iraqi soldiers, opined. "You'd try and tell 'em something and they'd go off and do something else." They did not pull guard duty and maintain security the way the Americans knew they must. The grunts had to be careful about correcting them, especially in front of their peers, because this would cause them to lose face. It was also shameful for them to admit that they did not know something. In response to questions, they would often shrug and say "Insha'Allah," a fatalistic phrase that means "God willing." The expression was a source of great frustration for the proactive, blunt-speaking Americans. "If you ask an Iraqi if he's gonna do something, if he says yes, it might get done," Lieutenant Colonel Funk commented drily. "If he says no, obviously, it won't get done. If he says Insha'Allah that means it ain't gonna get done. It's the universal Arabic way to say if God wills it, it will get done but don't count on me, buddy."

Soldiers and Ministry of the Interior (MOI) commandos often participated in American raids and patrols. The police maintained traffic control points (TCPs). By and large, the quality of all these security people got better as the months wore on, but they were still not all that good or as reliable as they needed to be. Most of the Americans did not completely trust them. More important, many of the locals did not like or trust them. Often, the Americans found themselves trying to persuade residents to change their negative perceptions of the ISF and their own government. Still, in a larger sense, they were an asset because, as Lieutenant Colonel Funk pointed out, "[they] don't have to be as good as us. They just have to be better than the insurgents they're fighting." In southwest Baghdad, by the fall of 2005, they were significantly better than most of the guerrillas.[9]

In spite of 3-7's wise approach to counterinsurgency in Rashid, there was no way a battalion of eight hundred soldiers could hope to truly control such a densely populated area. The danger of IEDs and suicide bombers was always profound. For the troops, this urban environment was stressful and unforgiving. The 3-7 Infantry spent many months intensively patrolling Route Irish, a stretch of road that had gotten out of control over the course of the previous year (reporters routinely referred to it as the most dangerous road on Earth). The highway bristled with IEDs of all varieties. The most common were drop-and-go types. Insurgents would cut a hole in a van, slow down a bit, and simply drop the IED on or alongside the road. Others were hidden in trash or buried in curbs or in the grassy median between the eastbound and westbound lanes. The Cottonbalers found and detonated countless IEDs on Route Irish. They also outlived all too many explosions. "We were on Route Irish a lot," Lieutenant Cantrell said. "We realized that you can survive IEDs." The soldiers weathered many near misses. "We saw a flash," one Alpha Company soldier remembered about an IED that exploded near his Humvee one night. "The IED went off . . . about four or five feet in front of our vehicle. Thank God . . . I stopped in the middle of the road and it blew up about four or five feet in front of us."

Eventually, new technology and new tactics took Route Irish away from the insurgents. The Americans began to equip most of their Humvees with the Warlock system, a piece of equipment capable of jamming the signals of cell phones and garage door openers that the terrorists used to detonate IEDs. Even more than Warlock, though, new tactics secured Route Irish. Not only did they saturate the road with patrols night and day, but they began to restrict access to the road. Engineers built concrete barriers and wire screens to prevent pedestrians from walking along the road. Then the Iraqi Army maintained checkpoints at every possible vehicular access route. To top it all off,

SEAL and Cottonbaler sniper teams performed overwatch missions, shooting anyone they could positively establish as planting an IED. Before long, Route Irish got dramatically better, to the point of almost complete safety. "That's why you really don't hear about Route Irish anymore," one soldier said, with disgust dripping from his voice.

Throughout the rest of Rashid, the best way to defeat IEDs was to know the area. Over time, the Cottonbalers got to know their neighborhoods so well that they could spot anything that was amiss. "You have to patrol the same area over and over," Lieutenant Peter Robinson, a platoon leader in Easy Company, said. "My guys could look at the curb and tell you the cinder block's been moved." They came to know instinctively what was normal and what was threatening. "There's absolutely no way to replicate that except by patrolling over and over." The only problem was that, once the Americans came to dominate one part of Rashid, the insurgents would simply relocate to another, creating a whack-a-mole scenario. There simply were not anywhere near enough soldiers in the battalion to control the whole AO.

The battalion's worst incident occurred on April 19 when a suicide bomber attacked a dismounted patrol from Alpha Company's 1st Platoon. The grunts had just dismounted from their vehicles and were on their way to a school in the Jihad neighborhood when a car drove into the middle of their formation and detonated. The hellish blast instantly killed Corporal Jacob Pfister and Specialist Kevin Wessel. Four other soldiers were wounded, two of whom had to be evacuated out of Iraq. Just moments after the blast, the platoon's vehicles turned around and roared back to the terrible scene. "People in the buildings around us were shooting at us," Sergeant James Malugin, a gunner on one of the Humvees, recalled. The gunners returned fire. As they did, medics did everything they could for the wounded and other soldiers policed up the remains of the two dead soldiers.

Several other Cottonbaler patrols, and many Iraqi policemen, scrambled to the scene. The standard procedure in these tragic instances was to seal off the entire site. Eventually, the shooting from the buildings petered out. "Once we got there, quickly everything was cordoned off," Staff Sergeant Gerard Leo, a gunner from Charlie Company, recalled. "We were watching the buildings. We weren't letting anyone walk near. The kids were trying to come out and play and we were chasing 'em back into their homes. The . . . guys were medevacked and gone within minutes." In addition to Pfister and Wessel, two other battalion soldiers lost their lives during the year in Iraq—Corporal Stanley Lapinski of Bravo Company and Corporal Manuel Lopez from Delta Company.

In another harrowing incident, a suicide car bomber attacked a Charlie Company traffic control point. The soldiers had set up barbed wire and orange traffic cones to maintain at least one hundred meters of standoff between themselves and the traffic. The troops were in the process of questioning a man whom they suspected of selling illegal gasoline. All of a sudden a white car veered around the cones. "I'll never forget it until the day I die," Staff Sergeant Michael Baroni said. He was standing several yards away from his Humvee, watching the terrible scene unfold, as if in a dream. "As soon as he swerved around the cones, it was all like slow motion. You could just hear the vehicle just gassing down [accelerating]. He hit the wire. As soon as he hit the wire . . . we pulled our weapons. By that time my gunner and my loader just started opening up on him. I remember just seeing the guy [suicide bomber] go down . . . on the windshield and then the fireball, and feeling the heat. It detonated . . . about fifteen feet or ten feet behind my Humvee . . . so close, the wreckage was . . . underneath my Humvee."

At that moment, Baroni could think of little else except the welfare of his men. He had promised their families that he would bring them home safely. Amid the smoke and flames, not to mention the concussion from the explosion, he had trouble figuring out where they were. One man was lying on the ground, shaken but okay. Another was inside the Humvee, slumped over. For a horrible instant, Staff Sergeant Baroni thought he was dead. The NCO began screaming for him to wake up and get out of the vehicle. "He gets out of the Humvee and he's okay. He said he was waiting for a second one [suicide bomber] so he ducked down. You could see the whole back of his helmet from his neck and his IBA [interceptor body armor] was all burnt up. Debris was all over the Humvee. He got out and grabbed his weapon. You get mad because now they've attacked *you*." Fortunately no Americans were hurt in this near miss.[10]

Suicide bombings spiked in May and June. Most of them were carried out by foreign jihadis or, in a few instances, Iraqis handcuffed to the steering wheel (the terrorists would threaten to kill the person's family if they did not carry out the attack). In one day alone, fourteen of them detonated in the brigade's area of operations (3-7 Infantry was attached to the 4th Brigade

Combat Team of the 3rd Infantry Division). From that point onward, though, they diminished substantially. Nonetheless, in response to the threat of such attacks, the Americans began implementing a greater standoff distance between themselves, local vehicles, and even the people they encountered on dismounted patrols.

For the average grunt, the life-and-death pressure of preventing the bombings was nearly overwhelming. That pressure was especially heavy on Humvee and Bradley gunners and dismounted soldiers. "There's a kind of courage that you don't really think about when you talk about combat operations," Staff Sergeant Keith Orr, a Bravo Company rifle squad leader and veteran of the Gulf War, said. "You've got these gunners up there and they're young and Iraqis are the stupidest drivers. I mean, they'd just do some dumb shit and you've got this kid . . . on the trigger. He's watching this car come up. Is that a VBIED? Is that a bad guy doing something or is that a family of five . . . not paying attention. It takes a lot of discipline and courage to hold your fire for that extra second to verify before you put . . . a half a pound of lead into a car."

At the exact same time, the gunner was responsible not only for the lives of his friends but also the Iraqis around him. On the one hand, the soldiers always knew that if they made the wrong choice, they could be court-martialed. On the other hand, if they held their fire too long, it could cost their lives and the lives of their buddies. Their momentous decisions had to be made in seconds. Every incident, no matter how small, could be a strategic event. Most of the gunners were not even twenty-one yet. "We literally are asking more of our soldiers today than ever in history," Lieutenant Colonel Funk asserted. "I have corporals on the ground literally making strategic decisions. There are young corporals and sergeants on the ground who are learning to interact with people, who are learning to determine very quickly the essence of a military problem and work their way through it. I know when I was a young man coming up, I wasn't nearly as talented as we ask our young platoon leaders and captains to be nowadays."

Truly, the stakes were immense. When they made the wrong choices, it poisoned relations with the locals and, often as not, it turned into a media event. One ugly tragedy could undo months of good relations. For instance, in June, at the height of the suicide bombings, a Cottonbaler opened fire at a car in the Sadiyah neighborhood and killed an innocent fifty-seven-year-old woman who was a local teacher. "To them, killing a human being is nothing," a furious bystander said of the soldiers. "When an American soldier gets killed, they make a big fuss. When an Iraqi gets killed in the street, it means nothing to them." Unfair though this perception certainly was, it resonated with many people in the wake of this incident.

The scathing media coverage that resulted from the tragic shooting only exacerbated bad feelings all the way around. The Cottonbalers respected reporters who would embed themselves with the unit and patrol with them, but they were few and far between. Truthfully, though, most of the soldiers were predisposed to distrust and dislike reporters. Negative coverage only fueled their disdain all the more. They would return to the FOB, watch television, and be amazed at what they believed was completely inaccurate, slanted reporting of the war. By their estimate, only 10 to 20 percent of what they saw was accurate or fair. "The media is a business," Lieutenant Follansbee said. "It's not really so much the pursuit of truth as meeting the bottom line as a lively institution. Blood is sexy. That's what sells so that's what they show. They don't show the MEDCAPs [medical patrols that dispensed free health care throughout Rashid] or the food distros [distributions] or us walking around talking to people, dropping off school supplies . . . because that's not sexy."

But, like it or not, in the modern age, a story would be told in the mass media. "The question is whose story is it gonna be?" Funk rhetorically asked. "You can ignore the media, get pissed off at 'em and say you're not gonna engage these guys anymore or you can try your level best to get the truth out to them." Even though Funk understood the importance of media relations, he too reached a point of exasperation in the wake of the accidental killing of the teacher. He was outraged by one story in particular, written by a reporter who spoke with the Iraqis at the scene of the shooting but had never patrolled with 3-7. "I should have been suspect when she was interviewing me over the phone. Well, when the article came out . . . it really, really, really painted us in a bad light." Lieutenant Colonel Funk challenged the substance and accuracy of the story. He also decided that, from then on, he would only deal with reporters who actually spent time with his soldiers. "I . . . made it clear to her that I would not be talking to her on the phone anymore but . . . if you want to join us on a patrol, I welcome you down anytime. Of course, she never took us up on it." Nor did many others, and that was fairly standard for most reporters in Iraq.

So, for 3-7 Infantry, the media gap was never really bridged. The battalion did not control the modern information war well enough. The soldiers continued to nurture the anger and mistrust they felt toward media members, in effect choosing to isolate themselves. This was a dysfunctional and self-defeating choice. In that sense, they were very typical of most combat units in Iraq at that time. Fair or unfair, the print and electronic media reported the war as they saw fit. That often did not work to the advantage of the American position in Iraq.[11]

What, if anything, did 3-7 accomplish during its year of counterinsurgent warfare in Baghdad? On the face of it, they had many successes. By and large, the soldiers comported themselves with discipline and compassion. The Iraqi Army and police in Rashid clearly got better over the course of 2005. The Cottonbalers of 3-7 participated in several large raids and operations that captured dozens of insurgents. The soldiers forged many positive relationships with sheiks, imams, and everyday people in southwest Baghdad. The Americans improved the schools, dispensed food and medical care, and generally enhanced the lives of some in Rashid. Route Irish improved dramatically on 3-7's watch. The battalion also presided over two peaceful and successful elections in October and December.

On the downside, there were accidental killings, raids that targeted the wrong people, and everyday insults dispensed by culturally ignorant GIs. The isolation of living on an FOB and commuting to war only served to deepen that ignorance. It also undermined the security of those Iraqis who wanted to help the Americans. A significant amount of bad will also came from the heavy-handed presence of military vehicles on the crowded streets of Rashid. Many civilians were terrified of the American convoys. At times, the heavy Bradleys and tanks could damage infrastructure. The American concern with standoff and force protection sometimes led to traffic snarls and overly aggressive driving by Cottonbaler drivers. To some locals, the mere presence of foreigners was offensive, no matter how well or poorly behaved they might have been.

Overall, 3-7 Infantry left Rashid a better place than they found it, but this was not good enough. By the time the Cottonbalers went home in early 2006, the American position in Iraq was deteriorating, mainly because of the poor strategic decisions made by American leaders. The political and military decision makers still did not understand that counterinsurgency war requires a saturation, troop-intensive presence, cultural outreach, and a willingness to sacrifice troop safety for the security of the population. This sort of war, like most, could not be won the easy way by technology and long-range weaponry. Political will, and everyday engagement, human being to human being, counted for much more.

Both 2-7 and 3-7 did the best they could within the confines of the flawed American strategic outlook in 2005–2006. Venturing forth from their FOBs, operating with pathetically small numbers, there was only so much they could do. Both units enjoyed some level of success, but this hardly mattered because their efforts did not lead to victory in the overall war effort. Their experience was actually a cautionary tale. Although nowhere near as bloody, the 7th Infantry's tour of duty was quite similar, in one sense, to the bitter experience of the soldiers at Masher/White Wing and Dak To: even the success of grunts on the ground can mean little in the face of the flawed strategies of generals and politicians.

EPILOGUE
A Plea for Change

I WILL END WITH A plea, extended to whoever has the power, or even casual interest, to heed it. We must learn from the lessons of recent history. For the United States, from World War II onward, technology has been a major asset, but not a magic-bullet solution to all security problems. Warfare remained what it has always been—an elemental, wasteful, tragic contest of wills. Contrary to the predictions of techno-vangelists, ground soldiers have done almost all of the fighting and dying in America's modern wars. Upon their overworked shoulders, the outcome of those wars rested. There were rarely enough of them. Nor was there, in general, enough national emphasis on them as the leading weapon in the American arsenal. Instead, the United States invested the bulk of its power and resources in technological weaponry, too often at the expense of the ground pounders. This must change, or we risk more Pelelius, more Dak Tos, and more Iraqs.

In the early twenty-first century, with wars raging in Afghanistan and Iraq, stretching both the Marine Corps and the Army to the breaking point, politicians of both parties talked of placing a new emphasis on building up the ground combat services. They spoke of expanding the Army to over 700,000 active duty soldiers and the Marine Corps to a strength of over 200,000. This was a step in the right direction, although only barely adequate to meet the considerable global responsibilities of the soldiers and leathernecks. The budget appropriations for the Army and Marines did rise, if only out of the sheer necessity that resulted from the two vexing wars and the obvious fact that these two services were doing almost all of the fighting and dying. Plus, the Air Force and Navy were both working diligently to assist the ground troops in Iraq and Afghanistan.

However, the good intentions for expanding ground combat forces did not survive the recession that began in 2008. With the Obama administration seeking to curtail defense spending, the Army took a 17 percent cut in its projected 2010 budget, while the Navy got a nice increase and the Air Force stayed more or less the same. By this time, after eight years of tough ground warfare, the Army and Marines still accounted for only about 31 percent of the defense budget, the Navy and Air Force over half of the rest. The historical pattern that had held true since World War II had not, then, really changed by the twenty-first century, even in the face of bloody ground wars. "Our prime weapon in our struggles with terrorists, insurgents, and warriors of every patchwork remains the soldier or Marine," Lieutenant Colonel Ralph Peters wrote. "Yet, confronted with reality's bloody evidence, we simply pretend that other, future, hypothetical wars will justify the systems we adore."

In the wake of the cuts, the Army now had to reconsider its plan to create three new combat brigades. I do not pretend to be an expert or an insider on the intricacies of Washington budget policies. But I do think it is fair to say that any cut in the Army's operating expenses is not likely to achieve the goal of adding to the number of ground combat soldiers in America's defense arsenal. S. L. A. Marshall once wrote that "we in the United States . . . have made a habit of believing that national security lies at the end of a production line." This indeed has been the American way of war—the material over the corporeal. Marshall understood that infantrymen cannot be cranked out of a production line or hatched from a lab. Not just anyone can become a combat soldier. They are a unique group, always the minority within their society, even within the armed forces, too. They represent the ultimate weapon of war for the mundane reason that no technology has yet eclipsed the human brain, the human will, and the human spirit in potency.[1]

The explosion of information-age technology since Marshall's time has only exacerbated American material predilections and techno-vangelism all the more. If that does not change, then the Americans risk more unhappy reality checks amid a troubling world that continues to rapidly urbanize, an internationalist media whose Net-centric, anti-U.S. hostility seemingly hardens by the day, and the power of terrorist groups such as al-Qaeda, Hezbollah, and FARC grows. These are the lessons of recent history, from Guam to Baghdad. In the absence of any meaningful change, the grunts, as always, will pay the steepest price, for it is they who most fully experience war's unforgiving cruelty.

To them, war is personal, animal, disturbing, and affecting beyond description. For them, war cannot possibly be seen as clinical, calculating, or material. They view it only through the prism of "the blood-soaked bandages, the smell of gunpowders, the horrendous din of the weaponry, the pain and numbness of a wound and the medic's syrette, all never to be forgotten, but to play forever within the memory of a 'Grunt,'" in the estimation of one Dak To veteran. As one Marine grunt put it, "Until you have physically experienced looking an enemy soldier in the face and pulling the trigger, the sensation in your hand as the k-bar [knife] cuts [through] the windpipe, the actual smell of burning flesh, or the human rage, and competition for life that allows a soldier to kill another soldier, you will never fully be able to feel or describe, or convey the emotions" of modern war.

They know, firsthand, the unhappy reality of war's viciousness—the anger, the desperation of small, frightened groups of men trying to kill one another, the survivor's guilt, the lust for revenge and destruction, the intensity of living with fear, boredom, physical discomfort, and danger for days, weeks, years on end. "Men get blown to bits, or shot, men that you know, men who are your friends," a World War II rifle platoon leader wrote. At the same time, the grunts experience "near shell hits, so close that you hear the fragments screaming, while you wonder . . . why you weren't hit; closing so near to the enemy that you can see his body jar under small, precise blows as somebody empties a BAR magazine into him; disappointment, maybe, at the difference between what Hollywood has taught you a battle should look like and the seemingly disjointed series of action that the thing really is; and somewhere in the middle of it, the desire to lie down in sheer disgust . . . and forget the whole business." Through it all, they come to know firsthand the strange nobility that sometimes grows, like a beautiful flower in the wild, out of the desperate, horrible world of combat. They see that, amid the worst of circumstances, human beings are capable of decency, honor, and amazing selflessness. They understand to their very core that all grunts fight primarily for one another, nothing more, nothing less. This brotherhood marks them forever. For many, it is the most powerful phenomenon they will experience in their lives.[2]

Some say that humanity is divided into three groups—sheep, wolves, and sheepdogs. The majority are sheep. They are peaceful, compliant, with small capacity for violence and not much ability to defend themselves. The minority are wolves or sheepdogs. Wolves will always prowl, plunder, and defile the sheep. They thrive on destruction, domination, and bloodshed. Only the sheepdogs can protect the flock from these preying wolves, men like Hitler, Zarqawi, and their ilk. The sheepdogs' job is to protect the sheep. To do so, they will use violence if necessary. They must maintain constant vigilance. Robots and machines cannot stand in for the sheepdogs. Technology can only assist them. They are a special breed. Theirs is a self-sacrificial struggle to the death to keep the wolves at bay. If necessary, they will lay down their lives so that the sheep might live. Without the sheepdogs, the wolves would rule. The grunts are America's sheepdogs. May they never go away. May there be peace on earth . . . but don't count on it.[3]

ACKNOWLEDGMENTS

This book was a monumental undertaking. It is the product of much travel, research, study, and quite a bit of plain old-fashioned listening. I could not possibly have written it without the considerable assistance of a great many people. For every individual I mention here, there are probably several others I am omitting, so I apologize in advance for those omissions. I also would like to make clear that any mistakes or errors of judgment are mine alone.

At the World War II Museum in New Orleans, Marty Morgan and Tommy Lofton were kind enough to guide me through the museum's extensive collection of firsthand accounts from World War II veterans. The 99th Infantry Division memoirs were especially useful. The staff at the National Archives in College Park, Maryland, was persistently patient and professional during my many visits. Rich Boylan went above and beyond the call of duty to access some excellent Masher/White Wing and Dak To material for me. Mark Reardon at the U.S. Army Center of Military History parceled out much good advice and guidance, for which I am very thankful. At the Cantigny First Division Foundation library in Chicago, Eric Gillespie and Andrew Woods went out of their way to make me feel comfortable. Thanks to Andrew, I was able to find a rich vein of excellent material on the 26th Infantry at Aachen, plus some first-rate photographs. The redoubtable Cynthia Tinker was her usual dedicated, insightful self during my visit to the Center for the Study of War and Society at the University of Tennessee. The same was true of Bill Eigelesbach and the staff at Special Collections down the hall. During my extended visit to the United States Army Military Institute at Carlisle, Pennsylvania, David Keough and the research staff did everything they possibly could to help me. David's knowledge of the modern U.S. Army and the archival collection at Carlisle is a potent combination. He was kind enough to share both realms of expertise with me. At the Library of Congress Veteran's History

Project, Alexa Potter did a fine job of accessing a treasure trove of memoirs, oral histories, and diaries for me. This material was especially useful for the World War II chapters.

I hold a special place in my heart for the staff at the Infantry School library, Fort Benning, Georgia. Ericka Loze and Genoa Stanford do the jobs of a staff three or four times their number, and they do it with courtesy and kindness. They never treated me like the pest I probably was. Genoa invested much of her own time to make sure I accessed the library's wonderful collection of infantry small-unit leader experience monographs. Dave Stiegan, the infantry branch historian, was nice enough to meet with me, explain the breadth of the library's historical collection, and impart his considerable wisdom on infantry history. I would like to extend a special word of thanks to Lieutenant Colonels Todd Wood and Dave Funk, who both welcomed me into the world of the 7th Infantry Regiment and facilitated many interviews. They also provided me unlimited access to their soldiers, something they did not necessarily have to do. I especially appreciate the willingness of the soldiers to share their experiences with such candor, humor, and sagacity. Thank you!

In my opinion, the Marines appreciate and preserve their history better than any other service. At Quantico, Virginia, the United States Marine Corps History and Museums Division, and its first-rate staff, certainly reflect that emphasis on the value of the past. Lieutenant Colonel Kurt Wheeler, an embedded historian, and Captain Cam Wilson of the reference branch provided me with a nice entrée to the division as a whole. Jim Ginther at the division's Gray Research Center patiently helped me mine the center's considerable archive, which is chock-full of the personal papers of famous and not so famous Marines. These sources greatly enriched the Guam, Peleliu, and combined action platoon chapters. Rob Taglianetti of the oral history branch worked closely with me to make sure I made use of every possible firsthand account at his disposal. Through his personal intercession, I was able to access the branch's extensive collection of Fallujah oral histories, a first for a non-Marine historian. Thank you, Rob. I will always be grateful. Annette Amerman is the soul of the division's reference branch. She is as knowledgeable on Corps history as anyone I have ever met. Through her cheerful professionalism, she helped me in more ways than I can count. Most notably, she took the time to go through the branch's relevant files with me, one by one. She also went out of her way to give me a tremendous amount of excellent information on the Marine combined action platoons in Vietnam. That chapter is better because of her efforts, and I cannot think of any greater compliment. Thanks, Annette!

Veterans' associations were especially important in the preparation of this book. I was consistently amazed at how welcoming and accommodating most of them were to me. The associations were my entrée to countless veterans, whose stories were so crucial to my depiction of the world of combat. By dredging up painful memories, these veterans were trusting me, as a historian, to portray their stories accurately, objectively, and honestly. I hope I have kept the faith.

A few, in particular, stand out. At the 3rd Marine Division Association, Don Gee was kind enough to place my ad in *CALTRAPS*, the association newsletter. Much to my surprise, I found a large number of Guam veterans in this fashion. Frank "Blackie" Hall also assisted me greatly in finding fellow veterans of that battle and, in particular, survivors of the Japanese banzai attack on the evening of July 25–26, 1944. Colonel Rudy Eggersdorfer of the 26th Infantry Regiment Association sent me several dozen back copies of their newsletter, and it was a source of excellent information for the Aachen chapter. Dave Garcia of the 5th Cavalry Regiment Association put me in touch with several other Vietnam veterans from the unit. Colonel Jim Brigham did the same for the 7th Cavalry Regiment. Larry Gwin, the author of one of the great Vietnam combat memoirs, sent me a specially signed copy of his excellent book and shared some forthright observations in his personal correspondence with me. Another Vietnam veteran, Paul Clifford, worked hard to keep me up-to-date on anything he thought might be relevant to this book. Bob Babcock, the 4th Infantry Division's historian, shared much of his expertise with me, including a signed copy of his fine book. Roger Hill, another 4th Division veteran, generously forwarded me much valuable information on the unit's role in the Battle of Dak To. Speaking of Dak To, Al Undiemi, Rocky Stone, and Dave Watson all sent me compelling, and useful, recollections. Watson put me in touch with more of his 173rd Airborne brothers than I could ever count, and I appreciate his efforts. My fellow military historian Pat O'Donnell lent me much insight into the Battle of Fallujah by relating his experiences to me. Ed Laughlin, a dear friend and distinguished World War II veteran of the 82nd Airborne, expended much effort to send me large amounts of useful research material on modern combat and military affairs in general.

I appreciate the assistance of my own place of employment, Missouri University of Science and Technology, for financial support that covered many of my considerable research costs. My colleagues in the Department of History and Political Science are a constant source of support and inspiration: Diana Ahmad, Mike Bruening, Petra DeWitt, Shannon Fogg, Pat Huber, Tseggai Isaac, Michael Meagher, and Jeff Schramm. A special word of thanks goes to Russ Buhite for being such a good friend and mentor, and department chair Larry Gragg for being a daily example of hard work, good fellowship, fine scholarship, and outstanding leadership. Robin Collier also deserves appreciation for being a great secretary and a great person. Garrett Martin, my student research assistant (and a newly commissioned Air Force officer), did a tremendous job of tracking down public domain maps and photographs for this book. In particular, his efforts yielded a treasure trove of combined action platoon pictures. Thank you, Garrett!

For the original maps in this book, I was fortunate once again to draw on the considerable talents of my friend Rick Britton, a master cartographer. In my opinion, Rick's maps create a new and powerful dimension for my prose. He is a true artist and his work has strengthened *Grunts*.

I owe Brent Howard, outstanding editor at NAL, special recognition. From the start, he believed in *Grunts* and the story we both knew we had to tell. He was a great sounding board and he dispensed so much good advice from his considerable reservoir of military expertise. Thank you to my literary agent Ted Chichak, a man of total integrity who has never steered me wrong. I am very grateful for his wise counsel and his hard work on my behalf.

I would like to express a special word of thanks to my good friend, comrade, and fellow military historian Kevin Hymel. Kevin shared his home with me during my numerous visits to Washington. He helped with the photo research for the book. He also provided much-needed comic relief and was a constant source of considerable expertise on the modern U.S. Army.

I am blessed with so many other good friends who helped me in some way, shape, or form, whether they realize it or not: Chris Anderson, Sean Roarty, Mike Chopp, Thad O'Donnell, Bob Kaemmerlen, John Villier, Steve Kutheis, Joe Carcagno, Ron Kurtz, Beth Fites, Tim Combs, Steve Vincent, Roland Merson, Tom Fleming, Chuck Hemann, Steve Loher, and Big Davey Cohen.

Family is my greatest blessing. Nelson and Ruth Woody are the best in-laws anyone could ever hope for. They are a constant source of love and affirmation. The same is true for Doug, Tonya, and the boys, David, Angee, and the girls, plus Nancy, and Charlie, too. Thank you! I would like to express my gratitude to my brother Mike and my sister Nancy not just for their willingness to tolerate their baby brother's workaholic tendencies but for their friendship, too. The same goes for John, my brother-in-law, who may have been raised in Cub country but was smart enough to become a Cardinal fan. My nephew Michael and my nieces Kelly and Erin are a source of joy and plenty of good laughs, too. My parents, Mike and Mary Jane, have no peer. They sacrificed so much for me that I cannot repay them in any meaningful way. The word "thanks" is too small but appropriate nonetheless. My wife, Nancy, is the foundation of everything for me. I do not know why I am so lucky as to be her husband. I just know that I appreciate her more each day. As usual, she assisted me in the photo research for *Grunts* and provided enough moral support to fill the Grand Canyon. Writing this book required total dedication. It was an emotional and sometimes gut-wrenching experience. Nancy understood this just as she understands so many other things about me. The only way I can repay her is with my enduring love.

John C. McManus

St. Louis, MO

BIBLIOGRAPHY

In researching this book, I gathered and read many thousands of pages of documents. I conducted hundreds of hours of interviews, along with the requisite transcriptions. I read several hundred books and articles, some of them multiple times. I consulted several dozen Web sites and blogs. While all of this material informed my thinking, the bibliography below only consists of material I directly used in the preparation of this book. If a book was not specifically applicable to one chapter, or if it was useful for more than one chapter, I included it in the General Works section.

ARCHIVES AND MANUSCRIPT COLLECTIONS

Carlisle, PA. United States Army Military History Institute
College Park, MD. National Archives and Records Administration (II)
Columbia, MO. Western Historical Manuscript Collection, University of Missouri
Columbus, GA. Donovan Infantry Library, Fort Benning
Knoxville, TN. University of Tennessee Special Collections Library (repository of the
    Center for the Study of War and Society)
New Orleans, LA. National World War II Museum
Quantico, VA. U.S. Marine Corps History and Museums Division, Reference, Oral
    History, and Gray Research Center branches
Washington, D.C. U.S. Army Center of Military History
Washington, D.C. Library of Congress, Veterans History Project
Wheaton, IL. Cantigny First Division Foundation Library, McCormick Research Center

JOURNALS, MAGAZINES, NEWSPAPERS, PERIODICALS

After the Battle
American Spectator
Armor
Army
Army Times
Associated Press
Atlantic
Atlantic Monthly
Buffalo News
The Bulge Bugle
Checkerboard: Newsletter of the 99th Infantry Division Association
Cottonbaler
Eyewitness to War
Field Artillery Journal
Infantry Journal
Infantry School Quarterly
Knight-Ridder Newspapers
Leatherneck
London Daily Telegraph
Marine Corps Gazette
McLean's
Military Affairs
Military and Aerospace Electronics
Military History Quarterly
Military Review
Newsweek
New York Times
Philadelphia Inquirer
Popular Mechanics
Rolling Stone
San Francisco Chronicle
Saturday Evening Post
Spectator
Time
United States Naval Institute Proceedings
U.S. Navy Medicine

U.S. News & World Report
VFW Magazine
Vietnam
VVA Veteran Magazine
Wall Street Journal
Washington Post
Washington Star
Weekly Standard
World War II
Yank

BOOKS

General Works

Bolger, Daniel. *Death Ground: Today's American Infantry in Battle.* Novato, CA: Presidio Press, 1999.

DeGroot, Gerald. *A Noble Cause? America and the Vietnam War.* Essex, England: Longman, 2000.

Gordon, Michael, and Bernard Trainer. *Cobra II: The Inside Story of the Invasion and Occupation of Iraq.* New York: Vintage, 2007.

Grossman, Dave. *On Killing: The Psychological Cost of Learning to Kill in War and Society.* New York: Back Bay Books, 1995

———, and Loren Christensen. *On Combat: The Psychology and Physiology of Deadly Conflict in War and in Peace.* Portland, OR: PPCT Research Publications, 2007.

Hough, Frank. *The Island War: The United States Marine Corps in the Pacific.* Philadelphia and New York: J. B. Lippincott Company, 1947.

Kagan, Frederick. *Finding the Target: The Transformation of American Military Policy.* New York: Encounter Books, 2006.

Karnow, Stanley. *Vietnam: A History.* New York: Viking, 1983.

Keegan, John. *The Face of Battle: A Study of Agincourt, Waterloo, and the Somme.* London: Penguin Books, 1976.

Kindsvatter, Peter. *American Soldiers: Ground Combat in the World Wars, Korea and Vietnam.* Lawrence, KS: University Press of Kansas, 2003.

Krulak, Victor. *First to Fight: An Inside View of the U.S. Marine Corps.* Annapolis, MD: Naval Institute Press, 1999.

Lewis, Adrian. *The American Culture of War: The History of U.S. Military Force from World War II to Operation Iraqi Freedom.* New York: Routledge, 2007.

Linn, Brian. *Echo of Battle: The Army's Way of War.* Cambridge, MA: Harvard University Press, 2007.

Mahan, Alfred Thayer. *The Influence of Sea Power upon History.* Newport, RI: Naval War College Press, 1991.

Maitland, Terrence, and Peter McInerney. *The Vietnam Experience: A Contagion of War.* Boston: Boston Publishing Company, 1983.

Marshall, S. L. A. *Men Against Fire: The Problem of Command in Future War.* Alexandria, VA: Byrrd Enterprises, 1947.

McManus, John C. *American Courage, American Carnage: The 7th Infantry Chronicles, the 7th Infantry Regiment's Combat Experience, 1812 Through World War II.* New York: Forge, 2009.

———. *The Deadly Brotherhood: The American Combat Soldier in World War II.* Novato, CA: Presidio Press, 1998.

———. *The 7th Infantry Regiment: Combat in an Age of Terror, the Korean War Through the Present.* New York: Forge, 2008.

People's Army of Vietnam. *Victory in Vietnam: The Official History of the People's Army of Vietnam, 1954–1975.* Lawrence, KS: University Press of Kansas, 2002.

Ricks, Thomas. *Fiasco: The American Military Adventure in Iraq.* New York: The Penguin Press, 2006.

West, Bing. *The Strongest Tribe: War, Politics and the Endgame in Iraq.* New York: Random House, 2008.

Westmoreland, William. *A Soldier Reports.* Garden City, NY: Doubleday & Company, Inc., 1976.

Woodward, Bob. *Plan of Attack.* New York: Simon & Schuster, 2004.

Guam

Arthur, Robert, and Kenneth Cohlmia. *The Third Marine Division.* Washington, D.C.: Infantry Journal Press, 1948.

Crowl, Philip. *The United States Army in World War II: The War in the Pacific, Campaign in the Marianas.* Washington, D.C.: Department of the Army, 1960.

Gailey, Harry. *The Liberation of Guam, 21 July–10 August, 1944.* Novato, CA: Presidio Press, 1988.

Josephy, Alvin. *The Long and the Short and the Tall: Marines in Combat on Guam and Iwo Jima.* Short Hills, NJ: Burford Books, 1946.

Lodge, Major O. R. *The Recapture of Guam.* Washington, D.C.: Historical Branch, U.S. Marine Corps, 1954.

O'Brien, Cyril. *Liberation: Marines in the Recapture of Guam.* Washington, D.C.: Marine Corps Historical Center, 1994.

Putney, William. *Always Faithful: A Memoir of the Marine Dogs of WWII*. Washington, D.C.: Brassey's, 2001.

Shaw, Henry, Bernard Nalty, and Edwin Turnbladh. *History of U.S. Marine Corps Operations in World War II: Central Pacific Drive*. Washington, D.C.: Historical Branch, 1966.

Peleliu

Camp, Dick. *Last Man Standing: The 1st Marine Regiment on Peleliu, September 15–21, 1944*. Minneapolis, MN: Zenith Press, 2008.

Davis, Burke. *Marine! The Life of Chesty Puller*. New York: Bantam, 1991.

Davis, Ray. *The Story of Ray Davis, General of Marines*. Fuquay Varina, NC: Research Triangle Publishing, 1995.

Davis, Russell. *Marine at War*. Boston: Little, Brown & Company, 1961.

81st Infantry Division Wildcat Historical Committee. *The 81st Infantry Wildcat Division in World War II*. Washington, D.C.: Infantry Journal Press, 1948.

Gailey, Harry. *Peleliu 1944*. Annapolis, MD: The Nautical and Aviation Publishing Company of America, 1983.

Garand, George, and Truman Strobridge. *History of U.S. Marine Corps Operations in World War II: Western Pacific Operations*. Washington, D.C.: U.S. Marine Corps Historical Division, 1971.

Gayle, Gordon. *Bloody Beaches: The Marines at Peleliu*. Washington, D.C.: Marine Corps Historical Center, 1996.

Hoffman, Jon. *Chesty: The Story of Lieutenant General Lewis B. Puller, USMC*. New York: Random House, 2001.

Hough, Major Frank. *The Assault on Peleliu*. Washington, D.C.: U.S. Marine Corps Historical Branch, 1950.

Hunt, George. *Coral Comes High*. New York: Signet, 1946.

Johnston, James. *The Long Road of War: A Marine's Story of Pacific Combat*. Lincoln, NE: University of Nebraska Press, 1998.

Kennard, Major Richard. *Combat Letters Home*. Bryn Mawr, PA: Dorrance & Company, Inc., 1985.

Leckie, Robert. *Helmet for My Pillow*. New York: Bantam Books, 1957.

McMillan, George. *The Old Breed: A History of the First Marine Division in World War II*. Washington, D.C.: Infantry Journal Press, 1949.

Ross, Bill. *A Special Piece of Hell: The Untold Story of Peleliu—The Pacific War's Forgotten Battle*. New York: St. Martin's, 1991.

Sledge, E. B. *With the Old Breed at Peleliu and Okinawa*. New York: Oxford University Press, 1990.

Sloan, Bill. *Brotherhood of Heroes: The Marines at Peleliu, 1944—The Bloodiest Battle of the Pacific War*. New York: Simon & Schuster, 2005.

Smith, Robert Ross. *The U.S. Army in World War II: The Approach to the Philippines*. Washington, D.C.: Department of the Army, 1953.

Aachen

MacDonald, Charles. *The U.S. Army in World War II: The Siegfried Line Campaign*. Washington, D.C.: Department of the Army, 1963.

Whiting, Charles. *Bloody Aachen*. New York: Playboy Press, 1976.

Battle of the Bulge

Cavanagh, William C. C. *The Battle East of Elsenborn & the Twin Villages*. South Yorkshire, England: Pen & Sword Books, Limited, 2004.

Cole, Hugh. *The United States Army in World War II: The Ardennes*. Washington, D.C.: Department of the Army, 1965.

Keefer, Louis. *Scholars in Foxholes: The Story of the Army Specialized Training Program in World War II*. Jefferson, NC: McFarland & Co., Inc., Publishers, 1988.

Lauer, Walter. *Battle Babies: The Story of the 99th Infantry Division in World War II*. Nashville, TN: The Battery Press, 1950.

MacDonald, Charles. *Company Commander*. New York: Bantam, 1947.

———. *A Time for Trumpets: The Untold Story of the Battle of the Bulge*. New York: Bantam Books, 1984.

Murphy, Edward. *Heroes of World War II*. New York: Ballantine Books, 1990.

Roland, Charles. *My Odyssey Through History: Memoirs of War and Academe*. Baton Rouge, LA: Louisiana State University Press, 2004.

Vannoy, Allyn, and Jay Karamales. *Against the Panzers: United States Infantry Versus German Tanks, 1944–1945*. Jefferson, NC: McFarland & Company Publishers, 1996.

Masher/White Wing

Carland, John. "How We Got There: Air Assault and the Emergence of the 1st Cavalry Division (Airmobile), 1950–1965." Arlington, VA: Association of the United States Army, 2003.

———. *The United States Army in Vietnam: Stemming the Tide, May 1965 to October 1966*. Washington, D.C.: Center of Military History, 2000.

Gwin, Larry. *Baptism: A Vietnam Memoir*. New York: Ivy Books, 1999.

Hymoff, Edward. *The First Air Cavalry Division in Vietnam*. New York: MW Lads Publishing Co., 1967.

Kinney, Charles. *Borrowed Time: A Medic's View of the Vietnam War*. Victoria, Canada: Trafford, 2003.

Laurence, John. *The Cat from Hue: A Vietnam War Story.* New York: Public Affairs, 2002.

Mason, Robert. *Chickenhawk: A Shattering Personal Account of the Helicopter War in Vietnam.* New York: Penguin Books, 1984.

Mertel, Kenneth. *Year of the Horse—Vietnam, 1st Air Cavalry in the Highlands.* New York: Bantam Books, 1990.

Moore, Harold, and Joe Galloway. *We Are Soldiers Still: A Journey to the Battlefields of Vietnam.* New York: HarperCollins Publishers, 2008.

———. *We Were Soldiers Once . . . and Young.* New York: HarperCollins, 1992.

Tolson, Lieutenant General John. *Vietnam Studies: Airmobility, 1961–1971.* Washington, D.C.: Department of the Army, 1989.

Combined Action Platoons

Akins, John. *Nam Au Go Go: Falling for the Vietnamese Goddess of War.* Port Jefferson, NY: The Vineyard Press, 2005.

Corson, William. *The Betrayal.* New York: W. W. Norton, 1968.

Cosmas, Graham, and Lieutenant Colonel Terrence Murray. *U.S. Marines in Vietnam: Vietnamization and Redeployment, 1970–1971.* Washington, D.C.: U.S. Marine Corps History and Museums Division, 1986.

Estes, Jackson. *A Field of Innocence.* Portland, OR: Breitenbush Books, 1987.

Flynn, Thomas. *A Voice of Hope.* Baltimore, MD: American Literary Press, Inc., 1994.

Goodson, Barry. *CAP Mot: The Story of a Marine Special Forces Unit in Vietnam, 1968–1969.* Denton, TX: University of North Texas Press, 1997.

Hemingway, Al. *Our War Was Different: Marine Combined Action Platoons in Vietnam.* Annapolis, MD: Naval Institute Press, 1994.

Peterson, Michael. *The Combined Action Platoons: The U.S. Marines' Other War in Vietnam.* New York: Praeger, 1989.

Shulimson, Jack, and Major Charles Johnson. *U.S. Marines in Vietnam: The Defining Year, 1968.* Washington, D.C.: U.S. Marine Corps History and Museums Division, 1997.

———, Lieutenant Colonel Leonard Blaison, Charles Smith, and Captain David Dawson. *U.S. Marines in Vietnam: The Landing and the Buildup, 1965.* Washington, D.C.: U.S. Marine Corps History and Museums Division, 1978.

Smith, Charles. *U.S. Marines in Vietnam: High Mobility and Standdown, 1969.* Washington, D.C.: U.S. Marine Corps History and Museums Division, 1988.

Telfer, Major Gary, Lieutenant Colonel Lane Rogers, and V. Keith Fleming. *U.S. Marines in Vietnam: Fighting the North Vietnamese, 1967.* Washington, D.C.: U.S. Marine Corps History and Museums Division, 1984.

Trullinger, James. *Village at War: An Account of Revolution in Vietnam*. New York: Longman, 1980.

Walt, Lewis. *Strange War, Strange Strategy: A General's Report on Vietnam*. New York: Funk & Wagnalls, 1970.

West, Bing. *The Village*. New York: Pocket Books, 2000.

Dak To

Arthurs, Ted. *Land with No Sun: A Year in Vietnam with the 173rd Airborne*. Mechanicsburg, PA: Stackpole Books, 2006.

Atkinson, Rick. *The Long Gray Line: The American Journey of West Point's Class of 1966*. New York: Owl Books, 1989.

Babcock, Robert, ed. *War Stories: Utah Beach to Pleiku*. Marietta, GA: Deeds Publishing, 2001.

Garland, Lieutenant Colonel Albert. *A Distant Challenge: The U.S. Infantryman in Vietnam*. New York: Jove Books, 1983.

Murphy, Edward. *Dak To: America's Sky Soldiers in South Vietnam's Central Highlands*. New York: Ballantine Books, 2007.

Pierce, Ivan. *An Infantry Lieutenant's Vietnam*. El Dorado Springs, MO: Capsarge Publishing, 2004.

Stanton, Shelby. *The Rise and Fall of an American Army: U.S. Ground Forces in Vietnam, 1965–1973*. New York: Ballantine Books, 2003.

Gulf War

Atkinson, Rick. *Crusade: The Untold Story of the Persian Gulf War*. Boston: Houghton Mifflin, 1993.

Bin, Alberto, Richard Hill, and Archer Jones. *Desert Storm: A Forgotten War*. Westport, CT: Praeger, 1998.

Bourque, Stephen. *Jayhawk! The VII Corps in the Persian Gulf War*. Washington, D.C.: Department of the Army, 2002.

Flanagan, Lieutenant General Edward. *Lightning: The 101st in the Gulf War*. Washington, D.C.: Brassey's, 1994.

Hallion, Richard. *Storm over Iraq: Air Power and the Gulf War*. Washington, D.C.: Smithsonian Institution Press, 1992.

Hartzog, William. *American Military Heritage*. Washington, D.C.: Center of Military History, 2001.

Houlahan, Thomas. *Gulf War: The Complete History*. New London, NH: Schrenker Military Publishing, 1999.

Lehrack, Otto, ed. *America's Battalion: Marines in the First Gulf War*. Tuscaloosa, AL: The University of Alabama Press, 2005.

Macgregor, Douglas. *Warrior's Rage: The Great Tank Battle of 73 Easting*. Annapolis, MD: Naval Institute Press, 2009.

Millett, Allan. *Semper Fidelis: The History of the United States Marine Corps*. New York: The Free Press, 1991.

Santoli, Al, ed. *Leading the Way: How Vietnam Veterans Rebuilt the U.S. Military, an Oral History*. New York: Ballantine Books, 1993.

Scales, Robert. *Certain Victory: The U.S. Army in the Gulf War*. Washington, D.C.: Office of the Chief of Staff, United States Army, 1993.

Shubert, Frank, and Theresa Kraus, general eds. *The Whirlwind War: The United States Army in Operations Desert Shield and Desert Storm*. Washington, D.C.: Center of Military History, 2001.

Swain, Richard. *"Lucky War": Third Army in Desert Storm*. Fort Leavenworth, KS: U.S. Army Command and General Staff College Press, 1997.

Taylor, Thomas. *Lightning in the Storm: The 101st Air Assault Division in the Gulf War*. New York: Hippocrene Books, 1994.

Vernon, Alex. *Most Succinctly Bred*. Kent, OH: Kent State University Press, 2006.

Fallujah

Afon, Milo. *Hogs in the Shadows: Combat Stories from Marine Snipers in Iraq*. New York: Berkley Caliber, 2007.

Bellavia, David, and John Bruning. *House to House: An Epic Memoir of War*. New York: Free Press, 2007.

Camp, Dick. *Operation Phantom Fury: The Assault and Capture of Fallujah, Iraq*. Minneapolis, MN: Zenith Press, 2009.

Danelo, David. *Blood Stripes: The Grunt's View of the War in Iraq*. Mechanicsburg, PA: Stackpole Books, 2006.

Gott, Kendall, ed. *Eyewitness to War, Volume I: The U.S. Army in Operation Al Fajr, an Oral History*. Fort Leavenworth, KS: Combat Studies Institute Press, 2007.

———. *Eyewitness to War, Volume II: The U.S. Army in Operation Al Fajr, an Oral History*. Fort Leavenworth, KS: Combat Studies Institute Press, 2007.

Jadick, Richard. *On Call in Hell: A Doctor's Iraq War Story*. New York: NAL Caliber, 2007.

Kaplan, Robert. *Imperial Grunts*. New York: Vintage, 2005.

Kasal, Brad, and Nathaniel Helms. *My Men Are My Heroes: The Brad Kasal Story*. Des Moines, IA: Meredith Books, 2007.

Livingston, Gary. *Fallujah with Honor: First Battalion, Eighth Marines in Operation Phantom Fury*. North Topsail Beach, NC: Caisson Press, 2006.

Matthews, Matt. *Operation Al Fajr: A Study in Army and Marine Corps Joint Operations*. Fort Leavenworth, KS: Combat Studies Institute Press, 2006.

O'Donnell, Patrick. *We Were One: Shoulder to Shoulder with the Marines Who Took Fallujah*. New York: DaCapo, 2006.

Pantano, Ilario, and Malcolm McConnell. *Warlord: No Better Friend, No Worse Enemy*. New York: Threshold Editions, 2006.

West, Bing. *No True Glory: A Frontline Account of the Battle for Fallujah*. New York: Bantam Books, 2005.

Wright, David, and Timothy Reese. *On Point II: Transition to the New Campaign, the United States Army in Operation Iraqi Freedom, May 2003–January 2005*. Fort Leavenworth, KS: Combat Studies Institute Press, 2008.

7th Infantry Counterinsurgency War

Mansoor, Peter. *Baghdad at Sunrise: A Brigade Commander's War in Iraq*. New Haven & London: Yale University Press, 2008.

ENDNOTES

Introduction

1. Captain William Whyte, "Will the Queen Die?" *Marine Corps Gazette*, January 1946, p. 10. In an article arguing for the infantry's continued importance, Whyte quoted another commentator who claimed that the infantry would soon be "extinct as the dodo bird"; Captain William C. Boehm, letter to the editor, *Infantry Journal*, September 1947.

2. S. L. A. Marshall, *Men Against Fire: The Problem of Command in Future War* (Alexandria, VA: Byrrd Enterprises, Inc., 1947), p. 15; Ralph Peters, "The Counterrevolution in Military Affairs," *Weekly Standard*, February 6, 2006, p. 18.

3. For more on the American notion of war as a logistical or engineering problem, see Brian Linn, *The Echo of Battle: The Army's Way of War* (Cambridge, MA: Harvard University Press, 2007). Linn trenchantly identifies three major intellectual groups that have dominated the Army's thinking since the earliest days of American history. The Guardians see war as primarily a science that is subject to natural laws and principles. In the nineteenth century, they favored coastal defense fortifications; in the twentieth, they argued for missile defense. The Managers think of warfare as a question of national mobilization, resource management, and the employment of overwhelming force. The Heroes argue that the human factor is paramount in war. They believe that battles, and wars, are decided by the fighting spirit of soldiers along with the inspirational leadership that motivates them to fight.

4. Department of Defense Web site, Fiscal Year 2007 Budget by Service; Bing West, *The Strongest Tribe: War, Politics and the Endgame in Iraq* (New York: Random

House, 2008), pp. 155, 346; August Cole and Yochi Dreazen, "Boots on the Ground or Weapons in the Sky?" *Wall Street Journal*, October 30, 2008, p. A14. The reference to inadequate equipment and weaponry for ground combat soldiers comes from my own Group Combat After Action Interview with Task Force 2-7 Infantry, enlisted soldiers, May 23, 2006. This problem is also general knowledge.

5.   I am by no means the first author to make this case about the importance of ground forces. Marshall and Peters have, of course, emphasized these same points, albeit many decades apart. More recently, Daniel Bolger, *Death Ground: Today's American Infantry in Battle* (Novato, CA: Presidio Press, 1999), Frederick Kagan, *Finding the Target: The Transformation of American Military Policy* (New York: Encounter Books, 2006), and Adrian Lewis, *The American Culture of War: The History of U.S. Military Force from World War II to Operation Iraqi Freedom* (New York: Routledge, 2007), all articulated similar arguments.

6.   Lieutenant Colonel Bruce Palmer, "Infantry and VT Fires," *Infantry School Quarterly*, October 1950, p. 8.

7.   The numbers on urban population come from a United Nations habitat study at www.unhabitat.org. According to the study, over half the world's population lived in urban areas by 2007. For more on the planning of the Iraq War, see Michael Gordon and Bernard Trainor, *Cobra II: The Inside Story of the Invasion and Occupation of Iraq* (New York: Vintage, 2007), Bob Woodward, *Plan of Attack* (New York: Simon & Schuster, 2004), and Tom Ricks, *Fiasco: The American Military Adventure in Iraq* (New York: The Penguin Press, 2006).

8.   For an excellent, groundbreaking study on killing in combat and its psychological effects, see Lieutenant Colonel Dave Grossman, *On Killing: The Psychological Cost of Learning to Kill in War and Society* (New York: Back Bay Books, 1995). Grossman made the salient point that, as a society, we know much about the phenomenon of warfare but very little about actual killing in combat. He equates this to knowing much about relationships but nothing of sex.

9.   Alfred Thayer Mahan, *The Influence of Sea Power upon History* (Newport, RI: Naval War College Press, 1991); the World War II statistics come from John C. McManus, *The Deadly Brotherhood: The American Combat Soldier in World War II* (New York: Ballantine Books, 2003), p. 154. The other statistics, compiled as of May 14, 2008, are at www.fas.org under "American War and Military Operations Casualties: Lists and Statistics."

10. John Keegan, *The Face of Battle: A Study of Agincourt, Waterloo, and the Somme* (London: Penguin Books, 1976).

11. *The Checkerboard: Newsletter of the 99th Infantry Division Association*, February 1993, p. 11.

Chapter 1

1. Task Force 53, After Action Report (AAR), Record Group (RG) 127, U.S. Marine Corps Records, Guam, Box 49, Folder 3; Lieutenant Colonel W. F. Coleman to Major O. R. Lodge, September 23, 1952, U.S. Marine Corps History and Museums Division, Publication Background Files, "The Recapture of Guam," RG 127, Box 12, Folder 5; Colonel Edward Craig to Commandant, November 19, 1952, RG 127, Box 12, Folder 5, all at National Archives, College Park, MD; Major O. R. Lodge, *The Recapture of Guam* (Washington, D.C.: Historical Branch, U.S. Marine Corps, 1954), pp. 34–35; Harry Gailey, *The Liberation of Guam, 21 July–10 August, 1944* (Novato, CA: Presidio Press, 1988), pp. 87–88.

2. 3rd Marine Division, Invasion plan and landing diagrams, RG 127, U.S. Marine Corps Records, Guam, Box 65, Folder 7, National Archives; Lieutenant Colonel C. H. Kuhn, "The Guam Operation, 21 July–10 August 1944: The Importance of Planning," U.S. Marine Corps Amphibious Warfare School Paper, 1947–1948, found at the Gray Research Center (GRC), U.S. Marine Corps History and Museums Division (USMCHMD), Quantico, VA; Cyril O'Brien, *Liberation: Marines in the Recapture of Guam* (Washington, D.C.: Marine Corps Historical Center, 1994), pp. 5–8; Robert Arthur and Kenneth Cohlmia, *The Third Marine Division* (Washington, D.C.: Infantry Journal Press, 1948), pp. 142–46; and Lodge, *Recapture of Guam*, pp. 16–20.

3. 3rd Marine Division, Special Report, Medics, Guam Operation, Enclosure I, RG 127, U.S. Marine Corps Records, Guam, Box 50, Folder 10; "Report on Guam Operations," Box 50, Folder 8, both at National Archives; Staff Sergeant John O'Neill, personal diary, John O'Neill Papers, Box 1, Folder 2, GRC, USMCHMD; William Morgan, oral history, William Morgan Collection, #30140, Veterans History Project (VHP), American Folklife Center (AFC), Library of Congress, Washington, D.C.; the spud locker quote is in Louis Metzger, "Guam 1944," *Marine Corps Gazette*, July 1994, p. 93.

4. Jack Kerins, "The Last Banzai" (self-published, 1992), pp. 76–77. For the bombardment ship order of battle and their placement off the beaches, see appendix chart in Lodge, *Recapture of Guam*.

5. 3rd Marine Division, "Report on Guam Operations"; Eugene Peterson, unpublished memoir, pp. 76–77, Eugene Peterson Collection, #477, VHP, AFC, Library of Congress; Philip Johnson, unpublished memoir, p. 1, copy in author's possession, courtesy of Mr. Johnson. Peterson and his colonel shared the meat loaf that night. Both men agreed that it was the best meal they ate on Guam.

6. 3rd Marine Division, D3 (Operations) Comments on Naval Gunfire Support, Annex C, RG 127, U.S. Marine Corps Records, Guam, Box 50, Folder 9; Task Force

53, AAR, both at National Archives; Philip Crowl, *The United States Army in World War II: The War in the Pacific, Campaign in the Marianas* (Washington, D.C.: Department of the Army, 1960), pp. 324–25; William Putney, *Always Faithful: A Memoir of the Marine Dogs of WWII* (Washington, D.C.: Brassey's, 2001), pp. 140–41; Lodge, *Recapture of Guam*, pp. 37, 106.

7.   3rd Marine Division, D3 Comments on Air Support, Annex D, RG 127, U.S. Marine Corps Records, Guam, Box 50, Folder 9; Lieutenant Colonel J. R. Spooner, close air support officer, to Major O. R. Lodge, August 12, 1952, U.S. Marine Corps History and Museums Division, Publication Background Files, "The Recapture of Guam," RG 127, Box 12, Folder 8, both at National Archives; Maury T. Williams, unpublished memoir, no pagination, John G. Balas Papers, Box 1, Folder 6, United States Army Military History Institute, Carlisle, PA (hereafter referred to as USAMHI); William Welch, unpublished memoir, in author's possession, courtesy of Mr. Welch; Crowl, *Campaign in the Marianas*, p. 324.

8.   Major L. A. Gilson to Major O. R. Lodge, February 11, 1952, U.S. Marine Corps History and Museums Division, Publication Background Files, "The Recapture of Guam," RG 127, Box 12, Folder 8; Admiral Richard Conolly to Commandant, November 12, 1952, also in Publication Background Files, RG 127, Box 12, Folder 5; Lieutenant Colonel Hideyuki Takeda to Marine Corps Historical Center, February 20, 1952, U.S. Marine Corps Records, Guam, RG 127, Box 68, Folder 17, all at National Archives; I. E. McMillan, "Naval Gunfire at Guam," *Marine Corps Gazette*, September 1948, p. 56; Crowl, *Campaign in the Marianas*, pp. 325–26; Lodge, *Recapture of Guam*, pp. 106–07.

9.   3rd Marine Division, AAR, RG 127, U.S. Marine Corps Records, Guam, Box 50, Folder 9; "Report on Guam Operations," both at National Archives; *War Dogs of the Pacific*, documentary by Harris Done, copy in author's possession, courtesy of Mr. Done; Williams, unpublished memoir, USAMHI; Kerins, "Last Banzai," p. 79; Bill Conley, interview with the author, March 21, 2008; Henry Shaw, Bernard Nalty, and Edwin Turnbladh, *History of U.S. Marine Corps Operations in World War II: Central Pacific Drive* (Washington, D.C.: Historical Branch, 1966), pp. 457–58; for more on the physiological effects of fear in combat, see Lieutenant Colonel Dave Grossman with Loren W. Christensen, *On Combat: The Psychology and Physiology of Deadly Conflict in War and in Peace* (Portland, OR: PPCT Research Publications, 2007), pp. 16–49.

10.   1st Provisional Marine Brigade, War Diary, RG 127, Marine Corps Records, Guam, Box 57, Folder 11; Unit Report, July 21, 1944, Box 57, Folder 13; 22nd Marine Regiment, Journal, July 21, 1944, Box 61, Folder 1; Tank Company, Special Action Report (SAR), Box 61, Folder 9; Lieutenant Colonel Robert Shaw to Commandant, September 29, 1952, RG 127, U.S. Marine Corps History and Museums Division,

Publication Background Files, "The Recapture of Guam," Box 12, Folder, all at National Archives; O'Neill, diary, GRC; Shaw et al., *Central Pacific Drive*, p. 461; O'Brien, *Liberation*, pp. 11–17; Lodge, *Recapture of Guam*, pp. 47–53.

11. 9th Marine Regiment, SAR, RG 127, Marine Corps Records, Guam, Box 50, Folder 10; R3 Journal, July 21, 1944, Box 59, Folder 3, both at National Archives; Welch memoir.

12. 21st Marine Regiment, SAR, RG 127, Marine Corps Records, Guam, Box 50, Folder 10; Operation Report, Box 51, Folder 2; Anthony Frances, "The Battle of Banzai Ridge," unpublished manuscript, pp. 4–7, USMCHMD, Reference Branch Files; Frank Hall, interview with the author, March 24, 2008; Frank Goodwin, interview with the author, March 25, 2008; Conley interview; Paul Jones, unpublished memoir, p. 19, Paul Jones Collection, #41436, VHP, AFC, Library of Congress; Lodge, *Recapture of Guam*, pp. 40–42. Jones's memoir provided firsthand context and description that added to my account of the 21st Marines' ascent up the cliff.

13. 3rd Marine Regiment, SAR, RG 127, U.S. Marine Corps Records, Guam, Box 50, Folder 10; Operation Report, Box 51, Folder 2; Unit Journal, July 21, 1944, Box 58, Folder 5; 1st Battalion, 3rd Marine Regiment, Journal, July 21, 1944, Box 58, Folder 8; Lieutenant Colonel Royal Bastion to USMCHMD, August 23, 1952, RG 127, U.S. Marine Corps History and Museums Division, Publication Background Files, "The Recapture of Guam," Box 12, Folder 5, all at National Archives; Pete Gilhooly, interview with the author, March 17, 2008; Mack Drake, unpublished journal, p. 7, copy in author's possession, courtesy of Drake family; Alvin Josephy, *The Long and the Short and the Tall: Marines in Combat on Guam and Iwo Jima* (Short Hills, NJ: Burford Books, 1946), pp. 43–45; Gailey, *Liberation of Guam*, pp. 95–97; Lodge, *Recapture of Guam*, pp. 42–47.

14. Takeda letter, National Archives; Major General Haruo Umezawa and Colonel Louis Metzger, "The Defense of Guam," *Marine Corps Gazette*, August 1964, p. 38; Lieutenant Colonel Hideyuki Takeda, "The Outline of Japanese Defense Plan and Battle of Guam Island," in Lester Dessez Papers, Box 1, Folder 11, GRC. In the quoted passage, Takeda was referring specifically to the 38th Infantry Regiment, but the sentiment applied equally to the entire Japanese garrison.

15. 1st Provisional Marine Brigade, War Diary, Journal, July 22, 1944; 22nd Marine Regiment, Journal, July 22, 1944; Tank Company, SAR; Captain Ben Read to Major O. R. Lodge, January 3, 1952, RG 127, U.S. Marine Corps History and Museums Division, Publication Background Files, "The Recapture of Guam," Box 12, Folder 8, all at National Archives; Takeda, "Outline of Japanese Defense Plan," pp. 3, 5; O'Neill, diary, both at GRC; First Lieutenant Millard Kaufman, "Attack on Guam," *Marine Corps Gazette*, April 1945; Sergeant Boondocks, "Facts from a Foxhole," *Infantry Journal*, September 1945, p. 20; Corporal Fred Travis, "75s on Guam," *Field*

Artillery Journal, April 1945, pp. 233–34; Umezawa and Metzger, "The Defense of Guam," pp. 40–41; Welch memoir; Shaw et al., *Central Pacific Drive*, pp. 471–76; O'Brien, *Liberation*, pp. 17–18; Gailey, *Liberation of Guam*, pp. 104–06; Lodge, *Recapture of Guam*, pp. 54–56.

16. Takeda letter, National Archives; Umezawa and Metzger, "Defense of Guam," pp. 41–42; Lodge, *Recapture of Guam*, pp. 79–80; Lieutenant P. W. "Bill" Lanier in a letter printed in the *Washington Star*, November 26, 1944, claimed to have found hypodermic needles and narcotics on the bodies of several dead Japanese.

17. Provisional War Dog Company, SAR, RG 127, U.S. Marine Corps Records, Guam, Box 50, Folder 11; 21st Marine Regiment, SAR, both at National Archives; *War Dogs of the Pacific*; Ed Adamski, interview with the author, March 7, 2008; Roger Belanger, interview with the author, March 4, 2008; Frank Goodwin, unpublished memoir, p. 1, in author's possession, courtesy of Mr. Goodwin; Goodwin interview; Putney, *Always Faithful*, pp. 168–69.

18. 21st Marine Regiment, SAR, National Archives; Bill Karpowicz, e-mail to author, June 10, 2008; Lanier letter; Kaufman, "Attack on Guam," p. 61; Bob Glenn, interview with the author, March 31, 2008; Lodge, *Recapture of Guam*, pp. 78–79; Grossman, *On Killing*, pp. 5–9.

19. 3rd Marine Division, Report on Guam Operations and AAR, Provisional War Dog Company, AAR, all at National Archives; *War Dogs of the Pacific*; Adamski, Goodwin interviews; Putney, *Always Faithful*, pp. 170–71.

20. 3rd Marine Division, D3 (Operations) Journal, July 26, 1944, RG 127, U.S. Marine Corps Records, Guam, Box 54, Folder 3; 21st Marine Regiment, SAR, both at National Archives; Drake, unpublished journal, p. 7; Belanger interview.

21. 12th Marine Regiment, SAR, RG 127, U.S. Marine Corps Records, Guam, Box 59, Folder 8; 21st Marine Regiment, SAR; Lieutenant Colonel R. R. Van Stockum to Lieutenant Colonel Harry Edwards, October 15, 1952, RG 127, U.S. Marine Corps History and Museums Division, Publication Background Files, "The Recapture of Guam," Box 12, Folder 7, all at National Archives; Frances, "Battle of Banzai Ridge," pp. 27–29, USMCHMD; Staff Sergeant James Hague, combat correspondent, untitled article on Banzai Ridge; Jim Headley, interview with the author, March 3, 2008; Walt Fischer, unpublished memoir, p. 3, copy in author's possession, courtesy of Mr. Fischer; Walt Fischer, interview with the author, March 18, 2008.

22. 3rd Marine Division, D3 Journal, July 26, 1944; 21st Marine Regiment, SAR, both at National Archives; Conley interview; Karpowicz e-mail; Lanier letter; Lodge, *Recapture of Guam*, pp. 80–81.

23. 1st Provisional Marine Brigade, War Diary, National Archives; O'Neill, diary, GRC; Lieutenant General Alpha Bowser, oral history, USMCHMD; Kaufman, "Attack on Guam," p. 61; Lodge, *Recapture of Guam*, pp. 78–79, 81; Kerins, "Last Banzai," pp. 120–24.

24. 3rd Marine Division, Report on Guam Operations, D3 Journal, July 26, 1944; 21st Marine Regiment, SAR, all at National Archives; Lodge, *Recapture of Guam*, pp. 81, 85.

25. 3rd Marine Division, Report on Guam Operations, AAR; 2nd Battalion, 12th Marine Regiment, "Account of Action Opposing Nip Breakthrough," RG 127, U.S. Marine Corps Records, Guam, Box 60, Folder 5, all at National Archives; Frank Hough, *The Island War: The United States Marine Corps in the Pacific* (Philadelphia and New York: J. B. Lippincott Company, 1947), p. 274.

26. Frances, "Battle of Banzai Ridge," p. 30, USMCHMD (in June 1945, Frances published part of this paper in the *Marine Corps Gazette*); Lanier letter; O'Neill, diary, GRC; Lodge, *Recapture of Guam*, p. 87.

27. 3rd Marine Division, AAR; D3 Periodic Report, July 26, 1944, RG 127, U.S. Marine Corps Records, Guam, Box 54, Folder 3; 21st Marine Regiment, SAR, all at National Archives; Goodwin memoir, interview; Kerins, "Last Banzai," p. 129.

28. Frances, "Battle of Banzai Ridge," p. 30, USMCHMD; Jim Headley to author, March 12, 2008.

29. The handbill is reprinted in Sgt. H. N. Oliphant, "Combat in the Marianas," *Yank*, October 13, 1944; S. L. A. Marshall, *Men Against Fire: The Problem of Battle Command in Future War* (Alexandria, VA: Byrrd Enterprises, Inc., 1947), pp. 50–84; Grossman, in *On Killing*, also discusses the reluctance to kill and the psychological cost of doing so. Although Grossman's book is a brilliant, landmark piece of work, he places way too much emphasis on Marshall's debunked ratio-of-fire claims. In an earlier book, *The Deadly Brotherhood: The American Combat Soldier in World War II* (New York: Ballantine Books, 2003), pp. 116–21, I discussed the problems with Marshall's claims and the work of several other historians who have cast doubt on his contentions. Since publishing that book, I have further examined Marshall's surviving records, and I have interviewed one of the key historians who worked with him during the war, but found no concrete evidence to support his theories. In researching this Guam chapter, I estimate that I have reviewed about five thousand pages of documents and firsthand accounts. Yet I found *not one* recorded instance of an American refusing to fire his weapon or preferring his own death to killing an enemy soldier.

30. 3rd Marine Division, Report on Guam Operations, AAR; Takeda letter, all at National Archives; Lanier letter; Josephy, *Long and the Short and the Tall*, p. 65; Lodge, *Recapture of Guam*, pp. 86–87.

Chapter 2

1. Joseph Alexander, "What Was Nimitz Thinking?" *United States Naval Institute Proceedings*, November 1998, pp. 42–47; Alexander, "'Everything about Peleliu Left a Bad Taste,'" *Leatherneck*, September 2004, pp. 28–30; Major Jon T. Hoffman, "The Legacy and Lessons of Peleliu," *Marine Corps Gazette*, September 1994, pp. 90–91; George Garand and Truman Strobridge, *History of U.S. Marine Corps Operations in World War II: Western Pacific Operations* (Washington, D.C.: U.S. Marine Corps Historical Division, 1971), pp. 63–65; Bill Ross, *A Special Piece of Hell: The Untold Story of Peleliu—The Pacific War's Forgotten Battle* (New York: St. Martin's, 1991), pp. 134–41.

2. 1st Marine Division, Special Action Report (SAR), Annex A, Infantry, Record Group (RG) 127, U.S. Marine Corps Records, Peleliu, Box 298, Folder 19; Sergeant Major Masao Kurihara et al., prisoner interrogations, provided to U.S. Marine Corps History and Museums Division by Major General Paul Mueller, RG 127, U.S. Marine Corps History and Museums Division, Publication Background Files, Assault on Peleliu, Box 6, Folder 2, all at National Archives, College Park, MD; Interrogation of Colonel Tokechi Tada and Lieutenant General Sadae Inoue regarding the Palau Campaign, both in Rex Beasley Papers, Box 1, Folder 1, United States Army Military History Institute (USAMHI), Carlisle, PA; Major Frank Hough, *The Assault on Peleliu* (Washington, D.C.: U.S. Marine Corps Historical Branch, 1950), pp. 192–97, 200–203; Harry Gailey, *Peleliu 1944* (Annapolis, MD: The Nautical and Aviation Publishing Company of America, 1983), pp. 37–51; Garand and Strobridge, *Western Pacific Operations*, pp. 66–72; David Green, "Peleliu," *After the Battle*, Number 78, 1992, pp. 8–9; Alexander, "'Bad Taste,'" pp. 28–31; Hoffman, "Legacy and Lessons," pp. 90–91. In speaking to his postwar interrogators, General Inoue said that another reason he sent General Murai to Peleliu was to make sure that Colonel Nakagawa did not "make any mistakes." However, General Inoue, according to the interrogator, said this "with a twinkle in his eye" and was probably joking.

3. 3rd Fleet, Naval Gunfire Report, RG 127, U.S. Marine Corps Records, Peleliu, Box 297, Folder 3; III Marine Amphibious Corps, Operation Report, Enclosure B, Naval Gunfire and Tactics, Box 298, Folder 4; Operation Report, Enclosure G, Naval Bombardment, Box 298, Folder 9; 1st Marine Division, SAR, Annex K, Naval Bombardment, Box 298, Folder 19; Rear Admiral George Fort to Major General Orlando Ward, November 15, 1950, RG 319, Records of the Office of the Chief of Military History, History Division, Approach to the Philippines, Box 306, Folder 4; Rear Admiral George Fort to Brigadier General Clayton Jerome, March 20, 1950, RG 127, U.S. Marine Corps History and Museums Division, Publication Background Files, Assault on Peleliu, Box 6, Folder 1; Admiral Jesse Oldendorf to Jerome, March 25, 1950, Box 6, Folder 2; Lieutenant Colonel Lewis Field to Commandant, March 17, 1950,

Box 6, Folder 1; Lieutenant Colonel Frederick Ramsay to Commandant, February 20, 1950, Box 6, Folder 1, all at National Archives; Vice Admiral Theodore Wilkinson to Major General Roy Geiger, August 17, 1944, Roy Geiger Papers, Box 5, Folder 99; Brigadier General Oliver Smith, unpublished memoir, p. 14, Oliver P. Smith Papers, Box 2, Folder 1, both at U.S. Marine Corps History and Museums Division (USMCHMD), Gray Research Center (GRC), Quantico, VA; Burke Davis, *Marine! The Life of Chesty Puller* (New York: Bantam, 1991), pp. 190–95; Gailey, *Peleliu*, pp. 65–68; Garand and Strobridge, *Western Pacific Operations*, pp. 102–05.

4.   1st Marine Division, SAR; D3 Journal, September 15, 1944, RG 127, U.S. Marine Corps Records, Peleliu, Box 299, Folder 6; 1st Battalion, 1st Marine Regiment, History, Box 300, Folder 6; 7th Marine Regiment, AAR, Box 299, Folder 4; Oldendorf to Jerome, all at National Archives.

5.   1st Marine Division, SAR, and Annex J, Tanks, RG 127, U.S. Marine Corps Records, Peleliu, Box 298, Folder 19, National Archives; Hough, *Seizure of Peleliu*, pp. 60–64. This description also is derived from my analysis of literally hundreds of firsthand accounts and official reports. Citing them all would be ponderous.

6.   1st Marine Regiment, History, RG 127, U.S. Marine Corps Records, Peleliu, Box 300, Folder 5; 1st Battalion, 1st Marines, History; 7th Marine Regiment, AAR, all at National Archives; Corporal Leo Zitko to Mom and Dad, Collection Number 68, World War II Letters, Box 40, Folder 3463, Western Historical Manuscript Collection, University of Missouri, Columbia, MO (hereafter WHMC); Henry Andrasovsky, oral history, Henry Andrasovsky Collection, #23434, and Alexander Costella, unpublished memoir, pp. 7–8, Alexander Costella Collection, #30258, both at Veterans History Project (VHP), American Folklife Center (AFC), Library of Congress, Washington, D.C.; William Martin, unpublished memoir, pp. 1–2, copy in author's possession, courtesy of Mr. Martin.

7.   5th Marine Regiment, AAR, RG 127, U.S. Marine Corps Records, Peleliu, Box 299, Folder 4, National Archives; E. B. Sledge, *With the Old Breed at Peleliu and Okinawa* (New York: Oxford University Press, 1990), pp. 59–60; Richard Bruce Watkins, "With the 1st Marine Division on Peleliu: The First Day," *Marine Corps Gazette*, August 2004, pp. 63–64. Watkins also posted this account on a Web site, www.brothersinbattle.net: Garand and Strobridge, *Western Pacific Operations*, p. 115.

8.   1st Marine Division, SAR, and Annex D, Medical, RG 127, U.S. Marine Corps Records, Peleliu, Box 298, Folder 19; III Marine Amphibious Corps, Operation Report, Enclosure J, Medical, Box 298, Folder 13; Captain James Flagg, personal diary, September 15, 1944, Box 307, Folder 12; 1st Battalion, 1st Marine Regiment, History, all at National Archives; Lieutenant Commander William Turney, "1st Medical Battalion in Action—Peleliu, 1 May 1944–20 October 1944," Amphibious Warfare School, 1947–1948, USMCHMD; Leslie Harrold, oral history, copy in au-

thor's possession, courtesy of Mr. Harrold; Leslie Harrold, conversation with the author, May 5, 2008.

9.   1st Marine Division, SAR; 1st Marine Regiment, AAR, both at National Archives; Fred Harris, unpublished memoir, p. 2, Peleliu accounts, Folder #2149, GRC; Charles H. Owen, "Capture of Peleliu: Bravery on the Beach," *World War II*, September 1998, pp. 35–40; Russell Davis, *Marine at War* (Boston: Little, Brown and Company, 1961), pp. 29–31; Colonel Dave Grossman with Loren W. Christensen, *On Combat: The Psychology and Physiology of Deadly Conflict in War and in Peace* (Portland, OR: PPCT Research Publications, 2007), pp. 30–49.

10. 1st Marine Regiment, AAR, History, Intelligence Section History, all at National Archives; George Hunt, *Coral Comes High* (New York: Signet, 1946), pp. 56–58; George Peto, interview with the author, April 25, 2008.

11. 3rd Battalion, 1st Marine Regiment, Record of Events, U.S. Marine Corps Records, Peleliu, Box 300, Folder 8; 1st Marine Regiment, AAR and History, all at National Archives; "Marines of K-3-1 Killed in Action During the Peleliu Operation," USMCHMD, Reference Branch Files; Braswell Deen, "Trial by Combat!" (self-published), pp. 246–48; Hunt, *Coral Comes High*, p. 74; Captain George Hunt, "Point Secured," *Marine Corps Gazette*, January 1945, pp. 39–40; Colonel Joseph Alexander, "Peleliu 1944: 'King' Company's Battle for 'The Point,'" *Leatherneck*, November 1996, pp. 18–21.

12. 1st Marine Regiment, AAR, Record of Events, both at National Archives; Fred Fox to General C. C. Krulak, September 9, 1996; Fox, unpublished memoir, pp. 7–8, both at USMCHMD, Reference Branch Files; Alexander, "Peleliu 1944," p. 21; Hunt, "Point Secured," p. 40; Hunt, *Coral Comes High*, pp. 59–61.

13. 1st Marine Regiment, Record of Events, National Archives; Alexander, "Peleliu," pp. 21–22; Hunt, "Point Secured," p. 40; Hunt, *Coral Comes High*, p. 54.

14. 1st Marine Regiment, AAR, History, Record of Events, all at National Archives; Fox, unpublished memoir, pp. 9–10, USMCHMD; Alexander, "Peleliu," pp. 22–23; Hunt, "Point Secured," p. 40.

15. 1st Marine Regiment, AAR, History, National Archives; Fox, unpublished memoir, pp. 12–14, USMCHMD; George Peto, unpublished memoir, pp. 1–2, copy in author's possession, courtesy of Mr. Peto; Peto interview; Hunt, *Coral Comes High*, pp. 91–93.

16. 1st Marine Regiment, AAR, History, Record of Events, National Archives; Albert Mikel, unpublished memoir, p. 4, Peleliu accounts, #2221; Russell Honsowetz, oral history, both at GRC; Fox, unpublished memoir, pp. 16–18; "Marines of K-3-1 Killed in Action During the Peleliu Operation," both at USMCHMD; Peto, unpublished memoir, p. 2; Peto interview; Alexander, "Peleliu," pp. 23–25; Hunt, "Point

Secured," pp. 40–42; Hunt, *Coral Comes High*, pp. 115–22; Matthew Stevenson, "Personal Perspectives on Peleliu," *Military History Quarterly*, Winter 1999, pp. 78–79; Jon Hoffman, *Chesty: The Story of Lieutenant General Lewis B. Puller, USMC* (New York: Random House, 2001), pp. 273–80. After the war, Captain Hunt taught at the Marine Corps Education Center in Quantico, VA. With his assistance, the school built an exact replica of the Point and used it to educate young officers on how to assault fortified positions. Not only was this educational process instructive, it preserved the Point battle in Marine Corps lore. Hunt left the Corps and returned to his prewar job with *Fortune* magazine. Over the years, he wrote many articles about the men of his company. Fred Fox returned to Peleliu, and the Point, four separate times after the war.

17. 1st Marine Division, SAR; D3 Journal, September 15, 1944; 5th Marine Regiment, AAR, all at National Archives; Technical Sergeant Joseph Alli, "First Two Days of Hell on Peleliu Described by Marine Combat Correspondent," dispatch found at USMCHMD, Reference Branch Files. There are literally dozens of accounts of the Japanese tank attack. I have consulted them all but have only listed the ones upon which I relied most heavily.

18. 1st Marine Division, SAR; 1st Marine Regiment, History; Major Waite Worden to Commandant, April 6, 1950, RG 127, U.S. Marine Corps History and Museums Division, Publication Background Files, Assault on Peleliu, Box 6, Folder 3, all at National Archives; Robert "Pepper" Martin, *Time*, October 16, 1944; *Webster's II New Riverside Dictionary* (New York: Berkley, 1984), p. 231; Robert Leckie, *Helmet for My Pillow* (New York: Bantam Books, 1957), p. 273; Davis, *Marine at War*, p. 99.

19. 1st Marine Division, SAR, Annex D, Medical, Annex I, Engineers; Lieutenant Colonel Theodore Drummond to Commandant, March 14, 1950, RG 127, U.S. Marine Corps History and Museums Division, Publication Background Files, Assault on Peleliu, Box 6, Folder 1, all at National Archives; George Parker, unpublished memoir, p. 49, George Parker Collection, #5375, Veterans History Project (VHP), American Folklife Center (AFC), Library of Congress; John Arthur Huber, unpublished memoir, p. 8, Peleliu Accounts, #3856, GRC; James W. Johnston, *The Long Road of War: A Marine's Story of Pacific Combat* (Lincoln, NE: University of Nebraska Press, 1998), pp. 78, 88; Hough, *Assault on Peleliu*, pp. 94–97; Leckie, *Helmet for My Pillow*, p. 273; Sledge, *With the Old Breed*, p. 76; Charlie Burchett, interview with the author, March 6, 1995; Harrold, oral history.

20. 1st Marine Division, SAR, Annex A, Infantry, Annex B, Intelligence; D2 Journal, September 16, 1944, RG 127, U.S. Marine Corps Records, Peleliu, Box 299, Folder 2; 1st Marine Regiment, History, all at National Archives; Peto interview.

21. III Marine Amphibious Corps, Operation Report, Enclosure A, Strength Report, RG 127, U.S. Marine Corps Records, Peleliu, Box 298, Folder 5; 2nd Battalion, 7th

Marine Regiment, War Diary, Box 301, Folder 2; 1st Marine Regiment, History; Record of Events, all at National Archives; Parker, unpublished memoir, pp. 50–51, Library of Congress; Brigadier General Gordon Gayle, *Bloody Beaches: The Marines at Peleliu* (Washington, D.C.: Marine Corps Historical Center, 1996), p. 20; Davis, *Marine at War*, pp. 103–04. Gene Burns was a professor of mine in graduate school. He told me this story in November 1989.

22. 1st Marine Division, SAR, Annex L, Air Support, Annex J, Tanks; 2nd Battalion, 11th Marine Regiment, Operation Report, RG 127, U.S. Marine Corps Records, Peleliu, Box 301, Folder 8; Lieutenant Colonel Arthur Stuart to Commandant, April 25, 1950, RG 127, U.S. Marine Corps History and Museums Division, Publication Background Files, Assault on Peleliu, Box 6, Folder 3, all at National Archives; Major Richard Kennard, *Combat Letters Home* (Bryn Mawr, PA: Dorrance & Company, Inc., 1985), pp. 16–17; Davis, *Marine at War*, p. 104.

23. 1st Marine Regiment, History; 1st Battalion, 1st Marine Regiment, History; Captain Everett Pope to Commandant, March 8, 1950, RG 127, U.S. Marine Corps History and Museums Division, Publication Background Files, Assault on Peleliu, Box 6, Folder 2, all at National Archives; Everett Pope, interview with Rob Taglianetti, USMCHMD, August 3, 2006, interview made available to author by Mr. Taglianetti; Martin, unpublished memoir, pp. 2–3; Ray Davis, *The Story of Ray Davis, General of Marines* (Fuquay Varina, NC: Research Triangle Publishing, 1995), pp. 68–70; Garand and Strobridge, *Western Pacific Operations*, pp. 146–48, 156–61; Davis, *Marine at War*, pp. 108–14; Kennard, *Combat Letters Home*, p. 17; Hoffman, *Chesty*, pp. 279–87. Many men in the 1st Marines, particularly the C Company survivors, felt that Hill 100 should have been named Pope's Ridge.

24. Hoffman, *Chesty*, pp. 284–85; Bill Ross, *Special Piece of Hell*, pp. 235–40; Peto, unpublished memoir, p. 3; Oliver Butler, unpublished memoir, p. 67, copy in author's possession, courtesy of Mr. Butler.

25. Oliver Smith, Ray Davis, Russell Honsowetz, Harold Deakin, oral histories, GRC; Bill Sloan, *Brotherhood of Heroes: The Marines at Peleliu, 1944—The Bloodiest Battle of the Pacific War* (New York: Simon & Schuster, 2005), pp. 340–41; Dick Camp, *Last Man Standing: The 1st Marine Regiment on Peleliu, September 15–21, 1944* (Minneapolis, MN: Zenith Press, 2008), p. 269; Hoffman, *Chesty*, pp. 285–88; Davis, *The Story of Ray Davis*, pp. 72–73; Gailey, *Peleliu 1944*, pp. 123–124; Ross, *Special Piece of Hell*, pp. 244–50, 261; Jon Hoffman, "The Truth about Peleliu," *Naval Institute Proceedings*, November 2002, pp. 51–54; Stevenson, "Personal Perspectives on Peleliu," *MHQ*, pp. 81–82.

26. Smith, Honsowetz, Deakin, oral histories, GRC; Hoffman, *Chesty*, pp. 296–98; Gailey, *Peleliu 1944*, pp. 133–35; Ross, *Special Piece of Hell*, pp. 261–64; Hoffman, "Truth about Peleliu," pp. 53–54; biography of Major General William Rupertus at www

.arlingtoncemetery.net. General Geiger later told General Smith that, had he known about Rupertus's broken ankle, he would have relieved him before the invasion.

27. Colonel Walter Wachtler to Commandant, March 1, 1950, RG 127, U.S. Marine Corps History and Museums Division, Publication Background Files, Assault on Peleliu, Box 6, Folder 3; Colonel William Coleman to Commandant, no date, Box 6, Folder 1, both at National Archives; Oliver Smith, unpublished memoir, pp. 61–62; Smith, Deakin, oral histories, all at GRC; George McMillan, *The Old Breed: A History of the First Marine Division in World War II* (Washington, D.C.: Infantry Journal Press, 1949), pp. 318–19; Gailey, *Peleliu 1944*, pp. 134–35; Kennard, *Combat Letters Home*, p. 31; Hoffman, *Chesty*, pp. 281–91; Ross, *Special Piece of Hell*, pp. 264–72; Davis, *Marine at War*, p. 116; Hoffman, "Truth about Peleliu," p. 54. Joe Rosenthal, the famous photographer, witnessed the meeting between Geiger and Puller. In Rosenthal's opinion, Chesty looked like "a tired guy."

28. 321st Infantry Regiment, AAR, RG 407, Box 12324, Folder 8; 1st Battalion, 1st Marine Regiment, History; 1st Marine Division, D2 Journal, September 23, 1944, all at National Archives; Thomas Climie, unpublished memoir, p. 22, World War II Questionnaire #10149; Robert Francis Heatley, "Breathes There a Soldier" (self-published), p. 9, World War II Questionnaire #12720; George Pasula, World War II Questionnaire #4333, all at USAMHI; Honsowetz, oral history, GRC; Peto, unpublished memoir, p. 3, interview; Hoffman, *Chesty*, p. 289.

29. 81st Infantry Division, History of Operations, RG 127, U.S. Marine Corps Records, Peleliu, Box 300, Folder 4; 321st Infantry Regiment, AAR, both at National Archives; "The 321st Infantry Regiment from Camp Rucker to Guadalcanal, Angaur, Peleliu, New Caledonia, Leyte and Japan"; Pasula, questionnaire; Heatley, "Breathes There a Soldier," p. 11, all at USAMHI; Captain Pierce Irby, "The Operations of Company 'L,' 321st Infantry (81st Infantry Division) in the Capture of the Island of Peleliu, 23–29 September, 1944, Personal Experience of a Company Commander," pp. 17–18, Advanced Infantry Officer's Course, 1948–1949, Donovan Library, Fort Benning, Columbus, Georgia.

30. 3rd Battalion, 7th Marines, War Diary, RG 127, U.S. Marine Corps Records, Peleliu, Box 301, Folder 5; Operation Report, Box 301, Folder 14; 321st Infantry Regiment, AAR, all at National Archives; Irby, "The Operations of Company 'L,' 321st," pp. 14–17; Robert Ross Smith, *The U.S. Army in World War II: The Approach to the Philippines* (Washington, D.C.: Department of the Army, 1953), pp. 537–38; Garand and Strobridge, *Western Pacific Operations*, pp. 197–98; Ross, *A Special Piece of Hell*, p. 277; Camp, *Last Man Standing*, pp. 290–91; Smith, oral history, GRC. General Paul Mueller, the commander of the 81st Division, believed, with some justification, that his soldiers never got the credit they deserved for their part in the Battle of Peleliu. He felt that Marine publicity overshadowed the Army's vital role in the battle. Sensi-

tive to any criticism of his troops, Mueller downplayed K Company's problems in an April 14, 1950, letter to Brigadier General Clayton Jerome, head of the Corps' History and Museums Division. Mueller felt that "the incident was exaggerated." The letter is in the National Archives at RG 127, U.S. Marine Corps History and Museums Division, Publication Background Files, Assault on Peleliu, Box 6, Folder 2.

31.   81st Infantry Division, History of Operations; 321st Infantry Regiment, AAR; 1st Marine Division, SAR, Annex H, Artillery, Annex L, Air Support; 11th Marine Regiment, Operation Report, all at National Archives; General Oliver Smith, "Comments and Recommendations as a Result of the Peleliu Campaign," Box 22, Folder 5, Oliver Smith Papers; William Burnett, unpublished memoir, p. 9, Peleliu Accounts, #3723, both at GRC; Kennard, *Combat Letters Home*, p. 25; Staff Sergeant Ward Walker, "Marine Tells of Cave Fighting on Peleliu," USMCHMD, Reference Branch Files; Lieutenant Colonel Lewis Walt, "The Closer the Better," *Marine Corps Gazette*, September 1946, pp. 38–39.

32.   321st Infantry Regiment, AAR; 1st Marine Division, SAR, Annex A, Infantry, Annex J, Tanks; 5th Marine Regiment, AAR; 3rd Battalion, 5th Marines, Record of Events; Captain James Flagg, diary entries, October 1–10, 1944; Stuart letter, all at National Archives; U.S. Armored School, "Armor in Island Warfare," p. 86, Donovan Library, Fort Benning; Climie, unpublished memoir, p. 25, USAMHI; Huber, unpublished memoir, pp. 13–14, GRC; Burchett interview.

33.   1st Marine Division, SAR, Annex D, Medical; 5th Marine Regiment, AAR; 321st Infantry Regiment, AAR, all at National Archives; Edward Thul, unpublished memoir, p. 12, Edward Thul Collection, #19069, VHP, AFC, Library of Congress; Climie, unpublished memoir, p. 24; Heatley, "Breathes There a Soldier," p. 11, both at USAMHI; Sledge, *With the Old Breed*, pp. 129–32, 142–44; Burchett interview.

34.   1st Marine Division, SAR; 81st Infantry Division, AAR; 323rd Infantry Regiment, AAR; Terrain and Intelligence Summary, RG 407, Box 12338, Folder 7, all at National Archives; "History of Cannon Company"; "History of E Company," both with 81st Infantry Division material at USAMHI; The 81st Wildcat Division Historical Committee, *The 81st Infantry Wildcat Division in World War II* (Washington, D.C.: Infantry Journal Press, 1948), pp. 200–201; Smith, *Approach to the Philippines*, pp. 573–75; Gailey, *Peleliu 1944*, p. 192.

Chapter 3

1.   General J. Lawton Collins, interview with Charles B. MacDonald, January 25, 1954, Record Group 319, Records of the Office of the Chief of Military History, History Division, The Siegfried Line, Box 184, Folder 4, National Archives, College Park,

MD; 1st Lieutenant Harry Condren, "The Fall of Aachen," located in World War II Combat Interviews Collection #4, microfiche copy of the entire collection in the author's possession (hereafter referred to as CI); Christopher Gabel, "'Knock 'Em All Down': The Reduction of Aachen, October 1944," paper prepared for the Combat Studies Institute, Fort Leavenworth, KS, copy in author's possession; Captain Monte Parrish, "The Battle of Aachen," *Field Artillery Journal*, September/October 1976, pp. 25–27; Charles B. MacDonald, *The U.S. Army in World War II: The Siegfried Line Campaign* (Washington, D.C.: Department of the Army, 1963), pp. 280–308.

2. Derrill Daniel, biography, Charles B. MacDonald Papers, Box 2, Folder 2, United States Army Military History Institute (USAMHI), Carlisle, PA; John Corley file, McCormick Research Center (MRC), Cantigny 1st Infantry Division Foundation, Wheaton, IL; Michael D. Runey, "Chaos, Cohesion, and Leadership: An American Infantry Battalion in Europe, October–December 1944," Master's thesis, Pennsylvania State University, pp. 13–17.

3. "Combat in Towns," RG 407, Entry 427, Box 14193, Folder 1, National Archives; 26th Infantry Regiment, "Battle of Aachen," Combat Interview, CI-4; Lieutenant Colonel Derrill Daniel, "The Infantry Battalion in Offensive Action, Aachen, 8–20 October 1944," pp. 3–4, Box 89, MRC; Matthew D. Bacik, "White Battalion Draws Red Blood at Aachen," unpublished paper, United States Military Academy, p. 3, copy in author's possession; Gabel, "'Knock 'Em All Down'"; Captain Harold Keebaugh, "Offensive Action in Cities," p. 9, Advanced Infantry Officer's Course, 1955–1956, Donovan Library, Fort Benning, Columbus, Georgia; "The Battle for Aachen," *After the Battle*, Number 42, pp. 6–13.

4. 26th Infantry Regiment, AAR; S2 Journal, October 10–12, 1944; S3 Journal, October 10–12, 1944, all at RG 407, Entry 427, Box 5268, Folder 2, National Archives; Periodic Report 128, "The Ultimatum Presented to the City of Aachen," CI-4; "1106th Engineer Group South of Aachen," Combat Interview; "The Fall of Aachen," both in CI-4; "Aachen: 26th Infantry Regimental Combat Team, Operations in Urban Terrain, October 1944," copy in author's possession; John Curran, oral history, MRC; Ed Wilcox, "Battle for Aachen: Death of a City," *Stars and Stripes*, October 28, 1944. Technically, at the time the Americans extended their ultimatum, Lieutenant Colonel Maximilian Leyherr, one of Wilck's regimental commanders in the 246th Volksgrenadier Division, was in charge at Aachen. However, Wilck soon arrived and, as division commander, he assumed responsibility for the defense of Aachen.

5. 26th Infantry Regiment, AAR; S3 Journal, October 13–14, 1944, both at National Archives; 3rd Battalion, 26th Infantry Regiment Unit Journal, October 13–14, 1944, copy in author's possession; 26th Infantry Regiment Combat Interview, CI-4; Daniel, "Aachen," pp. 4–5, 7–8, MRC; "Aachen: 26th Infantry, Operations in Urban

Terrain"; Bacik, "White Battalion Draws Red Blood," pp. 6–7; Charles Dye, interview with Doug Canin, July 16, 1992, MRC.

6.   26th Infantry Regiment, AAR, National Archives; 3rd Battalion, 26th Infantry Regiment Unit Journal, October 13–14, 1944; 26th Infantry Regiment Combat Interview, CI-4; "Aachen: 26th Infantry, Operations in Urban Terrain"; Leroy Stewart, unpublished memoir, pp. 58–59, 1st Infantry Division Survey Material, Box 2, USAMHI; Richard Tregaskis, "House to House and Room to Room," *Saturday Evening Post*, February 28, 1945, pp. 18–19; Mack Morris, "The Fight for Aachen," *Yank*, October 29, 1944, p. 5; Captain L. G. Lawton, "Tank Infantry Team," *Marine Corps Gazette*, November 1945, p. 32.

7.   26th Infantry Regiment, AAR; S3 Journal, October 13–14, 1944, both at National Archives; F Company, 26th Infantry Regiment, "The Battle of Aachen," AAR, Box 89; Daniel, "Aachen," pp. 8–9, both at MRC; "Aachen: 26th Infantry, Operations in Urban Terrain"; Tregaskis, "House to House and Room to Room," pp. 19–20.

8.   26th Infantry Regiment, S3 Journal, National Archives; "Evacuation of Civilians from Aachen," CI-4; Dick Lang, oral history; Dye interview, both at MRC; Morris, "The Fight for Aachen," p. 6.

9.   "Mines and Booby Traps in Aachen Operation," contained in 1106th Engineer Combat Group records, RG 407, Entry 427, Box 14119, Folder 1, National Archives; "1106th Engineer Combat Group South of Aachen"; 26th Infantry, Combat Interview, both in CI-4; Curran, oral history; Dye interview, both at MRC; Stewart, unpublished memoir, pp. 60–63, USAMHI; Captain Amos Cahan, "Battalion Surgeon, Infantry," *Infantry Journal*, May 1945, pp. 19–20; Tregaskis, "House to House, Room to Room," pp. 101–02. The evidence of self-inflicted wounds is recorded in the 3rd Battalion, 26th Infantry Regiment, journal, October 16–20, 1944. All accounts and records agree that veterans were more susceptible to combat fatigue than new men.

10.   26th Infantry Regiment, AAR; S3 Journal, October 15 and 16, 1944, both at National Archives; 26th Infantry Regiment, Combat Interview, CI-4; 3rd Battalion, 26th Infantry Regiment, unit journal, October 15 and 16, 1944; Lieutenant Colonel John Corley, "Farwick Park, Aachen," p. 1, Box 89; Curran, oral history, both at MRC; Runey, "Chaos, Cohesion and Leadership," pp. 69–78; Charles Whiting, *Bloody Aachen* (New York: Playboy Press, 1976), pp. 152–55.

11.   634th Tank Destroyer Battalion, Daily Reports, RG 407, Box 23602, Folder 1; 26th Infantry Regiment, AAR; S2 Journal, October 18 through 20, 1944; S3 Journal, October 18 through 20, 1944, all at National Archives; 26th Infantry Regiment, Combat Interview, CI-4; F Company, 26th Infantry Regiment, "Battle of Aachen";

"Employment of Armored Vehicles in Street Warfare as seen by an Infantryman," both in Box 89; Daniel, "Aachen," pp. 11–12; Corley, "Farwick Park," pp. 3–4, all at MRC; Stewart, unpublished memoir, pp. 63–65, USAMHI; 3rd Battalion, 26th Infantry Regiment, unit journal, October 18 through 20, 1944; "Aachen: 26th Infantry, Operations in Urban Terrain"; Runey, "Chaos, Cohesion, and Leadership," pp. 80–84; Tregaskis, "House to House, Room to Room," p. 102.

12.   26th Infantry Regiment, AAR; S3 Journal, October 21, 1944, both at National Archives; 26th Infantry Regiment, Combat Interview; "Experiences of Two American Prisoners of War Held in Aachen, Germany," Combat Interview, both in CI-4; 3rd Battalion, 26th Infantry Regiment, unit journal, October 21, 1944; "Aachen: 26th Infantry, Operations in Urban Terrain"; Runey, "Chaos, Cohesion, and Leadership," pp. 85–87; Keebaugh, "Offensive Action in Cities," p. 10; Frederich Koechling, "The Battle of Aachen Sector," Foreign Military Studies, Box 9, Folder A-989; Stewart, unpublished memoir, pp. 63–64, both at USAMHI; MacDonald, *The Siegfried Line Campaign*, pp. 316–20.

Chapter 4

1.   99th Infantry Division, After Action Report (AAR), December 1944, Record Group (RG) 407, Entry 427, Box 14120, Folder 1, National Archives, College Park, MD; 99th Infantry Division, "The German Breakthrough," Combat Interview (CI) #209, located in author's personal collection; Hugh Cole, *The United States Army in World War II: The Ardennes* (Washington, D.C.: Department of the Army, 1965), pp. 19–47; Walter E. Lauer, *Battle Babies: The Story of the 99th Infantry Division in World War II* (Nashville, TN: The Battery Press, 1950), pp. 1–12; Charles B. MacDonald, *A Time for Trumpets: The Untold Story of the Battle of the Bulge* (New York: Bantam Books, 1984), p. 83. For more on the ASTP program, see Louis Keefer, *Scholars in Foxholes: The Story of the Army Specialized Training Program in World War II* (Jefferson, NC: McFarland & Co., Inc., Publishers, 1988).

2.   1st Battalion, 394th Infantry Regiment, Recommendation for Unit Citation, RG 407, Entry 427, Box 14199, Folder 1, National Archives; Lloyd Long to Roger Foehringer, December 15, 1992, World War II Questionnaire #7320, 394th Infantry Regiment Material, Box 2; Milton Kitchens to Roger Foehringer, December 16, 1992, World War II Questionnaire #7065, 394th Infantry Regiment Material, Box 2, both at the United States Army Military History Institute (USAMHI), Carlisle, PA; Major William Kempton, S3, 394th Infantry, Combat Interview with Captain William Fox, January 30, 1945, CI-209; Captain Wesley Simmons, "The Operations of Company K, 394th Infantry (99th Infantry Division), in Defensive Action Near

Elsenborn, Belgium, 16–21 December 1944, Personal Experience of a Company Commander," Advanced Infantry Officer's Course, 1949–1950, Donovan Library, Fort Benning, Columbus, Georgia.

3.   3rd Battalion, 394th Infantry Regiment, Combat Interview with Master Sergeant Forrest Pogue, January 29, 1945, CI-209; John Thornburg, unpublished memoir, pp. 1–2, World War II Questionnaire #7315, 394th Infantry Regiment Material, Box 3; John Kuhn, unpublished memoir, p. 157, World War II Questionnaire #7108, 394th Infantry Regiment Material, Box 2, both at USAMHI; Simmons, "The Operations of Company K"; Charles Roland, unpublished memoir, located in the archival collection of the National World War II Museum, New Orleans, LA. He later published this under the title *My Odyssey Through History: Memoirs of War and Academe* (Baton Rouge, LA: Louisiana State University Press, 2004); William C. C. Cavanagh, *The Battle East of Elsenborn & the Twin Villages* (South Yorkshire, England: Pen & Sword Books, Limited, 2004), pp. 39–42. Although the Americans called the railroad station Buckholz Station, it was actually Losheimergraben Station.

4.   1st Battalion, 394th Infantry Regiment, Recommendation for Unit Citation, National Archives; 1st Battalion, 394th Infantry Regiment, Combat Interview with Captain John Howe; 2nd Battalion, 394th Infantry Regiment, Combat Interview, both in CI-209; 1st Battalion, 394th Infantry, History, World War II Questionnaire #10226, 394th Infantry Material, Box 1; Combs is quoted in "The Fight for Losheimergraben," Richard H. Byers Papers, Box 1; Danny Dalyai to Charles, February 17, 1991, World War II Questionnaire #6789, 394th Infantry Material, Box 1; Bob Newbrough, unpublished memoir, p. 2, Charles B. MacDonald Papers, Box 4, Folder 2, all at USAMHI; Cavanagh, *Battle East of Elsenborn*, pp. 34–38; Cole, *The Ardennes*, pp. 82–86; MacDonald, *A Time for Trumpets*, pp. 169–70; Lauer, *Battle Babies*, p. 23.

5.   1st Battalion, 394th Infantry Regiment, Recommendation for Unit Citation, National Archives; 394th Infantry Regiment, Combat Interview; 1st and 2nd Battalion, 394th Infantry Regiment, Combat Interviews, all in CI-209; I SS Panzer Corps, AAR, MS #B-779, Charles B. MacDonald Papers, Box 8, Folder 4; Ralph Gamber to Raphael D'Amico-Geran, no date, World War II Questionnaire #1897, 394th Infantry Material, Box 1; Gamber to Joe Doherty, no date, Battle of the Bulge Historical Foundation Papers, Box 14, 99th Infantry Division Folder; John Hilliard to Dick Byers, February 26, 1990; William Kirkbride, unpublished memoir, pp. 1–3, both in Richard H. Byers Papers, Box 1; Kitchens to Foehringer; Harold Schaefer, unpublished memoir, pp. 1–5, World War II Questionnaire #6787, 394th Infantry Material, Box 3, all at USAMHI; Steve Kallas, oral history, Steve Kallas Collection, #110, Veterans History Project (VHP), American Folklife Center (AFC), Library of Congress (LOC), Washington, D.C. Cavanagh, *Battle East of Elsenborn*, pp. 73–86; Cole, *The Ardennes*, pp. 85–86, 90–94. Along the lines of screwups: During the retreat, Colonel Riley rashly

ordered his men to abandon their vehicles, rather than reconnoiter, when they encountered machine-gun fire near the twin villages of Krinkelt and Rocherath. As it turned out, a battle was raging in the towns and some of the fire was friendly. The order had the effect of dispersing and disorganizing the survivors of the 394th. In a memoir that is housed in the World War II Museum Archives, Lieutenant Henry Reath, an artillery liaison officer, harshly criticized Colonel Riley for this order.

6. 393rd Infantry Regiment, AAR, December 1944, RG 407, Entry 427, Box 14190, Folder 2, National Archives; 1st Battalion, 393rd Infantry Regiment, Combat Interview with Captain William Fox, January 27, 1945; 2nd Platoon, B Company, 393rd Infantry, Combat Interview with Captain William Fox, January 27, 1945, both in CI-209; Sergeant Ben Nawrocki, "Battle of the Bulge, 1944," unpublished memoir, pp. 1–5, World War II Questionnaire #7895, 393rd Infantry Material, Box 2; Alvin Boeger, World War II Questionnaire #1637; Roy House, World War II Questionnaire #1499, both in 393rd Infantry Material, Box 1; Bernie Macay to Will Cavanagh, no date, Box 4, Folder 3, Charles B. MacDonald Papers, all at USAMHI; Lionel Adda, *The Bulge Bugle*, November 1990, pp. 16–17; Cole, *The Ardennes*, pp. 95–98; Dave Grossman and Loren Christensen, *On Combat: The Psychology and Physiology of Deadly Conflict in War and in Peace* (Portland, OR: PPCT Research Publications, 2007), pp. 30–46.

7. 393rd Infantry Regiment, AAR, December 1944, National Archives; 3rd Battalion, 393rd Infantry Regiment, Combat Interview with Captain William Fox, January 27, 1945, CI-209; Earl Wiseman to family, no date, World War II Questionnaire #7305; "History of Company M," World War II Questionnaire #2485, both in 393rd Infantry Material, Box 3, USAMHI; Robert Dettor, diary, December 16, 1944, *The Bulge Bugle*, November 1994, p. 19; Cole, *The Ardennes*, pp. 96–97.

8. 393rd Infantry Regiment, Unit History, RG 407, Entry 427, Box 14189, Folder 2; AAR, December 1944, both at National Archives; Major Elmer Schmierer, S3, 393rd Infantry, Combat Interview with Captain William Fox; 2nd Platoon, B Company, 393rd, Combat Interview; 1st Battalion, 393rd Infantry, Combat Interview; 3rd Battalion, 393rd Infantry, Combat Interview, all at CI-209; "History of Company M," USAMHI; James Langford, unpublished memoir, pp. 2–4, James Langford Collection, #7983, LOC; Allyn Vannoy and Jay Karamales, *Against the Panzers: United States Infantry Versus German Tanks, 1944–1945* (Jefferson, NC: McFarland & Company Publishers, 1996), pp. 238–39; Cavanagh, *Battle East of Elsenborn*, pp. 88–89; Cole, *The Ardennes*, pp. 99–100. The 1st Battalion of the 393rd withdrew later on December 17.

9. 23rd Infantry Regiment, Unit History, December 1944, RG 407, Entry 427, Box 5366, Folder 1; 393rd Infantry Regiment, Unit History, AAR, December 1944, all at National Archives; all 393rd Infantry Combat Interviews, CI-209; Major General

Walter Robertson, Combat Interview with Captain Francis Phelps, March 19, 1945; 3rd Battalion, 23rd Infantry, Combat Interview; Major Vernon Joseph, XO, 3rd Battalion, 23rd Infantry, Combat Interview with Captain Francis Phelps, March 3, 1945, all at CI-20-21; Long Goffigan, Interview with Charles MacDonald, March 11, 1982, Charles B. MacDonald Papers, Box 2, Folder 3; Ewell Lee Smith to Charles MacDonald, June 23, 1975, Ewell Smith Papers, Box 1, Folder 2; Ewell Lee Smith to Colonel Cecil Roberts, September 10, 1985, Ewell Smith Papers, Box 1, Folder 3, all at USAMHI; Edward Bartkiewicz, oral history, Edward Bartkiewicz Collection, #18257, LOC; Charles MacDonald, *Company Commander* (New York: Bantam, 1947), pp. 119–22; MacDonald, *A Time for Trumpets*, pp. 376–77.

10.   23rd Infantry Regiment, Unit Journal, December 17, 1944, RG 407, Entry 427, Box 5368, Folder 1; 23rd Infantry Regiment, Unit History, December 1944; 741st Tank Battalion, AAR, December 1944; Unit Journal, December 17, 1944, RG 407, Entry 427, Box 16703, Folder 8, all at National Archives; 3rd Battalion, 23rd Infantry Combat Interview, CI-20-21; Ewell Lee Smith, unpublished memoir, pp. 16-2 through 16-4, Ewell Smith Papers, Box 1, Folder 2; Smith to MacDonald, Smith to Roberts, Smith Papers; Ewell Smith to Charles MacDonald, March 26, 1982, Box 2, Folder 3; Hugh Burger to Charles MacDonald, Box 2, Folder 3; Goffigan interview, all in Charles B. MacDonald Papers, USAMHI; Bartkiewicz, oral history, LOC; Patrick Hargreaves, "With the Company Commander," *After the Battle*, Number 73, pp. 4–10; Cavanagh, *Battle East of Elsenborn*, pp. 91–98; Vannoy and Karamales, *Against the Panzers*, pp. 240–42; MacDonald, *A Time for Trumpets*, pp. 378–80; Mac-Donald, *Company Commander*, pp. 122–37. Most of the records list Smith as the commander of K Company during the battle, confirming his recollection that his CO was gone. However, MacDonald, in *Company Commander*, a book he published in 1947 while the battle was fresh in his mind, wrote about interacting with K Company's original commander throughout the battle. Yet, forty years later, in *A Time for Trumpets*, MacDonald listed Smith as the CO. Because of these conflicting accounts, I have elected not to list the original K Company commander's name.

11.   38th Infantry Regiment, Unit Histories, RG 407, Entry 427, Box 5375, Folder 7, and Box 5376, Folder 3, both at National Archives; "The German Breakthrough, V Corps Sector," 2nd Infantry Division Combat Interview; 1st Battalion, 9th Infantry, Combat Interview; Major William Hancock, Executive Officer, and Staff Sergeant Norman Bernstein, Operations Sergeant, Combat Interview with Captain Francis Phelps, March 17, 1945; Robertson interview, all at CI-20-21; Major General Walter Robertson, Record of Events, Box 2, Folder 3; Ralph Steele to Charles MacDonald, June 27, 1983, Box 2, Folder 3; Ralph Steele to Joe Doherty, April 8, 1982, Box 2, Folder 4, all in Charles B. MacDonald Papers, USAMHI; Cavanagh, *Battle East of Elsenborn*, pp. 107–11; MacDonald, *A Time for Trumpets*, pp. 380–81.

12. Statement by First Lieutenant Roy Allen concerning "B" Company, 9th Inf engage-ment east of Rocherath, Belgium, on 17 and 18 December, 1944; 1st Battalion, 9th Infantry Combat Interview; Hancock, Bernstein, Combat Interview, all at CI-20-21; Herbert Hunt, unpublished memoir, pp. 4–13; Herbert Hunt to Charles Mac-Donald, December 5, 1981, both in Box 2, Folder 5, Charles B. MacDonald Papers, USAMHI; Frank Royer, unpublished memoir, pp. 4–5, Frank Royer Collec-tion, #3858, LOC; Cole, *The Ardennes*, pp. 109–11; Cavanagh, *Battle East of Elsen-born*, pp. 110–16; MacDonald, *A Time for Trumpets*, pp. 380–83; Vannoy and Karamales, *Against the Panzers*, pp. 244–48. The accounts differ as to what kind of tanks attacked on the evening of December 17. Some claim they were Jagdpanzers; others refer to "Tigers"; still others claim that the Germans attacked with Mark V Panthers. Because of this confusion, I have elected to refrain from describing what sort of tanks attacked. Also, I would be remiss if I did not mention that large ele-ments of the 1st Battalion, 38th Infantry Regiment, under Lieutenant Colonel Frank Mildren were in the twin villages that evening and helped stave off the enemy attack. For the sake of clarity and brevity, I have chosen to focus exclusively on McKinley's 1st Battalion of the 9th Infantry.

13. Allen statement; 1st Battalion, 9th Infantry, Combat Interview; Hancock, Bern-stein, Combat Interview, all in CI-20-21; "AGF Report No. 559—Comments on Anti-tank Weapons," p. 4, Donovan Library, Fort Benning, Columbus, Georgia; Lieutenant Colonel Charles McMillan, "Manchus at the Crossroads: Defending the Northern Shoulder of the Bulge," Army War College Paper; Brigadier General John Hinds, Commander, 2nd Infantry Division artillery to Will Cavanagh, September 30, 1982, Box 2, Folder 3; Steele to MacDonald, Box 2, Folder 3; Hunt, unpublished memoir, pp. 13–15, Box 2, Folder 5; First Sergeant Henry Albin to Scotty, Septem-ber 14, 1981, Box 2, Folder 5, all in Charles B. MacDonald Papers, USAMHI; Royer, unpublished memoir, p. 5, LOC; Edward Murphy, *Heroes of World War II* (New York: Ballantine Books, 1990), pp. 249–51; Cole, *The Ardennes*, pp. 110–16; Ca-vanagh, *Battle East of Elsenborn*, pp. 137–40; MacDonald, *A Time for Trumpets*, pp. 395–98; Vannoy and Karamales, *Against the Panzers*, pp. 248–52. McKinley re-ported that mines destroyed four of the German tanks; bazookas killed eleven; fire wrecked the other two.

14. 23rd Infantry Regiment, Unit History; 38th Infantry Regiment, Unit Histories; 1944 History, RG 407, Entry 427, Box 5377, Folder 1, all at National Archives; 38th Infantry Regiment, AAR; Lieutenant Colonel Tom Morris, Executive Officer, 38th Infantry, interview with Captain Francis Phelps, February 23, 1945; 3rd Battalion, 38th Infantry, Combat Interview with Captain Francis Phelps, March 15, 1945, all at CI-20-21; Kenneth Myers, unpublished memoir, pp. 1–2, Box 13, Folder 7, Battle of the Bulge Historical Foundation; Byron Reburn, World War II Questionnaire

#3075, 394th Infantry material, Box 3; Daniel Franklin to Charles MacDonald, Box 2, Folder 3, Charles B. MacDonald Papers, all at USAMHI; Cavanagh, *Battle East of Elsenborn*, pp. 154–60; Cole, *The Ardennes*, pp. 113–16.

15. 23rd Infantry Regiment, Unit History; 38th Infantry Regiment, Unit Histories, National Archives; 3rd Battalion, 23rd Infantry, Combat Interview; 38th Infantry, AAR; Captain Ralph Stallworth, Headquarters Company, 38th Infantry, Combat Interview with Captain Francis Phelps, February 24, 1945; 1st Battalion, 38th Infantry, Combat Interview with Captain Francis Phelps, February 25, 1945; Lieutenant George Adams, Combat Interview with Captain Francis Phelps, February 25, 1945, all at CI-20-21; John Savard, unpublished memoir, pp. 33–35, World War II Questionnaire #7702, 2nd Infantry Division Material, Box 1; Burger to MacDonald, both at USAMHI; John Savard, *The Bulge Bugle*, February 1992, pp. 15–16; Merrill Huntzinger, Interview with Lesley Reser, Merrill Huntzinger Collection, #6793, LOC; MacDonald, *A Time for Trumpets*, pp. 399–400; Cavanagh, *Battle East of Elsenborn*, pp. 156–64.

16. Colonel Richard Schulze to Hubert Meyer, Box 9, Folder 10; C Company, 12th SS Panzer Regiment, 12th SS Panzer Division, unpublished memoirs, Box 9, Folder 10; I SS Panzer Corps, AAR, Box 8, Folder 4, all in Charles B. MacDonald Papers; "Operations of the Sixth Panzer Army," Foreign Military Studies, Box 5, #A-924, all at USAMHI.

17. 703rd Tank Destroyer Battalion, Summary of Operations, December 1944, RG 407, Entry 427, Box 23715, Folder 3; 741st Tank Battalion, AAR, December 1944; 23rd Infantry Regiment, Unit History; 38th Infantry Regiment, Unit Histories, S3 Artillery Reports, RG 407, Entry 427, Box 5383, Folder 5, all at National Archives; Adams Combat Interview, CI-20-21; Captain Halland Hankel, "Operations of Company M, 38th Infantry (2nd ID) in the Vicinity of Krinkelt, Belgium, 17–20 December 1944, Personal Experiences of a Company Commander," Advanced Infantry Officer's Course, 1948–1949, found at Box 2, Folder 3, Charles B. MacDonald Papers; Hunt to MacDonald, both at USAMHI; Howard Daniels, Jr., "Tanks Versus the Infantry—No Quarrel," letter to the editor in *Infantry Journal*, June 1950, p. 32; Major Robert Bateman, "An Infantryman's Thoughts on Armor," *Armor*, January–February 2001, pp. 11–12; Joseph Kiss, *The Bulge Bugle*, February 1993, pp. 16–17; Vannoy and Karamales, *Against the Panzers*, pp. 255–62.

18. 99th Infantry Division, AAR; 741st Tank Battalion, AAR; 38th Infantry Regiment, Unit Histories, all at National Archives; 99th Infantry Division Combat Interview, CI-209; 2nd Infantry Division Combat Interview; 38th Infantry, AAR; 23rd Infantry Regiment list of casualties, all at CI-20-21; I SS Panzer Corps, AAR; Robertson, Record of Events, both in MacDonald Papers, USAMHI; Harold Etter to Mother, Collection Number 68, World War II Letters, Western Historical Manu-

script Collection, University of Missouri, Columbia, MO; Lauer, *Battle Babies*, pp. 68–72; MacDonald, *A Time for Trumpets*, pp. 400–402; Vannoy and Karamales, *Against the Panzers*, pp. 264–72; Cole, *The Ardennes*, pp. 120–28.

Chapter 5

1. Plans and Policy Division, Office of the Chief of Information, "Analysis of Public Statements on Ten Selected Issues of General William C. Westmoreland," Record Group (RG) 319, Records of the Office of the Chief of Military History, William C. Westmoreland Papers, Box 42, Folder 1, National Archives, College Park, MD; Gerard DeGroot, *A Noble Cause? America and the Vietnam War* (Essex, England: Longman, 2000), pp. 134–42; Stanley Karnow, *Vietnam: A History* (New York: Viking, 1983), p. 361; William Westmoreland, *A Soldier Reports* (Garden City, NY: Doubleday & Company, Inc., 1976), pp. 145–50; Brian Linn, *The Echo of Battle: The Army's Way of War* (Cambridge, MA: Harvard University Press, 2007). In my opinion, Westmoreland is an example of a "Manager," one of the intellectual groups Linn describes as influential in the Army since the early nineteenth century.

2. Lieutenant Colonel John "Skip" Fesmire, oral history, Vietnam Company Command Oral Histories, Box 12, Folder 3; Lieutenant General Harry Kinnard, oral history, Harry Kinnard Papers, Box 1, Folder 1, both at United States Army Military History Institute (USAMHI), Carlisle, PA; Lieutenant General John Tolson, *Vietnam Studies: Airmobility, 1961–1971* (Washington, D.C.: Department of the Army, 1989), pp. 51–92; John Carland, "How We Got There: Air Assault and the Emergence of the 1st Cavalry Division (Airmobile), 1950–1965" (Arlington, VA: Association of the United States Army, 2003), pp. 10–15.

3. 3rd Brigade, 1st Cavalry Division, AAR, Masher/White Wing, March 10, 1966, RG 472, MAC-V J3 Evaluation and Analysis Division, Box 3, Folder 2; 1st Battalion, 7th Cavalry, Organizational History, RG 472, Box 194, Folder 2, both at National Archives; Kinnard, oral history, USAMHI; John Prados, "Operation Masher: The Boundaries of Force," *VVA Veteran Magazine*, February/March 2002; Lieutenant General Hal Moore, interview with the author, April 25, 2005; John Carland, *The United States Army in Vietnam: Stemming the Tide, May 1965 to October 1966* (Washington, D.C.: Center of Military History, 2000), pp. 201–03; Terrence Maitland and Peter McInerney, *The Vietnam Experience: A Contagion of War* (Boston: Boston Publishing Company, 1983), pp. 34–35; Harold Moore and Joseph Galloway, *We Are Soldiers Still: A Journey to the Battlefields of Vietnam* (New York: HarperCollins Publishers, 2008), pp. 157–70. Moore is a legend in the history of the modern U.S. Army. For more on the Battle of Ia Drang, see the classic book he authored with Galloway entitled *We Were Soldiers Once . . . and Young* (New York:

HarperCollins, 1992). The book was, of course, the subject of the 2002 feature film *We Were Soldiers*. Mel Gibson starred as Moore.

4. 2nd Battalion, 7th Cavalry, Organizational History, 1966, RG 472, Box 205, Folder 1; 2nd Battalion, 7th Cavalry, AAR, January 25 through February 16, 1966, RG 472, Records of the 3rd Military History Detachment, Box 1, Folder 1; 3rd Brigade, 1st Cavalry Division, AAR, Masher/White Wing, all at National Archives; Charles Kinney, *Borrowed Time: A Medic's View of the Vietnam War* (Victoria, Canada: Trafford, 2003), pp. 19–21; Kenneth Mertel, *Year of the Horse—Vietnam, 1st Air Cavalry in the Highlands* (New York: Bantam Books, 1990), pp. 241–42; Larry Gwin, *Baptism: A Vietnam Memoir* (New York: Ivy Books, 1999), pp. 185–89; Carland, *Stemming the Tide*, pp. 203–04; Maitland and McInerney, *Contagion of War*, p. 35; Tammy Bryant, message board post at www.virtualwall.org. Interestingly enough, although all the records speak of January 25 as an overcast, drizzly morning, General Moore told me that he remembers it as a sunny day.

5. 3rd Brigade, 1st Cavalry Division, AAR, Masher/White Wing, National Archives; 1st Cavalry Division, AAR, Operation Masher/White Wing, copy in author's possession; 1st Cavalry Division, Artillery, AAR, Donovan Library, Fort Benning, Columbus, Georgia; Kinney, *Borrowed Time*, p. 23; Moore interview; Moore and Galloway, *We Were Soldiers Once*, pp. 403–04.

6. 3rd Brigade, 1st Cavalry Division, AAR, Masher/White Wing; 2nd Battalion, 7th Cavalry, Organizational History, AAR, all at National Archives; 1st Cavalry Division, AAR; Fesmire, oral history, USAMHI; Al Hemingway, "'Graveyard' at LZ 4," *VFW Magazine*, January 2004; Prados, "Operation Masher"; Moore interview; Robert Mason, *Chickenhawk: A Shattering Personal Account of the Helicopter War in Vietnam* (New York: Penguin Books, 1984), pp. 266–68; Kinney, *Borrowed Time*, pp. 23–30, 42; Carland, *Stemming the Tide*, pp. 203–08; Maitland and McInerney, *Contagion of War*, pp. 36–40.

7. 2nd Battalion, 12th Cavalry, Organizational History, RG 472, Box 339, Folder 1; 1st Battalion, 7th Cavalry, Organizational History, RG 472, Box 194, Folder 2; 1st Battalion, 7th Cavalry, AAR, February 22, 1966; 1st Cavalry Division After Action Critique, March 9, 1966, both in Records of the 3rd Military History Detachment, Box 1, Folder 1; 2nd Battalion, 7th Cavalry, Organizational History and AAR; 3rd Brigade, 1st Cavalry Division, AAR, Masher/White Wing, all at National Archives; Fesmire, oral history, USAMHI; 1st Cavalry Division, AAR; 1st Cavalry Division Artillery, AAR, Donovan Library; Prados, "Operation Masher"; Moore interview; John Laurence, *The Cat from Hue: A Vietnam War Story* (New York: Public Affairs, 2002), p. 315; Kinney, *Borrowed Time*, pp. 29–33; Carland, *Stemming the Tide*, pp. 207–08; Maitland and McInerney, *Contagion of War*, pp. 42–46. Bruce Crandall eventually earned the Medal of Honor for his courageous actions in the Ia Drang

battle. His exploits at Luong Tho are not as well known, but they earned him a well-deserved Distinguished Flying Cross.

8.   1st Cavalry Division, AAR; Kinnard, oral history, USAMHI; Carland, *Stemming the Tide*, p. 203; Maitland and McInerney, *Contagion of War*, p. 46; Westmoreland, *A Soldier Reports*, p. 164; Prados, "Operation Masher." In discussing the name change many years later, Kinnard had an interesting Freudian slip. He mistakenly said that he renamed the operation "White Feather," which is a common term for surrender. Perhaps, in his mind, the presidential order to change the name equated to a surrender of sorts.

9.   2nd Battalion, 12th Cavalry, Organizational History; 3rd Brigade, 1st Cavalry Division, AAR, Masher/White Wing; 2nd Brigade, 1st Cavalry Division, AAR, Masher/White Wing, RG 472, MAC-V J3 Evaluation and Analysis Division, Box 3, Folder 2, all at National Archives; 1st Cavalry Division, AAR; 1st Battalion, 12th Cavalry, Organizational History, 1966, Donovan Library; Moore interview; Swanson Hudson, "Deadly Fight in the Eagle's Claw," *Eyewitness to War*, 2002, p. 85; Edward Hymoff, *The First Air Cavalry Division in Vietnam* (New York: MW Lads Publishing Co., 1967), pp. 66–68; Mason, *Chickenhawk*, p. 292; Carland, *Stemming the Tide*, pp. 208–09; Maitland and McInerney, *Contagion of War*, pp. 40–41, 46; Hiner's account is at www.projectdelta.net. Oddly enough, the Special Forces after action report is missing from the National Archives.

10.   2nd Battalion, 7th Cavalry, Organizational History and AAR; 3rd Brigade, 1st Cavalry Division, AAR, Masher/White Wing, all at National Archives; 1st Cavalry Division, AAR; Fesmire, oral history, USAMHI; Moore interview; Captain Myron Diduryk, "Operations of Company B, 2nd Battalion, 7th Cavalry, 1st Cavalry Division (Airmobile), in a search-and-destroy mission on 15 February 1966 during Operation White Wing (Eagle's Claw) in Binh Dinh Province, Republic of Vietnam (Personal Experience of a Company Commander)," Career Officer Class No. 1, February 7, 1967, Donovan Library; Captain Myron Diduryk and Captain Anthony Hartle, "Momentum in the Attack," *Army*, May 1967, pp. 35–38; Carland, *Stemming the Tide*, pp. 208–10; Maitland and McInerney, *Contagion of War*, pp. 46–47; Mason, *Chickenhawk*, pp. 299–300. Captain Diduryk was killed in 1970, during a subsequent tour of duty in Vietnam.

11.   2nd Brigade, 1st Cavalry Division, AAR, Masher/White Wing, National Archives; 1st Cavalry Division, AAR; Captain Robert McMahon, "Operations of Company B, 2nd Battalion, 5th Cavalry, 1st Cavalry Division (Airmobile), in the Attack upon a Main Force Viet Cong Heavy Weapons Battalion in the Vicinity of Bong Son, South Vietnam, 16–17 February 1966 (Personal Experience of a Company Commander)"; Captain Hubert Fincher, "Operations of Company A, 2nd Battalion, 5th Cavalry, 1st Cavalry Division (Airmobile), in the Relief of Company B, 2nd Battalion, 5th

Cavalry, 1st Cavalry Division (Airmobile), in Vicinity of Bong-Son, South Vietnam, 16–17 February 1966," both at Donovan Library; Jack Danner, oral history, Jack Danner Collection, #6052, Veterans History Project (VHP), American Folklife Center (AFC), Library of Congress (LOC), Washington, D.C.; Carland, *Stemming the Tide*, pp. 211–12; Hymoff, *First Air Cavalry Division in Vietnam*, pp. 69–70. Danner was executive officer of A Company.

12. 1st Brigade, 1st Cavalry Division, AAR, Masher/White Wing, RG 472, MAC-V J3 Evaluation and Analysis Division, Box 1, Folder 1; 1st Battalion, 5th Cavalry, Unit Journal, February 20 through 23, 1966, RG 472, Box 139, Folder 8; Company A, 2nd Battalion, 8th Cavalry, AAR, February 25 through March 6, 1966, and February 18 through 25, 1966, both in RG 472, Box 258, Folder 2, all at National Archives; 1st Cavalry Division, AAR; "Honor and Courage: A Combat Chronicle by the Paratroopers of Alpha Company, 2nd Battalion, 8th Cavalry," at www.honorand courage.net; 1st Battalion, 12th Cavalry, Organizational History, Donovan Library; Hudson, "Deadly Fight in the Eagle's Claw," pp. 85–88; Jim Grayson, e-mail to author, circa 2007; Carland, *Stemming the Tide*, pp. 212–14. Regrettably, the official history of the People's Army in Vietnam (called NVA by the Americans), titled *Victory in Vietnam*, is next to worthless on Masher/White Wing. It contains only a few vague, propaganda-laced paragraphs.

13. 1st Cavalry Division Artillery, After Action Comments, March 3, 1966, RG 472, MAC-V J3 Evaluation and Analysis Division, Box 1, Folder 1; 1st Cavalry Division, After Action Critique, both at National Archives; 1st Cavalry Division Artillery, AAR, Donovan Library; 1st Cavalry Division, AAR; Robert Crosson, oral history, Vietnam Veterans Interviews, Box 1, Folder 9, USAMHI; Moore interview; Robert Graham, "Vietnam: An Infantryman's View of Our Failure," *Military Affairs*, July 1984, p. 135; Carland, *Stemming the Tide*, pp. 214–15; Laurence, *Cat from Hue*, pp. 342–52; Maitland and McInerney, *Contagion of War*, p. 48; Moore and Galloway, *We Were Soldiers Once*, p. 404. With regard to the number of fire missions and shells fired, there is a slight discrepancy between the division artillery after action report and the division after action report. I believe that the artillery report is the better source for this information, so I drew my numbers from it. ARVN forces and the Korean Marines claimed to have killed another 808 enemy soldiers.

Chapter 6

1. Lieutenant General Victor Krulak, "A Strategic Appraisal, Vietnam"; Krulak to General Wallace Greene, Commandant of the Marine Corps, no date, both in Box 1, Folder 6, Victor Krulak Papers; Lieutenant General Victor Krulak, Marine Corps oral history interview, June 1970, Box 3, Folder 22, Victory H. Krulak Papers; Gen-

eral William Westmoreland, oral history interview with Marine Corps Historical Center, April 4, 1983, all at U.S. Marine Corps History and Museums Division (USMCHMD), Gray Research Center (GRC), Quantico, VA; Victor Krulak, *First to Fight: An Inside View of the U.S. Marine Corps* (Annapolis, MD: Naval Institute Press, 1999), pp. 195–200.

2. Westmoreland, oral history, GRC; Lieutenant Colonel Raymond Damm, "The Combined Action Program: A Tool for the Future," *Marine Corps Gazette*, October 1998, p. 50; Captain Keith Kopets, "The Combined Action Program: Vietnam," *Small Wars Journal*, no date, pp. 1–3; Jim Donovan, "Combined Action Program: Marines' Alternative to Search and Destroy," *Vietnam*, August 2004, pp. 26–29 (Jim also sent me a rough draft copy of his article); Peter Brush, "Civic Action: The Marine Corps Experience in Vietnam, Part I," located at The Sixties Project Web site; Victor Krulak, obituary, *Wall Street Journal*, January 3–4, 2009, p. A5; Victor Krulak, *First to Fight*, pp. 195–200; William Westmoreland, *A Soldier Reports* (Garden City, NY: Doubleday and Co., 1976), pp. 144–46; 164–66; William Corson, *The Betrayal* (New York: W. W. Norton, 1968), p. 177; Gerald DeGroot, *A Noble Cause? America and the Vietnam War* (Essex, England: Longman, 2000), p. 156; Michael Peterson, *The Combined Action Platoons: The U.S. Marines' Other War in Vietnam* (New York: Praeger, 1989), p. 19. The conflict between Westy and the Marine commanders is sometimes portrayed as an interservice rift between the Army and Marines with the Army supposedly being exclusively wedded to conventional, big-unit war, with no interest in pacification. This is demonstrably untrue. From the earliest American intervention in Vietnam to the end of the war, the Army was heavily involved in pacification, primarily through Special Forces units, embedded advisors, mobile advisory teams, and civic action teams. In some instances, Army infantry battalions even carried out combined unit operations with the South Vietnamese Army. For more on the experiences of one unit in such operations, see John C. McManus, *The 7th Infantry Regiment: Combat in an Age of Terror* (New York: Forge, 2008), pp. 115–16. The difference between the Marines and the Army is that the Corps placed a higher priority on pacification and earmarked more of its regular infantrymen for that purpose.

3. "The Marine Combined Action Program, Vietnam," Record Group (RG) 127, U.S. Marine Corps History and Museums Division, Records of Units, Fleet Marine Force, Pacific (FMFPAC), Box 146, Folder 6, National Archives, College Park, MD; Robert Klyman, "The Combined Action Program: An Alternative Not Taken," honors thesis, Department of History, University of Michigan, 1986, copy in author's possession; Sergeant Frank Beardsley, "Combined Action," *Leatherneck*, April 1966, pp. 20–24; Kopets, "Combined Action Program," p. 4; Lewis Walt, *Strange War, Strange Strategy: A General's Report on Vietnam* (New York: Funk & Wagnalls,

1970), pp. 105–07; Al Hemingway, *Our War Was Different: Marine Combined Action Platoons in Vietnam* (Annapolis, MD: Naval Institute Press, 1994), pp. 22–25; Jack Shulimson and Major Charles M. Johnson, *U.S. Marines in Vietnam: The Landing and the Buildup, 1965* (Washington, D.C.: U.S. Marine Corps History and Museums Division, 1978), pp. 133–38; Graham Cosmas and Lieutenant Colonel Terrence Murray, *U.S. Marines in Vietnam: Vietnamization and Redeployment, 1970–1971* (Washington, D.C.: U.S. Marine Corps History and Museums Division, 1986), p. 139; Peterson, *The Combined Action Platoons*, pp. 23–27. The combined action units were known, during their various stages of growth, by several names, including CAC (combined action company), JAC (joint action companies), CAG (combined action groups), and CUPP (Combined Unit Pacification Program). For the sake of clarity, I have chosen to refer to them as combined action platoons (CAPs). The complicated administrative history of the program is beyond the purview of this chapter. For more on that aspect of the CAPs, see all the sources listed above.

4.   "Marine Combined Action Program, Vietnam," National Archives; Lieutenant Colonel William Corson, "Marine Combined Action Program in Vietnam," Reference Branch Files, USMCHMD; Staff Sergeant Calvin Brown, oral histories, #707 and 1603, USMCHMD; Klyman, "An Alternative Not Taken"; David Sherman, "One Man's CAP," *Marine Corps Gazette*, February 1989, p. 58; Edward Palm, "Tiger Papa Three: A Memoir of the Combined Action Program, Part I," *Marine Corps Gazette*, January 1988, p. 37; John Akins, *Nam Au Go Go: Falling for the Vietnamese Goddess of War* (Port Jefferson, NY: The Vineyard Press, 2005), pp. 51–53; Thomas Flynn, *A Voice of Hope* (Baltimore, MD: American Literary Press, Inc., 1994), pp. 32–33; Jackson Estes, *A Field of Innocence* (Portland, OR: Breitenbush Books, 1987), p. 117; Barry Goodson, *CAP Mot: The Story of a Marine Special Forces Unit in Vietnam, 1968–1969* (Denton, TX: University of North Texas Press, 1997), p. 10; Corson, *The Betrayal*, pp. 183–84, 193–94; Hemingway, *Our War Was Different*, pp. 49–51, 105–07; Peterson, *The Combined Action Platoons*, pp. 31–44.

5.   FMFPAC, Operations Report, February 1967, copy in author's possession, courtesy of Annette Amerman; Corson, "Combined Action Program in Vietnam," Reference Branch Files; Gunnery Sergeant John Brockaway, oral history, #638; First Lieutenant Thomas Eagan, oral history, #707; Staff Sergeant Edward Evans, interview with Corporal Joseph Trainer and other CAP members at Thuy Phu village, #2341; Brown, oral history, #1603, all at USMCHMD; Klyman, "An Alternative Not Taken"; Major Gary Telfer, Lieutenant Colonel Lane Rogers, and V. Keith Fleming, Jr., *U.S. Marines in Vietnam: Fighting the North Vietnamese, 1967* (Washington, D.C.: U.S. Marine Corps History and Museums Division, 1984), pp. 188–92; Peterson, *Combined Action Platoons*, pp. 44–45; Hemingway, *Our War Was Different*, pp. 99, 120.

6. Brockaway, oral history, Thuy Phu village interview, USMCHMD; Jim Donovan, interview with the author, July 3, 2008; Hemingway, *Our War Was Different*, p. 99; Flynn, *Voice of Hope*, p. 54; Goodson, *CAP Mot*, p. 53.

7. "The Marine Combined Action Program," National Archives; Corson, "Combined Action Program, Vietnam," Reference Branch Files; Thuy Phu village interview, both at USMCHMD; Klyman, "An Alternative Not Taken"; Sherman, "One Man's CAP," pp. 60–61; Donovan interview; Peterson, *Combined Action Platoons*, pp. 44–50. Nearly every report and every study on the program speaks of the language gap as a serious, protracted issue. This point is so beyond dispute that I saw little need to cite them all.

8. Lieutenant General Victor Krulak to Lieutenant General Lew Walt, December 2, 1966, enclosure, comments from the troops, Box 1, Folder 15, Victor H. Krulak Papers, GRC; Eagan, oral history, USMCHMD; Captain Nick Grosz, oral history, Vietnam Company Command Oral History, Box 16, Folder 1, United States Army Military History Institute (USAMHI), Carlisle, PA (Grosz commanded a combined action company); Klyman, "An Alternative Not Taken"; Lieutenant Commander Lawrence Metcalf, "Corpsman Numbah One Bac Si!" *Marine Corps Gazette*, July 1970, pp. 12–13; Lawrence Metcalf, "The CAP Corpsman," *U.S. Navy Medicine*, December 1970, pp. 8–9; Sherman, "One Man's CAP," p. 60; Hemingway, *Our War Was Different*, pp. 122–35; Peterson, *The Combined Action Platoons*, pp. 116–18. Most scholars agree that the MEDCAPs were the most successful aspect of civic action. Too much of the other American civic action efforts amounted to giveaways that engendered suspicion among the Vietnamese and did little to further the goal of pacification. The Vietnamese did value and appreciate the medical treatment, though. Lieutenant Eck put this best when he remarked: "When you give people material things, you don't give them much. When you give them yourself, that's something." The CAP corpsmen gave generously of themselves.

9. "The Marine Combined Action Program," National Archives; Corson, "Combined Action Program, Vietnam," Reference Branch Files, USMCHMD; III Marine Amphibious Force, Presidential Unit Citation Recommendation, 1968, copy in author's possession, courtesy of Annette Amerman; Klyman, "An Alternative Not Taken"; Corson, *The Betrayal*, pp. 183–84; Telfer, Rogers, and Fleming, *U.S. Marines in Vietnam, 1967*, pp. 187–91. The best single source on the daily patrols, firefights, and general war of wits between the CAPs and the VC is Bing West, *The Village* (New York: Pocket Books, 2000). The book covers the activities of one CAP in Binh Nghia over the course of several years. As a young officer, West was a participant as well as an observer/chronicler of the team's actions. Despite being overrun twice, the Binh Nghia CAP succeeded in forging strong ties of kinship with the villagers.

Because West's fine book has been so heavily utilized by other CAP historians, I have chosen to rely upon other, lesser-known sources.

10. Eagan, oral history, USMCHMD; Edward Palm, "Tiger Papa Three: The Fire Next Time, Part Two," *Marine Corps Gazette*, February 1988, pp. 67–73; Palm, "Tiger Papa Three, Part One"; Donovan interview; Hemingway, *Our War Was Different*, pp. 35–37; Goodson, *CAP Mot*, pp. 222–31, 84–88.

11. FMFPAC, AAR, April 1967; 1st Combined Action Group, AAR, February 1969; III Marine Amphibious Force citation recommendation, all copies in author's possession, courtesy of Annette Amerman; Corson, "Combined Action Program, Vietnam," Reference Branch Files; "Interview with survivors of CAP 6, 3rd CAG," oral history, #3222, both at USMCHMD; Jack Shulimson, Lieutenant Colonel Leonard Blasiol, Charles Smith, and Captain David Dawson, *U.S. Marines in Vietnam: The Defining Year, 1968* (Washington, D.C.: U.S. Marine Corps History and Museums Division, 1997), pp. 620–22; Flynn, *A Voice of Hope*, pp. 68–73; Hemingway, *Our War Was Different*, pp. 59–60, 86–92; Peterson, *The Combined Action Platoons*, pp. 56–59; Goodson, *CAP Mot*, pp. 91–107.

12. Donovan, "Combined Action Program," pp. 31–32; Charles Smith, *U.S. Marines in Vietnam: High Mobility and Standdown, 1969* (Washington, D.C.: U.S. Marine Corps History and Museums Division, 1988), pp. 291–94; Cosmas and Murray, *Vietnamization and Redeployment, 1970–1971*, pp. 144–47; Hemingway, *Our War Was Different*, pp. 95–96, 166–69; Goodson, *CAP Mot*, p. 29; Peterson, *The Combined Action Platoons*, pp. 60–62.

13. "The Marine Combined Action Program," National Archives; FMFPAC Monthly Operations Reports and Command Chronologies, 1965–1967 (these reports are of such questionable veracity that they are still known as "Krulak's Fables"); III Marine Amphibious Force, Command Chronologies, 1965–1966, all copies in author's possession, courtesy of Annette Amerman; Major R. D. King, "Future of Combined Action," October 12, 1970; Corson, "Combined Action Program, Vietnam," both in Reference Branch Files, USMCHMD; T. P. Schwartz, "The Combined Action Program: A Different Perspective," *Marine Corps Gazette*, February 1999, pp. 64–68; Palm, "Tiger Papa Three: The Fire Next Time," p. 76; Sherman, "One Man's CAP," p. 62; Donovan, "Combined Action Program," pp. 31–32; Kopets, "The Combined Action Program," pp. 8–9; Donovan interview; Klyman, "An Alternative Not Taken"; James Trullinger, *Village at War: An Account of Revolution in Vietnam* (New York: Longman, 1980), pp. 115–32; Westmoreland, *A Soldier Reports*, p. 166; Cosmas and Murray, *Vietnamization and Redeployment, 1970–1971*, pp. 148–49; Walt, *Strange War, Strange Strategy*, p. 105; Hemingway, *Our War Was Different*, pp. 56, 83, 177–78; Peterson, *The Combined Action Platoons*, pp. 86–94. The North Vietnamese Army official history, *Victory in Vietnam*, is completely si-

lent on the combined action platoons. Given the propagandistic tone that is prevalent in much of the work, perhaps this absence of commentary on the CAPs is a
veiled recognition that they had some success.

Chapter 7

1. 4th Infantry Division, "Battle of Dak To," After Action Report (AAR), Record
    Group (RG) 472, Records of the 29th Military History Detachment, Box 200, Folder
    2; General William Westmoreland, National Press Club Press Conference, Novem-
    ber 21, 1967, RG 319, Records of the Office of the Chief of Military History, William
    C. Westmoreland Papers, Box 32, Folder 4; General William Westmoreland mes-
    sage to Admiral Ulysses Grant Sharp, November 22, 1967, RG 319, Records of the
    Office of the Chief of Military History, William C. Westmoreland Papers, Box 32,
    Folder 5; General William Westmoreland to Admiral Sharp, December 10, 1967,
    Records of the Office of the Chief of Military History, William C. Westmoreland
    Papers, Box 33, Folder 1, all at National Archives, College Park, MD; William West-
    moreland, *A Soldier Reports* (Garden City, NY: Doubleday & Company, Inc., 1976),
    pp. 236–38; Victor Krulak, *First to Fight: An Inside View of the U.S. Marine Corps*
    (Annapolis, MD: Naval Institute Press, 1999), p. 201; Ted Arthurs, command ser-
    geant major of the 4th Battalion, 503rd Parachute Infantry, claims in *Land with No
    Sun: A Year in Vietnam with the 173rd Airborne* (Mechanicsburg, PA: Stackpole
    Books, 2006) that the soldiers of his unit coined that unhappy moniker for Dak To;
    Robert Barr Smith, "A Lousy Place to Fight a War," *Vietnam*, October 2005, pp.
    28–30; Dale Andrade, "Why Westmoreland Was Right," *Vietnam*, April 2009, offers
    a spirited defense of the general and his attrition strategy. The official People's
    Army of Vietnam (NVA) history, *Victory in Vietnam: The Official History of the
    People's Army of Vietnam, 1954–1975* (Lawrence, KS: University Press of Kansas,
    2002), hardly mentions the 1967 Dak To battle. Some historians believe that the
    NVA lured the Americans to Dak To so that they would not be in place to oppose
    the massive Tet Offensive of 1968, which mainly focused on populated areas.
    The NVA history does not specifically confirm this, though.

2. 4th Infantry Division, AAR; 1st Brigade, 4th Infantry Division, December 9, 1967,
    AAR, Box 200, Folder 5; 5th Special Forces Group, November 6–December 3,
    1967, AAR, Box 200, Folder 6; 173rd Airborne Brigade, "The Battle of Dak
    To," AAR, Box 200, Folder 3, all in RG 472, Records of the 29th Military History
    Detachment; General William Peers, briefing to MAC-V commander's conference,
    December 3, 1967, RG 319, Records of the Office of the Chief of Military History,
    William C. Westmoreland Papers, Box 33, Folder 1, this and all previous sources at
    National Archives; William Peers, oral history, Box 1, Folder 1, William R. Peers

Papers, United States Army Military History Institute (USAMHI), Carlisle, PA; Barr, "A Lousy Place to Fight a War," p. 28; Shelby Stanton, *The Rise and Fall of an American Army: U.S. Ground Forces in Vietnam, 1965–1973* (New York: Ballantine Books, 2003), pp. 136–38, 166–69; Edward Murphy, *Dak To: America's Sky Soldiers in South Vietnam's Central Highlands* (New York: Ballantine Books, 2007), pp. 56–81, 133–34; *Victory in Vietnam*, p. 212.

3.   4th Infantry Division, AAR; 1st Brigade, 4th Infantry Division, AAR; Major John Ramsay, G3 Air, AAR, Box 200, Folder 6; 4th Infantry Division, Artillery, AAR, Box 200, Folder 3; General Order #404, PFC Clinton Bacon, Army Commendation Medal Citation; General Order #361, Spec-4 Cecil Millspaugh, Bronze Star Medal Citation, Box 205, Folder 6, all in RG 472, Records of the 29th Military History Detachment; 1st Brigade, 4th Infantry Division, Presidential Unit Citation (PUC), RG 472, U.S. Army Vietnam, Adjutant General, Awards Branch, Box 9, Folder 4, this and all previous sources at National Archives; Bill Vigil, interview with the author, April 7, 2008; Steve Edmunds, unpublished memoir, pp. 1–2, copy in author's possession, courtesy of Mr. Edmunds; www.ivydragoons.org Web site.

4.   4th Infantry Division, AAR; 1st Brigade, 4th Infantry Division, AAR; General Order #4563, PFC Nathaniel Thompson, Bronze Star with "V" for Valor Medal Citation; General Order #4561, PFC William Muir, Bronze Star with "V" for Valor Medal Citation; General Order #320, Spec-4 John Kind, Bronze Star with "V" for Valor Medal Citation; General Order #94, PFC John Trahan, Bronze Star with "V" for Valor Medal Citation, all citations in RG 472, Box 205, Folder 6, Records of the 29th Military History Detachment; 1st Brigade, 4th Division, PUC, RG 472, U.S. Army Vietnam, Adjutant General, Awards Branch, Box 9, Folder 4, this and all previous sources at National Archives; Bob Walkowiak, e-mail to the author, March 25, 2008; Robert Babcock, ed., *War Stories: Utah Beach to Pleiku* (Marietta, GA: Deeds Publishing, 2001), pp. 566–71.

5.   4th Infantry Division, AAR; 1st Brigade, 4th Infantry Division, AAR; G3 Air, AAR; 4th Infantry Division, Artillery, AAR; 4th Aviation Battalion, Box 200, Folder 3; 52nd Combat Aviation Battalion, AAR, Box 200, Folder 3; 4th Infantry Division, Outline and Statistical Summary, Dak To Operation, Box 200, Folder 4; General Order #4502, Captain John Falcone, Silver Star Medal Citation; General Order #370, Lieutenant William Gauff, Bronze Star with "V" for Valor Medal Citation; General Order #4285, Staff Sergeant Raymond Ortiz, Silver Star Medal Citation; General Order #1187, Captain John Mirus, Silver Star Medal Citation; General Order #148, Spec-4 Stephen Edmunds, Bronze Star with "V" for Valor Medal Citation, Box 205, Folder 6, all in RG 472, Records of the 29th Military History Detachment; 1st Brigade, 4th Infantry Division, PUC, all at National Archives; Walkowiak e-mail; Steve Edmunds, unpublished memoir, pp. 1–3; Larry Skogler, interview

with the author, April 18, 2008; Babcock, *War Stories*, pp. 571–77; www.ivydra goons.org; www.virtualwall.org, John Falcone entry. Lieutenant Colonel Belknap was killed in a helicopter accident a couple weeks after the Battle of Hill 724. Several Ivy Dragoons told me that the crash destroyed many of the battle records, making 724 somewhat anonymous in the history of the Dak To campaign. I hope that my account has redressed that anonymity somewhat.

6.   173rd Airborne Brigade, Dak To, AAR, RG 472, Records of the 29th Military History Detachment, Box 200, Folder 3; 173rd Airborne Brigade, Presidential Unit Citation, Dak To, RG 472, Adjutant General Award's Branch, Box 5, Folder 9; 1st Battalion, 503rd Parachute Infantry Regiment, Operation MacArthur, AAR, RG 472, Box 1101, Folder 1, all at National Archives; Thomas McElwain, interview with the author, March 2, 2008; Ken Lambertson, interview with the author, April 9, 2008; David Watson, interview with the author, January 25, 2008; Terrence Maitland and Peter McInerney, *The Vietnam Experience: A Contagion of War* (Boston: Boston Publishing Company, 1983), pp. 170–71; Arthurs, *Land with No Sun*, p. 159; Murphy, *Dak To*, pp. 56–81, 174–84. Every Task Force Black veteran with whom I spoke was effusive in their praise for McElwain.

7.   173rd Airborne Brigade, Dak To, AAR; PUC, National Archives; Jerry Cecil, interview with the author, January 10, 2008; Ken Cox, interview with the author, April 21, 2008; McElwain interview; Jerry Cecil, e-mail to the author, February 16, 2009; Rick Atkinson, *The Long Gray Line: The American Journey of West Point's Class of 1966* (New York: Owl Books, 1989), p. 241; Murphy, *Dak To*, pp. 184–88; Maitland and McInerney, *Contagion of War*, pp. 170–71.

8.   173rd Airborne Brigade, Dak To, AAR; PUC, National Archives; McElwain, Cecil, and Cox interviews; Murphy, *Dak To*, pp. 187–89; Maitland and McInerney, *Contagion of War*, pp. 170–71. The critique on the strategic implications of the defensive tactics is purely my interpretation. McElwain advanced no such opinions.

9.   173rd Airborne Brigade, Dak To, AAR; PUC; 1st Battalion, 503rd Parachute Infantry Regiment, Operation MacArthur, AAR, all at National Archives; Ed Kelley, interview with the author, April 4, 2008; Jerry Curry, interview with the author, April 15, 2008; McElwain, Lambertson, Watson interviews; Murphy, *Dak To*, pp. 190–91; Maitland and McInerney, *Contagion of War*, pp. 171–72. Kelley told me that he has never forgiven himself for bypassing the machine gun and, as of 2008, he still felt enormous guilt about it.

10. John Barnes, Medal of Honor citation material, RG 472, Medal of Honor Awards, Case Files, Box 2, Folder 11; 173rd Airborne Brigade, Dak To, AAR; PUC, all at National Archives; McElwain, Cecil, Cox interviews; Murphy, *Dak To*, pp. 193–94. Cecil received the Distinguished Service Cross for his actions.

11. Barnes, Medal of Honor citation material; 173rd Airborne Brigade, Dak To, AAR; PUC, all at National Archives; Kelley, Curry, McElwain, Lambertson, Cox, Watson interviews; Murphy, *Dak To*, p. 193. To make sure that the vaporized men would not be listed as missing in action, Curry later signed a sworn statement attesting to the fact that he had seen them die. The after action reports claim that Hardy was hit twice in the chest, rather than three times in various places, as Watson recalled. Because Watson was so close to the captain when he was hit, I have relied on his account.

12. 173rd Airborne Brigade, Dak To, AAR; PUC; sworn statements of Lieutenant George Brown, Sergeant Robert Lampkin, Spec-4 James Townsend, and Spec-4 Robert Ferry, located within Barnes Medal of Honor citation material, all at National Archives; Jim Stanzak, interview with the author, January 28, 2008; Lambertson, Curry, Watson, Kelley interviews; Maitland and McInerney, *Contagion of War*, pp. 171–73. The grenade that killed Barnes was a Chinese "Chicom" pineapple grenade. By this point in the battle, though, the NVA were also using American grenades. They had captured them when helicopter crews attempted to resupply hard-pressed Task Force Black but, under heavy fire, dropped their loads outside the perimeter, in terrain controlled by the enemy. The Task Force Black survivors have nothing but deep respect for the bravery of the aviators that day, especially Warrant Officer Gary Bass (code-named Flower Power), who routinely risked his life to help the grunts.

13. 173rd Airborne Brigade, Dak To, AAR; PUC; 1st Battalion, 503rd Parachute Infantry Regiment, Operation MacArthur, AAR, all at National Archives; Chuck Clutter, interview with the author, January 15, 2008; Jacques "Jack" deRemer, interview with the author, February 8, 2008; McElwain, Kelley, Curry interviews; Murphy, *Dak To*, pp. 191–93. Every Task Force Black survivor with whom I spoke expressed considerable dislike for Schumacher. In my interview with McElwain, he was quite forthright in describing his disdain for the battalion commander. He also told me that he did not have a very high opinion of Captain Jesmer, whom he thought of as overly cautious and a bit disingenuous. McElwain, and some of his men, resented Task Force Blue's inability to provide any help on November 11. From the Task Force Black point of view, Jesmer's unit was only dealing with moderate sniper fire and should have put forth a much more aggressive effort to relieve Task Force Black. Some of the men even told me that, a couple weeks after the battle, a grieving McElwain picked a fight with Jesmer and beat him up at the officer's club.

14. 173rd Airborne Brigade, Dak To, AAR; PUC, National Archives; Mike Tanner, interview with the author, April 18, 2008; Mike Tanner, unpublished memoir, pp. 67–68, 168, copy in author's possession, courtesy of Mr. Tanner; Bill Connolly, interview with the author, July 2, 2008; Lynne Morse, interview with the author, June

17, 2008; McElwain, deRemer interviews; Murphy, *Dak To*, pp. 200–204; Maitland and McInerney, *Contagion of War*, pp. 173–75. Task Force Black actually lost at least twenty-two killed because the two missing men were the machine gunners whom Staff Sergeant Curry saw disintegrated by a rocket. Apparently two more men were missing as well and many of the survivors were tormented by guilt for years because they thought the missing men might have become POWs. These two men were later confirmed as killed, though. The artillery support on the evening of November 11 disfigured some of the Task Force Black bodies that were lying throughout the battle area. Several of the men said that Captain Hardy's body was headless when they recovered it the next day. Ivan Pierce, the forward personnel officer, later confirmed this. His job was to process and account for all casualties. He personally saw Hardy's remains and wrote about this in his memoir, *An Infantry Lieutenant's Vietnam* (El Dorado Springs, MO: Capsarge Publishing, 2004), pp. 78–79.

15. 173rd Airborne Brigade, Dak To, AAR; PUC, National Archives; McElwain, Kelley, Stanzak, Watson, Curry, Cecil, deRemer, Lambertson, Clutter interviews; Murphy, *Dak To*, pp. 204–06; Maitland and McInerney, *Contagion of War*, p. 174. In the weeks following the battle, McElwain quarreled again with Schumacher when the colonel tried to turn down PFC Barnes's Medal of Honor citation because "we don't decorate people who commit suicide." Fortunately, McElwain did not back down in the face of such disrespectful idiocy and the young soldier received the medal he so richly deserved. McElwain later told me: "I'm kind of surprised that he didn't relieve me."

16. 2nd Battalion, 503rd Parachute Infantry Regiment, Operation MacArthur, AAR, RG 472, Box 1125, Folder 1; Carlos Lozada, Medal of Honor material, RG 472, Medal of Honor Awards, Box 14, Folder 3; 5th Special Forces Group, Dak To, AAR; 173rd Airborne Brigade, Dak To, AAR; PUC, all at National Archives; Leonard B. Scott, "The Battle for Hill 875, Dak To, Vietnam 1967," paper prepared for Army War College, USAMHI; *Combat Zone: Hill 875, Vietnam*, Military Channel documentary, 2007; Murphy, *Dak To*, pp. 248–58; Maitland and McInerney, *Contagion of War*, pp. 179–80. Typical of many battalion commanders in Vietnam, Steverson was in a helicopter above the action and thus did not have much feel for what was happening on the ground.

17. 2nd Battalion, 503rd Parachute Infantry Regiment, AAR; sworn statements of Spec-4 James Kelley, PFC Anthony Romano, and First Lieutenant Joseph Sheridan, in Carlos Lozada Medal of Honor material; 173rd Airborne Brigade, Dak To, AAR; PUC, all at National Archives; *Combat Zone: Hill 875*; John Steer, "True Valor at Hill 875," *Vietnam*, June 1990, pp. 42–43; Murphy, *Dak To*, pp. 261–64; Maitland and McInerney, *Contagion of War*, p. 180. Lozada left behind a young wife and baby girl.

18. 2nd Battalion, 503rd Parachute Infantry Regiment, AAR; 173rd Airborne Brigade, Dak To, AAR; PUC; sworn statements of First Lieutenant Bryan McDonough, Staff

Sergeant John Gentry, Sergeant Paul Ramirez, Sergeant Jimmy Stacey, and Lieutenant Colonel John Hulme, RG 472, Medal of Honor Awards, Box 23, Folder 18, all at National Archives; Scott, "Battle for Hill 875," USAMHI; *Combat Zone: Hill 875*; Kelley interview; Murphy, *Dak To*, pp. 266–67, 269, 274–75. Scott claims that eleven out of thirteen of the 2nd Battalion medics were killed and the other two wounded. There is no way to be sure when the eleven were killed.

19. 2nd Battalion, 503rd Parachute Infantry Regiment, AAR; 173rd Airborne Brigade, Dak To, AAR; PUC; 4th Infantry Division, G3 Air, AAR, all at National Archives; Scott, "Battle for Hill 875," USAMHI; *Combat Zone: Hill 875*; Clarence Johnson, interview with the author, February 1, 2008; Steer, "True Valor at Hill 875," pp. 43–44; Lawrence Okendo, *Sky Soldier: Battles of Dak To* (self-published, 1988), pp. 107–08; Atkinson, *Long Gray Line*, pp. 248–50; Murphy, *Dak To*, pp. 272–82; Maitland and McInerney, *Contagion of War*, pp. 180–81. As of this writing, the identity of the pilot and plane that made the tragic mistake at Hill 875 is still not definite. 2nd Battalion records claim that F-100 Super Sabres and A-1Es provided the close air support that day, indicating that the Air Force was responsible. Other accounts claim that the plane was a Marine jet. Because there is still no certainty over this, I felt that my account should reflect that. In the summer of 2008, while researching the friendly fire bombing at the National Archives, I met Joe Nigro, a Vietnam veteran and retired police officer who is also investigating the incident, but without definitive information. For the sake of closure for the veterans, he is hoping to find the elusive answers.

20. 2nd Battalion, 503rd Parachute Infantry Regiment, AAR; 173rd Airborne Brigade, Dak To, AAR; PUC, all at National Archives; Captain Ron Leonard, oral history, Vietnam Company Command Oral History, Box 21, Folder 8 (Leonard commanded Bravo Company); Scott, "Battle for Hill 875," both at USAMHI; *Combat Zone: Hill 875*; 4th Battalion, 503rd Parachute Infantry Regiment, Battle of Dak To, Hill 875, AAR, copy in author's possession; Johnson interview; Rocky Stone, e-mails to author, January 8 and 10, 2008; Murphy, *Dak To*, pp. 277–94.

21. 173rd Airborne Brigade, Dak To, AAR; PUC, National Archives; 4th Battalion, 503rd Parachute Infantry Regiment, Hill 875, AAR; Scott, "Battle for Hill 875," USAMHI; Connolly, Morse interviews; Stone, e-mails to author, January 8 and 10, 2008; Murphy, *Dak To*, pp. 298–03; Maitland and McInerney, *Contagion of War*, p. 182.

22. 4th Infantry Division, AAR; 173rd Airborne Brigade, Dak To, AAR; PUC, all at National Archives; Scott, "Battle for Hill 875"; Leonard, Peers, oral histories, all at USAMHI; 4th Battalion, 503rd Parachute Infantry Regiment, Hill 875, AAR; Connolly, Morse, Tanner interviews; Tanner, unpublished memoir, pp. 75–77; Stone, e-mails to author, January 8, 10, and 12, 2008; Murphy, *Dak To*, pp. 304–11; Maitland and McInerney, *Contagion of War*, p. 182.

23. 4th Infantry Division, AAR; 173rd Airborne Brigade, Dak To, AAR; PUC, all at National Archives; Scott, "Battle for Hill 875"; Leonard, oral history, both at USAMHI; 4th Battalion, 503rd Parachute Infantry Regiment, Hill 875, AAR; George Wilkins, interview with the author, March 10, 2008; Larry Cousins, interview with the author, February 26, 2008; Hal Birch to the author, March 14 and May 4, 2008 (Birch was the commander of 1st Battalion, 12th Infantry); Connolly, Tanner interviews; Tanner, unpublished memoir, pp. 83–87; Stone, e-mails to author, January 10 and 12, 2008; Al Undiemi, e-mail to author, January 11, 2008; "Dak To: The Battle for Hill 875, 1st Battalion, 12th Infantry Regiment, 4th Infantry Division," after action report and firsthand accounts compiled by Roger Hill, copy in author's possession, courtesy of Mr. Hill; Murphy, *Dak To*, pp. 315–20; Maitland and McInerney, *Contagion of War*, pp. 182–83.

24. Public Statements of General William Westmoreland, RG 472, Box 42, Folder 1; General William Westmoreland, National Press Club, Q&A, November 21, 1967, Box 32, Folder 4, both in Records of the Office of the Chief of Military History, William Westmoreland Papers; 4th Infantry Division, AAR; G3 Air, AAR; Division Artillery, AAR; Peers Briefing; Outline and Statistical Summary; 173rd Airborne Brigade, Dak To, AAR; PUC, all at National Archives; Scott, "Battle for Hill 875"; Leonard, Peers, oral histories, all at USAMHI; 4th Battalion, 503rd Parachute Infantry Regiment, Hill 875, AAR; Bill Ballard, interview with the author, January 22, 2008; Tanner, Morse, Connolly, Wilkins, Cousins interviews; Tanner, unpublished memoir, pp. 88–89; Dennis Lewallen, e-mail to author, January 9, 2008; Hill, "Dak To: Battle for Hill 875"; Birch to author, May 4, 2008; Stone, e-mails to author, January 8, 10, and 12, 2008; Undiemi, e-mail to author, January 11, 2008; Major George P. Long, S3, 1st Battalion, 12th Infantry, "Battle for Dak To," pp. 41–43, in Lieutenant Colonel Albert Garland, *A Distant Challenge: The U.S. Infantryman in Vietnam* (New York: Jove Books, 1983); Murphy, *Dak To*, pp. 321–32; Westmoreland, *A Soldier Reports*, pp. 238–39; Maitland and McInerney, *Contagion of War*, pp. 182–83. Rocky Stone was one of the men who adamantly opposed the turkey dinner as an insult to the memory of dead comrades. For the next forty years, he had trouble even eating turkey, much less sitting down to Thanksgiving dinner with his family. After the passage of several decades, he could finally bring himself to enjoy a Thanksgiving meal with the family, but he insisted that they eat ham.

Chapter 8

1. United States General Accounting Office, "Report to the Ranking Minority Member, Committee on Commerce, House of Representatives: Operation Desert Storm, Evaluation of the Air Campaign," pp. 19–41 (June 1997); Lieutenant Colonel Daniel

Bolger, "What Happened at Khafji: Learning the Wrong Lesson," paper prepared for the Army War College, United States Army Military History Institute (USAMHI), Carlisle, PA; Rick Atkinson, *Crusade: The Untold Story of the Persian Gulf War* (Boston: Houghton Mifflin, 1993), pp. 227–28; Alex Vernon, *Most Succinctly Bred* (Kent, OH: Kent State University Press, 2006), p. 44; Adrian Lewis, *The American Culture of War: The History of U.S. Military Forces from World War II Through Operation Iraqi Freedom* (New York: Routledge, 2007), pp. 367–74; Stephen Bourque, *Jayhawk! The VII Corps in the Persian Gulf War* (Washington, D.C.: Department of the Army, 2002), p. 455; Richard Hallion, *Storm over Iraq: Air Power and the Gulf War* (Washington, D.C.: Smithsonian Institution Press, 1992), p. 1. For a reasonably balanced, albeit slightly air-centric look at air power in the war, see Lieutenant Colonel Jerome Martin, "Victory from Above: Air Power Theory and the Conduct of Operations Desert Shield and Desert Storm." As of this writing, Bolger is a two-star general in command of the 1st Cavalry Division.

2.   Robert Scales, *Certain Victory: The U.S. Army in the Gulf War* (Washington, D.C.: Office of the Chief of Staff, United States Army, 1993), pp. 15–36; William Hartzog, *American Military Heritage* (Washington, D.C.: Center of Military History, 2001), pp. 220–24; Frank Shubert and Theresa Krauss, general eds., *The Whirlwind War: The United States Army in Operations Desert Shield and Desert Storm* (Washington, D.C.: Center of Military History, 2001), pp. 208–15; Allan Millett, *Semper Fidelis: The History of the United States Marine Corps* (New York: Free Press, 1991), pp. 644–52. For a close look at what the transformation to an all-volunteer force was like in one mechanized infantry unit, see my own *The 7th Infantry Regiment: Combat in an Age of Terror, the Korean War Through the Present* (New York: Forge, 2008), pp. 170–74.

3.   U.S. Army Field Manual 3-21.71, "Mechanized Infantry Platoon and Squad (Bradley), available on www.globalsecurity.org; Kurt Dabb, rifleman, Alpha 2-7 Infantry, Desert Storm, interview with the author, June 13, 2001; Rick Averna, commander, Charlie 2-7 Infantry, Desert Storm, interview with the author, June 25, 2001; Bradley Fighting Vehicle, personal knowledge; Daniel Bolger, *Death Ground: Today's American Infantry in Battle* (Novato, CA: Presidio Press, 1999), pp. 126–29.

4.   Colonel Michael Krause, Ph.D., "The Battle of 73 Easting, 26 February 1991"; 2nd Armored Cavalry Regiment, After Action Report (AAR), Gulf War Collection, Box 1, Folder 5, both at USAMHI; Richard Bohannon, "Dragon's Roar: 1–37 Armor in the Battle of 73 Easting," *Armor*, May–June 1992, pp. 11–17; Daniel Davis, "2nd Armored Cavalry Regiment at the Battle of 73 Easting," *Field Artillery*, April 1992, pp. 48–53; Vince Crowley, "Ghost Troop's Battle at 73 Easting," *Armor*, May–June 1991, pp. 7–12; Douglas Macgregor, *Warrior's Rage: The Great Tank Battle of 73*

Easting (Annapolis, MD: Naval Institute Press, 2009), pp. 139–81. Macgregor was S3 of Cougar Squadron, the parent unit for both Eagle and Ghost Troops; Alberto Bin, Richard Hill, and Archer Jones, *Desert Storm: A Forgotten War* (Westport, CT: Praeger, 1998), pp. 193–99; Thomas Houlahan, *Gulf War: The Complete History* (New London, NH: Schrenker Military Publishing, 1999), pp. 325–32; Atkinson, *Crusade!*, pp. 441–48; Scales, *Certain Victory*, pp. 1–5; Bourque, *Jayhawk!*, pp. 325–31. McMaster holds a Ph.D. in history from the University of North Carolina and is a leading scholar on the American war in Vietnam. As of this writing, he is a brigadier general with a distinguished record of combat command, not just in the Gulf War but in the Iraq War as well.

5. Father (Captain) David Kenehan, personal diary, February 26–27, 1991, Box 1, Folder 1, David Kenehan Papers; Lieutenant Colonel James Hillman, "Task Force 1-41 Infantry: Fratricide Experience in Southwest Asia," Army War College Paper; "1st Brigade, 1st Infantry Division Desert Shield/Desert Storm History," all at USAMHI; Captain Douglas Robbins, "Operation Desert Storm: Battle of Norfolk, Scout Platoon, Task Force 5-16, 1ID"; First Lieutenant Donald Murray, "Desert Storm Monograph"; Captain James Petro, "Operations of the 5th Battalion, 16th Infantry Regiment (1st Infantry Division) During Breaching Operations of the Iraqi Main Defenses, 24–28 February 1991," all at Donovan Library, Fort Benning, Columbus, Georgia; John S. Brown, "Desert Reckoning: Historical Continuities and the Battle for Norfolk, 1991," U.S. Naval War College, Newport, RI; Colonel Lon Maggart, "A Leap of Faith," *Armor*, January–February 1992, pp. 24–32; Steve Vogel, "'Fast and Hard': The Big Red One's Race Through Iraq," *Army Times*, March 25, 1991, pp. 2, 13; "Hell Night: For the Second Armored Division It Was No Clean War," *Army Times*, October 7, 1991, pp. 8, 14–18, 24, 69; Scott Rutter, commander, Charlie 2-16 Infantry, Desert Storm, interview with the author, February 10, 2008; Houlahan, *Gulf War*, pp. 333–54; Scales, *Certain Victory*, pp. 276–84; Bourque, *Jayhawk!*, pp. 331–37. Houlahan's study is particularly strong on the fratricide incidents. Rutter was not in the Norfolk battle, but his perspective as an infantry company commander in the same division enhanced my understanding of the battle.

6. Captain Daniel Stempniak, "The Battle of the Al Mutlaa Police Post, 26 February, 1991," Donovan Library, copy in author's possession, courtesy of Ms. Genoa Stanford; J. Paul Scicchitano, "Eye of the Tiger," *Army Times*, June 10, 1991, pp. 18, 61; Stephen Bourque and John Burdan, "A Nervous Night on the Basrah Road," *Military History Quarterly*, Autumn 1999, pp. 88–97; Al Santoli, ed., *Leading the Way: How Vietnam Veterans Rebuilt the U.S. Military, an Oral History* (New York: Ballantine Books, 1993), pp. 337–39; Richard Swain, *"Lucky War": Third Army in Desert Storm* (Fort Leavenworth, KS: U.S. Army Command and General Staff College Press, 1997), p. 265; Bolger, *Death Ground*, pp. 118–52.

7. Lieutenant Colonel John Garrett, CO, and Major Craig Huddleston, XO, interview with Lieutenant Colonel Charles Cureton, March 5, 1991, Box 170, Folder 3; Lieutenant Colonel Timothy Hannigan, CO, and Major Brad Washabaugh, S3, interview with Lieutenant Colonel Charles Cureton, March 5, 1991, Box 170, Folder 4; Task Force Ripper, group interview with Lieutenant Colonel Charles Cureton, March 11, 1991, Box 165, Folder 7; Task Force Papa Bear, combat engineers, interview with Lieutenant Colonel Charles Cureton, no date, Box 165, Folder 15, all at oral history collection, U.S. Marine Corps History and Museums Division, Quantico, VA; John Admire, "The 3rd Marines in Desert Storm," *Marine Corps Gazette*, September 1991, pp. 69–71; Major General Michael Myatt, "Close Air Support and Fire Support in Desert Shield and Desert Storm," *Marine Corps Gazette*, May 1998, pp. 72–73; Staff Sergeant Lee Tibbetts, "Squad Leader Awarded Medal for Gallantry," *Marines*, March 1992, pp. 23–24; Otto Kreisher, "Marines' Minefield Assault," *Military History Quarterly*, Summer 2002, pp. 6–15; Otto Lehrack, ed., *America's Battalion: Marines in the First Gulf War* (Tuscaloosa, AL: The University of Alabama Press, 2005), pp. 168–95; Bin et al., *Desert Storm*, pp. 159, 165–71; Santoli, *Leading the Way*, pp. 322–26.

8. Lieutenant Colonel Frank Hancock, personal narrative, Frank Hancock Papers, Box 1, Folder 2; Lieutenant Colonel Frank Hancock, "North to the Euphrates: Part One, the Taking of Cobra," Army War College Paper; Colonel Tom Hill, 1st Brigade, 101st Air Assault Division AAR, Gulf War Collection, Box 1, Folder 6, all at USAMHI; Captain Mark Esper, "The Screaming Eagles of Desert Storm," Donovan Library; Sean Naylor, "Flight of Eagles: The 101st Airborne Division's Raids into Iraq," *Army Times*, July 22, 1991, p. 14; Lieutenant General Edward Flanagan, *Lightning: The 101st in the Gulf War* (Washington, D.C.: Brassey's, 1994), pp. 165–201; Thomas Taylor, *Lightning in the Storm: The 101st Air Assault Division in the Gulf War* (New York: Hippocrene Books, 1994), pp. 305–79; Houlahan, *Gulf War*, pp. 241–51; Santoli, *Leading the Way*, pp. 332–33; Bolger, *Death Ground*, pp. 75–97.

9. Bolger, "What Happened at Khafji," Army War College Paper, USAMHI; Lewis, *The American Culture of War*, pp. 374, 386–91. Modern insurgent groups have often employed jungles and mountains quite effectively. Usually, they only come to power, though, when they seize control of cities or waterways. Fidel Castro's Cuban revolutionary movement and the Viet Cong are classic examples of this.

Chapter 9

1. Owen West, "Dispatches from Fallujah," July 30, 2004, www.slate.com. Most of this passage is derived from a mixture of common knowledge and my own opinion. The Cheney quote is at www.wikiquote.com. The best single book on the planning and

initial execution of the Iraq War is Tom Ricks's *Fiasco: The American Military Adventure in Iraq* (New York: Penguin Press, 2006). The Schwarzkopf quote is from page 83 of that book.

2. Gunnery Sergeant Mark Oliva, "Shutting Down Fallujah," *Leatherneck*, June 2004, p. 18; Jonathan Keiler, "Who Won the Battle of Fallujah?" *Naval Institute Proceedings*, January 2005, pp. 1–2; Bing West, *No True Glory: A Frontline Account of the Battle for Fallujah* (New York: Bantam Books, 2005), pp. 26–63; David Danelo, *Blood Stripes: The Grunt's View of the War in Iraq* (Mechanicsburg, PA: Stackpole Books, 2006), pp. 88–90; Robert Kaplan, *Imperial Grunts* (New York: Vintage, 2005), pp. 345–48. Like most religions, Islam also forbids the mutilation of bodies. At the prodding of the Americans, Fallujah's sheiks, imams, and elders publicly condemned the mutilations, but they refused to denounce the terrorists in their midst. This reflected popular opinion in Fallujah, which was quite anti-American and, at this point, supportive of the insurgents.

3. Eric Schmitt, "Marines Battle Guerrillas in Streets of Fallujah," *New York Times*, April 9, 2004; Sergeants Earl Catagnus, Jr. & Brad Edison & Lance Corporals James Keeling & David Moon, "Infantry Squad Tactics: Some of the Lessons Learned During MOUT in the Battle for Fallujah," *Marine Corps Gazette*, September 2005, pp. 80–82; Ross Simpson, "Fallujah: A Four-Letter Word," *Leatherneck*, February 2005, pp. 16–19; Captain Michael Skaggs, "Tank-Infantry Integration," *Marine Corps Gazette*, June 2005, pp. 41–42; Patrick Finnigan, interview with the author, February 23, 2008; West, *No True Glory*, pp. 63–68; Kaplan, *Imperial Grunts*, pp. 360–66. Several years after being wounded in Fallujah, Finnigan was still finding fragments in his body. I told him that I knew many World War II veterans who still had pieces in their bodies sixty years after the fact.

4. Bing West, "The Road to Haditha," *Atlantic Monthly*, October 2006; Christine Hauser, "War Reports from Civilians Stir up Iraqis against U.S.," *New York Times*, April 14, 2004; Christine Hauser and Jeff Warzer, "Siege Defined on Stones Set in Haste in the Dirt," *New York Times*, April 28, 2004; Edward Wong, "Battle for Fallujah Rouses the Anger of Iraqis Weary of the U.S. Occupation," *New York Times*, April 22, 2004; John Burns, "U.S. Pummels Rebel Positions as Fierce Clash Shakes Fallujah," *New York Times*, April 28, 2004; Ilario Pantano with Malcolm McConnell, *Warlord: No Better Friend, No Worse Enemy* (New York: Threshold Editions, 2006), pp. 197–99; West, *No True Glory*, pp. 68–73, 90–93, 118–21.

5. Ross Simpson, "In the Crosshairs: USMC Snipers in Iraq," *Leatherneck*, June 2004, pp. 24, 27; Jeffrey Gettleman, "Marines in Fallujah Still Face and Return Relentless Fire," *New York Times*, April 14, 2004; Finnegan interview; Milo Afong, *Hogs in the Shadows: Combat Stories from Marine Snipers in Iraq* (New York: Berkley Caliber, 2007), pp. 98–112; West, *No True Glory*, pp. 172–77. For a good discussion of the

moral struggle inherent in sniping, see Dave Grossman, *On Killing: The Psychological Cost of Learning to Kill in War and Society* (Boston: Little, Brown, 1996), pp. 108–10, 254–55. For his effective sniping, Finnigan earned a Navy Commendation Medal with a Combat "V" for Valor.

6. Adnan Khan, "After the Siege," *McLean's*, May 17, 2004; Paul Quinn-Judge, "Life on the Front Lines," *Time*, May 10, 2004; Finnigan interview; Pantano, *Warlord*, pp. 199, 232; Kaplan, *Imperial Grunts*, pp. 368–69; Afong, *Hogs in the Shadows*, pp. 111–12; West, *No True Glory*, pp. 208–25. Bellon was a high school classmate and football teammate of mine at Chaminade College Preparatory in St. Louis.

7. Lieutenant Colonel Willard Buhl, interview with Captain Steven "Joe" Winslow, October 28, 2004, declassified oral history at U.S. Marine Corps History and Museums Division (USMCHMD), Quantico, VA; Lieutenant Colonel Dave Bellon to Dad, November 8, 2004, originally posted at www.thegreenzone.com, copy in author's possession; Gunnery Sergeant Matt Hevezi, "'Battle for Fallujah: They've Chosen a Path of Violence,'" *Leatherneck*, December 2005, pp. 40–42; Lieutenant General John Sattler and Lieutenant Colonel Daniel Wilson, "Operation Al Fajr: The Battle of Fallujah, Part II," *Marine Corps Gazette*, July 2005, pp. 12–14; Keiler, "Who Won the Battle of Fallujah?"; "The Battle for Fallujah," at www.talking proud.us; Donald Wright and Timothy Reese, *On Point II: Transition to the New Campaign, the United States Army in Operation Iraqi Freedom, May 2003–January 2005* (Fort Leavenworth, KS: Combat Studies Institute Press, 2008), pp. 345–51; West, *No True Glory*, pp. 227–32.

8. Major General Richard Natonski, interview with Lieutenant Colonel John Way, March 16, 2005; Colonel Craig Tucker, interview with Major Steven "Joe" Winslow, August 11, 2006; Lieutenant General John Sattler, interview with Lieutenant Colonel John Way, April 8, 2005; Buhl interview, all at USMCHMD; Keiler, "Who Won the Battle of Fallujah?"; "Battle for Fallujah," at www.talkingproud.us; Kendall Gott, ed., *Eyewitness to War, Volume I: The U.S. Army in Operation Al Fajr, an Oral History* (Fort Leavenworth, KS: Combat Studies Institute Press, 2007), pp. 4–8, 159; West, *No True Glory*, pp. 250–60. By the time of the Tucker interview, Winslow had been promoted to major.

9. Colonel Michael Shupp, interview with Lieutenant Colonel John Way, March 27, 2005; Sattler, Natonski, Tucker interviews, all at USMCHMD; Richard Oppel, Jr., "Early Target of Offensive Is a Hospital," *New York Times*, November 8, 2004; Keiler, "Who Won the Battle of Fallujah?"; Sattler and Wilson, "Operation Al Fajr," pp. 14–19; Matt Matthews, *Operation Al Fajr: A Study in Army and Marine Corps Joint Operations* (Fort Leavenworth, KS: Combat Studies Institute Press, 2006), pp. 13–36; David Bellavia with John Bruning, *House to House: An Epic Memoir of War* (New York: Free Press, 2007), pp. 47–48; Gott, ed., *Eyewitness to War, Volume I*, pp. 8–10; Wright and Reese,

On Point II, pp. 344–52; West, *No True Glory*, pp. 257–67. The Americans used several names for the Iraqi Army soldiers who fought with them at Fallujah: Iraqi Intervention Force, Iraqi National Guard, and Iraqi Armed Forces. For the sake of simplicity, I have chosen to call them the Iraqi Army.

10. Shupp interview, USMCHMD; Lieutenant Colonel Pete Newell, interview with the author, January 11, 2008; Task Force 2-2 Infantry, "Operation Phantom Fury," AAR; Unit Journal and Timeline, copies in author's possession, courtesy of LTC Newell; Lieutenant Colonel Dave Bellon to Dad, November 20, 2004, www. thegreenzone.com, copy in author's possession; Hevezi, "'They've Chosen a Path of Violence,'" pp. 42–43; Sattler and Wilson, "Operation Al Fajr," pp. 20–23; Patrick O'Donnell, *We Were One: Shoulder to Shoulder with the Marines who took Fallujah* (New York: DaCapo, 2006), pp. 62–63; Gary Livingston, *Fallujah with Honor: First Battalion, Eighth Marines in Operation Phantom Fury* (North Topsail Beach, NC: Caisson Press, 2006), pp. 37–38; Matthews, *Operation Al Fajr*, p. 39; Bellavia, *House to House*, pp. 60–62, 73–75; Gott, ed., *Eyewitness to War, Volume I*, pp. 92–94; Gott, ed., *Eyewitness to War, Volume II*, pp. 250–52. Command Sergeant Major Faulkenberg was killed on the first night of the battle. He was leading a group of Iraqi soldiers into the city, under intense fire, when a bullet caught him just above the right eye. He later died at the battalion aid station.

11. Gunnery Sergeant Duanne Walters, interview with Captain Stephen "Joe" Winslow, January 6, 2005; Shupp, Tucker, Natonski interviews, all at USMCHMD; TF 2-2 Infantry, AAR, journal and timeline; Newell interview; "Battle for Fallujah," at www.talkingproud.us; O'Donnell, *We Were One*, pp. 73–77; Wright and Reese, *On Point II*, pp. 352–55; Bellavia, *House to House*, pp. 74–96; Matthews, *Operation Al Fajr*, pp. 39–45; Gott, ed., *Eyewitness to War, Volume I*, pp. 9–10, 52–57, 91–95, 144–45; Gott, ed., *Eyewitness to War, Volume II*, pp. 229–31, 251–54; Livingston, *Fallujah, with Honor*, pp. 44–45. For the diagnosis of acoustic trauma, I consulted my wife, Nancy, an audiology clinician with a doctorate (Aud.) in her field. The Americans took significant criticism in world media reports for using white phosphorous, as if they were employing some sort of new and heinous chemical weapon. The criticism only increased when the State Department ignorantly denied that the commanders at Fallujah were using it. Army and Marine spokesmen readily admitted its use, and they were anything but apologetic about it. For those who knew anything about modern American military history, the employment of white phosphorous was nothing new.

12. TF 2-2 Infantry, AAR, journal and timeline; Newell interview; Michael Ware, "Into the Hot Zone," *Time*, November 22, 2004, p. 35; Sattler and Wilson, "Operation Al Fajr," pp. 21–22; Gott, ed., *Eyewitness to War, Volume I*, pp. 10–11; Gott, ed., *Eyewitness to War, Volume II*, pp. 31–32, 254–57; Bellavia, *House to House*, pp. 112–27,

144–63; Grossman, *On Killing*, pp. 87–93, 282–85; Wright and Reese, *On Point II*, pp. 353–54; Matthews, *Operation Al Fajr*, pp. 44–46. By 2004, most squad leaders and team leaders were equipped with portable and/or headset radios to communicate with other leaders at the platoon and company level.

13. Sattler, Natonski, Shupp, Tucker interviews, all at USMCHMD; TF 2-2 Infantry, AAR, journal and timeline; Newell interview; Toby Harnden, "70 Insurgents Killed in Mosque Battle," *London Daily Telegraph*, November 11, 2004; Toby Harnden, "A Cat Ate the Face of a Corpse," *Spectator*, November 20, 2004; Gott, ed., *Eyewitness to War, Volume I*, pp. 56–61, 227–28, 302–04; Gott, ed., *Eyewitness to War, Volume II*, pp. 32-34, 155–57, 257–60; Bellavia, *House to House*, pp. 191–201; Matthews, *Operation Al Fajr*, pp. 45–47. The senior commanders, Marine and Army, all seemed to appreciate the respective strengths and weaknesses of their units. For instance, Lieutenant Colonel Newell fully understood that his mechanized formations would penetrate Fallujah faster than the Marine light infantry and he planned for that. General Sattler understood the very same thing—he had requested the two Army mech battalions because of their capabilities, albeit with the expectation that his Marines would end up clearing most of Fallujah's buildings. The negative perceptions about Marine and Army capabilities came mainly from junior officers and NCOs who were not as well versed in the big picture.

14. Ware, "Into the Hot Zone," pp. 32–36; Gott, ed., *Eyewitness to War, Volume I*, pp. 10–12, 256–59; Gott, ed., *Eyewitness to War, Volume II*, pp. 259–69; Grossman, *On Killing*, pp. 114–37; Bellavia, *House to House*, pp. 201–72. Lawson's quotes are from a CNN interview. Multiple firsthand accounts from Bellavia about this harrowing experience are posted on www.youtube.com. According to Bellavia, the men in the hell house were Palestinians who were affiliated with Hezbollah. He and the other grunts found drug paraphernalia that indicated the insurgents had shot themselves up with atoprine and epinephrine, drugs that produced a stimulant effect roughly similar to PCP (angel dust). This was common in Fallujah and it made the mujahideen especially hard to kill. Bellavia earned a Silver Star and Bronze Star for his actions in Iraq. He also was nominated for the Medal of Honor. The status of his case is pending. He left the Army in 2005.

15. TF 2-2 Infantry, AAR, timeline and journal; Ilana Ozernoy, "Taking It to the Mean Streets, Fallujah, Iraq," *U.S. News & World Report*, November 22, 2004; Ilana Ozernoy and Julian Barnes, "Taking Fallujah: U.S. Forces Strike Iraq's Hard-core Insurgents," *U.S. News & World Report*, November 22, 2004; Janet Reitman, "Surviving Fallujah," *Rolling Stone*, March 10, 2005; Lieutenant Colonel Scott Rutter, USA (Ret.), interview with the author, February 10, 2008; Newell interview; Camarda's recollections are posted at www.fallenheroes.com; Wright and Reese, *On Point II*, pp. 354–57; Matthews, *Operation Al Fajr*, pp. 47–57; Gott, ed., *Eyewitness to*

War, Volume I, pp. 10–13, 148–53, 244–49; Gott, ed., *Eyewitness to War, Volume II*, pp. 116–21; 202–04; 294–300, 306–12. Rutter commanded an infantry company in the Gulf War and an infantry battalion in 2003, during the initial invasion of Iraq. He subsequently retired and covered Fallujah for FoxNews. In that capacity, he was in the middle of the insurgent ambush that claimed Iwan's life, and he was kind enough to confirm for me many of the details related by other eyewitnesses. Another battalion surgeon, Commander Richard Jadick of 1/8 Marines, also located his aid station close to the fighting in hopes of providing rapid treatment to save as many lives as possible. See his book *On Call in Hell: A Doctor's Iraq War Story* (New York: NAL/Caliber, 2007), for many powerful details about his experiences in Fallujah.

16. First Lieutenant Tim Strabbing, interview with Captain Stephen "Joe" Winslow, January 8, 2005; Corporal Matthew Spencer, interview with Captain Stephen "Joe" Winslow, January 7, 2005; Corporal Frances Wolf, interview with Captain Stephen "Joe" Winslow, January 8, 2005; Shupp, Buhl interviews, all at USMCHMD; Major Joe Winslow, interview with the author, August 4, 2008; Lieutenant Colonel Dave Bellon to father, November 20, 2004, copy in author's possession; Colonel Gary Anderson, "Fallujah and the Future of Urban Operations," *Marine Corps Gazette*, November 2004, p. 57; Bing West and Owen West, "Victory in Fallujah," *Popular Mechanics*, August 2005; Catagnus et al., "Infantry Squad Tactics," pp. 80–87; Brad Kasal and Nathaniel Helms, *My Men Are My Heroes: The Brad Kasal Story* (Des Moines, IA: Meredith Books, 2007), pp. 166–67; Gott, ed., *Eyewitness to War, Volume I*, pp. 10–13, 52–56; West, *No True Glory*, pp. 268–73; O'Donnell, *We Were One*, pp. 79–81, 89–95, 107. The reporter was Kevin Sites, an experienced war correspondent affiliated with NBC News. The shooter was a scout sniper attached to Lieutenant Strabbing's platoon. The description of Marine grunts comes from my own observations.

17. First Lieutenant John Jacobs, interview with Captain Stephen "Joe" Winslow, January 7, 2005; Sergeant Joseph Nazario, interview with Captain Stephen "Joe" Winslow, January 8, 2005; Lance Corporal Justin Boswood, interview with Lieutenant Colonel Tim Crowley, October 21, 2005; Wolf interview, all at USMCHMD; Staff Sergeant Nathaniel Garcia, "Battalion Tells Squad Leader 'You've Done Enough,'" *Leatherneck*, February 2005, pp. 25–26; Jed Babbin, "Forty Minutes in Fallujah," *American Spectator*, May 2005, pp. 18–22; Catagnus et al., "Infantry Squad Tactics," pp. 82–87; Patrick O'Donnell, multiple conversations with the author, circa 2008-2009; O'Donnell, *We Were One*, pp. 82–90, 165–81, 221–23; Kasal and Helms, *My Men Are My Heroes*, pp. 200–280; West, *No True Glory*, pp. 293–303.

18. Staff Sergeant Shawn Ryan, interview with Captain Stephen "Joe" Winslow, January 8, 2005; Lieutenant Trustin Connor, interview with Captain Stephen "Joe" Winslow, January 8, 2005; Captain Vaughn, interview with Captain Stephen "Joe"

Winslow, January 7, 2005; Buhl, Strabbing, Shupp, Walters, Boswood interviews, all at USMCHMD; Winslow interview; Bellon letter; "Tanks and Doughboys," *Infantry Journal*, July 1945, pp. 8–10; First Lieutenant Carin Calvin, "The Assaultman in the Urban Environment," *Marine Corps Gazette*, July 2005, pp. 30–31; West and West, "Victory in Fallujah"; Catagnus et al., "Infantry Squad Tactics," pp. 87–89; Kasal, *My Men Are My Heroes*, pp. 169–80; O'Donnell, *We Were One*, pp. 69–70, 107.

19.   First Sergeant Miller, interview with Captain Stephen "Joe" Winslow, January 8, 2005; Corporal Ricardo Orozco, interview with Captain Stephen "Joe" Winslow, January 8, 2005; Natonski, Shupp, Buhl, Boswood interviews, all at USMCHMD; Winslow interview; Lieutenant General John Sattler, interview with Patrecia Slayden Hollis, "Second Battle of Fallujah: Urban Operations in a New Kind of War," *Field Artillery Journal*, March–April 2006, pp. 4–7; Tim Dyhouse, "Fallujah: Battle for the 'City of Mosques,'" *VFW*, February 2005, pp. 12–14; Ilana Ozernoy, Amer Saleh, and Julian Barnes, "Destroying It to Save It? With the Insurgents Routed, the Next Task Is to Rebuild Fallujah," *U.S. News & World Report*, November 29, 2004; Rod Nordland and Babak Dehghanpisheh, "Rules of Engagement," *Newsweek*, November 29, 2004; Sattler and Wilson, "Operation Al Fajr," pp. 22–24; Keiler, "Who Won the Battle of Fallujah?"; Bing West, *The Strongest Tribe: War, Politics, and the Endgame in Iraq* (New York: Random House, 2008), pp. 55–60; West, *No True Glory*, pp. 315–24; Gott, ed., *Eyewitness to War, Volume I*, pp. 12–16; Wright and Reese, *On Point II*, pp. 356–58; Matthews, *Operation Al Fajr*, pp. 75–79; Bellavia, *House to House*, p. 273; Ricks, *Fiasco*, pp. 398–405.

Chapter 10

1.   James Cross, "What Is the Army's Job?" *Military Review*, June 1956 (although Cross wrote in the 1950s, his words apply very well to the early twenty-first century); David Bolgiano, "Deadly Double Standards," *Wall Street Journal*, July 3, 2007; Peter Mansoor, *Baghdad at Sunrise: A Brigade Commander's War in Iraq* (New Haven & London: Yale University Press, 2008), pp. 345–46; Tom Ricks, *Fiasco: The American Military Adventure in Iraq* (New York: Penguin, 2006), p. 144; Adrian Lewis, *The American Culture of War: The History of U.S. Military Force from World War II to Operation Iraqi Freedom* (New York: Routledge, 2007), pp. 387–88. The *Washington Post* estimated that IEDs caused 61 percent of American deaths. A French study estimated that they caused 41 percent. As a rough estimate, I have chosen to split the difference.

2.   "AIF Cells Operating in Tikrit" (the Americans called the insurgents Anti Iraqi Forces, or AIF); "Enemy Threat"; "Tikrit Tribal Breakdown"; "2-7 Infantry, Disper-

sion of Forces"; Lieutenant Colonel Todd Wood, personal biography, multiple conversations circa 2004–2006; A/2-7 Infantry Summary of Operations During OIF III; B/2-7 Infantry, After Action Report (AAR), these and all subsequent documents in author's possession, courtesy of 2-7 Infantry; 2-7 Infantry, Officer's Group Combat After Action Interview with the author, May 22, 2006; Ricks, *Fiasco*, p. 233. The information on the 7th Infantry Regiment's lineage comes from my own personal knowledge as the official regimental historian. For more on the unit's compelling battle history, see my two books on the topic: *The 7th Infantry Regiment: Combat in an Age of Terror, the Korean War Through the Present* (New York: Forge, 2008), and *American Courage, American Carnage: The 7th Infantry Chronicles, the 7th Infantry Regiment's Combat Experience, 1812 Through World War II* (New York: Forge, 2009). During the Iraq War, every company had a nickname, such as "Rage" or "Bushmasters." To avoid confusion, I have chosen to refer to all of the companies in this chapter by their designated names, rather than their nicknames.

3. D/2-7 Infantry, AAR; E/2-7 Infantry, AAR; F/2-7 Infantry, AAR; B/2-7 Infantry, AAR; A/2-7 Infantry, Summary of Operations; First Lieutenant Jon Godwin to family and friends, July 25, 2005, copy of this and all subsequent letters in author's possession, courtesy of Lieutenant Godwin; 2-7 Infantry, Enlisted Group Combat After Action Interview with the author, May 23, 2006; 2-7 Infantry, Officer's interview; *The Cottonbaler: 7th Infantry Regiment Association*, Spring 2005, p. 7; Lieutenant Colonel David Kilcullen, "Twenty-Eight Articles: Fundamentals of Company-level Counterinsurgency," copy of this paper in author's possession.

4. A/2-7 Infantry, AAR; D/2-7 Infantry, AAR; E/2-7 Infantry, AAR and Memorandum for Easy Co 2-7 IN transition into 2-7 IN and missions in Iraq, May 19, 2006; "2-7 Infantry, Company Mission Set," "Daily Operations," and "Troop to Task Schedule"; 2-7 Infantry, Officer's interview; Enlisted interview; conversation with Specialist Dan Driss, May 2006.

5. 2-7 Infantry, Officer's interview; Enlisted interview; "7th Infantry Regiment: Fallen Soldiers, 2005"; Captain Diogo Tavares, casualty notifications, 2005; PFC Travis Anderson, Sergeant Kurtis Arcala, Lieutenant David Giaimo, Sergeant Carl Morgain, Private Wesley Riggs, biographies; Godwin to family and friends, September 26, 2005. Tavares was 2-7's rear detachment commander back at Fort Stewart, Georgia. One of his responsibilities was to notify families and the public of battalion casualties.

6. "Tikrit Tribal Breakdown"; A/2-7 Infantry, AAR; B/2-7 Infantry, AAR; Lieutenant Colonel Todd Wood, update, April 2, 2005; 2-7 Infantry, Officer's interview; Enlisted interview; Anna Badkhen, "Colonel's Toughest Duty," *San Francisco Chronicle*, October 14, 2005; "Unity Pulls Battalion Through Anxiety, Loss," *San Francisco Chronicle*, October 31, 2005; Godwin to family and friends, April 11, 2005.

7.   "IA Takes Over"; "IA Conducts Counterinsurgency Ops"; "Iraqi Police Partner-
     ship"; "2-7 AO Attacks, Pattern Analysis"; "2-7 AO MSR Attacks"; "Operation Able
     Delaware (Elections)"; A/2-7 Infantry, AAR, Summary of Operations; B/2-7 Infan-
     try, AAR; C/2-7 Infantry, AAR; D/2-7 Infantry, AAR; E/2-7 Infantry, AAR; 2-7
     Infantry, Officer's interview; Enlisted interview; Godwin to family and friends,
     April 18, May 8 and 16, 2005; Lieutenant Colonel Todd Wood, comments, *The Cot-
     tonbaler*, Spring 2006, p. 6, Wood conversations. In my group interviews, the
     enlisted soldiers were significantly more skeptical and cynical than the Cottonbaler
     officers about the quality of Iraqi Army soldiers and policemen. Thus, in my assess-
     ment, I tried to strike a balance between the differing shades of opinion.

8.   A/3-7 Infantry, Unit History, copy in author's possession, courtesy of Major Ike
     Sallee; 3-7 Infantry, Officer's Group Combat After Action Interview with the au-
     thor, May 22, 2006; 3-7 Infantry, Enlisted Group 1 Combat After Action Interview
     with the author, May 23, 2006; Lieutenant Reeon Brown and Sergeant First Class
     Joe Benavides, letter to the author, March 4, 2005; First Sergeant Michael Shirley,
     e-mail to Father Phil Salois, March 11, 2005, copy in author's possession, courtesy
     of Fr. Salois; Captain Ike Sallee to Roland and Team Alpha, March 26, 2005, copy
     in author's possession as a member of Team Alpha; Kilcullen, "Twenty-Eight Ar-
     ticles"; Captain Irvin Oliver, Jr., "Death Before Dismount: A Relic," *Armor*, July–
     August 2006, pp. 11–14.

9.   A/3-7 Infantry, Unit History; 3-7 Infantry, Enlisted Group 2 Combat After Action
     Interview with the author, May 24, 2006; Officer's interview; Enlisted, Group 1
     interview; Staff Sergeant Jason Vandegrift, e-mail to author, May 4, 2005; Captain
     Ike Sallee to Attack Families, June 2, 2005, copy in author's possession; Sallee to
     Roland and Team Alpha; Richard Chin, "Army Captain Knows Firepower Alone
     Won't Win War," Knight-Ridder Newspapers, August 20, 2005. Alpha Company's
     nickname was "Attack." As with 2-7 Infantry, the enlisted soldiers of 3-7 were more
     skeptical than the officers about the usefulness and dedication of the ISF men.
     Everyone respected the MOI commandos, though.

10. A/3-7 Infantry, Unit History; Officer's interview; Enlisted, Group 2 interview; Lieu-
     tenant Colonel Funk, update, circa June 2005; Funk, memorial services speeches;
     Captain Eric Hooper, casualty notifications, 2005; "7th Infantry Regiment Fallen
     Soldiers, 2005"; Vandegrift e-mail; Sallee to Attack Families; T. J. Pignataro, "Two
     Soldiers from Area Are Killed," *Buffalo News*, April 22, 2005; First Lieutenant
     Ken Segelhorst, "Small-Unit Kill Teams and IED Interdiction," *Armor*, January–
     February 2008, pp. 26–33. Hooper was the rear detachment commander for 3-7
     during the deployment.

11. A/3-7 Infantry, Unit History; Officer's interview; Enlisted Group 1 interview; En-
     listed Group 2 interview; Kilcullen, "Twenty-Eight Articles"; Colonel Ed Cardon and

Command Sergeant Major Louis Torres, 4th Brigade update, October 17, 2005; Lieutenant Colonel Funk, update, November 8, 2005; Nancy Youssef, "Fatal Shooting of Teacher Illustrates Why Iraqis Fear U.S. Convoys," Knight-Ridder, June 16, 2005; "Fatal Error Deepens Mistrust of U.S.," *Philadelphia Inquirer*, July 6, 2005; Captain David Connolly, "Media on the Battlefield: 'A Nonlethal Fire,'" *Infantry*, May–June 2004, pp. 31–37. The Youssef story included a heartbreaking portrait photo of the slain teacher and her widowed husband.

Epilogue

1. Department of Defense Web site, Fiscal Year 2010 Budget by Service; Mackubin Thomas Owens, "Let's Have Flexible Armed Forces," editorial, *Wall Street Journal*, January 27, 2009; Richard Lardner, "Aging Air Force Wants Big Bucks Fix," Associated Press, February 18, 2008; August Cole and Yochi Dreazen, "Boots on the Ground or Weapons in the Sky?" *Wall Street Journal*, October 30, 2008; Ann Scott Tyson, "Army, Marines to Seek More Troops," *Washington Post*, December 13, 2006; John Keller, "2010 DOD Budget Proposes Increases for Navy, DARPA Spending; Army Faces Big Cuts," *Military & Aerospace Electronics*, May 22, 2009; Ralph Peters, "The Counterrevolution in Military Affairs," *Weekly Standard*, February 6, 2006, p. 18; Tom Donnelly, "The Army We Need," *Weekly Standard*, June 4, 2007, pp. 21–28; Brian Mockenhaupt, "The Army We Have," *Atlantic*, June 2007, pp. 86–99; S. L. A. Marshall, *Men Against Fire: The Problem of Command in Future War* (Alexandria, VA: Byrrd Enterprises, Inc., 1947), pp. 208–09. As of early 2008, the Army's active duty strength was about 512,000 soldiers. Mockenhaupt, in his research, found that among seventeen- to twenty-four-year-olds, the prime group the Army relies upon for its recruits, only three in ten are eligible for service under Army standards. The rest are disqualified for physical, mental, or criminal reasons. The pool of available infantry recruits is obviously, then, even smaller and more elite.

2. David Watson, e-mail to the author, January 4, 2008; Robert Harriman, e-mail to the author, March 4, 2008; Robert Kaplan, "Modern Heroes," editorial, *Wall Street Journal*, October 4, 2007; Lieutenant Donald Taggart, "You're Part of the Infantry," *Infantry*, July 1944, p. 21; Charles Edmunson, "Why Warriors Fight," *Marine Corps Gazette*, September 1944, pp. 3–10; Adrian Lewis, *The American Culture of War: The History of U.S. Military Force from World War II Through Operation Iraqi Freedom* (New York: Routledge, 2007), p. 457.

3. Lieutenant Colonel Dave Grossman, "On Sheep, Wolves, and Sheepdogs," extracted from *On Combat: The Psychology and Physiology of Deadly Conflict in War and Peace* (Portland, OR: PPCT Publications, 2007).

INDEX